THE GREEN GUIDE

Ch. Bastin – J. Evrard/MICHELIN

Belgium
Grand Duchy
of Luxembourg

Director	David Brabis
Editorial	Nadia Bosquès, Sandra Darbé
English Edition	Mike Brammer, Theo Gott, Michael Ivory
Practical Points	Theo Gott, Michael Ivory
Mapping	Alain Baldet, Geneviève Corbic, Virginie Bruno, Fabienne Renard, Gaëlle Wachs
Picture Editor	Cathérine Guégan
Technical Assistance	Mathilde Vergnault, Robin Sawers, Lisa Guérard, Titus McCready
Lay-out	Frédéric Sardin
Graphics	Christiane Beylier
Cover	Agence Carré Noir
Production	Pierre Ballochard, Renaud Leblanc
Marketing	Ellie Griffith, Cécile Petiau
Sales	John Lewis (UK), Gayle Sparks (USA)
Public Relations	Gonzague de Jarnac, Paul Cordle

Contact

The Green Guide
Michelin Travel Publications
Hannay House
39 Clarendon Road
Watford
Herts
WD17 1JA
United Kingdom
☎ (01923) 205 240
Fax (01923) 205 241
www.ViaMichelin.com
TheGreenGuide-uk@uk.michelin.com

Published in 2004

The Green Guide:
Spirit of Discovery

Leisure time spent with **The Green Guide** is also a time for refreshing your spirit, enjoying yourself, and taking advantage of our selection of fine restaurants, hotels and other places for relaxing: immerse yourself in the local culture, discover new horizons, experience the local lifestyle. **The Green Guide** opens the door for you.

Each year our writers go touring: visiting the sights, devising the driving tours, identifying the highlights, selecting the most attractive hotels and restaurants, checking the routes for the maps and plans. Each title is compiled with great care, giving you the benefit of regular revisions and Michelin's first-hand knowledge. **The Green Guide** responds to changing circumstances and takes account of its readers' suggestions; all comments are welcome.

Share with us our enthusiasm for travel, which has led us to discover over 60 destinations in France and other countries. Like us, let yourself be guided by the desire to explore, which is the best motive for travel: the spirit of discovery.

Contents

B. Régent/PHOTONONSTOP

A traditional "Gille" from Binche.

Liège.

Selected Sights

Grand Duchy of Luxembourg

Chimay beer and cheese.

Traditional architecture in Leuven.

J.-D. Sudres/PHOTONONSTOP

M. Gurfinkel/MICHELIN

Maps
and Plans

Companion publications

Internet users can access personalised route plans, Michelin maps and town plans, and addresses of hotels and restaurants featured in *The Red Guide Benelux* through the website at www.ViaMichelin.com All Michelin publications are cross-referenced. For each sight covered in the Selected Sights section of the guide, a map reference is given under the heading "Location". From our range of products we recommend the following:

Plan no 44 and atlas no 2044 of Brussels:
– a complete plan of Brussels, including major thoroughfares, one-way streets, main car parks, post offices etc.
– an alphabetical street index
– practical information

Travelling around Belgium and the Grand Duchy of Luxembourg

Map of Belgium – Grand Duchy of Luxembourg no 716
– a 1:350 000 scale map with an index of place names and plans of Antwerp, Brussels and Liège.

Map of Grand Duchy of Luxembourg no 717
– a 1:150 000 scale map with an index of place names and a plan of the city of Luxembourg.

Map of Northern Belgium no 533
– a detailed 1:200 000 scale map with a list of place names and plans of Antwerp and Brussels.

Map of Southern Belgium no 534
– a detailed 1:200 000 scale map with a list of place names and plans of Charleroi, Liège, Mons and Namur.

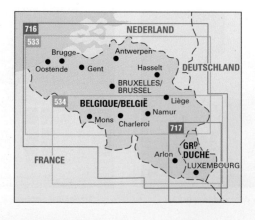

List of maps

Town plans

Plans of museums and monuments

Touring maps

Key

Selected monuments and sights

⊚ →]	Tour - Departure point
⛪ ⛫	Catholic church
⛪ ⛫	Protestant church, other temple
✡ ✉ ☪	Synagogue - Mosque
▮▮	Building
■	Statue, small building
⛉	Calvary, wayside cross
◎	Fountain
—•—■	Rampart - Tower - Gate
⋈	Château, castle, historic house
⸪	Ruins
⌣	Dam
☼	Factory, power plant
✩	Fort
⋒	Cave
ⴹ	Prehistoric site
▾	Viewing table
ⱴ	Viewpoint
▲	Other place of interest

Sports and recreation

🏇	Racecourse
⛸	Skating rink
≋ ⊞	Outdoor, indoor swimming pool
🎥	Multiplex Cinema
⛵	Marina, sailing centre
⌂	Trail refuge hut
□–■–■–□	Cable cars, gondolas
□++++++□	Funicular, rack railway
🚂	Tourist train
◆	Recreation area, park
🧜	Theme, amusement park
🦌	Wildlife park, zoo
⊛	Gardens, park, arboretum
◉	Bird sanctuary, aviary
🚶	Walking tour, footpath
👶	Of special interest to children

Special symbol

℞	Park and ride (Parking Relais)

Abbreviations

G, POL.	Police (Federale Politie)
H	Town hall (Hôtel de ville ou maison communale)
J	Law courts (Palais de justice)
M	Museum (Musée)
P	Provincial capital (Chef-lieu de province)
P	Local government offices (Gouvernement provincial)
T	Theatre (Théâtre)
U	University (Université)

	Sight	Seaside resort	Winter sports resort	Spa
Highly recommended	★★★	�☆☆☆	�֎�֎✖✖✖	⳾⳾⳾
Recommended	★★	☆☆	✖✖	⳾⳾
Interesting	★	☆	✖	⳾

Additional symbols

🔃		Tourist information
═══	═══	Motorway or other primary route
❶	❶	Junction: complete, limited
⊨	═══	Pedestrian street
⠶⠶⠶⠶		Unsuitable for traffic, street subject to restrictions
┉┉┉	----	Steps – Footpath
🚂	🚂	Train station – Auto-train station
🚌	S.N.C.F.	Coach (bus) station
┈┼┈		Tram
⌂		Metro, underground
P̱		Park-and-Ride
♿		Access for the disabled
✉		Post office
☎		Telephone
⌧		Covered market
⠶✕⠶		Barracks
△		Drawbridge
⋃		Quarry
✗		Mine
B	F	Car ferry (river or lake)
⛴		Ferry service: cars and passengers
⛴		Foot passengers only
③		Access route number common to Michelin maps and town plans
Bert (R.)...		Main shopping street
AZ B		Map co-ordinates
►►		Visit if time permits
⊘		Admission times and charges listed at the end of the guide

Hotels and restaurants

⊖	Price categories: Budget
⊖⊖	Moderate
⊖⊖⊖	Expensive
20 rooms: €*38/60*	Number of rooms: price for one person/ double room
half-board or full board: €*43*	Price per person, based on double occupancy
🍴 €*7.50*	Price of breakfast; when not given, it is included in the price of the room (i.e., for bed-and-breakfast)
120 sites: €*13*	Number of camp sites and cost for 2 people with a car
€*13 lunch-* €*16.50/39*	Restaurant: fixed-price menus served at lunch only – mini/maxi price fixed menu (lunch and dinner) or à la carte
rest. €*16.50/39*	Lodging where meals are served mini/maxi price fixed menu or à la carte
reserv	Reservation recommended
🚫	No credit cards accepted
P	Reserved parking for hotel patrons

Principal sights

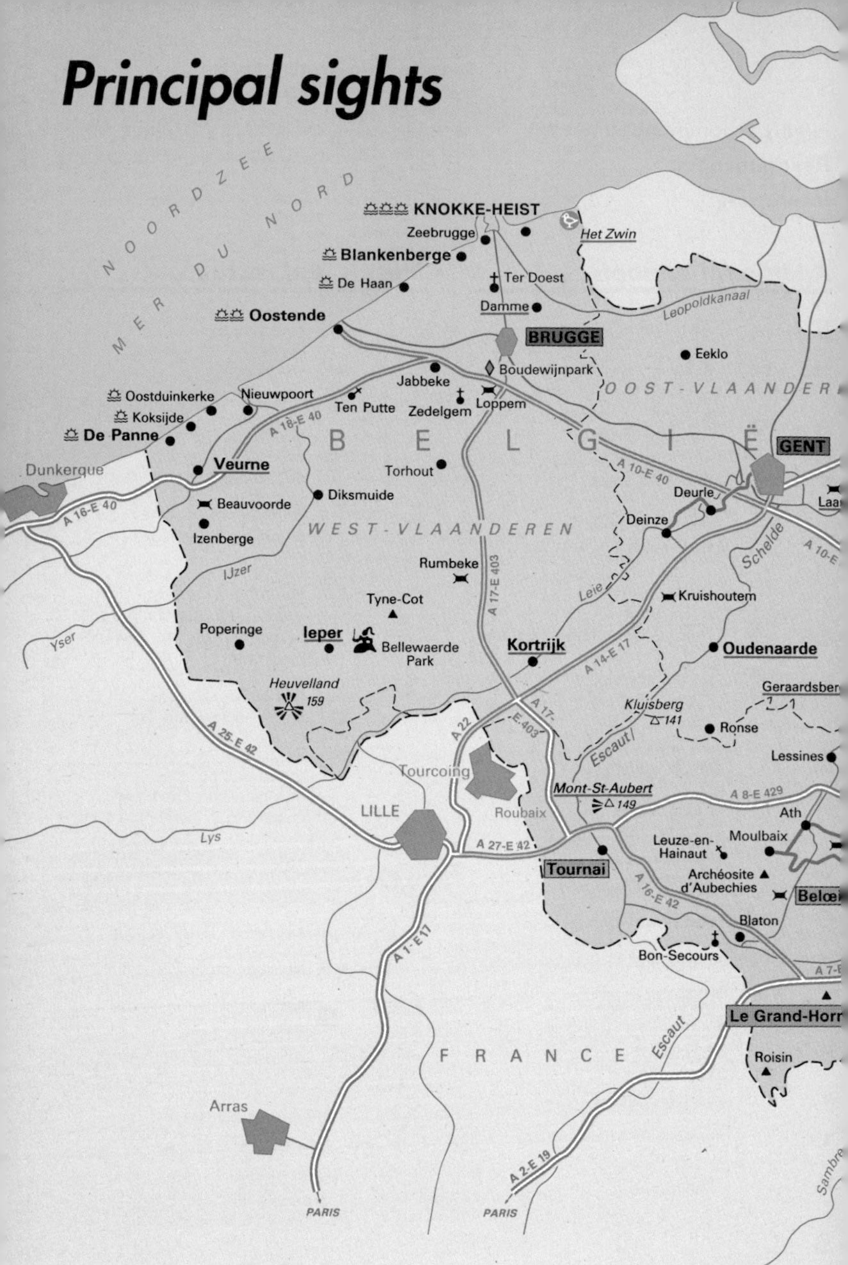

NOORDZEE / MER DU NORD

☆☆☆ **KNOKKE-HEIST**

Zeebrugge

Het Zwin

☆☆ **Blankenberge**

+ Ter Doest

☆ De Haan

Damme

Leopoldkanaal

☆☆ **Oostende**

BRUGGE

• Eeklo

Boudewijnpark

OOST-VLAANDEREN

☆ Oostduinkerke

Nieuwpoort

Jabbeke

Loppem

☆ Koksijde

Ten Putte

Zedelgem

GENT

☆ **De Panne**

B E L G I Ë

A 18-E 40

A 10-E 40

Dunkerque

Veurne

Torhout

Deurle

Laa

A 16-E 40

• Beauvoorde

Diksmuide

Deinze

A 10-E

Izenberge

W E S T - V L A A N D E R E N

Scheldе

IJzer

Rumbeke

A 17-E 403

Leie

Kruishoutem

Yser

Poperinge

Ieper

Tyne-Cot

Kortrijk

A 14-E 17

Oudenaarde

Bellewaerde Park

A 17-

Geraardsber

Heuvelland 159

A 22

Kluisberg
141

• Ronse

Lessines

A 25-E 42

E-403

Escaut

Tourcoing

Mont-St-Aubert
149

A 8-E 429

Ath

LILLE

Roubaix

Moulbaix

Lys

A 27-E 42

Leuze-en-Hainaut

Beloe

Tournai

Archéosite d'Aubechies

A 16-E 42

Blaton

+ Bon-Secours

A 7-E

A 1-E17

Le Grand-Horn

Roisin

F R A N C E

Escaut

Arras

A 2-E 19

Sambre

PARIS

PARIS

LAON

N 2

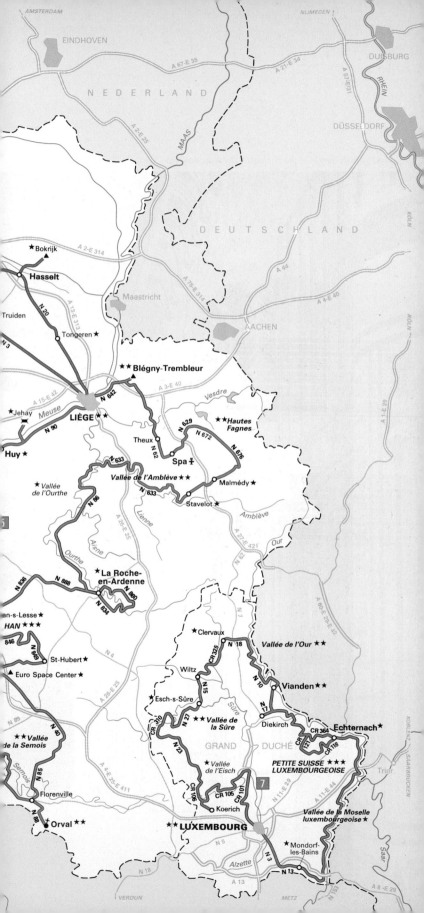

The Egyptian Temple in the Zoological Gardens, Antwerp

Practical Points

Planning your Trip

When to Go

Cultural activities may be enjoyed all year round. However, the countryside is at its best between April and October.

Spring – Burgeoning plant-life enhances avenues and squares, and the delicate foliage bordering canals makes a pretty scene, especially in cities like Bruges. The forests of the Ardennes and Luxembourg are cloaked in myriad shades of green. In April, Watermael-Boitsfort, a suburb of Brussels, is a vision in pink amid the blossom of its Japanese cherry trees.

Summer – The wide sandy beaches and sand dunes of the North Sea coast attract large crowds of holidaymakers. The rivers of the Ardennes cutting through their stunning backdrop of green hills are also extremely popular. In August the Lochristi region is resplendent with begonias in full bloom.

Autumn – This is the best time of year for visiting the Ardennes and Luxembourg, where richly stocked game forests take on magnificent seasonal hues. The city of Luxembourg is set jewel-like amid the russet foliage of its trees.

Winter – Snow often covers the evergreen forests of the Ardennes, lending a magical quality to the beauty of the landscape. What better setting for a winter sports holiday?

Useful Addresses

BELGIAN EMBASSIES

Belgian Embassy, 103-105 Eaton Square, London SW1W 9AB ☎ (020) 7470 3700; fax (020) 7259 6213; www.belgium-embassy.co.uk

Embassy of Belgium, 3330 Garfield St NW, Washington DC 20008 ☎ (202) 333 6900; fax (202) 333 3079; www.diplobel.us

LUXEMBOURG EMBASSIES

Luxembourg Embassy, 27 Wilton Crescent, London SW1X 8SD ☎ (020) 7235 6961.

Embassy of Luxembourg, 2200 Massachusetts Avenue NW, Washington DC 20008 ☎ (202) 265 4171.

FOREIGN EMBASSIES AND CONSULATES IN BELGIUM

American Embassy: 27, boulevard du Régent, 1000 Brussels ☎ 02 508 2111; www.usembassy.be

Australian Embassy: 6-8, rue Guimard, 1040 Brussels ☎ 02 286 0500.

British Embassy: 85, rue d'Arlon, 1040 Brussels ☎ 02 287 6211; www.british-embassy.be

British Consulate-General: Korte Klarenstraat 7, 2000 Antwerp ☎ 03 232 6940.

British Consulate: 45, rue Beeckman, 4000 Liège ☎ 042 235832.

Canadian Embassy: 2, avenue de Tervuren, 1040 Brussels ☎ 02 741 06 11.

Embassy of Ireland: 89/93, rue Froissart, 1040 Brussels ☎ 02 230 5337.

FOREIGN EMBASSIES IN LUXEMBOURG

American Embassy: 22, boulevard Emmanuel Servais, L-2535 ☎ 46 01 23.

British Embassy: 14, boulevard Roosevelt, L-2450 Luxembourg, ☎ 22 98 64/65/66.

Embassy of Ireland: 28, route d'Arlon, L-1140 Luxembourg ☎ 45 06 10/09.

BELGIAN NATIONAL TOURIST OFFICES

LONDON

Tourism Flanders-Brussels: 31 Pepper Street, EI4 9RW London, ☎ (020) 7458 0044 or (020) 7867 0311; www.visitflanders.com and Belgian Tourist Office (Brussels and Wallonia), 217 Marsh Wall, London E14 9FW, ☎ (020) 7531 0390, or 0800 954 5245 (brochure line); www.belgiumtheplaceto.be.

NEW YORK

Belgian Tourist Office, 780 Third Avenue, Suite 1501, New York, NY 10017, ☎ 212 758 8130; www.visitbelgium.com

BRUSSELS

Office de promotion du tourisme Wallonie-Bruxelles (OPT), rue du Marché-aux-Herbes 63, 1000 Bruxelles, ☎ 02 504 03 90; fax 02 504 02 70; www.belgique-tourisme.net Commissariat général au tourisme Région Wallonne-C.G.T., place de Wallonie 1 –Bât. III, 5100 Jambes, ☎ 081 33 40 70; fax 081 33 40 77. Toerisme Vlaanderen, Grasmarkt 61, 1000 Brussel, ☎ 02 504 03 90; fax 02 504 02 70; www.visitflanders.be

BELGIAN REGIONAL TOURIST OFFICES

Provinces in Belgium each have their own tourism organisations, which will provide any information you might require about a particular region. Their addresses are listed below. Local tourist information centres are listed in the Location sections in the main part of the guide.

Antwerp: Koningin Elisabethlei 16, 2018 Antwerpen, ☎ 03 240 63 73; fax 03 240 63 83; www.tourprovantwerp.be

Brabant wallon: Chaussée des Nerviens 25, 1300 Wavre, ☎ 03 351 12 00; www.brabantwallon.be

Hainaut: rue des Clercs 31, 7000 Mons, ☎ 065 36 04 64; fax 065 33 57 32; www.hainaut.be

Liège: boulevard de la Sauvenière 77, 4000 Liège, ☎ 04 232 65 10; fax 04 232 65 11; www.ftpl.be

Limburg: Willekensmolenlaan 140, 3500 Hasselt, ☎ 011 23 74 50; fax 011 23 74 66; www.toerismelimburg.be

Luxembourg: quai de l'Ourthe 9, 6980 La Roche-en-Ardenne, ☎ 084 41 10 11; fax 084 41 24 39; www.ftlb.be

Namur: avenue Reine Astrid 22/2, 5000 Namur, ☎ 081 74 99 00; fax 081 74 99 29; www.ftpn.be

Oost-Vlaanderen: Woodrow Wilsonplein 3, 9000 Gent, ☎ 09 267 70 20; fax 09 267 71 99; www.oost-vlaanderen.be/toerisme

Vlaams-Brabant: Diestsesteenweg 52, 3010 Leuven, ☎ 016 26 76 20; fax 016 26 76 76; www.vl-brabant.be

West-Vlaanderen: Westtoer, Koning Albert I-laan 120, 8200 Brugge, ☎ 050 30 55 00; fax 050 30 55 90; www.westtoerisme.be

LUXEMBOURG NATIONAL TOURIST OFFICES

London
Luxembourg Tourist Office, 122 Regent Street, London W1B 5SA, ☎ (020) 7434 2800; fax (020) 7734 1205; www.luxembourg.co.uk

New York
Luxembourg National Tourist Office, 17 Beekman Place, New York NY 10022, ☎ 212 935 8888; www.visitluxembourg.com

Luxembourg
Office National du Tourisme Luxembourgeois, B.P. 1001, 1010 Luxembourg, ☎ 42 82 82-1; fax 42 82 82-38; www.etat.lu/tourism; Gare Centrale, place de la Gare, Luxembourg, ☎ 42 82 82-20; Luxembourg-Findel Aéroport, ☎ 42 82 82-21.

Brussels
Office National du Tourisme Luxembourgeois, avenue Louise 104, 1050 Bruxelles, ☎ 02 646 03 70; fax 02 648 61 00.

In Belgium and Luxembourg, tourist information centres are indicated by the symbol **🛈**. They are called Office de Tourisme or Syndicat d'Initiative in French, and Dienst voor Toerisme or VVV (Vereniging voor Vreemdelingenverkeer) in Dutch. Addresses and telephone numbers are listed in the Admission Times and Charges section of the guide.

Formalities

Despite the law which came into force on 1 January 1993 authorising the free flow of goods and people within the EU, travellers from the UK, Ireland and countries outside the European Union require a **passport** to enter Belgium. Holders of British, Irish and US passports require no visa to enter Belgium and the Grand Duchy of Luxembourg, although visas may be necessary for visitors from some Commonwealth countries, and for those planning to stay for longer than three months. US citizens should obtain the booklet *Your Trip Abroad* which provides useful information on visa requirements, customs regulations, medical care etc for international travellers. Apply to the Superintendent of Documents, PO Box 371954, Pittsburgh, PA 15250-7954; ☎ (202)-512-1800; fax (202)-512-2250; www.access.gpo.gov

Customs regulations – Since the birth of the single European market and the abolition of the duty-free system on certain goods, allowances for various commodities within the EU have changed. A free leaflet, **Duty Paid**, is available from HM Customs and Excise, Finchley Excise Advice Centre, Berkeley House, 304 Regents Park Road, London N3 2JY, ☎ 0845 010 9000, www.hmce.gov.uk. The US Customs Service offers a free publication **Know Before You Go** for US citizens, ☎ (202) 927 6724; www.customs.gov

Travel insurance – British citizens should apply for **Form E 111**, issued by the Post Office, which entitles the holder to urgent treatment for accident or unexpected illness in EU countries. This form should be presented to the relevant medical services prior to receiving treatment. Visitors are strongly advised to take out additional travel insurance to cover against any expenses not covered by form E 111, as well as lost luggage, theft, cancellation, delayed departure etc.
Non-EU travellers are advised to check with their insurance companies about taking out supplementary medical insurance with specific overseas coverage.

Pets (cats and dogs) – A general health certificate and proof of rabies vaccination should be obtained from your local vet before departure. Under the Pet Travel Scheme (PETS) introduced by DEFRA (Department of Environment, Food and Rural Affairs), there are procedures which make it possible for UK residents to take their pets abroad and bring them back without the need for quarantine. www.defra.gov.uk/animalh/quarantine/pets/index.htm

Getting There

BY AIR
Various international airline companies operate regular services to Brussels International Airport at Zaventem, 14km/9mi from the city centre, and to Luxembourg. Other Belgian airports with international flights include Antwerp, Ostend-Bruges, and Charleroi/Brussels South.

British Airways: Waterside, PO Box 365, Harmondsworth, UB7 0GB, England; ☎ 0845 77 333 77; www.britishairways.com Reservations within the US and Canada: ☎ 1-800-AIRWAYS. British Midland: ☎ 0870 60 70555; www.flybmi.com SN Brussels Airlines: ☎ 0870 352345; www.brussels-airlines.com Ryanair: ☎ 0871 246 000; www.ryanair.com British European: ☎ 0870 567 6676; www.flybe.com VLM: ☎ 020 7476 6677; www.vlm-airlines.com Virgin Express: ☎ 0207 744 0004; www.virginexpress.com

By Sea

There are numerous cross-Channel services (passenger and car ferries, Sea Cat) from the United Kingdom. For details apply to travel agents or to: Hoverspeed: ☎ 0870 524 0241; www.hoverspeed.co.uk (Dover-Calais) P&O Ferries: ☎ 0870 600 0600; www.poferries.com (Dover-Calais check);☎ 0870 129 002; www.poferries.com (Hull-Zeebrugge) Sea France: ☎ 0870 571 1711; www.seafrance.com (Dover-Calais) Superfast Ferries: ☎ 0800 068 1676; www.viamare.com (Rosyth-Zeebrugge)

Gare Centrale in Antwerp

By Rail

With the opening of the first stage of the Channel Tunnel Rail Link between London and Folkestone, **Eurostar trains now take only 2hr 40min** to travel from London-Waterloo to Bruxelles-Midi. There are approximately eight trains a day from Monday to Saturday, and seven on Sundays. Change at Bruxelles-Midi station to travel on to Luxembourg; this journey usually takes about 3hr. ☎ (0990) 186 186; www.eurostar.com

By Road

When driving to the continent the ideal ports of entry for Belgium are **Zeebrugge** (from Hull and Felixstowe), **Ostend** (from Ramsgate) and **Calais** (from Dover). There is a wide choice of routes using motorways or national roads into Belgium and the Grand Duchy of Luxembourg.

Ostend to Bruges 28km/17mi, to Ghent 64km/40mi, to Brussels 115km/72mi; Zeebrugge to Bruges 14km/9mi, to Brussels 111km/69mi; Calais to Brussels 213km/132mi (via Ostend), 231km/144mi (via Lille); Brussels to Luxembourg 219km/136mi.

Eurotunnel vehicle-carrying shuttle trains link Calais and Folkestone through the Channel Tunnel in just 35min. The number of departures depends on the volume of traffic (there are three to four services every hour during the day and one to two every hour from midnight to 6am). ☎ (08705) 353 535; www.eurotunnel.com

The Channel Tunnel

This tunnel under the sea is the realisation of dreams of linking Britain to mainland Europe which date back over 200 years. The Channel link consists of two single-track rail tunnels (7.60m/24ft in diameter) for passenger and freight transport, and one service tunnel (4.80m/15ft in diameter) for safety and ventilation. The tunnels are 50.5km/31mi long, 37km/23mi of which are under the Channel. Most of the tunnel is 40m/131ft beneath the seabed, in a layer of blue chalk. The trains (800m/2 624ft long) have two levels for passenger cars (capacity 118 cars per shuttle) and one level for coaches and caravans. Special services operate for heavy goods vehicles.

Transport

By Car

DOCUMENTS

A valid **driving licence** is essential. Third party insurance is the minimum cover required by insurance legislation in Belgium, but it is advisable to take out additional insurance for fully comprehensive cover (Green Card).

DRIVING REGULATIONS

Traffic in Belgium and Luxembourg drives on the right! The minimum age for driving is 18 for cars and motorcycles and 16 for mopeds. Children under 12 are not allowed to travel in the front seat as long as there is room for them in the back. **Seatbelts** are compulsory in the back as well as the front of the car. Amber headlights are not necessary. Dipped headlights (not sidelights) are compulsory at night. Belgium has a highly developed road system, well-linked to all adjoining countries. Most towns are bypassed by main roads and there is lavish provision of motorways, all of which are toll-free and are lit at night. Motorway junctions are numbered and shown on Michelin maps. Main road signs are in blue with white lettering, motorway signs are in green with white lettering.

Maximum **speed limits** for cars, caravans and small trailers are 50kph/31mph in built-up areas, 90kph/55mph on the open road, and 120kph/75mph on motorways (minimum speed on motorways is 70kph/45mph).

Priority must be given to cars coming from the right at crossroads and on roundabouts, unless shown otherwise. Give way also to trams, pedestrians boarding or alighting from trams, and pedestrians crossing the road into which you are just turning.

The regulation **red warning triangle** must be carried, and displayed in the event of a breakdown. Dial 100 (in Belgium) for medical help for accidents involving injuries.

Motorcyclists – Crash helmets are compulsory for drivers and passengers of motorcycles of 50cc and over. Dipped headlights must be used at all times of the day or night.

MAPS AND PLANS

The **Michelin maps** which may be useful for your trip are no 705 (Europe), no 721 (France), no 717 (Grand Duchy of Luxembourg), no 716 (Belgium) and detailed maps of Belgium nos 533 and 534.

Route planning – Michelin has created a website to help motorists prepare their journey. The service enables browsers to select their preferred route (fastest, shortest etc) and to calculate distances between towns and cities: **www.michelin-travel.com**

ACCIDENTS

In the event of an accident the **emergency numbers** you can call are 100 (ambulance) and 101 (police) in Belgium, or 112 (ambulance) and 113 (police) in Luxembourg. Emergency telephones are to be found along main roads.

Breakdown service – The main organisations to call in the event of a breakdown are:
– **Touring Secours de Belgique**, ☎ 02 233 22 11. For help anywhere in Belgium call ☎ 070 344 777; this breakdown service operates round the clock. On motorways, however, it is best to use the emergency telephones.
– **Royal Automobile Club de Belgique**, ☎ 02 287 09 00.
– **Vlaamse Automobilistenbond**, ☎ 03 253 63 63.
– **Automobile Club du Grand Duché de Luxembourg**, ☎ 45 00 45-1.

Weather information – To find out about weather conditions or to enquire about weather forecasts for a particular area, call ☎ 0900 27 003 (Institut Royal Météorologique in Belgium) or 1818 (Luxembourg).

Road and traffic conditions – For any information concerning roads and traffic call ☎ 02 233 22 36 between 7am and 11pm (Touring Club) or ☎ 02 287 09 80 (Royal Automobile Club).

PETROL

In Belgium, you can buy four-star (super) petrol, lead-free petrol, diesel and LPG. Petrol is generally slightly more expensive in motorway service stations.

Although all major credit cards are generally accepted at petrol stations (Access, Barclaycard/Visa, Eurocard, American Express, Diners Club), visitors are strongly advised to have other means of payment with them.

Car hire – Vehicles in Belgium can be hired through the offices of all major international car hire companies around the world. Alternatively, cars can be hired at major airports, large hotels and in all major towns and cities in Belgium:
Avis ☎ 02 720 0944; www.avis.com
Europcar ☎ 02 721 05 92; www.europcar.com
Hertz ☎ 02 720 60 44; www.hertz.com
Most companies will only rent out vehicles to drivers over the age of 21. A valid driving licence is required.

Signposting – Bear in mind that in Flanders most towns are only signposted in Dutch: Luik for Liège, Parijs for Paris, Rijsel for Lille etc. Likewise in Wallonia, place-names appear in French: Anvers for Antwerp/Antwerpen, Gand for Ghent/Gent.

By Train

TICKETS AND FARES

The Belgian railway system is run by the **Société Nationale de Chemin de Fer de Belgique/Belgische Spoorwegen**, whose symbol is a "B" inscribed in an oval. It offers several cheap rates for train passengers meeting certain requirements. For details about the Go-Pass, Multi-Pass, Golden Rail Pass and Billet Week-End, contact ☎ 02 555 25 25.

In the UK, for further information and reservations apply to **Belgian Railways**, ☎ (020) 7593 2332; www.sncb.be

Where to Stay

Addresses Listed in the Guide

To offer you a pleasant stay we have scoured all regions of Belgium and Luxembourg in search of guesthouses, hotels, restaurants and campsites that best typify the area either for their striking location or traditional food, keeping all budgets in mind and not forgetting younger travellers.

CATEGORIES

Our selection is divided into three price brackets: **Budget**, represented by a ☺ symbol (€65 or under for a single room), **Moderate** ☺☺ (singles from €65 to €105) and **Expensive** ☺☺☺ (single rooms for over €105).

ACCOMMODATION

For regions and cities popular with tourists, it is advisable to book accommodation in advance, especially if you plan to go from April to October. You may find that, from November to March, prices are slightly lower and that some hotels offer discounts or special weekend deals.

For each establishment, the first figure refers to the price of a single room, the second figure to the price of a double room. Exceptions to this are highlighted (rural guesthouses, for example, which generally only have double rooms). Breakfast is usually included in the price although this may not be the case in smaller hotels. When not included in the price of the room, the cost of breakfast immediately follows the price of the room. Whatever type of accommodation you choose, it is advisable to check prices before booking, as rates can vary depending on the time of year and availability of rooms.

The Red Guide Benelux is revised annually and is an indispensable complement to this guide, with information on hotels and restaurants including category, price, degree of comfort and setting.

Booking a room – Hotel accommodation can be booked through the **Belgian Tourist Reservation** (**BTR**), 111, boulevard Anspach, 1000 Brussels, ☎ 02 513 74 84, fax 02 513 92 77. It is highly recommended to reserve hotel rooms in advance, especially for a weekend break, when visiting Bruges or any area where a local festival is being held.

BED & BREAKFAST

For information on Bed & Breakfast accommodation contact **Bed & Brussels**, 9, rue Kindermans, 1050 Bruxelles, ☎ 02 646 07 37 or **Taxistop**, 28/1, rue Fossé-aux-Loups, 1000 Bruxelles www.bnb.brussels.be, ☎ 02 223 22 31 www.taxistop.be

FARMHOUSE HOLIDAYS

The following organisations can provide information on farmhouse holidays and can also make reservations on your behalf:

– **Fédération du Tourisme Agricole de l'Alliance Agricole Belge (Fetourag)**, rue de la Science 23-25, 1040 Brussels, ☎ 02 230 72 95.

– **UPA Tourisme Rural**, 47, Chaussée de Namur, 5030 Gembloux, ☎ 081 60 00 60.

For Flanders, contact:

– **Vlaamse Federatie voor Hoeve-en Plattelandstoerisme**, Parijsstraat 52, 3000 Leuven, ☎ 016 24 21 58, www.hoevetoerisme.be; this organisation publishes a brochure listing details of accommodation.

For the Ardennes, contact the regional Tourist Information Centres in the provinces of Liège, Luxembourg and Namur *(see p 18)*.

For Luxembourg, contact:

– **Association pour la Promotion du Tourisme Rural au Grand-Duché de Luxembourg**, c/o Centrale Paysanne, 2980 Luxembourg, ☎ 48 81 61-1.

RURAL HOLIDAYS

Nature-based holidays can be enjoyed in *Stations Vertes de Vacances* resorts, which offer accommodation and some sporting and recreational activities. These resorts are particularly popular in the Ardennes and are indicated by a special sign.

CAMPING AND CARAVANNING

Belgium has over 500 camp sites, divided into four categories. They are extremely crowded in July and August. The Grand Duchy of Luxembourg numbers more than 100 camp sites. Independent camping is permitted in Belgium and Luxembourg, but do not forget to ask for permission from the landowner first! Further information from: Fédération Internationale de Camping et de Caravanning, rue Arenberg, 1000 Bruxelles, ☎ 02 513 87 83.

YOUTH HOSTELS

The main Belgian hostelling associations are:
– **Auberges de Jeunesse**, rue de la Sablonnière 28, 1000 Bruxelles, ☎ 02 219 56 76, www.laj.be.
– **Vlaamse Jeugdherbergcentrale**, Van Stralenstraat 40, 2060 Antwerp, ☎ 03 232 72 18, www.vjh.be.
The main Luxembourg Youth Hostel association is:
Centrale des Auberges de Jeunesse Luxembourgeoises, place de la Gare 24, 1616 Luxembourg, ☎ 26 29 35 00, www.youthhostels.lu

General Information

CURRENCY

The unit of currency in Belgium and Luxembourg is the Euro (€). Approximate exchange rate: £1 = €1.40.

CHANGING MONEY, CREDIT CARDS

Travellers' cheques and foreign cash can be exchanged at banks and exchange offices. International credit cards are accepted in most shops, hotels and restaurants.
The Red Guide Benelux gives details of which credit cards are accepted by the establishments listed. Visitors can also obtain cash from bank machines using credit and debit cards. A pin number will be required to use this service. In the event of credit card loss or theft, call the following numbers:
American Express ☎ 02 676 21 21;
Visa and **Eurocard** ☎ 070 344 344;
Diners Club ☎ 02 206 98 00.

OPENING HOURS AND PUBLIC HOLIDAYS

IN BELGIUM:

Banks open 9am to 12.30pm and 2pm to 3.30pm (4pm or even 6pm on Fridays in branches near major commercial centres); in town centres they open 8.30am to 3.30pm (4pm on Fridays); closed at weekends (some stay open on Saturday mornings).

Post offices open 9am to noon and 2.30pm to 5pm; in city centres 9am to 5pm; closed at weekends. Some post offices house telephone facilities, but check the town map or a telephone book for those that do not. Central telephone agency **Belgacom** in Brussels at 17, boulevard l'Impératrice is open 8.30am (10am Tuesday) to 6pm, Monday to Friday.

Shops open 9am to 6pm (7pm); closed on Sundays.

Public holidays are 1 January, Easter Monday, 1 May, Ascension Day, Whit Monday, 21 July (national holiday), 15 August, 1 November, 11 November and 25 December. Local festivals *(see Calendar of events)* can also mean that certain public facilities may be closed.

IN LUXEMBOURG:

Banks open 8.30am to 12.30pm and 1.30pm to 4.30pm; closed at weekends.

Post and telephone facilities are not always in the same place; consult a town map or the telephone book.

Shops open 9am to noon and 2pm to 6pm; they are often closed on Monday mornings.

Public holidays in Luxembourg are the same as those in Belgium *(see above)* except for the national holiday, which is 23 June, and 11 November, which is not a public holiday.

TELEPHONE CALLS

The international dialling code for Belgium is 32, and for Luxembourg 352. To call the United Kingdom from Belgium or Luxembourg, dial 00 + 44 + area code (minus preceding 0) + number.
If you need to call the operator or require information, dial 1307 in Belgium or 017 in Luxembourg. Phonecards for use in public telephone booths can be bought from post offices and stations as well as some newsagents. A few telephone boxes still accept coins.

TIPPING

It is customary to tip the waiter in cafés and restaurants.
Tips are included in the prices of Belgian **taxis**.

Conversion Tables

Weights and measures

| 1 kilogram (kg) | 2.2 pounds (lb) | 2.2 pounds |
| 1 metric ton (tn) | 1.1 tons | 1.1 tons |

to convert kilograms to pounds, multiply by 2.2

| 1 litre (l) | 2.1 pints (pt) | 1.8 pints |
| 1 litre | 0.3 gallon (gal) | 0.2 gallon |

to convert litres to gallons, multiply by 0.26 (US) or 0.22 (UK)

| 1 hectare (ha) | 2.5 acres | 2.5 acres |
| 1 square kilometre (km²) | 0.4 square miles (sq mi) | 0.4 square miles |

to convert hectares to acres, multiply by 2.4

1 centimetre (cm)	0.4 inches (in)	0.4 inches
1 metre (m)	3.3 feet (ft) - 39.4 inches - 1.1 yards (yd)	
1 kilometre (km)	0.6 miles (mi)	0.6 miles

to convert metres to feet, multiply by 3.28, kilometres to miles, multiply by 0.6

Clothing

Women	🇪🇺	🇺🇸	🇬🇧		🇪🇺	🇺🇸	🇬🇧	Men
	35	4	2½		40	7½	7	
	36	5	3½		41	8½	8	
	37	6	4½		42	9½	9	
Shoes	38	7	5½		43	10½	10	Shoes
	39	8	6½		44	11½	11	
	40	9	7½		45	12½	12	
	41	10	8½		46	13½	13	
	36	6	8		46	36	36	
	38	8	10		48	38	38	
Dresses &	40	10	12		50	40	40	Suits
suits	42	12	14		52	42	42	
	44	14	16		54	44	44	
	46	16	18		56	46	46	
	36	30	8		37	14½	14½	
	38	32	10		38	15	15	
Blouses &	40	34	12		39	15½	15½	Shirts
sweaters	42	36	14		40	15¾	15¾	
	44	38	16		41	16	16	
	46	40	18		42	16½	16½	

Sizes often vary depending on the designer. These equivalents are given for guidance only.

Speed

kph	10	30	50	70	80	90	100	110	120	130
mph	6	19	31	43	50	56	62	68	75	81

Temperature

Celsius (°C)	0°	5°	10°	15°	20°	25°	30°	40°	60°	80°	100°
Fahrenheit (°F)	32°	41°	50°	59°	68°	77°	86°	104°	140°	176°	212°

To convert Celsius into Fahrenheit, multiply °C by 9, divide by 5, and add 32.
To convert Fahrenheit into Celsius, subtract 32 from °F, multiply by 5, and divide by 9.

Notes and Coins

The euro banknotes were designed by Robert Kalinan, an Austrian artist. His designs were inspired by the theme "Ages and styles of European Architecture". Windows and gateways feature on the front of the banknotes, bridges feature on the reverse, symbolising the European spirit of openness and co-operation.
The images are stylised representations of the typical architectural style of each period, rather than specific structures.

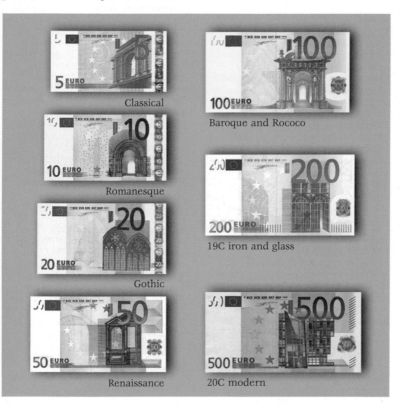

Classical

Baroque and Rococo

Romanesque

19C iron and glass

Gothic

Renaissance

20C modern

Euro coins have one face common to all 12 countries in the European single currency area or "Eurozone" (currently Austria, Belgium, Finland, France, Germany, Greece, Ireland, Italy, Luxembourg, The Netherlands, Portugal and Spain) and a reverse side specific to each country, created by their own national artists.

Euro banknotes look the same throughout the Eurozone. All Euro banknotes and coins can be used anywhere in this area.

Ideas for your Visit

Touring

The map of Touring Programmes at the front of the guide sets out the following recommended tours.

① ANTWERP AND THE KEMPEN

This tour starts at the attractive city of Antwerp, the dynamic "Metropolis of Flanders", then takes in the delightful villa suburbs of Brasschaat and the Kalmhout nature reserve. Step back in time at the superbly restored Beguin convent at Hoogstraten, then follow the Dutch-Belgian border, calling in at Baarle-Hertog, the tiny Belgian enclave in the Netherlands. Stop awhile at Turnhout, the world capital of the playing card, before continuing via the pleasant little towns of Geel and Herentals and reaching the end of the tour at Lier, one of the most charming small towns in Flanders, famous for its delicious tartlets.

② ALONG THE BANKS OF THE SCHELDT

From Antwerp, the capital of contemporary Belgian design, the tour leads to Sint-Niklaas in the heart of the Waasland, then to Temse with its metal bridge, the longest in Belgium, and on to Bornem with its imposing castle. Next comes St-Amands, the birthplace of the great poet Émile Verhaeren. Before coming to the end of the tour at the lovely historic city of Mechelen, the route passes by Fort Breendonk, used as a concentration camp in the Second World War.

③ BRUSSELS AND BRABANT

Despite its wealth of attractions, Brussels is still one of the least known capital cities of Europe. It is best explored using the Michelin Green Guide "Brussels". From the capital, the tour explores the gently undulating landscapes of Flemish and Walloon Brabant, stopping first at the fascinating botanical gardens at Meise. It then continues via Grimbergen with its Baroque abbey to one of the high points of any visit to Belgium, the ancient university city of Leuven. A visit to the Royal Museum of Central Africa is followed by a treat for art-lovers, the Fondation Foulon at La Hulpe. And who could fail to be moved by the battlefield of Waterloo with its memories of Wellington and Napoleon? The tour has its share of wonderful historic buildings, among them the lovely abbey ruins of Villers-la-Ville, the collegiate church at Nivelles, the glorious Baroque basilica at Halle, and last but not least the castles at Beersel and Gaasbeek.

④ HAINAUT

One of Belgium's finest old cities, Tournai, is the starting point of this exploration of the historic province of Hainaut. The route takes in Ath, famous for its parade of giants, Attre with its château, and Soignies with its austere collegiate church. After the formidable fortress of Ecaussinnes-Lalaing, the château of Seneffe with its superb silver collection, and the fascinating Mariemont Estate, the route enters Belgium's "Black Country" around La Louvière, with its capital, Charleroi. Nearby Mont-sur-Marchienne is home to the fascinating Museum of Photography. Little Thuin is the charming capital of the Thudinie area, whose highlight is the lovely ruin of Aulne Abbey on the banks of the River Sambre. Further south is the old fortified town of Walcourt and the dams and reservoirs of the Eau d'Heure with their tempting array of recreational and leisure facilities. Right on the border with France, the Château de Chimay has a magnificent little Rococo theatre where concerts are held. Now the route heads north again, to hilltop Beaumont and to Binche, world-famous for its carnival. The tour ends by visiting the Canal du Centre, a real jewel of industrial architecture, the city of Mons, dominated by its belfry, and the gorgeous moated castle of Beloeil.

⑤ THE ARDENNES

The city of Liège, where this tour begins, is a lively, welcoming place, with a wealth of historic memories. The area's rich industrial past is revisited at the fascinating mining complex of Blégny-Trembleur, before the route turns south via the delightful little town of Theux to the famous springs of Spa. No air is fresher than that of the cool uplands of the Hautes Fagnes nature park, while beyond, the towns of Malmédy and Stavelot were once a semi-independent ecclesiastical principality. The route penetrates deeper into the Ardennes along the green valleys of the Amblève and the Ourthe to reach one of the country's favourite summer resorts, La Roche-en-Ardenne. From here it is only a short distance to the celebrated caves at Han, the huntsman's capital of St-Hubert, and the Euro Space Center with its eye on the mysteries of the universe. Further south, the valley of the Semois is reached at Florenville on the border with France. The route follows the river past the abbey at Orval, famous for its beer, Bouillon dominated by its great medieval castle, and Vresse-sur-Semois, once known for its tobacco farms. North from here, the Meuse is reached; first comes picturesque Dinant clustered beneath its citadel, then, also dominated by a great fortress, Namur, the political capital of Wallonia.

⑥ THE NORTHEAST

From Liège, the birthplace of Inspector Maigret's creator, Georges Simenon, the tour leads to Tongeren, where the Gaulish chieftan Ambiorix won a great battle over the Romans. The next stop is Hasselt, capital of the province of Limburg and famous for its gin. The open-air museum at Bokrijk is a wonderful evocation of traditional life in Flanders, while the Beguin convent at Diest is one of the loveliest in Belgium. On the way to the sugar-town of Tienen the route passes through the hedge-country of the Hageland, before finishing at St-Truiden, best seen when its orchards are in blossom.

⑦ LUXEMBOURG

This tour of the Grand Duchy begins at its capital, the city of Luxembourg, whose fortifications and historic districts enjoy UNESCO World Heritage status. After a pause to sample the therapeutic waters at the little spa town of Mondorf-les-Bains, there are further tempting tastings to be enjoyed among the vineyards along the Luxembourg bank of the Moselle. Then, around Echternach on the border with Germany, the landscape changes, becoming densely wooded and more dramatic, earning it the name of Luxembourg's Little Switzerland. Beyond the brewery town of Diekirch and Vianden in the shadow of its great castle, the route follows the picturesque valley of the River Our to Clervaux, it too overlooked by a medieval stronghold. Here among the forests of the Luxembourg Ardennes there is the little upland town of Wiltz, together with the picturesque village of Esch-sur-Sûre, almost completely enclosed by a bend in the river. The return to Luxembourg city is via the peaceful villages strung out along the valley of the River Eisch.

⑧ ALONG THE RIVER LEIE

No visitor will remain unmoved by their experience of the starting point of this tour, the ancient city of Ghent. From here, the route takes in the tapestry town of Oudenaarde on the way to the prosperous and attractive town of Kortrijk. The Leie (or Lys) runs through a green and idyllic countryside studded with charming little villages, among them Machelen, Deinze, Ooidonk with its waterside castle, and Deurle and Sint-Martens-Latem, the inspiration of many an artist.

⑨ WEST FLANDERS

Lost in time, Bruges remains Belgium's most seductive city, with its ancient buildings, romantic canals, and superb museums and galleries. The road to the coast leads through delightful little Damme, the port of Bruges in medieval times. The Belgian seaside has a wonderful choice of resorts, among them Knokke-Heist, Blankenberge, De Haan, Ostend and Koksijde. Visitors should take time to explore the attractive far west of Flanders, the area known as Westhoek; here is Veurne, with its superb market square, and the hop-growing centre Poperinge. The way back to Bruges passes through the medieval cloth town of Ypres, martyred in the First World War, and through Torhout, dominated by its great church of St Peter.

Ch. Bastin – J. Evrard/MICHELIN

La plage à Koksijde.

More Themed Routes

As well as the itineraries described above, Belgium has over 60 signposted touring routes for motorists, identified by hexagonal-shaped signposts. They vary between 30-130km/18-80mi in length and link the main tourist centres or follow the scenic routes. Many focus on a special theme: literature (Pallieter-route), history (Routes 14 to 18), geography (Schelderoute or River Scheldt) or present a particular feature of a region, eg windmills (Molen Route or Route des Moulins) and vineyards (Druivenroute or Route du Raisin). Local bookshops and Tourist Information Centres can provide brochures and leaflets on these trails.

Sport and Leisure

Seaside Resorts

The beautiful sandy Belgian coast boasts a series of lively seaside resorts each with a character of its own. There are the well-known resorts featuring traditional facilities and entertainment; Blankenberg provides fun for all the family, whereas elegance and sophistication are the hallmarks of Knokke Heist and Ostend. Then come a series of family resorts such as De Haan, Koksijde and Middelkerke; and finally the tranquillity of more peaceful centres for the nature lover, including Westende and De Panne. There is free access to the dunes and beach almost everywhere and most beaches have hire facilities (deckchairs, sunloungers, parasols and windscreens). In the major resorts there are beach huts for rent per week or per month; the tourist office can provide the addresses of local rental firms.

All the resorts have one thing in common: great stretches of golden sandy beach which are sometimes 500m/1 600ft wide at low tide. These are ideal for strolling barefoot at the water's edge, for taking the dog for a brisk and invigorating walk, for an early morning or late evening ride, or for sand-yachting, speed sailing (windsurfing on the beach) and skim-boarding.

SWIMMING

Large signs on the beach or promenade indicate the areas supervised by lifeguards, and flags warn bathers of possible risks: green – safe bathing; yellow – be careful; red – bathing prohibited. When the yellow flag is up it is dangerous to take inflatable mattresses and dinghies into the sea; it is also dangerous to use them when the tide is receding. Lifeguards are normally on duty between 10am and 6pm.

WINDSURFING, SURFING AND SKIM-BOARDING

The Belgian coast is ideal for windsurfing, but for safety reasons, on popular beaches, windsurfers must set out from the specifically designated areas. The following resorts are popular with surfers: Bredene, De Panne, Knokke-Heist, Nieuwpoort, Ostend, Wenduine, Westende and Zeebrugge. Surfing is possible at Ostend and skim boarders can be seen "skimming along" at the water's edge.

SAND-YACHTING AND SPEED-SAILING

The great expanses of hard sand at low tide are ideal for sand-yachting and one of the more popular stretches of

Ch. Bastin – J. Evrard/MICHELIN

Planche à voile à Knokke.

coast for this sport is between De Panne and Oostduinkerke. Speed-sailing or windsurfing on wheels is growing in popularity.

Cycling

The flatter countryside of Flanders is good for cycling and has many cycle paths. A long-distance route, the Grote Route 5, links Bokrijk in Belgium to Bergen op Zoom in the Netherlands. There are a large number of brochures in Dutch for special cycling tours. A bicycle can be hired from one railway station and returned to another; it is best to book ahead. Reductions are offered to people with a railway ticket and to those who hire for more than three days.

Walking

Both Belgium and the Grand Duchy of Luxembourg have excellent networks of clearly marked footpaths, particularly in the Ardennes. Grande Randonnée or GR (long-distance) footpaths are marked on Michelin maps 533 and 534.

BELGIUM

The network of **marked footpaths** covers 4 750km/2 952mi. The main footpaths are: GR 5 (Holland-Mediterranean), linking Rotterdam to Nice via the province of Liège (Spa, Liège) and the Grand Duchy of Luxembourg; GR AE (Ardennes-Eifel, part of European footpath 3) crossing the Ardennes from west to east through the Semois Valley; GR 12 (Brussels-Paris); GR 56 (Eastern Townships, Hautes-Fagnes, Helle Valley); GR 57 (Ourthe footpath linking Liège to the Grand Duchy); GR 129 (Scheldt-Meuse) linking Bruges with the Meuse Valley; GR 126 linking Brussels to the Semois Valley. There is also an interesting

range of circular footpaths and footpaths in the Kempen region.
Two walking associations, **Sentiers de Grande Randonnée** (B.P. 10, 4000 Liège) and **Grote Routepaden** (Van Stralenstraat 40, 2060 Antwerpen, ☏ 03 232 72 18), publish the quarterly periodical *GR Infos Sentiers et Wandelen GR* and have maps and literature on all the footpaths.
Elsewhere, public woods and recreation centres often have footpaths indicated by a special symbol depicting hikers. At the entrance to several nature reserves, routes for walks are suggested, with an indication of the length of the walk and posts painted in bright colours to act as markers.

GRAND DUCHY OF LUXEMBOURG

The national network of **footpaths**, marked in yellow, covers about 720km/447mi and is at its most dense around the main tourist centres of Diekirch, Echternach and Clervaux. The GR 5 crosses the country *(see above)*.
Leaflets and small maps are available from tourist offices. Topographical maps (1:20 000) are on sale in bookshops or at the central office of the Youth Hostel Association *(see Accommodation)*.
Similarly there are 171 **drive-and-walk** routes and 25 **train-and-walk** routes. These vary in length from 5-15km/3-9mi and enable tourists to leave their car and go for a walk in areas of particular interest or natural beauty, using footpaths designed to return to the point of departure. There is a guide of such walks on sale in bookshops; the guide of the train-and-walk routes is available from the central office of the Youth Hostel Association and from bookshops.

Sport

CANOEING

Several stretches of river are suitable for canoeing. Canoes can be easily rented on the Ourthe, the Semois, the Sûre and the Amblève. Going down the River Lesse by canoe or boat is an unforgettable experience *(see DINANT: Excursions)*. The **Fédération Royale Belge de Canoë** can be contacted at Geerdegemvaart 79, 2800 Mechelen, ☏ 015 41 54 59.

WATER-SKIING

Water-skiing can be enjoyed on the Upper Meuse (at Wépion, Profondeville, Yvoir and Waulsort), in Liège, Mons, Manage and Ronquières, on Lake Eau d'Heure and on the Albert Canal. For further information contact the **Fédération Francophone du Ski Nautique Belge**, rue de Tervaete 11, 1040 Brussels, ☏ 02 734 93 73.

YACHTING

There are marinas along the coast at Zeebrugge, Blankenberge, Ostend and Nieuwpoort. Useful addresses include the **Ligue Régionale du Yachting Belge**, avenue du Parc d'Armée 90, 5100 Jambes, ☏ 081 30 49 79; **Landelijke Bond van Watersportverenigingen in België**, IJzerweglaan 72, 9050 Ledeberg, ☏ 09 232 36 24; **Vlaamse Vereniging voor Watersport**, Beatrijslaan 25, 2050 Antwerpen, ☏ 03 219 69 67.

SHOOTING AND WILDFOWLING

Small game and wildfowl are to be found mainly to the north of the valley of the Sambre and its continuation along the Meuse, while large game (boar, stags, roe-deer) is mostly confined to the Ardennes. It is compulsory to have either a shooting permit or game licence. For further information contact the **Royal St-Hubert Club**, 410, avenue Lambermont, 1030 Bruxelles, ☏ 02 248 25 85.

FISHING

Belgium offers opportunities for all sorts of angling. It is compulsory to have a fishing permit valid for a year, which can be obtained from a post office. Further details from: Service de la Pêche du Ministère de la Région Wallonne, avenue Gouverneur Bovesse 100, 5100 Jambes ☏ 081 32 74 88; www.wallonie.be

Cavaliers sur la plage.

Ch. Bastin – J. Evrard/MICHELIN

HORSE RIDING

There are riding stables throughout Belgium and Luxembourg. Certain agencies organise horse-riding weekends. Horse racing takes place at Ostend, Groenendael, Watermael-Boitsfort, Kuurne and Sterrebeek (trotting), Waregem (steeplechase). Belgium's national equestrian association is the **Fédération Belge des Sports Équestres**, Avenue Houba de Strooper 156, 1020 Brussels, ☏ 02 478 50 56. Information on horse races can be obtained from the **Jockey Club de Belgique**, Chaussée de La Hulpe 53, 1180 Brussels, ☏ 02 672 72 48.

ROCK CLIMBING
A few of the rock faces overhanging the rivers of the Ardennes are sheer enough for rock climbing. Details about rock-climbing *(alpinisme)* in Belgium can be obtained from the **Club Alpin Belge**, 129, avenue Albert I, 5000 Namur, ☎ 081 22 40 84, www.clubalpin.be

WINTER SPORTS
The Ardennes climate is harsh enough for there to be occasional substantial snowfalls between December and March, and in a number of places there are facilities for downhill and cross-country skiing and for tobogganing. For further information contact the tourist offices of the provinces of Liège and Luxembourg *(see Useful Addresses)*.

OTHER SPORTS
Belgians are passionate about cycle racing; one of the country's national heroes was Eddy Mercx, who won the Tour de France no fewer than five times. Among the many races and tournaments is the Tour of Flanders, which incorporates the notorious uphill section at Geraardsbergen known in French as the "Mur de Grammont".
Other popular sports and pastimes include swimming, tennis, bowling, pigeon-racing and **balle-pelote**, a ball game of ancient origin played, with some local variations, throughout Wallonia.
A brochure published by the national tourist office of the Grand Duchy of Luxembourg gives useful information about sports there.

Entertainment

CINEMA AND THEATRE
Films are usually shown in their original language with subtitles in Flanders, or dubbed into French in Wallonia. In Brussels and Wallonia, **plays** are staged in French. The Luxembourg tourist office publishes the Agenda Touristique six times a year which lists entertainments *(see Calendar of Events at the end of this section)*.

MUSIC
Belgians are great music-lovers and there are numerous **concerts** throughout the year, especially during festivals. From September to May, there is **opera** in Antwerp, Brussels, Ghent, Liège, Mons, Verviers and Charleroi, all of which have an opera house, as well as in Namur and Tournai.

ARTS FESTIVALS AND EVENTS
In summer and autumn there are two major festivals, the **Flanders Festival** and the **Wallonia Festival**. These include various types of performances (opera, concerts, recitals, ballet) in various towns throughout the country, usually set against the magnificent backdrop of an ecclesiastical building (church or cathedral) or a castle.

For further information on the Flanders Festival, contact the Secrétariat du Festival de Flandres, Kleine Gentstraat 46, 9051 St-Denijs-Westrem, ☎ 09 243 94 94. For further information on the Wallonia Festival contact the Secrétariat du Festival de Wallonie, 20, rue de l'Armée Grouchy, 5000 Namur, ☎ 081 73 37 81.

The **Europalia Festival** takes place every two years with a large number of events staged all over the country (theatre, music, literature, exhibitions, cinema, ballet). For details about the programme contact the Fondation Europalia International in Brussels on ☎ 02 507 85 94, or the Belgian Tourist Information Service on ☎ 0891 88 77 99 (60p per minute).

CASINOS
Last but not least, Belgium has no fewer than eight **casinos** open all year round in Blankenberge, Knokke, Ostend and Middelkerke on the coast, and Dinant, Chaudfontaine, Spa and Namur inland.

For entertainment in Luxembourg, consult the brochure available from the Luxembourg tourist office and the Calendar of Events section at the end of the guide.

Books

ART & ARCHITECTURE

Art Deco – A Duncan
(Thames & Hudson 1988)

Contemporary Architecture –
Geert Bekaert (Lannoo Publishers 1998)

*Flemish and Dutch Painting:
From Van Gogh, Ensor, Magritte
and Mondrian to Contemporary Artists* –
R Herman Fuchs (Ed), J Hoet (Ed),
R Fuchs (Ed) (Rizzoli Publications 1997)

The Art of the Northern Renaissance –
Craig Harbison (Weidenfeld Illustrated
1995)

Symbolism and Art Nouveau –
A MacKintosh (Barron's Educational
Series 1978)

From Van Eyck to Brueghel –
Max Friedlander (Phaidon Press 1998)

Art Nouveau in Belgium – Pierre Loze,
Francois Loze (Exhibitions International
1991)

Art Nouveau Architecture – Junichi
Shimomura (Academy Editions 1992)

Art Nouveau – Alastair Duncan
(Thames & Hudson 1994)

Art Nouveau – Stephen Escritt
(Phaidon Press 2000)

Rubens: A Double Life – Marie-Anne
Lescourret, Elfreda Powell (Trans)
(Ivan R Dee Publisher 1993)

Rubens – Kristin Lohse Belkin
(Phaidon Press 1998)

Early Flemish Painting – Jean-Claude
Frere (Editions Pierre Terrail 1997)

Brussels: Fin de Siècle – Philippe
Roberts-Jones (Taschen 1999)

LITERATURE & FICTION

Niccolò Rising – Dorothy Dunnett
(Penguin Books 1988)

Desire – Hugo Claus, Stacey Knecht
(Trans) (Viking Books 1997)

A House in Flanders – Michael Jenkins
(Minerva 1993)

The Folding Star – Alan Hollinghurst
(Vintage 1995)

Resistance – Anita Shreve
(Abacus 1996)

The Poisonwood Bible – Barbara
Kingsolver (Faber & Faber 2000)

Georges Simenon's famous "Maigret"
series are available in translation: some
are published in the Penguin Modern
Classics series.

GENERAL & TRAVEL

Blue Guide Belgium – Derek Blyth
(A & C Black 2000)

Flemish Cities Explored – Anthony
Blunt (Pallas Athene 1999)

A Tall Man in a Low Land – Harry
Pearson (Little, Brown & Co 1999)

The Great Beers of Belgium – Michael
Jackson (Prion Books Ltd 1997)

A Belgian Cookbook – Juliette Elkon
Hamelcourt (Hippocrene Books Inc
1996)

*Culture Shock! Belgium: A Guide to
Customs and Etiquette* – Mark Elliott
(Kuperard 2001)

Xenophobes Guide to the Belgians –
Anthony Mason (Ravette Books 1996)

Tintin, Hergé and his Creation –
H Thompson (Sceptre 1992)

Wallonia: Le Guide (Casterman 1994)
(in English)

HISTORY & POLITICS

Passchendaele – Robin Prior, Trevor
Wilson (Yale University Press 1997)

Civilisation – Kenneth Clark
(Penguin Books 1993)

Medieval Flanders – David Nicholas
(Longman Higher Education 1992)

The Dutch Revolt – Geoffrey Parker
(Penguin)

The Politics of Belgium – John
Fitzmaurice (C Hurst & Co 1996)

The King Incorporated – Neal Ascherson
(Granta Books 1999)

King Leopold's Ghost – Adam Hochschild
(Macmillan 2000)

Waterloo 1815 – Geoffrey Wooten, Brian
Fosten (Illustrator) (Osprey 1999)

*Outrageous Fortune: the Tragedy of King
Leopold of the Belgians 1901-1941* –
Roger Keyes (Secker & Warburg 1984)

*A New Guide to the Battlefields of
Northern France and the Low Countries*
– Michael Glover (Michael Joseph)

Events and Festivals

The following list includes the principal events among the many that take place. Other events are described in the main body of the text. Detailed lists are provided by the Belgian and Luxembourg tourist offices.

Belgium

Saturday, Sunday and Monday after Epiphany
Festival of Fools   **Ronse**

Thursday, Saturday, Sunday, Monday and Shrove Tuesday
Carnival★★ and Rosenmontag   **Eupen**

Saturday, Sunday, Monday and Shrove Tuesday
Carnival (*see BLANKENBERGE*)   **Blankenberge**
Carnival★ (*see MALMÉDY*)   **Malmédy**

Sunday, Monday, Shrove Tuesday
Carnival (*see AALST*)   **Aalst**
Carnival★★★ (*see BINCHE*)   **Binche**

Every Sunday in Lent
Passion Play at 3.30pm (booking advisable, **Ligny**
contact the Syndicat d'Initiative. ☎ 071 88 80 57

Refreshment Sunday (mid-Lent)
Carnival (*see HALLE*)   **Halle**
Carnival pageant with "Chinels"   **Fosses-la-Ville**
(*see NAMUR: Excursions*)
Carnival pageant (*see MAASEIK*) **Maaseik**
Carnival parade★★ with Blancs-Moussis **Stavelot**
(*see STAVELOT*)

Last Sunday in February
Folklore pageant and Krakelingen-throwing **Geraardsbergen**
(*see GERAARDSBERGEN*)

First Saturday in March
Dead Rat Ball (*see OOSTENDE*) **Ostend**

Good Friday
Procession of the Penitents at 8pm **Lessines**
(*see LESSINES*)

Easter Monday
Procession of the Divine Redeemer at 11am **Hakendover**
(*see HAKENDOVER*)

Second Sunday in May
Cat Festival (every three years: 2003) **Ypres**
(*see IEPER*)

Sunday before Ascension Day
Procession of Our Lady of Hanswijk **Mechelen**

Ascension Day
Holy Blood Procession★★★ (*see BRUGGE*) **Bruges**

Ascension to weekend after Ascension
Harbour Festivals (*see BLANKENBERGE*) **Blankenberge**

Third Sunday in May
St Roch military marches (*see THUIN*) **Thuin**

Last Sunday in May
Maitrank Festival (*see ARLON*)   **Arlon**

Whit Saturday, Sunday and Monday
Matrimonial meal (*see SOIGNIES: Excursions*) **Écaussines-Lalaing**

Whit Sunday
Procession at 3pm (*see HALLE*)   **Halle**

Whit Monday
Military march (*see CHARLEROI*)   **Gerpinnes**
Grand Tour and Historical Pageant **Soignies**
(*see SOIGNIES*)

The Lumeçon in Mons

Trinity Sunday (week after Whit Sunday)
Grand Tour and military march **Walcourt**
(see WALCOURT)
The "Lumeçon" and Chariot of Gold Procession **Mons**
(see MONS)
Fiertel Procession *(see RONSE)* **Ronse**

First weekend in June
Commemorative march celebrating **Ligny**
Napoleon's last victory

Second weekend in June
Day of Four Parades *(see TOURNAI)* **Tournai**

Last weekend in June
Fishermen's Folk Festival *(see KOKSIJDE)* **Koksijde**
Shrimp Festival *(see KOKSIJDE)* **Oostduinkerke**

July
"Juillet Musical" and Summer **St-Hubert**
Academy courses
(see ST-HUBERT)
Blessing of the Sea *(see BLANKENBERGE)* **Blankenberge**
Procession (every seven years: 2002) **Tongeren**
(see TONGEREN)

July – August
Theatre performances in the abbey **Villers-la-Ville**
Vacances-Théâtre, then Festival **Stavelot**
of Chamber Music *(see STAVELOT)*

First Thursday in July
Ommegang Procession at 9pm **Brussels**
(see BRUXELLES). Bookings via TIB, Grand-Place.
☎ 02 513 89 40

First Friday, Saturday and Sunday in July
International Open-Air Festival of Pop **Torhout-Werchter 533** *(1)*
and Rock Music **N17**

Sunday after 5 July
St Godelieve Procession **Gistel**
(see OOSTENDE: Excursions

Mid-July
World Folklore Festival **Schoten 533 L15** *(1)*
Francofolies Festival *(see SPA)* **Spa**

Third week in July
Fêtes Gantoises *(see GENT)* **Ghent**

Sunday nearest to 22 July
    Military march *(see CHARLEROI)*   **Jumet**

Last Sunday in July
    Procession of the Penitents★★ at 3.30pm   **Veurne**
    (see VEURNE)

August
    Spa Festival of Theatre *(see SPA)*   **Spa**
    Virga Jesse Madonna Procession   **Hasselt**
    (every seven years: 2003) *(see HASSELT)*

First or second Sunday in August
    "A Tribute to Flemish Painting" parade   **Koksijde**
    (see KOKSIJDE)

14, 15, 16 August
    Carpet of Flowers on the Grand-Place   **Brussels**
    (years ending in an even number)

15 August
    "Anno 1900" Festival *(see VEURNE)*   **Veurne**

Sunday after 15 August
    Military march *(see CHARLEROI)*   **Ham-sur-Heure**

Fourth Sunday in August
    Ducasse★★ *(see ATH)*   **Ath**

Thursday after the fourth Sunday in August
    Parade of Giants at 8pm   **Dendermonde**
    (see DENDERMONDE)

Last Sunday in August
    Brueghel Festival★★: parade in costume,   **Wingene 533 E16** *(1)*
    with some scenes reproducing paintings
    by Pieter Brueghel, followed
    by a Brueghel-style dinner
    Procession of floral floats   **Blankenberge**
    (see BLANKENBERGE)

End of August
    Grape Festival *(see LEUVEN: Excursions)*   **Overijse**

Tuesday following the last Sunday in August
    Flanders Steeplechase   **Waregem**
    (see OUDENAARDE: Excursion)

First weekend in September
    International Days of Hunting and Nature   **St-Hubert**
    (see ST-HUBERT)

Third weekend in September
    Wallonia Festival: Battle of the Stilt-walkers   **Namur**
    (see NAMUR)
    Hop Festival (every three years: 2002)   **Poperinge**

29 September or the following Sunday
    St Gertrude Procession *(see NIVELLES)*   **Nivelles**

Sunday after 11 October
    Procession *(see LIER)*   **Lier**

3 November
    St-Hubert's Festival *(see ST-HUBERT)*   **St-Hubert**

Sunday after 1 November
    Candlelit Procession at 2.30pm   **Scherpenheuvel**
    (see DIEST: Excursion)

Sunday before 14 November
    Pilgrimage *(see TONGERLO)*   **Tongerlo**

December

                           Bruges, Brussels,
                           Liège, Cantons de l'Est,
    Christmas markets   **Antwerp**
    Walnut Fair *(see BASTOGNE)*   **Bastogne**

Luxembourg

Easter Monday
"L'Emais'chen" Festival *(see LUXEMBOURG)*   **Luxembourg**

Tuesday after Whitsun
Dancing procession at 9.30am   **Echternach**
(see ECHTERNACH)

May – June
International Festival of Classical Music   **Echternach**
(see ECHTERNACH)

July (every Friday, Saturday and Sunday)
Festival of Theatre and Music *(see WILTZ)*   **Wiltz**

September
Wine Festival at **Grevenmacher**   **Moselle Valley**
and **Schwebsange** *(see Vallée de la MOSELLE LUXEMBOURGEOISE)*

(1) A reference number for the relevant Michelin map is given for sights not described in the guide.

Glossary

Some tips on pronunciation of Flemish:
The diversity of dialects in Belgium makes it difficult to give a exact guide to the spoken language. Some sounds do not occur in English: beginners can only listen carefully and try to match these approximations to the sounds they hear around them.

h: is sounded *(het = the)*
j: yeh *(kindje = small child)*
s: is soft *(except in "mus(z)eum")*
ng: more "n" than "ng" *(Tongeren)*
ch/g: guttural, as Scottish "loch" *(Mechelen)*; noticeably softer, with more "h", in S. Belgium.
sch: two sounds: s + ch as above *(Aarschot)*
sch (at end of word): sh *(toeristisch)*
n (at end of word): usually silent

aa, ae: ah *(Laarne, Verhaeren)*
ee: eh *(meer, zee)*
ie: ee *(Tienen, Ieper)*
oo: oh *(Oostende)*
ij: ay *(Kortrijk, Rijssel)*: -lijk is closer to (short), unstressed "look"
oe: oo *(Doest)*
ou: ow *(Oudenaarde, Turnhout)*
ui: in N. Dutch, a more 'pursed' "ow", sounded at the front of the mouth; some dialects separate the sounds slightly: u-ee *(Diksmuide, St.-Truiden)*

Common Words

NB For restaurant terminology, consult the current Michelin Red Guide Benelux.

Dutch	French	English
U	vous	you
mijnheer	monsieur	Mr
mevrouw	madame	Mrs, Ms
juffrouw	mademoiselle	Miss
toegang, ingang	entrée, accès	entry, access
uitgang	sortie	exit
rechts; links	droite; gauche	right; left
koffiehuis	café	café
ja; nee	oui; non	yes; no
goedemorgen	bonjour	good morning
goedemiddag	bonjour	good afternoon
goedenavond	bonsoir	good evening
tot ziens	au revoir	goodbye
alstublieft	s'il vous plaît	please
hoeveel?	combien?	how much?
dank u (wel)/bedankt	merci (bien)	thank you (very much)
zegel	timbre	stamp

Tourist vocabulary

abdij	abbaye	abbey
beeld	statue	statue
beiaard	carillon	chimes
begijnhof	béguinage	beguine convent
belfort	beffroi	belfry
beurs	bourse	stock exchange
burcht	forteresse	fortress
eeuw	siècle	century
gesloten	fermé	closed
gevel	façade	façade, front
gids	guide	guide
Grote Markt	Grand-Place	market square
haven	port	port
hof	cour	court(yard)
huis	maison	house
kaai	quai	quay
kapel	chapelle	chapel
kasteel	château	castle
kerk	église	church
kerkschat	trésor	treasury
koninklijk	royal	royal
koster	sacristain	sacristan

kunst	art	art
kursaal	casino	casino
lakenhalle	halle aux draps	cloth hall
meer; zee	lac; mer	lake; sea
molen	moulin	(wind)mill
museum	musée	museum
natuur-	réserve	nature
reservaat	naturelle	reserve
O.L.Vrouw	Notre-Dame	Our Lady
oost; west	est; ouest	east; west
oud, oude	vieux	old, former
pastoor	curé	priest
paleis	palais	palace
plein	place	square
poort	porte	gate
schilderij	peinture	painting
sleutel	clé	key
stadhuis	hôtel de ville	town hall
stedelijk	municipal	town-
straat	rue	road, street
toren	tour	tower
tuin	jardin	garden
uitzicht	vue, panorama	view
verdieping	étage	floor
vleeshuis	halle aux viandes	meat market
wandeling	promenade	walk

Road vocabulary

doorgaand verkeer	voie de traversée	through traffic
fiets; fietsen	bicyclette(s)	cycle(s)
ijzel	verglas	ice
let op, opgelet	attention	Look out!
moeilijke doorgang	passage difficile	poor road
schijf verpflicht	disque obligatoire	(parking) disc compulsory
uitgezonderd		
plaatselijk verkeer	excepté circulation locale	local traffic only
uitrit	sortie	exit
weg	chemin	path
wegomlegging	déviation	detour
werken, werkzaamheden	travaux	roadworks

The Ardennes.

K. Stratton/EXPLORER

Insights
and Images

Little countries with a lot to offer

At the heart of Europe in every sense, Belgium and Luxembourg are finally stepping out of the cultural shadows of their larger neighbours. First-time visitors will be surprised and delighted by what they find: green open spaces and bustling cities, a treasure-trove for art lovers and paradise for gourmets!

Ch. Bastin-J. Evrard/MICHELIN

Between North and South

Belgium and Luxembourg have been the meeting point of Roman and Germanic Europe for over 2 000 eventful years. Creative and ever-evolving, their culture is one of diversity and finds its truest expression in the nations' three official languages – Dutch, French and German in Belgium, Letzeburgesch, German and French in Luxembourg. While the delicate balancing act between two distinct language communities in Brussels has made the "compromis à la belge" a national metaphor, the Grand Duchy's own language, born on the banks of the Moselle, combines echoes of both French and German. In these outward-looking countries, tradition and local pride still run deep, and it was this spirit of openness and unity in variety which made Brussels and Luxembourg the natural choices for Europe's twin capitals of justice and government.

Young nations with a glorious past

Though it was only in the 19C that Belgium and Luxembourg became nations in their own right, their history has been filled with the illustrious ring of great names. This was the birthplace of the Crusader Godefroy de Bouillon, the "perfect Christian knight" and the mighty Charles V, who laid claim to the first empire "on which the sun never sets". Here, too, Julius Caesar won glory and crossed swords with "the bravest of all the Gaulish peoples". Tournai, Brussels, Bruges and Ghent were the prize possessions of the Burgundian lords; opulent trading towns built on matchless linen, lace and tapestries which were the envy of Europe. Hapsburgs, Spanish, Austrians, French and Dutch all fought for this vast fortune and strategic position, and each dynasty added to a wealth of culture and history.

An abundance of art and culture

Belgium's cities of art are a true revelation: Bruges' romantic canals and quiet convent, Ghent's mighty towers, Antwerp's Gothic cathedral and charming old town and, above all, the magnificent Grand-Place and Art Nouveau heritage of Brussels. These were the towns where Van Eyck, Brueghel and Rubens captivated kings and emperors with the richness and refinement of Flemish art. Nowadays, these fabulous treasures are no longer the privilege of princes, and

Time out in the Grand-Place, Brussels.

the perfectly preserved mediaeval towns are as breathtaking as ever. But why stop there when historic Liège, the citadel of Namur, Tournai cathedral, Luxembourg's Gründ and the castle of Vianden are all waiting to be discovered? Home to the world's finest Art Nouveau and Art Deco design, Belgium also fostered the painters of the Modernist avant-garde, firing the imaginations of Magritte, Ensor and Delvaux.

Sport and nature in perfect harmony

Between the North Sea sands and the highland forests of the Eifel, there is a huge variety of landscapes to explore. The well-known "flatlands" of dunes and polders, celebrated in song by Jaques Brel, give way to picturesque "Little Switzerland", the rolling landscapes of the Pajottenland and the unspoilt valleys of Wallonia. The great outdoors beckons: hire a bike and explore the coast, the pretty Limbourg countryside or the villages along the banks of the Scheldt, try rock-climbing at Marche-les-Dames, head for the Hautes Fagnes ski slopes, fish the lakes and streams of Luxembourg or strike out along one of the charming walking trails which criss-cross the countries.

A love of the good life

On both sides of the border, enthusiasm and imagination come to the fore at the dinner table, dispelling any myths that the Belgians and Luxembourgeois don't know how to enjoy themselves! Finely balanced dishes combine high culinary art with rich flavours from the medieval banquet, leading you off on a tour of regional delicacies in all their brilliant variety. Who could resist the sweetest, crispiest waffles from Brussels and Liège, delicious pralines from the world's best *chocolatiers*, a brisk shot of genever in a local bar, an effervescent abbey beer, overflowing with scents and flavours, or a cool, sparkling Moselle? Mussels are a must, and so too are authentic, twice-fried Belgian chips from a "friterie", with mayonnaise for the real connoisseur. But be warned: as with so much on offer in Belgium and Luxembourg, you may find yourself going back for more!

Language and Government

The administrative and political organisation of Belgium and the Grand Duchy of Luxembourg has been greatly influenced by the multilingualism of both countries. In the case of Belgium, this has led to state and local structures of considerable complexity.

Belgium

A Trilingual Country

Three languages are spoken in Belgium: Dutch *(nederlands)* in Flanders (60% of the Belgian population), French *(français)* in Wallonia (39%) and German *(deutsch)* in the Eupen area (slightly less than 1%). While the various dialects spoken in Flanders are referred to as Flemish *(vlaams)*, and there are numerous differences in vocabulary and pronounciation between the Dutch of the Netherlands and that of Flanders, there is no Flemish language as such. Walloon dialects are quite distinct from standard French, but are generally only spoken by older people. The linguistic border between Dutch and French corresponds roughly to the boundaries between the provinces of Flanders and those of Wallonia. Brussels is a sort of enclave within the Flemish region, being bilingual with a French-speaking majority.

The Linguistic Quarrel

The linguistic divide dates back as far as the 5C, when the Romans abandoned the north of the country to the Germanic tribes. The Gallo-Roman language in the south resisted Germanic influence despite occupation of the area by the Salian Franks. The Germanic term "Walha" (the origin of the words "Walloon" and "Welsh") meant "foreigner" to the Franks.

Literature in Dutch developed in Flanders from the 12C, but disappeared almost entirely after the break from the Netherlands at the end of the 16C. Spoken mostly by an uneducated rural population, the Dutch of Flanders degenerated into a jumble of local dialects. Its sudden elevation to an official language when Belgium formed part of the Kingdom of the Netherlands between 1814 and 1830 proved unpopular, and educated and ambitious Flemings continued to use French, the language of the court, government and high culture. The frequently fraught and always complex relationship between Belgium's two principal linguistic communities has tended to dominate the country's domestic history, with advances in the status of Dutch bitterly contested by French speakers and equally fiercely defended by adherents of the "Flemish Movement". The dates given below mark some of the key points in the evolution of this relationship.

The Equality Law (also called the Coremans-De Vriendt Law) of 1898 decreed that all laws should be promulgated in both French and Dutch, thereby making the latter the country's second official language.

In 1932 regional monolingualism replaced bilingualism for administrative purposes, except in Brussels.

Language laws passed in 1962-63 established linguistic borders, dividing the country into four linguistic regions: Flanders (Dutch-speaking), Wallonia (French-speaking), a German-speaking eastern district, and the bilingual Brussels-Capital area (Dutch- and French-speaking) comprising the 19 communes of the city of Brussels.

Violent demonstrations, typified by the slogan *"Walen buiten!"*: "Walloons out!", led in 1968 to the splitting of the University of Leuven/Louvain. The French-speaking section migrated to a new foundation at Louvain-la-Neuve.

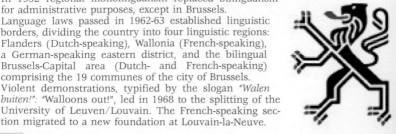

The reorganisation of the state in 1970 confirmed the existence of the four linguistic regions and recognised the existence of three cultural communities, French, Dutch, and German. Subsequent legislation has transformed what used to be a unitary state into a federation.

Federal Government

Belgium is a parliamentary, representative, constitutional monarchy. Its constitution dates from 1831 and has undergone several amendments, the last in 1993.

The king chooses the prime minister, who then forms his own government. Legislative power is exercised by the two chambers of parliament, the Senate (71 senators) and the Chamber of Representatives (150 deputies). Parliamentary elections are held by direct, universal suffrage every four years. The federal parliament is responsible for national finance, foreign policy, defence, justice, social security and the federal police force.

The Belgian state recognises three **communities**, Flemish, French and German. These communities are responsible for cultural matters, the use of language, education, and inter-community cooperation. They also oversee matters affecting the individual ie health and welfare. Except in the case of the German-speaking area in the east of the country, the communities are not defined in territorial terms.

The country is also divided into three **regions**, Flemish, Walloon, and the bilingual Brussels-Capital area. These regions are responsible for economic management, housing, employment, environment, agriculture, rural regeneration and nature conservation, planning and public works.

The Brussels-Capital Region consists of the 19 communes of the city of Brussels. The Wallonia Region comprises the five Walloon provinces of Hainaut, Namur, Liège, Walloon Brabant and Luxembourg, while the five provinces making up the Flanders Region are Antwerpen, Flemish Brabant, West Flanders, East Flanders and Limburg.

Each community and each region has a council or legislative assembly and an executive, except in the case of Flanders, where power is exercised by the council and the government of the Flemish community. Council representatives are elected every five years by universal suffrage.

Administrative divisions

Belgium is divided into 10 provinces. Each province has a capital with the seat of the provincial council.

Grand Duchy of Luxembourg

Languages

Three languages are spoken in the Grand Duchy of Luxembourg. Since 1984, Lëtzebuergesch, a variant of German similar to the Frankish dialect of the Moselle valley, has been the official language. High German is used for general purposes and is the first language for teaching. French is the literary and administrative language; it is taught in all schools and at all educational levels.

Political Organisation

The constitution dates from 17 October 1868 and has been revised several times, most recently in 1999. The Grand Duke holds executive power and is responsible for choosing a prime minister, who then appoints ministers and forms a government. Legislative power is exercised by the Chamber of Deputies, whose 60 members are elected every five years by direct universal suffrage.

Spellbinding Cities

Ch. Bastin – J. Evrard/MICHELIN

Fine civic structures such as belfries, town halls and covered markets are symbols of the municipal autonomy and medieval pride of Belgian cities, above all in the great art centres of Flanders. But it is not just on monuments like these that the country's urban charms depend; adding to their enchantment are tranquil canals, joyfully chiming carillons, peaceful convent precincts, and, not least, the cheerful atmosphere of the café and that characteristic Belgian institution, the estaminet.

Market Squares

The square (Grote Markt or Grand-Place) is lined by the town's main buildings, including the town hall, the covered market, the belfry and the guildhalls with their richly sculpted façades. This was once the focal point of the town, the place where the stocks were set up, where executions took place, and where markets, parades, fairs, festivals and major celebrations were held. The country's finest city squares are in Brussels, Bruges, Antwerp and Mechelen, though the biggest, 3.19ha/7.88 acres, is the Grote Markt in Sint Niklaas.

Bells

The carillon chimes regularly ring out their melodies in charming counterpoint to the rhythms of city life. Carillons were not always installed in the church tower (as at Antwerp and Mechelen), but sometimes in the municipal belfry (as at Bruges and Ghent).

The word "carillon" comes from the French *carignon*, meaning a group of four bells. The bells with their different chimes were connected to a clock (the first town clock appeared in 1370), and were set to play just before the sounding of the hour. They were tapped by hand with a hammer for many years. The first mechanical chimes, activated by the clock mechanism, were created in the 15C. The discovery of the manual keyboard, used for the first time in Oudenaarde in 1510, made it possible to increase the number of bells. In 1583 the invention of the pedal board in Mechelen enabled bass stops to be used, thus enriching the variety of sound possible. The art of founding the bells has been refined to a quite remarkable degree, so that most of the major carillons now consist of at least 47 bells. The most famous examples in Belgium are in Mechelen (49 bells), Bruges and Antwerp (47 bells), Nieuwpoort (67 bells), Ghent (52 bells) and Florenville (48 bells). The bell-ringers' school in Mechelen has an international reputation.

Jack-o'-the-clocks

From the 14C, many belfries were adorned with a clock incorporating a jack-o'-the-clock, a metal figure which strikes the hours by tapping a little bell with a hammer. Jack-o'-the-clocks are a delightful sight to be found in Kortrijk, Nivelles, Brussels (Mont des Arts), Virton, Lier and Sint-Truiden among other places.

Beguine Convents

The typical Beguine convent (begijnhof in Dutch, béguinage in French) is nowadays a place of great tranquillity, but this was not always so. Often sited a little off the beaten track and surrounded by walls, most Beguin convents were never-

The Begijnhof, Kortrijk.

theless hives of activity in their heyday, flourishing urban communities of widows and unmarried women. Their residents adhered to certain rules, wearing the approved costume, attending church services, and carrying out manual work. But unlike the religious orders, they were not obliged to swear vows of eternal poverty and chastity and were free to leave the community at any time. It was this that made the Beguine convents popular, particularly among single women, who were able to take refuge in them in troubled times. During the day, the residents were free to attend to various duties, caring for the sick, lace-making, sewing and knitting. As the convent closed its gates at nightfall they returned to the shelter of its walls. The community was led by a Superior known as the "grande demoiselle".

The origin of Beguine convents is unknown. The first establishment of this type is believed by some to have been founded by Lambert le Bègue in Liège at the end of the 12C, although their creation has traditionally been attributed to Saint Begga, who was the Mother Superior of a convent in Andenne, where she died in 694. By the 13C the typical Beguine convent had developed its definitive form as a little walled town within a town, with several gateways and with cottages laid out around a church. In 1566 many convents were destroyed by iconoclasts, but were then rebuilt at the end of the 16C and 17C.

Of the hundred or so 14C Beguine convents in the southern Low Countries, 25 have survived. Their Beguine sisterhoods are however no more, and they are now occupied by other religious communities (Benedictines in

Bruges), retired people, cultural institutions or, as at Leuven, by university students and lecturers. In 1998, thirteen Flemish Beguine convents were placed on the UNESCO World Heritage List: Hoogstraten, Lier, Mechelen, Turnhout, Sint-Truiden, Tongeren, Dendermonde, Ghent (Klein Begijnhof), Sint-Amandsberg, Diest, Leuven (Groot Begijnhof), Bruges and Kortrijk.

Almshouses

Financed by the guilds, these were a sort of sanctuary for the old or the poverty-stricken. They were rows of low, whitewashed

The Begijnhof, Bruges.

brick maisonettes, with a door and window surmounted by a high gable and chimney. Surviving almshouses include those at Bruges and the Alijn Children's Hospice in Ghent (now the Folklore Museum).

Estaminets

Estaminet is the Walloon word for a café. They are friendly places where people can meet and have a glass of beer, play cards and gossip. They are also a favourite gathering point for *coulonneux* (pigeon-fanciers). What better place to sit and watch the world go by over a cup of coffee? Famous Brussels estaminets include *In't Spinnekopke, La Grande Porte*, and *À la Bécasse*.

Land and Landscapes

From the coasts of Flanders facing the North Sea to the dense forests cladding the Ardennes, a great diversity of landscapes characterises Belgium, one of Europe's smaller countries. Beaches of fine sand, dunes, polders, undulating farmlands, heaths, valleys and uplands make up an ever-changing but harmonious picture. Likewise, little Luxembourg is an appealing combination of river valleys, glorious forests, and bold escarpments.

BELGIUM

Belgium covers an area of 30 513km2/11 781 sq mi, and has a population of 10 263 414 (January 2001). With 336 inhabitants per km^2, it is one of Europe's most densely populated countries. The movement of people and goods benefits from an excellent infrastructure, including numerous navigable waterways and a dense road network, and commuting between home and workplace is highly developed.
The country is divided into three regions.

Lower Belgium *(up to 100m/328ft in altitude)*

Lower Belgium consists of the provinces of **Antwerpen** (pop 1 645 652, capital Antwerp), **Limburg** (pop 794 785, captial Hasselt), **Oostvlaanderen/East Flanders** (pop 1 363 672, capital Ghent), and **Westvlaanderen/West Flanders** (pop 1 130 040, capital Bruges).

The coast
The 70km/44mi of straight coastline is the only part of Belgium which borders the sea. The beautiful beaches of fine white sand have made this coast a highly popular holiday venue, but have not made it easy to build ports. The only natural harbour is the mouth of the River IJzer (Yser) where the port town of Nieuwpoort is located. Zeebrugge is a man-made fishing port.
The coast has developed beyond recognition since the Middle Ages and is now bounded by sea-dikes or by a broad belt of dunes. In the past, it was marshy land criss-crossed by an infinite number of waterways. Over the years, these gradually became choked with mud, as in the case of the silting up of the Zwin tributary, which ruined Bruges as a centre of trade. Human effort completed the work of nature by creating a polder area on the landward side of the dunes.

The Polders
Although they are not the size of the Dutch ones, Belgian polders were created in the same way. They were once marshlands, which have been drained and dried out, and which are now protected against the tides by sluices. They extend over a vast area, their fertile soils the basis for a prosperous agriculture.

Kempen
These lowlands between the Scheldt, the Meuse and the Demer extend over the provinces of Antwerpen, Brabant and Limburg and into the Netherlands. Huge quantities of sands and pebbles deposited by the rivers have created a marshy and infertile landscape where only pines and heather grow on the poor soil.

The Belgian Coast.

Mesnil-Église.

Although the Kempen now has few inhabitants, it was once a favourite place for monks to build their monasteries (Postel, Westmalle and Tongerlo). Some of the land was reclaimed and cultivated in the 19C, while other areas were taken over by the armed forces (Leopoldsburg, founded in 1850). In the 20C, the region became the home of the Centre of Nuclear Studies at Mol (1952) as well as of a number of industrial concerns, attracted by the presence of the Albert Canal built in 1939. The only valuable natural resource is coal. This was discovered at the end of the 19C near Genk, but the coal seams have been gradually abandoned because it is no longer cost-effective to work them.

The sandy west

This region, with its occasional valleys, extends between the coast and the polders and the Leie and Scheldt. Several peaks are all that remain of the more resistant strata, among them the Kemmelberg, Kluisberg and Mont St Aubert.

The land is cultivated much more intensively here than in the Kempen, and the area is far more densely populated. The cultivated fields are bounded by lines of poplars.

It is easy to reach the ancient strata, making it possible to create many quarries (porphyry in Lessines and Tournai). Some areas, like the **Houtland** near Torhout, are densely wooded. In the Middle Ages, the existence of waterways helped the development of the textile industry, which continues to flourish today around Kortrijk, Tournai and Ghent.

Central Belgium *(100-200m/328-656ft in altitude)*

The provinces of **Flemish Brabant** (pop 1 018 403, capital Leuven), **Walloon Brabant** (pop 352 018, capital Wavre), and **Hainaut** (pop 1 279 823, capital Mons), together with the **Brussels Capital Region** (pop 964 405), constitute the heart of the country. The region consists of a cretaceous plain, rising gradually towards the Ardennes massif to the south, finally reaching an altitude of about 200m/656ft. Its relatively fertile soil supports both arable and livestock farming.

The Haspengouw/Hesbaye plateau to the east and the Hainaut to the west are covered with a layer of very fertile loess. This is arable country, where villages tuck themselves away in valleys, and farms are large and isolated. The limestone, sandstone or brick buildings (the latter often whitewashed) usually surround a vast central courtyard, which is reached through a single, sometimes monumental, gateway. Where Central Belgium meets the Ardennes, the long valley excavated by the rivers Sambre and Meuse between Charleroi and Liège extends further into the Borinage area around Mons. Here coal-bearing strata are exposed, the basis for Belgium's most important **mining area**, with its concomitant metal-working industries along the "Sambre-Meuse line" around Liège, Charleroi and La Louvière.

The Ardennes

Namur (pop 445 824, capital Namur), **Liège** (pop 1 020 042, capital Liège) and **Luxembourg** (pop 248 750, capital Arlon) are the three provinces constituting Upper Belgium (Haute Belgique). The remains of an ancient, much eroded massif, the Ardennes are the westward extension of the Eifel uplands in Germany. Famous for the forests dating from the Roman period (the name "Ardennes" comes from the name of a goddess, Arduinna), the region can be divided into the Lower and Upper Ardennes.

Lower Ardennes

This series of plateaux, at an average altitude of 200-500m/656-1 640ft, extend southward from the Meuse. The Condroz is a moderately fertile region, composed of limestone and schist. The main town is Ciney. Entre-Sambre-et-Meuse lies south of Charleroi. The broad depressions of Famenne (main town: Marche-en-Famenne) and Fagne are typically damp, wooded regions of sandstone and schist. Deep, narrow valleys gouged out by the Lesse, Ourthe and Meuse run between these plateaux.

The humid Herve region, consisting mostly of pastureland, together with the Verviers region, is part of the Lower Ardennes. The border region south of Couvin, known as the Pays des Rièzes et des Sarts, is over 300m/984ft in altitude, and is one of the areas where the ancient rock foundation of the Ardennes is exposed.

Upper Ardennes

The area consists of plateaux and gently rounded summits rising to more than 500m/1 640ft. The most resistant ridges make up the inhospitable area of Hautes Fagnes, which includes the highest point in Belgium, the **Signal de Botrange** (694m/2 277ft). Peat bogs have developed on the water-logged, poorly drained ground here.

Considerable tracts of the Upper Ardennes have been planted with coniferous trees. The winding river valleys, such as that of the Amblève, are more welcoming. Lacking in natural resources and ill-favoured by the harsh climate and difficult access, the region did not develop at the same pace as the rest of the country for many years. It has now opened up to tourism.

The Belgian Lorraine (Arlon) and the Gaume (Virton) regions belong geologically to the southern part of Luxembourg.

GRAND DUCHY OF LUXEMBOURG

Covering an area of 2 585km²/998sq mi, the Grand Duchy of Luxembourg has a population of 441 092 (January 2001), a fifth of whom live in the capital, Luxembourg city (pop 81 804). The country consists of two very different geographical regions.

In the north, the **Oesling** (the Luxembourg Ardennes) is a plateau linking the Ardennes with the Eifel. At its highest point it reaches 559m/1 833ft (Buurgplaatz). Thinly populated like the Belgian Ardennes because of its harsh climate, the region's principal economic activity is tourism.

Godinne.

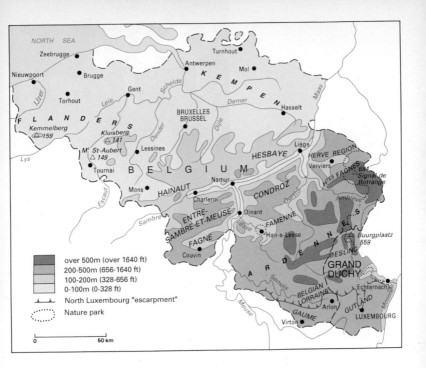

The **Gutland** (or "Bon Pays") to the south has a milder climate as it is at a lower altitude, sloping gently down towards French Lorraine. It is formed of superposed strata of sandstone and limestone, alternating with clay and marl which yield good arable soils. The Luxembourg vineyards are southeast of the Gutland, on the slopes overlooking the Moselle valley.

Where the hard rocks of the ancient upland massif meet softer formations, erosion has created "côtes", steep east-west running escarpments covered with beech forests. The northern escarpment stretches from the Arlon area to Echternach, running along the north of Luxembourg's "Little Switzerland". The southern escarpment extends along the border with France and carries on into Belgium to just south of Virton.

CAVES

The limestone areas of southern Belgium are famous for their caves, some of which have been an important tourist attraction for many years.

In the Lower Ardennes, an almost complete ring of rivers surrounds the Condroz plateau; the waters of the Meuse, Ourthe and Lesse have cut deep trenches through the schists and limestones and have hollowed out extensive cave systems, such as the Fondry des Chiens at Nismes or the Vallon des Chantoirs at Sougné-Remouchamps, where the caves are of the type known as "chantoirs".

Water percolating through the limestone dissolves it, forming subterranean rivers, which are sometimes just the underground stretch of a river which otherwise runs on the surface. The Lesse is an example of this, disappearing near Han to reappear 10km/6.25mi further on. It runs through the **Grotte de Han**, the most famous cavern in Belgium. The great chamber at the Grotte de Rochefort is equally impressive. In most cases the subterranean river has a tendency to cut deeper and deeper. Because of this, the old river bed higher up fills up only during floods. It can be a thrilling experience to take a boat along the course of an underground river, as at Remouchamps, where the trip covers about 1km/0.5mi.

The caves at Goyet, Furfooz, and Han were inhabited during the prehistoric period.

Concretions

Underground, the water deposits the limestone it has accumulated from filtering through the soil, thus forming the fantastic shapes of concretions. Stalactites, projections downwards from the roof, are the best known, along with stalagmites, columns rising up from the floor. Stalactites combine to form draperies, or fuse with a stalagmite to make a pillar.

Gravity-defying eccentrics are the delicate concretions produced by crystallisation, which often "grow" diagonally. Although they are generally white and formed of calcite, they are sometimes tinted with minerals: for example, iron oxide produces a reddish colour, and manganese gives a brownish one.

Festivals and Folklore

Archives Théâtre royal de Toone

From the colourful Fête des Chats in Ypres to the world-famous Carnival in Binche, popular festivals and local traditions continue to play an important part in Belgian life. Right through the year, fairs, processions, and pageants mark the red-letter days of the calendar and fill the streets and squares with crowds of convivial people.

See also the Calendar of Events in the Practical Points section

The religious or secular origin of these popular festivals often dates back many years and recalls legends or ancient mysteries. A history which has mixed people of diverse origin only serves to enrich this heritage, which is constantly being drawn upon; ancient customs are revived and new festivals added. In Flanders, the influence of the guilds has been strong, while in Wallonia, nearby Picardy has played an important role. Though non-locals are welcome to look on, visitors should remember that the festivals are not just for the tourists' sake; most reflect an old civic order, celebrate and reinforce the bonds of communities, guilds and associations and, as such, retain a private character and significance.

Everything is organised a long time in advance by the members of different "societies" or brotherhoods, who for several months pour their energies into preparing for the festival. When the big day comes, their members dress up in costume, meet old friends, have a meal and let the beer flow. Very little seems to have changed over the course of time; today's festivities would offer few surprises to Pieter Bruegel the Elder who painted the rollicking citizenry of the 16C with such verve.

Carnival

Carnival is celebrated almost all over Belgium. Probably of pagan origin, it takes place around Mardi Gras, or Shrove Tuesday, and was presented by the Catholic Church as a symbol of rejoicing before the period of Lenten fasting and penitence.

The three most famous carnivals in Belgium take place in **Binche**, **Eupen** and **Malmédy**. At Binche, the festivities last three whole days, with the celebrated **Gilles** only making their appearance on Shrove Tuesday. The privilege of wearing the Gilles' extraordinary costume is reserved for native-born male citizens of the town, who parade around the streets to the beat of the drum. In the afternoon, a huge procession takes place, with the Gilles hurling oranges among the spectators. The festival ends with a rondo in front of the town hall.

The German-speaking town of **Eupen** is known for its carnival, which resembles those in the nearby Rhineland. On the Monday **("Rosenmontag")** before Shrove Tuesday, cheerful bands of costumed revellers dance their way through the town, with the figure of Prince Carnival bringing up the rear.

Ch. Bastin – J. Evrard/MICHELIN

Traditional puppets at the Théâtre royal de Toone in Bruxelles.

As for **Malmédy**, the "Cwarmê" differs from other towns' carnivals with its satirical set-pieces performed in the local dialect. Best avoided are the town's infamous **Haguètes** who take great pleasure in pinching spectators' ankles with their long wooden pincers. Among the best-known carnivals in Flanders are those at Aalst and Ostend. In **Aalst**, the Sunday before Ash Wednesday is given over to a procession of giants as well as floats with tableaux passing satirical comment on the year's events. Monday is marked by **Ajuinworp**, a great throwing of onions, while Shrove Tuesday is dominated by the grotesquely costumed **Voil Jeannetten** ("mucky Janes" – men in drag). The carnival at **Ostend** takes place on the first weekend in March, and features a procession of a thousand lamps (Cimateirelichtstoet), a fancy-dress ball (the "Dead Rat Ball"), and a clog-hurling contest (Kloefenworp).

Lent

Mid-Lent, the Thursday of the third week in Lent, marks a break in this time of austerity and denial. It is celebrated enthusiastically at Stavelot with the **Blancs-Moussis**, droll figures in huge white hooded garments, with long red noses, who hark back to the period when the Stavelot Abbey monks participated in the carnival. They process through the town, scattering confetti and beating spectators with inflated pigs' bladders. The elegantly attired **Chinels**, irresistible Punch and Judy characters, parade in **Fosses-la-Ville**, tickling girls with their sabres and whipping the cigarettes from smokers' mouths. Mid-Lent is also celebrated with great gusto in Maaseik.

Every Sunday during Lent, **Ligny** stages a **Passion Play**, consisting of a series of tableaux inspired by the Gospels, which also make reference to the modern world. On Good Friday, **Lessines** is the scene of a famous **Penitents' Procession**; the participants, cloaked and hooded, carry the body of Christ and the Instruments of the Passion through the streets.

In the provinces of Antwerp and Liège, a Lenten custom is the beheading of a goose by horsemen. Other towns light great bonfires on which a guy is sometimes burnt. The most famous bonfire is the one at Geraardsbergen, the **"Tonnekensbrand"** involving the burning of a barrel and the throwing of Krakelingen biscuits.

Ch. Bastin – J. Evrard/MICHELIN

Giants and Puppets

Giants

Many festivals and carnival parades in Belgium feature giants. While the number of giants has increased since the beginning of the 20C, their popularity seems to date back to the 15C. The tradition began in Belgium and, because of the Spanish occupation, spread to Spain. The first giant character probably appeared in a religious procession or an Ommegang, in which he symbolised Goliath or St Christopher. Goliath is in fact still present at the great **ducasse** festival in **Ath**, where he is nicknamed Monsieur Gouyasse.

Secular characters gradually appeared at these events. Even Bayard the horse came to be included, ridden by the four Aymon sons (in Aalst, Dendermonde and Brussels). Giants appear also in Nivelles (Argayon, Argayonne, their son Lolo and the horse Godet), in Geraardsbergen, in Lier and in Arlon.

The more famous characters include Polydor, Polydra and little Polysorke in Aalst; Cagène and his companion Florentine in Belœil; Pie and Wanne and their son Jommeke in Tervuren; Count Baldwin IV the Builder and Alix of Namur in Braine-le-Comte.

Puppets

Puppet theatre appeared in Liège in the 19C and was a great success thanks to the famous Tchantchès character. The Liège puppet is moved by means of a rod fixed to the top of its head. It is carved out of wood, painted and covered with cloth. The repertoire draws as much on history as on legend and modern life, and is aimed mainly at adult audiences. Dating from the same period, the theatre founded by **Toone** in **Brussels** features the character Woltje, who speaks a wonderfully broad city dialect. Classics from the repetoire such as *The Four Aymon Brothers* and *Thyl Uylenspiegel* are complemented by newly-written items. Other dialect puppet theatres flourish in Antwerp, Ghent, and Mechelen.

Processions, Plays and Pageants

Processions

In the Middle Ages few people knew how to read, and over the course of the centuries the procession became a way of spreading knowledge of the Bible. In addition to the usual characters representing the Apostles, Prophets or Angels, there were also floats with tableaux illustrating biblical themes. Today, the processions often feature colourful episodes from secular history and in consequence have lost something of their original, strictly religious character.

The most impressive spectacle of this kind is undoubtedly the **Holy Blood Procession** in Bruges. Equally important is the festival of the **Virgin Virga Jesse** at Hasselt, held only once every seven years. Other festivals have a more rustic character, with the faithful following the statue or reliquary of the saint across the fields for quite long distances (over 30km/19mi in Ronse), praying and singing hymns as they go.

Plays and Pageants

Derived from religious and medieval origins, and bearing a resemblance to medieval mystery plays, these re-enact old legends during processions. Among the best-known is the one in **Rutten**, which evokes the death of St Evermeire in the 7C. In Mons, the Chariot of Gold (Car d'or) procession involves various guilds carrying figures of their patron saints and statues of the Virgin Mary. The Chariot of Gold itself, containing the relics of St Waudru, brings up the rear. Once the procession is over, the historic spectacle known as the **"Lumecon"** represents the struggle of Good with Evil.

At Ellezelles, the annual **Witches Sabbath** recalls the execution of five witches in 1610. In Vielsalm it is the **Macrâlles**, spell-casting witches, who star in a comic celebration, while in the **Fête des Chats** at **Ypres**, it is the witches' feline familiars who play the most important role, with toy cats being hurled from the town belfry in order to ward off witch-craft and the devil. In Wingene, the Bruegel Festival illustrates paintings by the great master.

Tchantchès.

The Blancs-Moussis

B. Foubert/GLOBAL PICTURES

Ducasses, Kermesses, and The May Tree

The Ducasse and the Kermesse
The words *ducasse* (from the Walloon *dédicace*) and *kermesse* (meaning "solemn Mass" in Dutch) now both designate a fête held in honour of the patron saint of a town or village. This holiday has retained certain aspects of its religious origins (Mass and procession) but now includes traditional games, competitions, and sometimes a fair and market. Mons and Ath are the settings for two well-known *ducasses*.

The May Tree
On 30 April, 1 May or during the month of May, certain towns such as Hasselt, Genk and Tongeren, solemnly plant a May tree as a symbol of renewal. In Brussels this tree is called the "Meyboom" or "Tree of Joy", and is planted every year in August.

Pageants and Military Parades

Historical Pageants
These vividly re-enacted, sumptuous pageants breathe new life into past grandeur. In Brussels, the annual Ommegang was first presided over by Emperor Charles V in 1549, while in Bruges, the quinquennial **Golden Tree Pageant** recalls the reign of the Dukes of Burgundy.

Military Parades
The military parades in the Entre-Sambre-et-Meuse region which begin at the end of May, date back to the 18C and probably owe their origin to the need to protect processions in troubled times. The strict ceremonial and the Napoleonic uniforms are very impressive. The best-known marches are those at Gerpinnes (35km), Ham-sur-Heure, and Thuin.

Festivals and Folk Customs
As well as the processions, parades and spectacles described above, Belgium has many other festivals and folk customs, for example the **Fêtes Gantoises** in Ghent, the **Fêtes de Wallonie** in Namur, and the **Fêtes d'Outremeuse** in Liège. For several days, the town is turned upside-down; strolling players and performers, marches, concerts, processions, puppets, stalls and stands, all create an atmosphere of extraordinary animation. A number of seaside places have Blessings of the Sea, while the resort of **Koksijde** stages an annual **Shrimp Festival** during which shrimping takes place in the traditional way on horseback.

Popular activities include **pigeon-fancying** and cock-crowing competitions. In the villages, people play skittles and balle-pelote, and indulge in archery. Virtuoso banner-waving and stilt-walking is a feature of historical pageants and popular festivals. Finally, the biggest children's event takes place on 6 December, when **St Nicholas**, accompanied by Bogeyman and his birch, brings them their presents.

The Delights of the Table

The Belgians are fond of the good life and appreciate the merits of a well-laden table. The famous "mussels and chips" are far from being the whole story; the country's cuisine

Waterzooi

offers an array of succulent, refined specialities, among them hearty "hochepot" stew, tasty Ardennes ham, delicious Flanders asparagus, spicy Herve cheese, divine "pralines", and waffles from Liège and Brussels – who could resist such temptations?

Belgium

For connoisseurs, the diversity and quality of Belgian food is no longer a secret. The country's culinary traditions have long been recognised as belonging to the finest in Europe, and while in many respects Belgian cuisine resembles that of France, its regional specialities lend it a special distinction.

Typical Dishes

Vegetable broth or clear beef or chicken soups known as **bouillons** are common starters to a meal, and are served with bread and butter. Ardennes ham or sausage, cold fish, seafood with mayonnaise, delicious shrimp rissoles or eels in a herb sauce, may also feature as an hors d'oeuvre.

The main course offers a choice of many regional specialities, including **waterzooi** from Ghent (chicken or fish stew), **Flanders hochepot** (casserole of pork, beef or mutton), **oie à la mode de Visé** (goose with a garlic sauce), or in the hunting season, a sample of the game in which the Ardennes abound.

Those who like fish and seafood will enjoy sole, trout, mussels, or **anguille au vert** (eel sautéed in butter with finely chopped parsley, chervil, sorrel, sage, citronella and tarragon). Fried to perfection, potato **chips** are a matter of national pride and may accompany virtually any main dish.

To end the meal on a deliciously sweet note, let yourself be tempted by a mouthwatering mixed fruit, rhubarb or sugar tart.

Meat, Fish and Poultry

The country's famous beers also feature in the preparation of a number of dishes, among them the **carbonades** of Flanders (beef braised in beer with onions, spices, vinegar and sugar) and **rabbit** stewed with prunes. Other meat dishes include choesels (offal with madeira sauce or mushrooms), filet américain (chopped raw beef), filet d'Anvers (smoked beef or horsemeat), and potjesvlees (terrine made from veal, rabbit or chicken). Coucou de Malines – Mechelen cuckoo – is a kind of chicken. Escavèche is fish fried and conserved in a marinade of herbs and spices, another speciality is Friture de la Moselle, small fried freshwater fish.

Vegetables

The country's tasty vegetable dishes include hop shoots in a mousseline sauce, a March speciality; chicory or Brussels witloof (endive) with ham, *au gratin* or braised; Brussels sprouts and Flanders asparagus, served with parsley or a chopped hardboiled egg.

Cheese

The country produces more than 80 delicious varieties of cheese. The best known are Herve, which since 1996 has had the status of an *Appellation d'Origine Protegée (AOP)*, Maredsous, Passchendaele, Chimay,

Nazareth, Orval and Brussels. Delicious cheesy snacks include doubles (pancakes with a Herve or Masedous filling) together with potkès or boulettes de Huy (salty cheese from Huy).

Bread and Cakes

Belgian chocolates and pralines (chocolates with creamy or nutty fillings) need no introduction, but Brussels and Liège waffles are appreciated just as much.

The country's bakeries offer a great variey of different kinds of **bread** and a number of regional specialities. They include couque (sugary, spicy bread from Brussels and hard spiced bread with honey from Dinant), craquelin (sugar-filled *brioche*), nœud (butter biscuit with brown sugar), cramique (milk bread with raisins), pistolet (small round loaf), and mastel (rusk bread with aniseed).

There are plenty of tasty **tarts**, among them Lierse vlaaikens (from Lier), tarte au maton (made with fromage frais, buttermilk and almonds), flamiche (made with local cheese and served hot), djote (with whitebeet, cheese, eggs, lardons and cream, served hot), and tarte au stofé (fromage frais, eggs, almonds and potato). Served with tea or coffee are speculoos (plain biscuit made with brown sugar), kletskoppen (fine butter biscuits with almonds and hazelnuts), mokken (macaroons flavoured with cinnamon or aniseed), spantôles (dessert biscuit perpetuating the name of a famous cannon), and lukken (small round buttery waffles). Also worth trying are manons (chocolates with a crème fraîche filling), babeluttes (hard toffees made with butter) and baisers de Malmédy – Malmédy kisses – (meringues filled with Chantilly cream).

Drinks

Beer is Belgium's national drink, *(see also The Land of Beer)* though most restaurant meals are accompanied by wine. A number of spirits and liqueurs are produced, notably Elixir d'Anvers (Antwerp elixir, a sweet and spicy liqueur), and Spa Elixir (rather like the *chartreuse* liqueur of France). Fruit (lemon, apple, gooseberry) and plain **gin** is distilled in Hasselt, while Liège gin is known as péket. The Maitrank from Arlon is an aperitif with a distinctive flavour.

Luxembourg

Among the gastronomic specialities of the Grand Duchy are sucking pig in aspic, smoked and cured ham from the Ardennes, and other smoked meats. The national dish is **Judd mat Gaardebounen**, smoked neck of pork with broad beans, which makes a hearty meal in itself. Game is eaten in season and freshwater fish are delicious fried or poached in Riesling.

These dishes are washed down with Moselle wines or with beer, the most popular drink. The liqueurs of Luxembourg – made with a variety of plums, blackcurrants, pears, elderberries and *marc* – have a good reputation.

In September, plum tart is eaten, and, in season, the little puff pastry crowns known as Veianer Kränzercher. **Kachkéis** is a salty country cheese.

Asparagus à la flamande
Belgian chips

The Land of Beer

Top or bottom fermented, pale or dark, sweet or bitter, light or heavy, fruity or spicy, clear or cloudy, Belgian beers

The Brasserie du Bocq in Purnode.

offer the drinker an unrivalled variety of tastes and textures.

Some 98 litres of beer are consumed by the average Belgian in the course of a year. The country boasts more than 100 breweries, the biggest being Stella Artois, Jupiler (part of the Interbrew group), and Alken-Maes. But in Belgium beer also comes from a number of abbeys, which continue a tradition dating back to the Middle Ages. Production was one of the privileges accorded to monasteries and for centuries beer was a far safer and more drinkable beverage than water.

The Brewing Process

Malt
Malt is obtained from barley, grown in huge quantities in northern Europe. The barley grains are germinated by soaking them in water; they are then dried and roasted in a kiln and milled, the whole process being known as **malting**; the resulting malt is the raw material of beer. Different kinds of malt are produced by variations in the drying process and it is these that give a beer its distinctive colour.

Brewing
Brewing consists of transforming the finely milled malt into a porridge-like **mash**. This is the most important stage in the process, involving the soaking of the mash in hot water and the consequent conversion of the starch in the malt into fermentable sugars. The type of beer obtained depends on the length of the period of infusion and the temperature chosen. Most breweries still use copper vats for this part of the process. The addition of hops gives beer its characteristic bitter taste.

Hops
The hop is a climbing plant which grows to a height of between five and seven metres. Hop-picking is carried out in September, the harvest consisting of the female flowers known as cones or strobiles. The main areas of hop-gardens in Belgium are around Aalst and Poperinge.

CANTILLON

Rosé de Gambrinus

Fermentation
Once the mash has cooled, fermentation begins, thanks to the action of yeast placed in the big fermentation vessels. The operation takes several days, during which alcohol is produced and carbon dioxide released. Depending on the temperature and the length of the fermentation process, three different kinds of beer are produced.

Types of Beer

Bottom-fermented beers
These are the pale beers commonly referred to as lagers or as "Pilsener" beers, "Pils" for short. Fermentation takes place at a low temperature (around 9 degrees), as does storage, or "lagering" (at 0 degrees). The best known Belgian lagers are Stella Artois, Jupiler, and Maes.

Top-fermented beers
These beers, or rather ales, are fermented at a relatively high temperature (around 24-28 degrees) and then undergo a kind of secondary fermentation in the cask or bottle (at around 13-16 degrees). Most so-called "special" beers are of this type.

Spontaneously fermented beers
In the case of these beers, which are unique to Belgium, fermentation is allowed to take place at its own pace, without the addition of yeast. The beer is matured over a long period, as much as three years, in old wine barrels, and is known as **Lambic**. According to the specialists, it is this process which produces the purest, most natural beer in the world.

Cheers!

There are more than 400 different beers in Belgium, promoted under more than 800 names. Make sure you never just ask for "a beer", but specify what it is you want, perhaps one of the almost infinite number of "specials".

Lambic
Lambic is used in the brewing of other kinds of beer. After being kept for a long period, the beer is drawn off into bottles in which a secondary fermentation takes place. The result is **Gueze**, a bubbly beer with a sharp taste. The red beer known as **Kriek**, gets its colour and its fruity taste from the cherries added to the lambic. **Framboise** is produced in a similar way, using raspberries. The best-known lambics are Belle Vue, St Louis and Gambrinus.

Trappist and Abbey Beers
The beers of Belgium's Trappist abbeys need no introduction. The five brews include Rochefort and Westfleteren, as well as Orval, Chimay and Westmalle with their worldwide reputation. But there are other abbey beers as well, among them Corsendonk, Leffe, Maredsous, Grimbergen and Affligem.

Other Special Beers
So-called **white beers** (Hoegaarden, Brugs Tarwebier) are light in colour and cloudy. Red beers (Rodenbach, Petrus) are typical of western Flanders and are bitter in taste. Brown beers (Liefmans) are rather sweet and are much used in cooking. Saisons de Wallonie are local craft brews, usually presented in wine bottles. Palm and De Koninck are **amber ales**, while the best-known ale in Wallonia is La Vieux Temps. Outstanding among strong beers are Duvel, Hapkin and Delerium Tremens. Then there are numerous local beers such as Brigand, Kasteelbier and Kwak in Flanders, Bush Beer and La Chouffe in Wallonia, to mention only a few.

Literature

Office de tourisme de Liège

Georges Simenon

The enormous extent and variety of Belgian literature is virtually unknown outside the country itself. Literary works, in particular those by Flemish speakers, have a pronounced local flavour and are characterised by unquestionable originality.

French-speaking Belgium

In earlier centuries the country produced some famous chroniclers. In the 14C, there was Froissart, who was born in Valenciennes and died at Chimay, in the 15C, Philippe de Commines, and in the 16C, Jean Lemaire de Belges, born in Bavay.

In the 18C the hallmark of the Maréchal de Ligne, a memorialist, was his cosmopolitan approach.

The 20C saw the development in Belgium of a highly original and active literary movement.

Following the great forerunner Charles de Coster (1827-79), author of the celebrated work *The Glorious Adventures of Tyl Ulenspiegel* (1867), came the group "La Jeune Belgique" (1881) and a period of upsurge in literary activity from novelists, such as the Antwerp writer Georges Eekhoud (1854-1927) and Camille Lemonnier (1844-1913) (*Un Mâle,* 1881); from poets, such as the Ghent author Van Lerberghe (1861-1907) who wrote the exquisite *Chanson d'Ève* in 1904, Max Elskamp (1862-1931) from Antwerp, and Georges Rodenbach (1855-98), made famous by his short stories entitled *Vies encloses* and his novel *Bruges la Morte* (1892). Some writers earned worldwide renown, among them the great poet Émile Verhaeren (1855-1916) and the Ghent writer **Maurice Maeterlinck** (1862-1949), who penned the mysterious and melancholy play *Pelleas and Melisande,* the basis of works by Debussy and Schoenberg, as well as essays (*La Vie des Abeilles*). He won the Nobel Prize in 1911.

From subsequent generations, outstanding writers include Maurice Carême (1899-1978), Robert Goffin (1898-1984), Jean de Boschère (1878-1953), Marcel Thiry (1897-1977), author of *Toi qui Pâlis au Nom de Vancouver,* Marie Gevers (1883-1975) who has been compared to the French author Colette, the Brussels writer Franz Hellens (1881-1972) who wrote mainly fantasy novels, and Pierre Nothomb (1887-1966), who also wrote a few novels, including *La Vie d'Adam.*

The Mons author Charles Plisnier (1896-1952) was a famous novelist and winner of the Prix Goncourt (*Faux Passeports*). Fernand Crommelynck (1886-1970) was best-known for an earthy play, *The Magnificent Cuckold,* and Michel De Ghelderode (1898-1962) was a prolific, audacious playwright.

Maurice Grevisse (1895-1980) wrote *Le Bon Usage* (1936), and M Joseph Hanse (1902-92) wrote *Nouveau Dictionnaire des Difficultés du Français Moderne,* both significant reference works in the field of grammar and linguistics.

Writers who have achieved international fame include the Namur author Henri Michaux (1899-1984), who took French nationality, the Liège writer of detective stories **Georges Simenon** (1903-89), creator of the famous Inspector Maigret in 1930 and author of many analytical novels, the essayist **Suzanne Lilar** (1901-92) who wrote works such as *Le Journal de l'Analogiste* and *Le Couple,* the historian **Carlo Bronne** (1901-87); and the novelist **Francoise Mallet-Joris** (b 1930) who lives in Paris.

The songwriter-composer **Jacques Brel** (*Le Plat Pays*) (1929-78) can be ranked among Belgium's poets. Also deserving of a mention is an author from Brussels, Pierre Mertens (b 1939), who in 1987 won the Prix Médicis for his novel *Les Éblouissements.* In 1966, this prestigious prize was awarded to the novelist, screenwriter and psychoanalyst Jaquelin Harpman (b 1929) for her *Orlanda.* Of Flemish origin, Liliane Wouters (b 1930) publishes plays and essays. The author of *La Place du Mort,* Jean-Luc Outers (b 1930) oversees the Service Général des Lettres et du Livre in the Ministry of Culture of the Francophone Community. Novels by Amélie Nothomb (born in Japan in 1967) are characterised by a simple, direct style.

There are a number of institutions which uphold French literature such as the Académie Royale de Langue et de Littérature Françaises de Belgique (1921) and the Association des Ecrivains Belges.

Dutch-speaking Belgium

Flemish literature was born in the 12C, and gained momentum first in the 13C with the poetess Hadewijch and the poet and moralist Jacob van Maerlant (c 1225-late 13C), then in the 14C, with the mystic Jan van Ruusbroec (1293-1381), considered to be the father of Dutch prose.

Writers who distinguished themselves in the 19C include the Antwerp citizen Hendrik Conscience (1812-83), Romantic author of novels and short stories, and the great Catholic poet Guido Gezelle (1830-99).

The 20C has had a number of outstanding poets such as the sensual, mystic Karel van de Woestijne (1878-1929), and the Expressionist Paul van Ostaijen (1896-1928). Cyriel Buysse (1859-1932) figures among the novelists, along with Stijn Streuvels (1871-1969), who drew inspiration from the flat landscapes in the southwest of the country (*De Vlaschaard* – The Flax Field), Herman Teirlinck (1879-1967), prolific novelist and dramatist, Willem Elsschot (1882-1960), Ernest Claes with his mischievous tales, as well as Félix Timmermans (1886-1947) and Gerard Walschap (1896-1989).

After 1930 poetry was dominated by Jan van Nijlen (1884-1965), Richard Minne (1891-1965), Karel Jonckheere (1906-33), Anton van Wilderode (1918-1998), and Christine D'Haen (b 1923).

A second wave of Modernist writers appeared around 1948, including the talented Bruges author Hugo Claus (b 1929), who is a dramatist (*Een bruid en de morgen* – A Bride in the Morning, 1955; *Vrijdag* – Friday, 1970), novelist (*Het Verdriet van België* – The Sorrow of Belgium, 1983) and poet. Other highly-acclaimed writers are Paul Snoek (1933-83) and Hugues Pernath (1931-76).

Contemporary Flemish novelists include Marnix Gijsen (1899-1984), who first rose to fame with his philosophical tale *Joachim van Babylon*. Louis Paul Boon (1912-79), a writer of realistic, passionate prose (*De Kapellensbaan* – Chapel Road, 1953; *Menuet* – Minuet, 1955) and also a painter. Johan Daisne (1912-78), some of whose works (*De man die zijn haar kort liet knippen* – The Man Who Had His Hair Cut Short, 1947; *De Trein der Traagheid*, 1950) inspired film-maker André Delvaux (1965 and 1968 respectively, the latter with the French title *Un Soir, un train*). As well as, André Demedts (1906-92); Hubert Lampo (b 1920); Ward Ruyslinck (b 1929); Jef Geeraerts (b 1930), interested by the Belgian Congo issue (*Ik ben maar een neger* – Black Ulysses, 1961; *Gangrene I-IV*, 1968-77); and Ivo Michiels (b 1923), whose formal research could be seen as part of the European avant-garde movement (*Book Alpha*, 1963).

Hugo Claus

M. Renders/GLOBAL PICTURES

Authors belonging to the younger generation include Leo Pleysier (b 1945), Walter van den Broeck (b 1941), Eriek Verpaele (b 1952), Erik de Kuyper (b 1942), Monica van Paemel (b 1945), Kristien Hemmerechts (b 1955), Herman Brusselmans (b 1957) and Tom Lanoye (b 1958). In poetry, two important names are Leonard Nolens (b 1947) and Herman de Coninck (1944-97), who is sadly missed.

Jean Ray (1887-1964), a native of Ghent, took the pen-name John Flanders. He wrote detective stories in Dutch and tales of the fantastic in French, including *Malpertuis* (1943) which was adapted for the cinema in 1972.

Luxembourg

Luxembourg has a few writers in the French language, such as Marcel Noppeney (1877-1966).

A poet expressing himself in the local language of Lëtzebuergesch, Michel Rodange (1827-76) wrote a version of the animal epic *Reynard the Fox*.

Frame from the album Bill est baboul by Roba. (Detail)

The Art of the Comic Strip

Some of the most famous figures to come out of Belgium are the heroes of the comic strips for which the country is renowned. The adventures of Tintin and the antics of the diminutive blue Smurfs have delighted generations of readers of all ages, justifying the Belgians' proud description of comic illustration as "the Ninth Art".

A World-beating Industry

An extraordinary total of 40 million comic books are published in Belgium every year. The majority – more than four-fifths – are in French, the remainder in Dutch, a difference which has its origins in the way comic strips were published in the 1930s, when they appeared in daily newspapers. In Wallonia, they came in the form of a weekly supplement, while in Flanders they were appeared every day in the main part of the paper. The outcome was that the comic book evolved rapidly in Wallonia and became part of mainstream publishing, whereas in Flanders the creators of cartoon characters remained dependent on newspapers.

The best way of finding out more about the history of the comic strip in Belgium is to visit the **Centre Belge de la Bande dessinée** in Brussels, where you can admire not only the original drawings of the great pioneers, but also the designs of their successors working today.

Contrasting Approaches

The production of a comic strip involves the work of a writer and designer, though sometimes the roles are combined. This was the case with Hergé, whose success forced him to take on assistants and to create the **Studios Hergé** on American lines, with a team of researchers, artists, draughtsmen, and designers specialising in clothes, vehicles etc. This system should have made it possible to continue the master's work even after his death (as happened with the figures created by Willy Vandersteen). But Hergé decided otherwise, and his creations accompanied him to the grave.

Belgium has two schools of thought in the field of comic books, one in Brussels, the other in Marcinelle. Both began by publishing in newspapers, invariably with a storyline involving a hero around whom secondary characters gravitated.

The Brussels School

Brussels is indelibly associated with the world-famous boy detective **Tintin**, who made his first appearance on 10 January 1929 in the weekly children's supplement of the Brussels newspaper *Le XX Siècle*. Tintin, the most famous figure in the Belgian cartoon pantheon, was the brainchild of Georges Rémi, alias Hergé, who also gave us the faithful Snowy, the irascible Captain Haddock and the dotty scientist Professor Calculus, all of whom are involved in the young reporter's many adventures around the globe.

Illustrations from Le Cosmoschtroumpf by Peyo.

Frame from the album
La Gardienne des clés de Thorgal.

Published by Hergé, the *Journal de Tintin* first appeared on 26 September 1946. It printed work by every member of the legendary "School of Brussels", including **EP Jacobs**, made famous by the exploits of the detectives Blake & Mortimer (1946); Jacques Martin, with his historic series *Alix l'Intrépide* (1948) and *Lefranc* (1952); Willy Vandersteen, who enjoyed his greatest success with *Bob & Bobette* (1945); and Bob De Moor, who was Hergé's main collaborator for more than 30 years.

The Brussels School is characterised by its realism, in terms of the storyline and the protagonists just as much as the settings. The relatively long texts are contained within rectangular speech bubbles, while the graphic design is meticulous and the figures precisely deliniated without the use of shading (the so-called "clear line").

The Marcinelle School

The great hero of the School of Marcinelle (a suburb of Charleroi) was **Spirou**. Drawn by Rob-Vel and making his first appearance on 21 April 1938 in the *Journal de Spirou*, this mischievous little chap was revived in 1941 by Jijé and in 1946 by Franquin. The guiding light of the Marcinelle School was Joseph Gillain (1914-1980), alias **Jijé**, who as well as Spirou created other series such as *Jerry Spring* and *Tanguy et Laverdure*. Among his pupils and associates the best-known are **Franquin**, the spiritual father of *Marsupilami* (1952) and the anti-hero *Gaston Lagaffe* (1957); Morris, whose cowboy *Lucky Luke* (1947) achieved world-wide fame; **Peyo**, who in 1958 invented the *Schtroumpfs*, or '**Smurfs'** to the English-speaking world; Roba, the creator of *Boule et Bil* (1959); and the writer Charlier.

Unlike the Brussels designers, the members of the Marcinelle School draw in a fluid way, with much use of shading. The texts are mostly humorous and appear in rounded speech balloons, while the settings are rudimentary or absent altogether.

Illustrations from La Route d'Armilia by Schuiten & Peeters.

Tintin in English

With his quiff and plus-fours, Tintin made his first appearance before an English-speaking public in 1952, when Hergé's publisher, Casterman, issued translations of *Le Secret de la Licorne* and *Le Trésor de Rackham le Rouge*. But the boy detective's popularity with an anglophone audience really only took off later in the decade, when the British publisher Metheun commissioned Leslie Lonsdale-Cooper and Michael Turner to translate and adapt the books. The work turned into a labour of love lasting 35 years, during which time the two Britons, Hergé and his team went to some lengths to make the work more convincing and appealing to the new readership. In one instance, a Belgian designer was sent to Scotland in order to redraw the Scottish settings in *The Black Island*; in another, the British bobbies who had been shown toting guns as a matter of course were effectively disarmed. The moment of Tintin's acceptance by the British establishment came when he received the accolade of a front-page article in *The Times Literary Supplement*.

Image from Les 3 formules du professeur Sato by E.P. Jacobs.

A Turbulent History

Celts and Romans

BC

The Roman advance into the Low Countries was resisted by the Celtic Belgae tribes, rallied by the chieftan Ambiorix. Their revolt was put down in 57 BC by **Julius Caesar**, who paid tribute to them as "the bravest of all the Gauls".

AD

● **1C-3C – Pax Romana**. To the south and west of the Rhine, Roman civilisation flourished. A great highway ran west from Cologne through the walled city of Tongeren to Bavai in today's France. Frankish tribes people settled in the infertile northern coastlands and retained their Germanic speech, in contrast to the Latinised Belgae to the south, thereby establishing the language frontier still largely in place today.

● **4C-5C** – As Roman rule collapsed, the Franks moved southwards. The Merovingians, the founders of the French monarchy, ruled from their capital Tournai, which the Christian ruler Clovis (c 465-511) made the seat of a bishop.

The Franks and the Rise of Flanders

● **8C/9C** – The territories making up today's Belgium flourished in their central position in the Holy Roman Empire ruled by **Charlemagne** (758-814). In 843, by the Treaty of Verdun, the Empire was divided between France (to the west of the Scheldt) and Germania. This left a narrow band of territory between the two which ran from the North Sea to the Mediterranean, this territory was given to Lothair I. Upon his death it was divided into three parts: Italy, Burgundy and Lotharingia. The frontiers of the latter correspond approximately to modern Belgium, minus Flanders (subject to the French crown).

● **862** – Baldwin Iron Arm became the first Count of Flanders. His son Baldwin II married a daughter of Alfred the Great, and the connection with England was maintained when Matilda, daughter of Baldwin V, shared the English throne with **William the Conqueror**.

● **963** – Count Sigefroi of the Moselle founded the county of Luxembourg.

● **980** – Notger, Prince-Bishop of Liège, gained temporal power over this province of the Holy Roman Empire, and his successors ruled over this important territory until 1794.

● **12C-13C** – Emancipation of the Flemish cities: The period from the 12C to the 14C is marked by the growth of trade and industry, particlarly the weaving of wool, mostly imported from England. Flanders was one of the most populous and industrialised regions of Europe. It enjoyed communal autonomy, its cities were among the continent's largest, with a teeming population of skilled workers often at odds with the ruling patrician class and the nobility. Local opposition to French claims on Flanders won the support of King John of England and Emperor Otto IV of Germany, but in 1214 the French were victorious at the Battle of Bouvines.

● **1300** – The French King Philip the Fair annexed Flanders, but the population revolted; on 11 July 1302 the **Battle of the Golden Spurs** near Kortrijk ended in victory for the Flemish citizen-soldiers over the flower of French chivalry.

● **1308** – The House of Luxembourg began several generations of rule over the Holy Roman Empire when Henry VII of Luxembourg was elected Emperor.

● **1337** – Beginning of the **Hundred Years War** between the English and the French, in dispute over the French crown. The Flemish cities allied themselves with their great trading partner, England.

● **1354** – The county of Luxembourg was raised to the status of duchy.

● **1369** – The marriage of Margaret, daughter of the Count of Flanders, to the Duke of Burgundy, **Philip the Bold**, marked the start of Burgundian interest in Flemish affairs.

Bust of Charles V, attributed to Konrad Meit, in the Gruuthuse, Bruges.

Foreign Rule

The Dukes of Burgundy

● **1384** – On the death of Margaret's father, Louis of Male, Flanders became part of the Duchy of Burgundy.

● **1429-77** – Reigns of the Dukes of Burgundy, Philip the Good and Charles the Bold. A great period of prosperity. Philip the Good founded the Order of the Golden Fleece at the time of his marriage with Isabella of Portugal. The Burgundian realm is consolidated with the acquisition of Luxembourg (1441), Liège (1468) and other territories. The dukes were major patrons of the arts and their court at Brussels was one of the most sumptuous in Europe.

On the death of Charles the Bold in 1477, his daughter Mary of Burgundy inherited his territories and married Maximilian of Austria. This opened the way to Habsburg rule of the Low Countries.

The Habsburgs

● **1482-1519** – On the death of Mary of Burgundy, Maximilian I became Regent of the Low Countries. In 1494 Maximilian gave the Low Countries to his son Philip the Handsome. In 1496 Philip married Joanna, daughter of the Catholic King of Spain. Their son Charles was born in Ghent in 1500; he became the Emperor **Charles V**. He was brought up in Flanders, partly by his aunt, Margaret of Austria, daughter of Maximilian, who became Governor after the death of Philip the Handsome in 1506.

● **1519-55** – **Reign of Emperor Charles V**: Charles I, King of Spain, became Emperor Charles V on the death of Maximilian. His empire, "on which the sun never sets", included the Burgundian lands, the Austrian Empire and Spain, together with all the American and Asian colonies. He extended the territory of the Low Countries both to the north and to the south.

The Spanish Netherlands

● **1555-98** – Reign of **Philip II** of Spain: in 1555 Emperor Charles V handed over the rule of the Low Countries to his son, Philip II. While Emperor Charles V had been strongly attached to the country of his birth and had protected it fiercely, his son was first and foremost a Spaniard. A fervent Catholic, he fought against the Protestants (iconoclasts), who ransacked the churches of his religion. During his reign, the nationalistic spirit of the Low Countries was rekindled and the struggle for political liberties kept pace with the battle of the Calvinists for religious tolerance. In 1567 Philip II appointed the fearsome Duke of Alba Governor of the Low Countries and charged him with quashing the Calvinistic "heresy" and with combatting the Dutch revolt, led by guerilla-style groups of "Geuzen" (rebel-nobility). The counts of **Egmont** and **Hornes** were executed in Brussels. In 1576 the "Spanish Fury" was unleashed in Antwerp, then in Ghent. In the wake of this Philip II was forced to concede the **Pacification of Ghent** which liberated the 17 provinces of the Low Countries from Spanish troops. In 1579, after the Confederation of Arras brought together the Catholic provinces that had chosen to stay under Spanish rule, the Protestant provinces formed the Union of Utrecht (the provinces of the present Netherlands), followed by the republic of the United Provinces.

● **1598-1621** – Reign of the "Archdukes" Albert and Isabella, daughter of Philip II.

● **1648** – End of the Thirty Years War. With the **Treaty of Münster** Philip IV of Spain recognised the independence of the United Provinces and granted them the north of Brabant, northern Limburg and Flemish Zeeland. Belgium's future territory began to take shape.

• **1659-95** – Following his marriage to Maria Theresa of Spain in 1659, Louis XIV of France laid claim to the Spanish Netherlands, aiming to extend his country's "natural frontiers" to the Rhine. Successive French invasions of the Low Countries met with varying success, opposed as they were by other European powers, particularly England. In 1659 France gained Artois and a number of strongpoints in southern Belgium.

The Treaty of Aachen awarded the French a number of frontier cities (Tournai, Kortrijk, Charleroi), and there were more acquisitions (Ypres) after the War of the Netherlands ended in 1678. Luxembourg was annexed in 1684. English opposition to French ambitions in the Low Countries was strengthened in 1689 when the Dutch monarch William of Orange became King of England. Nevertheless, Brussels was sacked in 1695 by French troops.

The Austrian Netherlands

War of the Spanish Succession: Charles II of Spain died with no direct descendants, leaving as heir Philip of Anjou, the grandson of Louis XIV. The renewed French claim on the Spanish Netherlands was resisted by a broad European alliance and the subsequent war was largely fought on Belgian soil, with the Duke of Marlborough winning notable victories at Ramillies (1706), Oudenaarde (1708) and Malplaquet (1709). By the **Treaty of Utrecht** (1713), the Spanish Netherlands were added to the lands ruled over by the Habsburg Emperor Charles VI of Austria, though France retained much of western Flanders, including the cities of Lille and Dunkirk.

• **1740-48** – **War of the Austrian Succession**. The French King Louis XV invaded Belgium, which was returned to Austria under the terms of the Treaty of Aachen.

• **1780-89** – Emperor Joseph II, an enlightened despot, nonetheless failed to take local idiosyncrasies into account, and his reforms sparked popular resistance: Belgian nationalism became a reality. In 1789 the Brabant Revolution drove out the Austrians and assembled the States General in Brussels. The Austrians were temporarily expelled.

French Rule

• **1795-1814** – After the victories at Jemappes (1792) and Fleurus (1794), Republican France annexed the Austrian Netherlands and the principality of Liège. French rule involved the persecution of the Church and conscription of young men for military service. The situation was eased under Napoleon, but French domination was only passively accepted when not actually rebelled against.

The Kingdom of the Netherlands

• **1814** – Napoleon's defeat: Belgium and Holland formed the United Kingdom of the Netherlands, with William I as sovereign. He also became Grand Duke of Luxembourg.

• **1815** – **The Battle of Waterloo**, followed by the Congress of Vienna. Eupen and Malmédy were annexed to Prussia.

• **1830** – The rule of the Protestant William I, with its insistence on Dutch as the official language, was unacceptable to many. Riots in Brussels were followed by successful resistance to Dutch troops. A National Congress was formed and Belgium won independence from Holland, renouncing its claims on Flemish Zeeland, northern Brabant and part of Limburg. The German-speaking part of Luxembourg remained under the rule of William I.

Independent Belgium

• **1831** – The London Conference recognised Belgian independence and the country became a constitutional monarchy. A French candidate for the crown was unacceptable to Britain, and it was given to Leopold of Saxe-Coburg-Gotha, a naturalised Englishman who was the widower of the heiress to the British throne, Princess Charlotte. He became **first King of the Belgians** under the name of **Leopold I** (1831-65). War broke out between the Belgians and the Dutch.

• **1839** – William I acknowledged Belgian independence. The country's neutrality was guaranteed by the European powers. Overcoming severe economic difficulties (famine in Flanders, 1845-1848), and with investment of British capital and know-how, Belgium became the pioneer of the Industrial Revolution on the European continent. Luxembourg, tied economically to Germany from 1842, also experienced substantial industrial growth.

• **1865-1909** – Reign of Leopold II. His personal ownership and exploitation of the Belgian Congo, in collaboration with the explorer HM Stanley, ended in accusations of maladministration and scandal. The immensely productive colony was taken over by the Belgian state in 1908.

- **1890** – Independence of Luxembourg: Adolf of Nassau was Grand Duke from 1890 to 1905. William IV succeeds him (1905-12).
- **1894** – Universal suffrage was established in Belgium.
- **1909** – Albert I became King of the Belgians.
- **1912** – Marie-Adelaïde became Grand Duchess of Luxembourg.
- **1914-18** – **First World War**: Germany dismissed the treaty that guaranteed Belgian neutrality as a "scrap of paper". Consequently, Germany invaded Belgium as well as Luxembourg, occupying virtually the whole of the country. The German advance was halted in western Flanders by the flooding of the polders, and Belgian resistance, led by **Albert I**, the "Soldier King" continued throughout the war. The **Ypres Salient**, mostly manned by British troops, was the scene of some of the bitterest fighting.
- **1919** – **Treaty of Versailles**: Belgium regained Eupen, Malmédy, Moresnet and St-Vith.

Grand Duchess Charlotte of Luxembourg succeeded her sister Marie-Adelaïde, who was forced to abdicate.
- **1922** – Economic union concluded between Belgium and Luxembourg.
- **1934** – The popular Albert I died in a climbing accident on the cliffs of the Meuse valley. Leopold III succeeded him (1934-44). His wife, Queen Astrid, died in a car crash in Switzerland the following year (1935).
- **1939-45** – **Second World War**: Belgian hopes of staying out of the war were nullified when In May 1940 Germany once again violated the country's neutrality (as well as that of Luxembourg). After fighting against overwhelming odds, Leopold III ordered the exhausted Belgian forces to surrender, and remained in the country, a virtual prisoner. A vigorous resistance movement developed. Following the break-out from Normandy in July 1944, British forces crossed the Belgian frontier on 3 September, liberating Brussels on the same day. Wallonia and Luxembourg were liberated by the Americans. In the winter of 1944-5, the German army temporarily retook part of the Ardennes in what became known as the "**Battle of the Bulge**".
- **1944-51** – Tainted, perhaps unjustly, by his war record, Leopold III was replaced by his brother Charles, who ruled as Regent.
- **1948** – The Customs & Excise Union of **Benelux** is concluded, linking Belgium, Netherlands and Luxembourg.
- **1951** – Faced with the threat of violent conflict between his supporters and opponents, Leopold III abdicated in favour of his son, who became King of the Belgians under the name of Baudouin I.
- **1957** – Belgium and Luxembourg became members of the **EEC** (European Economic Community). Brussels became the capital of the EEC.
- **1960** – The economic union of Benelux, instituted in 1958, came into effect.

The Eyskens government granted independence to the Belgian Congo, which became the Congo-Kinshasa, then Zaïre.

Marriage of King Baudouin with Doña Fabiola de Mora y Aragón.

To the Present Day

- **1964** – The heavy industries of Wallonia, in particular coal and steel, suffered a classic case of "rust-belt" decline, while Flanders prospered with the growth of light industry.

Jean of Nassau, Grand Duke of Luxembourg, succeeded Grand Duchess Charlotte.
- **1977** – Agreement drawn up which established three federal regions: Brussels, Flanders, Wallonia.
- **1980** – Referendum on regionalisation; new institutions in Flanders and Wallonia.
- **1989** – The Brussels conurbation was officially recognised as an autonomous region called Bruxelles-Capitale (Brussels-Capital Region).
- **1991-93** – Adoption (1991), ratification (1992) and enforcement (1993) of the Treaty of Maastricht setting up the **European Union**.
- **1993** – Baudouin I died and was succeeded by Albert II.

Belgium became a federal state.
- **1996** – The Dutroux scandal (kidnapping, rape and murder of young girls) provoked a crisis of confidence in Belgian institutions. Flemings and Walloons united in a mass protest march through the streets of Brussels.
- **2000** – Grand Duke Jean of Luxembourg abdicated in favour of his son, Grand Duke Henri.
- **2002** – Belgium and Luxembourg adopted the **Euro** as their currency.

ABC of Architecture

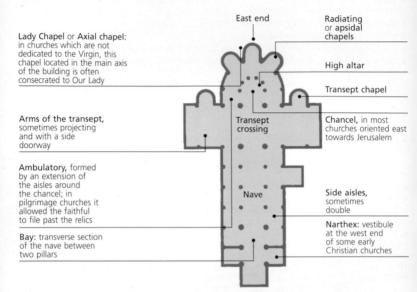

Lady Chapel or **Axial chapel:** in churches which are not dedicated to the Virgin, this chapel located in the main axis of the building is often consecrated to Our Lady

Arms of the transept, sometimes projecting and with a side doorway

Ambulatory, formed by an extension of the aisles around the chancel; in pilgrimage churches it allowed the faithful to file past the relics

Bay: transverse section of the nave between two pillars

East end

Radiating or apsidal chapels

High altar

Transept chapel

Transept crossing

Chancel, in most churches oriented east towards Jerusalem

Nave

Side aisles, sometimes double

Narthex: vestibule at the west end of some early Christian churches

ANTWERPEN - Cross-section of the Kathedraal (14C-16C), transept and chancel

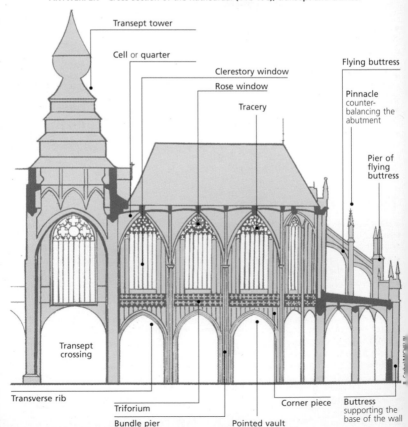

Transept tower

Cell or quarter

Clerestory window

Rose window

Tracery

Flying buttress

Pinnacle counter-balancing the abutment

Pier of flying buttress

Transept crossing

Transverse rib

Triforium

Bundle pier

Pointed vault

Corner piece

Buttress supporting the base of the wall

BRUXELLES - Façade of the Cathédrale des Saints-Michels-et-Gudule (14C-15C)

Blind bay window

Large stained-glass window

Tympanum

Bell-tower, sometimes crowned by a spire

Gallery with open-work balustrade

Gable

Upright post of a portal, usually adorned with a statue

Doorway or portal

Pinnacle

Buttress supporting the base of the wall

R. Corbel/MICHELIN

67

The Arts up to the end of the 19C

Over the centuries various peoples have flocked to Belgium and Luxembourg, bringing with them major artistic movements: the Romans, the French, the Germans, the Burgundians, the Austrians, the Spanish, the Dutch. Each of these civilisations was to leave its trace.

Nevertheless two very distinct and original styles, both of which gave rise to real masterpieces, were born and developed here: the Mosan School in the principality of Liège, and Flemish art, which flourished especially during the reign of the Dukes of Burgundy.

From Prehistory to the Carolingian Empire

A few megaliths have survived from the prehistoric era. Archaeological digs carried out in the towns once occupied by the Romans have brought to light a host of artefacts bearing witness to the skill of the craftsmen including pottery, glass, coins, bronze and terracotta statuettes, and jewellery. The area around **Tongeren** has been especially rich in finds, while the Treviri region (Arlon and Luxembourg) has produced innumerable statues, votive steles, and funerary monuments featuring low reliefs.

Funerary artefacts from the 5C to the 10C, in the regions ruled by the Salian Franks (Tournai) and the Ripuarian Franks (Arlon and Luxembourg), included damascene (inlaid) iron weapons, jewellery and brooches in bronze or gold, set with glass beads. Little of the architecture of the period has survived. The only examples are the Merovingian church at Arlon (5C) and the Nivelles abbey complex with its three 7C churches.

Charlemagne set up court at Aachen and introduced Christianity throughout his empire. He initiated a cultural revival which manifested itself above all in the art of illumination. The churches of Lobbes and Theux are characteristic of the Carolingian style with their avant-corps, wooden ceilings, square pillars and the gallery located west of the nave.

Romanesque Art (11C-12C)

Towns and abbeys flourished during this period. Belgium was divided into two parts: west of the River Scheldt, Flanders belonged to France, whereas regions to the east, through which the River Meuse flowed, belonged to the Holy Roman Empire. Romanesque art spread in particular along the trade routes through these two valleys. Two distinct movements formed: **Scaldian** art (from Scaldis, or the Scheldt) and **Mosan** art (named after the Meuse). Both movements were highly original, even though churches in both regions share many characteristics, such as basilical design, transept, chancel with a flat wooden ceiling and radiating chapels.

Scaldian Romanesque Art

In the Scaldian regions, devastated by the passage of hordes of marauding Vikings, Romanesque architecture is now evident only in isolated buildings such as the collegiate church of St Vincent in **Soignies**. The building of the **Cathédrale Notre-Dame** in **Tournai** led to the construction in the 12C of several churches

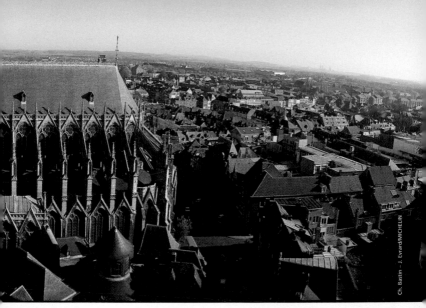

Tournai cathedral.

based on the same architectural style. The main features visible from the outside of these buildings are the tower at the transept crossing and turrets on the west front; inside, the Norman influence in the tribunes and galleries is also typical.

A number of civic buildings are also examples of Scaldian art. They include the Castle of the Counts of Flanders and the Spijker building in Ghent, the Burbant Tower at Ath, as well as several houses in Tournai. Above the ground floor with round-arched openings, the windows, divided into two by a colonnette, are aligned between two stone string courses.

Sculpture in the region from the 12C onwards, favoured by the availability of local Tournai stone, is quite remarkable. Outstanding examples can be seen on doorways and capitals (Tournai Cathedral) and fonts (Zedelgem, Dendermonde).

Mosan Romanesque Art

The art which developed in the diocese of Liège (the Meuse Valley and the surrounding countryside), in particular during the 11C and 12C, is known as Mosan Romanesque art. The **Principality of Liège**, which included Aachen, was already a leading area for arts and crafts during the Gallo-Roman period and it came very much under Carolingian influence. Later, owing to particularly close relations with the archbishopric of Cologne (on which the diocese of Liège depended) and the Rhine, the Rhenish Romanesque style began to exercise an influence as well. In the 13C, French style predominated. This put an end to Mosan influence on architecture.

Mosan Romanesque architecture retained a number of elements from Carolingian art, of which it is in some ways the continuation. First of all Ottonian architecture, which spread in Germany in the 10C and at the beginning of the 11C under Otto I, left its mark on part of the collegiate church in Nivelles, which was consecrated in 1046. Nivelles belonged at that time to the bishopric of Liège which was dependent on the Empire.

The avant-corps of the churches became more imposing in the 12C, being flanked with staircase turrets (Église St-Denis and Église St-Jean in Liège) or, in some cases, two square towers (Église St-Barthélemy, Liège). The outside of the church was decorated with Lombard arches. The apse occasionally included a second gallery on the outside (St-Pieterskerk, Sint-Truiden). There was often a crypt in the church, and sometimes beautiful cloisters (Nivelles, Tongeren).

Several of these characteristics can be seen in the later section of the collegiate church in Nivelles, as well as in many rural churches (Hastières-par-Delà, Celles, Xhignesse).

The art of melting and beating copper or brass was commonplace in the Meuse Valley, first in Huy, then in Dinant. It is probably the reason for the great liturgical goldsmithing tradition which was to spread throughout the Mosan region, resulting in the production of immensely ornate shrines, reliquaries, crucifixes and book bindings. From 1107 to 1118 **Renier de Huy** is believed to have made the famous brass font for the Église St-Barthélemy in Liège. Its classic perfection is quite exceptional for the period.

Thereafter the work became more complex, more elaborate in subject matter and more varied in materials used.

Godefroy de Huy used champlevé enamel for most of his work, in particular for the reliquary of the head of Pope St Alexander made for the Abbey of Stavelot and now exhibited in the Musée du Cinquantenaire in Brussels.

Nicolas de Verdun, who marked the transition from Romanesque to Gothic, created the reliquary of Our Lady for Tournai Cathedral in 1205.

The monk Hugo d'Oignies produced his delicate, sophisticated works at the beginning of the 13C. They are now on display in Namur, in Oignies Convent. There are also many anonymous works, such as the 12C Visé reliquary, or the 13C Stavelot reliquary. Both of them can be classed as Mosan art.

Mosan art also produced superb woodcarvings such as the *Tongeren Christ*, and the famous Virgins in Majesty known as the **Sedes Sapientiae**, or *Seat of Wisdom*. Further examples include the Walcourt carvings in the Museum of Religious and Mosan Art in Liège.

The sculptures in stone are equally interesting, especially the capitals (Tongeren) and the low reliefs (*Dom Rupert Madonna* in the Musée Curtius, Liège). Many Mosan church fonts have basins carved with heads on each of the four corners (Waha) and the lip decorated with ornamental foliage and animals (St-Séverin).

Gothic Art (13C-15C)

Religious Architecture

Rhenish art gradually gave way in ecclesiastical buildings to the French Gothic style, which was brought by the monastic communities from France and spread throughout the area from Tournai.

Nevertheless, Gothic art appears later in Belgium than in France. The first example was the chancel of the Cathédrale Notre-Dame in Tournai (1243), which was inspired by the cathedral in Soissons (Aisne, France). There are a number of clear variations peculiar to Belgium or to specific regions. The Gothic church is wider in Belgium than in France and is often not as high. On the other hand, the bell-tower reaches a very impressive height.

Scaldian Gothic – This style retains some Romanesque features such as a triforium and a square tower over the crossing, but its main feature is the development of triple lancet windows, or **triplets**. The finest example of the style is the St-Niklaaskirk in Ghent, another is the Onze-Lieve-Vrouwekerk van Pamele in Oudenaarde.

Brabant Gothic – It was not until the 14C that Gothic art appeared in Brabant. The architects drew inspiration from the great French cathedrals (Cathédrale des Saints-Michel-et-Gudule, Brussels). However, their modifications created a distinctive style which spread outside the province (Antwerp Cathedral).

The Brabant church is a large building with three aisles and an ambulatory with radiating chapels. Its main feature is the massive tower forming the west porch (the finest example being the St-Romboutskathedraal in Mechelen), and side aisle chapels surmounted by triangular gables lined up like a row of houses. There is often no transept (Halle Basilica), and the rose windows have commonly been replaced with larger windows.

The interior has a very distinctive style. The nave is supported by solid cylindrical pillars, whose capitals were originally decorated with a double row of kale leaves; large statues of the Apostles were later added to the other side of these pillars. The vaulting is of a fairly early Gothic style.

The side aisle chapels open into each other, creating new aisles. Finally, the triforium is sometimes replaced by a balustrade featuring intricate tracery, without a gallery. One of the loveliest examples is the basilica in Halle.

Belfries, Covered Markets, and Town Halls

From the end of the 13C, architectural originality manifested itself predominantly in civic buildings, especially in Flanders. Among these buildings were belfries, covered markets and town halls.

The flourishing cloth trade encouraged the creation and growth of towns. The inhabitants defended their prosperity by obtaining certain privileges, town charters providing guarantees for their industry. Such precious documents needed to

Belfry, Mons.

be kept in a safe place, notably in a belfry, while other impressive edifices were constructed for meetings and commercial activities. Witness to jealously defended local autonomy and busy community life, such buildings were arranged around the central market square (Grand-Place/Grote Markt).

Belfries – The belfry towers over the market square, symbolising civil power just as the belfry proclaims ecclesiastical power. It either stands alone (Tournai, Ghent) or is integrated into a public building, such as a covered market (Bruges, Ypres) or the town hall (Brussels).

It is designed as a keep with watch turrets and battlements. The prison is below ground level, with two rooms, one on top of the other, above it, with a cantilevered oriel window or balcony from which proclamations were read. The bell chamber is at the top, along with the lodge for the watchmen and heralds. Crowning everything is a weathervane symbolising the city, and shaped like a dragon (Ghent), the Flemish lion, a warrior, a saint (Brussels), or a local character (Oudenaarde).

Covered Markets – The community developed hand in hand with the cloth trade. In the 15C there were 4 000 weavers in Ghent out of a total population of 50 000. The covered market consisted of a rectangular building divided into spaces for stalls inside. The area used for meetings and storage was upstairs. The finest covered markets are those of Bruges, dating from the end of the 13C, and Ypres, dating from the same period and rebuilt after the First World War.

In both Bruges and Ypres the covered market contains the belfry because up to the end of the 14C it generally served as the town hall.

Town Halls – The finest town halls (Bruges, Leuven, Brussels, Oudenaarde) were built from the late 14C onwards, when the cloth trade was in decline. Bruges Town Hall, constructed in 1376, set an impressive precedent, the architecture still resembling that of a chapel. The town hall in Brussels followed. The town halls in Leuven and Ghent were built during the Renaissance. The one in Oudenaarde is a synthesis of its predecessors.

The reliquary of St-Remaclus.

Outside, the façade is decorated with recesses containing statues of Flemish counts and countesses and the town's patron saints.

On the first floor is the Great Hall, used for meetings and festivities and notable for its decor of tapestries and paintings depicting the history of the town or the life of its patron saint. A monumental fireplace is the single most imposing feature.

Town Houses and Guildhalls – The Gothic style is also evident in Flemish private houses and guildhalls. This is especially true of Bruges where the 16C saw the development of a distinctive style with many of the characteristics of Flamboyant architecture. Windows were surmounted by a more or less ornate tympanum. Later, the windows and tympanum were set adjacent to each other beneath an ogee arch, a feature known as the Bruges gable.

The guilds held their meetings in their halls, where their property, records and insignia were kept. Richly decorated facades graced with a statue of a patron saint or heraldic beast bear witness to the prominent role played by the guilds in the life of the city. The finest Gothic guildhalls still extant are those lining the Graslei in Ghent.

Altarpieces and Choir Stalls

A school of sculpture developed in Brabant (Brussels, Leuven) and in Antwerp and Mechelen during the second half of the 15C and the beginning of the 16C. It produced innumerable wooden altarpieces showing remarkably fine craftsmanship. They are also outstanding for the picturesque realism with traces of Gothic techniques.

An outstanding example of these Brabant altarpieces, apart from the one in Hakendover produced in 1430 (the oldest altarpiece in Belgium and also one of the most elegantly made), is the magnificent **St George Altarpiece** (1493) exhibited in the Musée du Cinquantenaire in Brussels.

The same picturesque quality marks the carving on choir stalls. The armrests and misericords (seat supports) in Brabant churches are decorated with satirical figures full of imagination, unforgiving illustrations of human vices. Those in Diest are among the most remarkable.

Decorative Arts – The Belgian Gothic style exhibits great originality particularly in the decoration of the interiors of ecclesiastical or civic buildings. The woodwork (altarpieces, statues, stalls, beams) is as remarkable as the stonecarving, as

Ch. Bastin – J. Evrard/MICHELIN

illustrated by the Flamboyant rood screens in Lier, Walcourt and Tessenderlo. Mosan gold- and silversmithing did not survive beyond the 13C. Copper-smithing, however, spread throughout the country, giving rise to magnificent chandeliers, fonts, and lecterns. Exceptional works were also produced in painting *(see below)* and tapestry *(see below)*.

The Renaissance (16C)

The Italian Renaissance had little impact on Belgium, and even then not until after 1530.

Architecture

Whereas ecclesiastical buildings retained the Gothic style, civic architecture gradually adopted the style of the Italian Renaissance.

Although the town hall in Oudenaarde (1526-30) and the courtyard of the Palais des Princes-Évêques in Liège largely upheld the Gothic tradition, they also herald the beginnings of the Renaissance. In Antwerp, the town hall (1564) designed by Cornelis Floris II de Vriendt (1514-75), as well as the guildhalls (late 16C) lining the Grote Markt, more fully reflect the change in taste.

The new style is particularly evident on the façades where there are engaged columns, pilasters and statues (town hall, Antwerp), friezes (Oude Griffie in Bruges), and gables trimmed with volutes and crowned with statues (town hall, Veurne). The windows often have moulded tympana above them, a regional characteristic inherited from the Gothic style.

The extent and exuberance of this decoration has earned Flemish Renaissance style the name pre-Baroque.

During the second half of the 16C, under Spanish rule, a style known as **Hispano-Flemish** developed in castle architecture. It is typified by onion domes such as those at Ooidonk, turrets as at Rumbeke, or crow-stepped gables like those in Beersel. These decorative elements give the buildings a characteristically picturesque appearance.

Sculpture

Renaissance sculpture in Belgium appears for the first time in the rood-screen of the Collégiale Ste-Waudru at Mons (the work of the local artist Jacques Du Brœucq (c 1500-84)), from which a number of reliefs and alabaster statues have been preserved. Despite his use of traditional iconography, Du Broeucq succeeded in developing a personal style.

Cornelis Floris II de Vriendt, the architect of the town hall in Antwerp, also created the magnificent tabernacle in Zoutleeuw.

The works of **Jérôme Duquesnoy the Elder** (c 1570-1641), renowned for his *Manneken Pis*, bear a resemblance to those of Cornelis Floris, especially the Aalst tabernacle.

Jean Mone (d 1548), sculptor to Emperor Charles V, was born in Metz. He specialised in funerary monuments (Enghien, Hoogstraten) and altarpieces (Halle) in the purest Italian tradition.

Baroque Art (17C)

The early 17C was a period of relative peace after the Wars of Religion and Independence. Spain was represented by the "Archdukes" Albert and Isabella, whose sumptuous court was in Brussels. These Catholic sovereigns had many ecclesiastical buildings constructed.

Until the middle of the century, however, the great artistic centre was still Antwerp, where Rubens died in 1640.

Religious Architecture

One of the buildings commissioned early in the century by Albert and Isabella was the domed pilgrimage church at Scherpenheuvel, its designer the prominent architect Wenceslas **Coebergher**. It is this building which marks the birth of the Baroque style in Belgium.

Numerous ecclesiastical buildings were constructed for the Society of Jesus (Jesuits), such as St-Carolus Borromeuskerk in Antwerp, Église St-Loup in Namur and St-Michielskerk in Leuven. They drew their inspiration from the Gesù Church built in Rome in the previous century.

By the end of the century several Premonstratensian abbey churches had adopted the Baroque style, among them Grimbergen, Averbode, and Ninove. They are grandiose buildings with a layout in the form of a trefoil cross and a particularly long chancel reserved for the monks. Sometimes the churches are crowned by a cupola, as is the case in Grimbergen.

Civic Architecture

Noteworthy buildings from this period include the **Mons belfry**. The most beautiful set of urban buildings in the Baroque style is to be found on the **Grand-Place, Brussels**. Rebuilt after the 1695 siege, the Grand-Place reveals decorative liveliness taken to excess but it nevertheless retained something of the Renaissance spirit in the Doric, Ionic and Corinthian orders which lend rhythm to the façades, as well as in the balustrades on some of the pediments.

In the Mosan region, 17C private houses are characteristically bereft of any flights of fancy. The brick walls are somewhat enlivened by courses of stone, between which there are tall mullion windows. The Musée Curtius in Liège is an excellent example.

Sculpture

Many churches dating from this period have interiors decorated with sculptures by Antwerp artist **Artus Quellin** the Elder (1609-68) who was strongly influenced by Rubens, or with works by his cousin Artus Quellin the Younger (1625-97).

Lucas Fayd'herbe (1617-97), the artist from Mechelen who was also a student of Rubens, produced huge statues resting against columns in the nave and on altarpieces.

Francois Duquesnoy (1597-1643), son of Jérôme *(see above)*, worked mainly in Rome. He was famous for his cherubs or *putti*, graceful figurines made of marble terracotta or ivory. He is also credited, together with his brother Jérôme Duquesnoy the Younger (1602-54), with producing numerous ivory crucifixes notable for their delicacy and the elegance of their craftsmanship (Château de Spontin).

In Liège, **Jean Delcour** (1627-1707), who had worked with Bernini in Rome sculpted elegant effigies of Madonnas and saints.

Antwerp artist Hendrik Frans Verbruggen (1655-1724) won renown for his woodcarvings. Examples include the Grimbergen confessionals decorated with life-size figures. They are outstanding for their remarkable vigour and sense of movement. They were frequently imitated.

For the Cathédrale des Saints-Michel-et-Gudule in Brussels, Verbruggen produced a prototype of the pulpits known in Belgium as **chaires de vérité** (truth pulpits) featuring the expulsion of Adam and Eve from Paradise.

The church stalls in Averbode, Floreffe and Vilvoorde, decorated with figures, are also remarkable examples of Belgian Baroque sculpture.

The 18C

Architecture

The Baroque style persisted in ecclesiastical buildings, but by the end of the century, under the rule of Charles of Lorraine (1744-80), the **neo-Classical** style had begun to spread. The **Place Royale** in Brussels was constructed in this style by French architects Barnabé Guimard and Nicolas Barré.

Laurent Dewez (1731-1812), architect to the governor, built the minster in Orval in 1760 in the same style (it has since been destroyed). He followed this with the abbey church at Gembloux (1762-79) and finally the Église de Bonne-Espérance (1770-76).

Sculpture
Baroque sculpture was still very much in evidence in churches. Pulpits tended more towards the Rococo, for example the elegant structure in oak and marble in St-Baafskathedraal in Ghent. It was the work of **Laurent Delvaux** (1696-1778), who thereafter adopted the neo-Classical style. **Theodoor Verhaegen** (1700-59) made several pulpits, and a splendid confessional with majestic figures carved in wood in Ninove.
Michiel Vervoort the Elder (1667-1737) produced pulpits and confessionals decorated with statues, such as the ones in St-Carolus Borromeuskerk in Antwerp.

Decorative Arts
The decorative arts came into their own in the 18C with tapestry and lace, ceramics in Tournai, and cabinet-making in Liège where fine items of furniture, drawing inspiration from the French style, adorned sumptuous interiors hung with painted leather or tapestries (Musée d'Ansembourg, Liège). In Liège, the lavish interior decoration of castles such as the Château d'Aigremont breaks with the austerity of local architecture.

The 19C and 20C

Architecture
At the beginning of the 19C, neo-Classicism triumphed in Brussels (Théâtre royal de la Monnaie, Hospice Pacheco), in Ghent (Grote Schouwburg, Law Courts and University), and in Antwerp (Bourla-Schouwburg). The end of the century saw a taste for **architectural revivalism**, the finest example being the Greco-Roman Law Courts in Brussels, designed by **Poelaert** (1817-79). Other examples include the Gothic Revival abbey at Maredsous (1872, JB Béthune), the neo-Renaissance Galeries St-Hubert in Brussels (1846, JP Cluysenaar), and the neo-Byzantine church of Ste-Marie at Schaarbeek (1845, L Van Overstraeten). Not satisfied with a single style, **eclectic** designers mingle historic elements taken from a wide architectural vocabulary. Antwerp's main **railway station** (1895-1905, L De la Censerie), together with the Zurenborg district (especially along the road known as the **Cogels-Osylei**) at nearby Berchem, are the outstanding examples. However, from 1890 onwards, certain architects rejected these copies of the past and sought new forms and materials. This consciously progressive movement rapidly developed a style we instantly recognise today as Art Nouveau.

The theatre, Ghent.

Ch. Bastin-J. Evrard/MICHELIN

Painting

Cussac/Musées royaux des Beaux-Arts, Bruxelles

Among the great painters who have made decisive contributions to the development of art in Western Europe, Belgium can point with pride to such names as Jan van Eyck, Peter Paul Rubens, James Ensor and René Magritte. A unique synthesis of the influences of their era, their works continue to fascinate the art lovers of today.

The Flemish Primitives

The 15C was the golden age of Flemish painting. A naturalist movement had already appeared by the end of the 14C, with Hennequin (or Jan) de Bruges, who drew the tapestry cartoons for *The Apocalypse* in Angers, and Melchior Broederlam of Ypres, painter of the altarpieces for the Champmol charterhouse in Burgundy.

Their art remained nonetheless closely related to the art of illumination in which the Flemings excelled under the patronage of the Dukes of Burgundy. In the early 15C the Pol friars, Jan and Herman van Limburg, miniaturists of *Les Très Riches Heures du Duc de Berry* (Château de Chantilly, France) displayed an astonishingly detailed and vivid realism in their art of illumination.

The greatest innovator in painting was **Jan van Eyck**, who was probably born in Maaseik and who died in Bruges in 1441. The ***Adoration of the Mystic Lamb Altarpiece*** remains one of the great wonders of painting of all time, due to Van Eyck's use of perspective, realistic detail and bright colours subdued by light. At one point, Van Eyck was incorrectly credited with the invention of oil painting.

Robert Campin, thought by some scholars to be the Master of Flémalle, worked in Tournai during the same period. One of his pupils was Rogier de la Pasture, known under the name of **Rogier van der Weyden** (c 1400-64), who was appointed official painter to the city of Brussels in 1436. His poignant compositions are steeped in mysticism and his portraits are remarkable for their neat, precise brushwork and an extraordinary eye for detail. Many painters were to imitate the manner in which he depicted the Virgin Mary: an oval face with soft, smooth features and a wide forehead.

After studying in Van der Weyden's studio, Dieric Bouts (1415-75), originally from Haarlem, settled in Leuven in 1468. Although his sober, spartan technique betrayed Weyden's influence, other characteristics testified to a more personal style generally associated with northern countries: impassive features, bold colours, delicate brushwork and minute attention to detail.

Van Eyck was succeeded by the Bruges School, which included Petrus Christus, (died c 1473) the great portraitist, and **Hans Memling** (c 1435-94), who offers a charming synthesis of the pictorial themes of his period in his work, as much in his calm sophisticated religious compositions as in his exceptional, masterfully executed portraits. Gerard David continued in a similar vein. In Ghent, Hugo van der Goes struck a fresh note with religious pictures populated by realistically painted common folk.

*Pietà,
Rogier Van der
Weyden.*

The Renaissance and Mannerism (16C)

At the beginning of the 16C, the influence of the Italian Renaissance is hardly felt in Flemish art. The dominant style is Flamboyant Gothic, its supremacy hardly disturbed by the occasional half-understood Renaissance feature. It is now that Antwerp takes over the leading cultural role hitherto played by Bruges. The first painter to reveal true Renaissance inspiration is Quentin Metsys (1466-1530), with a series of tasteful, sophisticated works. His followers Joachim Patinir *(1485-1524)* and Henri Bles *(d 1560)* devoted themselves to landscapes.

Artists such as **Jan Gossaert** (c 1478-1532) and Barend van Orley (c 1492-1542) travel to Italy and on their return promote an Italian style of painting which is further developed by Pieter Coecke van Aelst (1502-50, active in Antwerp) and Lambert Lombard (1505-66, working in Liège).

Around 1550, Mannerism comes to the fore, its principal representatives being the Antwerp painter **Frans Floris** (c 1516-70), his pupil Maarten de Vos (1532-1603) and the Bruges artist **Pieter Pourbus** (c 1523-84). **Pieter Bruegel the Elder** (c 1525-69), belongs to this generation, though his unique style lifts him far above the shoulders of his contemporaries. With their wealth of picturesque detail, his paintings reflect life as lived in the Brabant of the 16C. His son **Pieter Brueghel the Younger** (c 1564-1638), sometimes known as Hell Brueghel, imitated him with not inconsiderable talent.

The 17C and 18C

Like the 15C, the 17C was a golden age for painting, with Antwerp as its main focus. **Pieter Paul Rubens** (1577-1640) was a universal artist, his exuberant Baroque style expressive of sensuality and joie de vivre, his great achievement the fusion of Flemish realism and Italian harmony. He painted numerous religious pictures, but devoted himself also to the art of the portrait and to landscape. **Anthony van Dyck** (1599-1641), who lived in England from 1632 onwards, was far and away the most gifted pupil and collaborator of Rubens. A master of technique, with a superbly refined style, he was responsible for dark and melancholy works as well as religious scenes and elegant portraits.

Another of Rubens' assistants was **Jacob Jordaens** (1593-1678), who favoured colourful works depicting earthy, realistic scenes. Other contemporaries included the animal painter Frans Snyders (1579-1657) who also specialised in still lifes and who taught Paul de Vos, whose brother Cornelis de Vos was an exceptionally talented portraitist. **Jan Brueghel**, known as Velvet Brueghel, is known for his paintings of flowers and landscapes. His son-in-law **David Teniers the Younger** (1610-90) created a fashion in Belgium for scenes of peasant life, or genre painting. Jan Siberechts (1627-1703) is an important landscape painter, while Daniel Seghers (1590-1661) painted studies of flowers. The short-lived Adrian Brouwer (c 1605-38) was responsible for a series of magnificent genre paintings.

Developments slowed down somewhat in the 18C with the religious paintings of Pieter Jozef Verhaghen (1728-1811), who continued in Rubens' style.

The Adoration of the Magi, Rubens.

The 19C and 20C

The beginning of the 19C saw the triumph of neo-Classicism, its principal exponent the portraitist François-Joseph Navez (1787-1869), a pupil of the French painter Jacques-Louis David, in exile in Brussels. Romanticism makes its appearance in 1830 with Gustaaf Wappers (1803-74), Nicaise de Keyser (1813-87), and Antoine Wiertz (1806-65). Wiertz is considered by many to be the precursor of Belgian symbolism and surrealism.

In 1868 the Société Libre des Beaux-Arts in Brussels brought together the Realist painters Félicien Rops (1833-98), who subsequently devoted himself to painting works of an erotic character, the talented portraitist Alfred Stevens (1823-1906), as well as artists inspired by working-class life such as Charles de Groux (1867-1930) and Constantin Meunier (1831-1905). With the exception of **Émile Claus** (1848-1924) who painted quiet scenes of rural life and Théo van Rysselberghe (1862-1926), who adopted Seurat's Pointillist style, the painters of the late 19C paid no attention to new movements, in particular Impressionism. Henri Evenepoel (1872-99) studied daily life, whereas Henri de Braekeleer (1840-88) lent a luminous poetry to scenes of bourgeois life.

The Symbolist movement attracted William Degouves de Nuncques (1867-1935), Xavier Mellery (1845-1921) and Fernand Khnopff (1858-1921), who painted strange, sphinx-like women.

Still influenced by Impressionism, the canvases of the young **James Ensor** (1860-1949) reveal his exceptional talent and great originality. His later works, with their masks and skeletons, proclaim the arrival of Surrealism.

Around 1900, Belgian painting was given a fresh impulse thanks to the Sint Martens-Latem group, which took its name from a village near Ghent. The most important artists of the first Latem generation were Valerius de Saedeleer (1867-1941) who painted landscapes in the style of Brueghel, the sculptor Georges Minne, and Gustave van de Woestijne (1881-1947), who, with his depictions of ordinary people, was influenced by Symbolism. Between 1905 and 1910 it was the turn of the second, Expressionist generation, among them Albert Servaes (1883-1966), who tended towards mysticism, as well as Gust de Smet (1877-1943) and Frits Mayer van den Bergh (1883-1939), whose approach was more Surrealist in character. **Constant Permeke** (1886-1952) led this group. His landscapes and figures have a calm vigour about them and, like his sculptures, are endowed with a somewhat primitive lyricism. Fauvism was as important a movement in Brabant as Expressionism was in Flanders. The leading exponent was **Rik Wouters** (1882-1916), whose paintings showed a tendency towards Constructivism (influenced by Cézanne).

Surrealism made its mark with **René Magritte** (1898-1967) and his fantastic worlds in which his precise technique was put to the service of his imagination. Paul Delvaux (1897-1994) specialised in female nudes wandering about in theatrical settings.

Abstract painting had its Belgian theoreticians and practitioners, among them Joseph Peeters (1895-1960) and Victor Servranckx (1897-1965); the latter's non-figurative geometric works are reminiscent of Fernard Léger.

In July 1945, immediately after the end of the Second World War, a new abstract art movement began with the foundation of the association known as La Jeune Peinture Belge, bringing together Gaston Bertrand, Louis Van Lint, Anne Bonnet, Antoine Mortier and Marc Mendelson.

In 1948 the **CoBrA** group (Copenhagen, Brussels, Amsterdam) was founded by the Belgian writer **Christian Dotremont**. Principal exponents were the Dane Asger Jorn, the Dutchman Karel Appel and the Belgian Pierre Alechinsky (b 1927). CoBrA aimed to be a way of life, an art open to all types of experience.

Since 1960 Belgian painters have followed the great international movements without however losing their particular identity. The work of Roger Raveel (b 1921) is characterised by abstract silhouettes painted in bright colours. Together with Raoul De Keyser (b 1930), Raveel is a leading figure in the "Nouvelle Vision" movement, closely related to New Realism. Works by Marthe Wéry (b 1930) are monochrome in character, while Octave Landuyt (b 1922) creates a world of magic and fantasy. Among the Belgian artists with an international reputation, **Marcel Broodthaers** (1924-76) devoted himself to creating conceptual works that cocked a snook at convention, using such materials as eggs and mussels. The same kind of irony is evident in the output of Jacques Charlier (b 1939). The relationship between the individual and the universe is at the heart of the work of Thierry de Cordier (b 1954). Jan Fabre (b 1958) is best known for his drawings in blue biro, his assemblages, and his dramatic productions, while Lili Dujourie (b 1941) and Marie-Jo Lafontaine (b 1950) are exponents of the use of video.

Sculpture

Willem Geefs (1805-83), representing neo-Classicism, created the statue of Leopold I at the top of the Colonne du Congrès in Brussels.

From 1830, the influence of Romanticism and the taste for the Italian quattrocento are evident in the sculptures of Charles Fraikin (1817-93) and Julien Dillens (1849-1904) who participated with the exiled Rodin in decorating the Bourse in Brussels. Thomas Vinçotte (1850-1925) designed the group of charging horses on the triumphal arch in the Parc du Cinquantenaire, Brussels.

Jef Lambeaux (1852-1908) was popular for the surging passion emanating from his works, reminiscent of Jordaens (Brabo Fountain in Antwerp). Constantin Meunier (1831-1905) was a painter before turning to sculpture in 1885. He felt at one with the new industrial era and committed himself to representing working man, the miner at work.

The Impressionist period is mainly represented by Rik Wouters (1882-1916), whose spontaneity bursts out of boldly executed works such as the *Crazy Virgin.*

Georges Minne (1866-1941) pioneered Expressionism, whose principal representatives were to be Oscar Jespers (1887-1970) and Joseph Cantré. The works of Georges Grard (1901-84) celebrate the sensuality of the female form.

Notable post-war pioneers include Maurice Carlier and Félix Roulin (b 1931) who hammered out a highly personal world in copper, adding elements of the human body (hands, mouths, arms etc) to various reliefs. Pol Bury (b 1922) inherited the Surrealist tradition in addition to being close to the CoBrA group. Since the 1950s he has devoted himself to designing kinetic sculptures. The Antwerp sculptor **Panamarenko** (b 1940) explores the ties between art and modern science. His *aéronefs* and other curious flying machines are both poetic and amusing.

La repasseuse, Rik Wouters.

Koninklijk Museum voor Schone Kunsten, Antwerpen

Art Nouveau

With its swirling, organic forms, its love of elaborate ornament, and its meticulous attention to detail, the international artistic movement known as Art Nouveau reached a peak of development in Belgium. Breaking with the back-ward-looking historic styles which had dominated the scene at the end of the 19C, Belgian Art Nouveau created works which still fascinate today with their har-mony and controlled exuberance.

Ch. Bastin – J. Evrard/MICHELIN

La maison du peintre de St-Cyr *in Brus* designed by Gustave Strauven.

A Belgian Style

The version of Art Nouveau which developed in Belgium had little in common with conventional artistic styles. Its adherents were young, free-thinking intellectuals of the avant-garde, often with links to the Socialist movement. In 1896 it was they who commissioned the architect **Victor Horta** (1861-1947) to design the famous Maison du Peuple in Brussels, demolished in the 1960s despite a storm of protest. From Ghent, Horta had been responsible for the very first Art Nouveau building, the Hôtel Tassel, built in Brussels in 1893 for the university professor Émile Tassel. In the same year **Paul Hankar**, who favoured a more geometric version of the style, built a house for himself in the St-Gilles district of the capital. Then, two years later, **Henry van de Velde** (1863-1957) designed the Villa Bloemenwerf in English country-cottage style in the suburb of Uccle.

New Forms and New Materials

Until the advent of Art Nouveau, the new building materials of iron, steel and glass had been used only in structures like factories and railway stations. Now they began to feature in domestic buildings and were no longer clad in brick or stucco, but deliberately made visible, contributing in no small measure to the new architectural aesthetic. Designers developed new conceptions of internal space, Horta in particular revolutionising the plan of the house by creating a central light well around which all the other spaces were organised.

Art Nouveau also subscribed to the German idea of the **"Gesamtkunstwerk"**, the total or integral work of art. Since the form and structure of a building now diverged so completely from existing practice, the architects found themselves obliged to design every detail, from mosaic floor to stained glass, from door furniture to lighting fixtures, from banisters to carpets. Van der Velde went as far as attempting to match curtains, crockery, even the clothes worn by the ladies of the house to the design of his interiors. All these details, many of them beautifully curvilinear and of great complexity, had to be made by specialised craftsmen; in uncertain economic times, this contributed to the relatively short duration of the Art Nouveau period in architecture.

Art Nouveau in Brussels

Brussels is the undisputed capital of Belgian Art Nouveau. It has been calculated that the city has more than 500 edifices of outstanding quality dating from the period 1893-1914, more than anywhere else in the world. Most are in suburban locations. Among the surviving structures designed by Victor Horta are his own residence of 1898-1901 at St-Gilles, now the **Musée Horta**, the

Magasins Waucquez department store (1903-06) which is now the home of the Centre Belge de la Bande Desinée, and the Hôtel Van Eetvelde (1895-98). Other important buildings include **Old England** (1899) by Paul Saintenoy which now houses the Musée des Instruments de Musique, the **Maison du peintre de St-Cyr** (1900) by Gustave Strauven, notable for its extraordinarily narrow frontage and the exuberance of its decoration, and the Hôtel Hannon (1901) by Jules Brunfaut. Also outstanding is the interior by Paul Hamesse of the Maison Cohn-Donnay (1904), now the **"De Ultieme Hallucinatie"** café-restaurant.

The famous **Palais Stoclet** (1905-11), designed by the Austrian architect Josef Hoffmann and members of the **Wiener Werkstätte**, marks the end of Art Nouveau and the beginnings of Modernism.

Art Nouveau in Provincial Cities

The city of Antwerp is also famous for its magnificent Art Nouveau buildings, notably in the Zurenborg district, with its wonderful array of turn-of-the-century styles. Among the houses in this remarkably well-preserved area are houses by Jos Bascourt, Jules Hoffman and Frans Smet-Verhas. Smet-Verhas was also responsible for the **Cinq Continents** building (1901). Another splendid edifice is the **Help U zelve** hall (1881) by Van Averbeke and Van Asperen.

In Ghent, architects working in the new style included Geo Henderick and Achiel Van Hoecke-Dessel, while in Liège the most important designers were Paul Jaspar and Gustave Serrurier-Bovy, the latter a specialist in furniture and the decorative arts.

Le palais Stoclet à Woluwe-St-Pierre.

From Art Deco to the Contemporary Era

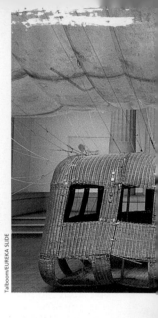

Talboom/EUREKA SLIDE

Horta and Van der Velde were outstanding figures in European architecture. In the decades that followed, few Belgian architects matched their stature; nevertheless, the country's location at the heart of Europe helped its architects and designers to achieve a remarkable synthesis of some of the continent's main stylistic currents.

Architecture

Hoffmann's Palais Stoclet had an enormous influence on the evolution of architecture in Belgium and elsewhere. White facades, flat roofs and geometric internal spaces heralded the arrival of a truly modern architecture and inspired designers everywhere. But the First World War slowed the advance of contemporary architecture, since the first priority was the rebuilding of the devastated towns, mostly in their original style in an attempt to reconnect with tradition and the certainties of the pre-war era. Nevertheless, development did occur, particularly in the styles which have come to be known as Art Deco and Modernism.

Art Deco

The term Art Deco was invented to describe the prevailing style of the artifacts shown at the great **International Exposition of Decorative Arts** held in Paris in 1925. The style combines elements of modern and traditional design, with uncompromisingly geometric forms set off by more traditional elements. Colourful tiles and mosaic brighten floors, and silver, steel and brass are much in vogue. As in the case of Art Nouveau, buildings and interiors are conceived as a harmonious whole. Among the Art Deco buildings gracing Brussels are the Koekelberg Basilica (1920-70) by **Albert Van Huffel**, the Town Hall at Forest (1925-36) by JB Dewin, the Institut National de Radiodiffusion on Place Flagey (1933-39) by Joseph Diongre and the Palais des Beaux-Arts (1919-28), one of the last works by Horta. Antoine Pompe and Jef Huygh were other important designers working in this style.

Modernism

Just as cast iron and steel had made new forms of construction possible in the 19C, so reinforced concrete and plate glass gave architects new challenges and opportunities in the 20C. Abstract lines, lack of ornamentation, pure and simple spaces were all characteristic of what came to be known as the Modern Movement. As well as new forms, new construction tasks came to the fore. The post-war housing shortage presented architects with the challenge of building social dwellings as quickly and cheaply as possible, sometimes in the form of garden cities and villages. Examples in the 1920s were "Floreal" and "Le Logis" at Watermael-Boisfort by the architects Jean J Eggerickx and Louis Van der Swaelmen, "Klein Rusland" at Zelzate and "Kapelleveld" and Woluwe-St-Lambert by Huib Hoste and the planned settlement at Berchem-St-Agathe by Victor Bourgeois. Other important representatives of Modernism included Henry Van de Velde (Ghent University Library 1932-35), Eduard Van Steenbergen (Athenée Royale at

Deurne, 1936), Louis Herman De Koninck, Gaston Eysselinck and Marcel Leborgne who built dwellings in the style of Le Corbusier, and Léon Stynen (Ostend casino, 1948).

1945 to the Present

After the Second World War, Brussels set about repairing and rebuilding herself with great zest. The long-planned North-South axis was finally completed and a number of monumental building complexes erected, among them a new building for the National Bank, the Cité Administrative (1958-84) and the World Trade Center (1969). The Mont des Arts was given a new look and work was begun on the Bibliothèque Royale (1949-64).

The high-rises of the 1950s, so symbolic of the era, were mostly residential, providing subsidised public housing (Kiel Estate, Antwerp). Among the architects working in the 1960s and 70s were the social militant Renaat Braem, Roger Bastin (Musée d'Art Moderne, Brussels, 1973), Jacques Dupuis, Claude Strebelle, and Charles Vandenhove (Sart Tilman University campus near Liège, 1960), André Jacqmain (Catholic University of Louvain at Louvain-la-Neuve, 1972), and Lucien Kroll (La Maison Médicale, part of the Catholic University of Louvain at Woluwe-St-Lambert, 1975). Bob Van Reeth ("Zuiderterras" Café at Anwerp, 1987), Bruno Albert (École des Hautes Études Commerciales at Liège, 1994), Jo Crepain and Willem-Jan Neutelings (barracks in Ghent, 1993-98).

Grand Designs

Of all Belgium's urban centres, Brussels can still claim to be the most architecturally diverse. Leopold II's determination to 'out-Haussmann' Paris as a European capital found expression in the exaggerated monumentalism of the Palais de Justice, and today's no less ambitious development of the European *quartier* bears his name. The visual rhetoric of its Hémicycle Européen, built as a business conference centre, is typical of the area's urban renewal programme, impressive, abrupt and forward-looking, but its shape, like a popular French cheese, inspired the scathing local nickname, *"Caprice des Dieux"*, "The Caprice of the Gods", a title only reinforced by the planners' readiness to sweep aside the old neighbourhood. Brussels is proof that an unsentimental confidence in shaping the built environment may not always succeed in willing an image of society into existence; it may even destroy as much as it hopes to create, as in the demolition of Horta's Maison du Peuple, but it can also produce striking works of art. While the motto of the 1958 Brussels World Fair – "Building the World for Mankind" – still sounds utopian, its symbol, the Atomium in Heysel, built to usher in a new atomic age, has become a city icon in its own right.

Art Deco and Art Nouveau, their proponents' motivations and manifestos now all too often overlooked, soon achieved international popularity and remain instantly recognisable and enduringly influential. Horta's trademark well of light, around which rooms and living spaces are centred, is only one example of the movements' elegant and simple design solutions, re-interpreted a thousand times, with parallels in contemporary interiors and the latest ultra-modern office block. No less revolutionary was the commitment to an integral, homogeneous whole, which was taken up in many later urban developments, and allowed such broadly applicable styles to influence so many aspects of architecture and the applied arts. Where Van de Velde's meticulous Art Nouveau fixtures and fittings called for high craftsmanship and generous patronage, mass production and new materials were to bring reflections of Art Deco shapes and colours to the most everyday objects, the first step in a democratisation of style which was to create countless "design classics", in Belgium and around the world.

Le Retour *(détail)*, René Magritte.

Selected Sights

Aalst

An important industrial and commercial town, Aalst once played a major role in the struggle of textile workers to assert their rights. Nowadays its great attraction for visitors is its famous and colourful carnival.

Location

Oost-Vlaanderen – Population 76 223 – Michelin maps 716 F 3 or 533 J 17 – Town plan in the current edition of The Red Guide Benelux.
Situated on the banks of the River Dender, Aalst lies halfway between Brussels and Ghent, just off the A 10/E 40 motorway.
🏛 *Belfort, Grote Markt, ☎ 053 73 22 70; www.aalst.be*

Directory

Where to Eat
🍽 **Borse van Amsterdam** – *Grote Markt –* ☎ *053 21 15 81 – Closed carnival fortnight, mid-Aug – early Sept, Wed eve, Thur – €9 lunch – €27.* Tavern-style restaurant in a fine 17C building in the shade of the town befry. Pleasant summer dining beneath the arcades. Honest traditional cuisine.

Where to Stay
🍽 **Host. Bovendael** – *Kuilstraat 1 – 9420 Erondegem –* ☎ *053 80 53 66 – bovendael @pandora.be –* 🅿 *– 20 rms: €53/84* 🍴 Tucked away in the village of Erondegem, this family hotel in an old farmstead has an attractively leafy setting. Simply furnished rooms. Summer terrace with pleasant view over garden and its lake.

Walking About

Grote Markt

The statue of **Dirk Martens**, a native of Aalst, stands in the middle of this irregularly shaped square; it was he who introduced the technique of printing to Flanders in 1473.

Schepenhuis★ (Aldermen's Hall)

This gracious building, formerly occupied by the deputy burgomasters, is thought to be the oldest of its kind in Belgium; it was extensively restored in the 19C following a fire. All that remains of the original 13C building are the façades on the right-hand side and at the rear, where it is possible to admire a crow-stepped gable and trefoil arcades.

On the right, a charming 16C Flamboyant oriel window brightens up the main façade. It once served as a backdrop against which bailiffs would read out new laws to the population.

The tall slender belfry dates from the 15C; it bears the town motto *"Nec spe nec metu"* ("neither by hope nor by fear") under two recesses containing two warriors. The statues represent the Count of Flanders and the Count of Aalst; the carillon consists of 52 bells.

Beurs van Amsterdam

This arcaded building, (the "Amsterdam Stock Exchange"), dates from the 17C. It boasts a beautiful brick-and-stone façade, with four scrolled pediments and an onion-domed campanile. It was in this building that the members of the **Chamber of Rhetoric** used to congregate.

Stadhuis

The 19C neo-Classical town hall has a gracious 18C Rococo façade on the far side of the courtyard.

St-Martinuskerk

Herman de Waghemakere and a member of the Keldermans family built this Flamboyant Gothic sandstone collegiate church in the Brabant style. The nave is unfinished, but the **east end★**, from the transepts to the apse with its ambulatory and radiating chapels is a particularly fine example of this style.

Interior – The inside of the church has a certain elegant simplicity. Note the round pillars and leaf-decorated capitals typical of the Brabant style, as

> ### NOT TO BE MISSED!
> Aalst's pre-Lenten carnival begins on the Sunday before Ash Wednesday. Three days of revelry start with a grand procession of giants together with floats passing satirical comment on the events of the past year. There's another parade on Monday, preceded by onion-hurling (*ajuinworp*) from the town hall and adjacent buildings. Carnival reaches a climax on Tuesday, with the appearance of the *"Voil Jeannetten"* (Dirty Janes), male citizens grotesquely attired in drag.

well as the side aisle in the transept and the triforium, confined merely to an open-work balustrade. A large work by Rubens, *St Roch, Patron Saint of the Plague-Stricken,* forms the altarpiece which can be seen in the south transept; the frame is said to have been made to a plan drawn by the artist.

Gaspar de Crayer's painting on the left demonstrates Rubenesque characteristics. On the north side of the chancel there is a splendid black and white marble **tabernacle★** carved in 1604 by Jerome Duquesnoy the Elder. The three juxtaposed turrets are decorated with charming statuettes (the Virtues, the Evangelists, the Fathers of the Church, angels bearing the instruments of Christ's Passion).

The first ambulatory chapel on the south side has an *Adoration of the Shepherds* attributed to Ambrosius Francken in which the Italian influence is obvious.

Dirk Martens's gravestone is in the fourth chapel, and the remains of delicate freely drawn late-15C frescoes can be seen in the axial chapel.

AALST AND THE SOCIAL STRUGGLE

The priest **Adolf Daens** and his brother, the printer and publisher **Pieter Daens**, both denounced the social injustice prevailing in Aalst at the end of the 19C. They spoke out openly against the exploitation of the local textile workers by their employers, and soon excited the wrath of the conservative Catholic authorities led by Charles Woeste. Among their achievements was the foundation of the Christelijke Volkspartij (Christian People's Party) in 1893, embodying the political and social movement of Daensism, which campaigned for the emancipation of workers and sought to reaffirm the importance of Flemish identity in social life.

Louis-Paul Boon (1921-79) drew inspiration from these issues in his novel *Pieter Daens* (subtitled *The Struggle of Aalst Workers against Poverty and Injustice in the 19C*). The work of this Aalst-born author and artist centres on the social history of the Flemish people, a theme already present in *Mijn Kleine Oorlog* (*My Little War,* 1946) which shows both the solidarity and the divisions in occupied Belgium. Although Aalst frequently features the work of this "tender anarchist" (in for example *De Kapellekensbaan,* translated into English as *Chapel Road),* his books must be seen as much more than simple regional chronicles; his name was even put forward for the Nobel Prize for Literature.

Worth a Visit

Oud-Hospitaal
In the street leading from the east end of St-Martinuskerk. Open Tues-Fri, 10am-noon and 2pm-5pm (7pm Wed); Sat-Sun, 2pm-5pm. Closed Mon, public holidays and between Christmas and New Year. No charge. ☎ 053 73 23 40.

Provisions and supplies used to be delivered to the Old Hospital by boat, as the River Dender once flowed just to the rear. The buildings, laid out around an inner courtyard, house a Museum of Regional Archaeology and Decorative Art, which also contains exhibits about local celebrities. Photographs and explanatory panels provide an interesting insight into Daensism. One room is devoted more specifically to the personality of Daens himself and shows scenes taken from the 1992 film *Daens* by Stijn Coninx, which was nominated for the Oscar awards. One room presents the work of the writer and artist LP Boon. The Dr Sierens room displays a fine collection of landscapes by Valerius de Saedeleer, a member of the very first Sint Martens-Latem School

Excursion

Ninove
11km S by N 45. 9am-5pm. ☎ 054 33 78 57 (Tourist Information Centre).
Ninove was renowned for its 12C Premonstratensian abbey, of which the lovely 17C-18C church survives and which contains some remarkable **wood panelling★**.

Aarschot

The collegiate church bell-tower overlooks the little town of Aarschot. The Austrians and Burgundians pillaged the town in the 15C, followed by the Spaniards in the 16C. Emperor Joseph II had the fortifications razed to the ground in 1782. The painter Pieter Jozef Verhaghen (1728-1811) was born here; he painted in the style of the great 17C masters, and his canvases adorn many a church, notably in Leuven, where he spent his final years.

Location

Vlaams-Brabant – Population 27 439 – Michelin maps 716 H 3 and 533 O 17. Aarschot lies in the **Hageland** ("hedgeland") region on the banks of the River Demer, between Diest and Leuven.
🄱 *Stadsfeestzaal, Demervallei 14,* ☏ *016 56 97 05.*

Walking About

Onze-Lieve-Vrouwkerk

For times and guided tours call ☏ 016 56 97 05 (Tourist Information Centre)
The chancel of this beautiful collegiate church built of local ferruginous sandstone dates from the 14C, and the nave from the beginning of the 15C. The tower comprising the façade rises to a height of 85m/279ft (by comparison, the tower in Mechelen has a height of 98m/321ft), its lower part brightened by alternate use of limestone and sandstone.

On entering there is a strikingly beautiful view of the nave; the upward sweep of its slender lines is heightened by the ribbing on the transverse arches. The same colouring as the tower is found in the chancel, which is concealed by a Late Gothic rood screen. This is surmounted by a 15C triumphal cross and decorated with scenes of the Passion and Resurrection.

The pulpit and the confessionals are in the 17C Flemish Baroque style.

The choir stalls (1515) in the chancel are decorated with satirical carvings. Note also the wrought-iron chandelier (1500) attributed to Quentin Metsys. A painting by PJ Verhaghen *(Disciples of Emmaus)* can be seen in a chapel on the south side of the ambulatory. In a chapel on the north side there is a remarkable painting on wood by an unknown 16C master of the Flemish School, *The Mystic Wine-Press*. The Seven Sacraments are on the predella. The miraculous statue of Our Lady of Aarschot (1596) lies in the north arm of the transept.

Begijnhof

Just past the Renaissance house by the church tower stands a row of 17C dwellings, all that remains of the former Beguine convent founded in 1259. The 16C **ducal mills** can be seen to the right on the banks of the Demer. There is an enclosure that forms a charming reconstruction of a Beguine convent on the left, now part of a hospice.

St-Rochustoren

On Grote Markt. The 14C brown sandstone tower was used in the Middle Ages as the law courts. It now houses the tourist office.

Viewpoint

There is a good view of the town and its surroundings from the **Orleans Tower** *(Orleanstoren)*, a remnant of the old fortifications.

Excursion

St-Pieters-Rode

8km/5mi S. Leave by the Leuven road. A short distance on, turn left on N 233 towards St-Joris-Winge, then turn right.
An attractive mansion surrounded by water, **Kasteel Horst** is about to undergo restoration. It is flanked by a 14C keep, which, together with the entrance porch, is the only remaining trace of the building which Emperor Maximilian's troops destroyed in 1489. The rest of the castle is built of brick with stone string courses and dates from the 16C and 17C. The outbuildings facing the château house a café and visitor centre.

Antwerpen ★★★

ANTWERP

A hive of creative activity, one of Europe's great ports and a diamond centre of world importance, Belgium's second city is still in many ways a typical old Flemish town. It is sheer pleasure to wander along the narrow streets or through the spacious squares, where fine old buildings, theatres, smart shops and boutiques, fashionable restaurants and art galleries give the city an irresistible charm.

Location

Antwerpen **P** *– Population 447 632 – Michelin maps 716 G 2, folds 8 and 9 for enlarged inset map, or 533 L 15.*
Antwerp lies on the east bank of the Scheldt, which flows into the North Sea 88km/54.5mi to the northwest; the town is linked to the west bank (Sint-Anneke) by three tunnels for motorists and one for cyclists and pedestrians.
Grote Markt 15, ☎ 03 232 01 03; www.visitantwerpen.be

Background

Mysterious origins – The first settlement on the present site dates back to the 3C. The name of the town seems to be derived from the word *aanwerpen*, which means "alluvial deposits". According to a 16C legend, however, the name comes from the exploit of a Roman soldier, Silvius Brabo. The story goes that Brabo challenged the giant Druon Antigon, who regularly pillaged ships on the Scheldt, ultimately cutting off the giant's hand and flinging it into the river. This explains why the city's coat-of-arms represents two severed hands next to a castle *(steen)*; the word *handwerpen* means "to throw a hand".

The golden age (15C-16C) – Antwerp built its first ramparts in the 11C, and began to flourish as a trading centre in the 13C, specialising in the trade of fish, salt and grain and in the import of English wool. The Hanseatic League established a branch here in the 15C. Antwerp was already in competition with Bruges, where the port was beginning to silt up.
The 16C decided the town's destiny. At the beginning of the century the Portuguese, who had discovered the Indian trade route, set up a European distribution centre here for spices and precious objects brought back from faraway lands. The first commodities exchange was created in 1515; the town was then under the protection of **Emperor Charles V** and had a population of more than 100 000. A new stock exchange set up in 1531, as well as the use of modern banking techniques (bills of exchange and letters of credit), made Antwerp a world centre of trade. Printing developed here in the middle of the century, largely through the efforts of Christopher Plantin. By 1560 Antwerp had become Europe's second largest city after Paris. This was a golden age too for architecture, with the construction of the cathedral, the butchers' and brewers' guildhalls and the town hall; and for art, with the Antwerp School represented by Quentin Metsys, Joachim Patinir, Gossaert and **Bruegel**.

Decline – Under Philip II, who was a staunch Catholic, the Inquisition led to the Wars of Religion, which put an end to this prosperity. In 1566 the cathedral was ransacked and desecrated by Calvinist iconoclasts. Harsh repression followed, led by the **Duke of Alba**, and then in 1576 the Spanish garrison launched a terrifying attack on the town known as the **"Spanish fury"**.
Antwerp's Calvinists had joined the revolt against the Spaniards; Alexander Farnese, Governor of the Low Countries, had to lay siege for a year before he could recapture the town in 1585. In 1648 the Treaty of Münster closed the Scheldt to traffic; it was not reopened until 1795.

Strategic prize – In 1794 the town fell into the hands of the French. When Napoleon came in 1803 he was immediately struck by Antwerp's strategic position, a "cocked pistol aimed at England". He developed the port and had the first dock excavated; today it is known as the Bonapartedok. In 1914 Antwerp resisted the German army from 28 September to 9 October, enabling Belgian troops to fall back to the River IJzer (Yser) at Nieuwpoort. Antwerp's port was fully functional shortly after the Liberation in September 1944, despite intensive bombardment by V1 flying bombs and V2 rockets.

Port development and economic growth – Antwerp is now **Belgium's largest port**, its main trading city and a major industrial centre. The port is being expanded northwards to the border with the Netherlands. It covers over 13 780ha/31 579 acres, comprising 127km/79mi of waterfront, 949km/590mi of

GETTING ABOUT

By car – It is never easy driving around a big city and Antwerp is no exception. You are strongly advised to leave your car in one of the central car parks.

Public transport – The Dagpas Stad (city day pass) permits unlimited travel on the whole of Antwerp's city's public transport network (bus, tram and Metro).
It is obtainable on board buses and trams and from De Lijn kiosks. Information: De Lijn, ☎ 03 218 14 11; www.delijn.be

SIGHTSEEING

Guided tours – In summer, the Tourist Information Centre offers individual guided tours in English. Antwerpen Averechts organise unusual walking tours in season. Haringrokerij, Kronenburgstraat 34, bus 1, ☎ 03 248 15 77.

Carriage rides – *Starts from Grote Markt. Mid-Apr - mid-Sept from midday, rest of year only in fine weather.* Pleasant tour around the old city of Antwerp.

Tourist tram – *Starts from Groenplaats. Mid-Apr - late Oct, hourly 11am-4pm; early and late season weekdays 1pm-4pm, weekend 11am-4pm* – ☎ 03 480 93 88. Practical, relaxing way of exploring the city.

Helicopter – *Antwerp Aviation,* ☎ 03 287 00 52 or Eurofly, ☎ 03 281 05 85. Bird's eye view of Antwerp.

Boat trip on the Scheldt – ☎ 03 231 31 00 – *www.flandriaboat.com – Starts from Steenplein 1pm, 2pm, 3pm and 4pm; May-Sept and weekends in Oct* – €7. A 50min excursion giving a fascinating glimpse of industrial Antwerp, its important chemical plants, the beach at Sainte-Anne, the mill and the marina.

Harbour tour – *☎ 03 231 31 00 – www.flandriaboat.com – Starts from Quay no 14, 2.30pm; May-Aug, weekends Sept-Oct and Easter* – €11.50. The port of Antwerp is most impressive, with great freighters and tankers, industrial plants, refineries, grain elevators, transporter bridges, dry docks and shipyards.

WHERE TO EAT

🍴 Grand Café Le Roy – *Kasteelpleinstraat 49* – ☎ 03 226 11 99 – ✂ – *€13.26.* Attractively intimate, bistro-like interior, contemporary chandeliers, generous wall-hangings, and candles. Dining in fine weather on the pleasant outdoor terrace with teak furniture.

🍴 Hungry Henrietta – *Lombardenvest 19* – ☎ 03 232 29 28 – ✂ – *€14.87.* This establishment has a 25-year reputation for excellent service. Determinedly up-to-date decor. Quiet rear terrace with view of the Bishop's Palace.

🍴 Arte – *Suikerrui 24* – ☎ 03 226 29 70 – ✂ – *€15/27.27.* In the heart of the old town, this "ristorante" offers Italian-style pizzas and other dishes. Decor featuring items of contemporary art. Good selection of Italian wine.

🍴 Zuiderterras – *E.Van Dijckkaai 37* – ☎ 03 234 12 75 – ✂ – *€17/44.* On the banks of the Scheldt, unusual contemporary architecture with a maritime touch. Bright and trendy mezzanine overlooking the main dining room. Seductive summer terrace with river views. The menu casts its net exceptionally wide.

Ch. Bastin – J. Evrard/MICHELIN

The Zuiderterras.

🍴 Dock's Café – *Jordaenskaai 7* – ☎ 03 226 63 30 – info@docks.be – *Closed 1 Jan, Sat midday* – *€21/27.* This brasserie and seafood specialist is extremely popular. It welcomes its guests in a futuristic ambience with a mock-Baroque touch. Superb stairway leading to an equally striking mezzanine. Reservation advisable.

🍴🍴 De Gulden Beer – *Grote Markt 14* – ☎ 03 226 08 41 – *€25 lunch* – *€35/62.* French and Italian food served in an old guildhall overlooking the main square. Lengthy Franco-Italian wine list. Some tables have a view of Town Hall and Brabo Fountain.

🍴🍴 Bizzie-Lizzie – *Vlaamse Kaai 16* – ☎ 03 238 61 97 – bizzielizzie@popmail.com – *closed Sun* – *€22 lunch* – *€37.* Fashionable location close to three of the city's more interesting museums. Good choice of traditional dishes with a local touch, blackboard with dishes of the day. Relaxed brasserie atmosphere.

🍴🍴 Pazzo – *Oude Leeuwenrui 12* – ☎ 03 232 86 82 – pazzo@skynet.be – *closed weekends and national holidays* – *€19 lunch* – *€38.* By the docks, loft-style brasserie in a converted warehouse, still with solid timber uprights supporting massive roof beams. Somewhat eclectic menu plus wines from around the globe.

🍴🍴 Panna Cotta – *Kasteelpleinstraat 64* – ☎ 03 237 07 86 – *€40.* This restaurant is in what used to be a bakery, with the old bread oven kept as a feature. But the decor is strictly contemporary. Menu and wine list offer a grand tour around Italy.

🍴🍴🍴 p.Zinc – *Veemarkt 9* – ☎ 03 213 19 08 – *closed Sat midday, Sun, public holidays* – *€20 lunch* – *€41/50.* Welcoming bistro with an array of traditional temptations. When the weather forecast gives the go-ahead, tables are set out on the quiet Veemarkt square overlooked by St Paul's church.

WHERE TO STAY

Rubenshof – *Amerikalei 115 –* ☎ *03 237 07 89 –* 🖷 *– €23.55/52.06* 🖵. Just a short hop from the Vogelmarkt (Bird Market), this hotel in the cardinal's old residence is full of nostalgic appeal. Attractive interior with plentiful turn-of-the-century features. Rooms of somewhat faded charm.

Bed & Breakfast Isabella – *Isabella Brantstraat 16 –* ☎ *03 237 61 91 –c.s@skynet.be –* 🖷 *– 2 rms: €38/50* 🖵. Close to the Law Courts, this century-old residence with its two guest rooms is the home of the welcoming Schoonbaert family. One room with balcony overlooking the garden.

Greta Stevens – *Molenstraat 35 –* ☎ *03 259 15 90 – greta.stevens@pandora.be –* 🖷 *– 3 rms: €40/50* 🖵. Highly recommended, not least for Mrs Stevens' attentive care of her guests. Immaculate rooms featuring contemporary artworks. Tiny courtyard and pleasant top-lit room where a fortifying breakfast is served.

Koen Ribbens en Marleen Engelen – *Justitiestraat 43 –* ☎ *03 248 15 39 – marleen.engelen@yucon.be –* 🖷 *– 3 rms: €42/50* 🖵. Well worth tracking down, this elegant 19C private hotel is close to the Law Courts. Spacious rooms named after historic grandes dames – Sissi, Victoria and Augusta. Friendly reception.

Marijke Vandepitte – *Britselei 49 building 6 –* ☎ *03 288 66 95 –* 🖷 *– 2 rms: €55/87* 🖵. Beautifully furnished penthouse atop a modern city centre building with huge bedrooms and ultramodern bathrooms. One room with terrace with views over Antwerp's rooftops.

Cammerpoorte – *Nationalestraat 40 –* ☎ *03 231 97 36 –* 🅿 *– 39 rms: €73/86* 🖵. The rooms are plain but more than adequate for a short stay. After a good night's rest, take time to visit the new Fashion Museum just opposite. Convenient private car park.

Industrie – *Emiel Banningstraat 52 –* ☎ *03 238 66 00 – hotelindustrie@pandora.be – 13 rms: €75/92* 🖵. Personalised and charmingly decorated rooms in a pair of patrician residences close to a trio of museums devoted to the arts and photography. Welcoming lounge.

Antigone – *Jordaenskai 11 –* ☎ *03 231 66 77 – 18 rms: €77/90* 🖵. This little establishment named after Sophocles' tragic heroine is just a step from the Steen Fortress. Plain but reasonably comfortable rooms, some with a view of the quayside.

Firean – *Karel Oomsstraat 6 –* ☎ *03 237 02 60 – info@hotelfirean.com – 15 rms: €126/150* 🖵. In Antwerp's Zuid district, this is a delightful Art Deco building, family-run with great competence. Stylish public rooms with a Twenties touch, charming patio and pretty bedrooms with choice furnishings.

T'Sandt – *Het Zand 17 –* ☎ *03 232 93 90 – info@hotel-sandt.be – 29 rms: €130/220* 🖵. Old Rococo-style residence with bright and attractive rooms guaranteeing a restful stay. Delightful Italian-style courtyard and rooftop summer terrace.

TAKING A BREAK

Fritkot Max – *Groenplaats 12 –* ☎ *03 234 37 88 – www.fritkotmax.be – noon-midnight – closed 1 Jan, 24 Dec.* Traditional chip-shop or friterie, serving Belgium's national speciality in the proper way, in cornets. A tiny first-floor museum pays homage to the culture of the chip.

L'entrepôt du Congo – *Vlaamse Kai 42 –* ☎ *03 257 16 48 – from 9am.* Much in favour with the city's jet-set. A splendid high-ceilinged interior with French-language newspapers on display. Pleasantly superannuated decor.

Pelgrom – *Pelgrimstraat 17 –* ☎ *03 234 08 09 – Mon-Thur midday-11pm, Fri-Sat midday-midnight.* Ideal for a drink or snack by the cathedral, this establishment consists of monumental vaulted cellars dating from the 15C. A number of archeological finds on display. Candle-lit atmosphere.

Del Rey – *Appelmansstraat 5 –* ☎ *03 233 29 37 – www.delrey.be – Mon-Sat 9am-6.30pm (meals 10am-6pm) – closed two weeks in Aug, public holidays.* A paradise for lovers of sweet things, close to the main station by the Keyserlei. The front of the building is an appetising dark chocolate colour, and the shop has a wide choice of of pralines and cakes and other home-made delicacies. Smart tea-room.

Hoedensalon – *Oude Koornmarkt 62 –* ☎ *03 233 59 28 – www.hoedensalon.com – Tues-Sat 10.30am-6pm.* Tea-room or hat-shop? You decide! The brainchild of a Dutch couple, this is an unusual combination of café, book-shop, and headgear specialist. Dally with a delicious cake to a background of classical music and admire the latest creations, on show from 2pm onwards.

De Groote Witte Arend – *Reynderstraat 18 –* ☎ *03 226 31 90 – Mon-Sat from 10am.* This typical bistro occupies the chapel of an 18C convent. Pretty courtyard with outside tables in summer. Dining room with solid timber furniture, classical music and quasi-monastic atmosphere.

The Groenplaats.

Grand Café Horta – *Hopland 2* – ☎ *03 232 28 15 – www.grandcafehorta.be – Mon-Thur 11am-11pm, Fri-Sat 11am-midnight*. Built in 2000 near the Rubenshuis, this vast and stylish café is a mixture of Art Nouveau architecture and designer furnishings, using material from Horta's famous Maison du Peuple in Brussels, demolished in the 1960s.

De Foyer – *Komedieplaats 18* – ☎ *03 233 55 17 – midday-midnight, Sat 11am-midnight, Sun and public holidays 11am-6pm*. The café of the Bourla Theatre is a distinguished rendezvous, much appreciated by those in search of a good brunch.

Café Het Elfde Gebod.

Ch. Bastin – J. Evrard/MICHELIN

Het Elfde Gebod – *Torfbrug 10* – ☎ *03 232 36 11 – from noon*. Behind the ivy-covered walls, this unusual bar – the Eleventh Commandment – encourages its guests to devote themselves to the serious contemplation of its excellent range of beers, beneath the gaze of a heavenly host of saintly statues.

Den Engel – *Grote Markt 3 – from 9am*. Antwerp's most famous café is a city institution, frequented by a cosmopolitan clientele.

ENTERTAINMENT AND NIGHTLIFE

De Keyserlei – The streets around the station are as busy by night as by day, with any number of places to eat, ethnic restaurants, cinemas, restaurants and discotheques. The Keyserlei is lined with one brasserie terrace after the other – Griffy's, Fouquets, Beverley Hills, the Windsor…

De Muze – *Melkmarkt 15 – noon-4am*. Founded in the 1960s and always crowded, this temple to jazz is in a converted warehouse building. There's live music almost every evening from 10pm, particularly on Tuesdays and Thursdays when the resident group perform. Concert room with mezzanine and exposed brickwork.

SHOPPING

Antwerp is a shoppers' paradise. Not surprisingly, the diamond district around the main station (Pelikanstraat, Appelmansstraat, Vestingstraat) is home to numerous jewellers. As well as the two shopping arcades of Century Center and Antwerp Tower, there are many clothes and shoe shops along De Keyserlei. Quellinstraat and Quellincentre lead to Frankrijklei with its prestigious fashion boutiques. With its splendid 19C and 20C facades and department stores (P&C, C&A, Esprit), the broad traffic-free Meir is undoubtedly the city's most important shopping artery. The Huidevetterstraat and adjoining streets like Wiegstraat, the Groendalstraat and the Korte Gasthuisstraat (sometimes dubbed De Wilde Zee – Stormy Sea) have been taken over by luxury fashion stores and little cafés. A number of famous Antwerp designers, such as Chris Mesdagh, Ann de Meulemeester and Dirk Bikkembergs, present their creations on Lombardenvest and Steenhouwersvest. Dries van Noten has settled a little further away in the Modepaleis on the Nationalestraat. Lovers of antique furniture and old things generally can browse in the shops along Klosterstraat and Steenhouwersvest. Another popular address is Hoogstraat. The Latin Quarter, not far from the Bourla Theatre, the Hopland and the Leopoldstraat are renowned for their shops selling expensive fashion ware and high-class antiques.

Diamondland – *Appelmansstraat 33a* – ☎ *03 229 29 90 – www.diamondland.com – Apr-Oct: 9.30am-5.30pm, Sun and public holidays 10am-5pm*. This establishment gives visitors the opportunity of watching diamond craftsmen at work and offers fascinating insights into this most precious of stones – its colour, purity, cutting, carats, certification… Bear in mind that what you see is also for sale!

Markets – The most famous market in Antwerp is unquestionably the **Vogelmarkt** (bird market), held on Theaterplein on Sunday mornings. Almost anything can be found here. Collectors in search of rare objects can browse at **Vrijdagmarkt** on Wednesday and Friday mornings.

Antwerp specialities – The city of Antwerp has another – more affordable – claim to fame besides diamonds: **Antwerpse handjes**, small chocolates with fillings. They also exist in biscuit form. **Antwerp Elixir** is a sweet liquor made with herbs. Beer drinkers should try **bolleke**, a traditional lager concocted by the renowned brewery De Koninck and named after the balloon-shaped glass in which it is served. It is the custom to have a *bolleke* or a *keuninkske* at the De Pelgrim café (Boomgaardstraat 8), said to be directly linked to the brewery opposite by an underground pipeline.

Boats moored along the Steen pontoon

R. van den Boom /EUREKA SLIDE

railway, 1 400ha/3 459 acres of docks, a large amount of stock handling equipment and enormous storage depots. The building of a large dock to the north of Kanaaldok has greatly increased mooring capacity. Seven locks connect the Scheldt with the docks. The Berendrecht lock, opened in 1988, is the biggest in the world: 763 000m³/791 994cu yd in volume, 500m/0.4mi long by 68m/74yd wide. The Zandvliet lock has a volume of 613 000m³/801 804cu yd.

The volume of traffic through Antwerp's port largely depends on Belgium's economy, but also on its being a transit point to Germany, France, the Netherlands, Switzerland and Italy. Imports consist of petroleum products, minerals, coal, timber, grain and raw chemicals; exports are usually fertilisers, cements, metallurgical and chemical products. As for storage, Antwerp has excellent warehouse installations making it a crucial link in the distribution chain. Sizeable industries have expanded near the port, dependent on its existence: oil refineries, car assembly plants, food industries, ship construction and repair.

Walking About

THE OLD CENTRE★★★

Antwerp's historic heart is a maze of squares, narrow streets and passageways, in which a remarkable number of niches containing statues of the Madonna are to be found; there are supposed to be more than 300 of them. Many were carved by sculptors seeking to obtain membership to the Guild of St Luke.

Start at Grote Markt

Grote Markt★

The cathedral's slender, graceful spire rises above the irregularly shaped Grote Markt, which is surrounded by 16C and 17C **guildhalls** with very tall façades consisting almost entirely of windows. They are crowned with crow-stepped or scrolled gables, often bristling with delicate pinnacles.

Look towards the Stadhuis and note the five beautiful guildhalls to the right, built mostly in Renaissance style and dating from the late 16C. They include the White Angel, appropriately surmounted by an angel, the Coopers' Hall with its statue of St Matthew, the very tall **Oude Handboog** (Old Crossbowmen's Hall) topped with an equestrian statue of St George, the Jonge Handboog (Young Crossbowmen's Hall) dating from 1500 and the Drapers' Hall, decorated with an eagle.

Stadhuis

Guided tours daily (exc Wed, Sat), 11am, 2pm, 3pm, Sat 2pm, 3pm. Closed Thur, Sun and public holidays. €0.75. ☎ 03 220 82 11.

The town hall was built in 1564 by Cornelis Floris. The façade is 76m/282ft long and displays an artful combination of Flemish influence (dormers, gables) and Italian Renaissance characteristics (a loggia just below the roof, pilasters between the windows, niches). The richly decorated central part lightens the austere orderly appearance of the tall mullioned windows. The interior was completely remodelled in the 19C.

Brabofontein

This spirited fountain by **Jef Lambeaux** (1887) depicts Silvius Brabo brandishing the giant Druon's hand in a legendary gesture. The water falls directly onto the cobblestones of the square.

Go along the Wisselstraat and cross Oude Beurs street into the Hofstraat

Oude Beurs

Mon-Fri, 8am-4.30pm. Closed Sat-Sun and public holidays. ☎ 03 220 85 15.

The former commodities exchange dates from 1515. Administrative offices occupy the building today. Behind the Classical façade there is a charming paved courtyard surrounded by porticoes and overlooked by a watchtower.

Go back along Oude Beurs and turn right into Vleeshouwersstraat, passing the Butchers' Hall. Continue as far as Veemarkt.

St-Pauluskerk

Entrance from the Veemarkt. Early May-late Sept, daily, 2-5pm. Kunstkamer €1. ☎ 03 232 32 67.

Right in the middle of the sailors' quarter, this Flamboyant Gothic church was once part of a vast monastic complex. Begun in the early 16C and completed in 1639, St Paul's is surmounted by a Baroque bell-tower (1680). It was badly damaged by a fire in 1968, but has been restored to its former glory. A rustic 18C Calvary is attached to the exterior.

The majestic interior★★ is embellished by Baroque furnishings and beautiful wooden panels on the confessionals, which are framed by huge expressive figures. In the north aisle are 15 paintings depicting the mysteries of the Rosary. This series of works was carried out by master painters of the Antwerp School, notably Rubens, Jordaens and Van Dyck. The superb *Flagellation* by Rubens is suffused with the most profound emotion. Statues surround the chancel, which is narrower than the nave, give an impression of depth further accentuated by the elevated position of the monumental marble altarpiece. There are two other works by Rubens in the transept, dating from about 1609: **Adoration of the Shepherds** (north transept) and **Dispute on the Nature of the Holy Sacrament** (south transept). The Kunstkamer houses religious objects and liturgical items.
Go back to Grote Markt

Gildekamersstraat

This narrow thoroughfare skirts the rear of the town hall and is bordered by beautiful old houses, one of which is the Folklore Museum.
Go back to the Grote Markt and into the Oude Koornmarkt.

Vlaaikensgang★

The porch at no 16 **Oude Koornmarkt** leads into this picturesque little lane, which has retained its village atmosphere.

Handschoenmarkt

This triangular square surrounded by old houses just in front of the cathedral used to be a glove market. The well is crowned with an elegant wrought-iron canopy, with Brabo on the top preparing to throw in the giant's hand. It stood in front of the town hall until 1565, and is attributed to Quentin Metsys, a wrought-iron worker said to have become a painter for love.

Kathedraal★★★

Open Mon-Fri, 10am-5pm, Sat 10am-3pm, Sun 1-4pm. Closed 1 Jan and during services. €2. ☎ 03 213 99 51.

The pride of Antwerp, the cathedral is also the largest in Belgium, covering an area of almost 1ha/2.5 acres. Although construction began with the east end in 1352 and was not completed until as late as 1521, the whole is nevertheless quite harmonious. Several generations of builders were committed to this major undertaking: Jacob Van Thienen, Jan Appelmans and his son Peeter, Jan Tac, Everaert Spoorwater, Herman and Dominique de Waghemakere and Rombout Keldermans. Recent restoration has exposed traces of the original Romanesque church, as well as some Gothic cellars (*archeological crypt in the choir*) and a number of 15C and 16C mural paintings.

The cathedral was originally the home of *Our Lady of the Tree*, a statue found in a tree after a Viking invasion. This statue was destroyed in 1580, but a copy still exists in the Église Notre-Dame-du-Sablon in Brussels.

Tower★★★ – A miracle of ornamentation and delicacy, the cathedral tower soars to a height of 123m/403ftIt was built over the course of a century by a number of different architects and houses a carillon of 47 chimes.

The second tower was left unfinished in the 16C. Four people seem to be busily at work at its foot. They were carved by Jef Lambeaux (1906) in honour of the architect Peeter Appelmans.

A curious onion dome has topped the transept crossing since the 16C.

Interior – The inside of the cathedral is exceptionally wide, comprising seven aisles, 125 pillars without capitals and a transept 117m/384ft long by 65m/213ft wide. There are many remarkable **works of art** contrasting with the cool majesty of the building itself.

In the central nave, the **pulpit** sculpted by Michel van der Voort in 1713 is a surprising sight, its effect heightened by flights of stairs crowned with birds and a ring of tumbling cherubs floating beneath a figure of Fame falling from heaven. The pulpit section itself is supported by four female figures representing four continents (Europe, Africa, Asia and America).

There are a great many works by **Rubens**. Above the high altar there is an *Assumption* (1626), one of his better representations on this theme, which captivates the viewer with its bold colours broken up by touches of light. The *Raising of the Cross* (1610) in the north transept, originally intended for St Walburga's church, is a violent, diagonal composition typical of the Baroque. The *Descent from the Cross* (1612) in the south transept is more classical in style: the body of the dead Christ and his white shroud stand out against the dark background and the red of St John's clothing; the blond hair of Mary Magdalene is resplendent while the martyred man seems to be slipping, barely supported, into the arms of a pale-faced Mary. Commissioned by the Harquebusiers' guild, of which St Christopher was patron saint, all the themes in this altarpiece represent the "bearers of Christ": St Christopher, Mary with Christ in her womb during the Visitation, Jesus being held by Simeon during the Presentation in the Temple, and the body of Christ being carried during the Descent from the Cross. Rubens' *Resurrection* (1612) is to the south in the second chapel in the ambulatory. De Backer's *Last Judgement* with panels depicting the Plantin family is in the fourth chapel in the ambulatory. Other notable works of art include Quellin the Younger's Baroque sarcophagus for Bishop Capello (1676), Frans Francken the Elder's triptych *Jesus among the Doctors of the Church* (1586), Murillo's *St Francis*, *The Last Supper* by Otto Venius and the *The Marriage at Cana* by Martin de Vos.

FROM THE LATIN QUARTER TO THE CHURCH OF ST CHARLES BORROMEUS

Start from the Komedieplaats

Bourlaschouwburg

In the heart of Antwerp's "Latin Quarter" with its numerous cafés and restaurants, the neo-Classical Bourla Theatre was designed by the city architect Pierre Bruno Bourla. The engaged columns on the façade frame the busts of famous

The Brabofontein and the guildhalls on the Grote Markt.

INDEX OF STREET NAMES AND SIGHTS IN ANTWERPEN

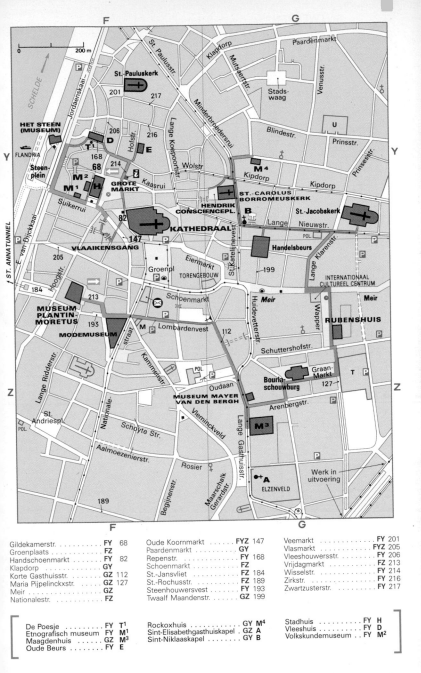

authors and composers, and from above the attic the Muses, accompanied by Apollo, hail the crowds below. The ceiling in the first entrance hall was decorated by the Antwerp artist Jan Vanriet.

Turn right, then right again and go along the Schuttershofstraat to the Wapper, the street on which the Rubens House is located (see below).

Meir – This is the city's main shopping street. The former Royal Palace dating from the 18C, in which a great many sovereigns resided, stands on the corner of the Meir (no 50) and the Wapper. The palace now houses a museum of cinematography, the Film Museum.

Go along the Lange Klarenstraat and turn right into the Lange Nieuwstraat.

St-Jacobskerk

Early Apr-late Oct, Mon-Sat, 2-5pm. €2 ☎ 03 225 04 14.

The **interior★** of this Late Gothic church is richly decorated in Baroque style. Among the paintings note Otto Venius's *Virgin Mary* in the south aisle and *The Calling of St Peter* by Jordaens in the ambulatory on the south side.

ANTWERPEN

Rubens' funerary chapel behind the chancel contains one of his last works, *The Virgin and the Saints* (1634); it is said that he depicted himself in St George's armour, the Virgin being Isabella Brant, and Mary Magdalene Hélène Fourment. Jordaens' *St Charles Healing the Plague-Stricken in Milan* hangs in the adjoining chapel.

The restored Gothic clock, believed to date from the second half of the 15C, is on display in a room at the back of the church.

Anyone wishing to visit the Begijnhof should turn left into the Parochiaanstraat. Go across St-Jacobsmarkt and the Frans Halsplein, then along the Rozenstraat and the Ossenmarkt.

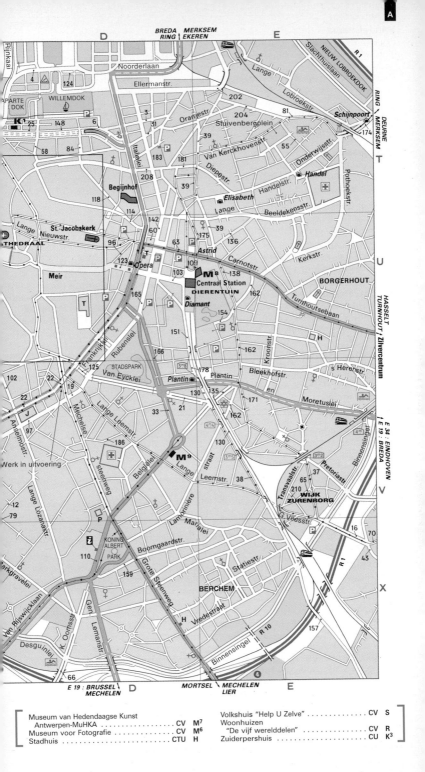

Museum van Hedendaagse Kunst		
Antwerpen-MuHKA	CV	M⁷
Museum voor Fotografie	CV	M⁶
Stadhuis	CTU	H
Volkshuis "Help U Zelve"	CV	S
Woonhuizen		
"De vijf werelddelen"	CV	R
Zuiderpershuis	CU	K³

Begijnhof

Rodestraat 39. Daily, 9am-5pm. Closed public holidays. No charge. ☎ 03 232 52 97.
The houses of the Beguine convent cluster together in their brick enclosure. A street of uneven cobblestones frames an orchard surrounded by hedges. The church, rebuilt in the 19C, is embellished with Jordaens and Van Noort paintings. Note the **Christ Bound** in the oratory.

Go back to St-Jacobskirk and then along the Lange Nieuwstraat towards the city centre.

Handelsbeurs

Open during exhibitions and events only. ☎ *03 232 41 73.*
The Stock Exchange stands at a crossroads, its glazed dome dominating the houses tightly packed around it.
Domien de Waghemakere built the first exchange, which soon became too crowded. He created a new one, which was inaugurated in 1531. It was very active throughout the 16C but was destroyed by fire in 1858. The architect Schadde rebuilt it in 1872 in the same style, and the present building consists of a hall with tiers of galleries beneath a superb glass roof.
Carry on along the Lange Nieuwstraat

St-Niklaaskapel

This 15C chapel is home to a puppet theatre (Poppenschouwburg). There is a charming little courtyard, surrounded by old buildings, tucked away behind it.
Turn right into the Sint-Katelijnevest, then turn left into the Wolstraat.

Hendrik Conscienceplein★

This quiet cobbled square blends harmoniously with the surrounding 17C and 19C buildings and with the façade of the church dedicated to St Charles Borromeus.

St-Carolus Borromeuskerk★ (Church of St Charles Borromeus)

Open Mon-Fri 10am-12.30pm, 2pm-5pm. Sat 10am-6pm. Closed Sun ☎ *03 231 37 51.*
The lovely Baroque façade of this "Jesuit-style" church is broken up horizontally into three registers with a central medallion based on a drawing by Rubens and two offset lantern turrets. Adjacent to the apse is an elegant Baroque bell-tower.
Built by the Jesuits Aguillon and Huyssens between 1615 and 1621 and initially dedicated to St Ignatius, the church was subsequently re-dedicated to St Charles Borromeus.
The interior is still striking, despite the fire of 1718 which destroyed most of the building. The ceilings painted by Rubens and Van Dyck unfortunately fell victim to the flames. The building is barrel-vaulted and has tribunes communicating with the nave through tall, brightly-lit galleries. The chancel has kept its marble ornamentation.
Rubens' painting The Assumption together with other pictures by him commissioned in 1620 for the decoration of the church are now in the Kunsthistorisches Museum in Vienna. The high altar has no fewer than three paintings. Thanks to an ingenious system still in use today it is possible to rotate them in accordance with liturgical needs.
There is 18C wood panelling running under the arcades; between each confessional guarded by four angels there are medallions tracing the lives of St Ignatius (south side) and St Francis Xavier (north side).
Museum – As well as the museum with its collections of antique lace, the gallery, funerary crypt and vestry with its reliefs in Hansche stucco are open to the public.
Return to the Wolstraat, then turn left into the Minderbroedersrui and then immediately right into the Keizersstraat.

Rockoxhuis★

Open Tue-Sun 10am-5pm. Closed Mon (except during Easter and Whitsun holidays), 1 and 2 Jan, 1 May, Ascension Day, 1 Nov, 25 Dec. €2.50. Free admission Fri. ☎ *03 201 92 50.*
Nikolas Rockox (1560-1640), a friend of Rubens, humanist and burgomaster of Antwerp, was an enthusiastic collector of objets d'art. His 17C patrician home has been restored and is now a museum. *(An audio-visual presentation in English, French and Dutch retraces Antwerp's cultural history from 1560 to 1640.)* Note the magnificent furniture (particularly the cupboards called *ribbanken*, and the finely decorated ebony cabinets), the beautiful pieces of ceramic ware, an extensive collection of paintings which includes works by Patinir, Van Dyck (two studies of a man's head), Jordaens, Teniers the Younger, Rubens, Momper, Snyders *(Antwerp Fish Market)* and Pieter Bruegel the Younger (copy of Bruegel the Elder's *Proverbs*).

Worth a visit

CITY CENTRE MUSEUMS AND MONUMENTS

South of the Schoenenmarkt and the Meir

Museum Plantin-Moretus★★★

Open daily except Mon 10am-5pm. Closed 1-2 Jan, 1 May, Ascension Day, 1-2 Nov, 25-26 Dec. €4. ☎ *03 221 14 50; www.antwerpen.be/cultuur/museum_plantinmoretus*
This magnificent museum occupies 34 rooms in the house and printing works built by the famous printer Plantin and enlarged in the 17C and 18C by his descendents, the Moretus family. It provides a fascinating history of humanism

Museum Plantin-Moretus.

and old books in 16C and 17C Netherlands, through its beautiful antique furniture, tapestries, gilded leatherwork, paintings, well-stocked libraries, collections of typography and drawings, engravings, old manuscripts and valuable editions.

Museum visit – *The rooms are numbered and should be visited in order.* Visitors are greeted by the pleasant tranquillity of the courtyard, surrounded by leaded stained-glass windows framed by a Virginia creeper. Go through the main drawing room decorated with portraits by Rubens, then the shop, the proof-reading room, Plantin's office and that of Justus Lipsius, Plantin's erudite friend. The presses in the printing shop date from the 16C, 17C and 18C; they still print *The Happiness of This World*, a sonnet by Plantin.

The famous *Biblia Regia* or *Biblia Polyglotta* is exhibited on the first floor, along with the Gutenberg Bible, of which there are only 13 copies left in the world. The wonderful libraries contain more than 25 000 old works, and the Max Horn Room has a collection of French literature from the 16C, 17C and 18C in magnificently bound first editions. The foundry is situated on the second floor.

The perfection of the publications produced on his 16 presses (the Estienne family in France had only four) and his reputation for culture and erudition earned him the admiration of the greatest men of his time, including Philip II who appointed him official Royal Printer and granted him the monopoly of sales of liturgical works in Spain and the Spanish colonies. Plantin created the famous Antwerp

> ### THE "PRINCE OF PRINTERS"
> **Christophe Plantin**, a native of the Tours area in France, arrived in Antwerp in 1549 and became a printer in 1555 under the sign of the Golden Compasses; this emblem illustrated his motto *"Labore et Constantia"*, the moving point representing work and the fixed point constancy.

School of Engraving, in collaboration with his friend, the governor and merchant Jerome Cook; Rubens himself would later head this institution. Plantin's greatest typographical achievement was his **Biblia Regia**, printed in five languages (Hebrew, Syrian, Greek, Latin and Aramaic). He died in 1589.

Modemuseum** (MOMU)
Tues-Sun 10am-6pm (Thur 9pm). Closed 1-2 Jan, 25, 26 and 31 Dec. Free admission Fri. €5. ☏ *03 470 27 70; www.momu.be*

Bang in the middle of an area made stylish by the younger generation of Belgian fashion designers, this sparkling new museum has been installed in a 19C building cleverly adapted by the architect Marie-Josée Van Hee. Material from the permanent collections is displayed in rotation and are arranged thematically, allowing fascinating comparisons to be made between historic and contemporary items (clothes, lovely old lace, accessories, textiles) and for the evolution of fashion to be followed through time. The building also houses the fashion department of the Academy of Fine Arts.

Museum Mayer van den Bergh**
Tue-Sun, 10am-5pm (last admission 4.30pm). Closed Mon (except during Easter and Whitsun holidays), 1 and 2 Jan, 1 May, Ascension Day, 1 and 2 Nov, 25 and 26 Dec. €4. Free admission Fri. ☏ *03 232 42 37; www.antwerpen.be/cultuur/museum_mvdb*

Antwerpen

This museum is located in a neo-Gothic house dating from the early 20C. It presents a remarkable collection of works of art, brought together by the collector **Fritz Mayer van den Bergh** (1858-1901), who showed real genius in his purchases of medieval sculpture, illuminated manuscripts, ivories, tapestries and paintings.

The ground floor has four lovely portraits by Cornelis de Vos, two 12C French statue-columns, as well as a 13C painted panel by Simeone and Machilone of Spoleto showing scenes from the life of the Virgin Mary. A 15C triptych of *Christ on the Cross* by Quentin Metsys testifies to the painter's talent. The beauty and serenity of the landscape forms a strong contrast to the apparent suffering of the figures.

The first floor has exceptionally fine Byzantine and Gothic ivories. Particularly arresting, however, is the carved group of *Jesus and St John* by the master Heinrich von Konstanz (c 1300), as is the small Dutch diptych (1400) – probably a travelling altar – representing the *Nativity and St Christopher* (the reverse side depicts the *Resurrection*).

The museum's finest exhibit is the painting entitled **Mad Meg★★** *(De Dulle Griet)* by Bruegel the Elder, an apocalyptic vision of war in remarkably bold, fiery colours. Next to it, the *Twelve Flemish Proverbs* demonstrates another facet of Bruegel's astounding talent. The *Census at Bethlehem* and *Winter Landscape* are the work of his sons.

Maagdenhuis

Open weekdays (exc Tues), 10am-5pm, Sat-Sun, 1pm-5pm. Closed public holidays, 2 Jan, 11 July and 26 Dec. €2.50. ☎ 03 223 56 10.
Part of this former orphanage for girls has been converted into a museum. There are many paintings by Rubens, *St Jerome* by Van Dyck, sculptures and a fine collection of 16C Antwerp ceramic bowls.

St-Elisabethgasthuiskapel

Open only to groups by prior arrangement. Apply to Maagdenhuismuseum, Lange Gasthuisstraat 45, 2000 Antwerpen. ☎ 03 232 56 20.
This chapel is part of the old 13C St Elizabeth's Hospital which was closed down in 1986 and subsequently restored as an arts centre (Elzenveld).
The Brabant Gothic nave has capitals decorated with motifs based on the crinkly leaves of kale; it dates from the early 15C. The chancel is the same length and was added on between 1442 and 1460. The black and white marble high altar by Artus Quellin the Younger dominates the Baroque decoration; above the altar is a statue portraying the Virgin Mary. Among the works of art note paintings by Godfried Maes and Frans Francken the Younger.

Rubenshuis★★

Open daily (except Mon), 10am-5pm. Closed 1 and 2 Jan, 1 May, 1 and 2 Nov, 25 and 26 Dec. €5. ☎ 03 201 15 55; www.antwerpen.be/cultuur/rubenshuis
Rubens' presence can be felt everywhere in the museums and churches of Antwerp, but it is perceived most strongly in this grand house bought in 1610, the year after he married Isabella Brant.

The Rubenshuis.

Ch. Bastin – J. Evrard/MICHELIN

ANTWERP'S GREATEST PAINTER

Rubens was born in exile near Cologne on 28 June 1577, where his father, an alderman of Antwerp, had been forced to take refuge when suspected of heresy. Rubens first saw Antwerp, in ruins, at the age of 12, after his father's death.

He studied with Verhaecht and Van Noort; from 1594 to 1598 he worked in the painter Otto Venius's studio and then he became a master in the Guild of St Luke.

He spent some time in Italy and returned to Antwerp in 1608, when the town was enjoying a period of peace under the reign of the "archdukes", Albert and Isabella. A flood of commissions led him to set up a studio-workshop. This was the apotheosis for Rubens and his school. Flemish and cosmopolitan, Catholic and Humanist, he embodied the city's vibrant spirit. A diplomat in the sovereigns' service, as a painter he succeeded in combining Italianate features with the Flemish tradition.

His students and assistants include the most prestigious names: Jan Brueghel, known as "Velvet" Brueghel; and the three Antwerp painters Jordaens, Van Dyck and Snyders. His influence extended both to sculpture (the Quellins and Verbruggen) and Baroque architecture.

He died in Antwerp in 1640 and was buried in St-Jacobskerk.

P. de Franqueville/MICHELIN

Rubens turned it into a sumptuous palace, after carrying out major extension work and the construction of a huge studio, and it was here that he spent most of his life and painted most of his works. Having borne him three children, his first wife died; four years after her death he married the very young Hélène Fourment. They had five more children who were brought up here.

Tour – *Tickets from the kiosk opposite.* The entire house was refurbished in 1946. In the north wing, the Flemish-style living quarters are embellished with gilded leatherwork, 17C furniture and numerous paintings (note Rubens' famous self-portrait in the dining room). In the south wing, the studio has a gallery from where visitors could contemplate his paintings.

The studio's Baroque façade with its philosophers' busts and mythological statuary can be admired from the courtyard. A portico links the two lodges and opens onto a garden through three arches which Rubens reproduced in some of his canvases. The 17C garden has been redesigned in accordance with period paintings and engravings.

Between the Scheldt and the Grote Markt

Etnografisch Museum★★

Suikerrui 19. &. Open daily (except Mon), 10am-5pm. Closed 1 and 2 Jan, 1 May, Ascension Day, 1 and 2 Nov, 25 and 26 Dec. €4. Free admission Fri. ☎ 03 220 86 00. Visitors are greeted by the statues and masks belonging to the Africa section, which displays both precious exhibits and everyday objects. Many of these carry magic symbolism and are used in ritual ceremonies and dances. The "mystical significance" of these so-called primitive objects is clearly reflected in the Songye masks and Mbuun bowls from the Congo. The South Sea Islands section highlights Melanesian tribes, in which ancestor worship and social hierarchy are essential concepts: note the drum from the New Hebrides with a vertical slit to symbolise high rank and the fine statues carved from tree-ferns. The latter are traditionally used in funerary rites, as are the Asmat sculptures (New Guinea), exemplified by the magnificent ancestors' post called "bis". Note the ancestral statues crowned by bowler hats from New Ireland and the macabre display with skulls of Sepik natives from the western part of New Guinea.

The Americas section on the first floor presents clothes and pipes associated with Native American culture. A child's kayak and its accessories evoke Inuit society in Greenland while a mask-crest in the shape of a salmon represents Canada. Numerous pre-Colombian earthenware pieces testify to South and Central American civilisations, along with fabrics, jewels, masks and decorative trappings; see also the brilliantly coloured Amazonian feather masks. The Indonesia section includes ancestral statues portraying reclining figures, firearms with elegantly chiselled ivory handles as well as batik cloth and jewellery items.

The collections on the second floor are devoted to the great religions of Asia: Buddhism, Hinduism and Jainism (a Hindu-inspired denomination advocating the salvation of man's soul). Japan is represented by the great Kannon Bosatsu (16C-17C) and by a Buddha in laquered wood. The objects from Tibet include a remarkable 19C map of Lhasa. The two 19C funerary towers from Nepal adorned with religious motifs, the work of Sherpas from Tibet, were part of the traditional rites which accompanied the dying. Note the Tibetan altarpiece for daily use and a unique series of 54 Chinese miniatures representing a meditation scene with mandalas. Indonesia is present with a collection of open-work dolls for shadow theatre performances.

The third floor displays Celadon porcelain ware (12C-17C), whose colour is reminiscent of jade. Besides Indian fabrics, there is an array of Japanese exhibits.

Volkskundemuseum

Open daily (except Mon), 10am-5pm (last admission 4.30pm). Closed 1 and 2 Jan, 1 May, Ascension Day, 1 and 2 Nov, 25 and 26 Dec. €2.50. Free admission Fri. ☎ 03 220 86 66; www.antwerpen.be/cultuur/volkskundemuseum

The extensive and varied collections displayed in the Folklore Museum are devoted to Flemish popular art. The ground floor concerns life outside the home: statues in gardens and parks, decorated façades, shop signs, street games, old posters and traditional funfair attractions such as the key exhibit, a wonderful Mortier street organ. The festive atmosphere continues into the stairway with the heads of the giants Druon Antigon and Pallas Athena, which take part in the procession that crosses the town every year. The first floor retraces the successive stages in human life, from birth through to death, covering childhood, school life, courtship and marriage. The reconstruction of an apothecary's shop and glass cabinets devoted to magic and superstition are also on view. The second floor illustrates home life and the community lifestyle that is so important to Belgium (De Poesje puppet theatre).

Vleeshuis★

Open daily (except Mon), 10am-4.45pm. Closed 1 and 2 Jan, 1 May, Ascension Day, 1 and 2 Nov, 25 and 26 Dec. €2.50. ☎ 03 233 64 04; www.antwerpen.be/cultuur/vleeshuis.

This imposing Gothic building is to be found in the old harbour district. Bands of white sandstone lighten the brick walls, which are framed by slender turrets. The **Butchers' Hall** was built between 1501 and 1504 by Herman de Waghemakere at the request of the guild members. Since 1913 it has housed the city museum.

In the great hall crowned by diagonal rib vaulting, the slabs for cutting up meat have been replaced by a huge collection of **musical instruments★**. In the 17C Antwerp was a famous centre for the manufacture of harpsicords. As well as a number of superb pieces which once belonged to the Ruckers family, there collection embraces a wide range of string and wind instruments. On the first floor a series of bourgeois interiors have been painstakingly reconstructed, as has the council chamber of the butchers' guild. The fine exhibits illustrate the artistry shown by Antwerp guilds and trades during the city's golden age: coins, faience, weapons, and panels of 16C Antwerp glazed earthenware tiles representing the conversion of St Paul (1547). There is also a model of the town centre around 1860 and a number of archeological finds. The museum also has a small collection of Egyptian art, including a remarkable sarcophagus dating from the 21st dynasty (10C BC), which housed the remains of Nesi-Chonsoe, known as the "opera singer from Amon-Rê".

Nationaal Scheepvaartmuseum (Het Steen)★

Open daily (except Mon), 10am-4.45pm. Closed 1 and 2 Jan, 1 May, Ascension Day, 1 and 2 Nov, 25 and 26 Dec. €4. ☎ 03 201 93 40; www.antwerpen.be/cultuur/scheepvaartmuseum

The Maritime Museum is in the Steen, the fortress originally built sometime after 843 on the Scheldt to defend the new frontier established by the Treaty of Verdun. Having been a prison since the early 14C, the castle was enlarged by Emperor Charles V around 1520, and subsequently restored in the 19C and 20C.

A fascinating exhibition retraces maritime and river life, with particular reference to Belgium, from its beginnings to the present time, aided by numerous pictures, models, instruments, sculptures and documents. There is also a department of industrial archaeology (maritime park) open to visitors where a collection of boats is on display. In front of the Steen stands a statue of the legendary mischievous imp of Antwerp, **Lange Wapper**.

Shipping activity on the estuary is visible from the terraces on the **Steenplein** promenade. Boat trips leave from here for the tour of the port. All along this quay structures in resolutely contemporary style (Van Roosmalenhuis, on the corner of Goede Hoopstraat and St-Michielskaai) alternate with superb older buildings.

Walk north to the Brouwershuis

Brouwershuis (Brewers' Hall)

Open by prior arrangment only, Tue-Sun 10am-5pm. Closed 1-2 Jan, 1 May, Ascension, 1-2 Nov, 25-26 Dec. €2.50. ☎ *03 232 65 11; www.antwerpen.be/cultuur/brouwershuis*

Gilbert van Schoonbeke erected this building around 1553 in order to supply water to the many breweries he had opened in the neighbourhood. In 1581 it became the seat of the brewers' guild. Visitors can see the refurbished stable, the horse treadmill and the water-raising system, as well as the reservoirs once connected to the canals. The workshop and more particularly the beautiful Council Room are upstairs; this room often figures in paintings by Henri De Braekeleer. It is furnished with antiques, the walls are clad with 17C gilded Mechelen leather and there is a beautiful fireplace decorated with twisted columns.

THE ZUID

Koninklijk Museum voor Schone Kunsten★★★

& *Open daily (except Mon), 10am-5pm. Closed 1 and 2 Jan, 1 May, Ascension Day and 25 Dec. €5.* ☎ *03 238 78 09; www.antwerpen.be/cultuur/kmska*

The Royal Museum of Fine Art is housed in a 19C building with a façade consisting of Corinthian columns crowned with bronze chariots by Vinçotte. The four allegorical figures adorning the façade symbolise the arts: architecture, painting, sculpture and engraving. Access to the upper floor is by a sweeping staircase profusely decorated by Nicaise de Keyser, which recounts the story of the Antwerp School of Painting. The museum's collections give an overview of the evolution of European painting from the 14C to the present day.

THE ZUID OR SOUTH TOWN

In 1875, construction of a new district began south of the city, not far from the Scheldt, on an area once occupied by the ramparts and the Zuiderkasteel, a Spanish stronghold built in the days of the Duke of Alba. The location was chosen twice to host the World Fair, first in 1885, then in 1894. The Museum of Fine Arts was inaugurated in 1890 and the Hippodroom Theatre opened its doors in 1894. After experiencing a difficult start, the district reached a peak of popularity between the two World Wars. It was made up of two very different areas: the lively, bustling south docks swarming with people and the quiet, residential neighbourhood around the museum. However, due to poor housing conditions, urban de-population and the fact that harbour activities gradually shifted to the north of the city, the Zuid entered a period of decline. The filling-in of basins in the 1960s and the pulling down of the Hippodroom in the early 1970s served to speed up the process. However, the trend was to be reversed at the beginning of the 1980s. The area saw an unexpected revival thanks to the opening of two new museums – the Museum of Photography and the Museum of Contemporary Art – in two former warehouses. People developed a taste for late 19C architecture and a great many buildings and monuments came to be restored. The most striking examples of this renovation movement are the Volkshuis "Help U Zelve", the corner building "De vijf werelddelen" and the Zuiderpershuis, as well as several buildings bordering the quays. Here fine old mansions can been seen alongside examples of uncompromisingly contemporary architecture, among them the Van Roosmalen building (corner of St-Michielskaai and Goede Hoopstraat), a black and white structure by Bob van Reeth dating from 1985-87, together with a timber edifice by Neutelings and Koning. At night, the many restaurants and cafés make the Zuid a popular and lively area. All the art galleries make a point of opening their exhibitions on the same day, enabling visitors to make a sort of "art tour" of the area. Of particular note is the Waterpoort in Gillisplaats, said to have been designed by Rubens, as well as the Lambermontplaats monument and the De Schelde Vrij statue on Marnixplaats.

Early painting (1300-1800) – The museum houses a superb array of early Flemish painting. Note especially two masterpieces by Jan Van Eyck: *St Barbara*, depicted in front of a meticulously detailed Gothic tower still under construction, and an exquisitely coloured *Madonna at the Fountain*. Van der Weyden's *Portrait of Philippe de Croÿ* is a work of great refinement, as is his *Seven Sacraments Triptych*, set against the backdrop of a huge Gothic church. Each sacrament (Baptism, Confirmation, the Eucharist, Repentance, Ordination, Marriage, Healing of the Sick) is embodied by an angel bearing a banner. The identity of the man depicted in Hans Memling's *Portrait of Man with Medal* has often given rise to controversy: some say he is the medal-maker Jean de Candida, others that he is an Italian collector. Of great appeal are four small panels by **Simone Martini** (14C), including one representing the Annunciation executed with a delicate touch reminiscent of miniature painting; the famous *Virgin Surrounded by Red and Blue Angels* which **Jean Fouquet** endowed with the lovely features of Agnès Sorel, mistress of Charles VII, King of France; splendid portraits by **Jean Clouet**, particularly that of the son of Francis I. The *Self-Portrait of the Artist and his Wife* by the Master of Frankfurt is one of the first non-religious double portraits in the history of the southern Low Countries.

Koninklijk Museum voor Schone Kunsten, Antwerpen

Virgin Surrounded by Red and Blue Angels,
by Jean Fouquet.

The painting of the 16C still has many of the characteristics of the Flemish Primitives but is nevertheless subject to Italian influence, as is quite clear in two works by **Quentin Metsys**, *Mary Magdalene* and his famous *Triptych of the Entombment of Christ,* painted for the joiners' guild. **Joachim Patinir**'s *Flight into Egypt* marks a turning-point in the history of landscape painting. The museum has many portraits (by Metsys, Pourbus and the Master of Antwerp), as well as landscapes and still lifes.

Four delightful small panels bearing the title *The Four Seasons*, are by Abel Grimmer.

17C Dutch painting is represented by works by Frans Hals, Ter Borch and Hobbema.

The **Rubens** room is completely given over to works by this master of the Antwerp Baroque, and it is possible to follow in great detail the way in which his style evolved. *The Baptism of Christ*, painted in Italy, and the triptych entitled *The Incredulity of St Thomas* are still Classical in inspiration. Then realism supervenes with the bloody *Christ in the Hay*, while pathos is conveyed in works such as the *Last Communion of St Francis*, the *Blow of the Spear*, and the *Trinity* with its striking perspective. Finally, the *Adoration of the Magi* (1624), with its vivid colours and expressive figures, represents a high point in Flemish painting of the 17C.

The Van Dyck and Jordaens rooms have distinguished portraits as well as religious works of great subtlety by **Van Dyck**, who at the age of 16 already had his own studio and a troop of apprentices. Works by **Jordaens** such as *The Family Concert* are splendidly full of life.

Modern art (1800-present) – One room is dedicated to **James Ensor** the famous painter, caricaturist and draughtsman from Ostend. It traces his career from his earliest work, often dubbed his "dark period", during which he concentrated on portraits and interiors; his style at this time is beautifully captured in *The Bourgeois Salon*. His fascination with strange masks is expressed in *Intrigue* (1890). Impressionism and Pointillism are represented with works by, among others, Émile Claus. The *Lady at the Window* is a fine example of a painting by the great architect Henry Van de Velde. The profound response of Meunier to the world of work finds expression in a number of pictures and sculptures. There is social concern too in *The Blind One* by Laermans. The very striking *Burgher of Calais* by Rodin, who settled in Brussels for a few years, is part of his famous group sculpture commissioned by Calais town council.

The museum's collections include many paintings and sculptures by the Brabant Fauvist artist **Rik Wouters**, who died prematurely. His wife Nel played a key role in his work, which was characterised by great expressiveness and luminosity, as in *Woman Ironing* and *Education*. The Sint-Martens-Latem group is well documented with works by the Expressionist Permeke and his arresting style *(Fisherman's Wife)*, the De Smet brothers and **Van den Berghe**. The two female figures in *Two Spring Seasons* by Van de Woestijne symbolise rural life and city life. The Constructivist movement can be seen in works by **Servrancks** and **De Peeters**. As for Surrealism, it is particularly well represented by **Magritte** *(16 September)*. Tribute is paid to several foreign artists such as Modigliani, Zadkine and Grosz. **Pierre Alechinsky**'s large canvas painted in 1964, *The Last Day*, can be seen as the ultimate expression of his involvement with the **CoBrA** group.

Woonhuizen "De vijf werelddelen"

Not far from the Museum of Fine Art on the corner of Plaatsnijderstraat and Schilderstraat is the remarkable "Five Continents" house dating from 1901. This Art Nouveau building designed by the architect Frans Smet-Verhas was built for a shipowner, hence the wooden ship's bow. A fine loggia above has stained-glass windows bearing the names of the world's five continents.

Volkshuis "Help U Zelve"

The architect Emiel van Averbeke, who was acclaimed as "Antwerp's Horta", built the Liberal People's House "Help U Zelve" in conjunction with Jan van Asperen in 1898. The splendid, recently restored façade is partially decorated with mosaics and has two gables topped with sculptures.

Zuiderpershuis

Beyond the neo-Baroque façade of the building designed by Emiel Dieltiens in 1881 stands a former hydraulic power station. The accumulators were housed in the twin towers. The building has been converted to serve as the home of the theatre troupe **De Internationale Nieuwe Scène** as well as an international cultural centre, a venue for concerts, dance and ballet, art shows and plays.

Museum van Hedendaags Kunst Antwerpen (MuHKA)

Leuvenstraat. Open daily (except Mon), 10am-5pm. Closed 1 Jan, 1 May, Ascension Day, and 25 Dec. €4. ☎ *03 238 59 60; www.muhka.be*

Housed in an old grain elevator, the Contemporary Art Gallery underwent extensive restoration work a few years ago. It is situated close to the river and displays an interesting collection of modern art from the 1970s onwards. Widely acclaimed artists from both Belgium (J Fabre, PH Van Snick, B Lohaus, J Deleu etc) and abroad (T Cragg, - B Nauman, A Charlton, Boltanski, D Flavin) exhibit their works here. Take the lift up to the top of the building to admire H Duchateau's *Growing Ladder*.

The museum's permanent exhibition is open to the public during the summer months only. The rest of the year MuHKA stages major temporary art shows.

Antwerpen Miniatuurstad (Magic World)

♿ *Open daily, 10am-6pm (5pm Mon). Closed 1 Jan and 25 Dec. €6.* ☎ *03 237 03 29.*

This miniature reconstruction of Antwerp *(still being completed)* has been laid out in an old shed on the wharf beside the Scheldt. A *son et lumière* brings the display to life. Note the workshops where new parts of the miniature town are built.

Museum voor Fotografie

Waalse Kaai 47. ♿ *Museum closed until Spring 2004 for renovation work.* ☎ *03 242 93 00; www.fotografiemuseum.be*

The Photography Museum has been established in an old warehouse dating back to 1902. The brick façade conceals a building with a reinforced concrete structure. Two galleries have been set aside for temporary exhibitions on the ground floor. One bears the name of **Lieven Gevaert**, an Antwerp industrialist who devoted much time to perfecting the quality of photographic paper.

The first floor traces each step in the history of photography from the camera obscura through a remarkable collection of equipment including daguerreotypes, dark rooms, detective cameras, spy cameras hidden in walking sticks or ties, panoramic devices, magic lanterns, folding equipment and more recent, sophisticated models. The most remarkable exhibit is undoubtedly the "Panorama Kaiser", commissioned by the Royal Zoological Society in 1905, a fine example of stereoscopic photography.

The second floor is devoted to artistic photography, with prints by some of the world's greatest names: Man Ray, Sander, Cartier-Bresson, Brassaï, Avedon, Irving Penn, Ansel Adams, Gilbert de Keyser etc. Note the monumental camera (c 1940) conceived for making plates used in the production of military maps.

Woonhuizen De Vijf Werelddelen

AROUND THE CENTRAL STATION

Centraal Station

Next to the Zoo, the main station (1900-05) was built to plans by L de La Censerie. The monumental neo-Baroque pile is topped by an enormous 60m/197ft high dome.

Dierentuin★★

Open daily Mar, Apr, Oct: 10am-5.30pm; May, Jun: 10am-6pm; Jul, Aug: 10am-7pm, Sept, Nov-Feb: 10am-4.30pm. €13.50. ☎ *03 202 45 40; www.zoo antwerpen.be*

The zoological gardens are located in a park covering an area of 10ha/25 acres between Centraal Station and the Natural History Museum which was built in 1885. A statue of the museum's founder astride a camel can be seen over the entrance. The zoo features some rare species among its 5 000 animals, such as white rhinoceros and okapis (Moorish building). The brightly coloured Egyptian temple (1856) houses elephants, giraffes, ostriches and Arabian oryx. The sculptor Rembrandt Bugatti often came here in search of inspiration. In the aviary nothing separates the tropical birds in the bright light from the public in the shadows. Visitors can see nocturnal beasts in their burrows from behind large windows in the Nocturama. The planetarium, aquarium, delphinarium and Natural History Museum offer additional attractions.

Provinciaal Diamantmuseum

Open daily May-Oct, 10am-6pm, Mon 1pm-6pm; Nov-Apr, 10am-5pm. Closed Jan, 25 and 26 Dec. €5. ☎ 03 202 48 90; www.diamantmuseum.be

The Provincial Diamond Museum is housed in a number of attractive early 20C buildings just a stone's throw from the diamond district and the main station. The museum explains the origin and properties of this crystal, formed between 150 and 200km/93-124mi beneath the surface of the earth at a temperature of 2 000 degrees C.

Up to the 18C, diamonds, the hardest known matter, whose weight is calculated in carats, came from India, but now the principal mines are in South Africa, West Africa and Australia.

The museum has displays on the industrial use of diamonds, the transformation of the raw stone into jewels, and the history of diamonds in Antwerp. A 19C diamond workshop has been reconstructed. The treasury houses an extraordinary collection of precious jewels which evoke changes in taste from the Middle Ages to today.

DIAMONDS: A TRADITIONAL INDUSTRY AND TRADE

In 1476 Louis de Berken, from Bruges, perfected the technique of diamond-cutting; this was to become a major industry in Antwerp. The arrival in the 16C of several Jewish families from Portugal gave it a new impetus. The trade in diamonds, mainly imported from the East Indies at that time, virtually became a Portuguese monopoly with Vasco da Gama's discovery of the Indian sea route. Antwerp's craftsmen rapidly won international renown. The South African diamond rush began in 1869, while at the same time the town underwent a major increase in its population with a large influx of Jews from Eastern Europe. Today the diamond trade (but not the actual cutting of stones) is handled by a number of Jewish families who have been established for centuries, as well as by traders from India, Zaïre, and Lebanon.

Museum Smidt van Gelder

Belgiëlei 91. Closed for restoration work. ☎ 03 239 06 52.

This museum is housed in a refined 18C interior, featuring beautiful furniture and valuable collections (Dutch painting, Chinese porcelain).

Excursions

Openluchtmuseum voor Beeldhouwkunst Middelheim★

S by Karel Oomsstraat. Follow Gerard Le Grellelaan, then Beukenlaan which runs along the edge of the park (Nachtegalenpark), then left onto Middelheimlaan. ⎣ Open early Oct-late Mar, daily (except Mon), 10am-5pm; Apr and Sept, 10am-7pm; May and Aug, 10am-8pm; June and July, 10am-9pm. Closed 1 and 2 Jan, 1 May, Ascension Day, 1 and 2 Nov, 25 and 26 Dec. No charge. ☎ 03 827 15 34; www.antwerpen.be /cultuur/museum_middelheim

The open-air Sculpture Museum is set against a backdrop of vast well-shaded lawns beneath huge trees in Middelheim Park (12ha/30 acres). It contains over 400 works by artists from Rodin to the present. The "Middelheim-Hoog" section contains modern sculptures by Belgian and foreign artists (Maillol, Bourdelle, Moore, Giacometti, Richier, Calder, Nevelson, Pompon, Jespers, Gentils etc). Note the fine sweeping lines of Henry Moore's *King and Queen* and the extremely dynamic *Mad Virgin* by Rik Wouters. Nature provided the inspiration for René Braem's white pavilion, which houses small or fragile sculptures in wood, terracotta, metal and plaster. "Middelheim-Laag" displays contemporary works; the most striking exhibits include two moving figures by Juan Muñoz, Richard Deacon's enigmatic creation and Panamarenko's *Poulet Préhistorique.*

Provinciaal Museum Sterckshof★ (Zilvercentrum)

Head east on Carnotstraat, then take Turnhoutsebaan to Borgerhout. Access by Cornelissenlaan. Open daily (except Mon), 10am-5.30pm. Closed 25 Dec to 2 Jan. No charge. ☎ 03 360 52 50; www.sterckshof.be

Nestling in the Rivierenhof Park in Deurne is the lovely mansion of Sterckshof (1938), built in Flemish neo-Renaissance tradition. Following extensive renovation it is now the home of the Silverware Museum.

On the first floor, visitors are offered practical information on various kinds of ore and silver mines as well as on how this precious metal is used in industry. The museum also presents a videotape on silverwork techniques, illustrated by a large collection of tools. Hallmarks reveal the origin of the object, the proportion of silver, the date when it was made and the identity of the silversmith. The most valuable

The White Bear by F. Pompon.

dishes and bowls are on display in the ornamental salon. The museum features a fine collection of liturgical objects, including a splendid holy water font (1833) by the Antwerp artist Verschuylen, portraying Jesus and the Samaritan beside the well. The bedroom contains jewellery pieces, toiletries and other miscellaneous items. The dining room, enhanced by a superb 16C coffered ceiling, traces the history of silver cutlery from the 14C to the 19C. The salon displays some pretty tea and coffee sets, presented alongside a magnificent Brussels plate embellished with an iris motif executed in the Art Nouveau style (c 1900). The greater part of the Lunden bequest is made up of silverware destined for household use.The workshop is devoted to restoring silver objects and to creating new designs.

Wijk Zurenborg★★

Near Berchem railway station. This splendid district, made up of several streets around **Cogels-Osylei** has been remarkably well-preserved. It takes its name from a 16C pleasure-garden. The area dates from the 19C and has a most impressive display of town houses built in revival, eclectic and Art Nouveau styles. A number of famous architects were employed in its construction, namely Jos Bascourt, Emiel Dieltiens, Frans Smet-Verhas and Jules Hofman. Certain groups of buildings look like veritable palaces, such as those at nos 32-36 Cogels-Osylei (1897-99), designed by the architect Dieltiens, and the three Flemish neo-Renaissance mansions at nos 25-29 on the same avenue, built to plans by J Bascourt. Also on this avenue stands the "Huize Zonnebleom" (Sunflower House) by Jules Hofman,

The Battle of Waterloo, Zurenborg.

striking on account of its sinuous lines. The house at no 80 is almost an exact copy of the painter Georges de St-Cyr's house in Brussels. The four houses at the corner of Generaal Van Merlenstraat and Waterloostraat are built in a more sober style and illustrate the four seasons. At no 11 Waterloostraat is the "Battle of Waterloo" residence ("De Slag van Waterloo") designed by F Smet-Verhas. Note the portraits of Napoleon and Wellington, the large bow-window and the small corner turret.

Brasschaat

15km north. This town has a large recreational centre in an extensive park with swimming pools and a zoo.

The **road** from Brasschaat to Schilde is most attractive. It is lined with banks of rhododendron bushes in several places, making a marvellous show in May and June when they are in full bloom, especially on the stretch of road flanking the Botermelk Estate on the other side of the swing bridge spanning the Antwerp canal at Turnhout. There are several mansions tucked amid the woods and flowers of **'s Gravenwezel**.

De Kalmthoutse Heide and Kalmthout Arboretum

25km/15.5mi N. Leave on Schijnpoortweg. Open late Jan-mid-Feb and mid-Mar to mid-Nov: 10am-5pm. €4. ☎ 03 666 67 41.

De Kalmthoutse Heide Nature Reserve *(natuurreservaat)* forms part of Kempen region, about 2km/1.25mi from the town of Kalmthout near the border. It covers 732ha/1 809 acres of sand dunes, heathland *(heide)*, pine forests and marshes, inhabited by numerous birds and crisscrossed by way-marked footpaths.

The Arboretum

Ch. Bastin – J. Evrard/MICHELIN

Kalmhout Arboretum *(off N 111)* dating from 1857, is a quiet place for a stroll as well as exceptionally interesting for botanists. A walk in the grounds *(no paths, sturdy footwear essential)* provides an opportunity to admire a wide variety of trees and shrubs, including many rare species. In addition to the many conifers, there are magnolias, rhododendrons and shrubs belonging to the rose family (prunus varieties). The presence of natural vegetation lends a particular charm to this beautifully laid-out park.

Lillo-Fort

15km/9.4mi along the east bank of the Scheldt.

Surrounded by water on all sides, the old stronghold of Lillo conceals a peaceful village behind its leafy ramparts. The church presides over a charming central square and a little harbour. This is one of the last three villages in the old polders area which is remembered in the **Polder en Zeemuseum** (Polders Museum).

The village of Doel can be seen from the dyke along the Scheldt.

Tour

ALONG THE SCHELDT TO DOEL

25 km. Head out of Antwerp on the Amerikalei, then take the Kennedy tunnel towards Hulst, then make for Antwerpen-Linkeroever (the left bank).

A little garden strewn with ships' propellers, anchors and lifebelts near the pedestrian and cyclist tunnel provides an interesting **view** of central Antwerp with its towering cathedral and skyscraper. The marina is tucked out of sight further north, along with a little mill and the St-Anne bathing beach. A boating lake lies to the south (Galgenweel).

Go back along the road towards Hulst, then head for Doel.

The road crosses a strange region where the polders, traditionally used for stock raising, lie next to Kallo's great industrial complexes *(see above)*, for which the ground had to be drained.

Doel

This small village, protected from the Scheldt by an enormous dike, has a tiny fishing port. A windmill stands on top of the dike. Lillo can be seen directly opposite, its white mill emerging from beyond the trees. Equally visible are the chimney-stacks of the industrial estate. A nuclear power plant has been built near Doel.

Arlon

Nowadays the attractive capital of the Belgian province of Luxembourg, Arlon is an ancient hilltop town. In Roman times it was one of the major towns (Orolaunum) on the road between Reims and Trier. Fortified in the late 3C, it still has a number of Roman remains. Arlon's exceptionally fine strategic position is revealed by the view from the tower of St Donat's church at the top of the hill. The panorama takes in the town's slate rooftops, St Martin's church and no fewer than four countries: Belgium, Luxembourg, France and Germany.

Location

Luxembourg P *– Population 24 685 – Michelin maps 716 K 6 and 534 T 24. Town plan in the current edition of The Red Guide Benelux.*
🛈 *Rue des Faubourgs 2 – 6700 – ☎ 063 21 63 60.*

Worth a Visit

Musée Luxembourgeois★

Closed for refurbishment. Due to re-open in 2004. Ring for details. ☎ *063 22 61 92; www.ial.be*

The museum contains fascinating regional archaeological and ethnographic collections.

The outstanding exhibits in the remarkable **Gallo-Roman lapidary section★★** on the ground floor are a unique collection of funerary monuments and fragments of civil architecture. The fragments are carved with low reliefs representing either mythological (Bacchus, Hercules) or allegorical figures (dancers), as well as domestic scenes offering detailed information on daily life in the first three centuries AD. Note in particular **The Travellers**, a magnificent, beautifully expressive low relief and also the very fine Vervicius monument discovered in 1979-80 (scenes including the combat between Achilles and Hector). There is also a Merovingian collection (tombs, jewels), medieval and Renaissance furniture and a 16C altarpiece.

The Travellers, low relief

Musée luxembourgeois, Arlon

Tour Romaine

Visitors should apply to the Café d'Alby, Grand-Place 1. €0.50. ☎ *063 21 64 47. Roman Baths open year-round, daily. No charge. Basilica open year-round, daily. No charge.*

Directory

⊜ **Au Capucin Gourmet** – *Rue Capucins 22* – ☎ *063 22 16 63* – *Closed Sat midday, Sun eve, Mon. €16 lunch* – *€43.*
A stone's throw from St Donat's church, this establishment has an attractively rustic character, with exposed stonework, massive beams, solid seating and a fine chimney piece. Prettily presented menu of the day. Summer terrace.

WHERE TO STAY

⊜ **Les Blés d'Or** – *Rue Blés d'Or 15 – 6780 Hondelange* – ☎ *063 22 52 34* – ▣ – *11 rms* ⊠ – *€50/55.* Ideally located for peace and quiet in a village. Family atmosphere. Rooms of somewhat faded charm and garden with lake.

SPECIALITY

Arlon's "maitrank" – May wine – consists of dry white wine flavoured with sprigs of woodruff (asperula) picked before flowering, full-bodied cognac and sugar; it is then served chilled with a slice of orange. Since 1954 the Maitrank Brotherhood has organised an important popular festival at the end of May.

The **Roman Tower** (*Grand-Place*) was part of a rampart, the structure of which can still be seen by visitors. The rampart was raised on large foundations consisting of fragments of demolished buildings, including the magnificent low reliefs which now have pride of place in the Musée Luxembourgeois. One of these sculptures, representing Neptune, is still in its place in the wall under the tower (*access by metal ladder*).

One can also see part of *The Travellers* low relief which is displayed in the museum.

Thermes

Free admission. ☎ *063 24 56 00.*
There are a few remains of the 4C **Roman Baths**, as well as the 5C foundations of Belgium's oldest Christian **Basilica**, near the **old cemetery** (*Rue des Thermes Romains*) with its beautiful stone crosses.

Ath

Ath lies at the confluence of two rivers, the eastern Dender and the western Dender. This strategic location on a traditional invasion route meant that it was besieged by the French in 1667. After it fell, Ath became the first town to be fortified by Louis XIV's great military engineer Vauban. He had a relief map made of Ath, the first of its type. The city underwent a second French siege in 1745 during the War of Austrian Succession and most of its fortifications were destroyed.

Location

Hainaut – Population 25 296 Michelin maps 716 E 4 or 533 H 19
Access to Ath is facilitated by its proximity to the A 8/E 429 Brussels-Tournai motorway.
🛈 *Rue Nazareth 2 – 7800 –* ☎ *068 26 92 30.*

Directory

WHERE TO EAT

⊜ **Arts et Terroir** – *Marché aux Toiles 5 –* ☎ *068 44 59 77 – artsetterroir@busmail.net – Closed Mon – €22/26.* New restaurant in two little houses backing on to the old town wall which can be seen from the dining room. Bright interior in designer style, tables made of blue stone. Good choice of traditional dishes.

WHERE TO STAY

⊜ **Du Parc** – *Rue de l'Esplanade 13 –* ☎ *068 28 69 77 – motel.parc@skynet.be – 11 rms: €52/62.* Overlooking a grassy esplanade, this family hotel near the town centre has the advantage of a reasonably quiet location. Plain but well-kept rooms. Mealtimes feature solid bourgeois food varied according to season.

SPECIALITY

One of Ath's gastronomic specialities is the *tarte à mastelles,* also known as *tarte Gouyasse,* a delicacy eaten mainly during the local fête (*ducasse*) and washed down with a glass of Bordeaux wine.

Madame Gouyasse.

E. Valenne/Geostory/MICHELIN

GIANTS ON PARADE

At the end of August the **ducasse**★★ (from the word meaning "dedication" or "consecration") is held with its parades of giants and other spectacular features. Festivities last for over two days. On Saturday at around 3pm, the marriage of Monsieur and Madame Gouyasse (local dialect for "Goliath") is solemnised in the Église St-Julien during the Gouyasse evensong, then David and Goliath confront each other before the town hall.

On Sunday at 10am and 3pm the giants, measuring over 4m/13ft in height and weighing more than 100kg/220lb, wend their way through the town, in a merry atmosphere of gaiety and fun. They include Monsieur and Madame Gouyasse, the four Aymon sons astride their horse Bayard, Samson symbolising military might, the Gaulish leader Ambiorix, and Mam'zelle Victoire, who symbolises Ath itself.

Walking About

The Grand-Place

The Grand-Place du Pays Vert (main square) has recently been refurbished and features two small fountains, a series of pretty benches and a carefully designed lighting system that creates a warm, cosy atmosphere. The Baroque **town hall** completed in 1624 was built to plans by **Coebergher** (c 1561-1634), an extraordinary character who worked for the "Archdukes", Albert and Isabella. An engineer and painter as well as an architect, he also introduced the first pawnshops into Flanders. A large part of the town hall was rebuilt during the 1980s. The imposing foyer boasts a splendid fireplace, a carved doorway and a sweeping staircase embellished with a stone balustrade.

The Église St-Julien can be glimpsed from here with its tall 15C tower, half-destroyed by fire in 1817, and its corner turrets. Also visible is the 16C **Église St-Martin** which has an oak *Crucifixion* outside consisting of a huge figure of Christ surrounded by the two thieves, the Virgin Mary and St John. Inside the building is a splendid *Entombment,* a monumental work believed to date back to the late 16C.

Walk along rue du Gouvernement, a lane leading off Grand-Place

Tour Burbant

The Burbant Tower is a massive, square, flat-buttressed keep. The Count of Hainaut, Baldwin IV the Builder, had it constructed in 1166 to serve as a base, defend Hainaut's northern border with Flanders and monitor the movements of the local nobility. The tower is a vestige of the old feudal lordship of Ath and it takes its name from the former Carolingian country of Brabant to which the region once belonged. It is a veritable military complex consisting of 4m/13ft thick walls and an interior laid out on four storeys. Note the lack of windows in the lower section and the impressive fireplace. During the 14C, the keep was mainly used as a prison. The surrounding enclosure, added during the 15C and 16C, has been restored and converted into an arts centre.

Worth a Visit

Maison des Géants

Rue de Pintamont 18. Open Tue-Sun, 10am-12pm, 1pm-5pm (Apr-Sept 6pm), weekends and public holidays 2pm-6pm. Closed Christmas-New Year. €4. ☎ 068 44 57 24; www.ath.be

Set out in a lovely late 18C residence, the museum's displays evoke the captivating world of festival giants: their history, how they are made, the story of the ducasse and its counterparts elsewhere in Europe.

Musée d'Histoire et de Folklore

Rue du Bouchain, access via the Esplanade. Open early Apr-end of Sept, daily (except Sat), 2-5pm (6pm Sun); rest of the year, by appointment only. €1.75. ☎ 068 26 92 30.

The first room in the Museum of History and Folklore is crammed with miscellaneous objects unearthed during local digs and dating from the Paleolithic era to the Bronze and Iron Ages. The next room takes the visitor back in time to the Middle Ages. Particularly noteworthy are an interesting late 14C *Entombment* from

Mainvault and a splendid collection of chasubles. On the second floor, one of the rooms is devoted to the folklore of Ath and its famous *ducasse*. Relief plans of the town trace the main stages in Ath's history, including its fortification by Vauban.

Espace Gallo-Romain

Rue de Nazareth 2. Open Tue-Fri, 10am-noon and 1-5pm, Sat 10am-noon and 2-6pm, Sun (holidays and Apr-Sept) 2pm-6pm. Closed Mon, fourth weekend in Aug and 25 Dec-1 Jan. €4. ☎ 068 26 92 33; www.ath.be/espace.gallo-romain.html

Displayed in an old drawing academy (1835-40), most of the museum's exhibits are the result of digs carried out in 1975 near Pommerœul, a small village next to the French border. The two most striking pieces are a barge dating from the 3C AD and a huge Roman **monoxylon★**, a boat made from a single tree-trunk. The museum also has a fine collection of fibulas, coins, weights, tools, ornaments and objects in baked clay. Video presentations explain old-fashioned crafts and trades.

Excursion

Musée de la Pierre et site des Carrières de Maffle

3km S on N 56, the road to Mons. Open July and Aug, Mon-Fri, 2-5pm; early Apr to end Sept, Sat-Sun and public holidays, 2.30-6.30pm. €1.75. ☎ 068 26 92 36.

The **Maffle quarries**, which now include a Stone Museum, cover approximately 10ha/25 acres in the valley of the eastern Dender. After closure around 1960, the area was overrun by vegetation. Although it has become a nature reserve, it has retained many traces of its former industrial activity.

The **Museum** is housed in the 19C quarry-master's house and the old workshops. It gives a comprehensive account of the history of stone working in Belgium, especially in the Ath region, through an exhibition of tools, machines and illustrated documents. The development of transport techniques and labourers' working conditions are also explained.

Tour

THE COUNTRYSIDE AROUND ATH

Leave Ath SW on N 527, then turn right towards Moulbaix.

The mixed-farming countryside around Ath is a landscape of wide horizons, broken only by lines of poplars, big farmsteads and the occasional hamlet.

Moulbaix

Sat 2pm-6pm. €0.75. ☎ 068 28 27 91. The "Moulin de la Marquise", a pretty timber **windmill★** (1614), is the last of its kind still in working order in the province of Hainaut. An unusual 19C Tudor-style residence is concealed in the extensive park near the church.

Go back the way you came, and cross N 527 towards Tongre-Notre-Dame.

Tongre-Notre-Dame

The 18C Renaissance-style basilica contains a Romanesque enthroned *Virgin* in polychrome wood. Since the 17C, the statue has often been draped in rich robes and ornaments concealing all but the Infant Jesus' face. The statue, which stands on an altar built on the spot where the Virgin was said to have appeared in February 1081, is highly venerated and is the object of pilgrimage twice a year.

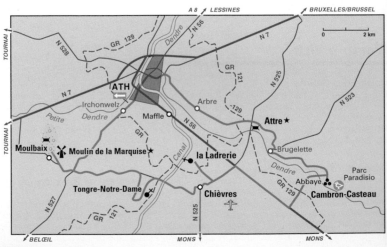

Aviary – Parc Paradisio

The most notable features in the church's harmonious interior are the chancel, the six low-relief sculptures in white stone recounting the church's history and the splendid pulpit.

Head towards Chièvres

Chièvres

This little town once belonged to the aristocratic Egmont family, one of whose members was beheaded in Brussels in 1568 for his role in resisting oppressive Spanish rule. The 15C/16C Gothic Église St-Martin has a bell-tower decorated with corner turrets. The church contains lovely funerary monuments and a 15C lectern. *Open early Apr-end Sept, daily, 10am-8pm; rest of the year, daily, 10am-6pm.* ☎ *068 65 72 47.*

The 15C **Tour de Gavre** is a remnant of the old ramparts. The tower's brick gable can be seen from the church.

La Ladrerie is a pretty Romanesque chapel just outside the town in a farmyard in the Hunelle Valley. It was once part of a leper hospital *(ladrerie)*.

Take N 56 towards Mons, then turn left into a lane.

Cambron-Casteau

The Cistercian **abbey** of Cambron-Casteau, founded in the 12C under the aegis of St Bernard, was one of the most prosperous in the land. It was rebuilt in the 18C, then destroyed by decree during the French Revolution. Now only the ruins remain.

At the far end of an avenue of lime-trees a Classical-style gateway forms the entrance to **Parc Paradisio**.

On the right of the entrance to the park is the abbey farm, the buildings of which include a strange barn *("charril")* that was once used to garage the farm carts. Above the barn is a dovecot. Beyond is the park itself, dominated by the tall **tower** (54m/177ft) of the abbey church. The four tombs with recesses containing recumbent figures, also in the church, recall that this was a cemetery for Hainaut's nobility during the Middle Ages.

The surrounding gardens planted with trees several centuries old contain an ornithological park which harbours over 2 500 birds belonging to a great many different species, including parrots, cranes, storks, ibis, penguins, ducks and owls. The birds are kept in **large aviaries** (1 500 and 3 000m^2/16 140 and 32 280sq ft), among artificially created marshland or quite simply live on the three lakes that can be seen from an impressive winding **flight of steps** (18C) edged with balustrades. *July-Aug: 10am-7pm (6pm late Mar-early Nov). €15.* ☎ *068 25 08 35; www.paradisio.be*

Attre

Built in 1752 by the Count of Gomegnies and completed by his son, Chamberlain to Emperor Joseph II, the charming **Château d'Attre**★ has kept its remarkably harmonious interior decoration. Four columns from the rood screen of the abbey in Cambron-Casteau stand before the entrance. Two sphinxes with female busts frame the doorway.

The entrance hall also served as a chapel; an altar has been set up in one of the corners. The very ornate handrail of the vestibule stairs is said to have been designed by the 18C Parisian architect Blondel.

Many works of art and valuable collections adorn the rooms. Lovely 18C paintings decorate the panelling of the main drawing room, in which there is also some very fine moulded plasterwork by the Italian Ferrari family. The Archducal Room is hung with the first painted wallpaper ever imported into Belgium (1760). The armchairs are covered in matching chintz. Chinese silk hangings decorate the walls and seats in the Chinese Room.

The River Dender cuts across the magnificent **park**. There is a 17C dovecot near the castle. The park's principal point of interest is the extraordinary "Rocher", the "Rock" or artificial hill, 24m/79ft high, pierced by underground passageways. It was built for the Austrian Archduchess Maria-Christina of Saxony-Teschen, who governed the Low Countries in the late 18C with her spouse Albert. She would use the small pavilion at the top as a hunting lodge. *Guided tour only (1hr), early Apr-end June and early Sept-end Oct, Sat, Sun and public holidays, 10am, 12pm and 2-6pm; July and Aug, daily (exc Wed) at same times. €4.50.* ☎ *068 45 44 60.*

Bastogne

High up on the Ardennes plateau at an altitude of 515m/1 689ft, Bastogne is an ancient stronghold with a long history of sieges. All that is left of its fortifications are a 14C tower and the Porte de Trèves (Trier Gate), the French having razed everything else after besieging the town in 1688. The latest, and most famous siege, occured in the harsh winter of 1944/45, when US forces held the German army at bay in what came to be known as the Battle of the Bulge.

Location

Luxembourg – Population 13 246. Michelin maps 716 K 5 and 534 T 22.
Bastogne is reached from Liège by the A 26/E 25 motorway and from Namur by the dual-carriageway N 4.
🛈 *Place McAuliffe –* ☎ *061 21 27 11; www.bastogne.be*

Background

The Battle of the Bulge – The Germans launched a counter-offensive against the Allied front on 16 December 1944, led by General von Rundstedt, whose objective was to take Antwerp. The element of surprise combined with the persistent bad weather (fog and snow) brought the Germans immediate success. General von Manteuffel headed for the Meuse, leaving the Allied front line in a "bulge" (from which the battle took its name) around Bastogne which was held by the Americans. Surrounded as it was, the town became a strategic point.

The commanding officer, **General McAuliffe**, was rudely awakened on 22 December and asked to surrender. His terse answer to this ultimatum was "Nuts!", and so began the siege of Bastogne.

The sky cleared on 23 December, allowing supplies to be air-dropped into Bastogne. By Christmas Day the Germans had advanced as far as the village of Celles near Dinant; however, this was as far as they were to get. The Allies threw everything they had into getting the upper hand. The US 3rd Army led by General Patton counter-attacked on the southeast flank and entered Bastogne on 26 December. Allied planes were able to prevent fuel supplies getting to the Germans for their tanks. At the beginning of January the US 1st Army reached Bastogne from the north. By 25 January, the "bulge" had been completely cleared of Germans.

Walking about

The tank gun turrets just outside the town on the main roads mark how closely the Germans surrounded the town in 1944.

Grand-Place (or Place McAuliffe)

An American tank stands next to a bust of General McAuliffe. Here too is one of the milestones which mark the "Liberation Route" which runs from Ste-Mère-Église in Normandy where the Americans first landed in June 1944 to the outskirts of Bastogne.

Église St-Pierre★
This 15C hall-church was built in Flamboyant Gothic style. It has a square tower in front of it (11C-12C) surmounted by a projecting timber gallery.

The **interior**★ is quite remarkable. The vaulting was painted in 1536 and depicts scenes from the Old and New Testaments, as well as patron saints of guilds and religious brotherhoods. Note also a Baroque pulpit by the sculptor Scholtus; a 16C wooden *Entombment*, still somewhat Gothic in style; a Romanesque font with four sculpted heads on the corners; and a beautiful 16C chandelier in beaten iron, also called a "crown of light".

Worth a visit

Bastogne Historical Center★
  Open Feb-Apr and Oct-Dec, daily, 10am-4.30pm; May, June and Sept, daily, 9.30am-5pm; July and Aug, daily, 9am-6pm. Closed Jan, 24, 25 and 31 Dec. €7.50. ☎ *061 21 14 13.*

This impressive building designed in the shape of a star is devoted to the Battle of the Bulge. It contains collections of uniforms and vehicles, and two battle scenes have been reconstructed, one from the German side, the other from the American side.

The course of the battle is traced on an illuminated model and small screens *(commentary in several languages)* in the central amphitheatre. Finally, a film featuring footage taken during the real battle is shown in the cinema.

Le Mardasson★
3km/1.75mi E on N 874. A gigantic monument honouring the American soldiers who died in the Battle of the Bulge stands on a hill, where it was erected in 1950. The final milestone of the "Liberation Route" is nearby.

"Le Mardasson" Memorial – The memorial is in the form of a five-pointed star, engraved with the story of the battle and the names of the various battalions that took part in it.

From the terrace at the top of the memorial, there is a **panoramic view** of Bastogne and the surrounding area; at each point of the star a viewing table indicates the main phases of the battle. The crypt, which was decorated by Fernand Léger, contains three altars.

Y. Vezant/GLOBAL PICTURES

Bastogne Historical Center.

Beaumont

With stretches of its medieval ramparts still intact, this little old hilltop town commands the approach to the 'Hainaut Boot', a sliver of land projecting southwards between the French frontier and the province of Namur. Delicious macaroons are made here using a recipe left by one of Napoleon's chefs when the French Emperor stayed in Beaumont on 14 June 1815, on his way to Waterloo.

Location

Hainaut – Population 6 541 – Michelin maps 716 F 5 or 534 K 21.
A number of main roads converge on Beaumont, including N 40 from Mons, N 53 from Charleroi, and D 936/N 597 from Maubeuge in France.
🛈 *Grand-Place 10 – ☎ 071 58 81 91; www.beaumont.be*

> ### An Unlucky Trio
> *"Beaumont town, woe begone,*
> *Come at noon, hung at one."*
> This was the fate of three vagabonds from the Auvergne, who stopped a man on horseback on the road to Beaumont and forced him to carry their heavy bags. Once in town the stranger revealed his identity: he was Emperor Charles V, come to visit the Low Countries (1549). The three wretches were soon hanging from the gibbet on the town square.

Worth a Visit

Tour Salamandre

Guided tours only (45min), May, June and Sept, daily, 9am-5pm; July and Aug, daily 10am-7pm; Oct, Sun, 10am-5pm. €1.50. ☎ 071 58 81 91.
On the slope of the hill, the Salamander Tower was once part of the 12C fortifications. It has been restored and now houses a Museum of Regional History.
The crest of the Cro family, the local aristocracy, can be seen crowning one of the doors, along with their motto and the neck chain of the Order of the Golden Fleece. From the terrace at the top of the tower, there is a view over the town, the valley of the River Hantes with its old watermill, and the attractive surrounding countryside. The park laid out on the site of the fortress destroyed in 1655 now belongs to a school.

Excursions

Solre-sur-Sambre

10km/6mi NW. Leave the town and head for Mons on N 40. Turn left shortly after Montignies.
A part-Roman **bridge** with 13 arches stands not far from the ancient Roman road from Bavay to Trier. It spans the River Hantes in a pretty setting, forming a dam. At the foot of the rock spur crowned by the village of Solre-sur-Sombre, a 13C-14C **castle** is defended by its well-shaded moat. The austere fortress consists of a square keep flanked by two great round towers with machicolations and pepper-pot roofs. *Currently closed ☎ 065 36 04 64.*

Rance

13km/8mi S on N 53. Rance was famous for its red marble of coralline origin, extracted from the now disused quarry and worked locally. The **Musée National du Marbre**, or National Marble Museum, is housed in the former town hall. Visitors can familiarise themselves here with the origins of the stone, see the types of marble most commonly found in Belgium, and the techniques used to extract and polish it *(marble polishing demonstration). Closed for restoration until end 2003 ☎ 060 41 20 48.*
Rance's **church** is adorned with many works carved in local marble.

Belœil★★

Belœil château has belonged to the Princes of Ligne since the 14C. The most illustrious member of the family was Field Marshal Charles Joseph de Ligne (1735-1814). known as the "Prince Charming of Europe", famous for his remark "Chaque homme a deux patries: la sienne et puis la France" (Every man has two countries, his own and France). The sumptuously furnished château is set in vast and splendid formal gardens which have earned it the name of the "Belgian Versailles".

Location

Hainaut – Population 13 236 – Michelin maps 716 E 4 or 534 H 19.
In a leafy setting close to the French border, Beloeil is 10km/6mi S of Ath via N 527 and N 526.

Highlight

Château★★

Open early Apr – mid-Oct daily, 10am-6pm. Mon-Fri Easter holidays: pre-booked group visits only. Château and grounds €5. ☎ 069 68 94 26.

There was a fortress here as early as the 12C, but the château which can be seen today was built in the early 16C and extensively modified in the 17C and 18C to create an elegant stately home. The main building, burnt down in 1900, was rebuilt in 1902. The wings and the entrance lodges with mansard roofs remained intact. They date from the end of the 17C. The château is a veritable museum containing **splendid collections★★★** although its interior has still retained a residential character. Valuable furniture, remarkable tapestries, paintings, sculptures and porcelain collections adorn the various rooms, while the many family mementoes evoke the course of European history from the 17C to the 19C. Certain rooms contain the Field Marshal's personal belongings, particularly the mementoes given to him by Marie-Antoinette and by Catherine the Great, who was a close friend. The **library★** contains more than 20 000 books dealing mainly with the sciences. The three large paintings in the Ambassadors' Drawing Room recalling the diplomatic missions entrusted to the De Ligne family illustrate high points in the life of Prince Claude-Lamoral I de Ligne, who was Ambassador to King Philip IV of Spain and Viceroy of Sicily in 1669. The **chapel** which occupies the former stables contains religious objets d'art and a collection of coral sculptures brought back from Sicily by Prince Claude-Lamoral I.

Park★★ – Work began on the grounds in the 16C; the gardens were altered on numerous occasions before Prince Claude-Lamoral II drew up the definitive plans in the 18C, acting on the advice of several landscape gardeners who specialised in

Château de Belœil.

French-style formal designs. The park was extended in the naturalistic English style by Prince Charles-Joseph. The central feature is a superb vista several miles in length, the **Grande Vue★★**, which leads to the **Great Neptune Basin**, an ornamental lake covering an area of 16ha/40 acres adorned with a group of statues dedicated to the Roman god of the sea (1761). Around the basin are alternating arbours and ponds providing an enticing setting for a stroll.

Excursion

Archéosite d'Aubechies

6km/4mi W on N 526, then turn right beyond Ellignies. & *Open year-round, Mon-Fri, 9am-5pm (Jul-Aug until 6pm); Sat-Sun and public holidays, Mar-Nov, 2-6pm (Jul-Aug until 7pm). Closed 1 Nov, 25 Dec-1 Jan. €5.* ☎ *069 67 11 16.*

After years of productive excavation on the archaeological site in Aubechies and the surrounding area, archaeologists have reconstructed the various types of dwellings which succeeded one another from the early Neolithic period until the days of the Gauls. The six wattle and daub houses with their furnishings and utensils give the visitor a good idea of life at the time. The first, very large buildings were in fact communal dwellings; single-family homes did not come into existence until the Bronze Age.

The **Roman House** in the centre of the village of Aubechies, beyond the Romanesque **church** (late 11C-early 12C) was built according to the plan of a 2C villa and now contains the finds unearthed during excavations of Gallo-Roman sites.

Blaton

13.5km/8.5mi SW. Blaton lies in a valley flanked by heather-covered hillsides (the Grande and Petite Bruyère). Three canals supply the town with water. Crowned by a tall 13C tower with a 17C onion dome, the **Église de Tous-les-Saints** is one of the oldest churches in the province of Hainaut. The austere nave has thick columns in two types of stone; the capitals are decorated with crockets and stylised foliage. Note the Gothic statues in the niches to the right of the entrance.

Bon Secours

16km/10mi SW. Bon-Secours is both a popular recreation area and a place of pilgrimage. Atop a hill on the Franco-Belgian border, the neo-Gothic basilica houses a statue of the Virgin Mary that has been venerated since 1606.

To the east and south, and partly in France, extends a lovely forest, in whose depths lies the Château de l'Hermitage

Stambruges

5km/3mi S. The pines and birches of the forest give way to an open tract of land known as the **Mer de Sable** (Sea of Sand).

Binche★

In the heart of the province of Hainaut, Binche is built on a rocky promontory once encircled by a meander of the River Samme. It is a pretty place, still ringed by its medieval ramparts. The town was partly destroyed by the French in 1554, and some of its fortifications were razed by Louis XIV in 1675. Binche is known for its brewery, its cheese-filled pancakes called "doubles", and above all for its world-famous Carnival★★★

Location
Hainaut – Population 32 185 – Michelin maps 716 F 4 or 534 J 20. Town plan in the current edition of The Red Guide Benelux.
Binche is at the junction of N 90 and N 55, approximately halfway between Mons and Charleroioiple.
🛈 *Grand-Place, 7130, ☎ 064 33 67 27; www.binche.be*

Directory

WHERE TO EAT	
😋 Éric – *Route de Mons 190 – 7131 Waudrez – ☎ 064 33 25 35 – Closed Mon except public holidays – €22/31.* Just outside the town's newly restored ramparts, this is a friendly establishment with a dining room in traditional style. Classic menu and a connoisseur's wine-list.	**😋😋 La Fermette des Pins** – *Rue Lustre 39 – 7133 Buvrinnes – ☎ 064 34 17 18 – Closed Mon evening, Tues, Wed. – €26 lunch – €32/42.* Pretty white-walled farmstead, cheerful rustic interior, open fireplace, welcoming summer terrace and garden in a countryside setting. Tasty traditional dishes.

Background

THE MOTHER OF ALL CARNIVALS
Carnival events are organised from January onwards: rehearsals for the drum corps, followed by four Sundays when the future "Gilles" can be seen wearing their *apertintailles* (belts hung with bells).

The **Trouilles de Nouilles Ball** takes place during the night of the Monday in the week before the beginning of Lent.

From 10pm onwards on the Sunday before Shrove Tuesday hundreds of people in fancy dress dance to the music of violas, barrel organs, accordions and drums. The high point of the afternoon is the parade of 1 500 local dancers. Monday is the day for groups of young people.

Shrove Tuesday is the day when people "play the Gille" in Binche, a privilege only accorded to native-born male citizens of the town. The legendary **Gilles** appear any time from dawn onwards. Large or small, they all wear a linen costume decorated with heraldic lions, trimmed with ribbons and brilliant white lace, featuring two humps, one on the chest and one on the back. Wearing a belt of bells and clogs on their feet, they brandish a bundle of sticks to ward off evil spirits. Together with Pierrots, Sailors and young beribboned Country Folk, they can be seen in the streets of the town dancing slowly to the beat of the drum as they go to join their brotherhood. At about 10am they dance on the town square (Grand-Place), wearing wax masks with green spectacles.

A 'Gille'.

They parade through the town in the afternoon, sporting their magnificent ostrich-feather hats, delving into a basket for oranges to give away or throw at the crowd (the windows along the route have been protected with grilles). This is followed by the **round dance** on Grand-Place, which by this time is packed with people.

The event is repeated at 7pm by the light of flares and ends in a glorious fireworks display. The Gilles dance all night, escorted by the town's inhabitants. Tradition has it that the Gilles may drink nothing but champagne.

In the late 19C these customs were said to be connected with the celebrations given in August 1549 by Mary of Hungary, Governor of the Low Countries, in honour of her brother Emperor Charles V, who had come to present his son, the future Philip II, to the country's nobility. The present Gilles are said to be descendants of the Indians crowned with feathers, who were supposed to have been brought before the emperor in honour of his recent conquest of Peru.

In fact Binche's carnival dates back at least as far as the 14C. The Gille is a serious figure cloaked in ritual. The customs – the dance of masked men, from which women are excluded, the giving of oranges (bread, apples or nuts in former times), the carrying of the bundle of sticks and the wearing of the belt hung with bells – are all very ancient, dating back to the days when dance carried religious and magical meaning.

Walking About

Grand-Place
The main square is dominated by the Gothic **town hall** which was altered in the 16C by Mons sculptor and architect Jacques Du Brœucq. The belfry with its onion dome was a later addition.
Walk along the narrow street to the right of the town hall.

Ramparts★
Just over 2km/1.4mi long, the recently restored 12C-14C town walls with their 25 towers are some of the finest in Belgium. It is best to start at the Tour St-Georges/St George's Tower and follow the walls round to the right; they are at their most imposing when seen from the south.
Return via the Posty gate and Rue Haute.
The **Chapelle St-André** (1537), which stands in the old cemetery on the left, contains sculpted modillions vividly illustrating the Dance of Death. *Guided tours only. Apply to the Tourist Information Centre.* ☎ 064 33 67 27.

Collégiale St-Ursmer
This collegiate church has a beautiful Renaissance rood screen and a 15C *Entombment*.

Parc Communal
There is a gilded bronze statue of a Gille at the entrance to the municipal park. The park was laid out in the ruins of the palace built by Du Brœucq in 1548 for Mary of Hungary. This impressive building, which was destroyed in 1554, overlooked the ramparts at the southernmost end of the town. There are some superb views from the top of the town walls.

Worth a Visit

Musée International du Carnavalet et du Masque★
& *Open year-round, Mon-Thur and Sun, 9.30am-12.30pm and 1.30-6pm, Sat, 1.30-6pm. Closed Fri, Sat am, Ash Wednesday, 1 Nov and 24 Dec to 2 Jan. €5.* ☎ *064 33 57 41; www.museedumasque.be*
The International Carnival and Mask Museum is housed in an old 18C Augustine school near the collegiate church. The collections take the visitor from carnival to carnival, from festival to festival, through many countries. The **mask collection**★★, with exhibits from countries all over the world, demonstrates the extent to which human imagination and creativity has been inspired by this art form in every age and every place: from the festival costumes of the South Sea Islands and the Amazon, to the astonishing masks from North America and Africa, to the theatre masks of Asia and the often macabre masks of Latin America. Another part of the museum takes us to Europe's winter festivals and carnivals held in Austria, Poland, Romania, Switzerland, Italy, Spain, France, and enlightens us on the masquerades of Austria, the Czech and Slovak Republics, and Bulgaria. A large part of the museum is set aside for Wallonia's traditional carnivals, especially the one in Binche, completed by an audio-visual presentation in several languages, giving explanations about the origins and details of the Gilles' strange costume.
Each year there is an exhibition on a chosen theme concerning masks or carnivals.

Domaine de Mariemont★★
10km/6mi NE. Leave Binche on N 55 towards Brussels, turn right on to N 563, then left at Morlanweiz.

Mariemont Estate is named after Mary of Hungary, who commissioned the sculptor and architect **Jacques du Brœucq** to build the castle on a wooded hillside in 1546. Henri II of France destroyed the castle in 1554, as he did the one in Binche, but it was almost immediately rebuilt and then extended by **Wenceslas Coeberger** under the 'Archdukes' Isabella and Albert. In the 18C, Charles of Lorraine built a second castle of which the ruins can still be seen in the park. It was burnt down during fighting in 1794. The **Warocqué** family, a dynasty of industrialists, remodelled the estate in the 19C and bequeathed it to the State in 1917, along with a large number of works of art taken from Raoul Warocqué's private collection. Although the family château was razed by a fire in 1960, its site was used in 1975 for a modern **museum** designed by Roger Bastin, the architect of the Museum of Modern Art in Brussels.

Park★ – The ruins of the old castle can still be seen in this beautiful 45ha/111 acre park which is dotted with a great many sculptures by Belgian artists such as Victor Rousseau, Constantin Meunier and Jef Lambeaux. Rodin's *Burghers of Calais* is another of the works displayed here, together with a huge Buddha dating from the early 20C. *Open Jan, Nov and Dec, daily, 9am-4pm; Feb, Mar and Oct, daily, 9am-5pm; Apr-Sept, daily, 9am-6pm (7pm Sun and public holidays from May-Aug). No charge. Guided tours available.* ☎ *064 21 21 93; www.musee-mariemont.be*

Musée★★ – The museum's rich collections of art and archaeology are displayed in a fascinating manner. The first floor is devoted to the great civilisations. The most outstanding exhibits come from Ancient Egypt (note the colossal head of a Hellenistic queen), Greece (a splendid marble head of Alexander the Great from the 3C BC), Rome (Boscoreale mural painting) and from the **Far East**: enamelwork, lacquerwork, jade and Chinese porcelain. A remarkable display of Gallo-Roman and Merovingian artefacts, unearthed during excavations carried out in the province of Hainaut, is on show in the basement, which also houses an exhibition lavishly illustrating the history of Mariemont Estate and another presenting a large collection of **Tournai porcelain**.

The second floor is used for temporary exhibitions. The museum has a valuable **library** of manuscripts, bound works etc. ♿ *Open year-round, daily (except Mon), 10am-6pm. Closed Mon (except public holidays), 1 Jan and 25 Dec. No charge. The library's special collection is open to the public by appointment only.* ☎ *064 21 21 93; www.musee-mariemont.be*

La Louvière
10km/6mi N. Leave Binche by N 55, heading for Brussels. The capital of Belgium's Centre Region, this industrial community saw its apogee in the 19C thanks to the Industrial Revolution and the presence of coal mines.

La Louvière played an active role in the Belgian Surrealist movement when the poet **Achille Chavée** founded the Groupe Surréaliste du Hainaut in 1939. Haine-St-Pierre, a small locality belonging to La Louvière, was the birthplace of the famous sculptor **Pol Bury** in 1922. A hydraulic fountain made by the artist decorates the esplanade fronting Château Gilson. The **Centre de la Gravure et de l'Image Imprimée** *(1 rue des Amours)* stages temporary exhibitions throughout the year. *Open during exhibitions only, Tues-Fri, noon-6pm, Sat-Sun and public holidays, 11am-6pm. Closed mid-Aug – mid-Sept.* €4.50. ☎ *064 28 87 27.*

Musée Ianchelevici – *Place Communale.* The neo-Classical law courts building now houses a museum devoted to the Romanian-born artist **Idel Ianchelevici** (1909-94). The drawings and sculptures displayed give a good overview of his work. The first floor is used for temporary exhibitions. *Open year-round, daily (except Mon), 2-5pm. Closed mid-Aug – mid-Sept and public holidays. No charge.* ☎ *064 28 25 30.*

Écomusée régional du Centre – *Rue St-Patrice 2B in Houdeng-Aimeries.* This museum has been established in the old coal mining area of Bois-du-Luc. Coal was first extracted here in 1685 and the last mine was closed down in 1973. Altogether 162 modest houses built for miners were constructed around the St-Emmanuel pit between 1838 and 1853. One of them is open to the public. Many of the buildings are still permeated with the highly distinctive atmosphere that reigned here in the days of mining: they include the offices (note the fine stained-glass window in the courtyard), the workshops where tools were made, the underground electrical plant, and the mine shaft. *Open Tue to Fri, 9am-5pm, Sat-Sun and public holidays, 10am-6pm. Closed public holidays and Sat-Sun from mid-Oct – mid-May, 25 Dec to 1 Jan.* €7.44; *www.ecomuseeboisduluc.be;* ☎ *064 28 20 00* The tour can be rounded off with a visit to the **Musée de la Mine**, a museum presenting the history of mining in the region *(5 rue St-Patrice). Open year-round, Mon-Fri, 9am-noon and 1-5pm, Sat-Sun and public holidays, 2-5pm. Closed 1 Jan, 25 Dec.* €3. ☎ *064 22 54 48.*

Abbaye de Bonne-Espérance

6km/4mi S on N 55, in the direction of Merbes-le-Château, then Vellereille-les-Brayeux.
Open early Apr – mid-Oct: guided tours Sun 3.30pm, 6pm. €1.50. ☎ 064 31 08 08.
A school now occupies this old Premonstratensian abbey, which Odo, a disciple of St Norbert, founded in 1126. Its 18C façade dominates the main courtyard. On the right is the 15C Gothic tower of the abbey church.
Enter by the central doorway, then turn immediately right.
The **cloisters**, which were altered in the 18C, have retained their Gothic vaulting; the refectory has paintings showing scenes from the life of St Norbert. A beautiful chapter house completes the abbey buildings.
The 18C neo-Classical **church** was designed by Laurent Dewez. The north transept chapel contains a *Virgin and Child*, a miraculous 14C statue with a warm smile and finely executed dress.

Blankenberge☼

This small fishing port is one of the most popular resorts on the Belgian coast. The casino with its glass façade, the pier offering pretty views of the sea, the sweeping beaches with fine sand and the traffic-free shopping streets are among Blankenberge's main attractions. Visitors can shelter from the sea breezes in the 100-year-old "Paravang", a splendid neo-Gothic structure with glazed tiles and seashell decoration.

Location
West Vlaanderen – Population 17 458 – Michelin maps 716 C 2 and 533 D 15.
Town plan in the current edition of The Red Guide Benelux.
On the east coast, Blankenberge can be reached on N 371 and on the main coast road N 34.
🛈 *Leopold III-plein, ☎ 050 41 22 27; www.blankenberge.be*

Worth a Visit

St-Antoniuskerk
The small brick church beside the station, dedicated to St Anthony, was consecrated in 1358. It was built on the site of the Église Notre-Dame, which suffered extensive damage during a violent storm in the winter of 1334-35.
The church has been restored on many occasions. The interior is adorned with beautiful 17C and 18C works of art including a communion pew, a confessional, a pulpit and an organ.

Sea-Life Centre
Koning Albertlaan 116. ♿ Open daily, 10am-6pm (last admission 5pm). Closed 1 Jan, 25 Dec. €9.50. ☎ 050 42 43 00.
Visitors can admire a great many types of fish and aquatic species from Belgian rivers and streams, as well as from the North Sea. At regular intervals, the marine laboratory stages presentations of sharks and ray fish which have been bred in special basins. The Ray Aquarium is peopled with flat fish which have developed the ability to hide in the marine depths, as well as other rays which seem to enjoy

Blankenberge pier.

Directory

Where to Eat

Kreeften-en oesterput – *Oude Wenduinsesteenweg 16* – ☎ *050 4286 35* – *Piet.devriend@skynet.be* – *closed Carnival, 11 Nov* – 🗷 – *€25*. This establishment dedicates itself to the gastronomic pleasures of the seaside. Close to the marina, it is like a huge shed, with tubs of oysters, lobster tanks, and long lines of tables covered in paper tablecloths. Go for the *plateaux de fruits de mer*.

Vijfwege – *Brugsebaan 12 (N 9)* – *8421 Vlissegem* – ☎ *059 23 31 96* – *Closed Tue, Wed* – 🗷 – *€25*. Eel, *côte à l'os*, and, in season, asparagus, have pride of place on the menu here, attracting a particularly faithful clientele who have been coming here for some time. Relaxed atmosphere.

Where To Stay

Hôtel Corner House – *Casinoplein 12* – ☎ *050 41 93 76* – 🗷 – *16 rms: €42/62* ☕. Just a spin of the wheel from the Casino, at the foot of the monumental stairway leading to the promenade, this establishment offers modern, well-kept rooms with good soundproofing.

Alfa Inn – *Kerkstraat 92* – ☎ *050 41 81 72* – *info@alfa-inn.com* – 🅿 – *65 rms: €75* ☕. Family hotel in an old convent on a shopping street midway between station and seafront. Functional rooms being systematically renovated.

Events and Festivals

Blankenberge doesn't lack for festivities. Its Carnival is particularly lively. The Harbour Festival in May involves a costumed parade followed by folk dancing. In July there is the **Blessing of the Sea** and in August, a famous **Floral Parade**.

---

coming to the surface and allowing themselves to be stroked. The underground tunnel allows visitors to follow the movements of the fish from down below, as if they were watching from the seabed. There is an adjacent seal sanctuary.

Excursions

THE COASTAL RESORTS

Wenduine

4.5km/3miSW. The Spioenkop, one of the highest dunes, is topped by a **viewpoint** giving a fine prospect of beaches, dunes and the resort with its old town hall rebuilt in traditional style. Note the small post windmill.

De Haan⌂

De Haan is a charming, flower-decked resort with turn-of-the-century villas nestling amid the woodland and sand dunes.

Klemskerke

This is a pretty village set in polderland. **St Clement's**, a hall-church (the nave and side aisles are all the same height), contains 17C woodwork including pews and confessionals. A post windmill stands nearby.

Blégny-Trembleur★★

The Blégny-Trembleur colliery, the last in the Liège coalfield, has been kept in working order since its closure in 1980 as a reminder of the miners' way of life. The mining tradition in this area goes back to the 16C, when the monks of Val-Dieu Abbey started to extract surface coal. The present shafts were sunk during the 19C. At that time the mine employed women and children, as well as the pit ponies which sometimes stayed below ground all their lives.

Location

Liège – Michelin maps 716 K 3 and 533 T 18.
In the countryside 12km/8mi NE of Liège. Follow signs from Exit 36 on the A 3/E 40 motorway.

Background

Life underground – The colliery consists of two shafts to ventilate the galleries, which descend through eight levels to a depth of 530m/1 739ft below the surface. In these galleries, the coal was mined using the "advancing face" technique which consists of cutting parallel to the steepest angle of the coal seam. The seams could be mined until they were only 30cm/12in thick. The miners worked in

J. Hanssens/GLOBAL PICTURES

Blégny-Mine.

three eight-hour shifts. The morning shift was responsible for cutting, which consisted of working the coal loose with a jackhammer. The afternoon shift shored up the area just worked, using timber or metal pit props. The night shift was responsible for backfilling (filling in holes with rubble) or caving (making the rocky roof cave in).

Worth a Visit

Guided tours only (2hr 30min), Easter – mid-Sept, daily 10am-4.30pm; early Mar – end Nov, Sat-Sun and public holidays, 10am-4.30pm. €7.56. ☎ 04 387 43 33; www.blegnymine.be

The Mine

The tour is made even more interesting and poignant by the fact that the guides are ex-miners, describing their own working conditions. There is also a film about the colliery and the lives of the men who worked there.

Puits Marie – The surface installations of "Pit Mary" are open to the public. They have remained unchanged since the pit closure in 1980. They consist of the lamp works, the baths, showers and changing rooms, the compressor station where air was compressed for the ventilation system and to power the jackhammers, and the sawmill where the pit props were made.

Puits no 1 – The 45m/148ft high concrete tower of Pit no.1 was rebuilt during the Second World War. The trucks were pulled halfway up the tower and their mineral load deposited on the tip.

The **underground workings** are reached by descending this shaft. The lift cage stops in a gallery 30m/98ft underground, and metal stairs lead along a passage, following a seam, to reach the next gallery 60m/196ft underground. The deafening sound of the ventilation system and the jackhammer worked by the guide, added to the narrowness of the coal face streaming with water, forcing the miners to lie down to work, combines to give a vivid picture of the miserable conditions in which the "gueules noires", or "black faces", laboured without a break for eight hours at a stretch.

Miners were liable to suffer from silicosis, rheumatism and deafness from a very early age. Added to this were the dangers of explosions, rock falls and pockets of water that could suddenly flood an entire gallery.

Tourist train

This little train chugs through the valleys and orchards of the Herve countryside to **Mortroux** and its **Musée de la Vie Rurale**. This Folk Museum demonstrates the traditional techniques used for making local products such as pear or apple syrup, cheese and butter. *From Apr-mid-Sept: train departs 2.30pm, 3.30pm, 4.30pm (Jul, Aug 5.30pm), Sat, Sun and public holidays until early Nov. (same times) €2.50. ☎ 04 387 43 33.*

Provinciaal domein van **Bokrijk**★

With its outstanding open-air museum and recreation facilities, the 550ha/1 359 acre Bokrijk provincial estate is one of the most popular visitor attractions in northeastern Belgium.

Location
Limburg – Michelin maps 716 J 3 and 533 R 17.
6.5km/4mi NE of Hasselt. From Brussels, leave A 2/E 314 motorway at Exit 30 (Park Midden Limburg) and follow N 726. From Hasselt, take N 75.

Worth a Visit

Recreation area★
This recreational centre includes the main amusement park, the **Speeltuin**, comprising an adventure playground, a sports complex and a mini-golf course, as well as **Natuurreservaat "Het Wiek"** (a nature reserve laid out around a string of lakes), a remarkably well-maintained 10ha/25 acre **arboretum★**, and several restaurants.
An easy way of getting round the extensive estate is aboard the 'Bokrijk-shuttle' which leaves from the 19C mansion of Kasteel Bokrijk.

Openluchtmuseum★★
Open end Mar-end Sept, daily, 10am-6pm; Mon-Fri €5 (Jul-Aug €10), Sat, Sun and public holidays €10. ☎ 011 22 53 00. www.bokrijk.be
The open-air museum consists of reconstructions of a hundred or so buildings on a 90ha/222 acre site. Together they give a wonderful picture of life lived in Flanders in days gone by. There are four sections, three rural and one urban. Each rural section corresponds to a particular region. The infertile heathland of the **Kempen region** is represented by a reconstructed village with public buildings (church, inn) flanking a triangular square. A southern Limburg village was taken as the model for the section devoted to the undulating fertile countryside of the **Haspengouw** and **Maasland regions**; it has a more "introverted" look to it than the Kempen village. The farmhouses from the fertile countryside of **Lower Belgium (Oost-Vlaanderen, West-Vlaanderen)** are not grouped in a village. They come from various regions in east and west Flanders, which explains why they are so different. The urban section **(Oude Stad)** features the facades of a number of 15C-18C houses from Antwerp.

The Open-air museum.

Bouillon★

From its rocky promontory above a broad bend in the river, an austere fortress looks down over the slate roofs of Bouillon, the little capital of the lovely **Semois Valley**, close to the French border. The town is one of the most popular places in the Ardennes, with canoeing on the river and wonderful walks in the surrounding countryside.

Location

Luxembourg – Population 5 463 – Michelin maps 716 I 6 and 534 P 24 – Local map see Vallée de la SEMOIS. Town plan in the current edition of The Red Guide Benelux.
In its wooded valley setting, Bouillon is accessible by the A 4/E 411 Brussels-Arlon motorway (exit 25), then by dual carriageway N 89. From Sedan in France, take N 58 and N 89.

🚩 *Château fort, 6830 ☎ 061 46 62 57; www.bouillon.be or www.sedan-bouillon.org*

Background

Godfrey of Bouillon – In a key position on one of the routes leading north from France to the Low Countries, the site of Bouillon was fortified at a very early date. The present stronghold seems to have been started in the 10C, and a century later was the residence of **Godfrey of Bouillon**, a pious knight who took a leading part in the First Crusade (1096-99), which he partly financed himself by selling the Duchy of Bouillon to the Prince-Bishop of Liège. Godfrey's troops were first to enter the Holy City, and he was acclaimed as the King of Jerusalem. He refused the offer, preferring the more modest title of Defender of the Holy Sepulchre. His exploits appealed to later writers, and he passed into legend as the perfect Christian knight. In subsequent years, Bouillon was fought over several times, its defences shattered, then restored and improved, most substantially by the great French military engineer Vauban.

Directory

EATING OUT

☕ **La Vieille Ardenne** – *Grand-rue 9 – ☎ 061 46 62 77 – Closed Wed except summer – ✒ – €13/23.* Friendly establishment much appreciated by local people, with a wonderful collection of beer mugs hanging from the ceiling. Menu features the best of local produce.

☕☕ **Le Feuillantin** – *Rue au-dessus de la Ville 25 – ☎ 061 46 61 38 – panorama@panoramahotels.be – Closed Wed, Thur except public and school holidays – €19 lunch – €38.* This restaurant benefits from its elevated position above the town and has fine views of Belgium's most famous castle and the spectacular bend in the river. Dishes coordinated with the changing seasons.

WHERE TO STAY

☕ **À la Cornette Chambre d'hôte** – *La Cornette 32 – ☎ 061 41 35 36 – ✒ – 5 rms: €50/90* ☑ Nestling in a lovely leafy setting, this is a good place to recharge your batteries. Contemporary, spacious rooms on two floors. Charming garden criss-crossed by little streams. Warm family atmosphere.

☕☕ **Ardennes** – *Rue Hate 1 – 6838 Corbion – ☎ 061 46 66 21 – contact@hoteldesardennes.be – ☐ – 29 rms: €80/105* ☑ – *restaurant €30/54.* Characterful Ardennes hostelry a few minutes from Bouillon in a quiet little village. Pleasantly old-fashioned lounge, delightful bedrooms, traditional restaurant and a garden to relax in with views of the rustic surroundings.

Worth a Visit

Château★★

Open Jan, Feb and Dec, Mon-Fri, 1-5pm (10am-5pm Sat-Sun); Mar, Oct and Nov, daily, 10am-5pm; Apr, May, June and Sept, daily, 10am-6pm (7pm Sat-Sun); July and Aug, daily, 10am-10pm (7pm Mon and Thur); during Christmas and Carnival holidays, daily, 10am-5pm. Closed 1 Jan and 25 Dec. €4. ☎ 061 46 62 57.

The castle is Belgium's largest remaining example of medieval military architecture. Its existence is recorded as early as the 10C. Three 17C stone drawbridges, separated by small forts, defended the castle entrances *(follow the numbered arrows)*. Beyond the second bridge is a staircase designed by Vauban with great attention to purity of line and built without either cement or mortar.

Visitors then come to the "Salle Primitive", a chamber with stout 12C walls, and the 13C Godfrey of Bouillon Chamber hollowed out of the rock and containing a large cross sunk into the floor as well as figures depicting the departure of Godfrey of Bouillon to the Crusades.

Le château de Bouillon.

Beyond is the main courtyard. The **Tour d'Autriche** (Austria Tower) was restored in 1551 by the Prince-Bishop of Liège, George of Austria; from it there are magnificent **views**★★ of the fortress, the meander of the River Semois, the town and the old bridge to the north.

The way back to the entrance is via the great underground passage which was both a means of reaching other parts of the castle and a warehouse. A cistern and a 54m/177ft deep well are indications that water was never in short supply here.

A **falconry demonstration** and torch-lit **night tour** take place in the summer months.

Musée Ducal★

Open mid-Apr – end Sept 10am-6pm (year-round Sat, Sun 10am-5pm). Closed 1 Jan, mid-Nov – Easter except school holidays. €3.30. ☎ *061 46 41 89.*

The **History and Folklore section** of the Ducal Museum is housed in a delightful 18C residence steeped in old-fashioned charm. It contains memorabilia of the Dukes of Bouillon and reminders of the region's folklore and crafts. There is a reconstruction of a typical Ardennes home (early 19C bedroom and kitchen) and of the study of Pierre Rousseau, an 18C printer of liberal views. A weaver's workshop and a clog maker's workshop can be seen in the attic.

The **Godfrey of Bouillon section** is in a restored court advisor's residence; it depicts life in the Middle Ages and the days of the Crusades. In addition to the mementoes brought back from the Levant by Crusaders, there is a model illustrating an attack on a fortress and another showing Bouillon castle as its was in the 12C. A further section is devoted to the area's industrial heritage.

Archéoscope Godefroid de Bouillon

 ♿ *Open Jul-Aug daily, 10am-5.30pm; Mar-June and Sep-Oct, daily, 10am-4pm (Sat, Sun 4.30pm); Feb, Nov-Dec, Tues to Fri, 1-4pm, Sat-Sun, 10am-4.30pm; Closed Jan (except school holidays). €5.95.* ☎ *061 46 87 58.*

Exhibits at this museum, housed in an old 17C convent on the riverbank, include an audio-visual presentation on the First Crusade and on Godfrey of Bouillon. Models and photos depict the various fortifications in the Bouillon region. Also worthy of note is the nuns' corridor, with its six small rooms.

Excursion

Cordemoy

3km/1.75mi W along a narrow road.

Follow the deep and narrow Semois Valley beyond the old **Gothic bridge** (Pont de la Poulie). The **Abbaye Notre-Dame-de-Clairefontaine** stands in a peaceful setting. It was built in 1935 in neo-Gothic style. It perpetuates the memory of a Cistercian abbey founded near Arlon by Ermesinde, the daughter of the Count of Luxembourg. The abbey was burnt down in 1794.

Brugge★★★

BRUGES

In winter or by moonlight, Bruges can seem a dream-like vision of the Middle Ages, with its houses of mellow time-worn brick, its majestic public buildings and its canals where swans glide gracefully over the dark waters. The medieval illusion is complete when melodious chimes ring out from the belfries of the city's ancient churches. In summer and even during out-of-season weekends a metamorphosis takes place, when visitors fill the streets and squares and the whole town buzzes with activity. Bruges' unique character was recognised by UNESCO in 2000 when it was placed on the World Heritage List. Two living traditions contribute to the city's fame; the production of exquisite bobbin lace, and the way in which its inhabitants celebrate Ascension Day with the renowned Holy Blood Procession.

Location

West-Vlaanderen – Population 115 991 – Michelin maps 716 C 2 and 533 E 15.
Bruges is near the coast just off the A 10/E 40 motorway between Brussels and Ostend.
🛈 *Burg 11, ☎ 050 44 86 86; www.brugge.be*

Background

A PROSPEROUS PAST

Like most of the towns in northern Flanders, Bruges was founded at a relatively late date and the exact details of its origin are obscure (it is first mentioned in 892). Count Baldwin Iron Arm built the castle in the late 9C to protect the coast which was under continuous attack from the Vikings.

The Rozenhoedkaai.

The Sea, Source of Wealth – Bruges was already a flourishing city when Robert the Frisian made it the capital of his duchy in 1093. The River Reie linked the port to the Zwin estuary. Like many other towns in Flanders, this was a cloth making community. Indeed, by the 12C it was a major importer of the English wool required for this industry, and it was during this period that Damme was built, as an outer harbour on the estuary of the Zwin.

By the 13C, Bruges was a great trading city, one of the most active members of the powerful **Hanseatic League**, an association of northern European towns with its headquarters in Lübeck and a monopoly on trade with Scandinavia and Russia. Commercial prosperity also brought artistic riches: the St-Jans Hospitaal was enlarged, as was the St-Salvatorskathedraal. The belfry, covered market and church dedicated to Our Lady were built. Bruges also constructed town walls, of which four gates still remain.

The town hall was built at the end of the 14C, then in the 15C a characteristic **architectural style** developed with tympana crowning rectangular windows and many of the doors and windows framed by elegant ogee moulding.

Europe's first stock exchange was held in Bruges, in the open air.

Princely Receptions – In 1280 conflict broke out in Flanders between the patricians who supported the King of France, known as **Leliaerts** (partisans of the fleur-de-lis), and the **Clauwaerts** (people with claws), referring to those of the lion of Flanders.

Philip the Fair took the opportunity of annexing Flanders. During the royal procession known as the Joyeuse Entrée (1301), his wife Queen Joan of Navarre cried out when she saw the richly dressed citizens of Bruges who had come to greet her: "I thought I alone was queen, but I can see hundreds of others around me!" The people were angered by the luxury of this reception, for which they were expected to pay. At dawn on 13 May 1302 the Clauwaerts, led by Pieter de Coninck, massacred the French garrison. The uprising was known as the **"Bruges Matins"**. It led to a general rebellion in Flanders and resulted in the Battle of the Golden Spurs.

In the 15C, the Dukes of Burgundy began to spend more and more time in Flanders. In January 1429, Philip the Good received his fiancée Isabella of Portugal in Bruges. The reception was unforgettably sumptuous. Philip founded the **Order of the Golden Fleece** during the marriage celebrations.

FLEMISH PAINTING AT ITS FINEST

Flemish Primitives in Bruges (15C) – Bruges is the cradle of Flemish painting. It was here that **Jan van Eyck** (born in Maaseik) painted the *Adoration of the Mystic Lamb Altarpiece* which has adorned Sint-Baafskathedraal in Ghent since 1432. His genius is apparent in other works displayed in Bruges, including his *Virgin Mary with Canon van der Paele*, a painting as remarkable for the richness of the decor as for the treatment of the portrait of the donor. His follower, **Petrus Christus**, who died c 1473, produced the famous *Portrait de Jeune Fille* in Berlin's Dahlem Museum.

Hugo Van der Goes (c 1440-82) worked in Ghent and ended his days near Brussels, but his last and greatest work, *Death of the Virgin*, can be seen in Bruges. The elaborate composition and emotional intensity are admirable for their rarity.

Hans Memling (c 1435-94) is to Bruges what Rubens is to Antwerp. Memling was of German origin, born near Frankfurt, but he settled in Bruges in 1465 after a stay in Cologne and perhaps also in Brussels. He completed a large number of commissioned works, including some for the St-Jans Hospitaal, for the town magistrates, as well as for wealthy foreigners. The most outstanding works are still in Bruges. The serenity of his paintings sets him apart from his contemporaries. This, combined with his warm palette and attention to detail, renders his works both charming and intense. He is the painter of gentle Madonnas, feminine figures that are calm, even ethereal. His portraits are often more idealised than those of Van Eyck.

Gerard David (c 1460-1523) was born in Oudewater in Holland and came to Bruges in 1483. David was a student of Memling, whose style he faithfully perpetuated, never renouncing the gravity and characteristic precision of his master's works *(Baptism of Christ)*.

During the Renaissance, a number of artists followed in his footsteps, including **Adriaen Isenbrandt** from Haarlem, the Lombard **Ambrosius Benson**, **Jan Provost**, originally from Mons, and **Pieter Pourbus** from Gouda. These were the last great talents of the Bruges School, although a few anonymous painters should also be acknowledged, for instance the Master of the Legend of St Ursula and the Master of the Legend of St Lucy.

DECLINE AND REVIVAL

"Sleeping Beauty" – Bruges' commerical demise began in the late 15C, due largely to the silting up of the Zwin and the decline in the cloth making industry, and it was soon supplanted by Antwerp. In 1488, the town revolted against Maximilian of Austria and took him prisoner. In 1520 it welcomed Emperor Charles V amid much pomp, a ceremonial organised by the painter Lancelot Blondeel.

The fury of the 16C Protestant iconoclasts, the bands of "Geuzen" revolting against Spanish rule, and later, the French invasion in 1794, hastened the town's decline and led to the disappearance of many historic buildings. The city's air of romantic decay appealed to visitors from abroad and inspired poets including Wordsworth and Longfellow. Georges Rodenbach called the moonlit town "Bruges la Morte".

Renewal – Major construction projects were undertaken in the late 19C. The building of a port at Zeebrugge on the coast linked by an 11km/7mi canal (finished in 1907) to Bruges' new inland harbour brought a certain degree of activity back to the town.

In the 1950s, new industries were established along Bruges' waterways. Nowadays the city's economy is very dependent on tourism.

The city is also a major educational centre thanks to the presence of the **Collège d'Europe** founded in 1949.

Walking About

THE HISTORIC CENTRE AND THE CANALS★★★

Markt★★

Life in Bruges centres on the spacious central market place, flanked by houses with crow-stepped gables, old guildhalls and the covered market in the shadow of the magnificent town belfry. The statue of Pieter de Coninck and Jan Breydel serves as a reminder of the heroes of the 1302 revolt *(see "Background" above)*.

Until the 18C a canal terminated at the Markt; it was here that boats used to berth. On the eastern side of the square stand two neo-Gothic buildings. One houses the post office, the other the seat of the provincial authorities.

FESTIVALS

The **Golden Tree Pageant** takes place in Bruges every five years. The pageant recalls the pomp and ceremony of the Burgundian period *(next procession in August 2006)*.

The **Reiefeest** is a canal festival, held every three years in August. *(Next festival in 2004)*. The **Holy Blood Procession** takes place on Ascension Day at 3pm when the Holy Blood reliquary is carried through the streets, preceded by the clergy, the innumerable religious brotherhoods and groups of people in costume. Some of them represent biblical scenes ranging from the original sin of Adam and Eve to the Passion of Christ; others represent the return from the Second Crusade, with Thierry of Alsace.

Directory

GETTING AROUND

By car – The municipality has made great efforts to discourage the use of cars in the town centre. Visitors are advised to leave their vehicle in one of the underground car parks in the central area or in one of the conventional car parks on the outskirts.

By bus – There is a frequent service between the railway station and the Markt. The Dagpas Brugge is a day pass entitling the holder to unlimited use of public transport for a whole day. Information from De Lijn: ☎ 059 56 53 53 or www.delijn.be

By bike – This is one of the best ways of exploring Bruges, particularly as traffic management measures in the centre favour cyclists. Bicycle hire from: the railway station, ☎ 050 38 58 71; Bauhaus Bike Rental, Langestraat 135, ☎ 050 34 10 93; De Ketting, Gentpoortstraat 23, ☎ 050 34 41 96; 't Koffieboontje, Hallestraat 14, ☎ 050 33 80 27; Eric Popelier, Mariastraat 26, ☎ 050 34 32 62. A number of hotels have bikes for use of guests. A Dutch-language brochure *5x op de fiets rond Brugge* ("5 times round Bruges by bike") is available from the Tourist Information Centre.

SIGHTSEEING

By bus – There is an hourly minibus tour of the town lasting 50min, starting from Burg. Information: Sightseeing Line Brugge, Kannunik Decoeneplein 6, 8310 St-Kruis, ☎ 050 35 50 24 (10am-noon).

Carriage rides – Horse-drawn carriages take visitors on a 30min tour of the centre, leaving from Markt (Wed am from Burg).

Guided tours – Daily at 3pm in July and August. Reservations from the Tourist Information Centre

Illuminations – Between April and September, the pleasures of a late evening stroll are enhanced immeasurably by sophisticated floodlighting of streets, canals, buildings and ramparts.

WHERE TO EAT

Chasse-Spleen – *Kleine Hoefijzerstraat 3* – ☎ *050 34 88 44 – Closed Wed, Thur* – *€12.39/34.71.* Welcoming establishment adept at extinguishing any traces of melancholy in its clientele. Mildly trendy dining room, blackboard with dishes of the day and a worthy wine list.

Steenhuyse – *Steenhuyse 29* – ☎ *050 33 23 24* – *€19.71/35.94.* This typical Bruges house has a charming dining room with long beams, brick walls, well-worn furniture, a venerable stove and a fireplace filled with blazing logs in winter. Easy parking beneath the 't Zand.

Soul Food – *Langestraat 15* – ☎ *050 33 41 13 – Closed Mon* – *€25/35.* Honourable little restaurant tucked away in a street linking the Burg area with the Kruispoort gateway. There are a number of vegetarian dishes in the contemporary menu. The dining room has an up to date look about it.

De Koetse – *Oude Brug 31* – ☎ *050 33 76 80 – Closed Thur, early July* – *€25/42.* Family enterprise in the town centre between the prestigious market hall and Simon Stevinplein. The food has a regional touch to it and goes well with the range of beers on offer. Bill unlikely to get you into trouble with the bank.

Terrasje – *Genthof 45* – ☎ *050 33 09 19 – Closed Mon, Tue* – *€25/42.* This pleasant restaurant in an 18C building extends on to an attractive little terrace – or terrasje – in summer. Range of dishes without too many frills and easily digestible bill.

Breydel – De Coninc – *Breidelstraat 24* – ☎ *050 33 97 46 – Closed Wed – €28/43.* A stone's throw from Burg and Markt, a seafood restaurant which is the final destination of any self-respecting lobster or eel. Mussels aplenty in season. Welcoming reception and friendly service.

't Apertje – *Damse Vaart Zuid 223* – *8310 Sint-Kruis* – ☎ *050 35 00 12 – Closed Mon* – *€33.* Bistro-style dishes designed to still your hunger in this delightful little canalside inn in polder country. Eels have pride of place in season.

Hof ter Doest – *Ter Doeststraat 4* – *8380 Lissewege* – ☎ *050 54 40 82* – *info@terdoest.be* – *€37/54* This rustic restaurant occupies the home farm of an old abbey, and the magnificent 13C tithe barn next door can be inspected. There are generous joints crackling on the spit and the offerings from the cellar would please the thirstiest medieval abbot!

Den Dyver – *Dijver 5* – ☎ *050 33 60 69 – Closed lunchtime Wed, Thur – €22 lunch – €42/50.* Solid traditional cuisine well marinated in beer, guaranteed to satisfy the heartiest appetite. Fine old 18C patrician residence and a dining room hung with lovely tapestries.

Cafedraal – *Zilverstraat 38* – ☎ *050 34 08 45 – Closed Sun, Mon – €10 lunch – €43.* Close to the Cathedral in a lovely historic group of buildings, this is a smart and lively brasserie with an exceptionally varied menu. Walled terrace for summer dining, and a Cuban bar where the lights burn brightly till late. Underground car park.

't Bourgoensche Cruyce – *Wollestraat 41* – ☎ *050 33 79 26* – *bour.cruyce@ssi.be – Closed Tue, Wed* – *€48/60.* This delightful eating place enjoys a picturesque canalside location. Up to date menu, well-stocked cellar, and a picture-postcard view. A number of bedrooms are available, also with superlative views.

WHERE TO STAY

Hanna Jaszyk – *Carmersstraat 16* – ☎ *050 34 17 35* – *2 rms: €38/50.* Typical 17C Flemish house steeped in the atmosphere created by music-loving Hanna Jaszyk and her husband. Two spacious bedrooms and a studio – all tastefully decorated – await guests in this residence well-favoured by the muses.

The secret garden – *Calvariestraat 10 –
☎ 050 31 18 06 – www.bedandbreakfast.be
– ✉ – 2 rms: €50/70.* This is a very
convenient place to stay despite its location
just outside the centre. The rooms are spread
over three floors and each has its own
character. Excellent English or Norwegian
breakfast. Delightful little walled garden at
the back.

Verdi – *Vlamingstraat 5 – ☎ 050 34
42 43 – restaurant closed Mon eve, Tue – ✉
– 3 rms: €65/75: – restaurant €22/28.* This
luxurious "tavern-restaurant-tea-room" with
five comfortable rooms close to the Markt
pays tribute to the celebrated composer with
its sign and its decor.

Maraboe – *Hofijzerlaan 9 – ☎ 050 33
81 55 – hotel@maraboe.be – 14 rms:
€70/90.* Just a step from the shopping
streets converging on 't Zand, this modest
family establishment offers simply furnished
but comfortable, reasonably-sized rooms.
Friendly reception.

't Putje – *'t Zand 31 – ☎ 050 33 28 47
– hotelputje@pandora.be – 24 rms:
€74/99 ☐ restaurant €22/39.* Convenient
place to stay and start your exploration of
Bruges, this family hotel-restaurant abuts 't
Zand and the new concert hall. Comfortable
rooms, quieter to the rear.

Malleberg – *Hoogstraat 7 – ☎ 050 34
41 11 – 8 rms: €87.* The ideal place to stay
for those who want to be as close as
possible to the architectural splendours of
the Burg. Functionally comfortable rooms.
Breakfast served in an attractive vaulted
cellar.

Gd H du Sablon – *Noordzandstraat 21
– ☎ 050 33 39 02 – info@sablon.be –
36 rms: €89/107.* A lovely Art Nouveau
cupola graces the foyer of the early 20C
hotel strategically located close to Grand-
Place and the shopping area. The whole
establishment has undergone recent
renovation.

Huyze de Maene –
*Markt 17 – ☎ 050 33 39 59 –
huyzedemaene@pandora.be – ✉ – 2 junior
suites and 1 suite: €112/220 – ☐ €8.80 –
restaurant €15/24.* Ideal location on the
Markt, this tavern-restaurant offers bistro-
style dining, two junior suites and a suite just
above them. Tables set out on the square in
summer.

A seat overlooking the Markt.

B. Juge/MICHELIN

Pandhotel – *Pandreitje 16 –
☎ 050 34 06 66 – info@pandhotel.com
– 24 rms: €120/300.* Elegant hotel occupying a
trio of typical Bruges houses in the heart of the
town. The attractive, comfortable rooms and
junior suites are individually decorated and
furnished. Excellent breakfast served in a
charming room.

TAKING A BREAK

Gran Kaffee de Passage – *Dweerstraat 26 –
☎ 050 34 13 27 – 5pm-midnight – closed
fortnight in Jan.* Affable welcome in this
candle-lit tavern with walls covered in old
photographs. Music from around the world.
Excellent lamb chops.

In 't Niuew Museum – *Hooistraat 42 –
☎ 050 33 12 80 – Thur-Mon 5pm-midnight.*
Cheerful atmosphere and typical Flemish
decor in this well-established local estaminet
close to the city's ring canal. Good choice of
beers and succulent steaks from the fireside
grille.

De Halve Maan – *Waalplein 26 –
☎ 050 33 26 97 – Dec-Feb: 10.30am-4pm,
Mar-Nov: 10.30-6.30pm.* This family
brasserie has been brewing its own beer
since 1856. Visitors can see the process
under way and, at the bar, sample the
product, called Straffe Hendrik (Stiff Henry).
Art gallery and outdoor seating in the
courtyard in summer. View over the city from
the top of the building.

Herberg Vlissinghe – *Blekersstraat 2 –
☎ 050 34 37 37 – Wed-Sat 11am-midnight,
Sun 11am-8pm.* Dating from the 16C, this is
Bruges' oldest estaminet, serving a range of
beers in a nostalgic atmosphere. There's a
lovely old stove for when it turns chilly.
Outside seating in the courtyard garden
where you can also have a go at playing
traditional *boules*.

Staminet de Garre – *De Gaare 1 –
☎ 050 34 10 29 – Fri noon-midnight, Sat
noon-1am, Sun 11am-midnight.* This
estaminet in a lovely old house is a haven of
peace, where the tone is set by classical
music. Excellent choice of beers.

HAVING A DRINK

Herberg Du Phare – *Sasplein 2 –
☎ 050 34 35 90 – Mon, Wed-Thur
11.30am-3am, Fri-Sat 11.30am-5am.* Blues
and jazz café, where the walls are hung with
accordions, cellos and zithers and old
sewing-machine stands serve as tables. Live
music twice monthly.

Wijnbar – *Nordzandstraat 34 – ☎ 050 33
38 39 – www.brugge.be – Sun-Mon, Thur
5pm-midnight, Fri, Sat 3pm-1am – Closed
Tue-Wed and fortnight in June.* Between 't
Zand and the Markt, 19C private hotel
converted into a wine bar with music. Wines
from around the world, cheese sampling and
jazz atmosphere. The owner was a
professional musician and plays a mean
guitar. Live music Sunday from 7.30pm.

SHOPPING

The main shopping streets are Steenstraat,
Zuidzandstraat, Zilverstraat with the Het
Zand shopping complex, Simon Stevinplein
and Vlamingstraat.

Markets – Traditional markets on the Markt on Wednesday and on 't Zand on Saturday morning. Flea-market on the Dijver Saturday and Sunday mid-March to mid-November.

Specialities – Apart from its famous **lace**, Bruges is renowned for its delicious **chocolate** specialities. Two brasseries, Straffe Hendrik and De Gouden Boom, still make their own **beer**, and the latter has a small brewing museum. *Straffe Hendrik: Walplein 26, ☎ 050 33 26 97; De Gouden Boom, Langestraat 47, ☎ 050 33 06 99.*

The Chocolate Line – *Simon Stevinplein 19 – ☎ 050 34 10 90 – 9.30am-6.30pm, Sun 10.30am-6.30pm.* The chocolate makers of Bruges are famous. This establishment has a shop window to make anyone's mouth water. Once inside, you can fill your lungs with the glorious aroma of cocoa, stock up with local pralines, and even take a look at how they are made.

't Apostelientje – *Balstraat 11 – ☎ 050 33 78 60 – 9.30am-6pm, Sun 10am-noon, 1.30pm-6pm.* A mother and her two daughters maintain Bruges' lace-making traditions in style in this boutique. As well as authentic hand-made lace, you can purchase all the necessary materials for this most meticulous of crafts.

LEISURE

Boat trips – *☎ 050 44 86 86 – Mar-Nov: 10am-6pm; otherwise only weekends, school and public holidays – €5.20.* A canal trip is probably the best and most relaxing way of experiencing Bruges' architectural heritage and unique atmosphere. Boats leave from five landing-stages in the city centre (see town plan).

Carriage rides – *Markt (Wed from the Burg) – Oct-Jun: 10am-6pm; July-Aug 10am-10pm – €27.50 per carriage (max 5 passengers).* A romantic horse-drawn carriage ride in the care of a friendly and informative coachman lasts 30 min and includes a short stop at the Beguinhof.

Boudewijnpark en Dolfinarium – *Alfons De Baeckestraat 12 – ☎ 050 40 84 08 – May-Aug 10am-6pm.* Extensive recreational park with lake, dolphinarium, ferris wheel, go-carts, shooting gallery, dodgems, stables and zoo.

ENTERTAINMENT

What's on – Full details of current events in the monthly periodical Exit, available at the Tourist Information Centre.

Brugge, anno 1468 – Participants share in the wedding feast of Charles the Bold and Margaret of York, and are royally entertained by jesters, fire-eaters, magicians and falconers. *Information: Celebrations Entertainment, Vlamingstraat 86, ☎ 050 34 75 72.*

Concert halls – **Concertgebouw** *'t Zand 34, ☎ 050 47 69 99; www.concertgebouw.be.* Opened in 2002, this magnificent red-brick edifice designed by Robbrecht and Daem has concerts of classical music. **De Werf**, Werfstraat 108, ☎ 050 33 05 29 (jazz and blues); **Cactusclub**, St-Jacobsstraat 36, ☎ 050 33 20 14 (jazz and blues).

EVENTS AND FESTIVALS

Festivals – The **Cactus festival** takes place in mid-July on the banks of the Minnewater, and features blues, pop, jazz and rock by the famous and the unknown. In late July/early August the city is home. to the prestigious **Ancient Music Festival**.

EXCURSION

Damme by boat – There are boat trips to Damme in summer from the Noorweegse kaai landing-stage just northeast of the town centre. The route takes you along the the lovely tree-lined waterway of the Napoleonkanaal dating from 1812.

Ghent by boat – Ghent can be reached by water, starting from Bargeweg. *Information: Rederij Hubrouck, ☎ 050 34 48 71.*

Belfort and Hallen★★★

Open Tue-Sun, 9.30am-5pm. Closed 1 Jan, Ascension (pm), 25 Dec. €5 ☎ 050 44 87 11. The belfry and covered market form a magnificent group of beautifully weathered brick buildings.

The **belfry** is the pride of the local population and is unquestionably the most impressive of its kind in Belgium. The massive tower dates from the 13C, but the corner turrets were added in the 14C, and the top octagonal storey at the end of the 15C. Above the entrance porch, a few statues frame the balcony, from where new laws used to be proclaimed. The climb up to the top of the belfry *(366 steps)* includes a visit to the second-floor **treasury**. The town seal and charters used to be kept behind beautiful wrought-iron grilles. The **carillon** is higher up. It consists of 47 bells which chime every quarter hour. Finally, the remarkable **view★★** from the top takes in all of Bruges and the surrounding countryside.

The **covered market** was constructed at the same time as the belfry and enlarged in the 14C and 16C. The four sections of the market surround a pretty courtyard.

Burg★★

This square is named after the castle (Burg) built by Baldwin Iron Arm. Excavations have uncovered remains of the early-9C ramparts. However these were pulled down in the 10C to enable the construction of **St-Donaaskerk**. Subsequently, the walls were replaced by brick ramparts. Vestiges of the fortified walls and church buildings have been incorporated into the basement of the adjoining hotel.

Brugge

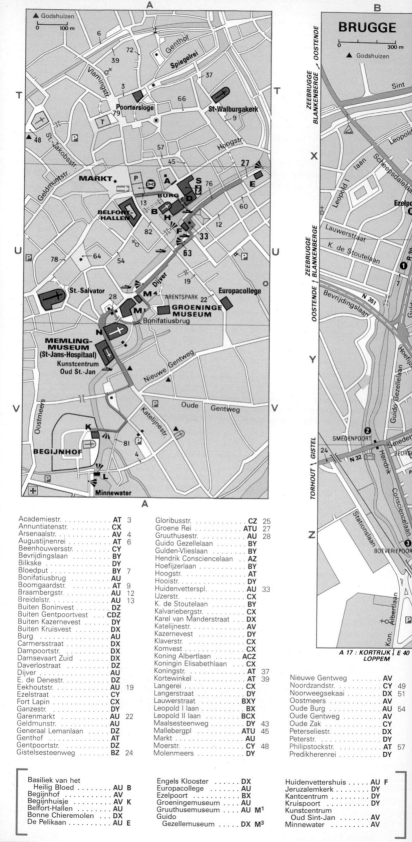

Predikherenstr.	**AU**	60
Rolweg	**DX**	61
Rozenhoedkaai	**AU**	63
Rubenslaan	**DZ**	
Schaarstr.	**DY**	
Scheepsdalelaan	**BX**	
Simon Stevinpl.	**AU**	64
Sint-Clarastr.	**CX**	
Sint-Jakobsstr.	**AT**	
Sint-Jansstr.	**AT**	66
Sint-Jorisstr.	**CXY**	

Sint-Pieterskaai	**BCX**	
Smedenstr.	**BY**	
Snaggaardstr.	**CDX**	
Spanjaardstr.	**AT**	72
Spiegelrei	**AT**	
Stationslaan	**AZ**	
Steenhouwersdijk	**AU**	76
Steenstr.	**AU**	78
Veemarkstr.	**BX**	
Vlamingdam	**CX**	
Vlamingstr.	**AT**	79

Vrijheidsstr.	**DZ**	
Wagnerstr.	**DZ**	
Weidestraat	**DZ**	
Werfstr.	**CX**	
Wijngaardstr.	**AV**	81
Wollestr.	**AU**	82
Wulpenstr.	**CX**	
'T Zand	**CY**	
Zuidervaartje	**DX**	
Zuidzandstr.	**CY**	84
Zwarte Leertouwersstr.	**DY**	85

Museum Arentshuis	**AU**	**M⁴**
Museum O.-L.-Vrouw ter Potterie	**CDX**	**M⁵**
Museum voor Volkskunde	**DY**	**M²**
O.-L.-Vrouwekerk	**AV**	**N**
Oude Griffie	**AU**	**D**

Paleis van het Brugse Vrije	**AU**	**S**
Poortersloge	**AT**	
Sashuis	**AV**	**L**
Schuttersgilde Sint-Sebastiaan	**DX**	**Y**
Sint-Annakerk	**DY**	

Sint-Donaaskerk	**AU**	**A**
Sint-Jans-Hospitaal (Memlingmuseum)	**AV**	
Sint-Janshuismolen	**DX**	
Sint-Salvator	**AU**	
Sint-Walburgakerk	**AT**	
Stadhuis	**AU**	**H**

Four of Bruges' main buildings surround this square: from right to left, the basilica church dedicated to the Holy Blood, the Gothic town hall, the Renaissance court record office, and opposite, the old law courts.

Basiliek van het Heilig Bloed★

The basilica church houses a reliquary said to contain the Holy Blood of Christ, brought back from the Holy Land by Thierry of Alsace, Count of Flanders, on his return from the second Crusade.

The Romanesque early 12C **lower chapel★** is dedicated to St Basil. It has retained its original character, as can be seen by the massive cylindrical pillars. Note the Romanesque low relief of the Baptism of Christ dating from 1300 on the reverse side of the tympanum over the door leading to a small chapel on the right. There is a wooden polychrome statue of the Virgin Mary in the south aisle.

A beautiful projecting doorway in a transitional Late Gothic-Renaissance style and a graceful 16C spiral staircase lead to the **chapel** dedicated to the Holy Blood. It was originally built in the Romanesque style but was altered in the 15C. It was decorated with murals in the 19C. Visitors' attention will be caught by the superb pulpit dating from 1728. *Apr-Sept: Upper and Lower chapel 9.30am-11.50am, 2pm-5.50pm; Oct-Mar 10am-11.50am, 2pm-3.50pm. Closed during services. (Upper chapel Wed-Sat 11am-11.50am, Lower chapel other days 11am-11.30am)* ☎ *050 44 86 86 (Tourist Information Centre).*

The little **museum** beside the chapel contains the reliquary of the Holy Blood (1617) which is carried through the streets during the famous procession. There are also two magnificent triptych panels by Pieter Pourbus representing members of the Brotherhood of the Holy Blood. *Apr-Sept: Upper and Lower chapel 9.30am-11.50am, 2pm-5.50pm; Oct-Mar 10am-11.50am, 2pm-3.50pm (not Wed). Closed 1 Jan, 1 Nov, 25 Dec. €1.50.*

Stadhuis

The town hall was built at the end of the 14C in the Late Gothic style and was restored in the 19C. The façade is unusual not only for its ornate decoration, but also for its sense of verticality, which is further accentuated by three turrets.

The **Gothic Room** on the upper floor has panelled rib vaulting, decorated at the intersection of the arches with beautiful hanging keystones. The late 19C neo-Gothic frescoes depict historical scenes and events. ♿ *Tue-Sun 9.30am-5pm. Closed 1 Jan, Ascension (pm), 25 Dec. €2.50.* ☎ *050 44 87 11.*

Oude Griffie – Now part of the law courts, the old municipal records office is a harmonious Renaissance building with a trio of graceful gables.

Paleis van de Brugse Vrije – The Liberty of Bruges Palace was built in neo-Classical style in the 18C on the site of a palace of 1520 which formed part of the Burg. A section of the early building has survived; it overlooks the canal. In the 14C the Liberty of Bruges was the council which administered an extensive area outside the city itself

From the Blinde Ezelstraat it is possible to see the beautiful window over the gallery, then the gables and turrets of the Brugse Vrije.

Take Steenhouwersdijk as far as the Groene Rei.

Groene Rei

To the right of this tree-lined quay ("Green Quay") stands **De Pelikaan** (1714), a low house with tall dormers. It is decorated with the emblem of a pelican. This used to be a hospital for the poor. The end of the wharf commands a beautiful **view** of the canal, the belfry and the spire of the church of Onze-Lieve-Vrouwekerke. The Steenhouwersdijk leads back to **Huidenvettersplaats**. This charming square, known by some Bruges residents as the small fish market, is embellished with a column sporting the emblem of the tanners' guild and surmounted by two lions. Nearby, the **Rozenhoedkaai**, literally "Rosary Quay", offers some of the most characteristic **views★★** of Bruges. The pretty 1630 **Huidenvettershuis** stands near the basin; it was the tanners' guildhall. Next to it is a turreted house. The tall roof of the chapel dedicated to the Holy Blood can be seen beyond, with the belfry to the left.

Dijver

The St-J Nepomucenusbrug is topped with a statue of the patron saint of bridges, St John of Nepomuk. From the end of the wharf lined with lime trees, there is a splendid **view★★** of an old bridge, the porch of the Gruuthusemuseum and the tower and spire of Onze-Lieve-Vrouwekerk.

By passing in front of the Groeningemuseum *(see description in "Worth a Visit")*

THE SWANS OF BRUGES

There is an old legend behind the graceful swans gliding across the peaceful waters bordering the Beguine Convent. In 1448 the citizens of Bruges imprisoned Maximilian of Austria in the Craenenburg House on the Markt, where he remained for several weeks. They also beheaded his councillor Pierre Lanchais, whose crest featured a swan. Once Maximilian had been set free, he ordered that the citizens of Bruges keep swans on the town's canals from that day onward, in order to expiate their crime.

and crossing the narrow street you come to the little Arentspark. Opposite the museum, there are sleighs and carriages in the windows of the Arentshuis *(see description in "Worth a Visit")*.

Cross the humpbacked **Bonifatiusbrug**, a bridge in a wonderfully poetic **setting★★**. A bust serves as a reminder of the 16C Spanish humanist, **Luis Vives**, who spent the last years of his life in Bruges.

Onze-Lieve-Vrouwekerk★

9am-12.30pm, 1.30pm-5pm (Sat 4pm), Sun 2pm-5pm. ☎ 050 34 53 14.

The Gothic church dedicated to Our Lady dates mainly from the 13C. The most remarkable feature is the slender brick **tower★★**, 122m/400ft tall.

Michelangelo's splendid white marble *Madonna and Child*★★ rests on the altar at the far end of the south aisle.

The Virgin and Child, by Michelangelo.

Chancel – The chancel contains the mausoleums of Charles the Bold and his daughter Mary of Burgundy. The Gothic **tomb★★** of Mary of Burgundy, who died at the age of 25, was designed by **Jan Borman** in 1498. The recumbent effigy is remarkable for its youthful face, graceful neck and long delicate hands with tapering fingers. The base is decorated with the crests of her ancestors.

The Renaissance monument to Charles the Bold dates from the 16C. B van Orley's triptych of the *Passion* decorates the high altar. Several funerary vaults decorated with frescoes were discovered beneath the chancel, among them Mary of Burgundy's original tomb. The ambulatory contains the beautiful *Seven Sorrows of the Virgin*, the masterpiece of the 16C artist Adriaen Isenbrandt. There is also a *Crucifixion* scene painted by Van Dyck, along with works by Gerard David and his students, and by Pieter Pourbus. A 15C carved wooden gallery leads to the Gruuthusemuseum.

Le tomb of Marie de Bourgogne.

The route leads past St John's Hospital which houses the Memling Museum *(see description in "Worth a Visit")*.

Begijnhof★★

The "Beguine Convent of the Vine" was founded in 1245 by Margaret of Constantinople, Countess of Flanders. The peaceful close lies beyond a beautiful Classical entrance near the canal. The 17C brick church and the white houses that were the Beguines' lodgings are set out around a vast green rectangle of lawn, brightened by a scattering of daffodils in the spring and planted with large trees. The Benedictines who took the place of the Beguine nuns retained the same style and colour of habit.

Begijnhuisje – Go through the kitchen and the simply furnished rooms of the Beguine House to reach a tiny garden with a well. ♿ *Open Apr to end Sept, daily, 10am-noon and 1.45-5pm (6pm Sun); Mar, Oct and Nov, daily, 10.30am-noon and 1.45-5pm; Dec to Feb, Wed, Thur and Sat-Sun, 2.45-4.15pm, Fri, 1.45-6pm. €2. ☎ 050 33 00 11 (Tourist Information Centre).*

The Begijnhof

The nearby bridge provides a beautiful **view** of the charming lock-keeper's house, *(sashuis)*, in front of the **Minnewater**, one of the basins in the old harbour. This is the famous Lake of Love. A tower (Poertoren) where gunpowder used to be kept can be seen to the right.

It is possible to return to the town centre by boat (see "Directory").

Worth a Visit

BRUGES' MAJOR MUSEUMS

Groeningemuseum★★★

Open Tue-Sun 9.30am-5pm. Closed 1 Jan, Ascension (pm), 25 Dec. €8 (includes admission to Arentshuis).

The museum presents a survey of Belgian painting from the 15C up to the present day, but it is particularly noted for its outstanding collections devoted to the **Flemish Primitives**. There are two fine works by **Jan van Eyck**. His *Madonna with Canon van der Paele* (1436) is striking for the brilliance of its colours and its fine details. The canon's portrait, in which Van Eyck depicts every wrinkle and wart, is truly remarkable. As for the *Portrait of Margaret van Eyck*, it illustrates the somewhat surly middle class dignity, sense of duty and piety of his wife, aged 33 at the time. The museum also has works by **Petrus Christus**, namely the *Annunciation*, the very first Dutch painting featuring a unified perspective. *Death of the Virgin* is a deeply poignant portrait by **Hugo van der Goes**. The famous *Moreel Triptych* by **Hans Memling** (1484) was commissioned by Willem Moreel and his wife Barbara van Vlaenderberch: the central panel depicting St Maur, St Christopher and St Giles is perhaps the painter's greatest masterpiece because of the mysticism, inner peace and contemplation which it conveys. Pictures by Gerard David include *The Judgement of Cambyses* and the *Baptism of Christ*, in which the impassive characters are set against a landscape of bold colours. The stunning *Last Judgement* is attributed to **Hieronymus Bosch**.

Part of the collection is devoted to Bruges painting after the mid-16C with works by **Isenbrant**, **Benson**, **Blondeel** and **Provoost**, all showing Italianate influence. One room is devoted exclusively to the work of the **Pourbus** family. Besides his religious pictures such as the *Last Judgement*, Pieter Pourbus produced many fine portraits (*Jan van Eyeewerve* and *Jacquemyne Buuck*). The 19C neo-Gothic wing is devoted to 17C to 19C painting. The ground-floor gallery concentrates on 17C and 18C paintings by artists from Bruges, as well as contemporary portraits and landscapes by Flemish and Dutch painters. The upstairs floor gives a survey of the various artistic movements that characterised the 19C. Neo-Classicism is represented with works by **Francois Kinsoen** and **Joseph Suvée**. **Fernand Khnopff**, who spent his childhood in Bruges, executed a mysterious painting bearing the title *Secret Reflexions*, the lower section of which depicts a side wall of St-Jans Hospitaal. A number of rooms are given over to modern and contemporary art from Belgium. The museum has works by **Rik Wouters** (*Household Concerns*) and by a great many Flemish Expressionists, namely **G van de Woestijne** (a huge *Last Supper*) and **Permeke** (*The Gruel Eater*). Visitors may also admire paintings by **Vantongerloo** (*Construction in Sphere 2*), **Delvaux**, **Magritte** (*The Attack*), **Raveel** and **Panamarenko**. The **Broodthaers** section contains all published works on the artist.

Memlingmuseum★★★

Access from Mariastraat. Tue-Sun 9.30am-5pm. Closed 1 Jan, Ascension (pm), 25 Dec €8 (includes admission to Onze-Lieve-Vrouw ter Potterie). ☎ 050 44 87 11.
This museum is housed in the old 12C St-Jans Hospitaal. The old wards for invalids have been superbly restored and now house works of art and other objects illustrating a variety of themes including the history of hospitals. The hospital's **church** has six works by Memling. Small **cloisters** housing a 17C **apothecary's shop** can be seen to the right of the entrance.

The **Reliquary of St Ursula** is probably the most famous of Memling's works. The highly detailed images describe the life and martyrdom of St Ursula and the 11 000 virgins who were her companions. It illustrates their arrival in Cologne and then Basle and depicts the Pope welcoming them to Rome. It shows their return to Basle with the Pope and their arrival in Cologne where the saint was killed by the Huns. On the end panels are the Virgin Mary and St Ursula. The saint is shown sheltering the virgins under her mantle.

The *Mystical Marriage of St Catherine of Alexandria* (also known as the *Triptych of St John the Baptist and St John the Evangelist*) depicts the Infant Jesus slipping a ring onto the saint's finger while St Barbara is deeply engrossed in reading a book. On either side of the painting are the following scenes: the beheading of St John the Baptist *(left)* and St John the Evangelist on the island of Patmos *(right)*. Memling reaches the height of grandeur with this highly symbolic triptych completed in 1479. Some believe that St Catherine and St Barbara are in fact portraits of Mary of Burgundy and Margaret of York.

The *Adoration of the Magi*, the central panel in **Jan Floreins'** 1479 triptych, is an important work if only for the perfect beauty of the Virgin Mary shown with her eyes lowered, and for the youthful beauty of the black king Balthazar.

The *Lamentation of Christ* triptych was executed in 1480 at the request of the Friarriest Adrien Reyns, who appears on his knees on the inside of the leaf to the right. St Barbara, a very popular saint at the time, is depicted on the inside of the leaf to the right. The chapel houses the perturbing *Portrait of a Young Woman*, diaphanous and enigmatic. The diptych of **Martin van Nieuwenhove**, with the portrait of the donor and *Virgin with Apple*, was painted in 1487 and has wonderfully sophisticated lines and tones.

A little staircase leads up to the lofts, the largest of which has kept its imposing oak timbers.

A number of 19C buildings house the **Oud St-Jan congress centre**.

OTHER MUSEUMS AND HISTORIC BUILDINGS

Around the Dijver and the Burg

Gruuthusemuseum★

Open Tue-Sun 9.30am-5pm. Closed 1 Jan, Ascension Day (pm), 25 Dec. €6. ☎ 050 44 87 11.
The Gothic Gruuthuse mansion was originally the building in which the municipality collected dues on *"grute"*, a mixture of flowers and dried plants which were added to the barley or wheat used for brewing beer. The vast 15C residence is built of warm red-toned brick; it houses a Museum of Decorative Arts at the end of the main courtyard.

The beautiful interior is very well kept and features splendid fireplaces. The past lives on through the thousand or so old Flemish objects, many from Bruges, among them fine furniture, sculpture, tapestries and paintings. The collection of musical instruments features a harpsichord and a spinet manufactured by the renowned Ruckers firm. There is also a **bust of Emperor Charles V★** (1520) at the age of 20, attributed to the German sculptor Konrad Meit.

Minnewater

The Mystical marriage of St. Catharine of Alexandria, by Hans Memling

Louis van Gruuthuse's wooden **oratory** (1472) used to lead directly to the chancel of Onze-Lieve-Vrouwekerk. This counsellor of Charles the Bold and Mary of Burgundy was not only a knight belonging to the Order of the Golden Fleece, he was also a seasoned diplomat whose skills were widely appreciated. The terrace at the top of the museum commands a lovely **view** of the city.

Museum Arentshuis★

Open Tue-Sun, 9.30am-5pm; Closed 1 Jan, Ascension Day (pm), 25 Dec. €8 (includes admission to the Groeningemuseum). ☎ *050 44 87 11.*

This late 18C town mansion is home to a beautiful collection of old Bruges landscapes (17C-19C) as well as a large collection of lace. Works by the English painter and engraver **Frank Brangwyn** (1867-1956) are displayed on the first floor.

St-Salvatorskathedraal

9am-noon (Sun 10.15am), 2-5.45pm (Sat 3.30pm), Mon, pm only. Closed Ascension Day. ☎ *050 33 68 41.*

The impressive Gothic brick cathedral, flanked by a 99m/325ft high tower, overlooks a shaded square. Building began in the 10C with the construction of the tower.

The cathedral burnt down several times and was not completed until the 16C; the last sections to be built were the chapels in the chancel. The pinnacle of the tower was finished in neo-Romanesque style in the 19C.

Inside, the nave is supported by tall, slender clustered columns. The triforium and 13C clerestory windows in the chancel rise above walls which were rebuilt in the 15C. The cathedral is richly decorated. At the far end of the nave is the late 17C Baroque rood screen, crowned by a beautiful statue of *God the Father* by Artus Quellin the Younger. The organ case above it dates from 1719. The pulpit was sculpted in 1785 by H Pulinx. Above the 15C choir stalls are the coats of arms of the Knights of the Golden Fleece. The 13th chapter of the Order was held here in 1478. Brussels tapestries dating from 1725 hang above them.

Treasury – *Access from the south transept.* In addition to a few liturgical objects, the treasury contains some fine paintings. Note Dieric Bouts' *Martyrdom of St Hippolytus.* The left panel of this triptych is attributed to Van der Goes. *Closed for restoration.*

Provinciaal Museum van het Brugse Vrije

In the Liberty of Bruges Palace. ♿ *Tue-Sun, 9.30am-12.30pm, 1.30pm-5pm. Closed 1 Jan, Ascension (pm), 25 Dec. €2.50.* ☎ *050 44 87 11.*

The museum contains the 16C **Liberty of Bruges fireplace★**, displayed in the Aldermen's Chamber. It was made according to designs by Lancelot Blondeel. The fireplace is Renaissance in style, built of black marble and oak, and decorated with an alabaster frieze recounting the story of Susannah and the Elders. The upper part depicts several Flemish sovereigns. Emperor Charles V is shown in the centre, his sword upraised. The other statues portray the ancestors of Charles V: Mary of Burgundy, Maximilian of Austria, Ferdinand of Aragon and Isabel of Castile. The copper handholds above the hearth were there for the aldermen to hold on to while drying their boots.

Around the Kruispoort

Museum voor Volkskunde★
Open Tue-Sun, 9.30am-5pm. Closed 1 Jan, Ascension Day (pm), 25 Dec. €3 (includes admission to Guido Gezelle museum). ☎ 050 44 87 11.
The entrance to the Folk Museum is at 40 Rolweg, by the sign for the Zwarte Kat (Black Cat Café). The folklore and traditions of Western Flanders are remembered in these charming old almshouses built by the cobblers' guild in the 17C. They display collections of everyday objects and tools, as well as reconstructed interiors: a classroom from the 1920s, a 19C apothecary's shop, a grocer's shop, workshops and even a confectioner's where sweets are still made on Thursday afternoons. The garden and its quaint white almshouses afford fine views of the lantern tower of the nearby Jeruzalemkerk.

Jeruzalemkerk
Open Mon-Sat, 10am-noon, 2-6pm (Sat 5pm). Closed public holidays.
The curious lantern tower of this church can be seen from the corner of Balstraat. The church was built in the 15C by the Adornes family, merchants from Genoa. Combining Gothic and Oriental characteristics, it is likely to have been inspired by the Church of the Holy Sepulchre in Jerusalem. The instruments of Christ's Passion can be seen on the altarpiece in the nave. The stained-glass windows date from the 16C and represent members of the Adornes family. The 15C recumbent effigies of Anselme Adornes and his wife are in the centre of the nave. There is a reconstructed tomb of Christ in the crypt. By the side of the church, the **Kantcentrum** (Lace Centre) organises courses and demonstrations in lacemaking. A small lace museum occupies the almshouses. *Mon-Sat 10am-noon, 2pm-6pm (5pm Sat). Closed public holidays, Christmas-New Year. €1.50. ☎ 050 33 00 72.*

Kruispoort
There are several sights to be seen in the vicinity of the Holy Cross Gate which was once part of the town walls.
Three post **windmills** stand on the old walls to the north. The first one, the **Bonne Chieremolen**, was brought here in 1911 from Olsene. The second one, **St-Janshuismolen**, dates from 1770. *Open early May – end Sept, Tue-Sun 9.30am-12.30pm and 1.30-5pm. Closed 1 Jan, Ascension (pm). €2. ☎ 050 44 87 11.*
The **Guido Gezellemuseum** is nearby, in the house where the poet was born. *Tue-Sun 9.30am-12.30pm and 1.30-5pm. Closed 1 Jan, Ascension Day (pm), 25 Dec. €2. ☎ 050 44 87 11.*
The beautiful 16C and 17C archers' guildhall in Camersstraat, the **Schuttersgilde St-Sebastiaan**, has portraits of the guild's "kings" and a collection of gold and silver plate. *Open early May – end Sept, Tue, Wed,Thu 10am-noon, Sat 2-5pm; Oct-Apr Tue, Wed, Thu, Sat €1.49. ☎ 050 33 16 26; www.sebastiaansgilde.be*
The **Engels Klooster** is in the same street. The domed chapel overlooking the socalled English convent dates from the 18C. ♿ *Guided tours. Mon-Sat. 2-3.30pm, 4.15-5.15pm. ☎ 050 33 24 28.*

St-Walburgakerk
This Jesuit church was built in Baroque style by Pieter Huyssens in 1643. It was originally dedicated to St Francis Xavier. A statue of the saint adorns the austere façade. The white Baroque interior houses a marble pew for communion ceremonies by H Verbrugghe, a pulpit from the 17C and a Rococo rood screen.
Cross the bridge to the Spiegelrei. At the end of this quay, on Jan van Eyckplein, there is a statue of Van Eyck and the 15C Poortersloge flanked by a little tower. This is the home of the state archives. In a niche by the Academiestraat there is a stone bear, the city's mascot, and, on the little square, the old tollhouse of 1477.

St-Annakerk
The interior of St Anne's Church was built in Gothic style in the 17C. It was embellished with beautiful Baroque furnishings including a rood screen, panelling and confessionals and a pulpit. It was in this church that Guido Gezelle was christened and made his first Communion.

Ezelpoort
The "Donkey Gate" stands in a pretty, shaded setting at the end of a canal. Swans glide along the peaceful waterway.

Godshuizen *(see key on town plan)*
The almshouses, of which there were many in Bruges from the 15C to the 18C, were financed by the guilds. They provided shelter for the elderly and the poverty-stricken. Most of them consist of rows of low, whitewashed and rather modest-looking brick houses. Each façade includes a door and a window with a tall dormer over it.

In addition to De Pelikaan *(see description in* "Walking About") and the little houses in the Folk Museum *(see description in "Worth a Visit")*, do not miss the houses in Gloribusstraat, Moerstraat, Zwarte-Leertouwersstraat, Nieuwe Gentweg and Sint-Katelijnestraat.

Museum Onze-Lieve-Vrouw ter Potterie
Tue-Sun, 9.30am-12.30pm, 1.30pm-5pm. Closed 1 Jan, Ascension Day (pm), 25 Dec. €8 (includes admission to Memlingmuseum) ☎ *050 44 87 11.*

The old 13C hospice of Our Lady of Pottery is at no 79 Potterierei. It had a similar purpose to that of St-Jans Hospitaal *(see above)*. Although it still operates as an old people's home, part of it is now a museum. This section includes the ward, the 14C-15C cloisters, and the passageway to the richly decorated little Baroque church. Exhibits include 15C, 16C and 17C furniture, paintings, Flemish books of hours and objects relating to religious life and the veneration of the miraculous Virgin known as Our Lady of Pottery.

Excursions

St-Michiels
3km/2mi S. Open Easter holiday, 11am-5pm; May-Jun, 10.30-5pm (Sun, public holidays 6pm); Jul-Aug, 10am-6pm; Sept, Wed, Sat, 10.30-5pm (Sun 6pm) €16. ☎ *050 38 38 38.*
The Boudewijnpark, named after King Baudouin, has a whole range of attractions and rides (switchback, pirate ship, mini-golf).
A vast building houses an enormous **astronomical clock**, the **Heirmanklok**. It is beautifully decorated and delights all visitors when its many automata come to life. The **Dolfinarium** facing the park entrance puts on shows featuring dolphins and seals. *(See "Entertainment")*
The forest of Tillegembos covers 44ha/108 acres and includes signposted footpaths and a pond, near which is a neo-Gothic château and an old horse-powered mill, or *rosmolen*.

Loppem
7km/4.3mi S. Open Apr-Oct; daily except Mon, Fri. 10am-noon, 2-6pm, €3.50. ☎ *050 82 22 45.*
The neo-Gothic **Kasteel** of Loppem was built in 1862 for Baron and Baroness Charles van Caloento designs by the London architect **Edward Welby Pugin** (1834-75) and **Baron Jean Béthune**, who also designed the Abbaye de Maredsous. King Albert and his family stayed here in October and November 1918, and it was here that the sovereign promised to establish universal suffrage and the conversion of Ghent University into a Flemish-language institution. Inside there is a fascinating collection of works of art. Among the paintings by the Dutch and Flemish Schools, note *De Burg te Brugge* (The Burg at Bruges), executed in the early 17C. Jan van Caloen's collection is exhibited upstairs. It includes religious sculptures (13C-16C) from the Netherlands, France, Italy, Spain and Germany.
In the English-style park there is a famous **maze** *(doolhof)*.

Zedelgem
10.5km/6.5mi SW. Leave Bruges on N 32.
The abbey known as **Zeven-kerken** comes into view on the right after crossing the A 10 motorway. It is a major missionary centre, built around an early 20C basilica with seven shrines.
The **St-Laurentiuskerk** in Zedelgem has a remarkable 11C-12C **font.**

Male
5km/3.1mi E on N 9. Open 9am (Sun, public holidays 10.30)-11.30am, 2.30-5pm. No charge. ☎ *050 36 70 22.*
Surrounded by its moat, Male's huge **Kasteel** has been occupied by the canonesses of St Trudo since 1954; it was once the residence of the Counts of Flanders.
The Knights' Hall and the church, which was rebuilt in 1965, are open to visitors.

Torhout
23km/14mi SW. Leave Bruges on N 32.
In the 12C Torhout was a prosperous town with a famous fair. Bombed in 1940, the **St-Pietersbandenkerk** has been rebuilt and has a lovely octagonal Romanesque belfry with a carillon. *Daily except Sat, Sun: 8.30am-noon, 3.30pm-6.30pm.* ☎ *050 22 07 70.* The harmonious **Stadhuis** of 1713 has widely spaced pilasters topped by a high roof.
3km/2mi to the west of the town stands **Wijnendale** (11C-19C), a moated castle begun by Robert the Frisian which became a favourite residence of the Counts of Flanders. It was here in 1482 that Mary of Burgundy fell to her death while riding in the surrounding woods.

Bruxelles★★★

BRUSSELS

At the heart of Belgium, Brussels is a place of contrast and paradox. Originally Flemish, the city was almost completely gallicised over the centuries, and today most of the population speak French. Despite suffering wholesale redevelopment between the 1950s and 1970s, Brussels has kept its human scale and convivial character. As well as priding itself on its unmatched heritage of Art Nouveau building, it is rich in museums and in architecture of all periods. Cosmopolitan Brussels is not limited to the "pentagon", the central area within the ring of boulevards; the 19 municipalities making up the Brussels Capital Region are attractive in their own right, among them Royal Laeken, bustling Ixelles, relaxed St-Gilles, Koekelberg with its imposing basilica, the smart southern districts...

Location

Brabant – Population 954 460 (conurbation).
Michelin maps 716 G 3, enlarged inset map on folds 21 and 22, and 533 L 17. Michelin plan 44 Bruxelles – See also Michelin Green Guide BRUSSELS. Brussels is at the centre of the national road and rail network, with motorways and main roads converging on the orbital expressway (RO) which almost encircles the city. Officially bilingual, the Brussels Capital Region is surrounded by the Flemish province of Vlaams Brabant.
🛈 *Hôtel de Ville, Grand Place,* ☎ *02 513 89 40; www.tib.be*
See also: WATERLOO.

Les galeries St-Hubert

Background

The medieval city – Brussels emerged at the end of the 10C when Charles, Duke of Lower Lotharingia, settled there. He had a castle built on Île St-Géry, an island formed by two branches of the little River Senne. It was a marshy site, and the settlement was named Bruocsella, a Frankish word meaning "the village in the marshes".
During the prosperous period of cloth making, Brussels developed as a trading city on the highway between Flanders and Cologne.
The Église Saint-Michel/St Michael's church, a sign of the town's prosperity, was built on a hill; it became a collegiate church in 1047. It was then dedicated to St Gudula, the virgin whose piety triumphed over the devil when he extinguished her lantern while she was on her way to pray.
The first ramparts were built in the 12C.
A new wall was built from 1357 to 1379. It was destroyed on the orders of Napoleon, and its location is now marked by the inner ring road, known as the Petite Ceinture. Only one of the original seven fortified gateways has survived, the Porte de Hal to the south.
Throughout the Middle Ages, conflicts divided craftsmen and merchants, but the community as a whole remained loyal to its prince.

Directory

ARRIVAL

By air – Brussels airport is at Zaventem, 12km/8mi north of the city centre. It is linked by the Airport City Express train to Bruxelles-Nord, Bruxelles-Centrale and Bruxelles-Midi stations: travel time 20-27min. Bus no 12 also runs between the airport and the city centre.

By train – Eurostar trains run via the Channel Tunnel between London Waterloo and Bruxelles-Midi: travel time 2hr 25min. Thalys high-speed trains link Brussels with cities in Holland, Germany and France.

GETTING AROUND

If you have arrived in Brussels by car, the best solution is to leave it in one of the many car parks; many of the principal sights are within walking distance of one another and others can be easily visited by bus, tram or underground railway (Métro). A plan of the public transport network can be obtained at ticket offices of the STIB (Société des Transports Intercommunaux de Bruxelles). As well as single tickets, there is a tram pass valid for 5 or 10 trips and a one-day pass giving unrestricted use of the network for 24hrs: Information: ☎ 02 515 2000 or *www.stib.irisnet.be*

Underground Art – Not many people know that the Brussels Métro is a veritable museum of modern art. Altogether forty stations have been adorned by the work of 54 different Belgian artists, including a number of famous names such as Pierre Alechinsky and Christian Dotremont (Annessens), Pol Bury and Paul Delvaux (Bourse), Jean-Michel Folon (Montgomery) and Roger Somville (Hankar).
The brochure *L'Art dans le métro* (in French) published by the STIB describes these works of art and the stations in which they can be found.

SIGHTSEEING

Guided tours – **La Fonderie** *(rue de Ransfort 27, ☎ 02 410 99 50)* concentrates on the city's social and industrial heritage. It offers a boat trip around the port of Brussels and visits to still active local firms. **De Boeck Sightseeing Tours** *(rue de la Colline 8, ☎ 02 513 77 44)* explores Brussels by bus. **ARAU** *(boulevard Adolphe Max 55, ☎ 02 219 33 45)* provides tours of Brussels Art Nouveau and Art Deco. **Arcadia** *(rue du Métal 58, ☎ 02 534 38 19)* and **Itinéraires** *(rue de l'Hôtel des Monnaies 157, ☎ 02 539 04 34)* organise guided tours on particular themes. In summer, **BI-TC** *(Grand-Place, 1000 Bruxelles, ☎ 02 513 89 40)* will arrange guided tours for individuals. **Pro-Vélo** *(rue de Londres 15, ☎ 02 502 73 55)* take the more energetic visitor by bicycle through the city streets in summer.

EATING OUT

☺ **Le Domaine de Lintillac** – *Rue de Flandre 25 – ☎ 02 511 51 23 – Closed Sun, Mon –⊟ – €13.36/26.38.* This dear little place between the Vismet and the 17C

Maison de la Bellone specialises in the fine food of southwestern France. There is foie gras, duck confit, potatoes done Sarlat-style, wines from Bergerac, and a bill without too many extras.

☺ **La Porteuse d'Eau** – *Avenue Jean Volders 48a – 1060 St-Gilles – ☎ 02 537 66 46 – €13.70/30.25* Here is an opportunity to try a selection of Belgian specialities in an Art Nouveau setting. The "Water-Carrier" also gives you the chance to quench your thirst in between times as it also functions as a tavern.

☺ **'t Kelderke** – *Grand-Place 15 – ☎ 02 513 73 44 – €8 lunch – €22/34.* Restaurant on the Grand-Place offering an appetising menu of Belgian and Brussels dishes including the ever-fashionable 'stoemp'. You dine in a charming little vaulted cellar (kelderke) beneath the House of the Dukes of Brabant.

☺ **Stekerlapatte** *Rue des Prêtres 4 – ☎ 02 512 86 81 – Closed lunchtime, Mon – ⊟ – €23.67/39.04.* This bustling place in a side-street in the Marolles district offers a range of dishes with plenty of local colour to them. The atmosphere is cheerful, the plates are well-filled and the bill is kept within bounds.

☺ **Yamayu Santasu** – *Chaussée d'Ixelles 141 – 1050 Ixelles – ☎ 02 513 53 12 – Closed 2nd week Feb, fortnight in Aug, Sun lunch, Mon – ⊟ – €11.40/32.23.* In the shopping district close to Avenue Louise, this long-established, soberly styled Japanese restaurant has earned a loyal following in the expat community. Sushi prepared at the counter before your very eyes.

☺ **Mano a Mano** – *Rue st-Boniface 8 – 1050 Ixelles – ☎ 02 502 08 01 – Closed lunchtime at weekends – ⊟ – €17/28.* This little Italian establishment beats off the competition with a friendly welcome, contemporary cooking with the flavours of the south, italianissimo wine list and home-made grappa, all at no-nonsense prices. Book in advance, if you can.

☺☺ **La Belle Maraîchère** – *Place Ste-Catherine 11 – ☎ 02 512 97 58 – Closed Wed, Thur – €31 lunch – €27/46.* One of the less expensive places to eat around St Catherine's Church. Pleasant surroundings, friendly service, tasty dishes frequently featuring fish, and wines to match the food. Highly recommendable.

☺☺ **Aux Armes de Bruxelles** – *Rue des Bouchers 13 – ☎ 02 511 55 98 – arbrux@beon.be – Closed Mon – €23 lunch – €29/45.* In a tourist thronged cul-de-sac just off the Grand-Place, this well-established restaurant was a favourite with the late King Leopold III, and celebrities such as Laurel and Hardy, Placido Domingo, and Jacques Brel have signed the visitors' book. Classic food from the Low Countries.

☺☺ **La Clef des Champs** – *Rue Rollebeek 23 – ☎ 02 512 11 93 – Closed Sun eve, Mon – €29/36* In the heart of the Sablons district, this is a friendly family establishment

La rue des Bouchers.

much appreciated for
its tasty Provencal cuisine, its well chosen
menus and its warm welcome. The owner
is an artist, and some of his works are
on show.

⊜⊜ **La Roue d'Or** – *Rue des Chapeliers 26
– ☎ 02 514 25 54 – €10 lunch – €43/52*.
Known for its Franco-Belgian cuisine, this
venerable café close to the Grand-Place is
also famous for the Surrealist murals which
pay homage to Magritte, and its pleasantly
unfussy style. A superb table-clock occupies
pride of place.

WHERE TO STAY

Reservations – A hotel room can be
booked through **BTR** (Belgian Tourist
Reservations), Boulevard Anspach 111,
1000 Bruxelles, ☎ 02 513 74 84.

⊜ **Les Bluets** – *Rue Berckmans 124 –
☎ 02 534 39 83 – ⌷ – 10 rms:
€37.18/44.62*. Family-run hotel close to the
Louise district which offers no frills but well-
kept accommodation. Not all rooms are en-
suite. Non-smoking establishment.

⊜ **La Légende** – *Rue du Lombard 35 –
☎ 02 512 82 90 – www.hotellalegende.com
– ⌷ – 26 rms; €70.65/97.92*. With an
enviable location between the Grand-Place
and the cheeky statue of the Manneken Pis,
this cheerful establishment makes an
excellent base for explorations of the city
centre. Comfortable rooms, fine for an
affordable long weekend, and an attractive
courtyard.

⊜ **À La Grande Cloche** –
*Place Rouppe 10 – ☎ 02 512 61 40 –
www.hotelgrandecloche.com – ⌷ –
37 rms: €73*. Not far from the Grand-Place
and just a stone's throw from one
of the capital's best places to eat,
this is a welcoming establishment
offering practical accommodation.
The best rooms have all facilities. Public car
park nearby.

⊜ **Lambeau** *Avenue Lambeau 150 –
1200 Woluwe St-Lambert – ☎ 02 732 51 70
– info@ hotellambeau.com – 24 rms:
€71/78*. Small hotel tucked away in a
residential area next to Square Vergote and
the busy thoroughfare of Boulevard Brand
Withlock with its good Metro connections.
Modest-sized, modern rooms and a pleasant
family atmosphere.

⊜⊜ **Matignon** – *Rue de la
Bourse 10 – ☎ 02 511 08 88 –
37 rms: €85/102*. Family hotel overlooking
the Bourse and the remains of an old
Franciscan convent converted into a
museum. Tavern-style restaurant with a
summer terrace on the street.

⊜⊜⊜ **Atlas** – *Rue du Vieux Marché-aux-
Grains 30 – ☎ 02 502 60 06 – info@atlas.be
– 83 rms: €145/168⌷*. This distinguished
18C patrician townhouse stands on a
peaceful little square close to the fashionable
Rue Antoine Dansaert. Tasteful contemporary
decor. Most of the rooms face the quiet
courtyard.

⊜⊜⊜ **Le Dixseptième** – *Rue de
la Madeleine 25 – ☎ 02 502 17 17 –
info@ledixseptieme.be – 18 rms: €170/240*.
Close to the Grand-Place and the Gare
Centrale, this charming hotel occupies
what in the 17C was the Spanish
ambassador's residence. Spacious rooms
with a personal touch, individually furnished
in a variety of styles.

⊜⊜⊜ **Manos Stephanie** – *Chaussée de
Charleroi 28 – ☎ 02 539 02 50 –
manos@manoshotel.com – 50 rms:
€234/259*. Lovely 19C residence with
unusually tasteful Louis XV and Louis XVI
decor. Smart, comfortable bedrooms and a
breakfast room beneath a glazed canopy.
Impeccable service.

⊜⊜⊜ **Métropole** – *Place de Brouckère 31
– ☎ 20 217 23 00 – info@metropolehotel.be
– 296 rms: €304/425*. Sumptuous palace
dating from 1895 on the vibrant Place de
Brouckère. Superb neo-Classical foyer, club-
style bar, café with exuberant decor, year-
round terrace, refined restaurant and
exquisite rooms. All in all, a legendary
establishment.

TAKING A BREAK

Wittamer – *Place du Grand-Sablon 6, 12,
13 – ☎ 02 512 37 42 – www.wittamer.be –
Mon 10am-6pm, Wed-Sat 7am-7pm,
Sun 7am-6.30pm*. This extremely chic
patisserie and chocolate shop has been
here since 1910. Clients can choose
between the tea-room and the attractive
terrace with its views of the
neighbourhood. Excellent lunchtime
snacks.

The Métropole.

Planète Chocolat – *Rue du Lombard 24 –* ☎ *02 511 07 55 – planetchocolat @hotmail.com – 10am-6.30pm, Sun 4pm-10pm – Closed Mon.* Planet Chocolate has been in orbit now for ten years and is well established in the constellation of Belgian chocolate shops. The bouquet de plaques is a must. Demonstrations every Saturday afternoon. Take your seat for a delicious cocoa-based snack.

La Bécasse – *Rue Tabora 11 –* ☎ *02 511 00 06 – 10am-1am.* Down a narrow lane, this establishment boasts retro decor and is famous for its draught lambic beer, as well as for its tasty slices of bread spread with cream cheese and accompanied by radishes.

HAVING A DRINK

Bar Dessiné – *Rue du Fossé aux Loups 47 –* ☎ *02 219 28 28 – Mon 11.30am-1am, Tue-Thur 5pm-1am, Fri-Sat 5pm-2am, Sun 11.30am-9pm.* The wonderful decor of the bar of the Hotel Radisson SAS takes as its theme the Belgian comic book; there are posters, sculptures and original designs. Cocktails and more than 100 brands of whisky.

L'Amadeus – *Rue Veydt 13 –* ☎ *02 538 34 27 – www.resto.be/amadeus – Tue-Sun noon-2am. Closed Mon, mid-July – late Aug.* This wine bar in what used to be an artist's studio is an absolute must, what with its Art Nouveau decor, its dim lighting and its highly individual menu.

La Fleur en papier doré – *Rue des Alexiens 53-55 –* ☎ *02 511 16 59 – 11am-1am.* Nothing has changed in this temple of Belgian Surrealism which has remained true to its heritage for more than 100 years. The walls are covered with items eloquent of its past. Excellent choice of gueze and fruit beers.

Le Cirio – *Rue de la Bourse 18 –* ☎ *02 12 13 95 – 10am-1am.* Superb 1900 brasserie with somewhat over the top turn-of-the-century decor. The spacious terrace gets very crowded in fine weather.

À la Mort Subite – *Rue de la Montagne-aux-Herbes-Potagères 7 –* ☎ *02 513 13 18 – 10am-3am, weekend 12pm-3am.* The "Sudden Death", the city's most celebrated café, boasts turn-of-the-century

Le Cirio.

decor, a convivial atmosphere, and a huge range of beers including faro, gueze and kriek. Cosmopolitan clientele.

À la Mort subite.

Le Poechenellekelder – *Rue du Chêne 5* ☎ *02 511 92 62 – 11am-midnight, Fri, Sat 11am-2am.* Tourists crowd into this typical Brussels café close to the Manneken Pis. The decor reflects its name – Punch's Cellar. Good selection of Belgian beers.

Le Roy d'Espagne – *Grand-Place 1 –* ☎ *02 513 08 07 – www.roydespagne.be – 10am-1am.* Famed tavern in a 17C building with a landmark dome. Vast, convivial interior and a terrace on the well-trodden cobblestones of the city's central square. Live music at the weekend in the "bierkelder".

Au Bon Vieux Temps – *Rue du Marché-aux-Herbes 12 –* ☎ *02 217 26 26 – from 10am.* Charming estaminet decorated in 17C style.

À l'imaige de Nostre-Dame – *Impasse des Cadeaux 6 –* ☎ *02 219 42 49 – from 10am.* Lovely wooden panelling and impeccable service are the strong points of this city centre café.

ENTERTAINMENT

LV la voix – *Rue du Lombard 1 –* ☎ *02 511 56 79 – lv-lavoix@hotmail.com – Thur-Mon 8pm-3am; aperitif bar 4.30pm-7pm – Closed Tue, Wed.* Unusual establishment where you dine while watching the show, in the course of which the singers wander about among the tables.

Goupil le Fol – *Rue de la Violette 22 –* ☎ *02 511 13 96.* A warren of little candle-lit rooms where French chanson reigns supreme. Fruit-based wines an unusual speciality!

Toone VII – *Petite rue des Bouchers-Impasse Schuddeveld 21 –* ☎ *02 511 71 37.* This extremely popular little theatre puts on delightful puppet plays in French, Dutch, English and German, as well as in Brussels dialect.

Opéra National – *Place de la Monnaie –* ☎ *02 217 22 11 – www.lamonnaie.be.* Opera, modern ballet and classical music.

Théatre National de la Communauté française de Belgique – *Boulevard Anspach 85* – ☎ *02 203 53 03* – *www.theatrenational.be* – *Closed July-Sept, Mon*. As its name implies, this institution puts on performances in French only, from both the classical and the contemporary repetoire.

Kaaitheater – *Place Sanctelette 20* – ☎ *02 201 59 59* – *www.kaaitheater.be* – *Box office Tue-Fri 11am-6pm, closed July.* Flemish community institution specialising in classical music and modern ballet.

SHOPPING

Shopping areas – In the lower part of town, traffic-free **rue Neuve** is thick with people on Saturdays. Department stores such as Inno and C&A are here, as well as fashion boutiques. At one end of the street, the indoor shopping centre **City 2** features numerous clothes shops and an enormous branch of the French FNAC media superstore. In the lively Marolles district, **rue Blaes** and **rue Haute** are the place to go for antique furniture. Bookworms will enjoy browsing in the **Galerie Bortier**. The **Galerie Agora** caters for a less demanding clientele in search of cheaper clothes and accessories. The magnificent **Galeries St-Hubert** are home to many exclusive fashion boutiques and bookshops (note the fine interiors of Tropismes and Librarie des Galeries). More antique furniture can be found in the **Sablon** district.

Rue Dansaert is an indispensable address for today's fashion world. The most prestigious establishments for designer wear and haute couture are located on **avenue Louise, avenue de la Toison d'Or, boulevard de Waterloo** and **rue de Namur**. Most shops are open from 9/10am to 6/6.30pm.

Chocolatier Mary – *Rue Royale 73* – ☎ *02 217 45 00* – *www.marychoc.com* – *9.30am-6pm* – *Closed Sun.* Founded in 1919, this venerable establishment is proud of its reputation, not least because of its "By Royal Appointment" status and a visit by a certain GW Bush. Its speciality is a delicate dark chocolate which comes in five grades of bitterness.

Dandoy – *Rue au Beurre 31* – ☎ *02 511 03 26* – *8am-6.30pm, Sun 10.30am-6.30pm* – *Closed Christmas and New Year.* Unmissable city centre biscuit specialist turning out quantities of "speculoos", the biscuit flavoured with brown sugar and cinnamon which are given to children on St Nicholas' Day (a tradition reinforced by the proximity of the church dedicated to the patron saint of school children). Home-made macaroons, "sablé" shortbread, and "Greek bread".

La Boutique de Tintin – *Rue de la Colline 13* – ☎ *02 514 51 52* – *www.tintin.com* – *10am-6pm, Sun 11am-5pm* – *Closed Christmas.* In a busy city centre alleyway, this establishment is entirely given over to the famous boy detective and his companions, with the complete range of the Tintin books and much else besides.

Specialities – Beneath the surface of this cosmopolitan and "European" city there are still layers of traditional joviality, even truculence, plus a number of old-established city specialities like **"caricoles"** (sea snails), **waffles, speculoos, pralines, "pistolets"** (bread rolls), **"cramiques"** and **"craquelins"**. For a more solid snack, turn to bread slices spread with **cream cheese** or of course **"moules-frites"** (mussels and chips). All this should be washed down with a glass or three of **gueze, lambic, faro, kriek** or **white beer,** known to the locals as **"witbier"** or **"bière blanche"**.

Markets – There is an **antiques and bric-à-brac** market every Saturday and Sunday morning at the Grand Sablon. Other markets include the morning **flea market** on place du Jeu-de-Balle (especially interesting on Sundays), the morning **flower market** on the Grand-Place, and Sunday's lively **Marché du Midi** close to the Gare du Midi (South Station)

The Flower market on the Grand-Place.

Ch. Bastin – J. Evrard/MICHELIN

LEISURE

Bruparck – *Boulevard du Centenaire 20* – ☎ *02 474 83 77* – *www.bruparck.com.* A few steps from the Atomium, this big entertainment complex offers all kinds of attractions including a giant multiplex cinema, Mini-Europe (models of famous buildings from all over Europe), Océade (pool, slides etc), and the Village with bars and restaurants.

EVENTS AND FESTIVALS

The capital's splendidly colourful **Ommegang** pageant takes place every year in July, when more than 1 000 courtiers, magistrates, guildsmen and soldiers, all in period finery, process through the city. This "Doing-The-Rounds" is a recreation of the ceremony of 1549 which was attended by Emperor Charles V and his sister Eleonor of Habsburg.

In even years, a **floral carpet** is laid out over the cobbles of the Grand-Place for several days in August.

C. Bastin and J. Evrard/MICHELIN

Lucien Kroll's" Mémé" in Woluwe-St-Lambert.

In the 15C Brussels turned to the arts, influenced by the merchant class and the Dukes of Burgundy. A magnificent town hall (Hôtel de Ville) was built, and decorated with paintings by **Rogier van der Weyden**. They were destroyed in 1695. The streets were adorned with fountains.

Brussels tapestry-makers produced marvellous works of art at the end of the 15C.

Capital of the Low Countries – In the 16C the city celebrated the arrival of the Emperor Charles V, who was crowned in St Gudula's Church *(now the Cathedral)* in 1516. The governor, Mary of Hungary, settled in Brussels in 1531, and the city gradually replaced Mechelen as the central seat of government of the Low Countries. Emperor Charles V abdicated at the Palais du Coudenberg in October 1555, handing over sovereignty of the Low Countries to his son Philip II.

Philip drew Brussels into the religious strife of the 16C. The merchant class staged an armed uprising against Spanish rule symbolised by the Duke of Alba. The Count of **Egmont** and his companion, the Count of Hornes (Hoorn), died on the scaffold on Grand-Place in 1568. Egmont, the military governor of Flanders, had been sentenced to death for having supported Hornes and William of Nassau, known as William the Silent (Willem de Zwijger), in the revolt of the Netherlands against Philip II.

In 1575 the city, which had shaken off Spanish rule, was recaptured. In 1695, in the course of the War of the Augsburg League, the French Marshal de Villeroi laid siege to Brussels on the orders of Louis XIV, who hoped that this action would end the siege of Namur. The town centre lay in ruins and extensive reconstruction was required.

For much of the 18C, Brussels was the seat of Austrian rule over the Low Countries. Governor Charles of Lorraine, the brother-in-law of Empress Maria Theresa, established a glittering court life and did a great deal to embellish the city. Austrian rule foundered at the end of the century; in 1795 the southern Netherlands became part of Republican France and Brussels was demoted from capital city to a mere "county town", the centre of the French-style *département* of Dyle. After the defeat of Napoleon at nearby Waterloo in 1815 the city once more became the capital of the reunited Netherlands, an honour it was to share alternately with The Hague for 15 years.

Capital of Belgium – Union with Holland proved unpopular. The European revolutions of 1830 had their counterpart here, and after the **"September Days"** uprising, the Belgian provinces separated from Holland and became independent. The Kingdom of Belgium was established with Brussels as its capital. **King Leopold I** made his ceremonial entry into the city on 21 July 1831 (21 July has been a national holiday ever since).

After 1830, the city grew rapidly, particularly as the 19C gave way to the 20C. The Université Libre was founded in 1834. Continental Europe's first passenger railway began operating in 1835, linking Brussels with Mechelen. The Congress Column was erected in 1859 to commemorate the National Congress which established Belgium's first constitution.

The Builder King – King Leopold II (1865-1909) launched several major projects which gave the town a new look. Lord Mayor Jules Anspach, who was to Brussels what Haussmann was to Paris, oversaw the building of the great central avenues. Several parks were created, including Laeken. A number of impressive buildings were erected: the Palais du Cinquantenaire with its arcade and the Tervuren Museum, linked together by Avenue de Tervuren; the basilica church on Koekelberg, which was completed in 1970. It stands on the grandiose Avenue Léopold-II.

Among the many other notable buildings are the Musée d'Art Ancien, the Bourse de Commerce, the Théâtre de la Monnaie, and the Law Courts. The façade of the Palais Royal dates from this period.

A new post-war city – A great many buildings were abandoned and hundreds of others were pulled down by property developers. A typical example of these practices was the demolition in the 1960s of the **Maison du Peuple** (designed by Horta), despite strong local resistance and an international outcry. Some of the poorer districts, including the Quartier Nord and the Quartier de l'Europe, were totally razed. The demolished buildings were replaced by far taller, multi-storey structures. The linking of the Gare du Midi to the Gare du Nord (1911-14 and 1935-52) by means of a tunnel transformed the district lying between the Upper and Lower Towns. New architectural projects were launched for blocks of flats and office buildings such as the Banque Nationale by Marcel van Goethem and the Cité Administrative (Groupe Alpha, 1958-84). Because of these changes the Mont des Arts district took on a whole new appearance.

The various buildings that make up the Palais du Centenaire had already been built on the Heysel Plateau for the 1935 **World Fair**. The successor to this event in 1958 saw the erection of the **Atomium** and the construction of tunnels for the city ring road, referred to as the **Petite Ceinture**. A plethora of civil and private buildings has contributed to the city's modernisation since then; the BBL building (1959) on Avenue Marnix, the Bibliothèque Royale (National Library, 1969), the EEC's Centre Berlaymont (1969) and the Museum of Modern Art (1973-84).

The ultra-modern, well-equipped medical faculty of the Université Catholique de Louvain-la-Neuve was built in Woluwe-St-Lambert. It was here that Lucien Kroll erected the highly colourful **Mémé** (Maison Médicale) and the Alma underground station. Watermael-Boitsfort is distinguished by some unusual office buildings set up along chaussée de la Hulpe and boulevard du Souverain: the circular Glaverbel construction (1963), the headquarters of the Royale Belge Bank (1966-67 and 1985), and the main branch of CBR (1968-70), notable for its open-work façade.

A new approach to urban planning – Opinions about architecture and town planning have evolved, in particular through the efforts of local organisations and community groups such as ARAU (Atelier de Recherche et d'Action Urbaines) and Sint-Lucas-archief. Several districts have been entirely renovated, with the exception of the Îlot Sacré, the ancient heart of the city spread out around Grand-Place, where many old houses were spared. A number of public buildings have been restored: the Botanique, La Luna, the Halles in Schaerbeek, the Église Notre-Dame-de-la-Chapelle, the Église Ste-Marie, the Cathédrale des Saints-Michel-et-Gudule, the former fire station on place du Jeu-de-Balle, the Kaaitheater studios, Old England etc. Besides the monumental structures scattered around Quartier Nord (Baudouin complex, North Gate), Quartier de l'Europe (European Parliament) and Quartier du Midi (terminus for high-speed trains), projects on a smaller scale have also been carried out, like the new residential and shopping complexes in rue de Laeken and rue du Marché-au-Charbon.

Highlight

GRAND-PLACE★★★

The "gigantic square" admired by Victor Hugo and "rich theatre" celebrated by Jean Cocteau is unparallelled anywhere else in the world. It is seen at its best during the early morning flower market, or at night when the floodlights throw the stunning gilded ornamentation of the buildings into sharp relief. The Grand-Place was given UNESCO World Heritage status in 1998.

GUILDHALLS

1-2 Le Roi d'Espagne
3 La Brouette
4 Le Sac
5 La Louve
6 Le Cornet
7 Le Renard
8 L'Étoile
9 Le Cygne
10 L'Arbre d'Or
11-12 La Rose et le Mont Thabor
13-19 Maison des Ducs de Brabant
20-23 Le Cerf, Joseph et Anne, l'Ange
24-25 La Chaloupe d'Or
26-27 Le Pigeon
28 La Chambrette de l'Amman
29-33 Maison du Roi
34-39 Le Heaume, Le Paon, Le Petit Renard et Le Chêne, Sainte Barbe, L'Âne

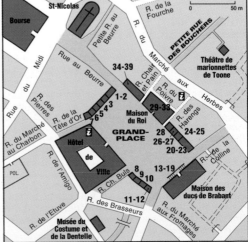

The Guildhalls

The guildhalls were built after the French destroyed the town in 1695 and then restored in the 19C. Their beautiful Baroque façades surround Grand-Place. They tend to have several storeys decorated in the three architectural orders – Doric, Ionic and Corinthian. Higher up the buildings are surmounted with scrolled gables and decorated with sculptures, gilded motifs and flame ornaments.

Walk round the Grand-Place anti-clockwise to see:

1-2 Le Roy d'Espagne – The King of Spain's Hall or Bakers' Guildhall. The building is topped with a dome and a gilded weather vane representing Fame.

3 La Brouette – The Wheelbarrow Hall of the Tallow Merchants' Guild.

4 Le Sac – The Sack Hall of the Coopers' and Cabinet-makers' Guild.

5 La Louve – The Wolf Hall of the Archers' Guild. This has a sculpture representing Romulus and Remus being suckled by the she-wolf. On the second storey there are four statues depicting Truth, Deceit, Peace and Discord.

6 Le Cornet – The Horn Hall of the Boatmen's Guild. Its gable is shaped like the bow of a 17C frigate.

7 Le Renard – The Fox Hall of the Haberdashers' Guild. In the low-relief sculptures on the mezzanine are cherubs undertaking the work of haberdashers. The gable is tipped by a statue of St Nicholas, the patron saint of the Haberdashers' Guild.

8 L'Étoile – The Star Hall, now a privately owned house. The 't Serclaes memorial by Dillens beneath the arcade is said to bring happiness to those who place their hands on the statue.

9 Le Cygne – The Swan Hall of the Butchers' Guild.

10 L'Arbre d'Or – The Golden Tree Hall of the Brewers' Guild. It is crowned by an equestrian statue of Charles of Lorraine. The **Musée de la Brasserie** is housed in the basement. The museum includes a reconstructed 17C tavern and all the equipment for preparing beer. A brand new display explains the latest brewing techniques. *Open daily, 10am-5pm. Closed 1 Jan and 25 Dec. €3.* ☎ *02 511 49 87.*

13-19 Maison des Ducs de Brabant – The House of the Dukes of Brabant, with its impressive façade (1698) surmounted by a beautiful carved pediment and an attic storey in the Palladio style, houses six guildhalls. A row of busts representing the Dukes of Brabant decorates the pilasters. No 13 is the home of the Musée du Cacao et du Chocolat. *Open daily July-Aug, closed Mon rest of year, 10am-4.30pm. €5.* ☎ *02 514 2048; www.mucc.be*

24-25 La Chaloupe d'Or – The Golden Boat Hall of the Tailors' Guild.

26-27 Le Pigeon – The Pigeon Hall of the Painters' Guild. This is where Victor Hugo stayed in 1851-2.

28 La Chambrette de l'Amman – The Amman's Garret. The *amman* was a magistrate representing the Duke of Brabant.

Hôtel de Ville

Guided tours only, Tues, Wed, 2.30pm, Sun (early Apr – end Sept only), 11.30am. €2.48. Closed 1 Jan, 1 May, 1, 11 Nov, 25 Dec. ☎ *02 279 43 65.*

In pure Gothic style, the town hall dates from the 13C and 15C. At the beginning of the 15C it consisted of no more than the south wing and the belfry. The present Escalier des Lions (Lions' Staircase) was then the main entrance. The slightly shorter north wing was added at a later date. On top of the building is a tower designed by Van Ruysbroeck, a marvel of daring elegance (96m/315ft), crowned with a gilded copper statue of St Michael.

Note the beautiful Brussels tapestries inside, especially the ones in the Maximilian Room.

Maison du Roi

Open Tue-Sun. 10am-5pm (Sat-Sun 1pm). Closed 1 Jan, 1 May, 1, 11 Nov, 25 Dec €2.48. ☎ *02 279 43 50.*

The King's House was rebuilt in the 19C, based on plans dating from 1515. It stands on the site of the former Bread Market, which was replaced in the 15C by the Duke's residence. No king has ever stayed here.

The **Musée de la Ville de Bruxelles** is housed here. It contains works of art and other items tracing the city's history and its role as a centre of the arts and crafts. *Tue-Sun 10am-5pm. Closed 1Jan, 1 May, 1 and 11 Nov, 25 Dec. €3*

Among the 15C and 16C paintings and altarpieces located on the ground floor are the *Wedding Procession* attributed to Pieter Bruegel the Elder, and the *Saluzzo Altarpiece*, a masterpiece dating from the early 16C. The Brussels tapestries include the outstanding representation of the legend of Notre-Dame-du-Sablon (1516-18) based on cartoons attributed to Bernard van Orley. The porcelain and silver collections contain beautiful examples of Brussels decorative art. Note the eight prophets from the town hall porch, in the room devoted to GoThe city's expansion and gradual transformation over the centuries are illustrated on the first floor by means of paintings, engravings, photographs and other objects, including a model of 13C Brussels.

thic sculpture.

Manneken Pis★★

The Manneken Pis fountain, also known as "Little Julian", was sculpted by **Jérôme Duquesnoy the Elder** in 1619. It provided the water supply for the district. The chubby little boy (*manneken* means little man), whose unselfconscious gesture has a certain cheeky charm, is said to symbolise the Brabant people's lively sense of humour and their vitality. The custom of giving him an outfit may have been established for reasons of decency, or more probably to honour Brussels' most famous and "oldest citizen". The donors range from Louis XV, who presented him with a beautiful French outfit, to the Military Police, who offered him a uniform. Almost every country has made a contribution to his wardrobe, which takes up an entire room in the Musée de la Ville de Bruxelles.

Walking About

FROM MAROLLES TO LE SABLON AND MONT DES ARTS★★

Between the Porte de Hal, the Notre-Dame-de-la-Chapelle Church and the Palais de Justice, the Marolles district was traditionally the domain of working folk and misfits. Nowadays, the typical "Marollien" has more or less died out and his colourful banter is hardly heard in the area's streets and cafés any more.

Place du Jeu-de-Balle

A **flea market** is held on this large square in the heart of the **Marolles**.
Turn into rue Blaes, then right into rue des Capucins, left into rue Haute and right into rue de l'Épée. From here take the lift up to place Poelaert.

Place Poelaert

This square lies at the top of Galgenberg (literally "Gallows Hill") where the gibbet once hung. Overlooking the square is the immense **Palais de Justice**, the Law Courts designed by Poelaert and built between 1866 and 1883. The main entrance consists of a huge peristyle leading into a majestic lobby. There is an extensive view from the terrace, of the Lower Town and the Marolles district with Notre-Dame-de-la-Chapelle. *Open Mon-Fri, 9am-3pm. Closed Public holidays.* ☎ *02 508 65 78.*
Go back to rue Haute and continue along it.

Église Notre-Dame-de-la-Chapelle★

Open Sat-Thur. 12.30-4.30pm. ☎ *02 513 53 48.*
Whereas the 13C transept is in the Romanesque style, most of the building is characteristic of Brabant Gothic architecture. In particular, note the alignment of side gables and the tower porch.
The painter Pieter Bruegel the Elder was buried in this church in 1569; his black marble memorial, surmounted by a copy of a work by Rubens entitled *Christ Giving the Keys to St Peter*, lies in the fourth chapel in the south aisle.
The visitor is immediately struck by the sharp

Église N.-D.-de-la-Chapelle.

contrast between the sombre transept and chancel and the well-lit nave. The columns in the central nave are embellished with capitals featuring curly cabbage leaf motifs and statues of the Apostles, several of which are attributed to Lucas Fayd'herbe and Jérôme Duquesnoy the Younger. The remarkably long neo-Gothic chancel is decorated with paintings by Charle-Albert, who also executed the nine stained-glass windows. The Chapelle du Saint-Sacrement, to the left of the chancel, houses the marble tomb of the Spinola family, dating from 1716. There is an fine triptych by Hendrik de Clerck in 1619 in the fifth chapel in the south aisle. In the fourth chapel in the north aisle, note the beautiful **wooden statue**★ of St Margaret of Antioch (c 1520).

Go along rue Joseph Stevens to place Grand-Sablon

Place du Grand-Sablon★

This is the most elegant square in Brussels, surrounded by old houses, antique shops, numerous cafés and smart restaurants.

Église Notre-Dame-du-Sablon★

Open Mon-Fri, 9am-5pm, Sat-Sun, 10am-5pm. Closed to visitors during services. ☎ *02 511 57 41.*

This beautiful Flamboyant Gothic church was originally the chapel of the Crossbowmen's guild. The story goes that in 1348 the pious Baet Soetkens saw a statue of the Virgin Mary in a dream. She brought it from Antwerp to Brussels in a small boat and presented it to the crossbowmen. The church became a place of pilgrimage and had to be enlarged in c 1400. The work was completed around 1550 with the main doorway. The "sacrarium", a small richly decorated structure built to house the Holy Sacrament, was added to the side of the apse in 1549.

Inside, the chancel is marvellously high and airy; delicate colonnettes rise between the tall stained-glass windows. The pulpit dates from 1697. The south transept is embellished with a beautiful rose window. The chapels in the side aisles are linked to each another in true Brabant fashion. Their lower arches, like the ones in the chancel, are decorated with squinches bearing narrative carvings. Above the entrance stands the statue of *Our Lady of the Tree*.

The **Chapelle Sépulcrale des Tour et Taxis** is near the chancel. It was this family of Lombard and German origin that founded the international postal system in 1516. The black and white marble decor was the work of Lucas Fayd'herbe. The white marble statue of St Ursula is by Jerome Duquesnoy the Younger.

Cross rue de la Régence.

Place du Petit-Sablon★

This square is surrounded by columns bearing 48 charming bronze statuettes representing the trades of Brussels. In the centre of the square are statues of Count Egmont and Count Hornes by Fraikin, together with statues of the great 16C humanists. The **Palais d'Egmont**, also known as the Palais d'Arenberg, is on the southeast side. It is used as a venue for international receptions. Attractive old houses have been restored in rue des Six-Jeunes-Hommes to the north.

Continue along rue de la Régence, passing the Musée d'Art ancien (See below under "Worth a Visit").

Place Royale★

This elegantly proportioned, Louis XVI style square lies at the top of the Coudenberg (the "cold hill") and is part of the district redeveloped at the end of the 18C by Charles of Lorraine. The square was designed by French architects Guimard and Barré and is overlooked by a church (Église St-Jacques-sur-Coudenberg).

The centre of the square with its statue of Godfrey of Bouillon commands a beautiful view of the Mont des Arts gardens, the tower of the town hall and the Palais de Justice.

Go along rue Royale, the turn immediately right.

Place des Palais

This is a vast esplanade, dominated by the **Palais Royal**. The curved, colonnaded façade of the palace was built during the reign of Leopold II. If there is a flag flying, it means that the sovereign is on Belgian soil. The sumptuous **Throne Room**★ dating from 1872 is decorated with huge chandeliers. *Generally open end July – Sept, daily (except Mon), 10.30am-4.30pm. No charge.* ☎ *02 513 89 40 (Tourist Information Centre).*

The **Palais des Académies** dating from 1823 stands at the eastern end of the square. This was once the residence of the Prince of Orange.

The **Palais des Beaux-Arts** built by Victor Horta between 1922 and 1928 stands discreetly to the west of the square, on the other side of rue Royale. It hosts many major cultural events (exhibitions, concerts, cinema, theatre) and also houses the **Musée du Cinéma**. *Open daily, 5.30-10.30pm. €2.* ☎ *02 507 83 70.*

Go across the place des Palais.

Parc de Bruxelles★

This is the former hunting ground of the Dukes of Brabant. It was laid out as formal gardens in the 18C by the Frenchman Barnabé Guimard and the Austrian Joachim Zinner, and dotted with statues including the delightful *Young Girl with a Shell* by A de Tombay.

Return to place Royale, then go down the street in front of the Musée des Instruments de Musique (see below under "Worth a Visit")

Hôtel Ravenstein
This 15-16C mansion on rue Ravenstein is flanked by a tower and has a charming inner courtyard.

Palais des Congrès
This building stands on the other side of rue Ravenstein. The **Palais de la Dynastie** is in one wing. There is a jack-o'-the-clock above the arcade portraying famous historic and folk figures.

From the top of the gardens, there is a beautiful view of the town hall spire, in front of which there is a row of houses rebuilt in Flemish style.

Go down the Mont des Arts, cross place de l'Albertine and go along rue de la Madeleine.

Galerie Bortier
The Bortier Arcade with its Renaissance style decor was built in 1848 to plans by the architect Jean-Pierre Cluysenaar and is now mainly occupied by bookshops.

The walk takes visitors past the **Tour Anneessens**, one of the towers built as part of the 12C fortifications. Anneessens, who represented the tradesmen rebelling against the Austrian government, is said to have been imprisoned here before his execution in 1719.

Musées Royaux des Beaux-Arts de Belgique★★★
The Royal Belgian Museums of Fine Art consist of the Museum of Ancient Art and the Museum of Modern Art *(see below)*.

BOURSE, MONNAIE AND CATHEDRAL★★
Allow half a day
Leave from place de la Bourse.

Bourse
The Stock Exchange (1868-73) is an impressive building reminiscent of Garnier's Paris Opera. It was designed by Léon Suys in neo-Classical style, but its basic simplicity is contradicted by an over abundance of ornamental features. A number of artists including Auguste Rodin were involved in its sculptural decoration.

Behind the Stock Exchange, hemmed in by old houses, stands the tiny **Église St-Nicolas** in rue au Beurre. Inside the church, the chancel is out of line with the nave. Note the canvas attributed to Rubens, *Virgin with Sleeping Child. 7.30am-6.30pm, Sat 9am-6pm, Sun 9am-7.30pm.* ☎ *02 513 80 22.*

Make for Grand-Place (see under "Highlight". Go along rue Chair-et-Pain which leads to petite rue des Bouchers.

Petite Rue des Bouchers★
The famous **Théâtre de marionnettes de Toone** is in this tiny street lined with tourist restaurants. *Performances Fri, Sat 8.30pm. For other days, call for details (☎ 02 217 04 64). Closed Sun, 1 Jan, Easter Mon, Whit Mon and 25 Dec.*

Galeries St-Hubert★★
The St-Hubert shopping arcades lead off rue de la Montagne. The elegant Classical façade decorated with pilasters was built in 1846 to plans by JP Cluysenaar. The central section is embellished with statues and bears the motto *"Omnibus Omnia"* ("Everything for Everybody").

The three-storied neo-Classical **Galerie du Roi** and **Galerie de la Reine** have glazed vaults supported by a slender metal framework.

View from the Mont des Arts.

The Galeries St-Hubert make a fine setting for luxury shops, elegant tea rooms and restaurants.

The **Galerie de la Reine** crosses rue des Bouchers with its many restaurants and leads into the **Galerie des Princes** on the left, which opens onto rue de l'Écuyer through a large façade echoing the architectural motifs of the square.

Return to rue des Bouchers, carry straight on along rue Grétry and turn right into rue des Fripiers.

Théâtre de la Monnaie★

Open Sept-Dec, Mar-Jun: guided tours Sat, noon. Closed public holidays. €6. ☎ 02 229 13 72; www.lamonnaie.be

After its destruction by fire in 1855 the theatre was rebuilt by Poelaert in 1855. From the square it is easy to appreciate how the auditorium was raised as part of the extensive renovation project carried out in 1985-86. In the entrance hall the brightly coloured,

> ### PRELUDE TO INDEPENDENCE
> On 25 August 1830, the Théâtre de la Monnaie was the scene of an extraordinary episode with dramatic political consequences. Outside the theatre a crowd had gathered, fired up by news of revolutionary events in France. Inside, Daniel Auber's opera *The Mute Girl of Portici* was being performed. As the tenor began to sing the rousingly patriotic song *"Sacred Love of the Fatherland"*, the audience responded with alacrity and rushed outside, joining the protesters in demonstrations which led to the "September Days" and the creation of the state of Belgium.

flowing forms on the ceiling by Sam Francis constrast sharply with the spartan lines of the floor by Sol LeWitt. The Royal Chamber, which is now used for official receptions, was decorated by Charles Vandenhove in association with two other internationally renowned artists, Daniel Buren and Giulio Paolini.

Cross over rue du Fossé-aux-Loups.

Rue Neuve

This is the main pedestrian shopping precinct, overlooked by the church of Notre-Dame du Finistère.

Go along rue aux Choux.

Place des Martyrs◆

This somewhat dilapidated square laid out on planned lines in 1774-75 has been under restoration for several years. At the centre of the square is Willem Geefs' monument (1838) dedicated to those who perished in the 1830 Revolution.

Go along rue du Persil and turn right into rue du Marais. Rue des Comédiens leads to boulevard de Berlaimont and the Banque nationale.

Cathédral des Saints-Michel-et-Gudule★★

Open 8.30am-6pm (Sat 3.30pm), Sun 2pm-6pm. ☎ 02 217 83 45.

The old collegiate church of St Michael and St Gudula has shared the title of cathedral of the Mechelen-Brussels archdiocese with the cathedral in Mechelen since 1962.

This beautiful Gothic building, the "ship anchored in the heart of Brussels", was built in several stages: the chancel dates from the 13C, the nave and side aisles from the 14C and 15C, and the towers from the 15C. The radiating chapels were added in the 16C and 17C. The façade's two lofty, powerful towers were designed by Van Ruysbroeck.

Starting at the east end, where the Brabant Gothic style made its first appearance, visitors arrive at the porch leading into the south transept. This is surmounted by a statue of St Gudula dating from the 15C.

Interior – The Brabant style nave is impressively austere in appearance. 17C statues of the Twelve Apostles adorn the columns. On the Baroque pulpit, by HF Verbruggen, are carvings of Adam and Eve being driven out of the Garden of Eden.

Note the difference between the 14C south aisle, supported by columns, and the 15C north aisle, which is striking for the seeming weightlessness of its ribbed vaulting. The chancel has great purity of line; it is the oldest part of the present building. The apsidal chapel has a fine altarpiece with scenes of Christ's Passion by the sculptor Jean Mone. The St-Sacrement Chapel houses the cathedral treasury, with precious items including a lovely *Virgin and Child* attributed to Conrad Meit.

The **stained-glass windows★** are marvellous. The gallery at the end of the nave is decorated with a brilliantly coloured *Last Judgement* dating from 1528. The deep blues and greens are particularly striking. The transept is lit by two sumptuous and beautifully designed 16C stained-glass windows, executed using cartoons by Bernard van Orley. The window in the north transept represents Emperor Charles V and Isabella of Portugal, while the one in the south transept depicts King Louis II of Hungary, with his wife Mary, the sister of Emperor Charles V. Wonderful 16C stained-glass windows decorate the Chapel of the Holy Sacrament on the north side of the chancel. Others from the 17C, designed in true Rubens style, decorate the Lady Chapel to the south of the chancel. They depict episodes from the Life of the Virgin Mary and, below, portraits of the donors.

Excavations have revealed the remains of the forepart of a Rhenish Mosan building in the nave, as well as the walls of an 11/12C Romanesque church.

Return to Grand-Place.

Worth a Visit

THE GREAT MUSEUMS OF THE CITY CENTRE

Around the Mont des Arts

Musée d'Art Ancien★★★

Open Tue-Sun 10am-5pm. Closed 1 Jan, second Thur in Jan, 1 May, 1 and 11 Nov and 25 Dec. €5 (includes Musée d'Art Moderne). No charge the first Wed of each month after 1pm. ☎ 02 508 32 11; www.fine-arts-museum.be

The Museum of Ancient Art is housed in a neo-Classical building designed by Alphonse Balat between 1874 and 1880, extending into a modern wing. The museum is famed throughout the world for its outstanding collections by Flemish Primitives and its famous masterpieces by Bruegel the Elder and Rubens.

15C-16C – This section exhibits some real treasures by the Flemish School as well as by the French, German, Dutch, Italian and Spanish Schools. One of the oldest paintings is *Scenes from the Life of the Virgin Mary* by an anonymous master from the Southern Low Countries (late 14C).

The work of the Tournai painter **Rogier van der Weyden** is represented by portraits such as *Antoine, Great Bastard of Burgundy* and *Laurent Froimont*, both marvels of simplicity, and by a magnificent *Pietà* (Room 11), its drama heightened by a reddish light. Also in this room is a work by the **Master of Flémalle**, thought by some scholars to be Van der Weyden's teacher, **Robert Campin**: his *Annunciation*, a variation on the central panel of the *Mérode Triptych* exhibited in The Cloisters, New York, is remarkable for the gentle features of the Virgin Mary's face, the choice of colour and the minute attention to detail. Van Eyck makes his influence felt in *Pietà*, one of the rare works by his student, **Petrus Christus**. The two panels of the *Justice of Emperor Otto III*, one of the major masterpieces by **Dieric Bouts**, were commissioned in 1468 for Leuven town hall as "paintings of justice"; in fact they depict a miscarriage of justice. Works on display by the Bruges artist **Hans Memling** include the tender *Virgin and Child* and the *Martyrdom of St Sebastian*, with a fine background evoking a Flemish town. **Hieronymus Bosch** is represented by *Calvary with Donor*, in which the landscape consists of chromatic nuances, and by a studio copy of his famous triptych, the *Temptation of St Anthony*. The *Virgin and Child* by **Hugo van der Goes** is on display, a magnificent work with a slightly cold feel to it because of the colours chosen by the artist. *Virgin with Milk Soup* by **Gérard David**, the last of the great Primitive painters, conveys a striking intimacy. **Quentin Metsys** still exhibits the main characteristics of the Flemish Primitives, but his works are tinged with Italian influence, heralding the Mannerism favoured by the Antwerp School; examples of his work include the *Triptych of the Holy Kindred*, *St Anne's Altarpiece* and several paintings of the *Virgin and Child*. **Jan Gossaert**, also known as Mabuse, was a portraitist and court painter, who reveals a different facet of his art here with *Venus and Cupid*, one of the first Flemish works to feature a mythological subject. There is also a panel from the *Altarpiece of the Holy Cross Brotherhood* by **Bernard van Orley**, painter to Margaret of Austria.

Landscape with the Fall of Icarus, by Pieter Bruegel the Elder.

BRUSSELS CAPITAL REGION

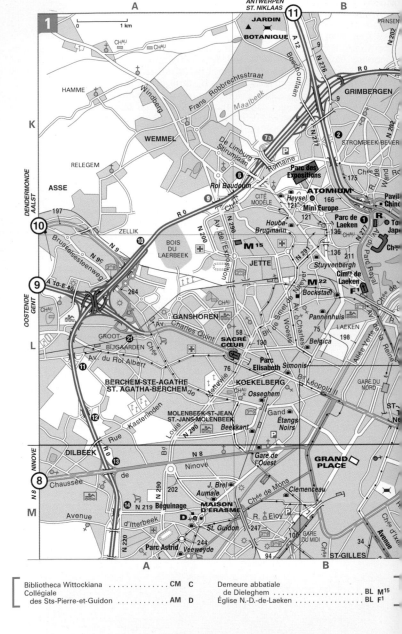

Room 31 is a veritable shrine to the work of **Bruegel the Elder**. Several of his masterpieces are exhibited here and they bear witness to the range of his talent and style. The *Fall of the Rebel Angels* shows the influence exerted by Hieronymus Bosch on Bruegel at the beginning of his career. Use of irony, realistic detail, and the tranquillity of the landscape, all of which are characteristic of Bruegel's work, are particularly evident in the famous *Census at Bethlehem* and *Fall of Icarus*, an unusual painting in which some people claim to see symbols from alchemy.

The rooms reserved for the **Delporte Legacy** include a Dutch Primitive panel *Calvary and Resurrection*, the pretty round panels by Grimmer depicting the *Seasons* and a lovely work by Bruegel the Elder, *Winter landscape with Skaters*.

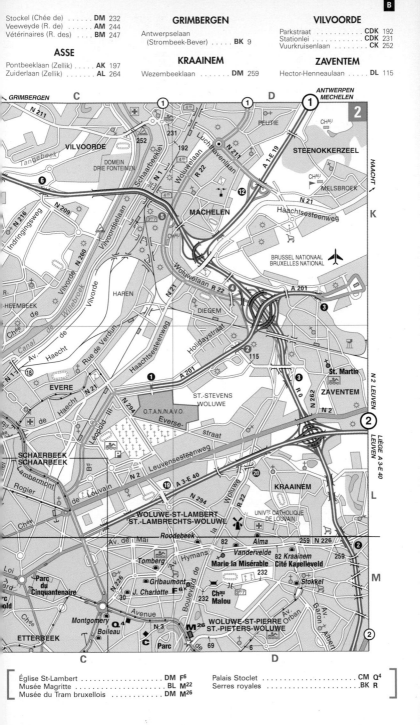

17C-18C – The works of this period hang in the rooms around the Great Hall in the renovated galleries. **Rubens** is represented by paintings of the highest quality. His talent for large religious works is obvious in his beautifully coloured *Adoration of the Magi*, his *Ascent to Calvary* and his *Martyrdom of St Livinus*. His skill in producing more personal works is manifest in the famous *Negro Heads* and the *Portrait of Hélène Fourment*, which exudes mischievousness and charm; they can be seen in Room 52. A good deal of space is also devoted to **Jordaens** and several of his works are on display in Room 57, including *Allegory of Fertility*, a lively painting with heightened sensuality. Among his other works are *The King Drinks* and *Susanna and the Elders*. There are also good works by Cornelis De Vos, Van Dyck, Teniers, Frans Hals. This exceptional collection is completed by works of Dutch landscape and genre painters.

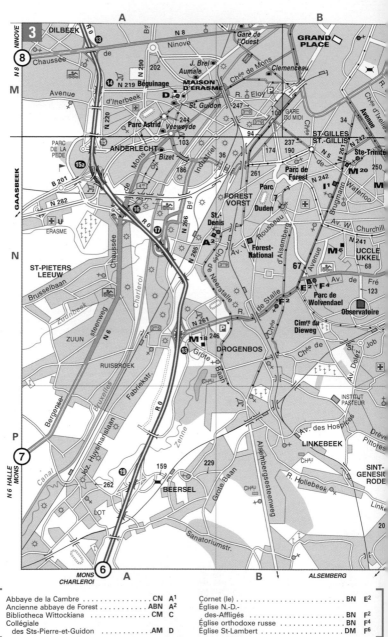

Musée d'Art Moderne★★

Access from Place Royale Open Tue-Sun 10am-5pm. Closed 1 Jan, 2nd Thur in Jan, 1 May, 1, 11 Nov, 25 Dec. €5 (includes entry to Musée d'Art ancien), free admission after 1pm 1st Wed in month. ☎ 02 508 32 11; www.fine-arts-museum.be

Opened in 1984, the Museum of Modern Art is divided into two parts. The neo-Classical building on Place Royale houses the 19C painting and sculpture collections, while the 20C statues, paintings and drawings are displayed in the below-ground section of the building on the Place du Musée, designed by the architects R Bastin and L Beek around an eight-storey deep light well.

19C – This section displays works illustrating **neo-Classicism** (Jacques-Louis David, *Death of Marat*, 1793 – level -2), **Romanticism** (level -2), **Realism** (level -1) and **Luminism** (*Portrait of Jenny Montigny* by Émile Claus – level -2). **Symbolism** (level +2) is represented by **Fernand Khnopff** with *Portrait of Marguerite*, *Memories* and the enigmatic *Carresses*. French Impressionist and neo-Impressionist works are on display on level +3 (Gauguin, Bonnard's *Nu à contre-jour*, Vuillard, Seurat), along with Rodin's famous statue *The Thinker*. A large area is devoted to the Flemish artist **James Ensor** (*The Colourist*, 1880; *Scandalised Masks*, 1883; *Skeletons Arguing over a Red Herring*, 1891), who embodied the transi-

BRUXELLES
BRUSSEL

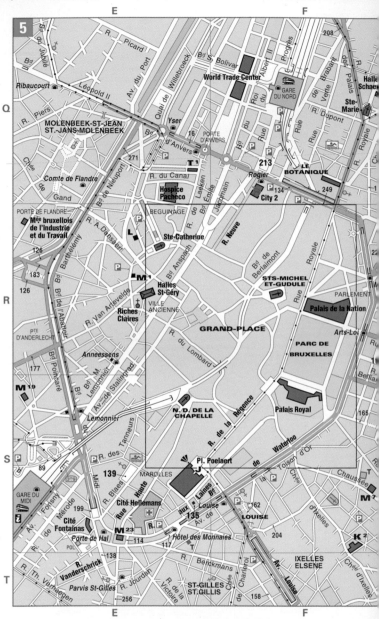

tion between the 19C and the 20C. Also exhibited on level +3 are works by Rik Wouters and a few moving statues by George Minne.

20C – Level -3, devoted to contemporary art, presents white life-size sculptures by Georges Segal (plaster figures moulded onto live models), works by Anselm Kiefer (*Bérénice*, 1989), Henry Moore, Pol Bury, Nam June Paik, Sam Francis, Claes Oldenburg and Francis Bacon.

Going down through the various levels, it is possible to follow the evolution of artistic movements such as Fauvism, Expressionism, Jeune Peinture Belge,

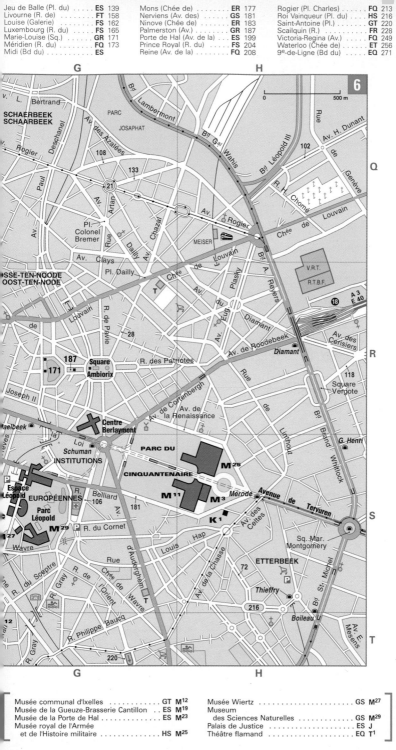

CoBrA, Phases, Surrealism, Groupe Zéro etc. Other particularly interesting works include those by **Rik Wouters** (*Lady in Blue before Mirror*, 1912; *Flute Player*, 1914). Note the beautiful group by **Leon Spilliaert** (*The Dike*, 1909; *Bather*, 1910), alongside representatives of the second Sint Martens-Latem School (**Permeke, Gustave De Smet** and **Frits van den Berghe**). The museum also contains Abstract art with **Servranckx**, Baugniet and Peeters; the Belgian Futurists (P. de Troyer and J Schmalzigaug) and the members of **CoBrA** (Pierre Alechinsky, Karel Appel). The works by **Delvaux** (*Night Trains; Pygmalion; Public Voice*) and

BRUXELLES
BRUSSEL

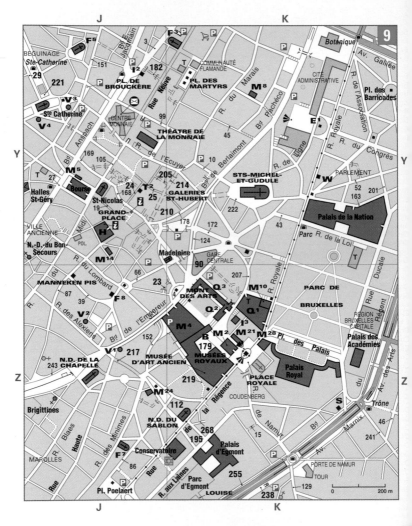

Bruxelles

ENVIRONS

ASSE

BEERSEL

DROGENBOS

GRIMBERGEN

HOEILAART

KRAAINEM

LINKEBEEK

MACHELEN

ST-GENESIUS-RODE

ST-PIETERS-LEEUW

STEENOKKERZEEL

VILVOORDE

WEMMEL

ZAVENTEM

Musées royaux des Beaux-Arts

Portrait of Marguerite by Fernand Khnopff

Magritte bear witness to the importance of Surrealism and Symbolism in Belgium in the 19C. One room is devoted to each of these artists. The Georgette and René Magritte Room shows works which were part of collections (*The Man of the Sea, Midnight Marriage, Empire of Lights, 1954, The Secret Gambler*) as well as those bequeathed to the museum by the artist's widow (*Black Magic Pebble, Arnhem Domain*). Note also works by Wilfredo Lam, Hans Hartung, Joan Miró, Max Ernst, Paul Klee, Giorgio de Chirico, **Marcel Broodthaers**, and Arman.

Level -8 is more particularly concerned with contemporary art, with works by Belgian artists (Michel Mouffe, Mark Luyten, Dan van Severen, Bernd Lohaus, Marthe Wéry, Jan Vercruysse, Walter Swennen, Jef Geys and Jan Fabre) as well as foreign painters (Dan Flavin, Don Judd, Ulrich Ruckriem, Tony Cragg).

Musée des Instruments de Musique★★★ (MIM)

Open Tue-Sun 9.30am-5pm (Thur 8pm), Sat, Sun 10am-5pm. Closed 1 Jan, 1 May, 1, 11 Nov, 25 Dec. €5, free admission after 1pm 1st Wed of month. ☎ 02 545 01 53, www.mim.fgov.be

The MIM occupies two buildings: the splendid Art Nouveau **Old England** by the architect Paul Saintenoy and the neo-Classical edifice by B Guimard. The former was built for the British firm of that name which established its Brussels branch in 1886. Renovation work has restored this fine old structures to their former glory.

The Museum of Musical Instruments has a prestigious collection of some 7 000 items from around the world. Infra-red devices allow the instruments on display to be heard by the individual visitor. Level -1 has mechanical instruments while Level 0 is devoted to folk instruments from Belgium and non-European countries; there are hurdy-gurdies, accordions, drums, and instruments used in Chinese opera. Level 1 gives a history of Western music from Antiquity to the present day. There is also a section devoted to Adolphe Sax, the Dinant man who revolutionised the design of brass wind instruments and had several named

after him, including of course the saxophone. String and keyboard instruments can be found on Level 2. In the past, pianos came in a whole variety of forms; note particularly the extraordinary Brussels tavern piano of 1830 built like a cupboard, with its mechanical parts hidden behind curtains. With beautifully carved details, some of the museum's harps are of great beauty. A lute-maker's workshop has been reconstructed, revealing the secrets of his craft. The mirror hall houses the museum's outstanding items, among them the Joachim Tielke's viola of 1701 with its wonderful incrustations of ivory. The 17C Ruckers-Taskin harpsicord is decorated with scenes of the

Casserole of Red Mussels by Marcel Broodthaers

Musées royaux des Beaux-Arts

towns conquered by Louis XIV. Note the sinuous lines of Nicola Papalini's 19C bass clarinet, as well as the striking Bible regal which, when folded, looks exactly like a real Bible. Level 3 has a small exhibition devoted to the work of the architect Saintenoy.

Concerts are held in the museum every Thursday evening.

Musées Bellevue★

Open Tue-Sun. 10am-5pm (last admission 4pm). Closed 1 Jan, Easter, 25 Dec. €6.20 (combined ticket with Palais du Coudenberg €7.40). ☎ 02 512 28 21.

Built between 1776 and 1777 as a luxury hotel, Hôtel Bellevue welcomed many famous names, before it was incorporated into the Palais Royal early in the 20C and used as a residence by Princess Clémentine, the daughter of Leopold II, and by the future Leopold III.

The building now houses two museums. The **Musée de la Dynastie** contains a fascinating collection of documents on the Belgian royal family from the 1830 revolution to the present day. The **Mémorial Roi Baudoin** is devoted entirely to this remarkable monarch, who played a prominent role in the history of the Belgian kingdom.

THE FORGOTTEN PALACE

Entry through the Musées Bellevue. Opening times same as Musées Bellevue. €5 (combined ticket with Musées Bellevue €7.40). ☎ 02 512 28 21.
The residence of the Dukes of Burgundy, the **Palais du Coudenberg** was destroyed by a terrible fire in 1731 and the memory of its glories passed into oblivion. But recent archeological excavations have revealed the vast ceremonial hall, the Magna Aula, the scene of Charles V's abdication in 1555. Nearby is the rue Isabelle, an underground street, used by Archduchess Isabelle on her way to Mass in the Cathedral.

Appartements de Charles de Lorraine

Open daily except Mon and Sun. 1pm (Sat 10am)-5pm. Closed public holidays, last week Aug, 25 Dec-1 Jan. €3. ☎ 02 519 53 11.
The neo-Classical palace of Charles of Lorraine stands on the northwest side of rue du Musée. This is in fact the only surviving wing of the building constructed under this Governor of the Low Countries. Work was carried out from 1756 to 1780, on the site of the old Hôtel de Nassau. The Prints Room and Chalcography Section of the Bibliothèque Royale are on the ground floor. A monumental staircase leads to the first floor. Note the statue at its foot, representing Hercules (1770) with the features of the Governor; it is by Laurent Delvaux. Do not miss the marvellous round drawing room decorated with a marble floor; the rose is made from 28 different types of Belgian marble. Equally interesting are the five refurbished rooms housing a **museum** devoted to the Low Countries under Austrian rule in the 18C.

Bibliothèque royale de Belgique

Guided tours only, pre-booked groups only: contact ☎ 02 519 53 57. Closed Sun and public holidays, last week in Aug, 2, 15 Nov, 25 Dec-1 Jan. www.kbr.be
The Albert I Royal Library was founded in the 15C during the reign of the Dukes of Burgundy. It has been open to the public since 1839 and was transferred to Mont des Arts in 1969. The magnificent collections number four million volumes available for consultation: manuscripts and printed material, prints and drawings, maps and plans, coins and medallions.

The building includes the **Chapelle de Nassau**, also known as St George's Chapel, which is a remnant of the old Palais de Nassau. This Flamboyant Gothic structure dates from 1520, and is now used for temporary exhibitions.

Musée du Livre and Cabinets de Donation – The donation rooms in the Book Museum include reconstructions of Émile Verhaeren's study in Saint-Cloud near Paris, Michel de Ghelderode's study in Schaerbeek, as well as a room in memory of Henry van de Velde and his friend Max Elskamp. The end room contains valuable manuscripts and printed material. *Mon, Wed, Sat, 2pm-4.50pm. ☎ 02 519 53 57; www.kbr.be*

Musée de l'Imprimerie – The Printing Museum exhibits a series of machines and printing presses dating from the late 18C to the early 20C. They illustrate the history of printing (typography, copperplate engraving, lithography, offset) and the art of bookbinding and gilding. *Open Mon-Fri 9am-5pm. Closed same dates as Bibliothèque royale. No charge. ☎ 02 519 53 56; www.kbr.be*

AROUND THE GRAND-PLACE

Bruxella 1238

To the left of the Bourse, rue de la Bourse. Guided tour Wed. 11.15am, 3pm. Meet at the Maison du Roi, Grand-Place. €2.48. ☎ 02 279 43 50.
This small archaeology museum is situated on the site of a former Franciscan friary founded in 1238. Archaeological digs carried out in 1988 uncovered the remains of the old church and monastery, numerous burial vaults, bones and fragments of pottery.

COMIC BOOK HEROES

People with a love of comic books will be delighted to find a trail around Brussels linking famous figures from "the Ninth Art". Over the past years, around a dozen famous characters taken from comic strips have made their appearance in the city, decorating several gable ends. The most striking are:

– Boule and Bill by Roba, rue du Chevreuil;
– Brousaille by Frank Pé, Plattesteen;
– Le Chat by Philippe Geluck, boulevard du Midi;
– Néron by Marc Sleen, in the Halles St-Géry;
– Ric Hochet by Tibet and Duchâteau, rue des Bons Secours;
– Bob and Bobette by Willy Vandersteen, rue de Laeken;
– Cubitus inspired by the Manneken Pis, rue de Flandre;
– Quick and Flupke with police officer 15 in rue Haute;
– Gaston Lagaffe, boulevard Pacheco, leading the way to the Centre Belge de la Bande Dessinée in rue des Sables, at the foot of the steps.

A brochure indicating the exact location of these murals can be obtained from the BI-TC Tourist Information Centre, on Grand-Place, ☎ 02 513 89 40.

"Broussaille" by Frank Pé

Ch. Bastin - J. Evrard/MICHELIN

Musée du Costume et de la Dentelle

Open daily (except Wed). 10am-12.30pm, 1.30-5pm, Sat-Sun 2-4.30pm. Closed 1 Jan, 1 May, 1, 11 Nov and 25 Dec. €3. ☎ 02 512 77 09.

The Costume and Lace Museum covers the various crafts related to costume-making from the 17C to the 20C, including Brussels lace, embroidery, and trimmings.

North of the City Centre

Centre Belge de la Bande Dessinée★★

  Open Tue-Sun 10am-6pm. Closed 1 Jan, 25 Dec. €6.20. ☎ 02 219 19 80.

The Belgian Centre for Comic Strip Art is housed in the magnificent Art Nouveau building designed by **Victor Horta** in 1903 for the textile wholesalers Waucquez. The vast entrance hall is lit by a street lamp, making the interior look like a public square. A bookshop, library and restaurant have been opened around the hall, and a monumental stone staircase with an ironwork balustrade leads up to the museum collections.

An exhibition on the mezzanine explains the various stages involved in the production of a comic strip (story board, drawing, colouring, printing). The "treasury" is a collection of more than 3 000 original plates by the greatest comic strip writers of all times, displayed in groups of 200 in rotating exhibitions. An area is devoted to the actual production process.

On the first floor, beneath the immense glass roof, the **Musée de l'Imaginaire** beckons the visitor into the world of the great heroes of Belgian comic strips and their creators: Tintin (Hergé), Gaston Lagaffe (André Franquin), Spirou (Rob Vel), Bob and Bobette (Willy Vandersteen), Blake and Mortimer (Edgar Pierre Jacobs), Lucky Luke (Morris), Boule and Bill (Roba), the Smurfs (Peyo) etc.

The top floor houses the **Musée de la Bande Dessinée Moderne** which looks at the development of this art form in Belgium between 1960 and 1990.

The Centre is also a major location for temporary exhibitions.

The Cinquantenaire

Parc du Cinquantenaire

The park was created for the 1880 exhibition celebrating the 50th anniversary of Belgium's independence. A large palace known as the Palais du Cinquantenaire stands in the grounds, its two wings joined by a monumental arcade designed by Charles Girault (1905). At the rear of the palace are two metal frame halls dating from 1888. The north wing and hall contain the Musée royal de l'Armée et de l'Histoire militaire; the south hall the Autoworld exhibition. The south wing contains the Musée du Cinquantenaire.

Musée du Cinquantenaire★★★

Part of the collection may be closed at certain times – ask at the information desk. Tue-Sun 9.30 (Sat, Sun, public holidays 10am)-5pm. Closed 1 Jan, 1 May, 1, 11 Nov, 25 Dec. €4. Free admission 1st Wed of the month after 1pm. ☎ 02 741 72 11; www.kmkg.mrah.be.

The collections are extremely diverse, especially as regards works from Antiquity, the decorative arts and non-European civilisations.

Antiquities (Near East, Greece, Rome, Egypt) – The civilisations of Palestine, Cyprus and Mesopotamia are brought to life on the ground floor (Level 0). A 1:400 scale **model of Rome** can be seen from the mezzanine, showing the capital of the Roman Empire in the 4C *(recorded commentary available with lighting)*. Level I is devoted to Ancient Rome. Level II focuses on **Rome** (portrait gallery), **Etruria** and **Greece** (vases with red and black figures). The great colonnade of Apamea has been reconstructed as a reminder of the Belgian missions in Syria. There is an overhead view of the famous Apamea mosaic in the centre of the great inner courtyard, a fabulous

Musées Royaux d'Art et d'Histoire, Bruxelles

Queen Tiy, bas relief

scene of hunters fighting wild beasts. Level III is devoted to Egypt. Note a fragment from one of the oldest Books of the Dead, the **Dame de Bruxelles** (a statue dating back to 2600 BC) and the very beautiful low relief representing **Queen Tiy**, wife of Amenhotep III. Level IV contains a plaster model of the burial complex of Djoser in Saqqarah.

Non-European Civilisations – The **America Rooms** (Level I) contain some splendid collections of pre-Columbian and ethnographic art. Note the magnificent feather cloak dating from the 16C, the monumental seated divinity from Mexico and a double scroll-shaped ornament (Columbia 600-1550).

Collections from **Micronesia and Polynesia** (Level I) include archaeological and ethnological objects which are exhibited by theme. The museum has one of the world-famous statues from Easter Island.

The **India, China and Southeast Asia** section (Level II) illustrates the arts, religions and traditions of India (13C bronze statue of Siva), China (two bodhisattvas from c 1200), Vietnam (pottery), Indonesia, Thailand and Tibet (extensive collection of thang-kas, religious and symbolic paintings by lamas).

Crafts – The **Salle aux Trésors** (Level 0) houses a treasure trove of ecclesiastical objets d'art, including the **Stavelot portable altar** (c 1150-60) made of brass and champlevé enamel, the main reliquary of Pope Alexander I, and some beautiful ivory pieces, including the **Genoels-Elderen diptych**.

The room devoted to decorative arts from the Middle Ages to the Baroque period (Level I) contains **tapestries** that vie with each other in the delicacy of their execution and the splendour of their colours. They include the early 16C *Legend of Notre-Dame-du-Sablon* and *The Story of Jacob*. The **St George Altarpiece** by Jan Borman the Elder (1493) stands out among the wooden **retables** because of the intensely life-like figures.

There is some extremely valuable furniture on display including fine Antwerp cabinets and a reconstruction of the shop window designed by Victor Horta in 1912 for the Wolfers jewellery store.

A number of rooms (Level II) display examples of glassware (101 pieces by M Marinot), textiles, pottery and lace (Archdukes Albert and Isabella's bedspread, 1599).

The **horsedrawn carriages** section (Level 0) houses a collection of coaches, sleighs, and saddles.

The **Musée du Cœur** (Heart Museum – Level I) presents an astonishing display of hearts donated by the famous heart specialist Boyadjian.

Statue of bodhisattva.

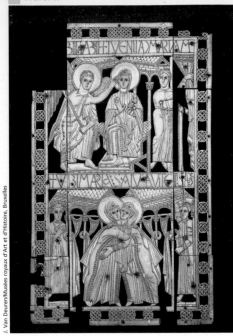

The Genoels-Elderen Diptych.

National Archaeology – The rooms (Level 0) display various objects (tools, jewels, fragments of pottery) of Paleolithic to Merovingian date uncovered during digs in Belgium, as well as various reconstructions, among them tombs and a Roman dwelling.

Musée royal de l'Armée et d'Histoire militaire

Open Tue-Sun, 9am-noon and 1-4.30pm. Closed 1 Jan, 1 May, 1 Nov and 25 Dec. No charge. ☎ *02 737 79 07; www.klm-mra.be*

The Royal Army and Military History Museum illustrates the country's military history from 1789 to the present, through an extensive collection of uniforms, decorations, weapons and pictures. It also has a fine **collection of arms and armour★**. Beneath the arcades, in a chamber resembling a vaulted cellar, the **Collection Titeca et Ribaucourt★** is a superb array of arms and helmets. The two terraces command a wonderful **panorama★** of the city. The **Air and Space Section★**, housed in a large hall, has about 100 planes. There is a little Nieuport, one of the mainstays of France's air force in the First World War, and a British Spitfire and Hurricane from the Second World War.

Autoworld★★

&. *Open early Apr – end Sept, 10am-6pm; the rest of the year, 9.30am-5pm. Closed 1 Jan, 25 Dec. €5.* ☎ *02 736 41 65; www.autoworld.be*

No fewer than 450 vehicles, mostly cars, are displayed beneath the high glass roof of the south hall of the Palais du Cinquantenaire. While the exhibitions include cars belonging to members of the Royal Veteran Car Club, most of the vehicles come from the prestigious **Ghislain Mahy Collection**.

Born in Ghent in 1901, Mahy assiduously collected more than 800 vehicles over a period of 40 years. They were often in pitiful condition when he purchased them, but they were always brought back to life in the collector's repair shop. There are now about 300 cars in perfect working order. Mahy bought his first car in 1944, a 1921 Ford, and the collection came to include many other American models. French vehicles include the little 1896 Léon Bollée, a 1908 Renault 14CV, a 1920 Delage and a 1935 Hispano-Suiza. Particularly fine examples of British car manufacture include Bentley, Daimler, Humber, Jaguar and Rolls-Royce; note the magnificent 1921 Silver Ghost. The German automobile industry is represented by Adler, Mercedes, Horch and Opel, while Alfa-Romeo, Fiat and Lancia provide examples of Italian sophistication.

The Belgian makes deserve particular attention. They include examples from

Emblem of Minerva.

Belga Rise, FN, Fondu, Hermes, Imperia, Miesse, Nagant and Vivinus, not to mention products from the famous **Sylvain de Jong** who started by building bicycles and motorcycles. The museum contains his 1902 prototype for the Minerva. Although the range initially consisted of only three models, it continued to expand until the 1930s. By 1911 the factory had taken on 1 600 workers. In 1912 the company offered electric lights as an option on their automobiles, and by 1914 electric ignition had become available. In 1922 all four wheels had brakes. The firm acquired a solid reputation for its range of enormously comfortable, superb quality automobiles, with very quiet engines. But by the beginning of the 1930s the golden age of the luxury car was drawing to a close, and customers were turning to less expensive makes. In 1934 the Minerva company went bankrupt.

The museum displays around 15 Minerva models. The oldest, dating from 1910, belonged to the Belgian Court during the reign of King Albert I.

Maison Cauchie★
Rue des Francs 5. Guided tours only (45min), the first Sat-Sun of each month, 11am-1pm 2-6pm. Closed 1 Jan and 25 Dec. €4. ☎ 02 673 15 06.
The home of architect and decorative artist **Paul Cauchie** dates from 1905 and has a remarkable façade almost entirely decorated in *sgraffito*, a technique similar to fresco painting.

Around the Parliament

Palais de la Nation
Guided tours (90 mins); groups only, advance bookings only – apply to Chambre des Représentants, Service des Relations publiques et internationales, 1008 Bruxelles, ☎ 02 549 81 36.
This palace was built during the days of Charles of Lorraine. It stands north of Brussels Park and was restored after a fire in 1883. It is the seat of the Chamber of Representatives and the Senate. The **Salle des Séances du Sénat★** is particularly finely decorated.

Colonne du Congrès
The Congress Column was designed and inaugurated by Poelaert in 1859 to commemorate the National Congress which proclaimed the Belgian Constitution after the 1830 Revolution. Willem Geefs' statue of Leopold II stands at its top. Two lions guard the tomb of the Unknown Soldier at the foot of the monument. There is an interesting overall view of the city from the "Esplanade" between the buildings of the Cité Administrative.

Musée Charlier★
Avenue des Arts 16. Mon-Fri, 1pm-5pm. Closed public holidays. €2.48 ☎ 02 218 53 82.
This museum occupies two semi-detached houses in St-Josse, which were purchased in 1890 by the wealthy art collector **Henri van Cutsem**. After having the two façades combined, Van Cutsem commissioned his friend Victor Horta to design glass roofs which would provide suitable lighting for his collections. He then asked the artist Guillaume Charlier (1854-1925) to move in. The artist, who was the sole heir to his patron's estate when the latter died in 1904, inherited the mansion and had a museum built by Victor Horta in Tournai to house Henri van Cutsem's collection of Impressionist oil paintings. The Charlier Museum contains a large number of paintings and sculptures by various artists, along with interesting collections of furniture, tapestries and decorative objects.

THE BÉGUINAGE DISTRICT

Église St-Jean-Baptiste-au-Béguinage
With its three-gabled Flemish Baroque façade, St John the Baptist's Church of 1676 is the centrepiece of the quiet Béguinage area.
The **interior** is beautifully proportioned, with Baroque decoration applied to the Gothic architecture. The boldly designed entablature above the arches rests on the heads of winged angels at the intersections of the arches.
Beneath the pulpit of 1757 there is a figure of St Dominic slaying Heresy. Note the marvellous paintings by the Brussels artist **Van Loon** and various other Flemish artists. The Beguine convent, which once housed no fewer than 1 200 nuns, disappeared in the 19C. *Tue-Sat 10am-5pm, Sun 11am-noon, 8pm-10pm*
Église Ste-Catherine stands nearby. It still has the **tower** from the old church, and the **Tour Noire**, which was once part of the town's first walls.

Maison de la Bellone
♿ Open Tue-Fri exc July and public holidays 10am-6pm. Free admission. ☎ 02 513 33 33.
This splendid patrician residence dating from the late 17C is not visible from the street. It is now the Maison du Spectacle, an exhibition and information centre about the world of theatre and entertainment.

THE "QUARTIER DE L'EUROPE"

Muséum des Sciences Naturelles (Institut Royal)★★

Rue Vautier 29. Tue-Sun. 9.30am-4.45pm, Sat-Sun and school holiays (except Jul-Aug) 10am-6pm. Closed 1 Jan, 1 May, 25 Dec. €4, no charge first Wed of the month after 1pm. ☎ *02 627 42 38; www.sciencesnaturelles.be*

The highlight of the dynamic Natural History Museum is its collection of **iguanodon skeletons**. In 1878 the well-preserved bones of 29 of these reptilian dinosaurs were discovered in a mine in Bernissart, in the west of the country. The animals were herbivores from the Cretaceous period.

Ten skeletons about 10m/33ft long have been rebuilt, whereas others are exhibited as they were found, lying in the sand. In addition to these authentic specimens there are also animated robots of the tyrannosaurus, triceratops and allosaurus. Other rooms provide an interesting insight into the life of invertebrates, the seas of the Jurassic and Cretaceous periods and polar animals. A vivarium gives the visitor a chance to observe a number of live species of giant spiders. The museum also presents a fine collection of minerals. The whale room has an impressive display of 18 skeletons of Cetecea, including that of the largest mammal of all times, the blue whale. There are also splendid collections of shells, insects, and minerals.

Musée Wiertz

Rue Vautier 62. Open Tue-Fri and alternate weekends (ring for information) 10am-noon, 1pm-5pm. Closed 1 Jan, second Thur in Jan, 1 May, 1, 11 Nov, 25 Dec. No charge. ☎ *02 508 32 11.*

Close to the Muséum des Sciences Naturelles, this museum occupies the former studio and home of the artist **Antoine Wiertz**, the visionary painter and forerunner of Belgian Symbolism and Surrealism. The compositions in the main room are striking for their monumental size. Note also the macabre *Premature Burial.*

Centre Berlaymont

Restoration work in progress.

This X-shaped complex of buildings (1967) on Rond-point Schuman was built on the site of a convent founded in the 17C by the Comtesse de Berlaymont. The Berlaymont was vacated by EU officials in late 1991 for safety reasons.

The Squares

Near the Centre Berlaymont is a district laid out from 1875 onwards by the architect Gédéon Bordiau. This example of advanced town planning with Eclectic and Art Nouveau style houses makes a fascinating stroll. Note the **Hôtel Van Eetvelde**★ (1895-98) at no 4 avenue Palmerston, a brilliant work by Victor Horta and the **Maison du Peintre de St-Cyr** (1900) at no 11 square Ambiorix, a remarkably narrow building designed by Gustave Strauven.

SOUTH OF THE CENTRE

St-Gilles

The great attraction for visitors to this municipality is its wealth of Art Nouveau buildings. The outstanding example is Victor Horta's own house.

Musée Horta★★

Open Tue-Sun 2-5.30pm. Closed public holidays. €4.95. ☎ *02 543 04 90.*

The Horta Museum occupies the two narrow houses that the architect **Victor Horta** built between 1898 and 1901 as his home and studio. He wrote in his Memoirs: "People should please realise that I drew and created the design for each piece of furniture, each hinge and door latch, the rugs and the wall decoration in each of the houses..." This tremendous amount of work resulted in a marvel of harmony and elegance, a remarkable tribute to Art Nouveau as a style in which glass and iron play the leading role and in which curves and countercurves are combined so gracefully. The **staircase** is one of Horta's most beautiful creations. The lightness of the metal structure is accentuated by the golden light diffused by the glazed ceiling and the reflections from the multitude of mirrors.

Hôtel Hannon

Avenue de la Jonction 1. From mid-Aug t- mid-Jul: open Tue-Sun. 1-6pm. Closed public holidays. €2.50. ☎ *02 538 42 20.*

This Art Nouveau residence was built in 1903 by the architect **Jules Brunfaut** (1852-1942) and decorated by the French artists Louis Majorelle and Émile Gallé, the founder of the Nancy School. It was neglected for many years and most of the furniture has been lost. The building is now occupied by a photographic gallery named after the industrialist **Édouard Hannon**, who was also a talented photographer. Nearby at avenue Brugmann 55 is the house known as **"Les Hiboux"** (The Owls) which was built by Édouard Pelseneer in 1899.

Ixelles

On the far side of Porte Louise, Ixelles is one of the largest municipalities in Greater Brussels. Avenue Louise was laid out in the middle of the 19C as a link between the city centre and the woodlands of the Bois de la Cambre. Nowadays it is lined with prestigious shops and boutiques.

Maison communale d'Ixelles

The town hall was formerly the residence of La Malibran, the famous singer who married the Belgian violinist Bériot in 1836 and died the same year after falling from a horse.

Musée communal d'Ixelles★★

Rue J-van-Volsem 71. Tue-Sun. 1-6.30pm, Sat, Sun 10am-5pm. Closed public holidays. Free admission to permanent collections. ☎ *02 515 64 21.*

The municipal museum was inaugurated in 1892 on the premises of a former slaughterhouse. It was extended in 1973 and partially restructured in 1994. The museum contains an excellent collection of 19C and 20C paintings and sculptures by famous Belgian and French artists. The display includes a sketch by Dürer, *The Stork*, and 29 original posters by Toulouse-Lautrec. Some rooms are devoted to temporary exhibitions.

Musée Constantin-Meunier★

Rue de l'Abbaye 59. Tue-Fri 10am-noon, 1pm-5pm, every other weekend at the same times (check in advance). Closed 1 Jan, 2nd Thur in Jan, 1 May, 1, 11 Nov, 25 Dec. Free admission. ☎ *02 508 32 11.*

The Constantin Meunier Museum is housed in the house studio of the artist (1831-1905). Alternately sculptor and painter, he devoted himself to depicting the world of work.

Abbaye Notre-Dame-de-la-Cambre★★

To the south of the Étangs (Lakes) d'Ixelles, this old Cistercian abbey now houses the École Nationale Supérieure d'Architecture et des Arts Décoratifs, the college otherwise known as "La Cambre" and the Institut Géographique National. The beautiful **main courtyard**, with the abbey building flanked by pavilions at the corners and outbuildings in a semicircular layout, forms a very harmonious 18C ensemble. *Open 9am-noon, 3pm-6pm*

The **church** dates from the 14C and there is a marvellous statue of *The Mocking of Christ*★ by Albert Bouts in the nave. The Stations of the Cross are by Anto Carte (1886-1954). The north transept contains the 17C reliquary of St Boniface, the Brussels citizen who became Bishop of Lausanne and died in the monastery in the 13C. *9am-noon, 3-6pm.* ☎ *02 648 11 21.*

The vaulting in the Lady Chapel (south transept) rests on brackets carved with human figures and symbolic animals.

Bois de la Cambre★

The woods form an oasis of greenery, with undulating countryside encircling an artificial lake suitable for boating.

Université Libre de Bruxelles

Part of this university, which was founded in 1834, lies to the east of the Bois de la Cambre. Another campus is situated near Ixelles cemetery.

Cimetière d'Ixelles

Several well-known figures are buried here, including French General Boulanger, who sought refuge in Brussels after his attempted *coup d'état*, and committed suicide in 1891 on the tomb of his mistress (avenue 3). There is a statue of Till Eulenspiegel on the tomb of Charles de Coster (avenue 1).

Forest

Église St-Denis★

Mon-Fri 10-11am, Thu-Fri also 3-4pm. At other times, ask at rue des Abbesses 15. ☎ *02 344 87 19.*

This charming Gothic church at the foot of the hill not far from the Forest-National multi-purpose hall, contains the tomb of St Alène (12C). The former **Abbaye de Forest** houses a cultural centre. On the side bordering Place St-Denis is a fine Louis XVI doorway.

Uccle

Musée David et Alice van Buuren★★

Avenue Léo-Errera 41. Open Mon 2pm (Sun 1pm)-5.45pm. Closed public holidays and 25 Dec-1 Jan. €10. ☎ *02 343 48 51; www.hmt.be/vanbuuren*

David van Buuren's house, built in 1928, is a worthy setting for this museum, which contains part of the rich collection which belonged to this Dutch financier and patron of the arts. There is a version of Bruegel the Elder's *Fall of Icarus*, as well as landscapes by Hercules Seghers and Patinir, still-life paintings by Fantin-Latour, several works by Permeke, a series of paintings by Van de Woestyne, sculptures by Georges Minne and Delft ceramic ware.

The magnificent Art Deco interior has retained the refined atmosphere created by the remarkable Van Buurens to display their array of works of art both ancient and modern.

Laid out by the landscape architect Réné Pechère, the grounds are full of charm. They include a Picturesque Garden, a Garden of the Heart and a Labyrinth, the various areas of which echo verses from the *Song of Solomon*.

Inside the 'Jardin du cœur'.

Parc de Wolvendael
Inside this vast park (10ha/25 acres), note the small Louis XVI style pavilion.
At the edge of the park is the **Cornet**, a charming inn built in 1570, in which Eulenspiegel is said to have stayed. The **Russian Orthodox Church** nearby is a copy of a church in Novgorod.

Église St-Clément
With its nave and its 12C Romanesque tower, St Clement's Church has preserved a certain rustic air.

Garden-cities of "Le Logis" and "Floréal"
Near Square des Archiducs. Built between 1921 and 1929 for tenant cooperatives, these garden-cities served as a model for public housing in Belgium. In late April or early May the many Japanese cherry-trees give a magnificent show of pink blossom.

EAST OF THE CENTRE
Having kept their rural character right up to the interwar period, the two Woluwe municipalities now consist mostly of residential suburbs sprawling over a vast area.

Woluwe-St-Lambert

Chapelle de Marie-la-Misérable
This charming chapel was built in 1360 in honour of a pious young girl who refused a young man's advances and was subsequently accused of theft by him. As punishment, she was buried alive. Miracles occurred on the spot where she had been killed.

An old post **windmill** stands in a small wood not far to the north *(access via avenue de la Chapelle-aux-Champs)*.

The 18C **Château Malou** stands overlooking a lake in a vast park to the south. It has a gallery of works of art available on loan and hosts temporary exhibitions.

The delightful area of lakes known as the **Étangs Mellaerts** in **Woluwe-St-Pierre** is very popular in summer.

Woluwe-St-Pierre

Palais Stoclet★
Avenue de Tervuren 279-281. Not open to the public.
This magnificent residence with its pure architectural lines was built by the renowned Austrian architect, **Josef Hoffmann**. The construction work, which involved the sculptors Powolny, Luksch and Metzner in addition to the famous painter **Gustav Klimt**, lasted for six years (1906-11). The exterior is a classical example of turn-of-the-century architecture. The quality of the construction and the modernity of the design have stood the test of time remarkably well. Note the magnificent staircase tower decorated with four figures and a half-circle in bronze by the sculptor Metzner.

Ch. Bastin et J. Evrard/MICHELIN

Bibliotheca Wittockiana★

Rue du Bémel 21. Guided tour with curator by appointment only, except for temporary exhibitions. Tue-Sat. 10am-5pm. Closed public holidays. €2.50. ☎ 02 770 53 33.

This museum contains an extensive collection of bound works belonging to the industrialist Michael Wittock. The valuable collection contains some 1 100 volumes, including some rare bound editions from the 16C to 20C.

The museum also owns a collection of baby rattles (the largest private collection in the world) spanning 40 centuries of history, beginning in the Hittite period.

The reading room on the first floor can be used to consult reference books.

Musée du Tram Bruxellois

Avenue de Tervuren 364b ♿ Apr-Sep: Sat, Sun, public holidays 1.30-7pm. €3.72 The admission ticket includes a return journey on a 1930s tram to Soignes Forest (Musée Royal de l'Afrique Centrale) or the Cinquantenaire (journey takes approximately 1hr). ☎ 02 515 31 08; www.mtub.be.

The Brussels Tram Museum is housed in a former depot of the STIB, the Brussels public transport undertaking. It provides an insight into the development of public transport through old trams and buses, information panels and documents.

Auderghem

Le Rouge Cloître

The monastery lies to the east of Auderghem in the Soignes Forest. The painter Hugo van der Goes stayed here until his death in 1482. The outbuildings house an **Art Centre** and a **Soignes Forest Visitor Centre**.

Not far from here in the woods south of the Wavre road stands the **Château forestier de Trois Fontaines** of which only a small red-brick building remains. A vast park to the north surrounds **Château de Val Duchesse,** where the Treaty of Rome was drawn up, and the delightful 12C **Chapelle Ste-Anne**.

WEST OF THE CENTRE

Anderlecht

Maison d'Érasme★★

Tue-Sun 10am-5pm. Closed 1 Jan, 25 Dec. €1.25. ☎ 02 521 13 83.

Erasmus' House, known as "The Swan", was built in 1468 and extended in 1515. It was one of the guest houses of the Anderlecht chapter, used to accommodate members of the community and their illustrious guests.

In 1521 the most famous of these guests, Erasmus Roterodamus (1469-1536) – otherwise known as **Erasmus** – gave his name to the house.

Behind the brick walls of the shady close, there are five rooms furnished with Gothic and Renaissance furniture. The natural lighting is subdued, apparently serving as a reminder of the "Prince of Humanists".

On the ground floor are the Chambre de rhétorique (Rhetoric Chamber), then the chapter house containing paintings by old masters such as Hieronymus Bosch's

Erasmus' study in Anderlecht.

superb *Adoration of the Magi*, **Erasmus' study** with its simple writing desk and the portraits of the philospher by Quentin Metsys, Dürer and Holbein (copy).

The 16C statue at the foot of the staircase is said to represent Erasmus as a pilgrim. The **Salle Blanche** upstairs, once a dormitory, contains valuable first editions, including that of *The Praise of Folly*, and engraved portraits of Erasmus and his contemporaries.

Collégiale des Saints-Pierre-et-Guidon★

Restoration work in progress. Mon-Fri, 9am-noon, 2pm-5.30pm. ☎ 02 521 74 38.

This beautiful Late Gothic collegiate church, dedicated to St Peter and St Guy of Anderlecht, dates from the 14C and the 15C. Its spire dates from the 19C.

Inside, there are traces of frescoes (c 1400) in the Chapelle Notre-Dame-de-Grâce. They illustrate the life of St Guy who died in 1012 and is greatly venerated as the patron saint of peasants and the protector of horses. The late 11C crypt contains the tombstone of St Guy.

Béguinage

This Beguine convent was founded in 1252, partially rebuilt in 1756, and has since been restored.

Musée de la Gueuze-Brasserie Cantillon★

Rue Gheude 56. Mon-Sat. 9am (Sat 10am)-5pm. Closed public holidays. €3. ☎ *02 521 49 28.*
The Beer Museum in the capital's last remaining family brewery gives visitors an insight into the different stages in the production of traditional beers such as *lambic, kriek, gueuze* and *faro*.

NORTH OF THE CENTRE

Koekelberg

Basilique nationale du Sacré-Cœur★

Access to the gallery walkway, dome and panoramic view; daily, 9am-5.15pm (summer) and 10am-4.15pm (winter). €2.50 (child). ☎ *02 425 88 22.*
Building began on the basilica church dedicated to the Sacred Heart in 1905. The church was consecrated in 1951 and finally completed in 1970. The dome of this immense brick, concrete and stone building rises to 90m/295ft above the Koekelberg hill. In the apse stands a huge *Crucifixion* by George Minne.
Inside, the walls are faced with golden-yellow terracotta. They enclose a vast space. The transept is 108m/354ft long. Notice especially the **ciborium** above the high altar. It is surmounted by a calvary and four bronze angels in a kneeling position, executed by Harry Elström. The many **stained-glass windows** diffuse a multi-coloured light. The windows in the nave were based on cartoons by Anto Carte.
It is possible to climb up to the **gallery walkway** and to the top of the **dome**, from where there is a **panoramic view** of Brussels.

Jette

Demeure Abbatiale de Dieleghem

Open early Jan – mid-Dec, Mon-Fri and first weekend of the month, 2-5pm, Closed public holidays. No charge. ☎ *02 476 04 39.*
This residence is all that remains of an 11C abbey; it now houses the small Moreau-Genot collection of fine Brussels, Delft and French 18C and 19C porcelain. The second floor houses the **Musée Communal du Comté de Jette** which traces the history of the town from prehistoric times.

Laeken

Église Notre-Dame-de-Laeken

Tue-Sun. 2-5pm. ☎ *02 478 20 95.* This huge church in neo-Gothic style was begun in 1854 by the architect of the Palais de Justice, Joseph Poelaert. The **crypt** contains the royal family's tombs. *Sun 2-5pm. No charge.* ☎ *02 478 20 95.*
The church also has a much venerated 13C statue of the Virgin Mary. The Gothic chancel of the old church can be seen in the cemetery in addition to the graves of several famous people. Rodin's statue *The Thinker* marks the tomb of Jef Dillens.

Château Royal de Laeken

The royal palace is located in the eastern section *(not open to the public)* of Laeken Park; this is the everyday residence of the Belgian sovereigns, though King Albert II has chosen to remain in the residence by the Belvédère. The façade, rebuilt in 1902 by the architect Girault, can be seen beyond the entrance gates. There is a monument opposite, in the public park, in memory of Leopold I.

Serres royales de Laeken★★

Open for a few days in spring (Apr and May). Dates vary each year. For further details contact: ☎ *02 513 89 40 (Tourist Information Centre).*
The royal greenhouses lie further to the north of the royal estate. Their architectural decor is splendid, and from a botanical point of view they are magnificent, but they are only rarely open to the public. The greenhouses were built towards the end of the 19C by the architect Alphonse Balat. A number of galleries and pavilions containing tropical plants link the two main areas, the Iron Church *(not open to the public)* and the marvellous Winter Garden which is impressive for its sheer size. This veritable palace of glass, iron, cast iron and steel is a bold synthesis of technical and aesthetic prowess.

Pavillon chinois

Tue-Sun. 10am-4.45pm. Closed 1 Jan, 1 May, 1, 11 Nov, 25 Dec. €3, free admission first Wed of the month after 1pm. ☎ *02 268 16 08; www.kmkg-mrah.be*
The elegant Chinese Pavilion (1901-09) opposite the Tour Japonaise was built by the architect Alexandre Marcel. The kiosk and exterior woodwork were made in Shanghai. On the ground floor, note the Delft Room decorated with drawings illustrating La Fontaine's fables. There is a fine collection of Sino-Japanese ware manufactured for export with pieces exhibited in rotation.
An underground passageway running under avenue J-van-Praet links the two buildings.

Basilique du Sacré-Cœur

Tour japonaise

Tue-Sun. 10am-4.45pm. Closed 1 Jan, 1 May, 1, 11 Nov, 25 Dec. €3, free admission first Wed of the month after 1pm. ☎ 02 268 16 08; www.kmkg-mrah.be

The entrance pavilion of this Buddhist pagoda known as the Japanese Tower (1901-04) is the reconstructed porch of the *Tour du Monde* from the 1900 World Fair in Paris. The porch was designed by Alexandre Marcel and bought by Leopold II at the close of the exhibition. The tower and wing housing the main staircase were built in Brussels by the same architect. The architectural decoration was made in Japan. The tower is used as a venue for temporary exhibitions. The nearby **fountain** is a reproduction of the famous *Neptune Fountain* in Bologna by Giambologna.

Heysel

Atomium★

Apr-Sept: 9am-8pm; Oct-Mar: 10am-5.30pm. €6. ☎ 02 475 47 77; www.atomium.be

A survivor of the 1958 World Fair, the 102m/335ft high Atomium dominates the Heysel plateau. It is a symbol of the atomic age, representing a molecule of iron crystal enlarged 165 billion times. The structure, made of steel sheathed in aluminum, consists of nine spheres 18m/59ft in diameter, linked by tubes 29m/95ft long and 3m/10ft in diameter, through which visitors move from one exhibition area to the next.

A lift leads to the uppermost sphere, from which there is a panoramic view of Brussels.

The **Bruparck** lies at the foot of the Atomium. This vast area contains Mini-Europe, the Kinepolis with nearly 30 cinemas, an IMAX auditorium with a 600m²/6 458sq ft screen, the Océade, a water sports complex, and The Village, a group of cafés and restaurants.

The **Palais du Centenaire** can be seen further away to the north in the Parc des Expositions, which was created for the 1935 World Fair.

Mini-Europe

& Apr-Sept: 9.30am-5pm; Jul-Aug: 9.30am-7pm (Fri-Sun 11pm); Oct-Dec: 10am-5pm. €11. ☎ 02 478 05 50; www.minieurope.com

All the countries in the European Union are represented here by 1:25 scale models of buildings with a socio-cultural, historic or symbolic value. They include the

Acropolis, Viking long-houses, the medieval town hall from Leuven, the austere El Escorial monastery outside Madrid, 17C canalside houses from Amsterdam, and the 18C extensions to the English town of Bath designed by John Wood Senior and Junior.

There are also a few contemporary creations in the park, such as the Ariane rocket, the French TGV high-speed train and a jumbo-ferry.

Excursions

WATERLOO
19km/11.75mi S.
Leave by W on the plan.19km/11.75mi S. Leave by W on the plan. For a description, see WATERLOO.

BEERSEL
14 km S
This market town has a splendid brick **castle** built between 1300 and 1310. It has been restored to its former glory using engravings depicting it as it was in the 17C. With its sentry-walks, watch-towers and crow-stepped gables reflected in the waters of its moat, it is a romantic-looking place. *Open late Mar – mid-Nov: Tue-Sun 10am-noon, 2pm-6pm; late Nov – late Feb: Sat, Sun 10am-noon, 2pm-6pm. Closed Jan. €2.50.* ☎ *02 331 00 24.*

ALSEMBERG
14km/9mi S.
Built in the 14C-16C in Late Gothic style, the **Église Notre-Dame** perches atop a hill in this commune which forms part of Bersel. The church was extensively restored by J and M van Ysendijck at the end of the 19C. Besides the Romanesque fonts (13C), the Rococo chancel and an imposing pulpit, the church also features a miraculous statuette of the Virgin Mary dating from c 1200.

The **Papiermolen Herisem** at Fabriekstraat 20 on the edge of the community of Dworp in the Molenbeek Valleyis an old paper mill dating back to 1536. In 1763 it became the property of the Winderickx family, who converted it into a cardboard factory. After 50 years of inactivity, the complex has recently been restored and is now open to the public. Thanks to the demonstrations, visitors can see how paper and cardboard were once made. *Mar-Nov: daily except Wed. 10am-4pm, first and third weekend of the month 10am-6pm. Closed public holidays. €4.46.* ☎ *02 381 07 70.*

HUIZINGEN
16km/10mi S.
The **Recreatiecentrum van het Provinciaal Domein** is a recreation area covering 90ha/220 acres. It is carefully maintained, and it constitutes a real oasis of greenery in the heart of a heavily industrialised region. ♿ *Apr-Sept: 9am-8pm (Nov-Jan 5pm; Feb, Oct 6pm; Mar 7pm). €2.48.* ☎ *02 383 00 20.*

GAASBEEK
12km/7.5mi SW.

Château et parc de Gaasbeek★★
Apr-Oct: open Tue-Thur, Sat, Sun. Jul-Aug also Mon. 10am-6pm. €2.50. ☎ *02 531 01 30.*
The castle in Gaasbeek, which stands on the edge of undulating grounds, was extensively restored in the late 19C and now houses a fascinating museum. The whole estate was bequeathed to the State by its owner in 1921, and has belonged to the Flemish community since 1981. The famous Count of Egmont spent the last three years of his life here.

The **museum** has fine furniture, paintings, numerous antiquities and magnificent **tapestries** (15C Tournai, 16C and 17C Brussels), some of them depicting the five episodes in the story of Tobias (main staircase). The Archives Room contains Rubens' will. The view over the surrounding countryside from the terrace is reminiscent of the works of Pieter Bruegel the Elder. Breugel was a frequent visitor to this part of the world (known as the Payottenland), and painted the area around St-Anna-Pede more than once; the village church can be seen in one of his paintings.

MEISE
14km/8.75mi N.

Plantentuin★★
♿ *9am-5pm (Nov-Mar 4pm). Closed 1 Jan, 25 Dec. €4.* ☎ *02 260 09 70; www.br.fgov.be*
Meise is famous for the Bouchot Estate, the home of the Botanical Gardens. The grounds are laid out with scientific precision, dense woodland areas alternating with lawns, lakes and remarkable individual trees. The variety of the collections means that there is always something to enjoy whatever the season. In the **Plantenpaleis** a waymarked route leads through the world of tropical and subtropical plants. Do not miss the "Victoria Greenhouse" with its "artists' palettes". Empress Charlotte, sister of Leopold II and widow of Maximilian, Emperor of Mexico, died in the castle which now houses temporary exhibitions. With its crenellated towers reflected in the calm waters of the old moat it is a particularly picturesque sight.

GRIMBERGEN
16km/10mi N.
Follow A 12 as far asMeise, then turn right.

Église Abbatiale des Prémontrés
The Premonstratensian minster is one of the finest examples of Baroque architecture and ornamentation in Belgium (1660-1725), though it was never completed. The chancel is very long and extends into a square tower. The interior owes its majestic proportions to the height of the vaulting and of the cupola. It still has its sumptuous furnishings, most notably four **confessionals★** carved with alternating allegories and characters from the Old and New Testament by the Antwerp sculptor Hendrik Frans Verbruggen. There are fine 17C **stalls**. The church also contains 15 paintings by Flemish old masters (17C-18C).
The **main sacristy** (1763) north of the chancel is decorated with remarkable panelling. The fresco and *grisaille* on the ceiling are dedicated to St Norbert, founder of the Order.
There are lovely 17C paintings in the small vestry.

ZAVENTEM
10km/6.25mi E.
Leave by Chaussée de Louvain, then turn left.

St-Martinus
The church dedicated to St Martin houses a fine painting by Van Dyck, *St Martin Dividing His Cloak*.

Tour

FORÊT DE SOIGNES★★
59km/37mi SE. Leave by ③ on the plan.

Tervuren★
Lying to the northeast of the Forêt de Soignes, **Tervuren Park★** was once a highly prized area for hunting; its attraction now lies in its carefully tended lawns and beautiful lakes. From the 13C to the 19C it saw a glorious succession of castles, manor houses and gardens.
Main entrance to the park for those in cars via place de l'Église.

Koninklijk Museum voor Midden-Afrika★★ (Musée royal de l'Afrique centrale)
Car park on Leuvensesteenweg ⚹ Tue-Sun. 10am-5pm (Sat, Sun 6pm). Closed 1 Jan, 1 May, 25 Dec. €4. ☏ 02 769 52 11; www.africamuseum.be
The Royal Museum of Central Africa originated in 1897 when King Leopold II of Belgium organised an exhibition in the Palais Colonial on the Congo, featuring the flora, fauna, art and ethnology of those faraway lands. It was such a success that it became a permanent museum, for which the architect Girault constructed the current building with its Louis XVI façade from 1904 to 1910.
The museum collections present a vast panoramic overview of Africa. The sculptures and other ethnographic exhibits represent various ethnic groups and, in particular, the two main centres of production of this form of artistic expression: Central Africa, especially the former Belgian Congo, and West Africa. The museum is also a centre for basic scientific research into the African continent.
Tour – Enter through the **rotunda**, from which there is a fine view of the park. The **great gallery** and a number of rooms leading off it to the right contain a remarkable selection of African objects and works of art. In the gallery to the left of the rotunda the collections are displayed thematically (hunting, agriculture, craftmanship or social events, such as marriage or death); in the gallery to the right the objects are arranged geographically (Congo, North Angola, Rwanda and Burundi). There is a variety of amazing sculptures in wood, ivory, stone and metal (especially in Room 4). There is also a marvellously rich collection of jewels and accessories (Room 6). The rest of the tour provides interesting glimpses of Africa's colonial history (Livingstone and Stanley have a place of honour among the great explorers), the African mountain landscape of Ruwenzori at various altitudes, and the region's zoology (enormous dioramas), geology and mineralogy.
Return to the centre of Tervuren and follow the signs to the Arboretum.

Arboretum
Open sunrise to sunset. Walks restricted to paths and lawns. No charge. ☏ 02 769 20 81.
Tervuren's geographical arboretum, created in 1902, takes up part of the woodland known as the Bois des Capucins. It is divided into two sections focusing on the New and Old World. Tree species include those from temperate climates, classified by region: oaks, elms, ashes, birches and coniferous trees, along with a few tropical varieties.
Note the huge conifers from the Pacific coast of North America (sequoias and Douglas firs).

Jezus-Eik

Walkers often stop at the "Jesus-Oak", known to French-speakers as Notre-Dame-au-Bois ("Our Lady in the Wood"), to rest a little and enjoy *une tartine au fromage blanc* – a slice of bread spread with soft white cheese and flavoured with onions and radishes.

Forêt de Soignes/Zoniënwoud★★

This superb forest extends over an area of 4 380ha/10 823 acres. It was once part of the ancient **charcoal-burners' forest** in the area west of the Ardennes forests, in which charcoal was produced in Roman times. Magnificent beech trees grow thickly in this rolling countryside which once echoed with the cries of hunters. Deep in the valleys, there are many traces of abbeys and their estates. One such valley is **Groenendael**, in a beautifully romantic **setting**★ dotted with lakes, famous from the 14C to the 18C for its abbey. The great mystic **Jan van Ruusbroec**, also called "The Admirable", lived here during the 14C. Away from the main roads, there are many attractive footpaths and bridle paths as well as a number of cycle routes.

La Hulpe

Stately homes and castles are widely scattered across the hills in this area. The 220ha/544 acre **Domaine Solvay**, an estate which once belonged to the family of the industrialist Solvay, was bequeathed to the State.

The magnificent **park**★★ dotted with lakes is overlooked by a **château** dating from 1840, which has been converted into an arts centre. *Park open 8am-9pm (winter 6pm). Free.* ☎ *02 653 64 04.* Further away, the home farm now houses the **Fondation Folon**★. It has been converted in a remarkable way to form a setting for a selection of some of the finest works kept in his possession by the artist Jean-Michel Folon (b 1934). *Tue-Sun 10am-6pm (last admission 5pm). €7.44.* ☎ *02 653 34 56.*

Lac de Genval

The people of Brussels often come to this lake at the weekend. The stretch of water is large enough to accommodate a variety of water sports. The wooded areas on the shores of the lake are a lovely setting for walks.

Château de Rixensart

Open mid-Apr – end Sept: guided tour (40 min) Sun 2-6pm. €4. ☎ *02 653 65 05.*

This is an impressive 17C square brick building in Renaissance style, with turrets at the corners.

The estate has belonged to the Mérode family for over a century; one of the family, Félix de Mérode, was a member of the 1830 provisional government. One of his daughters married Charles Montalembert, the famous French Catholic writer. Inside, there are beautiful tapestries (Beauvais, Gobelins), French paintings (Valentin, Nattier) and a collection of weapons brought back from the Egyptian campaign by the French mathematician Monge.

16km/10mi S.

Canal du CENTRE

The Canal du Centre was constructed between 1882 and 1917 to link the Meuse basin with that of the Scheldt and create a direct line of communication between Germany and France. The greatest problem was reducing the 90m/295ft difference in height between the two basins. This was finally resolved by the building of four canal lifts and six locks, all of which are still operational. In 1998 this magnificent example of industrial archeology was placed on UNESCO's World Heritage List.

Location

Hainaut – Michelin maps 716 F4 and 534 J20.
From Mons or Brussels take E 19, then follow signs
🛈 *Place Mansart 17, 7100 La Louvière,* ☎ *064 33 37 21; canal-du-centre.voies-hydrauliques.wallonie.be*

Background

The old hydraulic lifts – These beautiful metal structures were designed by a London firm, built in the Cockerill works, and put in place between 1888 and 1917. The principle is very simple: the barges enter two basins filled with water, one at the upper level of the canal, one at the lower. The two basins, fixed to enormous pistons, constitute a sort of huge pair of scales. The pistons slide along two cylinders filled with water, linked together by a pipe. The addition of extra water into the upper basin causes it to sink, while the principle of communicating vessels makes the other one rise.

> **Le Faitout** – *Av. Louis Goblet 161 – 7331 Baudour –* ☎ *065 64 48 57 – closed Mon and Tue eves – €24/26.* A pleasant place to stop off for a meal after a visit to the canal du Centre. A traditional menu features grills from the wood fire. Tables outside on fine summer days.

The new canal – From 1957 it became compulsory for major Belgian canals to accommodate barges of the European standard of 1 350t. The canal here was given a new course and the hydraulic lifts and locks were replaced by the Strépy-Thieu boat lift.

Worth a visit

Strépy-Thieu boat lift

Jul-Aug: Mon-Sat and public holidays, 9.30am-6.30pm (last admission 5pm); May-Oct: 9.30pm-6.30pm. €5. ☎ *064 67 12 00.*
Inside the lift, an audiovisual presentation gives a good idea of the scale and technical details of the project as it was finally carried out. Recently opened to navigation, the scheme chosen to resolve the problem of the 73.25m/240ft difference in height in the canal's new course has imposing dimensions: a height of 110m/361ft,

The boat lift

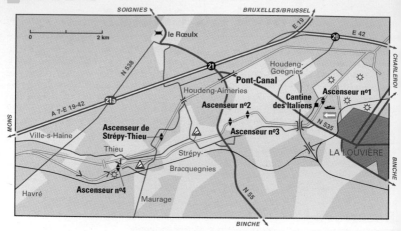

length of 130m/426ft, and width of 75m/246ft. The weight transferred to the ground can reach 300 000t. Two steel tanks measuring 112m/367ft by 12m/39ft, suspended by cables and balanced by counterweights, can move up or down independently in 6-7min. It takes a barge of up to 1 350t only 40min to negotiate the change in level. The old lifts and locks which the new lift has replaced could only take vessels of up to 300t and needed 5 hrs to move them from one level to the other, compared with the current 2 hrs.

At the top of the lift, the **Pays des Génies** display celebrates Belgian figures who have made a special contribution to the country's culture, economy, or sporting prestige. No one who has been here will ever have difficulty in answering the fatuous and all-too-frequent challenge to name '10 famous Belgians'.

From level 3 there is a fine **view** of the canal in its surroundings.

Boat trips

Allow 2hr for the trip; departure from the Cantine des Italiens or Strépy-Bracquenies. May-Oct: Sat 10am-2pm, Sun 10am-4pm (Jul-Aug, daily). ☎ *064 66 25 61.*

This pleasant trip along the old tree-lined canal gives an insight into the life of canal folk. The boat passes through some of the lifts as well as past turning or lifting bridges worked by bridgemen and lock-keepers. One of the landing stages is near the **Cantine des Italiens**, living quarters built in 1945 for Italian coal miners. The trip on lifts nos 2 and 3 shows exactly how these lifts work. In the machine room on the right bank near lift no 3, visitors can see how water is raised under high pressure and stored in the two towers to work the entrance gates to the lift, provide a watertight junction between the canal and the basin and operate the pistons.

The return journey is made on a little tourist train running along the towpath, giving a different view of the lifts.

Charleroi

The heavy industries which made Charleroi one of the powerhouses of the national economy may have declined, but busy streets, a lively atmosphere, and a spirited population make the old capital of Belgium's "Pays Noir" (Black Country) a place of more than passing interest. Two districts lie at the heart of the sprawling city: the upper town with town hall and belfry and, to the south, the lower town, the commercial district, standing on what was once an islet in the River Sambre, one branch of which has been filled in.

Location

Hainaut – Population 202 020 (conurbation) – Michelin maps 716 G4 and 534 L20. Town plan in the current edition of The Red Guide Benelux.

At the junction of the N 90 and the N 5, Charleroi also has good motorway connections, with the interchange just to the N of the town of the east-west E 42 with the A 54 to Brussels.

🛈 *Avenue Mascaux 100* ☎ *071 86 61 52; www.charleroi.be*

Background

A military past – In 1666 the government of the Spanish Low Countries, worried by the expansionist ambitions of the French under Louis XIV, had the village of Charnoy turned into a fortress; in homage to the Spanish king Charles II, it was renamed Charleroy. Nevertheless, the French succeeded in capturing it the following year; their great military engineer Vauban strengthened the ramparts of the upper town, then built the lower town to maintain economic activity. Industry (glass works) was attracted to the region because of the availability of coal. Charleroi became the prize at stake in many a hard fought battle until 1868, when the ramparts were turned into boulevards. The town was captured by the French revolutionary army in 1794 and subsequently served as a base in the Napoleonic wars.

In August 1914, one of the opening battles of the First World War took place here when, despite fierce resistance, the French failed to prevent the German army from crossing the Sambre on their westward march.

Industry – It was the presence of abundant reserves of coal that drew industry to the area. Glassmaking led the way, from 1577 onwards, followed by metalworking (foundries, nail-making, wire and rolled sheet metal). This sector underwent rapid expansion from the early 19C. Nowadays, the iron, steel and glass industries are still very much present, but manufacturing has diversified into electrical, electro-mechanical, chemical, pharmaceutical, printing and other industries. Two institutes of higher education train specialised technicians and engineers.

The Charleroi-Brussels canal links the navigable River Sambre to the Scheldt via Brussels and the Canal Maritime. From Charleroi, the Sambre flows east to meet the Meuse at Namur.

On parade – Countless wars have been fought over the region to the south of Charleroi between the rivers Sambre and Meuse, and its towns and villages retain many martial memories. The area features prominently in the Belgian calendar of traditional events, because of the military marches that have been held here since the 17C.

The marches probably hark back to the troubled days of the Reformation, when church processions were flanked by armed rural militias. Despite their military appearance, the events are organised in honour of a local patron saint.

On the saint's feast day a veritable army in miniature parades through the streets, sometimes escorting the statue of the saint. The "sappers" come first, then the drum corps, the fifes and the brass band. Then come the soldiers armed with guns, firing volleys into the air, accompanied by soldiers on horseback and even army victuallers. Forbidden by the French Revolutionaries, the parades were revived under Napoleon, and the uniforms worn date from this period.

About 40 towns organise military processions. The St Roch procession at **Ham-sur-Heure** includes more than 700 people, among them the "Mons Volunteers of the 1789 Brabant Revolution".

The military march in Ham-sur-Heure

The longest procession, covering a distance of 35km/28mi and involving 5 000 people, is in **Gerpinnes**. The small **Musée des Marches Folkloriques de l'Entre-Sambre-et-Meuse** in the village displays the marchers' military costumes. The **Fosses-la-Ville** procession is as infrequent as it is splendid, taking place only once every seven years.

Apart from the marches in the area between the Sambre and the Meuse, the Mary Magdalene procession in **Jumet** *(4km/2.5mi N of Charleroi)* is interesting too. This is the oldest procession in all of Wallonia, dating back to the year 1380. It is outstanding for the wide variety of costumes.

Directory

WHERE TO EAT

⌣ **La Vignerale** – *Avenue J.Henin 5 –* ☎ *071 31 32 27 – lunch only –* ⊟ *– €24/27.* Close to Square Hiernaux, this is a attractive little non-smoking restaurant linked to a wine merchant's. Traditional dishes complemented by no fewer than 400 different wines at extremely reasonable prices.

⌣⊟ **Piccolo Mondo** – *Grand'Rue 87 –* ☎ *071 42 00 17 – €9 lunch – €26.* Representing in great style the Italian presence in Charleroi, the lady owner of this establishment prepares her pasta according to a secret recipe.

Worth a Visit

THE UPPER TOWN

Hôtel de Ville

The town hall and its 70m/230ft belfry were built in 1936 to designs by Joseph André and Jules Cézar. The town hall features a splendid Art Deco interior and houses two museums.

Musée des Beaux-Arts – *Second floor of the town hall.* The Fine Arts Museum contains several pictures by **Francois-Joseph Navez**, a native of Charleroi and a student of David. The daily life of workers is evoked in paintings by Constantin Meunier and Pierre Paulus. The collections include works by Magritte and Delvaux as well as by local artists. The premises are also used to host temporary exhibitions. *Open Tue-Sun 9am-12.30pm, 1.15-5pm (Sat 6pm), Sun 10am-12.30pm, 1.15-6pm during exhibitions. Closed Sun (except during exhibitions) and public holidays. No charge, €4 during exhibitions.* ☎ *071 86 11 36; www.charleroi-museum.org*

Musée Jules-Destrée – *Upper floor of the town hall.* The multi-facetted career of the statesman, lawyer and socialist writer **Jules Destrée** is richly illustrated through a host of documents, early photographs, drawings, paintings and personal mementoes. A dedicated Walloon federalist, in 1912 he sent a famous letter to King Albert I on what he considered to be the irreconcilable divide between Wallonia and Flanders, in which he announced: "Sire, there are no more Belgians". *Open Tue-Sat (also Sun, Mon for temporary exhibitions). Permanent collections 9am-12.30pm, 1.15-5pm. Closed 1-2 Jan, Shrove Tuesday, Easter, 1 May, Ascension, Whitsun, 21 Jul, 15 Aug, 1-2 Nov, 25-26 Dec.* ☎ *071 86 11 38.*

Place du Manège

Part of the town's colourful Sunday market is held on this huge square, flanked by the Palais des Expositions (1954) and the Palais des Beaux-Arts, (used as a venue for exhibitions, concerts and various stage performances).

Excursions

Bois du Cazier industrial site

3km/2mi S. Access by A 54 or R 3, then on A 503 to exit 34 Marcinelles Haies. www.boisducazier.be

A metal gateway forms the entrance to this old colliery with its waste tips, winding gear, and array of industrial buildings. The **Espace du 8 août 1956★★** commemorates the 262 miners from 12 nationalities who perished in an underground fire at the St-Charles pit on 8 August 1956. One of Belgiums' worst-ever mining disasters, it is movingly evoked by photographs and interviews. The memorial also gives an insight into the Italian immigration into the coalfield and the working conditions in the mines. The **Musée de l'Industrie** illus-

> #### SPIROU
> In 1938 the comic strip *Spirou* was created in Marcinelle, a suburb of Charleroi. It was the work of first-rate writers, designers and draughtsmen, among them the Frenchman Robert Velter, alias Rob Bel; Jijé, the pen-name of Joseph Gillian; Morris and Roba; and André Franquin, the inventor of Marsupilami.

trates the rich industrial past of Wallonia. Among the most important items in the impressive collection of machinery is a steam engine of 1913 from the Zimmerman-Hanrez works and a rolling mill of 1883 from the old Anhée factory. The museum gives a fascinating account of the evolution of modern technology and of the way in which society has developed in the post-industrial age. The blue tiled changing rooms and baths plunge the visitor into the daily life of the "gueules noirs" (black faces), as the miners were known.

Mont-sur-Marchienne

3km/1.75mi S. Access via the Porte de la Villette exit on the ring road, or the Mont-sur-Marchienne exit on the R 3 ring road.

The **Musée de la Photographie**★ is housed in a neo-Gothic Carmelite convent. The history of photography is presented in the rooms surrounding the old cloisters. The visitor can follow the development of this art from its beginnings through the changes in equipment (from the camera obscura and daguerreotype to holography) and photographic style. Work by the world's greatest photographers illustrates this development. The museum aims to be a "living" institution, and has a library of more than 2 000 volumes on photography. It also organises temporary exhibitions of exceptional quality throughout the year. ♿ *Tue-Sun. 10am-6pm. Closed 1 Jan, 25 Dec. €3.72.* ☎ *071 43 58 10.*

© Library of Congress, Washington/Collection Musée de la Photographie à Charleroi

Dorothea Lange: Migrant Mother, Nipomo, California, 1936.

Chimay★

Little Chimay is famous for its Trappist beer and its castle, of which there is a lovely view from the bridge over the river known as the Eau Blanche, for the 14C chronicler Froissart, and for a celebrated beauty, Mme Tallien (1773-1835), the 'Princess of Chimay'. Of Spanish origin, this lady led a tempestuous life: having married a French aristocrat, she narrowly escaped the guillotine in the Revolution, then, after her jailer fell in love with her, became involved in the downfall of Robespierre. Finally she made what was her third marriage, to François-Joseph de Caraman, Prince of Chimay, and spent the rest of her days in the tranquillity of his castle.

Location

Hainaut – Population 9 755 – Michelin maps 716 G 5 or 534 K 22.
In a well-wooded setting, Chimay is close to the border with France at the southern end of the oddly-shaped stretch of Belgian territory known as the "Hainaut Boot".

Directory

WHERE TO EAT

☺☺☺ **Chez Edgard et Madeleine** – *Rue du Lac 35 – 6461 Virelles – ☎ 060 21 10 71 – Closed Mon eve, Wed (exc public holidays) – €42/51.* In an ideal location overlooking Virelles lake, this traditional inn has been pleasing discerning palates for four generations with its regional cuisine A number of dishes make good use of the town's Trappist beer.

WHERE TO STAY

☺☺ **Franc Bois** – *Courtil aux Martias 18 – 6463 Lompret – ☎ 060 21 44 75 – francbois@swing.be – 8 rms: ⌂ €69/74.* After your exploration of the fresh and charming valley of the Eau Blanche you will be able to sleep the sleep of the just in this pretty establishment built from the local stone. Contemporary, very comfortable rooms and cosy lounge.

Worth a Visit

Château

  Mar-Dec. Guided tour. €5. ☎ *060 21 28 23.*

The medieval castle passed into the ownership of the ancestors of the Prince de Chimay in the 15C. It was partly destroyed by a fire in 1935 and rebuilt according to old plansin late Renaissance style. Its bluish grey limestone façade lies at the end of a vast esplanade.

Inside, there is a drawing room with a terrace dropping 16m/53ft to the river. Two portraits recall Mme Tallien, one by Gerard, the other painted when she was older. In 1863 her first son Joseph had the charming Rococo-style theatre built and richly decorated with gilded stuccowork. A copy of the theatre in the royal palace of Fontainebleau to the southeast of Paris, it welcomed many an operatic celebrity to its stage.

The chapel with its delightful surbased vaulting contains a number of the banners of the French King Louis XI, who captured Chimay in 1477. A small room in the castle has a range of Napoleonic memorabilia.

Collégiale des Saints-Pierre-et-Paul

8am-6pm. ☎ *060 21 12 38.*

Extended in the 16C, this church built of freestone still has its beautiful 13C chancel. In it is a remarkable recumbent effigy of Charles de Croÿ, Chamberlain and godfather to Emperor Charles V (d 1552), as well as four plaques in memory of illustrious lords of Chimay. Note also the interesting 17C choir stalls and a triumphal cross (c 1550). The first chapel on the south side upon entering the church contains the Latin epitaph of the chronicler Froissart who was also a canon in Chimay and died there in 1410.

On the town squarae there is a monument with figures of the Chimay family. They include Mme Tallien and her husband, who wears a cape.

Excursions

Étang de Virelles★

3km/1.75mi NE. May-Sept: nature reserve 10am-6pm; Guided tours first and third Sun of the month (2hr) 10am, 3pm. Easter opening in good weather; ring for details. €2.50. ☎ *071 38 17 61.*

This nature reserve covers an area of 100ha/247 acres. The popular lake is surrounded by woods and is the largest natural stretch of water in Belgium. Leisure facilities include restaurants, pedalo hire and a children's adventure playground.

Abbaye Notre-Dame-de-Scourmont

10km/6mi S via Bourlers. Founded in 1850, the abbey is now a Trappist monastery. The austere buildings flank a central courtyard overlooked by the stark façade (1949) of the church.

It is here that the renowned **beer** known as *Trappiste de Chimay* is made.

Couvin

Charming Couvin's leafy riverbanks are lined with attractive slate-roofed buildings. Overlooking town and river – the Eau Noire – is a limestone crag on which a castle stood until its destruction by the French in 1672. In fine walking country among hills and woods, and with rivers well-stocked with fish, Couvin is a popular holiday place, proud of its gastronomic reputation and its local specialities; chicken '*à la Couvinoise*' and *escavèche*, a fried fish dish.

Location

Namur – Population 13 193 – Michelin maps 716 G5 and 534 L22.

Couvin is on N 5 between Philippeville and the French border and N 99 from Chimay.

🛈 *Rue de la Falaise 3,* ☎ *060 34 01 40; www.couvin.be*

See also CHIMAY.

Worth a visit

Cavernes de l'Abîme

Apr-Oct: guided tours, Sat, Sun and public holidays 10am-noon, 1.30-6pm; early Jul-mid-Sept: 10am-noon, 1.30-6pm. €4.34 (combined ticket including the Grottes de Neptune: €8.92). ☎ 071 55 88 11; www.abime.be

These caves were once inhabited by prehistoric people and were also used as a refuge during the Roman period and the Middle Ages. An audio-visual presentation on Belgian prehistory is shown in one of the most impressive caves. A small museum complements the visit. There is a delightful view of Couvin from the top of the steps outside. Couvin is on N 5 between Philippeville and the French border and N 99 from Chimay.

Tour

LES TROIS VALLÉES (THREE VALLEYS)

17km/11mi West. Take N 99, then left in Petigny.

Grottes de Neptune★

5km/3.25mi from Couvin. Apr-Sept: Guided tours (45min) 10.30-noon, 1.30-6pm. €6.82. ☎ 071 55 88 11; www.grottesneptune.be

The River Eau Noire, so called because of the black rocks lining its bed, disappears underground in the Adugeoir chasm before resurfacing near Nismes. Three tiers of galleries are open to the public with beautiful, well displayed rock formations. While the Eau Noire has not flowed through the upper gallery for centuries, it still fills the middle gallery when in spate. A pleasant boat trip takes visitors along the subterranean river in the lower gallery and gives them an opportunity to admire a spectacular **waterfall**. The end of the trip is enhanced by an exceptional *son et lumière* show.

Return to Pétigny, take N 99 again and turn left towards Nismes.

Nismes

After flowing through the Grottes de Neptune, the Eau Noire reappears above ground here and flows into the Eau Blanche to form the Viroin. Nismes is a popular summer holiday resort. There are many geological curiosities in the surrounding limestone area, including the **Fondry des Chiens** (*access by rue Orgeveau*), the most impressive of the twisting abysses bristling with monoliths dotted across the plateau east of the town. There is also a beautiful view of the surrounding countryside from here.

Mariembourg

This little town is named after **Mary of Hungary**, Governor of the Low Countries, who had it built in 1542. The geometrically laid out town was fortified (the walls have now totally disappeared) and faced the Maubert-Fontaine fortress on French territory opposite. Mariembourg was reputed to be impregnable, but was captured in 1554 by the French, forcing Emperor Charles V to create a new citadel, Philippeville. Mariembourg was recaptured by the Spanish in 1559 and then handed over to the French a century later. It remained French until 25 July 1815, the date on which the town's defenders were forced to capitulate to the Prussians, although they were granted the "honours of war" for their courage.

Mariembourg is the departure point of the **Chemin de Fer des Trois Vallées**, a tourist train that runs as far as Treignes via the picturesque **Viroin Valley**. It also goes through the Eau Blanche Valley on its way to Chimay. *Apr-Oct: Sat, Sun and public holidays (July-Aug daily) 10am-8pm. €7 round trip. ☎ 060 31 24 40.*

LE PAYS DES RIÈZES ET DES SARTS

20km/12mi S.

The Rièzes and Sarts country consists of marshy heaths and woodland stretching along the border with France. The otherwise infertile rièzes provide grazing and the area is known for its cheese and butter.

Take N 5 towards Rocroi, then N 964 and a turning to Brûly-de-Pesche.

Brûly-de-Pesche

In a wood near a spring, on the site of a traditional pilgrimage in honour of St Méen, is **Hitler's Bunker**. Hitler used it as his general headquarters from 6 June to 4 July 1940, directing the French campaign from here together with his staff. The small concrete bunker was built in great haste. *Apr-Sept, daily, 10.30am-6pm (last admission 5pm); Oct: Sat, Sun at same times. €2.97. ☎ 060 34 01 40 (low season) or 060 37 80 38 (high season).*

Damme★

This pretty but rather melancholy little place stretches out in a wonderfully leafy setting along the canal known as the Dammse Vaart. Popular with lovers of books and good food, it gets very busy at weekends; Damme is something of a 'book town', with a number of bookshops and a book fair every second Sunday of the month.

Location
West-Vlaanderen – Population 11 010 – Michelin maps 716 C2 and 533 E15.
Damme is close to both Bruges (7km/4mi to the S) and the coast. It is easy to get here from Bruges via Damport and then the Daamse Vaart.
🚹 *Huyse de Grote Sterre, Jacob van Maerlandtstraat 3, ☎ 050 35 33 19; www.damme-online.com*

Damme.

Background

On the estuary of the River Zwin, Damme served as Bruges' outport and owed its prosperity to the city whose history is so closely linked with its own. All sorts of merchandise passed through here, though Damme specialised in wine and herrings. In 1340, in the course of the Hundred Years War, the French fleet assembled at the mouth of the Zwin in preparation for an invasion of England, was destroyed in a suprise attack by a far smaller English force. In 1468, the marriage of Charles the Bold and Margaret of York was celebrated here with great pomp and ceremony; however, with the silting-up of the Zwin, the harbour became useless and Damme shared in the decline of Bruges.

One of the earliest Flemish writers, **Jacob van Maerlant** (probably between 1221-35 to late 13C) came from here, as did **Thyl Uylenspiegel**, the hero of the picaresque novel (1867) by **Charles de Coster**.

Worth a Visit

Stadhuis★
Jul-Aug, 10am-noon, 2pm-6pm. €0.99. ☎ 050 28 86 10 (Tourist Information Centre).
In Brabant Gothic style, the town hall dates from the 15C. The local market used to be held on the ground floor.
The fine façade, with its watch turrets and flight of steps, is decorated with charming 19C statues. In a niche is a statue of Charles the Bold offering a wedding ring to his fiancée, Margaret of York.
The interior has retained its magnificent carved beams. One of the figures is said to represent Jacob van Maerlant. A statue of the great medieval writer can be seen opposite the town hall.

Directory

Huyse de Grote Sterre

This picturesque twin-gabled 15C building (the "Great Star") by the town hall was almost completely rebuilt in the 1990s. It now houses the tourist information centre and the Maerlant-Uilenspiegel Literary Museum. The museum is largely devoted to the way in which the figure of Uilenspiegel developed over time, from outlaw to the popular hero of Charles De Coster's novel. *Mid-Apr – mid-Oct: 9am-noon, 1.30pm-6pm, Sat, Sun 10am-noon, 2-6pm; mid-Oct – mid-Apr: 9am-noon, 1-5pm, Sat, Sun 2-5pm. Closed 1 Jan, 25 Dec. €2.48. ☎ 050 28 06 10.*

Onze-Lieve-Vrouwekerk

Apr-Sept: 10.30-noon, 2.30-5.30. €0.50 (church), €1 (tower). ☎ 050 28 86 10 (Tourist Information Centre).

The church dates from the 13C and 14C. The apse, between the flat chevets of the two side chapels, has beautiful lancet windows. In the early 17C, when the harbour silted up and the town's population fell, it was decided that the church was too big, and the nave was demolished. The ruins still feature a gallery with Tournai-style triplet windows.

A series of late 13C wooden statues of the Apostles can be seen inside. Note also the Baroque altarpiece in the north aisle, and a statue of *Christ of Miracles* which is carried in religious processions such as the one dedicated to the Holy Blood in Bruges.

The tall square **tower★**, which has lost its spire, is most imposing. It overlooks a charming little square shaded by lime trees and flanked by the high roofs of the Hospital of St John. There is a **view** of the town from the top of the tower. Earth mounds mark the location of the 17C fortifications, long since demolished. The coast can be seen in clear weather.

St-Janshospital

Apr-Sept, daily (except Mon, Fri) 11am-noon, 2-6pm; Oct-Mar: as before (closes 4.30 Sat, Sun). Closed 1 Jan, 25 Dec. €1.50. ☎ 050 46 10 80.

The Hospital of St John was founded in the 13C, then later extended and turned into a hospice. The chapel and **museum** are open to the public.

The museum contains collections of furniture, paintings, faience, liturgical objects and sculptures (statuette of St Margaret of Antioch), testifying to the rich past of both the hospital and the town.

De Schellemolen

Jul-Aug: 10am-noon, 1-6pm; Jun, Sept, Sat 2-6pm, Sun and public holidays 10am-noon, 1-6pm. No charge. ☎ 056 25 49 74.

This mill on the banks of the canal has been restored and is in working order.

Dendermonde★

Dendermonde lies in what was once a strategic position at the confluence of the River Dender and the Scheldt; the town's name means 'mouth of the Dender'. Louis XIV was forced to abandon his siege of the town in 1667 because the defenders had flooded the surrounding countryside. "Accursed town!" he cried, "I would need an army of ducks to capture you!"

Location

Oost-Vlaanderen – Population 42 994 – Michelin maps 716 F2 and 533 J16.
Dendermonde is at the centre of the triangle formed by Ghent, Brussels and Antwerp. Access by N 17, N 41 or N 47.
🛈 *Stadhuis, Grote Markt,* ☎ *052 21 39 56; www.dendermonde.be*

WHERE TO EAT

Arte Shock – *Guldenhoofdstraat 2 –* ☎ *052 22 34 47 – info@arteshock.be –* *Closed Mon, Tue, Sat lunchtime – €34.* From the Grote Markt, a lane leads to this little restaurant in a 14C building. Contemporary cuisine, up to date decor and trendy atmosphere. Outdoor dining in summer.

Worth a Visit

Grote Markt

The square still retains its old charm even though part of it has been rebuilt. Two major buildings command attention.

Stadhuis – This former cloth market, now the town hall, was rebuilt in Flemish Renaissance style after the First World War. All that remained of the original was the square 14C belfry with its corner turrets.

There is a pretty view of the Dender (Oude Dender) from behind the Stadhuis.

Vleeshuismuseum – The municipal museum is located in the former meat market of 1460 with its octagonal tower. Collections evoking the town's archeology and history are exhibited in this fascinating medieval setting. ♿ *Tue-Fri 2pm-5.30pm, Sat, Sun and public holidays 10am-noon, 2pm-5pm. Closed 1 Jan, 25-26 Dec. €2.50.* ☎ *09 381 96 70.*

Onze-Lieve-Vrouwekerk★★

Jul-Aug: 10am-4.30pm; mid-Apr – end Sept, Sat, Sun 2-4.30pm. ☎ *052 21 39 56 (Tourist Information Centre).*
The church dedicated to Our Lady stands on a square surrounded by chestnut trees that can be seen from the rear of the museum. It was built in the 13C and 14C, and is surmounted by an octagonal tower above the transept crossing which is a blend of Gothic, Brabant and Scaldian styles.

There is a beautiful collection of **works of art★** inside. Note the Romanesque font in the south aisle, in blue Tournai stone. The sides are decorated with symbolic pictures on the subject of baptism. The main events in the life of St Paul the Apostle are on the two friezes. He is depicted among the other Apostles on one side of the basin. Two works by Van Dyck can be seen nearby, a Crucifixion scene and a painting depicting the Adoration of the Shepherds.

LOCAL FOLKLORE

Every year the town organises a parade of giants, but Dendermonde is most famous for its 10-yearly pageant led by Bayard the horse, ridden by the four Aymon sons *(see p. 51)*. Legend has it that the famous horse was drowned here in the Scheldt on Charlemagne's orders.

The north transept and chancel still have 15C and 17C wall paintings.

Begijnhof

Access via Brusselsestraat then turn right. Tall 17C houses encircle the inner courtyard of this Beguin convent. There are small **museums** at nos 11, 24 and 25. *Apr-Oct, Tue-Sun 9.30am-12.30pm, 1.30-6pm. Free.* ☎ *052 21 39 56 (Tourist Information Centre).*

Diest ★

On a bend in the River Demer, this charming old town is still surrounded by the remains of its medieval fortifications. Like Breda in the Netherlands, Dillenburg in Germany, and Orange in France, Diest was a possession of the House of Orange, of which the most illustrious member was William of Nassau or William the Silent (1533-84), who led the revolt of the Low Countries against Spain. Heir to his cousin René de Chalon, Prince of Orange, who was born in Diest, he founded the Orange-Nassau dynasty to which the present Queen Beatrix of the Netherlands belongs. Philip-William, William the Silent's eldest son, was buried in the town church dedicated to St Sulpicius.

Location

Vlaams Braban t– Population 22 046 – Michelin maps 716 I3 and 533 P17.
Mid-way between Leuven and Hasselt, Diest is served by the E 314 motorway and several main roads, notably N 2, N 10, N 29 and N 174.
🚹 *Stadhuis, Grote Markt,* ☎ *013 31 21 21; www.diest.be*

WHERE TO EAT
De Nieuwe Haan – *Grote Markt 19 –* ☎ *013 33 51 06 – de.nieuwe.haan@skynet.be – Closed Mon, Wed, except July-Aug –* 🚭 – €36.90. Family tavern-cum-restaurant in an imposing 17C building by the main square. Interior decor to match. Good selection of traditional dishes. Open-air dining when weather permits.

Walking About

Grote Markt

The town's attractive main square is lined with 17C and 18C buildings, among them the neo-Classical 18C town hall. In the middle of the square stands the church.

St-Sulpitiuskerk – This church was built from the 14C to the 16C. The successive stages of construction can be seen in the different types of stonework, from the local Carboniferous sandstone in the chancel and nave to the white stone of the unfinished 16C tower. The two-tiered steeple above the crossing, shaped somewhat like a windmill, is known as *mosterdpot* (mustard pot). It features a carillon with 32 bells.

Inside, there is an open-work triforium, a number of fine **works of art★**, and fine 18C woodwork (pulpit, organ). The 15C **choir stalls** have amusing misericords representing the Seven Deadly Sins and proverbs. Note the 17C tabernacle with niches decorated in Italian style, the 16C triptych entitled *Adoration of the Magi* and the 13C *Virgin and Child Enthroned* (Sedes Sapientiae). The church plate is kept in a room behind the chancel. *Jul-Aug, Tue-Sun. 2-5pm; Sept-Jun by prior arrangement. €1.25.* ☎ *013 35 32 71.*

Lakenhal – The façade of the linen market was rebuilt in the 19C. A 15C cannon called Holle Griet (Mother Meg) has been installed in front of the building.
Go round the building to see the old façade.

There are two picturesque 15C **houses** ('t Dambord and Het Fortuyn) with overhanging upper storeys at the junction of the nearby traffic-free streets (F Moonsstraat, Ketelstraat, G Gezellestraat and Schotelstraat).
From the square go along Zoutstraat and Demerstraat, then turn right into Refugie-straat.

Almshouses

A short way along Demerstraat, to the right and by a canal, are the 16C **Tongerlo abbey almshouses** known as Het Spijker.
The 15C **Averbode almshouses** are a little further along, half-hidden amid foliage. The outbuildings date from the 20C.
Go along Michael Theystraat and turn right into Schaffensestraat. The Begijnhof is on Begijnenstraat.

Begijnhof★★

The Beguine convent was founded in the 13C and is one of the largest in Belgium. It has a splendid Baroque entrance (1671), decorated with a niche housing a statue of the Madonna and Child.
The present buildings, ornamented with gables and niches, date from the 17C and 18C. The little Engelenconvent (Angels' Convent) (no 5 in the street of the same name) gives a good idea of daily life in the convent from the 16C to the 20C. The infirmary in the Apostelenconvent is now used as a venue for cultural events. A number of artists have established themselves in the Begijnhof and some of their work is on display.

M. Gurfinkel/MICHELIN

The door of the Begijnhof.

St Catherine's Church (**St-Katarinakerk**), built in the Gothic style characteristic of the Demer region, has lovely woodwork; note the pulpit dating from 1671 with its remarkably graceful sculptures, and the finely worked chancel screen from the same period. The church also has some fine statuary. *Early May – mid-Sept, guided tours 1.30-5pm. Free.* ☎ *013 35 32 74.*

Stop to admire the gables of the two old breweries at nos 72 and 74 Koning Albertstraat. They are decorated with carvings of brewer's tools.

Go back to Schaffensestraat to get to the watermill.

Watermolen van Oranje

The 16C mill stands in the shade of a weeping willow. With its crow-stepped gable reflected in the nearby canal, it makes a very pretty picture.

Schaffensepoort

This passageway was driven through successive lines of 19C fortifications.

Turn right onto the Leopoldvest.

Leopoldvest

This boulevard runs along the town walls (*vest* means rampart), providing a pretty **view** of the Beguine convent. Behind the brick walls are the convent gardens, with the closely packed, high-roofed buildings beyond.

The 18C **Lindenmolen**, a timber windmill brought here from the nearby village of Assent, stands by the **De Halve Maan** recreation area, with its outdoor pools, beach, tennis courts and lake.

Go along Parklaan.

St-Janskerk

The ivy-clad, red sandstone ruins of the Gothic chancel of this church stand in the middle of a square.

Go along St-Jansstraat to Verstappenplein.

H Verstappenplein

The main entrance to **Warande Park** can be seen from this square. Located on the hill where the castle once stood, this was the hunting ground of the Princes of Orange. It is overlooked by their palace, dating from 1516 and flanked by a turret.

St-Barbarakerk

9am-noon. ☎ *013 31 10 41.* This Baroque church has six sumptuous 17C carved wooden confessionals, one of them forming the base of the pulpit.

Worth a Visit

Stedelijk Museum★

Open Oct-Feb Mon-Sat 10am-noon, 1-5pm. Closed public holidays. €1.24. ☎ *013 35 32 74 (Tourist Information Centre).*

The Municipal Museum is housed in the town hall crypt *(right-hand door under the flight of steps)*. The medieval setting shows off the museum's displays to great advantage. A 15C painting on wood depicting the **Last Judgement** is exhibited beneath the 14C red sandstone Gothic vaulting. There is also the replica of a marble statue, *Madonna and Child*. The original work, dating from 1345, was brought here from the Beguine convent and is currently on show in the Metropolitan Museum in New York. The Gothic Room exhibits 15C and 16C armour.

The next room, which is clearly of Romanesque influence with brick cupolas set on short pillars, is believed to be an old seigneurial brewery; the well still exists. Notice the 15C chandelier made of deer horn, gold and silver.

The Aldermen's Chamber has been restored and embellished with intricately carved furniture; it also has a number of drawings showing Diest as it used to be. The beautiful 17C, 18C and 19C **guild chains of office** are among the most impressive pieces on display.

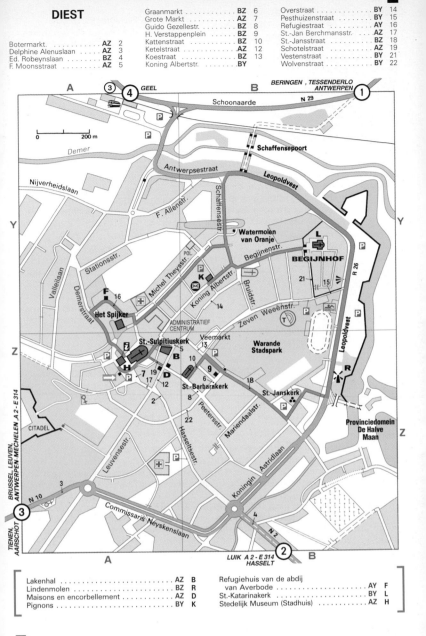

DIEST

Tour

FROM THE KEMPEN TO THE HAGELAND
37km/23mi – allow 2hr
Leave on ① on the town plan and turn left. Take N 174 north to Tessenderlo.

Tessenderlo
The attractive **St-Maartenskerk** has a beautiful 16C **rood screen★**. Its three finely carved arcades rest on six pillars. Eight large statues of the Evangelists and the Fathers of the Church stand in the arches. Small figures in medieval costume enliven the four medallions above the arches, depicting scenes from the Life of the Virgin. Higher still, but beneath the open-work canopies, are scenes from the Life of Christ. The font was sculpted in the 12C.
Leave Tenderlo towards Laakdal, then take N 165.

Averbode
Averbode Abbey is occupied by the Premonstratensians. It was founded by the Order in 1134-35 in an area of pine forest where the three provinces of Antwerp, Limburg and Brabant meet.

Abbey

Conventual buildings – Open year-round, daily, 7.30am-7.30pm. ☎ *013 78 04 40.*

Enter the courtyard through the 14C porch, surmounted by a ferruginous sandstone structure decorated with statues in Gothic niches. The abbot's house at the far end of the courtyard was rebuilt in the 18C style.

Church★ – This lovely abbey church, built from 1664 to 1672 by Van den Eynde, resembles those in Grimbergen and Ninove. The undulating façade displays statues of St Norbert on the right and St John the Baptist, patron of the abbey, on the left. The interior is majestic in scale; the chancel is longer than the nave and is separated from it by two altarpieces which once formed the rood screen. Visitors can see the richly carved 17C stalls beyond them.

Conventual buildings – These buildings were burned down in 1942, with the exception of the 18C cloisters, the chapter house and the vestry, which is decorated with fine 18C woodwork. Interesting paintings can be seen here: in the cloisters the portraits of abbots from the 17C are on view; in the chapter-house, there is a work by De Crayer. *7.30-11.30am, 2-6pm. Contact the Prior,* ☎ *013 78 04 40.*

Conventual cemetery – *Between the church and the road.* The tomb of **Ernest Claes** and his wife lies here. This Flemish author (1885-1968) was born in Zichem and was especially fond of Averbode Abbey.

Take N 212 towards Zichem

THE PREMONSTRATENSIANS

This religious Order was founded by **St Norbert**. In 1120 he established the first community of the Order which he based on the Rule of St Augustine, at Prémontré near Laon in France. The Order spread rapidly to the Low Countries where it proved to be a great success. This is still one of Belgium's largest orders, the principal abbeys being Averbode, Parc and Tongerlo. The Premonstratensians, or Norbertines, are regular canons. While living in their community, they devote themselves to pastoral work, which they conduct mostly in the parishes, dressed in their distinctive white habits.

Zichem

The Flemish author **Ernest Claes** was born in this small market town. The church has a fine 16C triptych illustrating the Life of St Eustace, its patron saint. The stained-glass window over the high altar, dating from 1397, is said to be the oldest in the country.

Take N 212.

Scherpeheuvel

Belgium's most visited pilgrimage site stands in a prominent position atop a low, wooded hill rising from the surrounding countryside. Pilgrimages began here in the Middle Ages, and were associated with a miraculous statue of the Virgin Mary. A candlelight procession takes place in the afternoon of the Sunday following All Saints' Day.

The great basilica crowning the hilltop was built between 1609 and 1627 by the court architect Coeberger on the orders of the "archdukes" Albert and Isabella. Its design, ornamentation, and the layout of its surroundings are conceived in terms of sacred geometry, and a tradition of mystic numerology is reflected in its seven sides, seven-pointed stars and seven converging avenues. The Baroque dome marks the advent of this style in Belgium.

Brightly coloured paintings by Van Loon, depicting the *Lives of St Anne and the Virgin*, are on display in the radiating chapels.

Diksmuide

In the Middle Ages Diksmuide was a port on the River IJzer and a cloth making town. In October/November 1914 it was one of the strategic points in the Battle of the IJzer, when Belgian and French units put up heroic resistance to the German advance. The bombardments were so intense that the town disappeared from the face of the earth. After 1918 it was rebuilt, like Ypres, in traditional style.

Location

West-Vlaanderen – Population 15 494 – Michelin maps 716 B2 and 533 C16.

Among the polderlands of the Westhoek area, Diksmuide is within easy reach of the coast. Access by N 35 and N 369.

🄱 *Grote Markt 28,* ☎ *051 51 91 46. www.toerismediksmuide.be*

Worth a Visit

Grote Markt
Dominated by the neo-Gothic town hall and St Nicholas' Church, the square is lined by buildings with crow-stepped gables.
Go past the entrance to the church, turn left at the Vismarkt and cross the little bridge.

Begijnhof
The Beguine convent has been rebuilt exactly as it was. The white houses are set out around a lawn on either side of a brick chapel.

IJzertoren
In Kaaskerke. Leave Diksmuide by IJzerlaan, the road to Nieuwport. 10am-6pm (Oct-Mar 5pm). Closed 1, 2 Jan, 3 weeks after Christmas holidays. €6. ☎ 051 50 02 86.
Built 1952-64, the 84m/275ft IJzer Tower stands on the opposite bank of the river as a memorial to the soldiers who fell in the First World War. It bears the initials A.V.V.-V.V.K., standing for *"Alles voor Vlaanderen, Vlaanderen voor Kristus"* ("All for Flanders, Flanders for Christ"), and has become an important symbol of the Flemish movement, the object of a well attended and sometimes controversial annual pilgimage.
There is a fine **panoramic view**★ from the top *(lift)* over the Flanders Plain, the winding course of the IJzer and the town of Diksmuide. On a clear day it is possible to see *(right to left)* the belfries of Bruges, Ostend, and Nieuwpoort, as well as various low but prominent summits much fought over in 1914-18 *(viewing table)*.
The tower houses a **museum** (22 storeys) devoted to the two world wars and the history of the Flemish movement.

Dodengang
3km/2mi NW on the west bank of the IJzer. Early Apr – early Oct, daily, 10am-5pm; Oct – mid-Nov, Mon-Fri, 10am-5pm. ☎ 050 44 54 01.
For four years (1914-18) Belgian soldiers resisted the German advance in these dug-outs, which became known as the Trench of Death. They were only a few yards away from the lines of the German troops who had managed to cross the IJzer here in October 1914.
Visitors can walk through the two long trenches, in which the sandbagged parapets have been faithfully reproduced in concrete.

Excursion

Vladslo German cemetery
6km/4mi E. In these leafy surroundings are buried 25 638 German soldiers. The statue *The Bereaved Parents* is the work of the German artist Käthe Kollwitz who lost her 17-year old son on the battlefield.

Dinant★★

Dinant lies in a remarkable **setting**★★ in the Meuse Valley. The massive citadel and the onion-domed collegiate church dominate the town, whose slate-roofed buildings stretch for 4km/2.5mi between river and rugged cliffs. Nowadays Dinant largely lives off tourism, but in the past it was an industrial town as well as a fortress, renowned for the chased copper- and brass-ware produced here since the 12C. The town's other speciality is the couque, a little honey cake baked in a decoratively carved wooden mould.

Location
Namur – Population 12 661 – Michelin maps 716 H5 and 534 O21 – Local maps see overleaf and La MEUSE NAMUROISE – Town plan in the current edition of The Red Guide Benelux.
Dinant is 30km/19mi S of Namur in the valley of the Meuse and is linked to the provincial capital by N 92.
🛈 *Rue Grande 37,* ☎ *082 22 28 70; www.dinant-tourisme.be*

FAMOUS FIGURES FROM DINANT
The artist **Joachim Patinir** (or Patenier) was born here in the late 15C. He set biblical scenes in vast landscapes recalling the scenery of the Meuse Valley. It was also the birthplace of **Antoine Wiertz** (1806-65), a visionary painter whose work heralded the advent of Symbolism and Surrealism in Belgium. **Adolphe Sax** (1814-94), as his name suggests, was the inventor of the saxophone.

Background

A turbulent past – Dinant was constantly in conflict with nearby Bouvignes, as well as with Namur, Liège and the Dukes of Burgundy, all of them rivals in the brass and copper industry. The town was destroyed for this reason in 1466 by **Charles the Bold**. Owing to its strategic position on the Meuse, it witnessed a succession of conquering armies – the French in 1554 and again 1675, the Germans in 1914 and again in 1940, then the liberating Americans in 1944. Destruction in both world wars was acute; in 1914, believing they had been fired on by civilians, the German army sacked the town and shot 674 people. Then in 1944 the Wehrmacht offered stiff resistance to the Americans attempting to cross the Meuse.

Directory

Where to Eat

La Broche – *Rue Grande 22,* ☎ *082 22 82 81 – Closed lunchtime Tue, Wed –* 🍽 *– €18.84/28.26.* Family restaurant in the heart of Dinant's main street, squeezed in between the river and the rocky escarpment. The up to date menu matches the contemporary décor; this is the place to come for grilled dishes.

Le Grill – *Rue des Rivages 88 (via N 95) –* ☎ *082 22 69 35 – Closed Mon eve, Tue – €31.* Discriminating meat eaters will appreciate the offerings coming off the wood-fired grill in this venerable town residence just a jump on horseback from the famous Bayard rock. Take your pick from three dining rooms.

Where to Stay

Le Gailly Chambre d'hôte – *Place du Baty 7 – 5500 Falmagne –* ☎ *082 74 51 03 – Closed Jan – 5 rms* ⚏ *€34/47.* Pretty, ivy-covered country house. Bedroom decor (and names) inspired by a palette of great painters – Gauguin, Van Gogh, Renoir, Klimt and Monet. Friendly welcome.

Les Crétias – *Rue des Crétias 99 – 5500 Falmignoul –* ☎ *082 74 42 11 –* 🍽 *– 10 rms* ⚏ *€45/65 – restaurant €25/50.* On the heights of Falmignoul, imposing country house offering sustenance as well as accommodation. Choice of classic dishes with a modern touch. Outdoor dining in summer overlooking the garden. Comfortable rooms.

Worth a Visit

Collégiale Notre-Dame

Nothing remains of the sanctuary that became a collegiate church as far back as the 10C. This building was replaced by a Romanesque church, of which the north door remains.

The present church was erected in a Gothic style imported from Burgundy and Champagne between the 13C and the late 14C. The onion dome and the elegant tower, both of which were originally designed to be topped by a belfry, date from the mid-16C.

Interior – *Enter by the north door.* Although the church is small because of its cramped site, it produces the impression of grandeur and austerity characteristic of the Mosan School. The layout is in the form of a Latin cross, and the identical elevations throughout lend the interior a great sense of harmony. The monolithic columns have octagonal capitals decorated with austere foliage in the regional style. The columns bear the weight of huge, moulded arches, a triforium with tre-foil arches and tall windows with Flamboyant Gothic tracery. The chancel has an ambulatory but no radiating chapels.

Citadelle★

Access by cable car, on foot (408 steps) or by car (N 936 Sorinnes road). Jul-Aug: guided tour (1hr) 10am-6pm; Jan, Sat, Sun and public holidays 10am-4.30pm; Feb-Dec: daily except Fri 10am-5pm. Closed one week in Jan, 1 Jan, 25 Dec. €5.20. ☎ *082 22 36 70.*

The fortress established here in 1051 was rebuilt by the Bishop of Liège in 1523 and destroyed by the French in 1703. Its present appearance dates from the Dutch occupation (1818-21).

The citadel has been turned into a **museum**. The various rooms contain tableaux of various kinds (some with audio commentary), dioramas, a medley of exhibits and a small collection of weapons recalling the main events in the history of the citadel and the town.

The splendid **view★★** from the walls 100m/328ft above the Meuse takes in the town in its valley setting and extends downstream to Dinant's ancient rival, little Bouvignes.

Grotte la Merveilleuse★

West bank of the Meuse, Philippeville road. Apr-Oct and Christmas holidays: guided tours (50min) 10am-5pm; during Carnaval: 1-4pm. Closed Mon-Fri in winter, 1 Jan, 25 Dec. €5. ☎ *082 22 22 10.*

The Collégiale and the Citadelle

This cave is outstanding for the number of rock formations (drapes, waterfalls, colonnettes) and the range of colours (white, brown, blue and pink). Visitors are taken along galleries on three levels.

A gallery staircase with more than 120 steps brings visitors back out into the open air again.

Parc de Mont-Fat

Apr-Oct, 10.30am-7pm. €5. ☎ 082 22 27 83.

The **Tour de Mont-Fat**, which can be reached by chairlift, stands in the centre of this amusement park. There is a panoramic view of Dinant and the Meuse Valley from the top of the tower.

Grottes préhistoriques de Mont-Fat – The prehistoric caves lie halfway up the hillside. They can be reached by underground passageways and the aptly named Trou du Diable (literally "Devil's Hole") or via the gardens.

Water streaming off the plateau and into the fissures in the cliff face hollowed out these caverns which were inhabited in prehistoric times. Under the Romans they became a temple to Diana, hence perhaps the name of the town.

The various chambers are adorned with rock formations.

Excursions

Rocher Bayard★

1km/0.6mi S of the town on N 95. This 40m/130ft high rock is supposed to have been split open with one blow of his hoof by Bayard the famous horse as he fled from Charlemagne. In days gone by there was only a narrow path along here but it was widened in 1661, then again in 1698, for Louis XIV's troops.

Bouvignes★

2km/1.25mi N on N 96. Bouvignes and Dinant have merged to form a single built-up area. High above the town are the ruins of the Château de Crèvecoeur ("Heartbreak Castle"), so named after being razed by the troops of King Henri II of France in 1554. **Henri Bles**, the famous landscape painter who continued to work in the style of Patinir, was born here. His paintings are unusual because they all include the little owl that he used as his signature.

Maison Espagnole – The "Spanish House" with scrolled gables and Renaissance windows stands on Grand-Place. It was named after the period in which it was built (16C) and was once the town hall.

Église St-Lambert – The church dates from the 13C and 16C. It has been restored and contains some interesting works of art including the 16C *Christ Bound* and the 17C pulpit and lectern.

Near the church, current archaeological digs are revealing the remains of a castle thought to have been built in the 11C.

Guided tours by prior arrangement. Contact Révérend Raty, Presbytère de Bouvignes, rue des Potiers 1, 5500 Dinant. ☎ 0477 98 00 75.

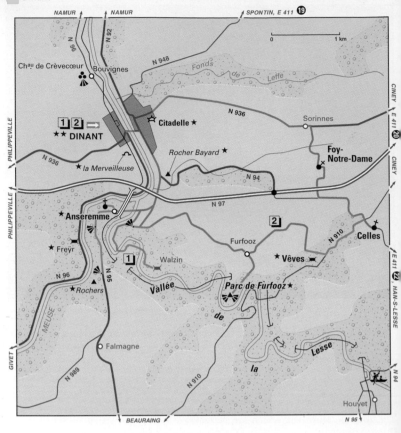

Château de Crèvecœur – *Access by the Sommière road (4km/2.5mi) or via a flight of steps.* A reminder of the old fortifications, a gate, can be seen opposite the bottom of the steps. There is a beautiful **view**★★ from the château of the town, the church, and the Spanish House, as well as of the Meuse Valley with Dinant in the distance.

Beauraing
20km/12mi S on N 95. Beauraing has been a famous place of pilgrimage ever since five local children claimed to have seen the Virgin Mary on several occasions between 29 November 1932 and 3 January 1933.

The sanctuaries – These have increased in number since 1943. There is a statue of the Virgin Mary in the garden, under the hawthorn where the apparitions took place; some of the stones the children kneeled on are set in a pavement nearby. The **Crypte St-Jean** is a little further down the street. Max van der Linden's Stations of the Cross, executed in colourful naïve-style ceramics, add life to the bare stone walls of the crypt. The thick walled **monumental chapel** is lit by stained-glass windows erected in 1963-64. The glass façade of the concrete complex built in 1968 to plans by the architect Roger Bastin overlooks the esplanade and its tiers of seats. Bastin's work comprises the **great crypt** and the **upper church** which can hold 7 000 worshippers. It is accessible to the ill or disabled thanks to a special entrance ramp.

Tours

BY BOAT DOWN THE RIVER LESSE
4.5km/3mi S on N 95.

Anseremme★
This little town, stretching along the right bank of the river to join Dinant, is a well situated tourist centre at the confluence of the Lesse and Meuse. Note in particular the 16C bridge, the **Pont St-Jean**, spanning the Lesse. To the south on the river bank in Old Anseremme is a 15C **priory** *(private property)* and its church surrounded by a graveyard.

Lesse valley

From Anseremme a very narrow road runs through the steep sided, verdant valley to the rocky spur topped by the Château de Walzin.

The best way of experiencing the lovely **valley of the Lesse**★ is on the water. It is possible to go down the river from Houyet to Anseremme by canoe or as a passenger in a boat. Houyet can be reached by train or bus from Anseremme. *Canoe hire: Lesse Kayaks, place de l'Église 2, Dinant,* ☎ *082 22 43 97; Kayaks Ansiaux, rue du Vélodrome 15, Dinant,* ☎ *082 22 23 25. Boat trip: Libert Frères, quai de Meuse 1, Anseremme,* ☎ *082 21 35 35.*

Cross the Lesse where it flows into the Meuse.

The Freÿr viewpoint on a bend near a café provides a fine **view**★ of the lovely formal gardens of the Château de Freÿr far below. Further along the road, admire the **panoramic view**★ over the valley from another viewpoint, taking in the Freÿr crags and the château.

FROM FURFOOZ TO FOY-NOTRE-DAME

30km/19mi.

Take N 92 S and turn left onto the Furfooz road.

The road climbs and soon comes to a junction with a road on the right. A few yards from the fork there is a pretty **view**★ down over Anseremme.

Furfooz

Just to the south of the village of Furfooz, part of a limestone massif enclosed by a bend in the river is now protected as the **Parc national de Furfooz**★. One branch of the river passes beneath the massif itself, an underground waterway which has been subject to exploration since 1962. A 3.5km/2mi waymarked footpath enables visitors to explore the area with its fascinating limestone vegetation and evidence of human occupation from prehistoric to medieval times. *Jul-Aug: 9am-6pm; mid-Feb – March: Sat-Sun 10am-4pm; April – mid-Nov: 10am-5pm. €2.50.* ☎ *082 22 34 77 or 081 22 47 65.*

This site was a natural fortress and was occupied until the 10C, a fact recalled by the reconstructed Roman baths with hypocaust and the ruins at the top of the plateau (from which there is a beautiful view of the wooded Lesse Valley). The promontory is pitted with caves in which traces of prehistoric habitation have been found.

Vêves

An elegant **château**★ stands out dramatically against the woods and overlooks the hamlet. Since the 12C it has belonged first to the Beaufort line, then to that of the counts of Liedekerke Beaufort. The fortress was destroyed by the people of Dinant in revenge for its owner's involvement in the 1466 siege of the town. It was immediately rebuilt and was then altered during the Renaissance, and again in the early 18C. The courtyard has an arcaded gallery with half-timbered balconies above 18C French furniture and family mementoes decorate the carefully restored interior. *Jul-Aug: guided tours (50min) 10am-6pm; Apr-Nov: Tue-Sun 10am-5pm (May and Sept 6pm). €5.* ☎ *082 66 63 95.*

Continue to Celles on N 910

Celles

A German tank at the north entrance to this village marks the furthest point of the German advance during the Battle of the Bulge in late 1944. The 11C **Romanesque church** dedicated to St Hadelin is an excellent example of the Mosan style: massive tower-façade flanked by two turrets, pilaster strips decorating the façade and half-domed vaulting in the apse. Inside there is 17C *grisaille* and 13C choir stalls, the oldest in Belgium, along with a superb 16C **tombstone**★ made of black Dinant marble, depicting Louis de Beaufort and his wife on either side of the Cross. The church still has two 11C crypts.

Foy-Notre-Dame

A statue of the Virgin Mary was found in an old oak tree in Foy in 1609. Its miraculous gifts were acknowledged by the Prince-Bishop of Liège, and the village became a popular place of pilgrimage. The church dates from 1623. There is Louis XIII panelling inside and a remarkable coffered **ceiling**★ decorated with 145 paintings (17C) by the Stilmant brothers and Guillaume Goblet, all of them Dinant artists. The works were given to the church by pilgrims; they depict the Lives of the Virgin Mary and of Christ, the Evangelists, the Doctors of the Church and the Saints.

Return to Dinant via Sorinnes. This route skirts the citadel.

Barrages de l'**Eau d'Heure**★

The well-watered, undulating countryside to the north of Chimay was chosen for a series of reservoirs designed to supply the River Sambre and the Charleroi Canal, in which the volume of water was insufficient once it was made accessible to large international vessels. Two huge dams have been created: Eau d'Heure, a vast rock-filled dam with a crest 250m/0.23mi long and La Plate-Taille, which has a hydroelectric plant. Plate-Taille is higher but the water supply is inadequate and it has to be filled by pumps during the night, using the Eau d'Heure turbines. Three "fore-dams", Féronval, Ry-Jaune and Falemprise, were built to make the larger projects easier to carry out. They have also made it possible to create a new road network. An extensive tourist development programme is in progress on the shores of the lake, including various types of accommodation and sporting and recreational facilities. The area is crisscrossed by more than 100km/62mi of footpaths.

Directory

WHERE TO EAT

⌂ **Relais du Surmoy** – *Rue Bironfosse 38 – 5630 Soumoy* – ☎ *071 64 32 13 – relaissurmoy@belgacom.net* – 🅿 *– 24 rms: €51/59* ⌷ *– restaurant €21/24.* What a pleasant surprise to find this hotel established in a huge early 19C farmhouse. Rustic surroundings, comfortable rooms and country-style dining room with exposed beams and stonework and brick vaults.

⌂ **Le Domaine de la Carrauterie** – *Rue de la Station 11 – 6470 Sautin* – ☎ *060 45 53 52 – carrauterie@bmedia.be* – 🅿 *– 5 rms: €65/90* ⌷. Not far from Chimay, this lovely cottage-style residence is tucked away in a leafy setting. Pretty, tastefully decorated rooms for guests to relax and spoil themselves – there is a pool, sauna and jacuzzi. Friendly, personal welcome.

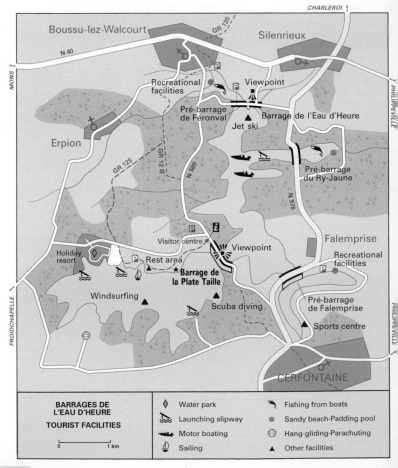

Location

Hainaut-Namur – Michelin maps 716 G5 and 534 L21amur.
Between Beaumont and Philippeville and 32km/20mi S of Charleroi, the reservoirs are on the border between the provinces of Namur and Hainaut. Access by N 40 or N 978.
🛈 *Place de l'Église 9, 5630 Cerfontaine,* ☎ *071 64 46 67.*

Barrage de la Plate-Taille★

Access by a wide road from Boussu-lez-Walcourt.
The dam was built in 1977 and is the largest in Belgium. It is a gravity dam with a crest 790m/0.5mi long. The reservoir itself covers an area of 351ha/867 acres and has a capacity of 68.4 million m^3/2 416 million cu ft of water. It is used for sailing, windsurfing and sub-aqua. A **viewing tower** 107m/351ft high has been built on the crest.

Visitor centre

There are audio-visual presentations about the dams and aquariums filled with fish from the region.

Enghien

On the border between the French- and Dutch-speaking areas of Belgium, Enghien was granted to the Arenberg family in 1606 by King Henri IV of France. Once famous for the manufacture of "verdures", tapestries representing leafy vegetation or other natural scenes, it is an attractive little place, worth visiting above all for its superb park.

Location

Hainaut – Population 10 751 – Michelin maps 716 F3 and 534 J18.
Enghien is 30km/19mi W of Brussels on the A 8/E 429 motorway linking the capital with Tournai.
🛈 *Grand-Place 50,* ☎ *02 395 83 60; www-enghien-edingen.be*

Worth a Visit

Park★

10am to 6pm (Nov – Mar 5pm). €3. ☎ *02 395 83 60.*
The park was originally laid out in the 15C but it was not until the 17C, when Charles d'Arenberg was the owner of the estate, that it became one of the finest in Europe, celebrated at the time as "the most beautiful and extraordinary thing in the world". The original stately home was demolished in the 19C and the tower from the chapel is all that remains of the building. The present house was built in 1913 on the site of the former orangery. The grounds include woodland, lawns, flowerbeds, and lakes, laid out around the 18C stables, the Chinese Pavilion, and the Pavilion of the Seven Stars.

Église St-Nicolas

This vast Gothic church on the Grand-Place has a carillon of 51 bells. Lovely modern stained-glass windows (1964) by **Max Ingrand** can be seen inside. The main window represents the Apostolate. The Chapel of Our Lady of Messines, originally known as Chapelle St-Éloi, is the oldest part of the building. It contains a beautiful 16C altarpiece of uncertain origin, decorated with scenes depicting the Life of the Virgin Mary.

Église des Capucins

Access via the Ninove road then via rue des Capucins on the left.
This church (1616) features a splendid Renaissance mausoleum in one of its chapels. It was designed by Emperor Charles V's sculptor, Jean Mone, for Guillaume de Cro, Cardinal-Bishop of Toledo. The chapel on the opposite side is dedicated to Our Lady of Grace. Her statue, believed to possess miraculous powers, stands on the altar; it was a gift from Archduke Albert and Archduchess Isabella to Marie de Medici. On the high altar, there is an ebony and ivory altarpiece (17C) framing an *Adoration of the Magi* on which 51 of the figures are portraits of Arenburg family members.

The Chinese Pavilion

The convent also includes a number of rooms which have been turned into the **Musée de la Maison d'Arenberg**. The small museum displays sculptures, paintings, tapestries and family archives.

Maison de Jonathas
Oct-May: Wed, Sat, Sun 2-5pm (last admission 4.30pm); Jun-Sept: 2-6pm (last entry 5.30pm). No charge. ☎ 02 395 83 60.
This 12C Romanesque keep only a few yards from the church was turned into a patrician residence in the 16C, unlike the Burbant Tower in Ath which has retained its military appearance. The small **Musée de la Tapisserie** serves as a reminder of the fact that Enghien had a number of major tapestry workshops from the 15C to the 18C. Note the fine series of five 16C Enghien tapestries, *Children's Games Among the Greenery.*

Eupen

The capital of Belgium's German-language minority, Eupen is an industrial town of some importance with factories lining the banks of the River Vesdre. The town dates from the 18C, a period when its beautiful patrician houses were built by rich wool merchants from Ghent who saw possibilities in the abundant soft waters of the Vesdre. The Church of St Nicolas with its green onion domes and exuberant Baroque altars also dates from this time. Eupen belonged to Germany for a century and was only allocated to Belgium by the Treaty of Versailles in 1919, along with Moresnet, Malmédy and St-Vith.

Location
Liège – Population 17 429 – Michelin maps 716 K4 and 534 V19 – Town plan in the current edition of The Red Guide Benelux.
Close to the border with Germany, Eupen spreads along the slopes of the valley of the River Vesdre, on the edge of the Hautes Fagnes and the Herve area. Acces from Liège and Aachen by the A 3/E 40 motorway or N 61, N 67 and N 68.
🛈 *Marktplatz 7, ☎ 087 55 34 50; www.eupen.be*

< />
Directory

Worth a Visit

Stadtmuseum
Gospertstrasse 52. Tue-Sun. 9.30-noon, 1-4pm, Sat 2-5pm, Sun 10am-noon, 2-5pm. Closed public holidays, third weekend in Jun, 25 Dec to 1 Jan. €1.25. ☎ 087 74 00 05.
The Municipal Museum is in a picturesque 17C house and features watch and clockmaking, local history, the development of fashion, as well as a silver and goldsmith's workshop and a collection of Raeren potteries.

Excursions

Barrage de la Vesdre★
5km/3.25mi. Head SE from Eupen on N 67 and turn left, following signs for Wesertalsperre.
This dam lies upstream from the town, at the confluence of the Vesdre – or Weser to German-speakers – and the Getzbach. It was inaugurated in 1950 and is one of the largest projects of this type in Belgium, along with the Gileppe dam and the Eau d'Heure complex.
It is a gravity dam, more than 63m/207ft high and nearly 410m/0.25mi long, and is 55m/180ft thick at the base. It has a capacity of 25 million m^3/883 million cu ft. Like the Gileppe dam, it was designed to supply water to the Eupen and Liège areas. It has water-treatment plant and a small hydro-electric power station. Sailing is permitted on the reservoir, at the Yacht Club de la Vesdre, but motorboats, fishing and swimming are prohibited.
Panoramic drive – this is a good way of appreciating the lake and the beautiful spruces and birches of the surrounding Hertogenwald forest. *Mar to Oct: 11am-6pm. ☎ 087 21 39 11.*

Henri-Chapelle
11km/7mi NW on N 67 then N 3 on the left.
There is an **American Cemetery** about 4.5km/2.75mi north of **Henri-Chapelle**, in Vogelsang-Hombourg. The remarkably well-maintained site blooms with roses and rhododendrons. It contains the graves of 7 989 American soldiers who died in 1944-45 in the Ardennes or Germany. White marble crosses or stones carved with the Star of David converge across the gently sloping lawns on a memorial. Inside the memorial, there is a small **museum**, with the story of the campaign carved into the marble. *9am-6pm (Nov-Mar 5pm). ☎ 087 68 71 73 (American Cemetery).*
From the terrace opposite the cemetery there is a **panoramic view**★ of the fields and hedgerows of the Herve plateau. The area is densely populated, though with a widely dispersed settlement pattern.

Les Trois Bornes★ – (Drielandenpunt)
18km/11.25mi N on N 68.
After leaving N 68 at Kettenis, the road goes through Walhorn and Astenet, where there is a small sanctuary to honour the memory of St Catherine of Siena. Beyond Kelmis-La Calamine, it reaches Gemmenich via the Moresnet-Chapelle shrine to the Virgin Mary with its monumental calvary set amid the trees. From here a series of hairpin bends leads to the wooded plateau where the borders of the Netherlands, Belgium and Germany meet. From 1816 until the end of the First World War, the borders also marked out the little neutral town of Moresnet, a tiny quirk of geography which is now part of Belgian territory. This is also the highest point in the Netherlands, with an altitude of 321m/1 053ft. There is a fine **panoramic view**★ of the region from the top of the **Tour Baudouin**, a tall metal structure. The view encompasses the urban sprawl of Aachen and the forests of the Eifel in Germany, as well as the Dutch town of Maastricht in the distance, nestling amid wooded hills. ♿ *Apr-Oct: 10am-6pm; Nov-Mar: 11am-5pm. €2.50. ☎ 087 78 76 10.*
On the right, about 500m/0.3mi further along the Vaals (Netherlands) road, there is a fine **view**★ over Aachen and the German plain.

Founeau-St-Michel ★★

Fourneau-St-Michel lies among the wonderfully wooded hills of the Ardennes in the delightful Masblette Valley, a spot favoured by the Benedictines when they founded the abbey of St-Hubert. In the 18C the last abbot, Nicolas Spirlet, set up a metal works here. The valley is now the site of a trio of fascinating museums.

Location
Luxembourg – Michelin maps 716 J5 and 534 R22.
The museums are a few kilometres to the N of St-Hubert on N 849.
🛈 *Rue St-Gilles 12, 6870 St-Hubert, ☎ 061 61 30 10; www.saint-hubert-tourisme.be*
See also ST-HUBERT.

Worth a Visit

Musée de la Vie Rurale en Wallonie★★
There are two entrances. Allow 3hr for this pleasant outing, with a stop for refreshment at the 18C Prévost inn or at the Tahons cafeteria (play facilities). Early Mar – mid-Nov: 9am-5pm (Jul-Aug 6pm). €2.50. ☎ 084 21 08 90 or 084 21 06 44.
This extensive open-air museum consists of around 50 old rural buildings representing the various regions in Wallonia. Removed from their original sites and rebuilt here along a 2km/1.25mi trail, they include a small school, a chapel, a printers, tobacco sheds, a wash-house, and workshops. A large traditional Ardennes building is home to the **Musée du Cheval de Trait Ardennais** which is devoted to the Ardennes draught horse and has an exhibition of the implements that this powerful working animal used to pull.

Musée du Fer et de la Métallurgie Ancienne★
Allow 1hr. Mar-Dec: 9am-5pm (Jul-Aug 6pm). €2.50. ☎ 084 21 08 90 or 084 21 06 13.
Now the Museum of Iron and Metal-Working, this building was once the home of the owner of the ironworks. As well as objects made of iron (firebacks, locks, religious objects, traps etc), there are old tools employed by the various tradesmen who made use of the metal, such as nail makers, blacksmiths, coopers and wheelwrights.
The blast furnace and the forge with its different types of bellows help to explain how iron was produced in the 18C and 19C. The old coal house is now a museum dedicated to the history of the Ardenne forest (**Musée de l'Histoire de la forêt d'Ardenne**).

Musée P-J Redouté
Closed for restoration. ☎ 084 21 08 90.
This museum occupies another part of the iron-master's house, and is devoted to **Pierre-Joseph Redouté**, the "Raphael of flowers" who was born in St-Hubert in 1759, and to his brother Henri-Joseph, who took part in Napoleon's campaign in Egypt and became famous for his finely observed pictures of the natural world.

Gembloux

Set in much prized farmland, Gembloux was once more famous for its important Benedictine abbey founded in the 10C. The abbey was dissolved during the French Revolution, and since 1860 the building has been occupied by an agricultural college. The town still has remnants of its 12C ramparts.

Location
Namur – Population 20 294 – Michelin maps 716 H4 and 534 N19.
On the River Orneau, the town stands at the junction of the N 4 and N 29.
🖪 *Caves du Château du Bailli 15,* ☎ *081 62 63 39; www.gembloux.be*

Worth a Visit

Former Abbey
This group of buildings was constructed to designs by the architect Dewez from 1759 to 1779. Note the beautiful layout of the **main courtyard** with the abbot's palace at the end. The sculptures on the pediment recall the abbot's powerful position as Count of Gembloux. The cloisters have been restored. They lead into a Romanesque chamber that is the only surviving part of the medieval abbey.
The 18C **abbey church**, now the parish church, is nearby.

Maison du Bailli
This 12C fortified house was extensively modified in the 16C. It is now as the town hall.

Excursions

Corroy-le-Château
5km/3.25mi SW. Take N 29 towards Charleroi and turn left on a minor road.
This 13C **castle★** is surrounded by woods and reflected in the moat spanned by a stone bridge. Its design is based on the castles built for King Philippe-Auguste, of France, and, with its barbican and seven cylindrical towers, it still makes a formidable impression.
The interior has been altered over the course of the centuries. The Gothic chapel on the mezzanine of the 7th tower in the outer wall was restored in the 19C. The apartments have 17C and 18C furniture and are decorated with marble and with paintings, some of them depicting Flemish festivals. There is a beautiful collection of *jolités* (little painted boxes) from Spa. *May-Sept: guided tour (1hr) Sat, Sun and public holidays 10am-noon, 2pm-6pm. €3.80.* ☎ *081 63 32 32.*

Corroy-le-Château

Grand-Leez

8km/5mi NE. Take N 4 towards Namur and turn left by Lonzée.

The only working mill left in the province of Namur, the Defrenne **mill** dates from 1830 and is still grinding corn. It is shaped like a truncated cone, with a rotating cap.

Gentinnes

12km/7.5mi E. Take N 29 towards Charleroiand turn right after 3.5km/2mi.

Gentinnes has had a seminary and study centre for prospective missionaries belonging to the congregation of the Fathers of the Holy Spirit since 1904.

The **Mémorial Kongolo** is a chapel built in 1967 in memory of the 21 Belgian missionaries belonging to this order who were massacred in 1962 during a revolt in Kongolo in what is now the Democratic Republic of the Congo. Their names are carved on the façade with the names of 196 other victims, religious or lay people, Catholic or Protestant.

Genk

In the heart of an old coalfield, with its waste tips and miners' housing, Genk is now a centre of modern industry, the most important in the province of Limburg. It is known for the **Molenvijver**, superb public gardens covering an area of 15ha/37 acres including a vast lake and a watermill, as well as recreation parks such as the Kattevennen, or sports complexes such as Kattevenia.

Location

Limburg – Population 62 654 – Michelin maps 716 J3 and 533 S17 – Town plan in the current edition of The Red Guide Benelux.

On the edge of the Kempen region, Genk is conveniently close to the Albert Canal, the A 2/E 314 motorway and to N 75.

🛈 *Dieplaan 2, ☎ 089 30 95 62.*

Excursions

Natuurreservaat De Maten

2km/1.25m SW. Take N 75 towards Hasseltand turn left after the railway bridge. Jul-Feb: open sunrise to sunset. ☎ 089 30 95 62.

The marshy area stretching among the heather-clad hills contains a string of lakes that are home to numerous species of water fowl *(footpaths).*

Natuurreservaat De Mechelse Heide

7km/4.5mi NE on N 75, then N 763 towards Maasmechelen.

Bounded by woodland, this nature reserve is a vast area of heathland (400ha/988 acres), a rare and splendid relic of the Kempen area's natural vegetation. *(signposted footpaths).*

Gent★★★

GHENT

Ghent is the spiritual citadel of Flanders, a university city, the second largest Belgian port and a major industrial centre. In short, a place full of vitality, thanks not least to the 43 000 students who live here and whose bicycles fill the streets. **Emperor Charles V** (1500-58) was born here, and Ghent is steeped in history and rich in historical buildings. In the old districts and along the quaysides between the cathedral and the castle of the Counts of Flanders, there reigns a poetic, intimate atmosphere. Among the many famous citizens of Ghent are the great poet, playwright and Nobel Prize winner **Maurice Maeterlinck** (1862-1949), and the Van de Woestijne brothers: Karel, a writer, and Gustave, a painter.

Location

Oost-Vlaanderen. Population 224 074. Michelin maps 716 E2 and 533 H 16
Built at the confluence of the Leie, or Lys, and the Scheldt, Ghent has many canals and waterways. It enjoys easy access from Bruges and Brussels via the A 10/E 40 motorway and from Antwerp and Kortrijk via the A 14/E 17. For some years a **"mobility plan"** has been in operation: the city centre is completely closed to cars and motorists are guided to one of nine car parks – just follow the 'P' for Parking signs. Other signs at entry points into the town indicate the number of spaces available in the car parks.
🖪 *Belfry crypt, Botermarkt 17,* ☎ *09 266 52 32; www.gent.be*

Background

Ghent was one of the last bastions of paganism in Gaul, and St Amand, who came to evangelise the town in the 7C, was thrown into the Scheldt. Amand persevered, however, and founded the abbey of St Bavo which, with the abbey of St-Peter near Mount Blandin (Blandijnberg), became the centre of the developing town. Baldwin II erected a stone fort in about 940 on the site of the present Gravensteen, the Castle of the Counts, which was the focal point of a third urban settlement.
At the end of the 12C the cloth-making industry was flourishing. The city acquired borough status and gained important privileges, and a wealthy mercantile class built fortified stone residences called *stenen*. Count Philip of Alsace, determined to demonstrate his supremacy over the influential cloth traders, had the castle rebuilt in 1180.
A rebel city – Ghent soon succumbed to fierce internal conflicts. As in Bruges, the wool workers backed by Guy of Dampierre, Count of Flanders, rebelled in 1280 against the merchants who had sided with the King of France. It was only after the Battle of the Golden Spurs in 1302 that the patricians' supremacy was finally overcome.
In the 14C, during the Hundred Years War, the struggle with France was renewed. The Count of Flanders, Louis of Nevers, supported the King of France against England. As this blocked imports of English wool into Flanders, the citizens of Ghent revolted again. As their leader they chose **Jacob van Artevelde**, who allied himself with Edward III of England, whose son John of Gaunt (or 'Ghent') was born here. Artevelde placed himself at the head of the league of Flemish towns, but, following a series of internal conflicts, he was assassinated in 1345 by the head of the weavers' guild. Nevertheless his son Philip managed to impose the supremacy of Ghent throughout Flanders. Finally however the Flemish were defeated by the French at the Battle of Westrozebeke in 1382.
In the 15C, when Ghent was ruled by the Dukes of Burgundy, the city rebelled against Philip the Good and his ideas of a new tax (1452). The citizens of Ghent were defeated at Gavere *(18km/11mi southwest)* and surrendered in 1453. The rebel city fought once more against Charles the Bold in 1469, and in 1477 against Mary of Burgundy who was compelled to grant new privileges to the Low Countries.
By the end of the century the cloth-making industry was in decline. However, Ghent managed to become Europe's principal marketplace for grain, and this ensured renewed prosperity.
In the 16C the citizens were up in arms yet again, this time against Emperor Charles V, who had himself been born here and who had proudly proclaimed "I could put the whole of Paris into a corner of my town of Ghent". The townspeople refused to pay heavy taxes; Charles V responded with the **Caroline Concession** (1540) which stripped the city of its privileges.

CHARLES V AND THE 'STROPPENDRAGERS'

On 24 February 1500, the city bells chimed and the cannon thundered to announce the birth of a new prince. In the Hof ten Walle, soon renamed Prinsenhof by the local population, Joanna, daughter of the Catholic King of Spain, had just given birth to a son, Charles of Luxembourg. The future ruler of the Holy Roman Empire left Ghent in 1506, but he was never to forget his hometown. Under his rule, the power of the cities was curbed, not always with the results desired. Rebellious Ghent reacted violently. Requests for money were staunchly denied and tax officials were regularly thrown into prison. All attempts to reach a solution were rejected by the citizenry. Drastic measures were needed and the Council decided to muzzle the city once and for all. To do so, the Emperor himself travelled to Ghent in 1540. He promulgated the Caroline Concession, collected the taxes that were overdue, stripped the town of its privileges and had the rebel leaders prosecuted. However, he could not bring himself to destroy his birthplace. He showed great magnanimity, confining his punishment to the levelling of the ramparts and the building of a citadel dubbed the "Spanish Castle", but still wished to teach the proud people of Ghent a lesson. He therefore insisted that the leading citizens beg forgiveness in public and walk through the city barefoot, wearing a white hair shirt, with a hangman's noose around their neck. Because of this public act of humiliation, the Ghent people were to be called "carriers of the noose" or 'Stroppendragers'. While this nickname was considered to be an insult in the past, today they are proud of it, especially during the Gentse Feesten, when these historical events are duly celebrated.

Religious strife disrupted community life at the end of the century. The Duke of Alba put down a revolt by Calvinist iconoclasts in 1567, but the Protestants reacted strongly; four days after the "Spanish Fury" in Antwerp, Philip II was forced to concede the **Pacification of Ghent** (1576) which freed the 17 provinces of the Low Countries of Spanish troops.

The town became a Republic in 1577, having revolted against the Spanish, but it was recaptured by Farnese in 1584. On 24 December 1814, the Treaty of Ghent was signed here, bringing to an end the war between Britain and the United States; the delegates sat down together the following day to eat their Christmas dinner.

From decline to revival – Ghent's economic decline continued during the 17C. The closure of the Scheldt by the Dutch in 1648 dealt a fatal blow to its commercial and industrial activities. However, at the start of the 19C, a new cycle of prosperity was initiated by a local man, **Lieven Bauwens**. His success in smuggling in a mule-jenny from England through the blockade imposed by France revived the textile industry and heralded the Industrial Revolution in continental Europe. Ghent became known as the "continental Manchester". The Belgian city spun and wove linen as well as cotton, since the waters of the Leie were suitable for the retting of flax.

At the instigation of King William I of the Netherlands, the 33km/21mi long canal from Ghent to Terneuzen was built in 1827, linking the **port** to the Western Scheldt. In 1968 it was made capable of handling 80 000t vessels, and its international cargo traffic reached 20 million tons in 1996.

Over the years, new industries have sprung up along the canal, including metalworking, chemicals and car assembly. The Sidmar complex in the port area north of the city produces several million tons of steel per year.

Ghent has also developed a prosperous local horticultural industry which has earned it the nickname "city of flowers": these activities involve around 2 000 companies within a 15km/9.5mi radius (mainly northeast of the town). A large proportion of its production is exported to countries all over the world.

Every five years the town hosts the famous **Gentse Floraliën** flower show in the Flanders Expo exhibition hall.

Directory

GETTING ABOUT

Drivers should be aware that Ghent discourages traffic in the city centre, and that it makes sense for visitors to leave their cars in one of the central car parks. The main city centre attractions are close to one another and are best explored on foot.

SIGHTSEEING

By carriage – *St Baafsplein – Easter-Oct, Sat, Sun, public holidays and daily in school holidays 10am-6pm – €24 per carriage.* Enjoyable tour in a horse-drawn carriage through the streets of this fine old city, taking in the main points of interest in the historic centre.

Boat trips – *Graslei or Korenlei – Mar-Nov: 10am-6pm – €5. From Graslei: information from Gent Watertoerist – ☎ 09 266 05 22 – www.gentwatertoerist.be. From Korenlei: information from Bootjes van Gent – ☎ 09 223 88 53 – www.bootjesvangent.be.* These two companies run trips by boat which give visitors an unusual view of old Ghent and its many attractions.

Minerva Boat Company – *Coupure Rechts-Lindenlei 2a – ☎ 09 233 79 17 – www.minervaboten.be – Jun-Aug: 10am-8pm; May, Oct: 1pm-7pm – 42, €14/114.* This company will hire you a little boat with a pleasantly silent motor, enabling you to explore the city waterways on your own. No licence necessary. Map of the river and canal network provided.

Illuminations – Floodlighting of the old town creates an extraordinary spectacle.

WHERE TO EAT

⊖ **Horta's Eethuis** – *Zwarte Zusterstraat 32 – ☎ 09 234 15 38 – Closed lunchtime Sat, Sun – €27.* This little place – Horta's Eating House – dedicated to the memory of the famous architect, serves no-frills cooking ideal for filling stomachs hollow from too much sightseeing. Outdoor dining in summer in a walled courtyard. Friendly service.

⊖⊖ **Pakhuis** – *Schuurkenstraat 4 – ☎ 09 223 55 55 – info@pakhuis.be – lunch €11 – €27.* In an old industrial warehouse, the Pakhuis is a brasserie and oyster bar with a spacious dining room and gallery. Closely packed tables and a faithfully recreated 1900 bistro ambience.

⊖⊖ **Kasteel van Laarne** – *Eekhoekstraat 7 – 9270 Laarne – ☎ 09 230 71 78 – Closed Mon, Tue and 3 wks in July – lunch €24 – €37/55.* Pleasant restaurant in the outbuildings of Laarne Castle, a few minutes from Ghent. When the sun allows there is outdoor dining by of the moat with a fine view of the fortress itself.

⊖⊖⊖ **Le Tête à Tête** – *Jan Breydelstraat 32 – ☎ 09 233 95 00 – Closed lunchtime Mon and Tue – ⊄ – €42.* An ideally located place to eat just a step from the Hoofdbrug. Selection of contemporary dishes. Weather permitting, meals are served outdoors with the river Leie and the Gravensteen as the background.

⊖⊖⊖ **De Blauwe Zalm** – *Vrouwebroerstraat 2 – ☎ 09 224 08 52 – Closed lunchtime Sat, Sun, lunchtime Mon, mid-July – mid-Aug – lunch €28 – €45.* The "Blue Salmon" lives up to its name with fine seafood served in the charming, contemporary-style interior, or in the courtyard in summer. Friendly reception and good service.

WHERE TO STAY

⊖ **Cecilia Jaime** – *Kraanlei 55 – ☎ 09 225 75 32 – rojaime@skynet.be – ⊄ – 2 rms: €40/70:* In the heart of one of the city's most historic districts, family bed & breakfast establishment with one bright and spacious room and two studios with a view of the river lined with historic buildings. Breakfast served in your room.

⊖ **La Maison de Claudine** – *Pussemierstraat 20 – ☎ 09 225 75 08 – ⊄ – 3 rms: €70/90 – ⊑ €12.40 – meals €16.10/24.80.* Claudine welcomes guests to her home in what used to be a 17C convent. Tasteful decor and attractive bedrooms. You are welcome to relax in the garden in fine weather.

⊖ **Chambre d'ami(e)s** – *Schoolstraat 14 – 9040 Sint-Amandsberg – ☎ 09 238 43 47 – jan.de.baets@pandora.be – ⊄ – 2 rms:*

€45/50⊑. On the edge of town, not far from the Groot Begijnhof, this guesthouse in an old patrician house accommodates its guests in fine rooms, each with a special theme (opera, belfry, the River Leie). Exquisite walled garden for lazing in.

⊖⊖ **Cour St-Georges** – *Botermarkt 2 – ☎ 09 224 24 24 – courstgeorges@skynet.be – ▣ – 36 rms: €89/125 – €11 – restaurant €28/39.* Stylish traditional inn next to the town hall. Those who have stayed here include Mary of Burgundy, Emperor Charles V and Napoleon. Attractive rooms with antique furnishings. The superb hall in Flemish Gothic style is gradually being returned to its former glory.

⊖⊖ **PoortAckere Monasterium** – *Oude Houtlei 58 – ☎ 09 269 22 10 – info@poortackere.com – ▣ – 34 rms: €95/120⊑.* This former convent has a very special atmosphere. Cloister garden, cosy bedrooms with more than monkish comforts and breakfast served in the old chapter house.

TAKING A BREAK

Pâtisserie Alsacienne Bloch – *Veldstraat 60-62 – ☎ 09 225 70 85 – 8am-7.30pm, Fri 8am-7.45pm, Sat 7.30am-7.45pm.* This establishment has been run by the same family from Alsace since 1898, and is famous for its traditional cakes, tarts and Viennese patisserie. Simple lunches and a tea room which attracts a good crowd in the afternoon.

HAVING A DRINK

't Dreupelkot – *Groentenmarkt 12 – ☎ 09 224 21 20 – 4pm-1am, Fri-Sat 5am.* Convivial little bar specialising in gin, with almost 200 varieties on offer. The owner is an inexhaustible source of wisdom about the juniper berry and the product derived from it. Outdoor drinking in summer by the canal.

't Velootje – *Kalversteeg – ☎ 09 223 28 34 – 8pm-3am.* With bicycles hanging from the ceiling, bric-à-brac scattered around and the occasional cobwebby statue, this establishment is as much a cabinet of curiosities as a bar. 'Celtic' music.

The Vrijdagmarkt.

Ch. Bastin – J. Evrard/MICHELIN

ENTERTAINMENT

What's On – List obtainable from the Tourist Information Centre.

De Vlaamse Opera – *Schouwburgstraat 3 – ☎ 09 225 24 25 – www.vlaamseopera.be – Box-office Tue-Sat 11am-5.45pm.* Magnificent theatre, with opera, dance and classical music.

Handelsbeurs – *Kouter 29 – ☎ 09 265 91 60 – www.handelsbeurs.be* Completely new concert hall in an historic setting devoted to music from around the world.

Vooruit *St-Pietersnieuwstraat 23 – ☎ 09 267 28 48 – www.vooruit.be – 11.30am-2am, Fri, Sat 3am, Sun 4pm-1am.* This striking Art Nouveau palace, "Forwards!", was originally built in 1914 as a centre of the local socialist movement. Nowadays all sorts of activities go on behind its splendid facade – theatre, dance, concerts… It is a city institution, with a bar much frequented by artists and students.

Ch. Bastin – J. Evrard/MICHELIN

Vooruit

Damberd Jazz Café – *Korenmarkt 19 – ☎ 09 329 53 37 – www.damberd.be – 11am-4am.* This venerable old building on Ghent's Cornmarket has been turned into a bar specialising in jazz. Plenty of buzz, walls decorated with pictures of the city, summer terrace. Live music most Tuesdays and Wednesdays.

Den Turk – *Botermarkt 3 – ☎ 09 233 01 97 – 11am-3am.* A popular rendezvous for local jazz fans. Just a few steps from the town hall and the belfry, it is in a building dating back to the 12C, though only since the 16C has it been possible to get a drink here.

SHOPPING

Ghent's department stores (C&A, H&M, Inno, FNAC) are in the pedestrian area bordered by **Veldstraat** and **Langemunt**, luxury fashion boutiques in **Brabantdam**, **Mageleinstraat** and in the vicinity of **Koestraat**. Collectors of antiques and rare objects will enjoy browsing in **Burgstraat** and in the quarter around the St-Jacobskerk. Exotic objects can be purchased in **Jan Breydelstraat** and the surrounding streets.

Markets – On weekdays a **fruit and vegetable market** is held on Groentenmarkt. The **flower market** is situated on Kouter, a popular meeting place

for Ghent people on Sundays. The **Vrijdagmarkt** *(Friday market)* offers all kinds of products on Fridays and Saturdays. There is also a friendly **flea market** around the Sint-Jacobskerk on Fridays, Saturdays and Sundays.

Specialities – Besides its delicious **waterzooi**, a clear chicken or fish soup, and **carbonades flamandes**, beef stew cooked in beer, Ghent is also famous for its strong mustard from Tierenteyn (Groentenmarkt 3) and its potent Bruggeman **genever** (gin). Those with a sweet tooth will enjoy the **confectionery** *(babbeluttes, mokken, stropkes).*

Temmerman – *Kraanlei 79 – ☎ 09 224 00 41 – Wed-Sat 11am-6pm.* This lovely confectioner's deals in a number of local specialities. There are *wippers* (toffees), *mokken* (biscuits with almonds or flavoured with aniseed), *babbelaars* and *trientjes* (sugary sweets), as well as spiced bread and candied flowers.

Vve Tierenteijn-Verlent – *Groentenmarkt 3 – ☎ 09 225 83 36 – Mon-Sat 8.30am-6pm.* A deliciously stimulating aroma fills the nostrils on entering this establishment, where mustard-making expertise has been practised for more than a century. The celebrated condiment is stored here in wooden barrels, and in addition there are unusual products such as fruit preserved in mustard and elderflower syrup.

't Vlaams Wandtapijt – *St-Baafsplein 6 – ☎ 09 223 16 43 – Mon-Sat 10am-6pm except Wed 2pm-6pm.* In the shadow of Ghent's famous belfry, this little shop specialises in Flemish tapestry, which is offered in various forms such as carpets, cushions and items of luggage. Friendly service.

Home Linen – *Korenlei 3 – ☎ 09 223 60 93 – 10am-6pm.* This attractive boutique offers lace from both Ghent (bobbin lace) and Brussels (needlepoint lace) as well as exporting its "designer home linen" to all parts of the world. Every kind of motif is available to enhance the appeal of clothes, tablecloths, sheets, duvets etc.

FESTIVALS AND EVENTS

Festivals – Ghent is a lively city in which many festivals are held:
Festival van Vlaanderen (opening ceremony in September); **Internationaal Filmfestival** (cinema, October), and of course the **Gentse Feesten** *(information: ☎ 09 269 46 00; www.gentsefeesten.be).* This is the most popular event of all, a famous street festival lasting for 10 days in the second fortnight of July, which has become the biggest of its kind in Europe. Every year over one million visitors flock to Ghent to soak up the local atmosphere and enjoy the many different events: music, theatre, mime, puppet shows, folklore etc.
Every five years, the **Gentse Floraliën** garden festival is held in the Flanders Expo complex *(next event 2005).*

Walking About

THE OLD TOWN★★★
Start at St-Baafsplein.

St-Baafskathedraal★★
8.30am-6pm (Nov-Mar 5pm), Sun 1pm-5pm.

The cathedral stands on the site of the 12C Church of St John. A few traces of this Romanesque church have survived in the crypt. In 1540 Emperor Charles V had the church of the Abbey of St Bavo pulled down to make way for the Spanish Palace. It was on this occasion that the Church of St John took on the name of the collegiate church of St Bavo. It became a cathedral in 1561.

The cathedral was built in stages and shows various tendencies. There are elements of Scaldian or Scheldt Gothic (chancel), Brabant Gothic (tower) and Late Gothic (nave). Yet despite this diversity, it conveys an overall impression of harmony and sober elegance.

The remarkable **tower** on the west side of the church is also the entrance, as is the rule in Brabant Gothic architecture. There is an extensive **view** of Ghent and its surroundings from the top of the tower.

The majestic effect of the **interior** is somewhat undermined by the neo-Classical marble choir screen, which disrupts the harmony of the elevations. The lofty chancel built of Tournai stone, which is slightly higher than the nave, dates from the 14C. It was extended in the 15C by five radiating chapels and surmounted by a triforium. A certain rhythmic regularity is added to the ambulatory by marble columns and finely worked Baroque doors. The plain sandstone and brick nave dates from the 16C and harmonises well with the elegant Late Gothic balustrades and the fine ribbed vaulting. The cathedral contains many valuable works of art.

Adoration of the Mystic Lamb Altarpiece★★★ – *In the chapel on the left as you enter.*

This superb polyptych has had many an adventure. It was donated to the church by Joos Vijd, a wealthy local patrician, and was solemnly placed in the first radiating chapel to the right of the ambulatory in 1432. Philip II wanted to take possession of it, while the Protestants wanted to burn it in 1566, Emperor Joseph II had the paintings of Adam and Eve removed as he found them shocking, and the French Directoire had it sent to Paris where it remained until 1815. It then lost several of its panels which were exhibited in the Berlin Museum. It was re-assembled in 1920, but the panel of the Righteous Judges *(below, to the left)* was stolen in 1934. In 1941 it was replaced by a copy. The polyptych was first entrusted to the French during the Second World War, but the German authorities transferred it to Austria, where American troops found it in 1945 in a salt mine. The work was returned once more to the original chapel, but was moved again in 1986 to a more secure location where viewing it would be easier. It is now exhibited in the former baptistery which has been converted into a strong room.

The authorship of the work has given rise to many a controversy. Is it the work of **Jan van Eyck** alone? Or are we to believe the Latin inscription on the frame, which claims that it was executed in collaboration with Van Eyck's older brother Hubert, although no other painting by this artist is known? In any case, the colossal work depicts no fewer than 248 characters. As was the case in the original chapel, the scene is illuminated by a single source of light coming from the right, reflected in the many precious stones and other jewels adorning the figures. The polyptych displays incomparable style and technique; it is a vivid illustration of the Christian ideals of the Middle Ages.

The **paintings on the lower level** depict the Mystic Lamb on an altar surrounded by angels. Approaching the altar from either side of the Fountain of

BRIDGEMAN-GIRAUDON

Adoration of the Mystic Lamb Altarpiece by Jan van Eyck – Detail

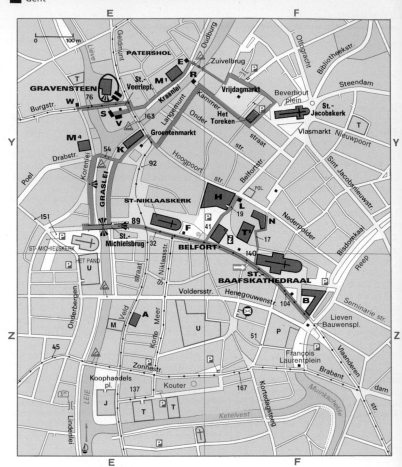

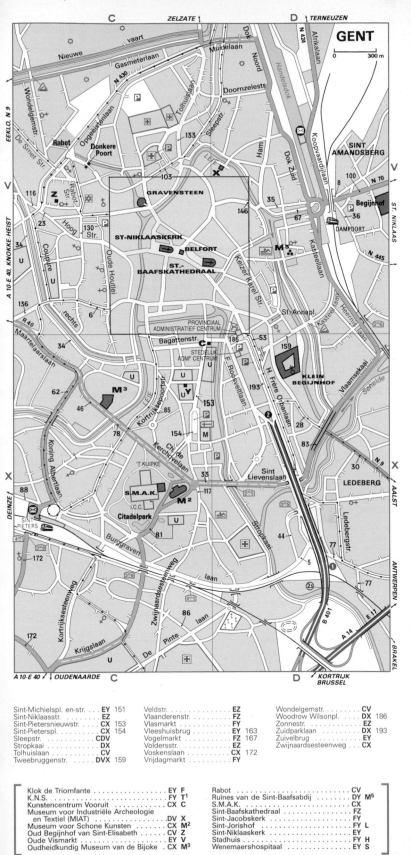

Life are the Knights and the Righteous Judges, from the left, and the Hermits and Pilgrims, from the right. In the background the Virgins are gathered on the right, and the Martyrs and Confessors on the left.

The vegetation is shown in luminous colours, and in minute detail; botanists have identified 42 species of plants and flowers.

In the **upper register** we see Christ Triumphant, enthroned as the Great High Priest. To the left of Him are the Virgin Mary, a choir of angels and Adam. To the right, St John the Baptist, a group of angel musicians, and Eve. The vivid realism of the figures and the decorative beauty of the fabrics are truly stunning.

When closed, the panels represent the Annunciation in the centre, with the Prophets and the Sibyls above, and St John the Baptist, St John the Evangelist and the donors, Joos Vijd and his wife Elisabeth Borluut, below. *Apr-Oct: 9.30am (Sun 1pm)-5pm; Nov-Mar: 10.30am-4pm, Sun 2-5pm (last admission 45min before closing). Closed religious holidays.* €2.50. ☎ 09 225 16 26.

Cathedral furniture and works of art – The monumental Rococo pulpit (1741) with its marble statues is by L Delvaux. HF Verbruggen made the high altar in the chancel in the Baroque style. It depicts the *Apotheosis of St Bavo*. Left of the chancel stands the mausoleum of Monsignor Triest (1654) by Jérôme Duquesnoy the Younger, who was to become famous for his **Manneken Pis** statue. The figure's weary expression is striking.

The altarpiece of *Jesus Among the Doctors* (1751), by Frans Pourbus the Elder is in the first ambulatory chapel to the south. Many famous figures feature on it, including Emperor Charles V in the lower left corner. Rubens' depiction of the *Vocation of St Bavo* (1624) can be seen in the 10th ambulatory chapel. The artist represented himself as a convert in a red cloak.

Crypt★ – This, the largest crypt in Flanders, has the same layout as the chancel above it. The oldest part (1150) is marked out in black tiles on the floor. 15C and 16C naive ex-votos are painted on the pillars and the Romanesque vaulting taken from the Church of St John. There is also a valuable collection of church plate in the crypt including a silver reliquary of St Macarius by Hugo de la Vigne (1616), a 9C gospel book and a necrological scroll describing monastic life in the Middle Ages. One of the chapels containing tombstones also includes the remarkable **Calvary triptych★** painted by Justus van Gent, a major work executed by the artist in 1466, before he left for Italy. The influence of Van Eyck and Van der Weyden is very clear (group of holy women in front of the Cross). This work is striking for the subtlety of the often acidic colours.

The 13C castle that belonged to Gerard the Devil, **Geraard de Duivelsteen**, is behind the east end of the cathedral. This austere medieval dwelling was extensively restored in the 19C and belonged to a Ghent lord of this name. It currently houses the Royal Archives. The bronze statues fronting the Steen were erected in 1913 to pay tribute to the Van Eyck brothers. On the rotunda, to the right, stands the statue portraying Liévin Bauwens (1769-1822) *(see below)*.

Go along Biezekapelstraat to the left of the cathedral.

De Achtersikkel

With its turrets and arcaded courtyard, this splendid 16C patrician's residence forms a fine ensemble. The premises have been home to the Academy of Music since 1900.

Note the series of old façades in Hoogpoortstraat, a little further along.

Return to Sint-Baafsplein.

Opposite the neo-Renaissance **Koninklijke Vlaamse Schouwburg** (1897), in the centre of an ornamental pond, stands a memorial to **Jan Frans Willems** (1793-1846), the "father of the Flemish Movement".

Belfort and Lakenhalle★★★

Mid-Mar to mid-Nov: 10am-1pm, 2-6pm (last admission 30 mins before closing). €3. ☎ 09 233 07 72.

Ghent's formidable belfry (91m/298ft), topped with a gilded copper dragon, symbolises the power of the city's guilds during the Middle Ages. It was built in the 13C and 14C and has frequently been altered and restored. Adjoining it is the 15C Cloth Hall or **Lakenhalle**. The carillon consists of 52 chimes.

Inside the **belfry**, the room called "The Secret" once contained documents defining the privileged status of the town. Today there is a statue of a wild-looking man-at-arms, the only survivor of the four that once decorated the belfry's corners.

There is a fine **view** of the town from the upper platform. At the foot of the belfry is the sculpture entitled the *Fountain of Kneeling People* by George Minne.

Walk round the belfry to see the door (1741) of the **old prison** embellished with the "suckling man ", the **mammelokker**. This Baroque low relief is a symbol of Christian charity. Cimon, an old Roman who was condemned to die of hunger, was suckled by his own daughter.

Continue to Botermarkt.

Stadhuis

May-Oct: guided tours (2hrs) Mon-Thur 2.30pm. Closed public holidays. €6. ☎ 09 233 07 72.

Building work on a new town hall on the site of its predecessor began in 1518 to plans by Dominique de Waghemakere and Rombaut Keldermans. It was interrupted in 1535, however, and resumed 60 years later, hence the two different styles.

The 16C **Huis van de Schepenen van de Keure** (Charterhouse) on the right is decorated with a corner turret and built in Late Gothic style. The chapel, a little balcony (for proclamations) and a flight of steps project from the north façade *(Hoogpoortstraat)*. The Bollaerts Room, a fine example of Mannerist architecture, and the Baroque conciergerie are subsequent additions. The left section, built at a later date (early 17C), took its inspiration from the Italian Renaissance. This is the **Huis van de Schepenen van Gedele**, named after the aldermen responsible for settling disputes. Finally, the south façade giving onto Poelijemarkt was completed towards the mid 18C.

Part of the Charterhouse is open to the public. The visit includes the Hall of Justice with its labyrinth pavement, which leads onto the balcony from which the Pacification of Ghent was proclaimed and into a chapel with beautiful Gothic vaulting. The Throne Room upstairs features Renaissance vaulting.

The 15C crossbowmen's guildhall, **St-Jorishof**, stands opposite the town hall. In the past it was also used as a post house for carriages and now houses a hotel and restaurant.

Go to the apse of St-Niklaaskerk

To the left is a bell called **De Triomfante** (The Triumphant One), which once adorned the belfry with the saying: "This bell carries the name of Roeland; when it chimes, it brings bad news ". The bell cracked in 1914; it was taken down from the belfry and brought here.

St-Niklaaskerk★

The construction on Romanesque foundations of this monumental parish church in Tournai stone started in 1200. A second phase of building took place between 1220 and 1250.

During this period, the sturdy tower over the crossing was used as a belfry and decorated with imposing stone figures depicting watchmen. Soon afterwards the side aisles were covered with vaulting and the interior saw considerable changes. Later still, the chancel was reinforced with flying buttresses. During the Wars of Religion in the 16C, the interior was entirely demolished, then replaced by a Baroque interior in the 17C.

The east façade of the church overlooks **Korenmarkt** (Corn Market), a popular meeting place with many cafés and restaurants which is the heart of the Cuve district. In summer it is pleasant to relax on a terrace and watch the bustle of daily life and the stream of shoppers in search of a good bargain.

Walk to the left of the post office to the St-Michielsbrug.

St-Michielsbrug

There is a stunning **view★★★** of the old town's historic buildings from St Michael's Bridge. Turn round to admire the towers of St Nicholas' Church, the belfry and the Cathedral.

From the centre of the bridge, the view to the right reveals the Late Gothic apse of St-Michielskerk and the old 15C Dominican convent next to it which is now a university building (Het Pand); to the left are the crenellations of the Gravensteen and, in front of it, the houses on the quays known as Graslei and Korenlei.

Continue to Graslei.

Graslei★★★

There is a good view of the house fronts from Korenlei.

In the Middle Ages, this used to be Ghent's harbour, the backbone of the city. The Graslei (Herb Quay) is lined with 12C to 17C houses, in a very pure architectural style. From left to right, the most interesting houses are:

– the 16C Gildehuis van de Metselaars, the (rebuilt) masons' guildhall which has a tall stone façade crowned with graceful pinnacles;

– the first Korenmetershuis (15C), the Grain Weighers' hall, presenting a typical Flemish crow-stepped gable;

– the large, sombre Koornstapelhuis in local Romanesque style, which was a warehouse for grain taken as payment in kind for customs duty.

– the tiny Tolhuisje (1682), the smallest building in the town, where customs officers were lodged;

– the second Gildehuis der Graanmeters (1698) with 14C vaulted cellars;

– the Gildehuis der Vrije Schippers, the Free Boatmen's hall. The doorway is surmounted with the figure of a ship, and the wonderful façade is crowned with a Brabant Gothic gable with gently flowing lines, which dates from 1531.

Return to Graslei and continue to Groentenmarkt.

Groentenmarkt

On the left-hand side of the vegetable market stands the meat market, the **Groot Vleeshuis**, a building dating from 1404 which features an impressive oak structure and crow-stepped dormer windows. The wooden stalls leaning against the façade were used for selling offal. On the corner stands **'t Galgenhuyseken** (Little Gibbet House), where gallows were set up in former times.

Go along Langemunt and Kammerstraat to Vrijdagmarkt.

Dulle Griet

This huge 15C cannon ('Mad Meg') was brought to Ghent in 1578 to defend the town against the Spanish occupying forces. However, when it arrived, it turned out to be impossible to use.

Vrijdagmarkt

The enormous Friday Market was the scene of many historical episodes. The sovereigns of Flanders would come here to address the people. Weavers and wool workers fought bloody battles here in May 1345. During one of these violent encounters, Jacob van Artevelde *(see above)* was assassinated; he is commemorated by a statue.

North of the square, the imposing Ons Huis-Bond Moyson house (1897-1902) was built in eclectic style by F Dierkens. The left section accommodated a poorhouse; the right section was a warehouse used to store by Socialist welfare organisations to store clothes.

The house with the turret on the far side of the marketplace is **Het Toreken**. It dates from 1451-58 and belonged to the tanners' guild. It was used mainly for selling cotton and linen cloth. When lengths of cloth failed to measure up to standard in terms of quality and size, they were put out to hang from the balustrade of the turret as a sign of disgrace.

Further east are the three towers of **St-Jacobskerk**. The two towers on the west front are Romanesque, but one of them was given a sandstone roof with crockets in the 15C. The small square adjoining the church is the setting for a lively flea market on Fridays, Saturdays and Sundays.

Cross the River Leie by the Zuivelbrug (Dairy Bridge).

Patershol

Take Rodekoningstraat to reach the heart of Patershol, one of the most attractive and picturesque districts of Ghent. It is also one of the oldest.

Return the way you came and go along the Kraanlei bordering the River Leie.

Kraanlei

Interesting houses line Crane Quay, in particular the one known as **'t Vliegend Hert**, or Kite House. Next door is a house decorated with low reliefs representing works of mercy.

Continue to St-Veerleplein.

St-Veerleplein

This square, which was once used for executions, is surrounded by old houses. The **Wenemaershospitaal**, a hospice named after St Lawrence, has a façade dating from 1564. The old Baroque Fish Market, **Oude Vismarkt**, dating from 1689, has beautifully modelled reliefs crowning the portico; they represent Neptune as well as the Leie and Scheldt.

PATERSHOL

Between Lange Steenstraat, Het Sluizeken, Geldmunt and the River Leie, Patershol takes its name from a narrow tunnel located beneath the Carmelite convent which enabled local residents to fetch water from the Ploter Canal. Architecturally speaking, this area is characterised by smallish houses occupied by artisans; the earliest date back to the 12C. It also features imposing town houses and two medieval convents.

Patershol has had an eventful past. Home to religious institutions and craftsmen in medieval times, in the 17C and 18C it became a fashionable district, home to many of Ghent's lawyers and magistrates. However, during the 19C, it fell into decline and acquired the reputation of a bad and dangerous place. It was only in the 1980s that serious renovation work on Patershol actually began. Although a great many cafés and restaurants have been established here, it remains above all a residential area, much frequented by the city's students and artists. During the weekend around 15 August, it is the setting for the local festival called the Patersholfeesten.

A street in the Patershol.

Ch. Bastin et J. Evrard/MICHELIN

The Gravensteen.

Gravensteen★★

9am-6pm (Oct-Mar 5pm). Closed 1-2 Jan, 25-26 Dec; €6.20. ☎ 09 225 93 06 or 09 269 37 30.

The Castle of the Counts was built in 1180 by the Count of Flanders, Philip of Alsace, on the site of an older keep. It was extensively restored in the early 20C. At the time there was nothing left but a few ruins occupied by a spinning mill. Its architecture drew inspiration from the Crusader castles in Syria. Its ring of curtain walls features oriels, watch turrets and merlons, all reflected in the waters of the Leie.

Highlights of the interior include the "Romanesque gallery" with twin windows in the east wall of the keep, and the splendid rooms in the Count's Residence, one of which was used by the seventh chapter of the Order of the Golden Fleece in 1445, presided over by Philip the Good. Another chamber now contains a collection of instruments of torture, recalling that the castle served as a prison for many years.

From the top of the keep there is a superb **view★** of Ghent and the surrounding area.

Go round the keep to enter the old stables, a vaulted crypt with a well.

On leaving the castle, note the **Huis der Gekroonde Hoofden**, literally the "House of Crowned Heads", at the beginning of Burgstraat. It is decorated with medallions containing busts of the Counts of Flanders.

Worth a Visit

MONUMENTS AND MUSEUMS

The City Centre

Huis van Alijn★

Tue-Sun 11am-5pm. Closed 1 Jan, 25 Dec. €2.50. www.huisvanalijn.be; ☎09 269 23 50

The city's **Folk Museum** is housed in the cottages and Late Gothic chapel of the 14C almshouses called the Huis van Alijn or Hospitaal der Kindren Alyns. The inner **courtyard★** makes a pretty picture, surrounded by the delightful white houses and their tall dormer windows.

The museum is devoted to Flemish popular arts and traditions. Among the 40 or so rooms, there are remarkable reconstructions of shops (grocer's, estaminet, apothecary's), domestic interiors, craftsmen's workshops (cobbler's, wax-taper maker's, wood-turner's) recalling life in Ghent in c 1900. Beneath the eaves there is a **Puppet Theatre** starring the legendary Ghent hero Pierke Pierlala. *Performances Wed and Sat 2.30pm; during the Gentse Feesten (week of 21 Jul): 3pm, first Thur of Jan, Thur of Carnival holidays and Thur of Easter holidays 2.30pm. Closed Aug, 1 Jan, 25 Dec. €2.50. ☎ 09 269 23 67; www.huisvanalijn.be*

Designmuseum Gent★

Tue-Sun. 10am-6pm. Closed 1-2 Jan, 25-26 Dec. €2.50. ☎ 09 267 99 99; design.museum .gent.be

The Design Museum's **16C and 17C collections** are housed in the elegant rooms of the 18C Coninck Mansion. They include fine furniture grouped by period, tapestries and objets d'art which recreate the atmosphere of a patrician home of days gone by. Certain rooms are decorated with painted canvas panels. With its wooden chandelier, pretty furniture and fine Chinese porcelain, the **dining room** is truly a feast for the eyes.

The new wing at the rear of the building contains the **modern collections**, running from 1880 to the present day. The ground floor hosts temporary exhibitions while the first floor has works from between 1880 and 1950. Special attention should be paid to the exhibitions of Art Deco, the Modernist movement (E Lenoble, H Hoste, Le Corbusier) and Art Nouveau (superb interiors by Henry van de Velde and Paul Hankar). Other exhibits are arranged so as to explain various aspects of architectural and decorative

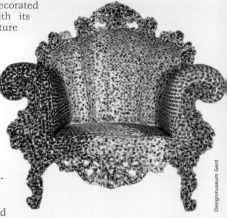

Alessandro Mendini – the 'Fauteuil Proust'.

Designmuseum Gent

design in Western Europe at the turn of the 20C. The upper floor gives a retrospective of decorative art in the 1970s and 1980s. The museum also introduces visitors to contemporary creations in the field of jewellery, furniture and ceramics. Note the extraordinary Kandissi armchair by the American designer and architect Alessandro Mendini.

South of the Centre

Museum voor Schone Kunsten★★
Tue-Sun (open Easter Mon) 10am-6pm. Closed 1˙2 Jan, 25-26 Dec. €2.50. ☎ *09 222 17 03.*

This large art gallery stands on the edge of the Citadelpark with its splendid octagonal bandstand dating from 1885. The gallery houses extensive and interesting collections of ancient and modern art from the 15C to the first half of the 20C. While the collection of sculptures and 18C Brussels tapestries is outstanding, it is the paintings in particular that make this a gallery well worth a visit.

Old Masters – The collection of old master paintings includes the delightful *Virgin with Carnation* by Rogier van der Weyden's pupils and the two paintings by **Hieronymus Bosch** that explore the theme of Good versus Evil. The first of the two, **St Jerome**, is a work from his early years. The foreground represents Evil, with the saint at prayer surrounded by terrifying objects and a menacing natural landscape; in the background, the peaceful landscape represents Good. The *Bearing of the Cross*, one of the great painter's last works, reveals an extraordinary modernism in the way the mass of bloated, demonic faces is depicted, with the serene countenance of Christ in the centre. The figure of Christ is set between two diagonals: one symbolises Evil with the beam of the Cross and the face of the bad thief on the lower right. The other links the face of the good thief with St Veronica withdrawing with the shroud.

Adriaan Isenbrant's *Virgin and Child* has a strikingly beautiful landscape. There are also some fine portraits by the 16C Ghent miniaturist Gheeraert Hoorenbaut.

The museum provides an interesting overview of **16C and 17C painting**, concentrating on artists from the Low Countries: Pieter Brueghel the Younger, Frans Pourbus the Elder *(Portrait of a Young Woman)*, Rubens, Jordaens *(Study of Heads)*, Van Heemskerck, Maarten de Vos, Gaspar de Crayer *(Study of Young Moor's Head)*, Philippe de Champaigne *(Disciples on the Road to Emmaus, Portrait of Pierre Camus)*, and Frans Hals *(Portrait)*.

Modern painting – This extensive collection presents a survey of Belgian painting from the **19C to the early 20C**. The influence of the 19C French School is demonstrated by Géricault's remarkable *Portrait of a Kleptomaniac* as well as by the landscapes of Corot, Courbet, Daubigny and Théodore Rousseau, illustrating both Realism and Romanticism. Belgian Expressionism and Surrealism are represented by Claus, Van Rysselberghe *(The Reading)*, Evenepoel *(Spaniard in Paris)*, Spilliaert and Khnopff. Visitors can also admire a great many works by Ensor, along with sculptures and sketches by the Ghent artist George Minne. The latter painter, like his contemporaries Gustave van de Woestijne and Valerius de Saedeleer, belonged to the second Sint Martens-Latem School. The spirit of Flemish Expressionism is expressed by the works of Albert Servaes, Constant Permeke *(Reclining Peasant)*, Gust de Smet, Frits van den Berghe and Rik Wouters. The collections also cover international Expressionism with paintings by Kokoschka, Rouault, Kirchner, Rohlfs and Heckel.

SMAK (Stedelijk Museum voor Actuele Kunst Gent)★★

 ♿ *Tue-Sun. 10am-6pm. Closed 25 Dec to 1 Jan. €4.96.* ☎ *09 221 17 03; www.smak.be*
Housed in the old exhbition halls, this museum was built on the occasion of the
World Fair in 1913 and completely renovated in 1999 by the architect Koen Van
Nieuwenhuyse. Its curator and director is Jan Hoet, an *enfant terrible* of the arts
world, an organiser of Documenta IX, a renowned annual show held in Kassel in
Germany. The fascinating collections are presented in rotation and portray the
evolution of art from the 1950s to the present day. Works include *Aeromodeller* by
Panamarenko, *Wirtschaftswerte (Economic Values)* by Joseph Beuys, *Two Watchmen*
by Juan Muñoz, *Le Gardien de notre potager* by Thierry De Cordier and *La Toilette*
by Ilya Kabakov. The museum also organises important temporary exhibitions.

Oudheidkundig Museum van de Bijloke★★

Thur 10am-1pm, 2-6pm, Sun 2-6pm. €2.50. ☎ *09 225 11 06.*
The Cistercians founded the Abbey of Bijloke in the 13C, though the present
remarkable group of buildings date from the 14C to the 18C. They are currently
undergoing restoration and only parts are open to the public.
The rooms off the cloisters have been furnished in a variety of styles and illustrate life in Ghent from the Middle Ages to the French Revolution. Two rooms are
devoted to the town's military guilds.
The marvellous 14C **refectory** on the first floor has a large coffered vault and
frescoes, one of which represents the *Last Supper*. The recumbent effigy in the
centre of the room is that of a Ghent nobleman who died in 1232. This room has
been turned into a treasury containing precious religious works.
The dormitory has magnificent 18C carved wooden *torchères* (torch-holders) symbolising the different trades.

Boekentoren

Rozier 9. The central library or "book tower" of the University of Ghent (1933-40)
lies in a bustling district of the city. An austere Modernist structure in concrete, it
was built to plans by Henry van de Velde (1863-1957), the founder of the
Kunstgewerbeschule in Weimar and forerunner of the Bauhaus movement. The
64m/210ft tower has 26 storeys including a wonderful reception room (Belvedere)
of particularly pure design.

Klein Begijnhof★

Lange Violettenstraat. This tranquil Beguine convent was founded in 1234 by
Joanna of Constantinople. It has not changed since the 17C. The charming brick
houses, with small front gardens and whitewashed walls, surround the church
and two lawns.

North of the Centre

Museum voor Industriële Archeologie en Textiel (MIAT)★

Minnemeers 9. ♿ *Tue-Sun 10am-6pm. Closed 1-2 Jan, 25-26 Dec. €2.50.* ☎ *09 269
42 00.* Housed in an old cotton mill (1905-13), the museum depicts the industrial
history of the city. The changes experienced over the centuries are illustrated by
miscellaneous objects and documents, reconstructed interiors and especially by a
great many machines, including the famous **mule-jenny** smuggled in from
England.
The first section *(fifth floor)* covers the period 1750-1900, with special emphasis
placed on the role played by women in society (there is also a splendid **view** of
the towers of the city from this part of the museum). The exhibitions devoted to
the period 1900-2000 *(fourth floor)* show the technological and economic changes
brought about by the 20C. The numerous machines related to the cotton industry
(third floor) allow visitors to follow the successive stages of production, viewing
old-fashioned techniques and seeing how rough cotton can be turned into the
final dyed fabric.
The modern wing of the museum hosts temporary exhibitions; the plants grown
in the garden were once used for dyeing material produced on the premises.

East of the Centre

St-Baafsabdij

Closed for reconstruction.
Now in ruins, the abbey dedicated to St Bavo was founded in the 7C and rebuilt in
the 10C.
In 1540, having proclaimed the Caroline Concession *(see above)*, Emperor
Charles V turned the abbey into a fortress known as the Spanish Citadel. It was
demolished in the 19C.
Nothing remains of the abbey buildings apart from one gallery of the Gothic cloisters, the beautiful Romanesque lavabo, the twin Romanesque windows in the chapter-house and above all the vast 12C **refectory★**, with its magnificent timber ceiling
shaped like a ship's hull. It contains Romanesque frescoes and a large collection of
tombstones. There is also Romanesque and Gothic stonework in the undercroft.

Oud Begijnhof St-Elisabeth

The large Beguine convent was founded, like the small one, in 1234. When it became inadequate for their needs in the 19C the nuns left it and moved to St-Amandsberg. All that now remains is a narrow, picturesque street, **Proveniersterstraat**, near the church dedicated to St Elizabeth. Around the church there are three pretty houses with crow-stepped gables which have been carefully restored.

Begijnhoflaan leads northwards to the **Rabot**. This gate (1489) with pointed roofs and crow-stepped gables is in fact an old lock into which the Lième disappears to flow partly underground. By following Bachterwalle, you will reach the **Donkere Poort**; the "Dark Gate" is all that remains of the palace (Prinsenhof) where Emperor Charles V was born on 24 February 1500.

Excursions

St-Amandsberg

1.5km/1mi NE on Land van Waaslaan. The entrance to the convent is in Schoolstraat, a narrow street leading off Land van Waaslaan.

Groot Begijnhof – In 1874 this replaced the old Beguine convent of St Elizabeth. It is a huge enclosure with the traditional layout of Beguine convents clustered around a neo-Gothic church like a small village. A few nuns still live here and a **museum** presents information on life in the convent. *Apr-Oct: Wed-Fri 9-11am, 2pm-5pm, Sat-Sun 2-5pm. €1. ☎ 09 228 19 13.*

Lochristi

9km/5.5mi NE on N 70. The cultivation of azaleas and summer-flowering begonias predominates in this large agricultural centre.

Laarne★

13km/8mi E. Leave on N 445 and turn left towards Heusden.

Magnificent properties can be seen along the road to Heusden. The grey walls of the **Kasteel van Laarne** are flanked with stone-roofed towers and a turreted keep. The castle is surrounded by a moat. It was built in the 12C to defend Ghent and was altered in the 17C. The main courtyard and present entrance, which is preceded by a stone bridge and surmounted by a loggia, date from this period.

The **interior** has been refurnished to recreate the atmosphere of a 17C stately home. The rooms have splendid fireplaces and Antwerp and French furniture of massive proportions. The walls are hung with marvellous tapestries. Two of these were woven in Brussels in the 16C. They were based on cartoons by B van Orley and belong to the series known as the *Hunts of Maximilian*. On the ground floor note the Renaissance vaulting in the gallery overlooking the inner courtyard. On the first floor there is an elegant 16C tapestry depicting aristocratic life. Finally, visitors should not miss the 15C-18C European **silver collection★** donated by M Claude Dallemagne. *Jul-Aug: daily except Mon and Fri, 1-5.30pm, mid-Apr to end Oct: Sun 1-5.30pm. €5. ☎ 09 230 91 55.*

Eeklo

20km/12.5mi NW on N 9. Eeklo has a pretty Renaissance **town hall**, with crow-stepped gables and dormers and brightly coloured shutters.

The 16C **Watervliet** church, *(29km/18mi north on N 456, near the border with the Netherlands)* has a beautiful 15C triptych painted on wood, and interesting Baroque furniture.

ALONG THE RIVER LEIE (LEIESTREEK)

28.5km/18mi. Leave on the Koningin Fabiolalaan, near the station (St-Pietersstation). The best way of exploring the river itself is by taking a boat trip: the tourist office in Ghent can advise on times and prices

Afsnee

This charming Romanesque church on the river bank has been the subject of countless paintings.

THE ARTISTS' COLONY

The banks of the Leie have inspired many a painter. At the end of the 19C a group of artists formed around sculptor George Minne, who had lived in the village of Sint Martens-Latem since 1897. Among the group's members were Gustave van de Woestijne (1881-1947), and the landscape painters Albijn Van den Abeele (1835-1918) and Valerius de Saedeleer (1867-1941).

After the first world war, their efforts led to the very marked Expressionism of the second Sint Martens-Latem group, of which the forerunner was **Albert Servaes** (1873-1967). The main representatives were Constant Permeke (1886-1952), the leading figure **Gustave de Smet** (1877-1943) and **Frits Mayer van den Bergh** (1883-1939).

Boat on the Leie.

Sint Martens-Latem

The area around this village near the Leie is understandably popular with people from Ghent; note the sumptuous villas nestling in their luxuriant setting. A 15C wooden windmill can be seen on the left from the road running through the village.

Deurle

Its prosperous villas nestling in well-stocked gardens, leafy Deurle stands on the banks of the Leie in the heart of the area dear to the hearts of the Expressionist painters of Sint Martens-Latem.

Museum Gust de Smet – The house to which the Ghent artist Gust (or Gustave) de Smet (1877-1943) retired to paint from 1935 until his death is now a museum. The studio and interior have remained unchanged and contain many works by this artist from the second group of Sint Martens-Latem artists. *Wed-Sun 2pm-6pm (Oct-Mar 5pm). Closed Jan. €2.50.* ☎ *09 282 77 42.*

Museum Léon de Smet – This house was built in 1969 by the last companion of Gust de Smet's brother, Léon (1881-1966). It contains the painter's furniture and the everyday objects that he depicted in his paintings. About 20 of his paintings and drawings are exhibited. *Sat-Sun 2.30-6pm (from early Nov to mid-Apr 5pm). Closed Jan, Jul, 1 Nov, 25 Dec.* ☎ *09 282 30 90.*

Museum Dhondt-Dhaenens – This long white brick building next to the Museum Léon de Smet was built in 1969. It offers a good general view of Flemish Expressionism, which was based on the Latem School.

The museum houses works by great masters such as Permeke *(Lady in the Green Hat, Golden Landscape)*, Van den Berghe, Gust de Smet *(Twilight, Farm, Shooting Gallery)* and their precursor Albert Servaes whose works are steeped in tragic mysticism *(Executioner, The Passion, The Tomb, Resurrection)*. Finally, there are also a few sculptures and an exhibition room. ♿ *Early Feb to mid-Dec: Tue-Sun 1pm (Sat, Sun and public holidays 11am)-5pm. €2.50.* ☎ *09 281 08 53.*

Beyond Deurle the route initially follows the Leie (pretty view on the left), before crossing a bridge. There is then a beautiful **view** of the river meandering lazily between rich green meadows.

Kasteel Ooidonk

Early Apr to mid-Sept: guided tour (1hr) Sun, public holidays, 2-5.30pm (Jul-Aug also Sat, same times). €5. ☎ *09 282 61 23.*

This late 16C castle stands in a bend of the River Leie, near the village of Bachte-Maria-Leerne. It replaced a medieval fortress that was inhabited by the Lords of Nevele and destroyed during the Wars of Religion.

The present castle, surrounded by water and a park, is still inhabited. It is characteristic of the Hispano-Flemish style, with crow-stepped gables and onion-domed towers. The interior was refurbished in the 19C and includes a beautiful suite of apartments. Among the 16C portraits are those of Philip of Montmorency, Count of Hornes and owner of the castle, and the Count of Egmont. Both were beheaded in Brussels in 1568.

Deinze

This small industrial town on the banks of the Leie has a fine **church** dedicated to Our Lady *(Onze-Lieve-Vrouwekerk)*. It dates from the 13C and is an excellent example of Scaldian Gothic. A work by Gaspar de Crayer depicting the Adoration of the Shepherds can be seen inside.

A little further along, the white building of the **Museum van Deinze en de Leiestreek** can be glimpsed. The Sint Martens-Latem group is well represented in the collections of paintings and sculptures by artists from the Ghent-Kortrijk area. The most striking works are *Beetroot Harvest* by Émile Claus, *Marshy Landscape* by Saedeleer and paintings by A Saverys, A Servaes, Van de Woestijne, George Minne, Van Rysselberghe, Van den Abeele and R Raveel. The museum also has an archaeology and folklore section.

Machelen

This quiet little village on the banks of the river was the birthplace of the celebrated artist Roger Raveel (1921-). In a resolutely modern building designed by Stéphane Beel, a **museum** gives a good overview of his work, which, combining figurative and abstract elements, is close to New Realism and draws on the realities of everyday life. *Wed-Sun, 11am-5pm. Closed Christmas-New Year.* ☎ 09 381 60 00.

Close to the river is *Het plein van de Nieuwe Visie* (The Square of the New Vision) depicting the artist and his wife.

Geraardsbergen★

In a prominent location★ on the steep slopes of the Oudenberg hill overlooking the River Dender, Geraardsbergen is famous in the world of cycle racing because of its "wall", the daunting and roughly cobbled ascent known as the "Kappelmuur", or "Mur de Grammont" in French. The local speciality is mattentaart, a delicious tart made with curd and fromage frais.

Location

Oost-Vlaanderen – Population 30 825 – Michelin maps 716 E3 and 533 I18.
On the N 42, Geraardsbergen is just on the Flanders side of the language border from the province of Hainaut.
🛈 *Markt,* ☎ *054 43 72 89; www. geraardsbergen.be*

Worth a Visit

Grote Markt

The town's main square is dominated by the St-Bartholomeuskerk. The church was renovated in the neo-Gothic style in the 19C, as was the 19C town hall with its toothed gables and corner turrets. The little Manneken Pis on the outside is said to be the oldest in Belgium (1455); his costumes are displayed in the museum on the ground floor of the building. In the centre of the square, the Gothic fountain called the Marbol dates from 1475.

St-Adriaansabdij

Follow Vredestraat to the left of the town hall, then turn right into Abdijstraat. Early Apr to mid-Sept: guided tours (1hr) Sun and public holidays, 2-5.30pm (Jul-Aug also Sat at same times). €5. ☎ *09 282 61 23.*
A Benedictine monastery was founded here in 1081. The 18C abbey buildings have now been turned into a **museum**, with old paintings and furniture from the St-Bartholomeuskerk in Geraardsbergen and from the Hane Steenhuyse in Ghent. There are also some old paintings. The exhibits are displayed in various rooms opening onto a wide vaulted corridor. The second floor presents exhibits relating to the cultivation of tobacco, a flourishing business in Geraardsbergen from 1840 until the Second World War. Another room has a display of black Chantilly lace which was made locally from 1870 onwards. There is also a collection of pipes from all over the world.

The waggon sheds in the park laid out around a lake have been restored to provide exhibition space.

Oudenberg

Access by car by Oude Steenweg then turn left into Driepikkel. A pilgrims' chapel containing a 17C statue of the Virgin Mary was built at the top of this hill, 110m/364ft high. There is a fine view of the surrounding countryside from the chapel. The **Krakelingenworp Festival** (literally "sugar bun throwing") takes place here. A procession of 800 people dressed up in costumes begins to climb the hill at 3pm. When they reach the top 8 000 sugar buns **(krakelingen)** are thrown out over the crowd and the local celebrities must drink little live fish from a silver goblet. In the evening, a cask filled with tar and wrapped in straw is set on fire during the **Tonnekensbrand**. There are numerous stories and legends which claim to explain the origin of this event, which is thought to be very old, yet despite them it still remains a mystery.

Le Grand-Hornu ★

Hornu lies in the Borinage region near Mons, where coal was still mined until the 1970s. This small community features a remarkable example of industrial architecture called Le Grand-Hornu, now the home of the MAC's, a museum devoted to the contemporary arts of Belgium's francophone community.

Location
Hainaut – Michelin maps 716 E4 and 534 I20.
Close to the border with France and a short distance from Mons, the Grand-Hornu is easily accessible off the E 19 motorway (exit 25 – St-Gislain, then follow signs to the MAC's).

Background

The Grand-Hornu complex was mostly built between 1816 and 1835 on the initiative of the industrialist **Henri de Gorge** (1774-1832), a native of Valenciennes just over the border in France. In 1810 he bought the concession with a view to working the coal mines. Three architects – François Obin, Pierre Cordona and Bruno Renard – were called upon to carry out the project. The complex consists of 435 houses built for workers (luxurious for the time), several workshops and warehouses and a building to house the administrative quarters. It is generally thought

The Grand-Hornu.

that Bruno Renard designed the two inner courtyards and the so-called château of the De Gorge family. It is likely that he drew inspiration from the architect Ledoux' famous salt-works of 1779 at Arc-et-Senans in France. The Grand-Hornu complex was built in the neo-Classical tradition, evidenced by the presence of arcades, pediments, colonnades and half-moon windows.

Le Grand-Hornu ceased its activites in 1954 and the site gradually fell into disrepair. In 1969 permission was given for its demolition. Then in 1971 an architect from Le Grand-Hornu, **Henri Guchez**, bought the ruins of the site and undertook its restoration. Since 2002 the complex has housed the prestigious MAC's – Musée des Arts contemporains de la communauté française (Museum of Contemporary Arts of the French Community)

Worth a Visit

Tue-Sun 10am-6pm. €2. ☎ *065 77 07 12.*
On the right, the large entrance gate gives access to the **Museum of Contemporary Arts** *(open during temporary exhibitions; www.mac-s.be)*. The architect Pierre Hebbelinck has succeeded in harmonising the new buildings in black brick with the existing structures. The stark but beautifully designed interior spaces make a fine setting for works drawn from the collections, which are of international significance. They include paintings, sculpture, photos, and multimedia installations. On show in the great hall with its walls of exposed brickwork which was once the hay store, Christian Boltanski's *Les Registres du Grand-Hornu* pays impressive tribute to the miners who once worked here. The middle of the first courtyard is dominated by Pol Beury's 1991 work entitled *64 carrés*. Bounded by arcades and brick structures which once housed store-rooms and workshops, a huge ellipse-shaped space has been converted into offices. To the left, the main workshop, which once turned out steam engines, has kept the pillars which supported a series of domes. Around the factory, the hundreds of very basic workers' houses were laid out along the rectilinear streets of a planned industrial village, which was home to 2 500 people in the 1820s.

Halle★

Since the 13C life in Halle has centred on worship of a Black Virgin, the object of a famous pilgrimage. Every other year at Whitsun there is a historical pageant in which the statue is carried through the town. In addition, Halle's carnival on the third Sunday in Lent is noted for its particularly colourful procession.

Location
Vlaams-Brabant – Population 33 529. Michelin maps 716 F 3 or 533 K 18. Town plan in the current edition of The Red Guide Benelux
🗓 *Grote Markt 1,* ☎ *02 356 42 59; www.halle.be*

Worth a Visit

Grote Markt
The **town hall** was built in the early 17C in the Renaissance style. It was restored in the 19C, and now has a harmonious façade. A statue of the cellist **Adrien-Francois Servais** (1807-66), who was born in Halle, stands in the middle of the square. Servais was to achieve international fame: Berlioz called him the Paganini of the cello, and he was also solo cellist for Leopold I.

Basiliek★★
Allow 45min – 8am-6pm. ☎ *02 356 42 59 (Tourist Information Centre).*
The basilical church was built in the 14C. Its layout, without a projecting transept, is a good example of the early Brabant Gothic style. There is a powerful-looking square **tower** surmounted by pinnacles at the corners and, since 1775, also by a Baroque lantern. There is a little 15C baptistery on the south side, projecting from the main body of the basilica, with a bulbous roof. The carillon installed in 1973 consists of 54 chimes.

Note the **south doorway** and its carving of the Virgin and Child surrounded by angel musicians. A little further on, there is a little door decorated with a carving of the Coronation of the Virgin Mary. The harmoniously proportioned east end and the sides of the building are decorated with superb narrative corbels and two tiers of balustrades.

Interior – The elegant nave has a triforium with Flamboyant Gothic tracery. Above the porch, there is a double tier of windows, also in the Flamboyant Gothic style. There are many wonderful **objets d'art** in the church, as well as beautiful sculptures. The font *(chapel south of the tower)* dates from 1466. It is made of brass and has a cover sumptuously decorated with Apostles, horsemen and a group representing the Baptism of Christ. In the chancel there are statues of the Apostles dating from 1410. They were inspired by the work of Claus Sluter, the famous sculptor to the Dukes of Burgundy in Dijon. The famous Black Virgin is enthroned in the middle. The spandrels of the arches in the ambulatory are decorated with remarkable narrative carvings (15C).

An altarpiece in the Trazegnies chapel, which juts out from the basilica along the north aisle, represents the Seven Sacraments. It was made in the Italian Renaissance style by Jean Mone, sculptor to Emperor Charles V. Note also the tiny recumbent effigy of Joachim, the son of Louis XI, in a chapel on the north side of the chancel. The boy died in 1460, while his father, who was still Dauphin or heir apparent at that time, was in hiding in Genappe *(7km/4.75mi east)*.

Treasury – The finest items of church plate are displayed in the crypt, bearing witness to the generosity of illustrious donors. Particularly outstanding examples include two Brussels monstrances, one dating from the 15C and donated by Louis XI of France, the other from the 16C, bequeathed by England's Henry VIII.

Zuidwest-Brabants Museum

♿ *May-Aug: Sam 2-5pm, public holidays 10am-noon, 2pm-5pm; Apr-Oct: Sun 2-6pm, public holidays 10am-noon, 2pm-5pm. €1.* ☎ *02 356 42 59.*

The Museum of Southwest Brabant is housed in a 17C Jesuit school. It reflects the regional way of life in days gone by through objects found during archaeological excavations, among them early tools, baskets made in Halle in the 17C and 18C, and Huizingen porcelain.

Excursion

Rebecq

10km/6.25mi SW on N 6, then a road to the right.

A **tourist train** pulled by a little locomotive runs between the old Rebecq station and Rognon in the Senne Valley. *Allow 1hr.* ♿ *May-Sept: Sun and public holidays 2.30pm, 4pm and 5.30pm (last train if demand sufficient). €4.* ☎ *067 63 82 32 (Tourist Information Centre).*

Exhibitions are organised in the **Arenberg Mill** along the River Senne.

Han-Sur-Lesse★

In the heart of the Parc National de Lesse et Lomme, an extensive limestone upland crossed by two rivers, this village is a quiet little place out of season, famous for its magnificent cave and its wild animal reserve.

Location

Namur. Michelin maps 716 I 5 and 534 Q 22

In the heart of the well-wooded Famenne area, Han-sur-Lesse is accessible from the A 4/E 411 motorway linking Brussels and Arlon; leave the motorway at Exit 23 and follow N 86.

🛈 *Place Théo Lannoy 1,* ☎ *084 37 75 96.*

WHERE TO EAT
Bellevue-Chez Herman – *Rue Joseph Lamotte 2 –* ☎ *084 37 72 27 – Closed Mon – ⊘ – €14.75/38.42.* Successive generations of the Herman family have served up no-frills meals in traditional style ever since 1868. Country-style dining room. Outdoor dining, weather permitting.

Worth a Visit

Grotte de Han★★★

The entrance to the cave is at Le Trou de Salpêtre and can only be reached by tram. The return journey is made on foot (400m/0.3mi). Jul-Aug: guided tour (1hr 30min) 10am-noon, 1.30-5.30pm; Apr-Oct: 10am-noon, 1.30-4.30pm (May-Jun: Sat, Sun and public holidays 5.30pm); Open occasionally Nov, Mar: check for details. Closed Jan. €10.50. ☎ *084 37 72 13; www.han.be*

The tour takes visitors round one-fifth of the giant limestone cave eroded by the River Lesse over a distance of 15km/9.50mi. The cave served as a refuge from the end of the Neolithic period to the 18C. It is very damp, with a temperature of 13°C/55°F, and gigantic concretions have formed at a rate of 4-5cm/1.5-2in every 100 years. They include the graceful **Minaret** stalagmite which is 5m/16.25ft tall. Certain galleries have been open to the public since 1856 and have been blackened by the torches of the first visitors. The **Salle des Mystérieuses** has retained all the magic of a crystal palace, with its superb stalagmite in the shape of a tiara. The impressive **Salle d'Armes**, 50m/164ft across, is crossed by the Lesse and features an outstanding *son et lumière* show. Beyond it is the **Salle du Dôme** which is 129m/423ft high. A torch-bearer can be seen here, rushing down the huge pile of boulders. Then comes the **Salle des Draperies** in which the ceiling bristles with marbled stalactites.

Large boats pass along the subterranean stretch of the Lesse and emerge into daylight at the **Trou de Han** after a cannon has been fired to demonstrate the echo in the gallery.

Expothème

At the exit to the cave, in an upper room of the Ferme de Dry Hamptay. & Jul-Aug: part-guided tour (1hr) noon-7pm; Apr-Oct: noon-6pm (May-June: Sat, Sun and public holidays 7pm). €5. ☎ 084 37 72 13.

An audio-visual presentation shows the other caves and galleries of the system which are only open to experienced potholers.

Musée du Monde Souterrain

Apr: noon-5pm; May-Jun: noon-5pm (Sat, Sun and public holidays 6pm); Jul-Aug: noon-6pm; Sept-Oct: 2pm-5pm. €3. ☎ 084 37 72 13.

This museum displays the results of local archaeological digs, mainly those conducted in the Han Cave, on the river bed or on the banks. The exhibits include Neolithic shaped flints, a remarkable collection of pottery, tools, weapons, jewellery, some of it gold jewellery from the Bronze Age (1100-700 BC), fibulae from the Iron Age, a fragment of an **official diploma★** belonging to a Roman veteran consisting of two bronze tablets, and various Gallo-Roman, Merovingian and medieval objects.

Réserve d'Animaux Sauvages★

& *See Grotte de Han. €8.* ☎ *084 37 72 13.*

A little road train takes visitors through the magnificent Massif du Boine estate covering an area of 250ha/618 acres, where the Lesse flows underground. The reserve contains animals from the Ardennes forests (deer, stags, boars) and, in a vast clearing, the wild animals that would once have roamed the region: bison, brown bears, ibex, chamois, wolves, tarpans (small wild horses), wild oxen (this extinct species was "recreated" by breeding) and Przewalski horses which originally came from the Russian steppe.

The reserve.

Ch. Bastin – J. Evrard/MICHELIN

At the chasm known as the **Gouffre de Belvaux**, the Lesse disappears beneath a rocky arch on Mont de Boine then reappears at Le Trou de Han *(see above)*.

Excursion

Lavaux-Ste-Anne

10km/6.2mi W on the Dinant road. Still with an impregnable look about it, the medieval moated **castle** has retained its keep and its three massive 15C corner towers with their onion domes. The original curtain walls between the towers were replaced by a U-shaped building in the 17C and 18C.

The castle houses the **Musée de la Chasse et de la Conservation de la Nature**, a museum devoted to hunting and nature conservation. Stuffed animals, hunting trophies and documentation on European animals are on display. *9am-6pm (Jul-Aug 7pm). Closed 1 Jan. €4.96. ☎ 084 38 83 62.*

Hasselt

The thriving capital of the province of Limburg lies on the borders of the Kempen and Hesbaye regions. An ancient town, its name perhaps derived from an old word meaning "hazel wood", it belonged for centuries to the principality of Liège. Under Napoleon it was part of the French Department of Basse-Meuse, and then became the provincial capital when the Treaty of London divided Limburg between Belgium and Holland.

Location
Limburg P *– Population 67 777 – Michelin maps 716 I3 and 533 Q17.*
In eastern Belgium, Hasselt is reached from Antwerp or Liège by the A 13/E 313 motorway and from Brussels and Aachen by the A 2/E 314. Drivers are advised to leave their vehicles in one of the free car parks (Grenslandhallen or Alverberg) and take the free bus service to the town centre (no service Sundays and public holidays).
Town hall, Lombaardstraat 3, ☎ 011 23 95 40; www.hasselt.be

Directory

GETTING AROUND
Bus – Use of cars in the town centre has been discouraged by the provision of two free bus services, the "Centrumpendel" or CP between the station and Grote Markt, and the "Boulevardpendel" or BP between the station and the edge of town (no service Sundays or public holidays). Information: De Lijn Limburg, Grote Breemstraat 4, ☎ 011 85 03 03; www.delijn.be

WHERE TO EAT
't Kleine Genoegen – *Raamstraat 3 – ☎ 011 22 57 03 – Closed Sun, Mon and July – lunch €13 – €31/40.* Enjoy one of life's little pleasures in a fine old patrician house, conveniently placed between the Begijnhof and the cathedral. Bright dining room heated in winter by a splendid open fire. Well-chosen traditional dishes.

De Egge – *Walputstraat 23 – ☎ 011 22 49 51 – Closed second half Aug, lunchtime Sat, Sun – lunch €24 – €32.* This welcoming, family-run establishment ("The Harrow") occupies one of the town centre's venerable old buildings and serves up unpretentious but tasty cooking.

WHERE TO STAY
Century – *Leopoldplein 1 – ☎ 011 22 47 99 – www.century.be – ✗ – 17 rms: €45/70* ⌷ Just a short distance from the Markt, this hotel has recently given all its rooms a thoroughgoing refurbishment. Tavern-cum-restaurant with an attractive, shaded terrace on the square. The bill is kept to a reasonable size.

Den Oversten Mantel B&B – *Pastorijstraat 11 – 3590 Diepenbeek – ☎ 011 72 69 11 – ✗ – 2 rms: €27.50/47.10* ⌷ In a residential district just a 10-minute drive from Hasselt, farmhouse-like residence in a well-kept garden. The two rooms, one on the ground floor, one on the first floor, are simply furnished but have private facilities.

TAKING A BREAK
't Borrelius – *Witte Nonnenstraat 28 – ☎ 011 24 32 28 – 9.30am-1am, 2.30am Fri, 3am Sat.* This establishment in what was once a Franciscan monastery is next door to the Gin Museum, so no wonder that it specialises in serving some fifteen-plus varieties of Hasselt's favourite tipple. Attractive outdoor terrace in a cul-de-sac.

SHOPPING
Window-shoppers will find plenty of temptation in Hasselt, a town with numerous clothes shops and places selling luxury items as well as antique dealers. A Fashion Trail booklet is available at the Tourist Information Centre.
Speciality – The town is famous for its excellent gin *(genever)*. Several distilleries in the area still produce what is called locally "witteke", literally "little white". It is made in the traditional way in the Gin Museum. The statue of the Borrelmanneke, the little chap who symbolises Hasselt gin, stands in the Maastrichterstraat.

EVENTS AND FESTIVALS
Every year on 30 April, the **Meieavondviering folklore festival** is held on Grote Markt. The May Tree is brought here in a procession, then planted while witches dance and dummies representing the winter season are burned.
Every seven years in August *(see Calendar of events)* the Virgin **Virga Jesse**, patron saint of the town, is honoured by a large religious procession. August is also the month when the famous **Pukkelpop** pop festival is celebrated on the Kiewit. The third weekend in October is the occasion of the **Gin Festival**, with a variety of events and entertainments.

HASSELT

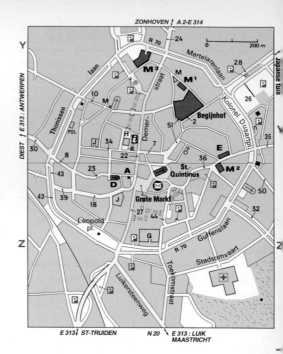

Walking About

Start at Grote Markt.

Grote Markt
A half-timbered house dating from 1659, now housing a chemist's shop, is named after its sign **Het Sweert**, The Sword.
St-Quintinuskathedraal stands nearby, marked by a squat 13C tower topped by an 18C spire. The nave and side aisles of the cathedral were built in the 15C and gradually enlarged with the chancel, the side chapels, then the ambulatory.
Turn left into Kapelstraat.

Onze Lieve Vrouwekerk
This 18C church dedicated to Our Lady contains marble sculptures brought here from the Cistercian Herkenrode Abbey *(5km/3mi northwest of Hasselt)* founded at the end of the 12C. The black and white marble **high altar** is a masterpiece by Liège sculptor **Jean Delcour**. The statues of St Bernard and the Virgin are also by Delcour. In the transepts there are two **mausoleums** of abbesses of Herkenrode. The one in the south transept *(Christ in the Tomb)* was by Artus Quellin the Younger (1625-1700), the one in the north *(Resurrection of Christ)* by Laurent Delvaux (1696-1778). The splendid polychrome statue of Virga Jesse (14C), the original of the one now carried in procession every seven years, is on display in the chancel.
Go back to Grote Markt and turn right into Maastrichterstraat.

Refugiehuis van de Abdij van Herkenrode
This lovely 16C Gothic-Renaissance building is now occupied by government offices. In times of trouble, this was a refuge for the Cistercians of Herkenrode.

Worth a Visit

Nationaal Jenevermuseum★
Nov-Mar: Tue-Sun 10am (Sat, Sun, public holidays 1pm)-5pm; Apr-Oct: Tue-Sun (Jul, Aug, daily) 10am-5pm. Closed Jan, 1, 2 and 11 Nov, 25 Dec. €3. ☎ 011 24 11 44.
The National Gin Museum is in the farmhouse of a former convent. It was turned into a distillery in 1803. The museum has resumed production using 19C techniques. A numbered trail takes visitors through the old ox stables to the kiln. On the ground floor is the impressive steam engine that runs the millstones and the macerator. The 19C distillation equipment can still be operated. The exhibits on display in the old house concern the history, packaging and manufacturers, advertising of genever. The tour ends with a tasting session.

THE MAKING OF GENEVER

Genever, a gin made with a base of barley and rye, has been produced in Flanders since the 16C. Sprouted barley is put on the perforated floor of a kiln to dry. Then the malted barley and rye are ground to release the starch, and the mix (2/3 rye to 1/3 malted barley) is left to macerate at about 63°C/145°F, so that the enzymes can turn starch into sucrose. Yeast is added to the sugars, turning them into alcohol, and the mix is distilled to separate the wort from the alcohol. A second distillation of this rough genever produces the gin with a taste that varies depending on the flavourings – juniper berries, for example – added during this distillation.

Ph. Gajic/MICHELIN

Begijnhof

The garden of the old Beguine convent is still bordered by rows of 18C nuns' houses. They are in the Mosan style with brick and stone walls and nowadays house provincial council offices. A modern building is home to the **Provinciaal Museum** which organises exhibitions of international contemporary art. Ivy-clad ruins and a few carved stones are all that remain of the church which was destroyed by an air raid in 1944.

Museum Stellingwerff-Waerdenhof

&. _Nov-Mar: Tue-Sun 10am (Sat, Sun public holidays 1pm)-5pm; Apr-Oct: Tue-Sun 10am-5pm. Closed Jan, 1, 2 andt 11 Nov, 24, 25, 26 and 31 Dec. €3. ☎ 011 24 10 70._
The collections in this museum illustrate the history and artistic life of the town of Hasselt and the surrounding area. Besides the liturgical objects, including the world's oldest monstrance dating from 1286, there are some marvellous locally made Art Nouveau ceramics, a collection of shop signs and some 19C and 20C paintings.

Stedelijk Modemuseum

&. _Apr-Oct: Tue-Sun 10am-5pm; Nov-Mar: Tue-Sun 10am (Sat, Sun and public holidays 1pm)-5pm. Closed Jan, 1, 2 and 11 Nov, 24, 25, 26 and 31 Dec. €3. ☎ 011 23 96 21._
The Museum of Fashion is housed in a 17C building that was both a convent and a hospital. Its exhibits reflect changes in fashion from the 18C to the present day, through documents, accessories and clothes. The museum also organises temporary exhibitions.

Modemuseum Hasselt

Corset.

Japanse Tuin

Northeast of the town between Koning Boudewijnlaan and Elfde Liniestraat. Apr-Oct: Tue-Sun 10am-5pm, Sat, Sun, public holidays 2-6pm. Closed Easter. €3. ☎ 011 23 95 40.
Carefully designed in accordance with 17C principles, this delightful Japanese garden was created with the assistance of Itami, Hasselt's twin town in Japan. In an enchanting setting of pools, rocks, winding paths, cherry trees and a waterfall, the tea house and the ceremonial house look like something from a fairy tale, especially in the spring when the cherries are in gorgeous blossom. Visitors can take part in the monthly **tea ceremony**.

Tour

THE KAMPEN

42km/26mi – allow 3hr.
Leave Hasselt to the N by Kempische Steenweg and turn right on to N 75 beyond the bridge over the Albert Canal.

Bokrijk Provincial Domain★ – _(See Provinciaal Domein van BOKRIJK.)_
Continue on N 75 towards Genk.

Genk – *(See GENK)*

Leave Genk on Westerring and take N 76.

The road soon crosses the magnificent heather-covered hills characteristic of the Kempen, before reaching the road from Houthalen to Zwartberg.

Continue towards Houthalen-Helchteren.

Kelchterhoef

This is an extensive wooded recreation area comprising a large lake with fishing and swimming facilities. An old half-timbered abbey far-mouse has been turned into an inn.

Continue towards Houthalen-Helchteren, then head towards Heusden-Zolder.

Heusen-Zolder

The Zolder International Motor Racing Circuit is south of the town near the pine-clad Bolderberg (alt 60m/197ft). It is 4.19km/2.6mi long, and is an important centre for competitive motor sports. The Belgian Formula One Grand Prix is run here when it is not held at Spa Francorchamps.

Leave Heusen-Zolder on N 719, then turn left by Helchteren on to N 715.

Ch. Bastin – J. Evrard/MICHELIN

The Japanese Garden

Molenheide

This 180-ha/445-acre woodland park has a good range of facilities. In the **Game Park** (Wild- en Wandelpark) animals such as deer and stags live in the wild. The park also provides many opportunities for sports (swimming, tennis, cycling).&. *Jul-Aug: 10am-5.30pm; May-Jun: 10am-5pm; Mar-Oct: 10am-4.30pm; Dec-Feb: 10am-4pm. €1.25. ☎ 011 52 14 17.*

Hautes Fagnes★★

This is the name given to the wind-swept uplands between Eupen and Malmédy, a melancholy stretch of peat bog, heath and moorland stretching as far as the eye can see. Here and there the vastness is broken up by the dark masses of spruce plantations and scattered clumps of beech, oak and birch. The Hautes Fagnes are now practically deserted, but this was not always so; traces have been found of a road, the Via Mansuerisca, which is thought to date back to the 7C.

Location

Liège – Michelin maps 716 L4 and 534 V20-W19.
The Hautes-Fagnes is part of the largely German-speaking area in the eastern part of the province of Liège. The area is crossed by several main roads including N 67, N 68, N 672 and N 676. It is accessible from Verviers by the A 27/E 42/E 421 motorway which runs along its western edge.

Background

NATURE RESERVE

Open dawn-dusk. The reserve is closed mid-Mar – mid-June to protect nesting birds. Some paths in Zone C are also closed mid-June – late July (accompanied visitors only at other times). More information from Centre Nature de Botrange, ☎ 080 44 03 00; www.ful.ac.be/Hotes/Cnatbotrange or Bureau Touristique Info, ☎ 080 44 72 73.
The Hautes Fagnes nature reserve was created in 1957. It covers an area of over 4 200ha/10 378 acres, providing protection for flora, fauna, soil and landscape within its boundaries. Most of the peat bogs lie within the nature reserve. The plateau is not particularly high, but its harsh climate favours the existence and natural regeneration of numerous plant and animal species otherwise confined to high mountains and northern latitudes.
The peat bogs in particular are threatened by two dangers: firstly, being trodden down by walkers stops their development and will ultimately lead to their destruction. This is why it is forbidden to stray from the signposted footpaths and why some areas are only accessible in the course of an accompanied visit. Secondly, fire is absolutely fatal to this environment, and unfortunately it occurs here all too often. Extreme caution is strongly recommended, especially in the dry season *(red flags = no admission).*

NATURE PARK

Since 1971 the reserve has been part of the **Parc Naturel Hautes Fagnes-Eifel**. This nature park includes the lakes at Robertville, Bütgenbach, Gileppe and Eupen, the Valley of the River Our and the Eifel. It runs into the German Nordeifel nature park. The whole area is called the **Deutsch-Belgischer Naturpark**, and covers an area of 2 400km^2/926sq mi, of which 700km^2/270sq mi are in Belgium. To the south, it joins the Parc Naturel Germano-Luxembourgeois.

Les Hautes Fagnes

Directory

WHERE TO EAT

⊖⊜ Ferme Libert – *Bévercé-Village 26 – 4960 Bévercé* – ☎ *080 33 02 47 – Closed after 8pm – lunch €24 – €46.* Inn-style restaurant occupying a prominent position in the village of Bévercé. Good choice of traditional and regional dishes, a variety of complete meals, 100% authentic Ardennes ambience and wonderful view down into the valley. No-frills, well-kept bedrooms.

⊖⊜⊜ du Moulin – *Grand'Rue 28 (Ligneuville) – 4960 Bellevaux-Ligneuville* – ☎ *080 57 00 81 – Closed Mar, late-Aug – mid-Sept, lunchtime Wed and Thur – €27/69.* Wonderful gourmet establishment in a 19C building typical of the Ardennes countryside. Fine contemporary cuisine, Rabelaisian wine list, refined decor, exquisite summer terrace and impeccable bedrooms.

Worth a Visit

Centre Nature de Botrange

& *10am-6pm. Closed 1 Jan, 25 Dec. €2.50. www.ful.ac.be/hotes/cnatbotrange* ☎ *080 44 03 00.*
This attractive stone building houses a visitor centre, a permanent exhibition on the Hautes Fagnes, audio-visual presentations and a bookshop.

Signal de Botrange

694m/2 277ft. This is the highest peak in Belgium. Together with the Baraque-Michel survey station it occupies the centre of this wild and marshy plateau speckled with tufts of white-plumed cotton grass.
There is a far-ranging panorama *(viewing tables)* from the top of the **tower.** On a clear day the **view★** is especially far-reaching to the northeast. Beyond the conifers, the moorland stretches into Germany towards Roetgen and Aachen.
Daily except Tue, 9am-6pm. ☎ *080 44 72 73.*

Nature trail★

1hr 15min on foot. Wellington boots or good walking shoes are recommended. The beginning of the path is opposite the Signal de Botrange on the other side of the road.
This fascinating trail on boardwalks laid out over the peat bogs makes it possible to appreciate both the immensity of the landscape and the variety of its bird and plant life, which includes bilberry and heather, birches, rowans, and coniferous species.

La Baraque-Michel

This is an old land-surveying station (1886-88) at an altitude of 675m/2 214ft. The University of Liège has set up a scientific study station on nearby **Mont Rigi**.

Herentals

Among the woods and heaths of the western Kempen, little Herentals lies between the Albert Canal and the Kleine Nete river. Once a flourishing centre of cloth manufacture, it has kept a few mementoes of its past, notably the south and east gateways (Zandpoort and Bovenpoort) from its 14C defences. The sculptor Charles Fraikin (1817-93) was born in the town.

Location

Population 25 427 – Michelin maps 716 H2 and 533 O15 – Antwerpen.
Herentals is on N 13 between Lier and Geel and just off the A 13/E 313 motorway between Antwerp and Hasselt
🗓 *Grote Markt 41,* ☎ *014 21 90 88; www.herentals.be*

't Ganzennest – *Watervoort 68 –* ☎ *014 21 64 56 – Closed Mon, Tue – lunch €14 – €20/26.* An old farmstead charmingly converted into a tavern-cum-restaurant. Summer terrace with countryside views. Relaxed atmosphere.

Walking About

Start at Grote Markt

Stadhuis

The town hall stands in the middle of the elongated Grote Markt and was once the cloth makers' guildhall. Dating from the 16C, and built in brick and sandstone, it is surmounted by a tiny belfry with a carillon.
Go along Kerkstraat.

St-Waldetrudiskerk

Jun-Sept: Guided tour Wed. (July-Aug) and Sat 2-5pm by prior arrangement with the Tourist Information Centre, ☎ 014 21 90 88.

This Brabant Gothic church dedicated to St Waudru still has its 14C square central tower. Inside are some fascinating furnishings. An early 16C wood carving by Pasquier Borremans, the **altarpiece★** represents the Martyrdom of St Crispin and St Crispinian, the patron saints of cobblers and tanners. Other fine works include the 17C carved choir stalls, 16C and 17C paintings by Ambrosius, by **Frans Francken the Elder**, who was born in Herentals, and by Pieter-Jozef Verhaghen (18C), also a local man. Note the Romanesque font.

Return to Grote Markt. Carry straight on along Hofkwartier, then turn right into Begijnenstraat.

Begijnhof

The Beguine convent was founded in the 13C and was very prosperous. However, the iconoclasts destroyed it in 1578, and it had to be rebuilt. The houses surround a garden in which there is a charming Gothic church (1614).

Tour

THE WESTERN KEMPEN

65km/40mi NE.

Leave Herentals to the SE on N 13. In about 4km/2.5mi, turn right on to a minor road.

Tongerlo

Founded around 1130, this famous Premonstratensian **abbey** is surrounded by its moat. Beyond the porch is the **courtyard** with the abbey farm (1640) and tithe barn (1618). The **prelacy** to the right has a splendid Classical façade dating from 1725. The 19C **abbey church** has an ebony reliquary containing the relics of St Siard. The **Leonardo da Vinci museum★** *(access via the prelacy)* has a huge canvas, a copy of the **Last Supper** painted by the great master on the walls of the convent of Santa Maria delle Grazie in Milan between 1495 and 1498. This faithful copy was executed less than 20 years later, and for many years graced the abbey church. *Apr-Oct: 2pm-5pm. Closed Easter. €1.50. ☎ 014 53 99 00.* From the garden in front of the museum there is a fine view of the rear of the prelacy and an elegant little watchtower of 1479.

Head for N 19.

Geel

The town has earned a reputation for its community of mentally ill people, who are boarded out with local families in order to give them a degree of freedom. This special function of Geel is said to have followed the decapitation of the Irish princess St Dympna (patron saint of the mentally ill) by her father, who had been driven mad by the devil.

On the Mol road on the outskirts of the town, the Flamboyant Gothic **St.-Dimfnakerk** has sumptuous furnishings. In the chancel, there is a beautiful black marble and alabaster **mausoleum★** dating from the 16C by Antwerp artist Cornelis II Floris. An altarpiece (1513) illustrates the life of the saint. A late-15C Brabant altarpiece in the south transept represents scenes from the Passion of Christ, and a 14C altarpiece in the first chapel of the ambulatory shows the Twelve Apostles.

A small building adjoining the church tower, called the Sieckencamere or Chamber of the Ill, features a pretty Renaissance façade. *Apr-Sept: Tue-Fri, Sun 2-5pm. ☎ 014 57 09 50.*

Leave Geel to the E on N 71.

Mol

Mol is known for the National Nuclear Research Centre established here in 1952. **St-Pieter-en-Pauluskerk** contains a thorn from Christ's crown. A procession is held in its honour (H Doornprocessie) every year. Near the church is a **pillory.**

Jakob Smits (1855-1928), who lived in the village of **Achterbos**, was the greatest of Kempen painters. The old presbytery in the neighbouring village of **Sluis** has been turned into the **Jakob Smits Museum**. *Wed-Sun 2-6pm. Closed 1 Jan, Easter, mid-end Aug, 25 Dec. €1. ☎ 014 31 74 35.*

Continue along N 71.

Ginderbuiten

The village has a striking modern church dedicated to St.-Jozef Ambachtsman (St Joseph the Workman).

Zilvermeer

This large public leisure area in the pine forests north of Sluis includes two lakes, one for swimming and boating, the other for sailing.

Head towards Lommel on N 71.

Lommel

This little Limburg town is known for the large **German Military Cemetery** in the pine forests just to the south. The 16ha/40acre cemetery contains the remains of all the German soldiers who fell in Belgium in the Second World War as well as some of those killed in eastern Germany or in the First World War. Almost 20 000 crosses (one for every two graves) are laid out in rows on a carpet of heather dotted with pines and birches and separated by grassy avenues.

The **Kattenbos nature reserve** is part of the 120km^2/75sq mi **Park der Lage Kempen**, the Lower Kempen Nature Park, together with the Pijnven Forest near Eksel and the Holven Forest to the east near Overpelt.

Near the road to the north of the Kattenbos there is a post windmill of 1809. This is the starting point for a number of waymarked footpaths through the pine forest.

Go back the way you came and before reaching Ginderbuiten, turn right on N 136 to Postel Abbey.

Abdij van Postel

This is a Premonstratensian abbey, founded in the 12C by the monks from Floreffe. The 18C buildings are flanked by a Renaissance tower with a carillon (concerts in summer). The Romanesque **church** dates from the 12C and 13C but was altered in the 17C. Organ concerts are given here.

Take N 123 towards Kasterlee.

Kasterlee

In the middle of the pinewoods, this is the main tourist centre in the western Kempen.

There is a pretty **windmill** to the south, opposite the little British Second World War cemetery profusely decorated with flowers. Further south, on the Kleine Nete river, there is a watermill that has been turned into a restaurant *(signposted "De Watermolen")*.

Continue along N 123.

Papekelders Viewpoint

Shortly before the railway line just outside Herentals, turn right towards the Bosbergen Wood and continue on foot. 10am-6pm (Oct-Apr Sat, Sun only). €0.60. ☎ 014 21 90 88 (Tourist Information Centre).

A 24m/74ft tower with viewing platform has been built at the wood's highest point (alt 40m/131ft). From it there is a panoramic view of the surrounding area.

Huy★★

At the confluence of the Meuse and the Houyoux, Huy (pronounced "oo-ee") is a charming little town huddled at the foot of its collegiate church and its citadel. In days gone by Huy's inhabitants boasted that they possessed four wonders: the bridge (Gothic, rebuilt in 1956); the rose window in the collegiate church; the fountain on Grand-Place; and the citadel. Huy was part of the principality of Liège from 985 to 1789. Its strategic location resulted in about 30 sieges and the town was destroyed many times over.

Location

Liège – Population 18 816 – Michelin maps 716 I14 and 533 Q19.
Midway between Namur and Liège, Huy stands on N 19, the main road hugging the Meuse.
🛈 *Quai de Namur 1,* ☎ *085 21 29 15; www.huy.be*

Walking About

Collégiale Notre-Dame★

Close to the river. Currently undergoing restoration.

This is a vast 14C church in Rayonnant Gothic style, though Flamboyant Gothic flourishes can be noted in the clerestory, which was completed at the end of the 15C. An impressive tower adorned with a

Ph. Gajic/MICHELIN

Fabri medallion "The Tree of Life", Treasury of the Collégiale Notre-Dame

Directory

SIGHTSEEING

By boat – *May-Aug: Tue-Sun 2pm, 3pm, 4.30pm (same times Sept weekends). €3.* ☎ *085 21 29 15.* Boat trips along the Meuse are a good way of getting to know the town from a different angle.

WHERE TO EAT

🍴 **La Tête du Chou** – *Rue Vierst-Godin 8 –* ☎ *085 23 59 65 – Closed lunchtime Mon and Sat – ✗ – €25/30.* A small, contemporary place with intimate atmosphere with dishes based on local produce. Meals served outside in summer. Limited seating, so get here early, if you can.

🍴🍴 *Les Colombes – Rue L'Apleit 9 –* ☎ *085 25 15 72 – lunch €20 – €26.* Diners can enjoy a meal in peace in what was once a pigeon-loft belonging to Huy's collegiate church. Appetising traditional dishes with a tasty local touch.

WHERE TO STAY

🛏🍴 *Sirius – Quai de Compiègne 47 –* ☎ *085 21 24 00 – hotel.sirius @proximedia.be –* 🅿 *– 24 rms; €68/97 –* ⊐ Away from the town centre on the left bank of the Meuse, this large modern hotel has been well integrated into the local townscape. Conventional but comfortable rooms, some with river views. Private car park.

🛏🛏 **Château la Motte en Gée** – *Chemin de St-Loup 1 – 4500 Tihange –* ☎ *085 21 18 03 – www.kasteelhotel.com – ✗ –* 🅿 *– 35 rms: €38.42 –* ⊐ *€9.92.* An aristocratic residence set in the distinctive countryside of the Condroz plateau, a good place to dine as well as to rest the weary head. Relax in the extensive park or enjoy a meal by the side of the swimming pool.

---

beautiful rose window, 9m/30ft in diameter, precedes the main body of the church. The apse is flanked by two square towers, a very unusual feature in Belgium.

The nave and side aisles inside are lofty, harmonising with the 20m/66ft lancet windows in the chancel which are filled with modern stained glass. The vaulting was rebuilt in the 16C and painted with Renaissance arabesques. A Romanesque crypt lies under the chancel.

Treasury★ – As well as some fascinating wooden statues of saints dating from the 14C and 16C, there is a rich collection of Mosan gold and silverware. The most outstanding pieces are the four magnificent **reliquaries** from the 12C and 13C. The ones made for relics of the town's patron saints St Domitian and St Mengold have been attributed to Godefroy de Huy but are unfortunately severely damaged. The reliquary of St Mark (probably 13C) is remarkable for the lively little figures whose fluid lines are highlighted by the use of champlevé enamel. There is alsoa reliquary of the Virgin Mary (c 1265) with repoussé copper figures set against a very ornate background. *Open by arrangement only.* ☎ *085 21 20 05*

Portail du Bethléem – *Go along the south side of the nave.* The 14C "Bethlehem Door" by the chevet once opened onto the cloisters. The carving on the tympanum represents the Nativity (shepherds to the left, the Magi to the right), with the Massacre of the Innocents above. The fluid folds of the drapery and the picturesque way in which certain details are rendered make this a very fine piece of work.

Go along the riverside on Quai de Namur.

Ancien Hospice d'Oultremont

The brick-built hospice at the foot of the citadel was constructed in the 16Cby Canon Gérard d'Oultremont. Note the beautiful staircase-tower. The building now houses the **Tourist Information Centre**. The **Maison de Batta** on the opposite bank is a house built in the Mosan Renaissance style.

Walk along Rue du Pont des Chaînes leading away from the collegiate church. Turn right into Avenue des Ardennes. On the left, narrow Rue Mounie leads to Grand-Place.

Grand-Place

The central feature of this attractive square is the lovely 18C **fountain** with its little bronze figures dating from 1406 and 1597. The elegant town hall was completed in 1766.

Charming little winding streets lead to **Place Verte** overlooked by the pretty little Gothic church dedicated to the town's patron saint St Mengold. The building is now a cultural centre.

Return to Avenue des Ardennes. Cross the Roi Baudouin bridge, go along Rue Neuve and turn right into Rue St-Pierre.

Église St-Pierre

Romanesque font decorated with symbolic animals (lion and dragon).

Return to Rue Neuve, turn right before the bridge and pass in front of the Maison Batta. La Sarte park is reached by cable-car.

La Sarte

The **recreation park** features children's play facilities. ♿ *Mid-Mar to end Oct: 10am-8pm. €3.75.* ☎ *085 23 29 96.*

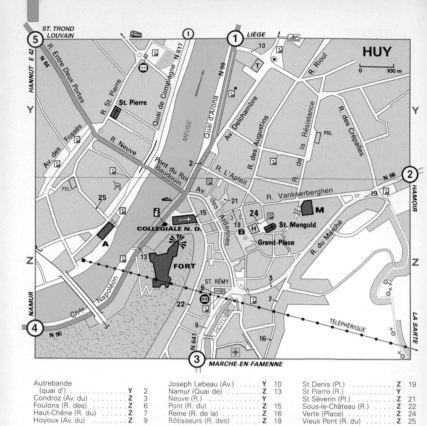

Worth a Visit

Musée Communal

Closed for renovation. For more information contact the Tourist Information Centre ☎ 085 21 29 15.

The museum is housed in the buildings and cloisters of the 17C Minorite Brothers monastery. It has large local history and folklore collections including a typical local interior with a beautiful sandstone fireplace (1621), archaeological finds, prints of the town, ceramics made in Huy in the 19C, pewter ware, and liturgical objects, including a 13C figure of Christ called the **"beau Dieu de Huy"★**.

Citadel★

Access by foot or by the La Sartre cable car Jul-Aug: 11am-7pm; Apr-Sept: 9am-12.30pm, 1-4.30pm, Sat, Sun, public holidays 11am-6pm (last admission 1hr before closing). €3. ☎ 085 21 29 15 (Tourist Information Centre) or 085 21 53 34.

The citadel was built from 1818 to 1823 by the Dutch, on the site of the old Prince-

Terrasses on the Grand-Place.

A. Kouprianoff/MICHELIN

Bishops' castle which had been demolished in 1717. It was used to imprison hostages and members of the Resistance from 1940 to 1944. More than 7 000 people were detained here. A signposted route leads visitors through the dungeons, the interrogation room and the **Musée de la Résistance et des Camps de Concentration**. From the glacis there is a splendid **view★★** of the old town, the River Meuse and surrounding area. The Tihange Nuclear Power Station (1975) can also be seen to the northeast.

Excursions

Amay
8km/5mi E on N 617 along the banks of the Meuse.
Collégiale St-Georges et Ste-Ode – This was originally a Romanesque church but it was restored in the 18C. The pride of its treasury is a masterpiece of Mosan goldsmiths' work: the **reliquary★** in silver and gilded copper of St Oda and St George, created in about 1230. There is also a **Merovingian sarcophagus★** *(beneath the chancel)* bearing the inscription "Santa Chrodoara", but which could in fact be that of St Oda, a Merovingian noblewoman.
The little **Musée Communal d'Archéologie et d'Art Religieux** in the cloisters is a museum of archaeology and religious art. *Closed for renvation.* ☎ 085 31 37 62.
About 2km/1.25mi from Amay, 17C/18C **Flône Abbey** stands between the rock face and the Meuse. There is a beautiful 12C Romanesque font in the church.

Château de Jehay★
12km/7.5mi E along the Meuse via N 617 and N 614. July-Aug: Tue-Sun 2pm (Sat, Sun 11am)-6pm, Jun, Sept: Sat, Sun 11am-6pm, Wed 2-5pm, Easter weekend, Ascension Thur, Whit Sunday, Monday. €5. ☎ 085 31 17 16.
The château makes a very romantic picture with its walls in a white and brown stone checkerboard pattern reflected in the water of the moat. The building which visitors see today dates from the 16C and 17C and is a beautiful example of a Mosan fortified manor house, but the site was inhabited much further back in time. Archaeological digs have unearthed traces of a Mesolithic lakeside town some 12 000 years old. The gardens were redesigned by the last owner of the castle, a sculptor and archaeologist.
There are marvellous **collections★** inside including furniture, tapestries, porcelain and gold and silverware. In the smoking room, note the beautiful collection of silver- and goldware and a human head shrunk by the Jivaros, headhunters from the Andes. The library contains a Brussels tapestry after Teniers and in the Queen Anne Drawing Room there is a rare 18C harpsichord.
The Gothic cellars house a museum of caving and archeology.
Near the château is the 16C Église St-Lambert.

Modave★
14 km S by N 641. 9am (mid-end Dec 2pm) -6pm. €5. ☎ 085 41 13 69.
The castle at Modave makes a striking first impression with its sheer scale, but there is little indication of the drama of its site, atop a cliff dropping some 60m/200ft to the River Hoyoux. Parts of the castle date back to the 13C, but its present appearance is mostly due to the Count of Marchin, who restored it between 1652 and 1673. In 1941 it was acquired by the Brussels Water Board, since considerable quantities of water are extracted from the estate. It was at Modave in 1667 that Rennequin Sualem constructed a hydraulic wheel, a model for the famous "Machine de Marly" which raised water to supply the fountains of Versailles.
A vast main courtyard precedes the classical façade. The rooms inside are elegantly furnished. Note **Jean-Christian Hansche**'s extraordinary multicoloured stuccowork. The stucco in the guard-room represents the family tree of the counts of Marchin with their crests; the stuccowork in Hercules' Room depicts the hero's Labours. The magnificent spiral staircase in oak in the round tower dates from the 17C. There is a fine **view★** over the wild and wooded Hoyoux Valley from the terrace outside the Duke of Montmorency's bedchamber. The bedchamber of the Duchess of Montmorency, who owned the castle in the late 18C, is upstairs. A model of the hydraulic wheel can be seen in the cellars.
7km/4mi southeast of Modave is the Romanesque **church** in Bois (10C), still with its beautiful late-14C to early-15C **frescoes★** illustrating the Coronation of the Virgin Mary, the Life of Christ and the legends of St Lambert and St Hubert on the vaulting and walls of the chancel and nave. *Apply to the parish priest, Rue de l'Abattoir 11, Bois-et-Borsu,* ☎ 086 34 41 02.
The village of **Ocquier** lies some 3.5km/2mi from Bois-et-Borsu. Its grey stone houses cluster around the Romanesque church of St Remaclus.

Ieper★

In the 13C, along with Bruges and Ghent, Ypres was one of the great cities of Flanders, though it later entered a long decline. In the First World War it was the fulcrum of the Ypres Salient, a bitterly fought-over enclave protruding into the German lines, and the town was almost completely destroyed. After the war it was rebuilt in traditional style. Today it is a focal point of commemoration of the terrible slaughter that took place between 1914-18, while the countryside around is a vast necropolis with around 170 military cemeteries and many other reminders of war.

Location

Westvlaanderen – Population 35 128 – Michelin maps 716 B3 and 533 C17.
Ypres is one of the towns of the rural Westhoek area in western Flanders, midway between Kortrijk and Poperinge. It is reached from Kortrijk by N 37 and the A 19 motorway (exit 4), from Poperinge on N 38, from Veurne on N 8, from Dixmuide on N 369 and from Comines on the border with France on N 336.
🛈 *Lakenhalle, Grote Markt, ☎ 057 22 85 84; www.ieper.be*

Background

A wealthy cloth town (12C-13C) – Founded in the 10C, Ypres is thought to have had a population of 40 000 by c 1260, making it one of the largest cities in Europe. The cloth market and the church dedicated to St Martin were built at this time. In the Hundred Years War Ypres sided with England, the country which provided it with the wool on which its economy depended; as a result, it suffered reprisals from the French. This was the beginning of the town's economic decline, and Bruges replaced it on the international market. Ypres suffered from local problems too. Conflict between patricians and craftsmen eventually put power in the hands of the latter, especially after the Battle of the Golden Spurs in 1302.

The decline of the town was accelerated by an outbreak of plague in 1316, then by the destruction of the workers' suburbs in 1383 during the siege by the people of Ghent and the English. By the 16C repression had given way to religious troubles; many weavers left the country altogether. Ypres became an ecclesiastical town in 1559, when it was made the seat of a new bishropic (abolished in 1801). Several convents were built. One of the bishops was the famous Jansenius.

A stronghold (17C-18C) – Ypres has been subjected to several sieges over the centuries. From the Middle Ages, the town was protected by ramparts; the old Rijselsepoort (Lille Gate) dates from this time.
The French captured the town in 1678 and Vauban surrounded it with bastions. During the reign of William I (1814-30), the fortifications of the town were restored. The ramparts were demolished in 1852. They have since been turned into attractive promenades.

The Kattenstoet Procession.

The Ypres Salient (1914-18) – In October 1914, after the Belgian army had frustrated the German advance by flooding the countryside inland from Nieuwpoort, the Germans tried to break the Allied line by attacking towards Ypres. They collided head-on with a mostly British force engaged in an offensive of their own. The bloody engagement which ensued became known as the First Battle of Ypres. The town was saved, but was half surrounded by a semicircle of German lines established on the low ridges to the east. From here artillery could begin the destruction of the town, while the ridgetop villages like Passchendaele (now Passendale) were to become bywords for death, mutilation, and mud. With comparatively little strategic value, Ypres took on huge significance as a symbol of the Allies' dogged determination not to give up this last remaining corner of Belgium. In Spring 1915, the Second Battle of Ypres saw the salient further reduced in size, as well as the first use of poison gas by German units. Gas was used again by the Germans in the Third Battle of Ypres in summer 1917, a largely futile offensive conducted by British and Empire troops who pushed back the German lines a few short kilometres. By the time of the final Allied offensive in 1918, more than 300 000 Allied soldiers, the vast majority of them from Britain and the Empire, had lost their lives at "Wipers", one of the "Great War's" most frightful killing grounds.

Directory

WHERE TO EAT

In 't klein stadhuis – *Grote Markt 32* – ☎ *057 21 55 42* – ✗ – *€20.95*. Popular establishment in one of the old buildings on the main square. Dine in the trendy interior or, when the sun shines, outside in the square. Concise and contemporary menu.

De Wijngaard – *Focklaan 8* – ☎ *057 20 42 30* – ✗ – *€30*. Family establishment with a straightforward style. Generously proportioned steaks served with a variety of sauces. Friendly service. The grape baskets hanging above the bar are a nice touch.

WHERE TO STAY

't Zweerd – *Grote Markt 2* – ☎ *057 20 04 75* – *zweerd@pandora.be* – ✗ – *17 rms: €58/68* – *restaurant €18/35*. This modest hotel on the main square has rooms with somewhat dated decor, but they are fine for an overnight stay. There's a friendly little bistro with an outdoor terrace on the ground floor.

Regina – *Grote Markt 45* – ☎ *057 21 88 88* – *info@hotelregina.be* – *17 rms: €17/100* – *restaurant €25/60*. In an historic building on a corner of the main square, this establishment has been run by the same family for more than 30 years. Classic but unpretentious cuisine in the restaurant, and straightforward accommodation on the first floor.

Walking About

Start at St-Maartensplein.

St-Maartenskathedraal

The cathedral was destroyed during the First World War, but rebuilt in its original style (13C-15C). Near the entrance, admire the 17C alabaster statues on the left on top of the parclose screen of the baptistery chapel. The chapel of the Holy Sacrament, behind the triumphal arch, houses a 16C polyptych representing the scenes of the Passion.)

Go past the theatre and turn left.

St George's Memorial Church

9am-6pm. ☎ *057 21 56 85.* Designed by Reginald Blomfeld in the style of an English parish church, this place of worship was completed in 1929 to commemorate the British servicemen who died during both World Wars. The interior contains many poignant memorials, among them that of Sir John French, commander of the British Expeditionary Force and later Earl of Ypres (on the cover of the font).

Return to St-Maartensplein. Go past the Lakenhalle, cross the Grote Markt and walk along Meensestraat which leads to the Menin Gate.

IEPER

Menenpoort

The **Menin Gate** was designed in the form of a Classical gateway by Sir Reginald Blomfeld and unveiled in 1927. The most important British memorial of the First World War, it commemorates the names of 54 896 soldiers who have no known grave. It stands on the site of the old Menenpoort, the gateway guarding the road from the little town of Menen (Menin in French) to the east; this was the route taken by countless thousands of soldiers marching to and from the front line. Every evening at 8pm, traffic stops and the buglers of the Ypres fire brigade sound the Last Post.

Worth a Visit

Lakenhalle★

One of Gothic Europe's grandest secular buildings, the cathedral-sized Cloth Hall symbolised the wealth and power of the medieval wool trade in Flanders. 133m/436 foot long and topped by a majestic turreted belfry, it had no fewer than 48 doorways opening on to the River Ieperle (then navigable and now in a culvert) and leading to the spacious market halls inside. The upper floor was used for storage. By 1918 four years of shelling had reduced the huge structure to a few stumps of masonry. In an heroic effort of reconstruction, it was meticulously rebuilt in sandstone in the original style. On the outside are statues of Earl Baldwin IX and Mary of Champagne (in whose reign building began) and of King Albert and Queen Elisabeth (in whose reign the restoration was completed).

To the right of the Cloth Hall is the **Nieuwerck** (Stadhuis), an elegant Renaissance building builtin 1619 as the town hall.

In Flanders Fields Museum★★

   Apr-Sept: 10am-6pm; Oct-Mar: Tue-Sun 10am-5pm. Closed for 3 weeks after Christmas holidays. €10 from April to mid-Nov (€7.50 at other times). ☏ *057 22 85 84 (Tourist Information Centre).*

This innovative museum, opened in 1998, retraces the history of the First World War in a most compelling way. The Battles of the Ypres Salient are explained through interactive terminals, miscellaneous documents and photographs, recordings, including the famous poem *In Flanders Fields* by John McCrae, and extracts from films. The museum pays particular attention to the experiences of ordinary people, evoking the terrible trench warfare and everyday life behind the front, such as the medical assistance given to the wounded in the mobile hospitals, and Talbot House in Poperinge, a popular meeting place for British soldiers.

Belle Godshuis Museum

Apr-Oct: Tue-Sun 10am-12.30pm, 2-6pm. €2.50. ☏ *057 22 85 84 (Tourist Information Centre).*

This museum is housed in the chapel of the **Hospice Belle**. The collection consists of antique furniture and works of art such as silver and goldwork, ecclesiastical garments, and paintings (including *Virgin and Donors*, a beautiful composition from 1420 set against a gold background).

Hotel-Museum Arthur Merghelynck

Guided tours (1hr 30min) by prior arrangement, 9am-noon, 1.30-5.30pm. €2.50. All enquiries to the Tourist Information Centre ☏ *057 22 85 84.*

This town residenceof 1774 was destroyed in 1915 and rebuilt in 1932. Fortunately, its collections were salvaged from the disaster. The beautiful furniture and objets d'art (paintings, porcelain) complement the refined 18C elegance of the reconstructed rooms.

Nearby, in Rijselsestraat, the lovely Templars' house dates back to the 13C.

Excursions

Bellewaerde Park

5km/3mi E. Leave by N 8. Beyond the Menin Gate are several military cemeteries, notably the **Hooghe Crater Cemetery** on the right, which contains over 6 800 British war graves. Near the Sanctuary Wood Cemetery is the Sanctuary Wood Museum with some preserved lengths of trench, and, atop fiercely contested Hill 62, a Canadian memorial.

In **Bellewaerde Park** visitors can wander among antelopes, ostriches, stags, llamas and zebras. They can take a safari-tram through the tiger and lion enclosure, see a show given by an elephant, have a boat trip through an African landscape after passing beneath a magical waterfall and much more.

Tyne Cot Military Cemetery

10km/6.25mi NE on N 332. In the Third Battle of Ypres, the British – mostly Australians and Canadians – paid for an advance of 8km/5mi towards the ruined village of Passchendaele/Passendale with almost 400 000 casualties. Tyne Cot ("cottage") was the ironic name given by men of the Royal Northumberland Fuseliers to a ridgetop German strongpoint. The cemetery here is the largest Commonwealth war cemetery anywhere, with 11 856 tombstones and the names of 35 000 missing soldiers inscribed on the enclosing semicircular wall. The view extends over the now tranquil countryside towards Ypres and, in clear conditions, to the English Channel.

Hundreds of years before the Ypres battles, on 11 July 1302, the village of **Westrozebeke** to the northeast *(13km/8mi)* was the site of another famous clash of arms, the Battle of the Golden Spurs *(see Kortrijk)*.

Heuvelland (Flanders Uplands)

Leave Ypres by ③ on the town plan. By the village of Wijtschate turn right. The Pool of Peace is off the road to the left.

Rising to the modest height of 90m/295ft, the ridge at Messines (now Mesen) was captured in the Third Battle of Ypres when the German defences were destroyed by huge mines, the detonation of which could be heard in England. One crater, 129m/423ft across, is now known as the Pool of Peace.

Continue W and cross N 331.

Kemmelberg – This wooded hill (alt 159m/522ft) is a part of the Flanders Uplands which extend along each side of the border. Bitter battles were fought around here in April 1918, at the beginning of the last major German offensive. The climb up the hill reveals extensive countryside views. Near the top there is a neo-Gothic **tower** commanding a panoramic view. An obelisk on the south slope marks the site of the **French ossuary** where more than 5 000 unknown soldiers are buried.

Cross N 375.

Rodeberg –The "Red Hill" reaches an altitude of 143m/469ft, and like the Zwarteberg (Black Hill) just over the border in France, is a popular spot. It is topped by a little windmill.

Knokke-Heist ♨♨♨

Heist, Duinbergen, Albert-Strand, Knokke and Het Zoute together constitute a single seaside resort, renowned for its elegance and what are considered the most beautiful villas on the coast, particularly in Het Zoute. The
resort offers an exceptionally wide variety of recreational, sporting and
entertainment facilities. Major exhibitions are held in the casino and the
Scharpoord cultural centre, which is also used for conferences. As well as
golf courses, swimming pools and tennis courts, there is the artificial lake
of the Zegemeer and a thalassotherapy centre.

Location

*Westvlaanderen – population 32 936 – Michelin maps 716 C1 and 533 E14 – town
plan in the current edition of The Red Guide Benelux.*
This smart seaside resort is close to the border with the Netherlands. Easily
accessible by N 49 from Antwerp or by the N 34 coastal road.
🖪 *Zeedijk 660, ☎ 050 63 03 80; www.knokke-heist.be*

Worth a Visit

Casino

The foyer of the casino has a beautiful Venetian crystal chandelier as well as
mural paintings by Magritte *(Le Domaine enchanté, 1953)* and Keith Haring. A
bronze statue (1965) by Zadkine, entitled *The Poet*, stands in front of the building.

Directory

PUBLIC TRANSPORT

An efficient coastal tramway serves all the
seaside resorts between Knokke in the
northeast and De Panne in the southwest.

SIGHTSEEING

Walking and cycling – There are several
pleasant walks starting from the resort,
which take visitors along willow-shaded
avenues past Het Zoute's luxury villas
nestling in their luxuriant gardens.
Several of the walks in the surrounding area
lead through green countryside scattered
with pretty white farmhouses with red-
tiled roofs.

WHERE TO EAT

☺ **'t Kantientje** – *Lippenslaan 103 –
☎ 050 60 54 11 – Closed 1 week Apr,
1 week Jul, mid-Nov to mid-Dec, Mon eve
except Jul-Aug, Tue – €21/40.*
This attractive little establishment is
one of the most reliable places to eat on
Knokke's main street, featuring tasty
traditional dishes at very than reasonable
prices, mussels in season and an outdoor
summer terrace where you can drink your
aperitif. It's best to book a table.

☺☺ **Marie Siska** – *Zoutelaan 177 –
☎ 050 60 17 64 – Sat, Sun and school
holidays Apr-Oct – lunch €12 – €28/38.*
Marie Siska has been Het Zoute's
unchallenged "Waffle Queen" since 1822.
This is a friendly, family-run restaurant,
with a tea-room, outdoor terraces, cosily
furnished bedrooms, and a garden with
children's play facilities and minigolf.

WHERE TO STAY

☺☺☺ **Villa 't Zonneke B&B** –
*Duinbergenlaan 78 – 8301 Duinbergen –
☎ 050 51 98 51 – villa.zonneke
@worldonline.be – ✍ – 3 rms, 3 apts:
€89/111* ☜ Next door to a chapel in a
residential area, this villa has spacious
and attractive bedrooms, all with
kitchenette. Breakfast is taken in the garden,
weather permitting. Bike storage. Book well
in advance.

☺☺☺ **Monterey** – *Bocheldreef 4 –
83-1 Duinbergen – ☎ 050 51 58 65 –
info@monterey.be – Closed mid-Nov
to end Dec – 🅿 – 8 rms: €104* ☜
Just a short step from the beach, this
villa is perched on top of a sand-dune.
Cosy lounge with open fireplace, attractive
bedrooms and bright and airy breakfast
room opening out on to a terrace with
a panoramic view.

TAKING A BREAK

Cambridge – *Zeedijk 649 – ☎ 050 60
71 17 – 9am-8.30pm.* This long-established
combination of tea room and inn is
appreciated by local people and
visitors alike, whom it has served well
and loyally for over three-quarters of
a century. Lounge with warm and
comfortable ambience. Well-sheltered
outdoor terrace on the sea-dike
in summer.

SHOPPING

Pâtisserie Gaelens – *Kustlaan 68 –
☎ 050 61 01 50 – Daily exc Mon
(Mon, Tue in winter) 7am-7.45pm;
take-away only – closed Jan, Oct.*
On Knokke's *"Triangle Square"*, this patisserie
is a must for every sweet-toothed visitor. Its
two great specialities are
rice Condé and the Misérable, a little
confection made from almond paste
and vanilla cream.

Market – There is a colourful Thursday
afternoon market in July and August at De
Bolle, close to the Tourist Information
Centre.

Het Zwin★

♿ *Mid-Apr to end Sept: 9am-7pm; early Oct to mid-Apr: Thur-Tue, 9am-5pm. €4.46.* ☎ *050 60 70 86; www.zwin.be*

An arm of the sea which is now silted up, the **Zwin** lies between the resort and the Belgian-Dutch border. It once served the ports of Sluis, Damme and Bruges.

This is a world of channels, tides and salt meadows, surrounded by dunes that isolate it from the sea and dikes that protect the countryside from flooding.

The Zwin is now a **nature reserve** (150ha/370 acres, of which 25ha/62 acres are situated in the Netherlands) and is home to some very interesting flora and fauna. Part of the reserve (60ha/148 acres) is open to the public.

The best times to visit are in spring, for the birds, and in summer, for the flowers. From mid-July to the end of August sea-lavender forms a marvellous mauve carpet.

Before beginning the walk, it is worth visiting the aviaries and the enclosure where storks nest and ducks splash about, and where it is possible to observe birds that come from the reserve itself. From the dike on the far side of the woodland there is a view of the whole of the reserve.

The innumerable species living in the Zwin include terns, waders such as the avocet with its fine curved beak, ducks such as the red-beaked sheldrake and several migratory birds such as the grey plover and various species of sandpiper.

The Zwin

Natuurcentrum Het Zwin

Excursions

Zeebrugge

8 km/5mi W on N 34.

Zeebrugge is the only Belgian deep-water coastal port. Inaugurated in 1907, it is linked to Bruges by the Baudouin Canal. The outer harbour, connected to the three basins of the inner harbour by a lock, can accommodate very large vessels. Like Ostend, Zeebrugge has scheduled car ferry services to England (Hull) as well as roll-on/roll-off and container facilities. It is also Belgium's major fishing port and a pleasant seaside resort complete with a small marina. Zeebrugge was a German submarine base during the First World War. It was made famous by the daring British raid during the night of 22-23 April 1918, when blockships were sunk in the harbour entrance, rendering the port virtually unusable.

Seafront

In this theme park devoted to the sea, visitors may venture on board the lightship *West-Hinder* or the Soviet Foxtrot class submarine B143.

The vast building of the fish market now houses **Aquastrip**, with interactive displays on the development of the port of Zeebrugge, the history of the North Sea and Belgian fisheries, and the 1917 raid. *10am-6pm (Jul-Aug 7pm). Closed Jan, 25 Dec. €9.95. ☎ 050 55 14 15.* The Maritieme Boulevard and the Viskade are lined with shops, cafés and restaurants.

Lissewege

4km/2.5mi by ② on the plan in TheRed Guide Benelux.
The white-painted houses of this delightful village are overlooked by the impressive brick **tower** of its church. Built in the 13C and rebuilt in the 16C to the 17C, the church has retained its original charm.

All that remains of the **Ter Doest** *(1km/0.5mi S of Lissewege)*, a daughterhouse of the "Abbey in the Dunes" in Koksijde, are the chapel, a turreted farmhouse (part of which has been turned into a restaurant) and the vast and beautiful **abbey barn★** (13C), decorated with Gothic brick mouldings and with a wonderful oak roof.

Koksijde ≋

This attractive seaside resort is made up of Koksijde-Bad, Sint-Idesbald and Oostduinkerke, and also includes the Hoge Blekker, the highest sand-dune on the Belgian coast (33m/108ft). A great many events are held in Koksijde throughout the year: among the most interesting are the large flower market, the fishermen's folk festival and a procession entitled "A Tribute to Flemish Painting". At Oostduinkerke, fishermen still catch shrimps in the traditional way, on horseback.

Location

Westvlaanderen – Population 19 618 – Michelin maps 716 A2 and 533 A16.
On Belgium's west coast, Koksijde is on the N 34 coastal road which runs from De Panne all the way to Knokke. From the E 40/A 18 motorway, take exits 1 or 2.
🛈 *Leopold II-laan 2, ☎ 058 53 21 21; www.koksijde.be*

Fishing for shrimps on horseback

A. Kouprianoff/MICHELIN

Worth a Visit

Duinenabdij

Open Tue-Sat 10am-6pm, Sun 2pm-6pm. Closed Jan €5 ☎ 058 52 16 65. www.tenduinen.be
Access by the museum (Abdijmuseum Ter Duinen) at no 8 Koninklijke Prinslaan.
The "Abbey in the Dunes" was founded in 1107 by the Benedictines and became Cistercian in 1138. The abbey reached its apogee around 1300, and under Abbot Elias van Koksijde it was to become one of the most important sanctuaries in western Europe. Subsequently it fell into decline and was eventually destroyed by the Calvinists in 1566.

Archaeological digs carried out since 1949 have uncovered certain **traces** of the original abbey, revealing the majestic lines of its church. The cloisters still have pretty corbels. The lovely sandstone columns which belonged to the chapter house and the lay-brothers' refectory still exist.

The finds uncovered during the digs are exhibited in the **museum** together with a model of the abbey in medieval days. Other collections are devoted to history as well as regional flora and fauna (dioramas).

Near the abbey there is a wooden post **windmill** (Zuid Abdijmolen), dating from 1773.

Directory

Onze-Lieve-Vrouwekerk-ter-Duinenkerk

J van Buggenhoutlaan.
This modern church was built in 1962. Its undulating form and the navy-blue colour of the roof recall the waves of the ocean, while the beige walls harmonise with the nearby dunes. The stained-glass windows diffuse an iridescent light inside. The crypt *(access from outside)* contains a relic of St Idesbald, the 12C Abbot of the Abbey in the Dunes.

Museum Paul Delvaux

Delvauxlaan 42, St-Idesbald ♿ *Apr-Dec: Tue-Sun 10.30am-5.30. Closed 25 Dec. €4.71.* ☎ *058 52 12 29.*
Visitors may follow the development of the Belgian artist **Paul Delvaux** through the paintings, watercolours, drawings, engravings and sketches gathered by the foundation bearing his name and exhibited here. The artist's career was to encompass Post-Impressionism, Expressionism and finally Surrealism, in which he developed a highly personal style. Delvaux's world can be described as hallucinatory and yet strangely poetic. Among his favourite themes were stations (note the eerie light in *Gare Forestière*), women, whom he portrayed in varying stages of undress, set against a backdrop of Greek or Roman temples, and skeletons. The visit ends with a display of glass cabinets containing personal mementoes of the artist: a set of toy trains and trams, the replica of his Brussels studio and an extensive collection of photographs.

Excursions

Oostduinkerke⌂

4.5km/2.75mi E. Leave by ① on the town plan.
A few people still fish on horseback for shrimps on the beach of **Oostduinkerke-Bad**. At low tide the horses pull heavy drag-nets deep into the water. At the end of June there is a Shrimp Festival and a Shrimp Parade.
Here, as well as in De Panne, the spacious beaches are ideal for sand yachting.

St-Niklaaskerk

Leopold II-laan. This brown brick church, built in 1955, has arcades linking it to a massive square tower reminiscent of the one in Lissewege.
The originality of the building lies in the absence of the chancel and the series of closely spaced lancet arches which spring up from below ground level. *For information contact Mr. Gruwet, Witte Burg 90, 8670 Oostduinkerke,* ☎ *058 51 23 33.*

Nationaal Visserijmuseum

Pastoor Schmitzstraat 5. The National Fishing Museum has a fine collection of model boats, nautical instruments, a model of a fishing harbour, displays on shrimp fishing, and paintings by artists who worked in Oostduinkerke c 1900, such as **Artan**, the Belgian painter born in The Hague (1837-90). Beside the museum are reconstructions of a typical fisherman's house and an estaminet of 1920. A lifeboat and a shrimp boat are displayed in the courtyard. ♿ *Tue-Sun (daily Jul-Aug) 10am-noon, 2-6pm. Closed 1 Jan, 1, 11 Nov, 25 Dec. €2.* ☎ *058 51 24 68; www.visserijmuseum.be*

Folklore Museum Florishof

Koksijdesteenweg 24 The museum includes a reconstruction of a traditional local interior, workshops, a chapel, a grocer's shop, a barn and a small school. ♿ *Mid-Apr to mid-Sept: Wed-Mon, 1.30-5.30pm; early Oct to mid-Apr: Sat, Sun, public holidays 1.30-5.30pm. €1.70.* ☎ *058 51 12 57.*

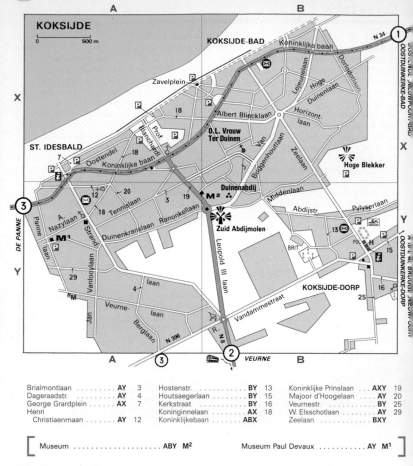

KOKSIJDE

Ten Bogaerde Farm

4km/2.5mi S by ③.

This farm, a lovely group of brick buildings that once belonged to the Abbey in the Dunes, is to the right of the road. The monumental barn, similar to the one in Ter Doest, now lies in ruins.

Nieuwpoort

5 km/3mi E by N 396.

This old fortified town at the mouth of the River IJzer was completely rebuilt in traditional style following its destruction in the First World War.

Nieuwpoort is also a seaside resort **(Nieuwpoort-Bad)** and a water sports centre. The town's focal point is the pretty Marktplein, lined with shops and cafés. Here too are the **market hall** and **town hall**, both meticulously rebuilt after 1918.

By the bridge over the River IJzer, the **Albert I monument** features an equestrian statue of the "warrior-king" whose tenacious leadership encouraged the depleted Belgian army to hold on to this westernmost tip of the country. From the top of the monument there is a **view** over the town and the surrounding countryside. *Mon-Fri 8.45am-noon, 1.15-6pm (mid-Oct to end Feb 5pm). Closed public holidays. €1.25 by lift, €1 on foot. ☎ 058 23 55 87 (Tourist Information Centre).*

The IJzermonding nature reserve extends north of the resort, along the estuary of the River IJzer. *Regular schedule of guided tours. Ring for more information ☎ 058 22 44 44 (Tourist Information Centre)*

THE BATTLE OF THE YSER

This is the name usually given to the fierce fighting which took place along the River IJzer (Yser in French) in the autumn of 1914 and which led to the stabilisation of this section of the Western Front. It was here that the hard-pressed Belgian army made a determined stand against the invading German forces and ensured that at least a portion of the national territory remained unoccupied. On 16 October the Germans launched an attack and succeeded in crossing the IJzer at Tervate, north of Diksmuide. As Allied reinforcements had still not arrived, the Belgians opened the sluice gates of the Veurne-Ambacht canal at Nieuwpoort on 28 October. The subsequent flooding of the surrounding polders immediately halted the German advance. The front line then settled south of Diksmuide until the end of the war, and the Germans turned their attention to the Ypres Salient.

Kortrijk★

On the River Leie, Kortrijk is a dynamic business centre at the heart of an industrial area often referred to as the Texas of Flanders. The attractive pedestrian streets and smart shops are perfect for a lesiurely stroll, while the renovation of the municipal theatre and the conversion of the Tack brewery into a cultural centre have given the town additional artistic flair.

Location
Westvlaanderen – Population 75 099 – Michelin maps 716 C3 and 533 E18 – Plan of the built-up area in the current edition of The Red Guide Benelux.
Only 28km/17mi from Lille just over the border in France, Kortrijk is served by two motorways, A 17/E 403 from Bruges and A 14/E 17 from Ghent or Lille. The town can also be reached on N 8, N 43 and N 50.
🅱 *Sint-Michielsplein,* ☎ *056 23 93 71; www.kortrijk.be*

Background

A prosperous place – Kortrijk has existed since the Roman period, but it reached the peak of its wealth in the 15C when its cloth trade flourished. Wool-weaving soon gave way to linen-making thanks to the River Leie, whose soft waters were ideal for retting flax. Kortrijk became famous for making linen, and damask linen became its speciality. The city has remained an internationally renowned textile centre (carpets, upholstery, off-the-peg clothing).
There are several other expanding sectors: metallurgy, electronics, gold and silverwork, oils, timber, chemical industries, construction.
The **Hallen** *(access by Doorniksewijk to the south)* date from 1967 and are used as a venue for conventions, exhibitions and concerts.
The town also plays an important role in education, largely because of its university campus, which is part of the Flemish Catholic University of Leuven.
The Battle of the Golden Spurs – On 11 July 1302, under the very walls of Kortrijk, a famous battle took place, a milestone in the Flemish struggle against the hegemony of the King of France.
The aristocratic cavalry of King Philip the Fair of Francewere humiliatingly defeated by the workers and weavers of Ypres and Bruges, under the command of Pieter de Coninck and Jan Breydel. The golden spurs picked up on the battlefield by the victors graced the vaults of the Church of Our Lady until 1382, when they were recaptured by the victorious French army who had just defeated the Flemish in the Battle of Westrozebeke.
It was at this time that Philip the Bold, Duke of Burgundy, is said to have stolen the jack-o'-the-clocks crowning the belfry and to have given them to the Church of Notre-Dame in his capital city of Dijon. The symbolic return of the statues took place on 23 September 1961, and Manten and his wife Kalle have resumed their place at the top of the belfry.

Walking About

Start at Grote Markt.

Grote Markt
This is the commercial hub of the town.
Belfort – The belfry, which dates from the 14C, stands in the middle of Grote Markt and is topped with four pointed turrets and the famous jack-o'-the-clocks at the very top.
The lovely tower of the 15C **St.-Maartenskerk** can be seen to the east of the square.
Stadhuis – The town hall has a restored Late Gothic façade. The statues, which were replaced in the 19C, portray the Counts of Flanders. *Mon-Fri 9am-noon, 2-5pm. Closed public holidays.* ☎ *056 23 93 71 (Tourist Information Centre).*
The modernised interior still has magnificent rooms. The **Schepenzaal★** or Aldermen's Chamber on the ground floor is decorated with a remarkable stone fireplace in Late Gothic style (1527), with alcoves containing statues of the Virgin Mary and the patron saints of towns in the region. The ends of the beams on the ceilings are decorated with picturesque polychrome scenes in which Justice, a crowned woman, features as the main character.
The **Oude Raadzaal★**, the former Council Chamber on the first floor, also has a fireplace dating from 1527. It is decorated with three rows of sculpture: at the top, the Virtues; in the middle, on either side of Emperor Charles V, the Vices; at the bottom, Idolatry and the Deadly Sins.
The carvings on the ceiling beams show droll scenes depicting the evil influence of woman over man, for instance in the illustration of the medieval poem *The Lay of Aristotle*, in which the philospher is being straddled by a woman.
The attractive courtyard, covered with a glass roof, is now used for receptions.
Go along Begijnhofstraat from the top left end of the square.

Directory

WHERE TO EAT

⊖⊜ **Bistro Aubergine** – *Groeningestraat 16-18 – ☎ 056 25 79 80 – v.beernaert @pandora.be – Closed Aug, Mon, midday Sat – lunch €12 – €31.* This friendly, slightly old-fashioned bistro right by the Church of Our Lady has a varied lunch-time menu as well as an inexpensive three-course set meal. Dining room with gallery and small courtyard where a table can be reserved in summer.

⊖⊜⊜ **Huyze Decock** – *Louis Verweestraat 1 – ☎ 056 25 28 54 – huyzedecock @pandora.be – Closed late Jan – early Feb, late July – early Aug, Mon, Tue – lunch €15 – €41.* Reliable establishment only a few steps from the Grote Markt. Bistro-style dining room divided into two sections. Traditional dishes and an inclusive handwritten menu changed monthly.

WHERE TO STAY

⊖ **Center Broel** – *Graanmarkt 6 – ☎ 056 21 97 21 – cbh@skynet.be – Closed mid-Dec – mid-Jan; restaurant closed Fri – 26 rms: €47/70 – €9 – restaurant €34/44.* On the riverside close to the Broeltorens, this establishment offers every comfort, while its decor brings to mind the stylish ambience of the hotels of yesteryear. Spacious public rooms, cosy bedrooms, fine cuisine, pretty summer terrace and a friendly bistro.

⊖ **Focus** – *Hovenierstraat 50 – ☎ 056 21 29 08 – focus@aletheia.be; €47/64:* Some distance from the town centre, this hotel is unusual in the decor of four of its rooms, which have been styled by local artists. Well-kept, friendly welcome, but only intermittent staffing of reception.

TAKING A BREAK

De Roadskelder – *Leiestraat 1 – ☎ 056 21 91 87 – 11am-1am, Sat 3pm-2am, Sun 3pm-1am.* Huge bar occupying the vaulted cellars of the 15C town hall.

SHOPPING

De Kaashalle – *Graanmarkt 18 – ☎ 056 22 59 98 – Mon 2pm-7pm, Tue-Sat 9am-7pm, Sun 9.30am-12.30pm.* A splendid cheesemonger's. The cheeses are matured here, and the establishment offers its own ready-made dishes, as well as jams and preserves.

Foque – *Doorniksestraat 8 – ☎ 056 22 06 81 – Thur-Tue 9am-6.30pm.* This patisserie is famous for delicacies such as *beschuiten* (milk bread) and *kalletaart*, an apple tart with almonds and apple brandy.

Begijnhof★

Between the churches of St.-Maarten and Onze-Lieve-Vrouw, the Beguine convent resembles a charming little village. Its tranquillity comes as a surprise amid the hustle and bustle of the surrounding district.

Founded in 1238, the convent was richly endowed by the Countess of Flanders, Joanna of Constantinople, in 1241. There is a statue of the Countess in the convent. The present 41 cottages date from the 17C. The Mother Superior's House stands out from the others because of its double gables. It houses a small museum, the **Begijnhofmuseum**, which recreates the atmosphere of the past. *Mar-Nov: Sat-Mon 2-5pm, Tue-Fri 1-5pm. €0.74. ☎ 056 24 48 02.*

Onze-Lieve-Vrouwekerk★

9.30am-6.30pm. ☎ 056 21 38 09.

The towers of the church dedicated to Our Lady look out over the picturesque little streets round nearby. Baldwin of Constantinople founded it in the 13C, and the poet **Guido Gezelle** was vicar in the 19C.

Begijnhof, Kortrijk

M. Gurfinkel/MICHELIN

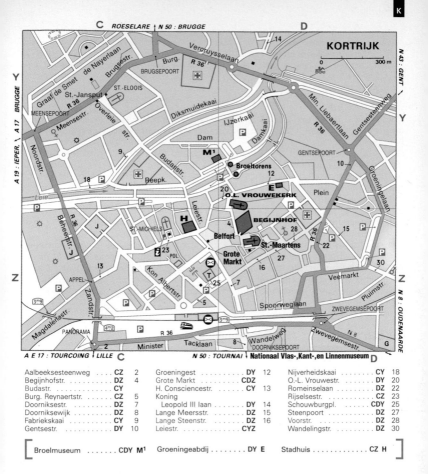

The 14C chapel of the counts of Flanders opens onto the south side of the ambulatory, and has arches with curiously sculpted spandrels. It contains an attractive alabaster **statue of St Catherine★** (1380) attributed to André Beauneveu.

A lovely Van Dyck canvas, **The Raising of the Cross★**, is in the north transept; Rubens' influence is obvious.

Go along Guido Gezellestraat.

Broeltorens

These towers were once part of the early fortifications destroyed by Louis XIV in 1684. They protected the bridge over the Leie (rebuilt after the First World War). The south tower dates from the 12C; the north one probably from the 14C or 15C.

Worth a Visit

Groenigeabdij

Tue-Sun 10am-noon, 2pm-5pm. Closed 24 Dec-2 Jan. ☎ 056 24 08 70.
The attractively restored brick buildings of the old abbey of Groeninge date back to 1597. They were occupied by Cistercian monks for two centuries and then by an order of Poor Clares from 1845. The ground floor houses the communal hall, with dormitories on the first floor. The museum is dedicated mainly to the history of Kortrijk, from prehistory to the beginning of the 20C, displaying a range of exhibits including a beautiful collection of silver, ceramics and damask, as well as information on the Battle of the Golden Spurs.

Broelmuseum

  Tue-Sun 10am-noon, 2-5pm. Closed 24 Dec – 2 Jan. ☎ 056 24 08 71.
This well laid-out museum, situated in an attractive riverside mansion, has a beautiful collection of ceramics, sculptures and an interesting series of paintings from the 16C to the present day. Note Roland Savery's *Pillaging of a Village.*

Nationaal Vlas-, Kant-, en Linnenmuseum

Etienne Sabbelaan 4. Via Doorniksewijk south of the town plan. & Mar-Nov: Tue-Sun 9am-12.30pm, 1.30-6pm, Sat, Sun 2-6pm. Closed 11 Jul, public holidays. €3. ☎ 056 21 01 38.

The National Linen and Lace Museum is housed in a 19C farm originally intended for growing flax, one of the most important activities in Flanders, especially in the Leie region.

The successive stages in the growing of flax and the production of linen cloth as well as the development of the industry up to the use of the first machines (c 1900), are evoked by paintings or life-size dummies dressed in traditional costume demonstrating each activity. One wing of the building illustrates the growing of flax and the production of linen, whereas the other one is devoted to crafts for household purposes.

Reconstructed interiors demonstrate the various steps: breaking, scutching, hackling, spinning and finally the weaving of linen.

A brand new building houses an interesting collection of lace, embroidery, damask and linen, in addition to tools and photos which evoke the life of days gone by. On the first floor, a number of paintings show how people lived in the period between 1880 and 1920. The models, which often portray well-known Flemish characters, also show the evolution of traditional costume made from lace and linen.

Excursion

Rumbeke

18km/11mi northwest towards Roeselare.

A lovely park (Sterrebos) surrounds **Kasteel Rumbeke** *(not open to the public).* The castle was given its array of crow-stepped gables and turrets in the 15C/16C. Much earlier, in 862, it provided a refuge for Baldwin Iron Arm, following his elopement with Judith, daughter of the French king Charles the Bald and widow of two Saxon princes. Pardoning Baldwin on condition that the pair were properly married, Charles granted him further territory in this area and made him the first Count of Flanders.

Lessines

Founded in medieval times, Lessines lies on the banks of the River Dender, in the middle of a region in which medicinal plants are grown. The town's once famous porphyry quarries are now deserted. Lessines' most celebrated son is the great master of Belgian Surrealism, René Magritte, born here in 1898.

Location

Hainaut – Population 17 020 – Michelin maps 716 E3 and 533 I 18.

Just south of the Dutch/French language border, Lessines is reached off the A 8/E 429 motorway between Tournai and Halle (exit 29, then N 57). It is also on N 42.

🚩 *Grand-Place 11,* 📞 *068 33 21 13; www.lessines.be*

Worth a Visit

Hôpital Notre-Dame-à-la- Rose★

Apr-Oct: Sat, Sun and public holidays 2-6pm; Jul, Aug, Tue-Sun at same times €6.50.
☏ *068 33 24 03 (museum) or 068 33 24 03.www.notredamealarose.com*

This hospital-monastery was founded in 1242 by Alix de Rosoit, lady-in-waiting to Blanche of Castile and widow of Arnold IV of Oudenaarde, Grand Bailiff of Flanders and Lord of Lessines. The buildings were reconstructed between the 16C and 18C in the Flemish Renaissance style around Gothic cloisters enclosing a delightful garden. The hospital is now a museum that serves as a reminder of everyday life in the monastery and hospital through the ages. Its exhibits include furniture, paintings, gold and silver ware, and porcelain, set out in the many rooms that have been restored and turned into the museum. The 18C church was built at the end of the hospital ward dating from the same period because of the principles on which care and treatment were based. They required that the soul and the body be treated at the same time, hence the close links between areas devoted to spiritual matters and those devoted to material ones. The equipment used to make *helkiase* (from the Greek word for "wound") can be seen in the 19C infirmary. It was a cream used to treat skin diseases and ulcers and was invented by Sister Marie-Rose Carouy in the late 19C. It enjoyed enormous popularity.

Excursion

Ellezelles

11km/6.75mi west.

This village is known for its **Witches' Sabbath**, held every year in June. To the right of the church is the **Maison du Pays des Collines**, a visitor centre explaining the flora, fauna and legends of the gently undulating hill country along the border with Flanders. The ridge 3km/1.75mi to the west of the village is crowned by the **Moulin du Cat Sauvage**, a picturesque timber-built post mill dating from 1751. *May-Sept: Sun p.m. on request only. €2.* ☏ *068 64 51 55.*

Leuven ★★

Leuven owes its fame to its university, the oldest in Belgium. The presence of thousands of students gives the city a lively and very special atmosphere, especially in the evening. Leuven is the dynamic capital of the recently formed province of Flemish Brabant; it is also celebrated for the beer brewed here since the 14C, and Stella Artois, the biggest Belgian brewery, has a worldwide reputation for the lager first produced in 1926. The little Domus brewery is still turning out a number of specialist beers, among them the white beer known as Leuvense Wit/Blanche de Louvain.

Location

Vlaams-Brabant ▯ *– Population 88 245 – Michelin maps 716 GH3 and 533 N17.*
On the banks of the River Dijle, Leuven is easily reached by the E 40/A 3 and E 314/A 2 motorways.
▯ *Stadhuis, Grote Markt 9, ☎ 016 21 15 39; www.leuven.be*

Directory

WHERE TO EAT

De Blauwe Schuit – *Vismarkt 16 –* ☎ *016 22 05 70 – €10/15.* This striking yellow edifice on Leuven's Fishmarket square offers a limited range of straightforward but tasty dishes. When the sun comes out, the walled outdoor section with its fountain is very popular.

't Zwart Schap – *Boekhandelstraat 1 –* ☎ *016 23 24 16 – Closed Carnival week, mid-Jul – mid-Aug, Sun, Mon, public holidays – lunch €15 – €25/43.* On the corner of a lane in the traffic-free town centre, close to the town hall, this old and very pretty building is known for classic cuisine brought subtly up to date. Panelled restaurant with close-packed tables and pleasant bistro-style ambience.

WHERE TO STAY

dewerf B&B – *Hogeschoolplein 5 –* ☎ *0476 96 42 41 – €22.31/35.94.* A fine place to stay when stopping off in Leuven, this centrally located bed and breakfast establishment is by a little square lined with bistros. Simply furnished but well-kept bedrooms. Shared facilities.

Jeff's Guesthouse B&B – *Kortstraat 2 –* ☎ *016 23 87 80 – 6 rms: €69.40/79.30 – €7.30 – meal €40.90.* A charming and original establishment, right in the historic centre. Ground floor olive oil boutique and restaurant with daily specials. Upper floor – a slippers-only zone! – opens onto a Moroccan lounge and bedrooms with very simple but attractive decor. Mediterranean atmosphere.

TAKING A BREAK

Gambrinus – *Grote Markt 13 –* ☎ *016 20 12 38 – 10am-midnight.* One of the oldest brasseries in Leuven, with a particularly convivial atmosphere. Outdoor drinking on the market place in fine weather.

De Wiering – *Wieringstraat 2 –* ☎ *016 29 15 45 – 11am-1.30am, 3am Fri, Sat.* Streamside café-restaurant on several floors of a lovely building decorated with all sorts of intriguing objects. Extremely popular, it greets its guests with a burst of Gregorian chant!

Background

Leuven's first stronghold was captured by the Normans. who were defeated by Arnulf of Carinthia. A new castle was built in the 11C by Lambert I the Bearded, Count of Leuven, forming the nucleus for the development of a town.

Capital of the Duchy of Brabant, and in an enviable position at the end of the navigable section of the Dijle and on the route linking the Rhineland to the sea, Leuven became a major cloth making town. City walls were built in the 12C, of which a few traces remain, especially in **St.-Donatuspark**. In the 13C a fortress was built to the north on **Cesarsberg**.

The **Joyeuse Entrée**, a charter of Brabant's liberties to which all new sovereigns had to swear fealty, was signed in Leuven in 1356 and remained effective until 1789.

Leuven surrounded itself with a second set of walls about 7km/4.25mi long. However, violent conflicts pitted the clothmakers' guilds against the patrician class, and a major riot broke out in 1378, culminating in the capture of the town hall. The nobles who had taken refuge there were unceremoniously defenestrated and impaled on the pikes of the citizens waiting below. With its cloth trade ruined by civil war, Leuven was subjected to competition from Brussels. Nevertheless, under Burgundian rule, the town decked itself out with a number of fine public buildings (the town hall was built at the end of the 15C) and a university. In the 18C, various commercial activities were developed, especially the brewing of beer.

In 1914, the invading German army sacked the town and set it on fire; 1 800 houses and the magnificent university library were destroyed. Leuven suffered again in the Second World War; there was heavy bombing in 1940, then in 1944 the library was destroyed once more, this time in an Allied air raid.

However, the city rapidly rose from its ashes.

Katholieke Universiteit Leuven – The Catholic University of Leuven was founded in 1425 at the instigation of Pope Martin V and at the request of John IV, Duke of Brabant. It soon became one of the most prestigious universities in Europe. In 1517 Erasmus founded the Collegium Trilingue, where Hebrew, Latin and Greek were taught. It was to serve as a model for the Collège de France in Paris. The University withstood the religious strife of the 16C and remained a steadfast champion of orthodoxy for many years. Several illustrious figures are associated with it: one of its rectors, the preceptor of Emperor Charles V, became Pope Adrian VI (1459-1523). In the 16C, Justus Lipsius and Mercator both taught here. In the 17C, **Jansenius** (1585-1638) was one of its lecturers. In 1640, after his death, his *Augustinus* was published here; condemned by the Pope, it was to give rise to the Jansenist movement.

The University has been split since the controversial linguistic divide of 1968, following which the French-speaking university, or Université Catholique de Louvain (UCL), moved to the new town of Louvain-la-Neuve in Wallonia. The Flemish Katholieke Universiteit Leuven (KUL) has 25 000 students, including some 2 000 from abroad. At the start of term, the professors parade through the city streets, decked out in full regalia.

Walking About

From Grote Markt, walk along Naamsestraat.

Naamsestraat
Several of the university colleges are to be found in this long street.

Universiteitshalle – In 1425 the University occupied this cloth hall built in the previous century. In the 17C the building was given an additional storey in Baroque style; it was reconstructed after its destruction in 1914.
It now houses the University offices.

Turn left into Standonckstraat which leads to Hogeschoolplein.

Pauscollege – The classical buildings of the **Pope's College**, founded by Pope Adrian VI, are clustered around the main courtyard, where you can admire two bronze statues (1985-91) by Olivier Strebelle.

Return to Naamsestraat.

St.-Michielskerk – This church, dedicated to St Michael, was designed by Father Hesius in the 17C. The splendid Baroque **facade**★ is harmoniously proportioned, and has beautiful flowing lines which draw the eye upwards.

Continue along Naamsestraat.

Groot Begijnhof

LEUVEN

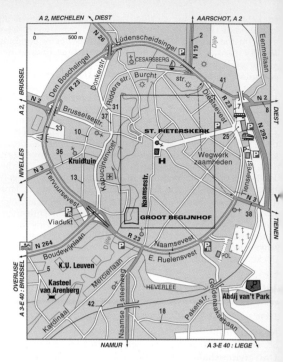

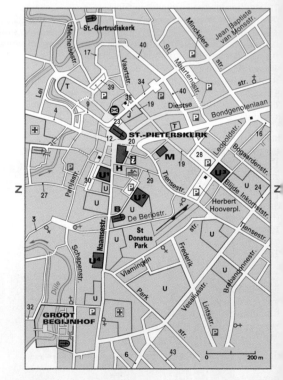

Van Dalecollege – The magnificent buildings of this college, which were recently restored, are in Renaissance style. They house the social services of Leuven University.

Turn into St-Beggaberg which leads to the Begijnhof.

Groot Begijnhof★★

Founded around 1230, the Beguine convent originally just consisted of the area around the church. In the 17C it was extended, covering an impressive area of approximately 7ha/15 acres. On the UNESCO World Heritage List since 1998, it is the largest Beguine convent in Belgium. The university bought the complex in 1962 and restored it as closely as possible to its original state. The houses have since provided accommodation for students and lecturers. The last nun died in 1988.

Behind its venerable brick walls, the Begijnhof consists of a picturesque group of buildings, crossed by two arms of the Dijle. The houses have small arched door-ways and some of them have quaint alcoves decorated with statues. Several of the dwellings have gardens. Whereas some of the richer nuns had their own homes (the 1634 Sint-Pauwel House at Middenstraat 65 is an example), others shared a convent.

The Gothic **church** is an austere building devoid of tower, transept and ambula-tory. The chevet is lit by a beautiful double-lancet window. The decoration of the interior dates from the 18C.

Worth a Visit

Stadhuis★★★

Apr-Sept: guided tours (45min) 11am, 3pm, Sat, Sun and public holidays 3pm; Oct-Mar: 3pm. Closed Christmas and New Year. €2. ☎ 016 21 15 39.

Leuven's extraordinary town hall was built in the mid-15C in the reign of Philip the Good in Flamboyant Gothic style by Matys de Layens. In some ways resembling a giant reliquary built in stone, it needs to be studied from a distance for its vertical lines to be fully appreciated, to say nothing of its profusion of gables, turrets and pinnacles, dormers, and almost 300 alcoves containing 19C statues. The alcove cor-bels are picturesquely decorated with naive little scenes illustrating biblical themes. Inside, several works by Constantin Meunier are exhibited in the lobby. Of the three reception rooms, the last two are richly decorated. Otto van Veen's *Resurrection of Christ* hangs in the Louis XVI Room. The large and small Gothic rooms on the first floor have oak ceilings. The archstones of the vaulting are dec-orated with scenes from the Old and New Testaments. Note also in the large room the 16C beams, on which the corbels are carved with biblical scenes.

St.-Pieterskerk★

The church dedicated to St Peter was built in the 15C and 16C in Brabant Gothic style, on the site of a Romanesque church.

The 16C façade was intended to have three tall towers, according to Joost Metsys' bold plans. The ground was unstable, however, and the west front remained unfinished.

The Gothic **interior** is outstanding because of its pure lines, with enormous pil-lars rising to the vaulting in a single sweep and a triforium extended by many tall lancet windows.

The 18C pulpit is exuberantly Baroque. St Norbert is seen struck down at the foot of a rock.

In front of the chancel are the three delicate arches of the **rood screen**★ (late 15C). Above it is a wooden Crucifix. In the front of the nave is a *Sedes Sapientiae* of 1442, the emblem of the University.

Treasury★★ – A veritable museum of religious art, the treasury contains magnifi-cent paintings and sculptures.

A remarkable **Head of Christ**★ in wood, called "from the twisted Cross", is of Romanesque date. A copy of the famous Van der Weyden triptych *Descent from the Cross* (now in the Prado, Madrid) dates from 1443.

Dieric Bouts' **Last Supper★★** (1464-67) is a calm, luminous masterpiece of decep-tive simplicity. The depth of perspective and the delicacy of the brushwork are combined with the use of a wide range of colours. The painter, who pictured him-self standing to the right in a red hat, chose to lay emphasis on the mystery of the Eucharist rather than on Judas' betrayal. Four richly coloured biblical scenes on the leaves of the altarpiece prefigure the introduction of this sacrament.

By the same artist, the triptych known as the *Martyrdom of St Erasmus* shows the executioners winding out the saint's entrails with a winch. St Erasmus is totally impassive.

A superb **tabernacle**★ stands in the chancel. The lace-like tracery of the tower was executed in Avesnes stone by de Layens (1450). The 15C choir stalls are carved with satirical subjects.

The 11C Romanesque crypt was a sepulchre for the Counts of Leuven. *10am-5pm. ☎ 016 22 69 06.*

Museum Vander Kelen-Mertens★

Tue-Sun 10am (Sun and public holidays 2pm)-5pm. €5. ☎ 016 22 69 06.
Entered through the Baroque doorway of the Savoy College, the town mansion of the Vander Kelen-Mertens family is now a museum with marvellous art collections. In the 19C, the burgomaster Vander Kelen had four of the ground-floor rooms restored in a variety of historic styles. The basement contains an archaeological collection which includes miscellaneous objects and terracotta pieces dating from prehistoric times to the Middle Ages. The section on fine arts has works from the studio of Albrecht Bouts, as well as paintings by Van der Weyden and Van Cleve. The 11/12C *Sedes Sapientiae* stands out among the sculptures. The collection gives an idea of the flourishing state of sculpture in Brabant in the 15C and 16C.

Part of the courtyard has been laid out as a medieval garden.

> **DIRK BOUTS**
>
> Dirk or Dieric Bouts ranks highly among the 15C Flemish Primitive painters. Having studied in Brussels in Van der Weyden's studio, this Haarlem-born artist settled in Leuven in 1450, where he became the official painter in 1468. His masterpiece, the *Last Supper*, can still be admired in St.-Pieterskerk. Dirk Bouts died in Leuven in 1475. Both his sons, Dirk and especially **Albrecht**, inherited his talent.

Universiteitsbibliotheek

After its wartime destruction in 1914, the university library was rebuilt, with generous funding from the United States, under the direction of the American architect Whitney Warren. Further restoration had to take place after 1945, and it was only in 1951 that the library, with its tower imitating the Giralda in Seville, was fully functional again.

St-Gertrudiskerk

Sat, Sun 1.30-4.30pm. ☎ 016 21 15 39 (Tourist Information Centre).
The church dedicated to St Gertrude has a beautiful mid-15C tower designed by Jan van Ruysbroeck, the architect of the town hall in Brussels. The tower is surmounted by an open-work stone spire. Inside there are some interesting 16C wooden **choir stalls** carved with biblical scenes.

Excursions

Abdij van 't Park

In Heverlee. Leave on Geldenaaksebaan and turn left after the railway bridge. Guided tour Sun 4pm. €3. ☎ 016 40 63 29.
The 16C-18C buildings of this Premonstratensian abbey stand on the edge of vast lakes fed by the Molenbeek stream. The abbey was founded in 1129 by Godfrey I the Bearded. Passing several dilapidated porches, the water mill and the farmhouse, one comes to the prelate's courtyard, guarded by two stone lions.
The guided tour of the abbey buildings provides an opportunity to admire the **ceilings**★ in the refectory (1679) and the library (1672). They are adorned with stucco high reliefs by Jean-Christian Hansche. The Romanesque church was altered in 1729. The Baroque interior is decorated with several canvases by **Pieter-Jozef Verhagen** (in the chancel and gallery).

Kasteel van Arenberg

In Heverlee. Leave SW on Kardinaal Mercierlaan.
This huge, early-16C castle has an impressive façade overlooking a wide lawn. It belongs to Leuven University, whose **Science Faculty** is situated in the grounds of the surrounding estate (120ha/296 acres).

Tour

VALLEY OF THE IJSE

25km/15.5mi SW.
Take N 264 and turn left onto N 253 towards Overijse.
The road soon passes through pleasant countryside with rows of poplars.

Korbeek-Dijle

The **St.-Bartholomeüskerk** has a superb sculpted wooden **altarpiece**★ (1522) with expressive figures and painted side panels. It illustrates the Martyrdom and Worship of St Stephen. *9am-5pm, visits by prior arrangement. €1. ☎ 016 47 77 42.*

't Zoet Water

3km/2mi beyond Korbeek-Dijle. This pretty wooded area has a succession of five lakes which are popular with tourists *(riding, fishing, boating, recreation park)*. Het Spaans Dak (The Spanish Roof), a remnant of a 16C manor house, has been turned into a restaurant. It is reflected in the waters of one of the lakes.
The road enters the valley of the IJse, a tributary of the Dyle, at Neerijse.
Continue along N 253.

Grapes under glass in the IJse valley

Huldenberg
The first **greenhouses** used for growing grapes come into view at this point. The cultivation of vines in heated greenhouses began in this area in 1865 and is now commonplace throughout the IJse Valley and around **Duisberg**.
Return to N 253

Overijse
The 16C humanist **Justus Lipsius** (1547-1606) was born here. He taught at Leuven and was a friend of the famous Antwerp printer Plantin.
Overijse, the heart of the wine-producing region, has an annual grape festival.
Continue on N 253.

Hoeilaart
Nicknamed "city of glass", Hoeilaart is built on hilly land where even the smallest plot is occupied by a greenhouse. A major grape harvest festival takes place here during the third weekend in September.

Liège★★

At the confluence of the Meuse and the Ourthe, surrounded by hills, this large and vital city is a major economic, commercial, and communications centre, famous for the friendliness and irreverent spirit of its inhabitants. The city's glorious history has endowed it with a large number of churches and museums, but Liège is also celebrated for its vibrant working-class district, the right-bank quarter known as Outremeuse.

Location
Liège 🅿 – *Population 187 538 – Michelin maps 716 J4 (enlarged inset map folds 17, 18) and 533 S19 – Local map see Vallée de l'Ourthe – Plan of the built-up area in the current edition of The Red Guide Benelux.*
An important inland port, Liège benefits from its proximity to Germany and the Netherlands. It is also an important hub in the European motorway network, served by E 40/A 3 (Brussels-Aachen), E 25 (Luxembourg-Maastricht), E 313/A 13 (Antwerp) and E 42/A 15 (Charleroi).
🅱 *Féronstrée 92,* ☎ *04 221 92 21; www.liege.be*
See also BLÉGNY-TREMBLEUR.

Background

It is thought that Liège was founded in 705 after the assassination of St Lambert, Bishop of Tongeren and Maastricht. The chapel built in his honour rapidly became a major place of pilgrimage, then the seat of a bishop, but it was not until the 10C that the town really began to gain importance.

The ecclesiastical principality (10C-18C) – At the end of the 10C **Bishop Notger** turned his territories into a principality dependent on the Holy German Empire. It covered two-thirds of present-day Wallonia. The history of this region was to be little more than a long series of battles. Some of the conflicts were instigated by princes anxious to retain their autonomy; others were rebellions by subjects against their prince.

Liège was granted certain privileges in 1316 and again in 1343. However, they were taken away in 1408 after the principality's communities revolted. Charles the Bold crushed another rebellion and had the town razed in 1468, sparing nothing but the churches. He later repented and presented Liège with the beautiful reliquary that is now part of the cathedral treasure.

In the 15C the ferocious Guillaume de la Marck, nicknamed "the Wild Boar of the Ardennes" because his followers wore boarskins, terrorised the principality and killed Prince-Bishop Louis de Bourbon (1482).

The town regained its prosperity during the reign of Erard de la Marck (1506-38). On his death the struggle between the Prince-Bishop's followers and opponents broke out again.

In the 18C Liège embraced the ideas of the Age of Enlightenment and welcomed the French Revolution of 1789. The rule of the prince-bishops ended in 1794, and the town became first French, then Dutch territory until 1830.

In August 1914, Liège as a fortress city presented a formidable obstacle to the invading German army. The heroic resistance of its citadel and ring of forts (including **Fort de Loncin**, of which the ruins can be seen 8km/5mi north of Liège) won the Allies an important breathing space. In the Second World War, much damage resulted when Liège was targeted by German V1 flying bombs and V2 rockets, more than 1500 of these missiles falling on the city in the winter of 1944/45.

A major centre of art – The Mosan School began to develop during the reign of Bishop Notger. It gained particular fame for its ivories in the 10C and 11C then, in the second half of the 11C, the 12C and the 13C, it began producing wonderful masterpieces in gold, silver, enamelwork and, most outstandingly, in cast iron, copper and brass.

During the Renaissance, **Lambert Lombard** (1505-66) excelled in both painting and architecture. **Jean Delcour** (1627-1707), who studied in Rome and is sometimes called the Bernini of Liège, was the most productive sculptor of the 17C. His innumerable statues with their flowing drapery, including several graceful Madonnas, decorate the town's churches and fountains.

Architecture came into its own in the 16C and the 18C. The Classical style triumphed but local particularities were retained, such as the use of brick relieved by white stone string courses and stone window mullions.

The great period of Liège cabinet-making was in the 18C when craftsmen sought inspiration from the Rococo style. Decorative carving was always done in the wood of the piece itself rather than being added on afterwards.

GEORGES SIMENON – THE BOY FROM OUTREMEUSE

The famous and prolific author Georges Simenon was born at 24 Rue Leopold on 13 February 1903. His family soon moved to Rue Pasteur, which has now been renamed Rue Simenon. in the Outremeuse district. By the age of 16, Simenon was already working as a junior reporter for the *Gazette de Liège*. He was still young when he left home to settle first in Paris, then in the United States and Switzerland. During his career Simenon produced a great many novels with psychological themes. Written with great economy of style, his books are always fascinating, conveying a tense, taut atmosphere and exposing the subtle and intricate web of human relationships. He is of course best known for his creation of the legendary pipe-smoking police inspector **Jules Maigret**. Simenon's home town has often played a key role in his stories such as *Pedigree, Je Me Souviens* and *Maigret and the 100 Gibbets*. The people of Liège are understandably proud of their writer, who died in Lausanne in 1989. Today a street, a hotel and a youth hostel carry his name. A bust of the author has been erected on Place du Congrès to honour his memory and a "Georges Simenon Trail" is available from the tourist office.

Famous musicians such as **André-Modeste Grétry** (1741-1813), **César Franck** (1822-90) and violinist **Eugène Ysaÿe** (1858-1931) were born here. One of the leading representatives of **Art Nouveau** in Belgium was decorator and cabinet-maker **Gustave Serrurier-Bovy** (1858-1910).

Liège was the birthplace of the novelist **Georges Simenon** (1903-89), who described his native city in several of his works.

Folklore is an important part of Liège life. There are three puppet theatres. The best-known character is **Tchantchès**, a good-natured incarnation of a typical citizen of Liège.

Economic growth – The rich seams of the Liège coalfield were first worked in the 12C, and from the 14C onwards metalworking flourished, with the city gaining a reputation for the manufacture of arms and armour. In the 19C, it was around Liège that the Industrial Revolution first took hold on the European continent, not least due to the presence of the English inventor and entrepreneur William Cockerill and his son John, the latter founding the industrial empire centred on the giant Seraing steelworks. The continent's first locomotive was built in Liège, and it was here that the Bessemer steel-making process was tested. The Fabrique Nationale d'Armes, the Belgian national armaments factory, was set up in Herstal in 1889.

Industrial growth was interrupted by the two World Wars, which hit Liège hard. Nevertheless, the building of the **Albert Canal** (1939) to link the Meuse and the Scheldt made Liège Europe's third-largest inland port. A tanker port was constructed between 1951 and 1964. Nowadays, metalworking remains one of the region's most important activities, and there are also chemical and plastics plants, glassworks (Val-St-Lambert), cement works and rubber manufacture.

Directory

WHERE TO EAT

L'Eureye – *Place du Marché 9 –* 04 223 28 13 – *Closed Sun, public holidays –* €16.10/27.80. This little place is close to the Perron and is much in favour among local people. Delightful dining room with exposed beams and rafters, faïence tiles and old prints. Traditional dishes with an individual touch.

Café Lequet – *Quai-sur-Meuse 17 –* 04 222 21 34 – *Closed Tue in summer –* – €4.70/17. Famous for its "boulets-frites" Liège-style *(see below)*, as well as for its cheerful atmosphere, this typical bistro is a city institution, which gets very busy indeed on Sunday mornings when the Batte market is in full swing.

Casa Paco – *Rue du Pot d'Or 30 –* 04 221 21 93 – *1130am-2am, Fri-Sat - 4am, Sun 4pm-midnight –* €6.20/29.70. Welcoming tapas bar with a restaurant on the upper floor specialising in paella. Old beams, bullfighting trophies and hams hanging from the ceiling add to the atmospheric Iberian ambience. Good choice of French and Spanish wines served by the glass.

Enoteca – *Rue de la Casquette 5 –* 04 222 24 64 – *Closed Sat midday, Sun – lunch €19 – €32.* Friendly service and tasty Franco-Italian cuisine, inexpensive lunches and wide selection of Italian wines are among the reasons for patronising this establishment right by the Carré and the Opera House. You can watch the chef at work in his open kitchen.

Le Bistrot d'en face – *Rue de la Goffe 8 –* 04 223 15 84 – *Closed early Aug – mid-Aug, Mon, Sat midday – €37.* Delightful bistro tucked away in a lane running at right angles to the riverside behind the old meat market. Fine Lyons-style food orchestrated by two brothers, one behind the scenes, the other out front. Tempting dishes of the day.

Max – *Place Verte 2 –* 04 222 08 59 – *Closed last fortnight Aug, Sat midday, Sun – lunch €31 – €39/69.* Elegant brasserie in front of the new St-Michel shopping centre, known for its range of seafood specialities. Designer decor, oyster bar and heated terrace for cold days.

WHERE TO STAY

L'Embrun – *Port des Yachts* – ☎ *04 221 11 20* – *www.penichehotel.com* – ⊠ – *10 rms: 38/85€* – ⊡ *€6.50*. This barge anchored in the yacht harbour by the Albert I bridge houses a small hotel. Eight double cabins with washbasins and shared bathrooms. Two others (including the captain's cabin) have their own facilities. Advance booking essential.

Le Berger – *Rue des Urbanistes 10* – ☎ *04 223 00 80* – ⊠ – *€50/65* ⊡. Warm family atmosphere in this well-kept and centrally located little establishment. Friendly reception. Public rooms decorated in what is best described as an eclectic style, functional bedrooms.

Passerelle – *Chaussée-des-Prés 24* – ☎ *04 341 20 20* – *15 rms: €55/62* – ⊡ *€7*. This hotel is just a few steps from the footbridge linking the city centre with what was once declared the "Free Republic" of Outremeuse on the far bank of the Meuse. Rooms are not particularly spacious but are always well-kept.

Le Cygne d'Argent – *Rue Beeckman 49* – ☎ *04 223 70 01* – *cygne@cybernet.be* – ⊡ – *22 rms: €60/71* – ⊡ *€7*. In a quiet little street close to the centre and the botanic gardens, this is a good place to park your suitcase. Some rooms have been completely refurbished. Bright and cheerful breakfast room.

L'Univers – *Rue des Guillemins 116* – ☎ *04 254 55 55* – *comfort.inn.liege @skynet.be* – ⊡ – *47 rms: €62/75* ⊡ Ideal for travellers worried about catching their train, this chain hotel overlooks the Guillemins railway station and has compact, functional rooms with efficient double glazing.

Apéritif time on the Boulevard de la Sauvenière.

Mahaux Photography/Office de tourisme Liège

TAKING A BREAK

Tchantchès et Nanesse – *Rue Grande Bêche 35* – ☎ *04 343 39 31* – *Mon-Sat from 5pm*. Typical Liège inn in the heart of the Outremeuse district. It occupies a lovely 17C building and is decorated with authentic old puppets, including of course Tchantchès and Nanessse. On offer is a range of beers, "pèkets" (gin), and light meals (including the famous Liège

meatballs known as "boulets"). Piano bar – and sometimes gypsy music – on Friday.

La Maison du Péket – *Rue de l'Épée 4* – ☎ *04 223 66 55* – *10am-2am, Fri-Sat – 5am*. The name on the door says it all: The House of Gin, near the town hall, specialises in the city's favourite tipple, served neat with its "original" flavour, or with the added kick of fruits and spices; you can even try it *flambé*. Rustic interiors, with an old well and a lovely open fireplace.

ENTERTAINMENT

En Roture – *Rue Roture*. With its medley of old and pretty buildings housing numerous small restaurants and bars, this little old street in the heart of working-class Outremeuse is up there with the Carré in terms of liveliness.

Chez Bouldou – *Rue Tête de Bœuf 15* – ☎ *04 221 31 22* – *11am-2am, Fri -4am, Sat 7pm-4am, Sun 8pm-2am*. One of the best bars on the Carré, always chock-full on weekend evenings. Trendy clientele, deliberately unusual decor and good atmosphere. Live music Sun eve from 10pm, "apéritif concert" 7pm first Thur of the month and, every Wed from 9.30pm, an evening presided over by ex-DJ Bouldou himself.

SHOPPING

Most large stores are clustered around Place St-Lambert. The first part of **Féronstrée** features a great many shops selling clothes. The true shopping area is located in the **Carré** and the **Île**, where most of the streets are traffic-free. This old quarter is home to the famous **Passage Lemonnier**, which is over 150 years old.

Markets – In Liège, on Sunday mornings, it is the custom to go to the **Marché de la Batte,** along Quai de Maastricht and Quai de la Batte, where clothes, antiques, poultry, fruit and vegetables are sold. On Friday mornings the **Brocante St-Pholien** offering second-hand antique furniture is held on Place Jehan le Bel.

Specialities from Liège – Visitors to Liège should make a point of tasting **péket**, a local type of gin served in a tumbler. A **salade liégeoise** combines green beans, potatoes and pieces of bacon and onion, sprinkled with parsley and seasoned with wine vinegar. Other traditional dishes are **boulets-frites** (meatballs and chips served in a syrup sauce), **matoufèt** (bacon pancake) and **Rodge tripe** (black pudding with apple slices). Péket and juniper berries lend a distinctive flavour to the celebrated **rognons à la liègeoise** (kidneys Liège-style).

Offices des produits wallons Asat – *Place des Carmes 8* – ☎ *04 223 19 60* – *Mon-Fri 9.30am-12.30pm and 2.30pm-5pm*. This little shop deals exclusively in products from Wallonia, including Liège syrup, Herve cheese, péket, sweet cider and local beers. It is located just below the Chiroux library at the entrance to a small shopping arcade by the Kennedy bridge.

Galler – *Rue du Pot d'Or 2 – ☎ 04 221 30 50 – galler.liege@skynet.be – 10am- 6pm; Fri, Sat 10am-6.30pm*. An "enfant terrible" of the chocolate world, Galler has a cream-coloured shop-front gracing the traffic-free Rue du Pot d'Or. This family firm was first established in the suburb of Vaux-sur-Chêvremont, and became suppliers of chocolate by appointment to the Belgian court. It's the place to try Langues de Chat ("cat's tongues") designed by the humorist Philippe Geluck.

Cristalleries du Val St-Lambert – *Rue du Val – 4100 Seraing – ☎ 04 337 09 60 – www.val-saint-lambert.com – 9am-noon, 1pm-5pm – tours 9.30am, 11am, 1pm, 2.30pm, 3.30pm – adults €6.*
The tour tells you all you ever wanted to know about Belgian crystal, a luxury product exported worldwide. The story began in 1825, when the first glass was blown on the site of Val Saint-Lambert Abbey.

Visitor trail, demonstrations of glass-making, exhibition and sales hall and reject shop. Purchases can be personalised.

The Meuse.

Mahaux Photography/Office de tourisme Liège

Walking About

Start at Place St-Lambert

Spacious **Place St-Lambert** is the historical cradle of Liège. St Lambert's Cathedral stood here until its was demolished during the French Revolution. Work carried out on the square has led to the discovery of some of the remains of this building dating from the time of Bishop Notger.

Palais des Princes-Évêques★

The Palace of the Prince-Bishops was built c 1000 by Bishop Notger, and was completely rebuilt from 1526 on the orders of Prince-Bishop Erard de la Marck. The main façade was replaced after a fire in 1734, and the left wing dates from the 1800s. The building is now occupied by provincial government offices and the law courts.

The **main courtyard★★** is surrounded by arcades with raised arches and 60 massive yet elegant columns with entasis, crowned by richly ornamented capitals. The variety of decoration on the columns is extraordinary. The **small courtyard**, which can be seen from the window of a corridor, seems more intimate.

Go along Rue de Bex to Place du Marché.

Détail from the façade of the Palais des Princes-Évêques.

Ch. Bastin – J. Evrard/MICHELIN

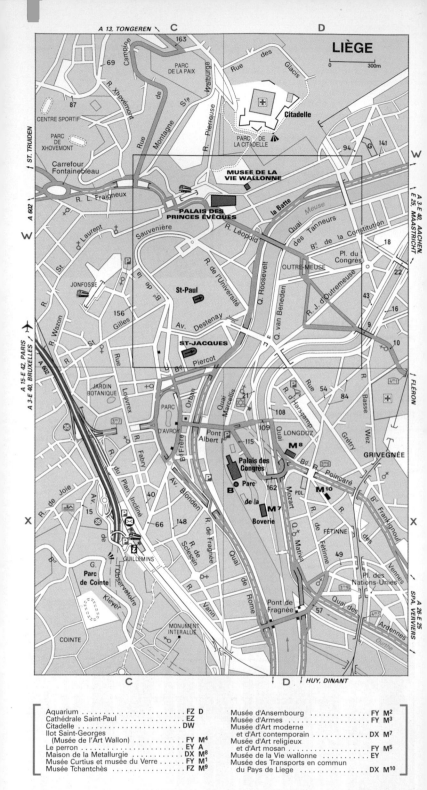

LIÈGE

Aquarium .... FZ **D**	Musée d'Ansembourg .... FY **M²**
Cathédrale Saint-Paul .... EZ	Musée d'Armes .... FY **M³**
Citadelle .... DW	Musée d'Art moderne
Ilot Saint-Georges	et d'Art contemporain .... DX **M⁷**
(Musée de l'Art Wallon) .... FY **M⁴**	Musée d'Art religieux
Le perron .... EY **A**	et d'Art mosan .... FY **M⁵**
Maison de la Metallurgie .... DX **M⁸**	Musée de la Vie wallonne .... EY
Musée Curtius et musée du Verre ..... FY **M¹**	Musée des Transports en commun
Musée Tchantchès .... FZ **M⁹**	du Pays de Liege .... DX **M¹⁰**

Place du Marché

On this pleasant square lined with many cafés and restaurants stands the **Fountain of Tradition** (1719) and the splendid 18C town hall, known as La Violette, whose hidden rear façade is worth a detour. The square is, however, unquestionably dominated by the monument known as **Le Perron★** perched on top of a huge fountain. Usually consisting of a column rising from a platform, a *perron* was originally the emblem of

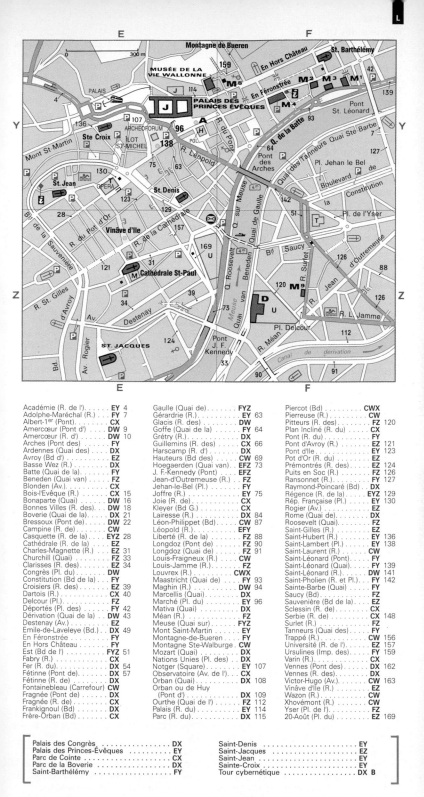

episcopal jurisdiction, but later became a symbol of civic liberties. There are a number of them in the province of Liège. This, the most famous of its kind in Belgium, has a group entitled *The Three Graces* by Jean Delcour, and was erected in 1677 on the site of a previous one destroyed in a storm. This original had been stolen in 1468 by Charles the Bold, taken to Bruges and not returned to Liège until 1478.

Turn left into Rue des Mineurs, then right into Rue Hors-Château.

Impasse des Ursulines

This street is named after the community of nuns from the **Old Beguine Convent of the Holy Spirit**. The beautiful half-timbered façades of the convent can be seen from the street. An old post stage has been rebuilt next door; it houses a reconstruction of the studio of the violinist Eugène Ysaïe.

Go along Rue Hors-Château.

Hors-Château

This 11C street derived its name (literally "Outside the castle") from the fact that it was situated beyond the town walls. It still features several narrow alleys. At nos 114-116, a small doorway flanked by modern Corinthian pillars gives access to the **Cour St-Antoine**, a courtyard beautifully restored by the architect **Charles Vandenhove** in the late 1970s. The monument carved in blue stone is the work of Anne and Patrick Poirier.

Église St-Barthélemy

Cathedral 8am-noon, 2pm-5pm. Treasury Mon 2-5pm. €4. ☎ 04 232 61 32; www.ulg. ac.be/trecatlg

This Romanesque church built in ferruginous sandstone has a massive avant-corps, or projecting section, surmounted by two towers, a feature characteristic of the 12C Rhineland-Mosan style.

Inside the church there is an outstanding brass **font★★★** attributed to the great master of Dinant **Renier de Huy**.

Go along the street known as En Féronstrée.

THE FONT OF ST –BARTHÉLEMY: A MASTERPIECE OF MOSAN ART?

This remarkable font was made between 1107 and 1118 for the Église Notre-Dame-aux-Fonts. It was originally supported on 12 statues of oxen (only 10 have survived) symbolising the Apostles. The basin has five scenes depicted on it, the main one being the Baptism of Jesus. The others represent the Preaching of St John the Baptist, the Baptism of the Catechumens, the Baptism of Cornelius the Centurion and the Baptism of the Philosopher Crato. High-relief figures stand out against the smooth background. The fluidity of the postures and their highly stylised forms elevate them to a level of technical perfection reminiscent of the art of Antiquity. The cover, embellished with figures portraying the Apostles and the Prophets, has unfortunately disappeared.

In recent years a controversy has broken out concerning the origin and authorship of the font. Some say that it is the work of Renier de Huy, others claim that it was executed by Lambert Patras, a pewter-beater from Dinant. Some experts have even suggested that the basin is not of Mosan origin at all but was crafted by Byzantine artisans. Despite these academic arguments, the issue is far from settled and the true origins of the font remain a mystery.

En Féronstrée

This busy shopping street is named after the *férons* or ironworkers who exercised their trade here in the Middle Ages

Îlot St-Georges

This complex includes the modern building housing the Musée d'Art Wallon *(Description under "Worth a visit")*

Go back to Place St-Lambert. Turn left into Rue Gérarderie, then go along Rue St-Etienne to Place St-Denis.

Église St-Denis

This church was founded in the 10C by Bishop Notger and now stands at the heart of the shopping district. It has been altered several times but still includes the base of a large 12C avant-corps.

The interior was renovated in the 18C. An early 16C wooden Brabant style **altarpiece★** in the south transept illustrates the Passion of Christ with a crowd of figures. The predella, dating from somewhat later, depicts the Life of St Denis.

Go along Rue de la Cathédrale to Place Vinâve d'Île.

Vinâve d'Île

There is a *Virgin and Child* by Delcour above the fountain in this square, in the heart of the pedestrianised shopping district.

Le Carré

Defined by Rue du Pot d'Or, Rue St-Adalbert, Rue St-Gilles and Boulevard de la Sauvenière, this area with its numerous cafés, bars and little restaurants is the favourite evening meeting-place for students from the Sart Tilman campus.

Continue to Place de la Cathédrale.

Cathédrale St-Paul

8am-noon, 2-5pm.

This Gothic cathedral has three lofty naves and a triforium. The superb foliage scrolls in the nave and transept date back to the 16C: the side aisles and chapels were decorated only in the 19C. The church presents some fine works of art

Liège From Above

To get an idea of the city in its setting along the Meuse, you can climb the 373 steps up Montagne de Beuren to the **Citadel**. Those with more time on their hands can take the charming Sentier des Coteaux (Hillside Path) at the end of Impasse des Ursulines. Another option is to reach the citadel by car. The viewing table near the Enclos des Fusillés offers a **sweeping panorama**★★ over Liège. The viewing table in **Parc de Cointe** also affords a fine general **view**★★ of the city.

including a *Madonna and Child* (late-12C to early-13C), an outstanding pulpit (mid-19C) by Willem Geefs portraying a diabolical Lucifer and a moving *Christ in the Tomb* showing Italianate influence by Jean Delcour.

Treasury★★ – *Access through the cloisters.* Laid out on several levels, this new complex houses the majestic silver-gilt **bust reliquary of St Lambert** (before 1512). 1.59m/5.3ft tall, it stands on an ornate pedestal decorated with scenes illustrating the life of the saint. Every 50 years, the reliquary is officially opened to check that his skull has remained intact. The **reliquary of Charles the Bold**★★ is made of gold enhanced by enamelwork and vermeil; it was a gift from the Duke to the cathedral in 1471. The nobleman is depicted on it next to St George, whose face is identical to his; a striking detail. Two 11C ivories, one Byzantine and the other Mosan, are also particularly worthy of note. *Tue-Sun 2-5pm. €4.* ☎ *04 232 61 32; www.ulg.ac.be/trecatlg From Place St-Paul go along Rue St-Remy and cross Rue Destenay to Place St-Jacques.*

Église St-Jacques★★

8am-noon, Sun 10am-noon (mid-Apr to mid-Jun 2-6pm). ☎ *04 222 14 41.*
Behind the west front of this Flamboyant Gothic church dedicated to St James is a Romanesque narthex that was once part of the Benedictine abbey church built here in the 11C. An interesting Renaissance façade (1558) attributed to Lambert Lombard was added to the north porch. There is a 1380 low relief inside the porch, depicting the *Coronation of the Virgin Mary*.
Inside, the sumptuous architectural decoration is awe-inspiring. The **star vaulting in the nave**★★ has a myriad of lierne and tierceron ribs framing painted portraits. There is a carved keystone at each intersection of the ribs. Great statues in painted limewood, most of them works by Delcour, back onto the line of columns. The chancel was decorated in an extraordinarily rich Flamboyant ogival style, with 16C stained-glass windows donated by the town's wealthy families.

Inside Église St-Jacques.

An altarpiece with a 15C *Pietà* in its centre can be seen in the chapel on the north side of the chancel. At the end of the nave there is a superb 17C organ.

Go back to Rue Destenay. Turn right into Avenue Rogier, then go along Rue du Pont d'Avroy. Turn left into Rue d'Amay. Go along Rue St-Jean-en-Île and cross over Rue de la Casquette. Continue along Rue du Diamant to Place Xavier Neujean.

Église St-Jean

Mid-Jun to mid-Sept and Easter holidays: visits by prior arrangement 10am-noon, 2pm-5pm.Inquiries to Madame Gérard (Thur. 1-4pm), ☏ *04 223 70 42.*

This church dedicated to St John was built in the shape of an octagon surmounted by a cupola, a design inspired by that of Aachen Cathedral. It was commissioned in the late 10C by Bishop Notger. The avant-corps was erected in c 1200 and the nave rebuilt in the 18C. The rotunda and chancel inside were decorated in Classical style at the end of the 18C. There is a 13C Calvary in the vestry, with lovely wooden **statues★** of the Virgin Mary and St John. There is a magnificent *Madonna and Child*, or **Sedes Sapientiae★**, in a side chapel. The statue was carved in wood in about 1220. The clothing is draped in a remarkably fluid manner and the face is delicately feminine.

Open-work was added to the cloisters in the 16C, and more modifications were made in the 18C. The south gallery still features beautiful 16C vaulting in which the ribs and liernes form graceful rose patterns.

Go via Boulevard de la Sauvenière and Place de l'Opéra to Rue Haute-Sauvenière.

Église Ste-Croix

8am-6pm. For visits to the treasury, apply to the vestry in the cloisters (no 9).

This is a hall-church, with three equally high aisles, dating from the 13C and 14C. The avant-corps is Romanesque in style. The church is unusual in that it has two chancels facing each other. The one at the west end is now used for christenings. The **treasury** includes valuable liturgical ornaments and some gold and silver plate. One of the most valuable exhibits is a symbolic bronze key given by Pope Gregory II to St Hubert in 722. There is also a 12C triptych reliquary in gilded repoussé brass, attributed to Godefroy de Huy.

Worth a Visit

THE CITY CENTRE MUSEUMS

Musée de la Vie Wallonne★★

Tue-Sun 10am-5pm (Sun, public holidays 4pm). Closed 1 Jan, 1 May, 1 Nov, 25 Dec. €2. ☏ *04 237 90 40.*

This museum, devoted to Walloon ethnography, popular art and folk art, is housed in an old Minorite monastery, a magnificent 17C Mosan Renaissance style residence elegantly combining brick and limestone. The museum illustrates life in the past through reconstructed interiors, workshops where clogs, candles and baskets were made, and traditional family scenes. It also has displays relating to regional art and local superstitions. Note the "nail oaks" in the room devoted to magic and popular beliefs. The sick would nail their bandages to these oaks to cure their ills.

An exceptional collection of sundials by the Antwerp poet Max Elskamp and a fine series of Liège puppets can be seen on the second floor. The museum also has a **puppet theatre** and a room with material on dialects.

Musée d'Art Religieux et d'Art Mosan★

Tue-Sun 11am-6pm (Sun 4pm). Closed 1 Jan, 1, 8 May, 1, 2, 11, 15 Nov, 24-26, 31 Dec. €3.80. ☏ *04 221 42 25.*

The museum collections illustrate the changes in religious art in the Liège diocese since the early Middle Ages and include several masterpieces.

The upper floor displays a model of the former St Lambert's Cathedral which once stood on the square bearing the same name. Mosan Romanesque art is represented by numerous sculptures and pieces of gold and silver plate. The exhibits include the **Évegnée Madonna**, a very early (late-11C) statue, and the **Rausa Christ**, a 13C wooden sculpture showing the transition from Romanesque (seated effigy) to Gothic (softness of the features and the folds of garments). Among the Gothic paintings note the **Virgin with Butterfly**, a rare 15C work by the Mosan School, and the marvellous **Virgin with Donor and St Mary Magdalene** (1475), attributed to the Master of St Gudula. The wooden **Berselius Madonna** carved in 1530 by Swabian artist Daniel Mauch, shows a wriggling Infant Jesus and cherubs playing among the skirts of a beautiful Madonna.

Musée Curtius and Musée du Verre★

This tall town mansion dates from the early 17C. Jean Curtius, a rich commissary to the Spanish armies, had it built in the Mosan Renaissance style. It now houses valuable archaeological and decorative arts collections. It contains in particular three remarkable Mosan works: the **Notger Gospels★★★**, a magnificent ivory dating from c 1000 that is decorated with 12C champlevé enamel work and copper plaques added later, the **Dom Rupert Virgin**, a 12C sandstone statue of the Virgin Mary which still shows Byzantine influence, and the **Mystery of Apollo**, a carved stone tympanum dating from the 12C.

The Glass Museum at the back of the courtyard has a large **collection of glass objects★** dating from the origins of glass-making to the present day. Particularly fine are the sets of Art Nouveau and Art Deco vases by Gallé, Lalique, Daum and Val-St-Lambert as well as furniture by the famous decorator and cabinet-maker from Liège, Gustave Serrurier-Bovy.

Musée d'Armes★

Closed for building works. ☎ *04 221 92 21 (Tourist Information Centre)*
The Arms Museum is housed in a fine 18C mansion. From 1800 to 1814 this was the *préfecture* of the Ourthe *département*, one of the adminstrative districts created when Belgium was ruled by Revolutionary France. Napoleon stayed here in 1803 and 1811. The museum displays to great advantage an exceptionally rich collection of weaponry, mainly firearms from the Middle Ages to the present, along with a large display of Napoleonic medals and decorations.

Musée d'Ansembourg★

Tue-Sun 1pm-6pm. Closed 1 Jan, 1, 8 May, 1, 2, 11, 15 Nov, 24-26, 31 déc. €3.80.
☎ *04 221 94 02.*
Now the Museum of Archaeology and Decorative Arts, this splendid 18C town house was built for the merchant and banker **Michel Willems**. Everything in the interior combines to give it the sophisticated atmosphere of the period. There are ceilings decorated with stuccowork, walls covered with Mechelen leather and Oudenaarde tapestries, furniture characteristic of Liège cabinet-making, and a kitchen adorned with Delft tiles.

Musée de l'Art Wallon

Tue-Sat, 1pm-6pm, Sun 11am-4.30pm. Closed 1 Jan, 1 May, 1 Nov, 24-26 Dec, 31 Dec. €2.50. ☎ *04 221 92 31.*
This museum is devoted to those painters and sculptors from Brussels and Wallonia who were involved in the major artistic movements of Europe from the 16C to the present. The works are displayed in chronological order, beginning on the 4th floor. They include works by Henri Blès (also known as Civetta), Lambert Lombard, Jean Delcour, Léonard Defrance, Antoine Wiertz, Félicien Rops, Henri Evenepoel, Constantin Meunier, as well as by 20C figures such as Anto Carte, Pierre Paulus, Léon Navez, Auguste Mambour, Pol Bury, Jo Delhaut, René Magritte and Paul Delvaux. There are also important temporary exhibitions.

THE EAST BANK

Parc de la Boverie

This park is at the extreme south end of the island, between the Meuse on one side and the canal on the other. The long façade of the **Palais des Congrès** conference centre is reflected in the water. Next to it is the **Tour Cybernétique** 52m/170ft high designed by Nicolas Schöffer. On the tower, a set of mobile blades indicates atmospheric changes.

Musée d'Art moderne et d'Art contemporain★

Tue-Sat, 1pm-6pm, Sun 11am-4.30pm. Closed 1 Jan, 1, 8 May, 1, 2, 11, 15 Nov, 24-26, 31 Dec. €3.80. ☎ *04 343 04 03.*

Le Sorcier d'Hiva-Oa, Gauguin.

Housed in a Louis XVI style building of 1905, this gallery has a fine collection of paintings and sculptures dating from the late 19C to the present day. Among the works by French artists, note particularly *Le Sorcier d'Hiva-Oa* by Gauguin, and the famous *Famille Soler* by Picasso, typical of his Blue Period. Belgian art is well represented with works by Van Rysselberghe, Claus, Ensor, Wouters, Khnopff, Evenepoel and the Flemish Expressionists. The gallery has an exhibition of works by contemporary artists including Magnelli, Arp and Ubac. In the basement, there is a collection of prints. This room is also used for temporary exhibitions.

MAMAC, Liège

Maison de la Métallurgie

Mid-Mar to end Oct: 9am-5pm, Sat, Sun 2-6pm. Closed public holidays. €4.96. ☎ 04 342 65 63.

Here, in enormous 19C workshops, are a forge with a 17C coal-burning iron smelting kiln and two huge 18C *makas* (hydraulic hammers). The traditional work of Liège's ironworkers is exhibited. They include firebacks and andirons. The history of energy is illustrated in another room through an extensive collection of machinery, models and motors.

Aquarium*

♿ *Easter holidays and Jul-Aug: 9am (Sat, Sun 10.30) -6pm; Sept-Jun: 9am-5pm. Closed 1 Jan, 24, 25, 31 Dec. €5. ☎ 04 366 50 21.*

This fine aquarium belongs to the university's Institute of Zoology. Visitors can admire fish from all over the world in the 26 tanks in the basement of the building, as well as marvel at the astonishing universe of the shark and the coral reef. On the first floor there is a fascinating collection of madrepores which were brought back from an expedition to the Great Barrier Reef in Australia.

The Republic across the River

No need to get your passport stamped when you arrive, but this former working-class suburb has kept its independent outlook on life. The best time to come to Liège's lively Outremeuse quarter is when its inhabitants celebrate their festival, on 15 August. It was in this part of town, declared a "Free Republic" in 1927, that André Grétry and Georges Simenon passed their youth. But Outremeuse's most popular character is undoubtedly the good-humoured puppet **Tchantchès**, whose monument stands on Place de l'Yser at the far end of Rue Surlet. An attractive feature of the streets here are the niches sheltering figures of saints and madonnas. Right at the heart of Outremeuse, the equivalent of the Carré on the other bank of the river, **Rue Roture** is lined with attractive premises housing little restaurants, music bars and "alternative" establishments of various kinds; it is reached via a gate by no 44 in the shopping street of Rue Puits-en-Soc.

Musée Tchantchès

♿ *Tue-Thur. 2-4pm. Closed 1 Jan, Easter Monday, Ascension, Whitsun, July, 1, 11 Nov. ☎ 04 342 75 75.*

This museum is devoted to the puppet Tchantchès (whose name is the Walloon dialect equivalent of François). The museum possesses all the costumes ever donated to this popular local character, as well as a collection of puppets from the Old Royal Imperial Theatre. **Puppet shows** are performed on the premises.

Musée des Transports en Commun du Pays de Liège

Rue Richard-Heintz 9. ♿ Mar-Nov: 10am-noon, 2-5pm, Sat, Sun and public holidays 2-6pm. €2.50. ☎ 04 361 94 19.

Housed in a vast shed, this splendid collection of vehicles tells the story of trams and buses from the horse-drawn era to the present.

Excursions

Sart Tilman

10km/6.25mi S.

The **University of Liège** and its centre for metallurgical research occupies a campus covering an area of 740ha/1 828 acres on this wooded plateau. The 17C Château de Colonster on the eastern edge of the campus has been turned into a conference centre and houses the **Simenon Foundation** containing the writer's archives, manuscripts and collection of books. The park also has an open-air museum.

Chaudfontaine

10km/6.25mi on the Verviers road.

Chaudfontaine in the Vesdre Valley has been a popular spa since the late 17C. It has the only hot springs (38.6°C/101.4°F) in Belgium. The water is used to treat rheumatism. Chaudfontaine also has an open-roofed hot-spring swimming pool and a **casino** with a crazy golf course.

The 17C restored **Maison Sauveur** in the park is home to the Tourist Information Centre. *Mon-Fri 9am-noon, 2-4pm. No charge. ☎ 04 361 56 30; www.chaudfontaine.be*

Château d'Aigremont

16km/10mi W, on E 42 motorway, leaving at junction 4. No group visits; ring for details of open days. ☎ 04 336 16 87.

Like the nearby Château de Chokier, this castle stands on the top of a sheer cliff overlooking the Meuse. It is said that it was built by the four Aymon brothers. During the 15C it was one of the lairs of Guillaume de la Marck. The castle was rebuilt in brick and stone in the early 18C. The interior is adorned with beautiful 18C furnishings. Its finest decorative feature is the stairwell with *trompe-l'œil* frescoes reproducing the architecture of an Italian palace. The kitchen walls are decorated with Delft tiles in more than 1 000 different patterns.

There is a pretty French-style garden on the terraces.

NEUVILLE-EN-CONDROZ AND ST-SÉVERIN

27km/16.75mi SW, in the Dinant direction.

Neuville-en-Condroz

This is the site of the Ardennes American Cemetery, set in a magnificent, well-tended park. The 5 310 soldiers buried here fell in the course of the Second World War, most of them during the Battle of the Bulge. The white gravestones are arranged in the form of an immense Greek cross. Maps carved inside the memorial describe the famous battle.

St-Séverin

The **church★** in this small town is a harmonious 12C Romanesque building that was once a priory of the great abbey of Cluny in France. Indeed, the tower above the octagonal transept crossing is a copy of the "Blessed Water" *(eau bénite)* bell-tower at Cluny. The attractively varied tiered structure of the building is best appreciated from the presbytery garden.

The ceiling in the nave is the same height as the vaulting in the transept and chancel whereas the ceilings in the apse and transept chapels are much lower. The discreet decor in the great nave consists of alternating columns or groups of colonnettes and pillars with twisted twinned columns above. The late-12C stone **font★** is original. The basin, supported by 12 colonnettes surrounding a central shaft, is sculpted with back-to-back lions. There is a head, of Syrian inspiration, at each of the four corners.

Visé

17km/10.5mi N on E 25 towards Maastricht.

Visé is a popular tourist resort on the banks of the Meuse. The town is well-known for its gastronomic speciality, goose prepared with a garlic sauce. It is also proud of its three guilds (crossbowmen, arquebusiers and free arquebusiers) who parade through the town during special events.

The town's collegiate church has a **reliquary of St Hadelin★** in the south transept. This 12C Mosan work in repoussé silver has end panels from an older reliquary (1046). They show Christ crushing the asp and the basilisk (a mythological beast) on one side, and Christ crowning the two friends St Remaclus and St Hadelin on the other side. Some of the scenes on the side panels, illustrating the life of St Hadelin, are attributed to Renier de Huy. St Hadelin was the founder of Celles monastery near Dinant in the 7C. The community moved to Visé in the 14C.

Lier★★

This attractive small town, often referred to as Lierke Plezierke (charming little Lier), is situated on the confluence of the Grande and Petite Nèthe rivers and is renowned for its many historical buildings and old façades. The town still has its 16C walls, which have been turned into esplanades and edged with a canal. Among the well-known people born here were the portrait painter Isidoor Opsomer (1878-1967), the writer Félix Timmermans (1886-1947) and the clock and watch maker, Louis Zimmer (1888-1970).

Location

Population 32 064 – Michelin maps 716 G 2 or 533 M 16 – Antwerp
Lier lies 22km from Antwerp and 15km from Mechelen and can be reached via the N 10, N 13 and N 14.
🛈 *Stadhuis, Grote Markt 57, ☎ 03 491 13 93; www.lier.be*

Walking About

Grote Markt

The **Stadhuis** in the centre is an elegant 18C structure, whose interior houses a magnificent Rococo spiral staircase. Beside the stadhuis is a slender Gothic **belfry** (1369) surmounted with four corner turrets. It includes a carillon which was once part of the old drapers' guildhall.

Several old guildhalls surround the square, where a market is held every Saturday. In the past, members of a rhetorical chamber met at the Eyken Boom (oak tree), which dates from 1709. Near the belfry the butchers' guildhall has retained its crowstepped gables and perron guarded by two heraldic lions.

St.-Gummaruskerk★★

This Brabant Gothic church was built between the 14C and the 16C. The Keldermans and the De Waghemakeres were involved in its construction *(see ANTWERPEN: Kathedraal)*.

Directory

WHERE TO EAT

Numerus Clausus – *Keldermansstraat 2 –* ☎ *03 480 51 62 – closed 1 week in Jun, 2weeks in Sep, Sat lunch, Sun, Mon –* €*25 lunch –* €*27.* Hidden away between the Académie des Beaux-Arts and the canal, this welcoming, family-run place offers full-flavoured cooking with daily specials, lunches and set menus. The walled terrace is lovely in summer.

De Fortuin – *Felix Timmermansplein 7 –* ☎ *03 480 29 51 – de_fortuin@hotmail.com –* €*29/49.60.* Near the Zimmertoren, a typical Lierse façade with painted shutters is reflected in the waters of the Petite Nèthe: dine on the moored barge and take in the view of the riverbank and the old houses. Traditional cuisine with a modern touch.

WHERE TO STAY

M. et Mme Guido Van den Bogaert Chambre d'hôte – *Antwerpsesteenweg 262 –* ☎ *03 480 85 43 – gvandenbogaert@provant.be –* ☑ *– 3 rms:* €*33.50/45.90* ☑. Family-run guesthouse, a little way out of the centre, offering three comfortable rooms: the best of them is in the annexe by the open-air pool. The hearty breakfasts will get your day off to a flying start.

Masia del Viento Chambre d'hôte – *Beatrijsstraat 123 – 2860 St-Katelijne-Waver –* ☎ *015 31 72 22 –* ☑ *– 2 rms:* €*44* ☑. In the heart of the village, in the countryside south of Lier, a pretty house with a summer terrace and delightful kitchen garden, where practically equipped bedrooms and fresh country air make for a good night's sleep. Carefully prepared breakfasts.

SPECIALITIES

Lier tartlets, known as *Lierse vlaaikens,* are a delicious local speciality made with spices.

Philip the Handsome married Joanna of Castile here in 1496.

The massive square tower, ending in an octagonal bell-tower, is known as the Pepperpot because of its shape.

There is a good view of the whole of the exterior from near the north transept.

The **interior** has some beautiful keystones, and the floor is paved with grave-stones. The thick columns with great statues of the Apostles leaning against them, and the traceried triforium are characteristic of the Brabant style.

The magnificent **rood screen**★★, a later work (1536) than its Flamboyant Gothic style suggests, was carved by sculptors from Mechelen. Statues of the Evangelists and the Fathers of the Church, which were restored in 1850, are displayed on columns; scenes from the Passion stand out against the rich decoration. The turret was added in 1850.

The church has a beautiful collection of windows. A 15C **stained-glass window**★ in the south aisle depicts the *Coronation of the Virgin* in a medallion. The fluid lines of the drawing recall the art of Van der Weyden. Maximilian of Austria presented the church with many of the stained-glass windows in the chancel during his visit in 1516. One of them shows him with his wife, Mary of Burgundy.

The choir stalls (1555) are carved with picturesque motifs. The Baroque pulpit is the work of two artists, one of whom was **Artus Quellin the Elder**. *The Marriage of the Virgin Mary* (1516), known as the *Colibrant Triptych* is attributed to Goswyn van der Weyden, grandson of Rogier. It's worth seeking out the *Descent of the Holy Spirit* in the south transept; this triptych dating from 1612 was painted by Rubens' master, Otto Venius.

Continue along Eikelstraat, cross the Zimmerplein and head along Begijnhofstraat

Begijnhof★

The Beguine convent was founded in the early 13C, although most of the buildings date from the 17C and beginning of the 18C.

A late-17C Renaissance portico marks the entrance. Above it is a statue of St Begga. There is a beautiful view from here of the Gevangenenpoort; the belfry is clearly visible in the distance.

The small, picturesque houses, some with gardens half-hidden behind low walls, line narrow paved streets. The houses are not numbered but bear evocative names, such as The Flight into Egypt and The Five Small Wounds. The church has a 17C Baroque façade topped with 18C scrolling and a lantern turret.

Worth a Visit

Zimmertoren

Jan-Feb and Nov-Dec: 10am-noon, 2-4pm; Mar, Oct: 10am-noon, 2-5pm; Apr-Sept: 10am-noon, 1-6pm. €*2.* ☎ *03 491 13 95.*

Two traces of the 14C fortifications stand on the Zimmerplein: the Prisoners' Gate, **Gevangenenpoort**, and the Zimmer Tower, once known as the Cornelius Tower.

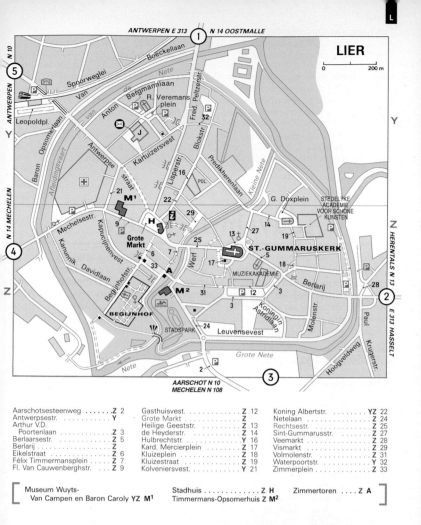

Museum Wuyts-
Van Campen en Baron Caroly **YZ M¹**   Stadhuis . . . . **Z H**   Zimmertoren . . . . **Z A**
Timmermans-Opsomerhuis **Z M²**

On the front of the tower is the **Astronomical Clock★** made in 1930 by Zimmer of Lier. It consists of 11 different dials and two spheres, the earth and the moon. Every day at noon there is a procession of clockwork figures, portraying various historical figures from Lier and Belgium, on the right side of the tower.

The **astronomical studio** inside the tower has 57 dials showing the lunar cycle, the tides, the zodiac and the main cosmic phenomena.

Another astronomical clock, the **Wonderklok**, can be visited in the pavilion to the right of tower. It has 93 dials and 14 automata. Zimmer's workshop is also open to visitors.

Museum Wuyts-Van Campen en Baron Caroly

Apr-Oct: Wed-Sun   10am-noon, 1.30-5.30pm. €1. ☎ 03 491 13 93.
This quaint museum boasts a collection of paintings, with works ranging from the 16C up to the present day, pieces of gold work and sculptures. Pieter Brueghel the Younger, Velvet Brueghel and Rubens feature among the Flemish painters; visitors should not miss **Frans Floris**' truly remarkable group portrait, *The Van Berchem Family*, paintings by Jan Steen, works from the Spanish (Murillo) and French (Poussin, Le Lorrain) Schools, as well as 19C and 20C Belgian art.

The Astronomical Clock

Ph. Gajic/MICHELIN

273

Timmermans-Opsomerhuis

Apr-Oct: Wed-Sun 10am-noon, 1.30-5.30pm. €1. ☎ *03 491 13 93.*

This museum is devoted to Lier artists. The **Van Boeckel** forge regroups, under a flowery chandelier, the works of art of the wrought ironsmith. The reconstructed artist's studio belonging to **Baron Opsomer** contains landscapes (*Lier Beguine Convent*) and numerous portraits (Albert I, and Opsomer himself).

There are several rooms upstairs devoted to the Flemish writer **Félix Timmermans**, who was also a painter and cartoonist. Among his most famous works are *Tales of the Beguine Convent*, *Pallieter* (1916, a powerful, spirited book) and *Peasants' Psalms*.

Another room contains works and mementoes associated with the musician **Renaat Veremans** (1894-1969), with the writer **Anton Bergmann**, the architect **Flor van Reeth** and the medieval author **Beatrijs van Nazareth**.

Louvain-la-Neuve★

On the Lauzelle plateau and part of the municipality of Ottignies, Louvain-la-Neuve is the only completely new town to have been established in Belgium since the foundation of Charleroi in 1666. In town planning terms it is highly original: an urban centre and also a university city, divided into four neighbourhoods – Hocaille, Biéreau, Bruyères, Lauzelle – but with an intermingling of shops, residential areas and academic institutions intended to integrate the student community with the urban population.

Location

Brabant-Wallon – Michelin maps 716 G4 and 533 M18.
7km/4mi south of Wavre, Louvain-la-Neuve is served by the A 4/E 411 Brussels-Namur motorway and by a branch railway running off the main Brussels-Namur line and terminating at an underground station.
🚹 *Grange du Douaire, Avenue des Combattants 2, 1340 Ottignies,* ☎ *010 41 83 11.*

Background

The Catholic University of Louvain (UCL) – Since the 1968 split in the Catholic University (founded in Leuven in 1425), the French-language university has been based in Louvain-la-Neuve, with the exception of the medical students, whose faculty is in **Woluwe-St-Lambert** in Brussels. The transfer took place from 1972 to 1979. The UCL has about 18 300 students, 14 000 of whom are in Louvain-la-Neuve.

Town and Gown – The **urban centre** in the heart of the town was designed as a meeting place and venue for special events, reserved exclusively for pedestrians: the railway, motor traffic and car parks have been banished underground.

A science park was created for research companies and laboratories on the outskirts of the town, along with the Cyclotron complex. The natural lie of the land was respected. The neighbourhoods are built on the Lauzelle plateau which overlooks the little Malaise Valley.

The river has been covered over with a concrete deck supporting the streets and buildings of the town centre, including the University's central building, the **Halles universitaires**.

Contemporary architecture serves town planning here, taking its inspiration from medieval towns and keeping everything on a human scale. Narrow streets, small squares, stairs and clever manipulation of the townscape create surprise and avoid monotony.

Several decorative elements have appeared since the town was created: a fountain (*Place de l'Université*) designed by a student and murals, including R Somville's great fresco (400m²/478sq yd), whose bright colours enliven one of the walls of the Halles universitaires(Rue des Wallons). There is a Bosquet mural in the underground railway station depicting a 16C university town, with enlarged versions of Paul Delvaux's paintings of railway stations.

Worth a Visit

Musée de Louvain-la-Neuve (Institut Supérieur d'Archéologie et d'Histoire de l'Art de l'U.C.L.)

Place Blaise-Pascal. 10am (Sun 2pm except Jul-Aug)-6pm. Closed public holidays, 24 Dec-1 Jan. €1.25. ☎ *010 47 48 41; www.muse.ucl.ac.be*
The university museum's collections include Egyptian, Greek and Roman antiquities, sculptures and masks representing African and South Sea primitive art, religious art (sculptures including a 16C *Christ and the Triumphal Entrance into*

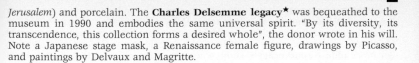

Jerusalem) and porcelain. The **Charles Delsemme legacy**★ was bequeathed to the museum in 1990 and embodies the same universal spirit. "By its diversity, its transcendence, this collection forms a desired whole", the donor wrote in his will. Note a Japanese stage mask, a Renaissance female figure, drawings by Picasso, and paintings by Delvaux and Magritte.

Excursion

Wavre
6km/4mi N by N 238.
The small town of Wavre lies amid hills in the valley of the River Dijle. The little statue of Maca, a laughing boy who symbolises the light-hearted spirit of the inhabitants, stands in front of the town hall which is housed in an old church.

The **Six Flags Belgium** theme park, spread over 50ha/123 acres, is the most popular in the country, offering a multitude of spectacular rides and attractions. *Apr-Oct. €28.50.* ☎ *010 42 15 00.*

The vast swimming pool complex called **Aqualibi**, set against a tropical backdrop, was inaugurated in 1987. ♿ *Wed-Sun 2pm-9pm (Fri 11pm), Sat 10am-11pm, Sun 10am-9pm. €13.50.* ☎ *010 42 16 00.*

Maaseik

In the heart of the Maasland, the country along the Flanders bank of the Meuse, the old town of Maaseik is said to be the birthplace of the Van Eyck brothers, Jan and Hubert. Maaseik's carnival procession (halfvastenstoet) halfway through Lent draws a considerable crowd. The town still has remains of the fortifications built in 1672, the year in which the French King Louis XIV set out to conquer the Netherlands. The local speciality is "knapkoek", a crisp kind of pastry.

Location
Limburg – Population 22 673 – Michelin maps 716 K2 and 533 T16.
On the banks of the Meuse in the extreme northeast of the Limburg Kempen region, Maaseik is reached by N 78.
🛈 *Markt 1,* ☎ *089 81 92 90; www.maaseik.be*

Worth a Visit

Grote Markt
This vast rectangular square, shaded by lime trees, is surrounded by 17C and 18C houses, their narrow windows embellished with leaded lights. The town hall (Stadhuis) is housed in a particularly fine 18C mansion. A statue of the brothers Jan and Hubert Van Eyck stands in the centre of the square.

Bosstraat
There are fine old buildings all along this street.
House no 7, a venerable brick-built edifice, is called De Verkeerde Wereld (The World Turned Upside Down). There is a half-timbered medieval house on the corner of the Halstraat.
No 19 has a white façade (1620), jettied out on arches, a characteristic feature of the region.
No 21, the Stenen- or Drossardshuis (Stone- or Baliff's House)has a more austere, classical façade.

St.-Catharinakerk
In the vestry of this 19C church is a remarkable **treasury** (kerkschat). Most of the items in it were brought from the abbey at Aldeneik Abbey. The most precious object of all is the Codex Eyckensis or St Harlinde's gospel book, dating from the 8C, and said to be the oldest book in Belgium. *Apr-Sept: Tue-Sun. (Jul-Aug daily) 1-5pm; Oct-Mar: Sat, Sun 1-5pm. Closed end Dec to mid-Jan, 1, 2, 11, 15 Nov, 24-26 Dec. €2.* ☎ *089 56 68 90.*

Museactron
Lekkerstraat 5. Apr-Sept: Tue-Sun (daily Jul-Aug) 10am-5pm; Oct-Mar: Tue-Sun 10am-noon, 2-5pm. Closed end Dec to mid-Jan, 1, 2, 11 and 15 Nov and 24-26 Dec. €2. ☎ *089 56 68 90.*

The Museactron houses a total of three museums. The collections displayed in the **Regionaal Archeologisch Museum** relate to local archaeology and the history of the town. They include prehistoric exhibits, a few objects from the Roman period (doctors' instruments), and some from the Middle Ages. Visitors can also see Belgium's **oldest apothecary's shop**, where the atmosphere of the past has been faithfully recreated. In the cellars is the **Bakkerijmuseum**, a museum of bakery.

Excursion

Aldeneik

2km/1.25mi E. May-Sept: guided tours Sun by prior arrangement with the Maaseik Tourist Information Centre ☎ 089 81 92 90.
The **church** in Aldeneik once formed part of a monastery founded in the 8C by St Harlinde and St Relinde. It was enlarged in the 12C, and a Gothic chancel was added in the 13C. Further restoration work was carried out in the 19C. The church still has its Romanesque central nave decorated with murals; it contains several Merovingian sarcophagi dating back to the 8C.

Malmédy ★

At the confluence of the Warthe and Warchenne, Malmédy stands in a picturesque valley **setting★** surrounded by steep wooded hills. Together with Stavelot, the town was a principality ruled by bishops until 1794. In 1815 it was annexed by Prussia and remained Prussian until 1919, when the Treaty of Versailles assigned it to Belgium. Between 1940 and 1944 it became part of Germany. During the Battle of the Bulge in the winter of 1944/45 the town centre was inadvertently destroyed in an Allied air raid.

Location

Liège – Population 11 060 – Michelin maps 716 L4 and 534 NW fold 9 – Local map see Spa.
Malmédy is in the southern part of the Hautes Fagnes. The town is served by N 62 (from St-Vith) and N 68 (from Eupen), as well as by motorway E 42/A 27 between Verviers and St-Vith (exit 11, then N 62).
🅱 *Place Albert I 29A, ☎ 080 33 02 50; www.malmedy.be*

THE MALMEDY CARNIVAL

Malmédy's pre-Lenten festival, **Cwarmê**, is one of the most riotous in Belgium, with the town in tumult for four days. On Saturday·afternoon a humorous procession accompanies the *"Trouv'Lê"*, a sort of carnival king who is enthroned at the town hall. Sunday is the day of the great parade after which the *banes corantes* (groups of running people) pursue the public. Steer clear of the **"haguètes"**, who are armed with long hinged pincers, and aren't afraid to use them! These characters have an Austrian eagle emblem emblazoned on their backs and wear a bicorn hat embellished with feathers. On Monday short satirical sketches in the local Wallon dialect are performed in the streets.

Carnival time in Malmédy.

Directory

WHERE TO EAT

⊖ **Au Petit Louvain** – *Chemin-rue 47 –* ☎ *080 33 04 15 – petitlouvain@yucom.be – Closed Mon eve, Wed – €24/36.* Small family establishment discreetly located in the town's main shopping street. Generous helpings of tempting, traditional dishes, with lots of local game in season.

WHERE TO STAY

⊖ **Maison Géron** – *Bévercé-Village 29 – 4960 Bévercé –* ☎ *080 33 00 06 – geron@busmail.net –* ▣ *– 10 rms: €52/79.* Only a couple of minutes out of town on the road winding its way up into the Haute Fagnes, this solid residence is located opposite a dear little chapel. No-frills bedrooms, stunning modern conservatory and garden terrace. Friendly reception.

SHOPPING

Speciality – Delicious *"Baisers de Malmédy"* (Malmédy kisses) are cream-filled meringues.

Worth a Visit

Cathédrale Saints-Pierre-Paul-et-Quirinn

Once a Benedictine abbey church, Malmédy's cathedral of 1782 has a west front framed by two tall towers.

Inside, the furniture is particularly interesting (carved 18C pulpit, late-17C confessionals), as are the works of art: the 17C *Virgin* by Delcour, the gilded wood St Quirin reliquary dating from 1698 and the 18C silver bust-reliquaries of St Gereon and his companions, who were Roman soldiers.

Excursions

Robertville

10km/6.25mi NE on N 681.

Robertville is part of the Hautes Fagnes-Eifel nature park. The town is best known for its **dam** built in 1928, which overlooks the Warche from a height of 55m/180ft. The reservoir forms a 62-ha/153-acre **lake★** which supplies Malmédy with drinking water and powers a hydroelectric plant in Bévercé. The lake is surrounded by a dense forest and offers many recreational opportunities. There is a fine **view★** of the reservoir from just outside Robertville.

Château de Reinhardstein★

Access along a path starting from the dam, or along the first road on the left beyond the dam (signposted), then 800m/0.5mi on foot beyond the car park.

Guided tours (1hr 15min) only. Jul, Aug: Tue, Thu, Sat 3.30pm, Sun, public hols (incl. Whitsun, Easter Sun, Ascension Day), 2.15pm, 3.15pm, 4.15pm, 5.15pm. Last Sun in Dec, 2.15pm, 3.15pm. To confirm dates and ask about trips on other days: ☎ *080 44 68 68.*

The keep, surrounded by walls and standing on a rocky spur in a magnificent forest setting, gives the impression that the centuries have left it untouched and ready to defy any attacker. However, in the early 1960s there was nothing on this site but ruins. Reinhardstein was resurrected thanks to the efforts of a Professor Overloop, who rebuilt it using 17C engravings showing the castle at the height of its splendour, when it was owned by the Metternich family.

The rooms with their stone walls and flagstone floors contain old furniture, tapestries, armour and works of art. The Knights' Hall and the chapel are particularly striking.

Bütgenbach

15km/9.3mi E on N 62 and N 632.

This dam (1928-32) spans the River Warche. Its vast 120-ha/296-acre reservoir is a popular visitor attraction with lots of water-based recreational facilities. Bütgenbach is also a winter sports centre.

Rocher de Falize★

3.4km/2mi SW. Leave by the Stavelot road. Take a minor road on the left before the viaduct, then a road on the right.

This magnificent pinnacle of rock with sheer sides overlooks the valley of the Warche. A spire on the opposite hilltop indicates Wavreumont Abbey, founded in 1950 by Benedictine monks from Leuven.

Château de Reinhardstein.

Bellevaux-Ligneuville
8.5km/5mi on N 62.
This village in the upper Amblève Valley still has a pretty half-timbered house typical of the region, the Maison Maraite of 1592.

Faymonville
11km/6.75mi SE by N 62 and N 632.
A very old legend led to the villagers here being known as "Turks". The name is reflected in the great carnival parade on the Monday before Shrove Tuesday.

Mechelen★★

A rich heritage of palaces, grand public buildings and fine old dwellings lining streets, squares and quaysides, testifies to Mechelen's splendid past. The old city centre is dominated by the magnificent cathedral towerwith its famous carillon. Traditional crafts such as lacemaking and weaving still flourish here; the tapestry Belgium presented to the United Nations for its building in New York in 1954 came from a Mechelen workshop. Mechelen is also a major centre of furniture-making and brewing, and the countryside around is famous for its market gardens which produce delicious asparagus and lettuce.

Location
Antwerpen – Population 75 418 – Michelin maps 716 G2 and 533 L16 – Plan of the built-up area in the current editon of The Red Guide Benelux.
Midway between Brussels and Antwerp, Mechelen is just off motorway A 1/E 19. Take exit 9 (from Antwerp) or 10 (from Brussels), then follow the Mechelen ring road (R 12) which leads to the city centre.
🗉 *Grote Markt 21,* ☏ *015 29 76 55; www.mechelen.be*

Background

Mechelen was a lakeside community in prehistoric times, and seems to have been converted to Christianity in the 8C by St Rumbald from Ireland. It then belonged to the Prince-Bishops of Liège who surrounded it with a defensive wall. Thanks to its location on the River Dijle, the town had a port and trade prospered, especially with the advent of cloth making. Mechelen gained a second set of ramparts around 1300.

The Golden Age – In the 14C, Mechelen belonged to the Count of Flanders, but legacies and bequests later brought it under the rule of the Dukes of Burgundy. This was the beginning of its most illustrious period. Charles the Bold established his Court of Accounts and the Parliament of Burgundian Estates here in 1473. The Parliament became the **Grand Council** in 1503, acting as a supreme court until the French Revolution.

The town enjoyed its greatest period of prosperity under **Margaret of Austria**, Emperor Charles V's aunt who governed until Charles came of age, then under Emperor Charles V himself from 1519 to 1530. The highly cultivated princess loved the arts and surrounded herself with the greatest minds of her time – philosophers Erasmus and Thomas More, historian Lemaire de Belges, musicians Pierre de la Rue and Josquin des Prés, and painters Gossaert and Van Orley. Much building was carried out in this period, including fine town mansions as well as a palace for Margaret herself, designed by the Mechelen architect Rombout Keldermans.

The 16C to the present – The Court moved to Brussels in 1531. Although the Grand Council remained in Mechelen, the city's influence waned, except as a religious centre. It was made an archbishopric in 1559 (a title shared with Brussels since 1961); Mechelen's prelate then became Archbishop of the Low Countries. The first man to sit on the episcopal throne was Cardinal de Granvelle, Philip II's minister.

In 1572 the Spanish set fire to the city and massacred its inhabitants. But Mechelen recovered; in the 17C and the 18C Mechelen lace enjoyed a wide reputation and Baroque furniture was produced in prolific quantities. The incomparable skills of Mechelen sculptors such as **Lucas Fayd'herbe** (1617-97), who studied under Rubens, or Fayd'herbe's student **Theodoor Verhaegen** (1700-59), became internationally famous. In 1835 the first railway train on the European continent set out from Mechelen on its way to Brussels.

Directory

WHERE TO EAT

Den Beer – *Grote Markt 32* – ☎ *015 20 97 06* – ✍ – *€23.75/47.75*. This resolutely contemporary brasserie on the main square has become the place to see and be seen in Mechelen. Tables are set out in a bright and spacious interior where a piano dominates the scene. In front there is a summer terrace with teak chairs and tables.

Brasserie Het Anker – *Guido Gezellelaan 49* – ☎ *015 20 38 80* – ✍ – *€45*. Authentic brasserie forming part of the De Anker establishment which is responsible for Carolus, the beer that is the pride of Mechelen, dispensed in no fewer than six varieties. The old bottling plant is now a fine 22-room hotel. Cuisine keeps faith with Belgian tradition.

WHERE TO STAY

Op Sinjoor B&B – *Leegheid 21* – ☎ *015 33 03 38* – ✍ – *3 rms: €28/45*▢ City centre establishment with three simply furnished and decorated guest rooms with shared bathroom and kitchenette. Dogs allowed.

Hobbit – *Battelsesteenweg 455F* – ☎ *015 27 20 27* – *hobbit.hotel@yucom.be* – ▣ – *21 rms: €44* – ▢ *€6*. What's in a name? Not much, at least for Tolkien fans. On the edge of town by the interchange of the Antwerp-Brussels motorway (A 1/E 19) and the Louvain Canal, this modern hotel has spacious and functional rooms with good soundproofing and no mythical beasts.

Walking About

Start at Grote Markt

Grote Markt★
Overlooked from the northwest by the cathedral's imposing tower, Mechelen's main square is lined with lovely 16C and 18C buildings and has a statue of Margaret of Austria at its centre.

Stadhuis★ – The town hall stands on the east side of the square, occupying three adjacent buildings.
Construction work began on the Late Gothic **Palais du Grand Conseil** (Grand Council Building) on the left in the early 16C. It remained unfinished until the early 20C, when it was completed using Rombout Keldermans' original plans. A statue of Emperor Charles V stands in one of the alcoves. The building has been the town hall since 1913. The central façade with its corbelled turrets is in fact the front of the never completed 14C belfry.
The former cloth hall, or **Lakenhalle** (to the right) also dates from the 14C, although the gable was added in the 17C.

De Beyaert – This extensively restored mansion, now the General Post Office, used to be the town hall.

Schepenhuis – Facing De Beyaert is the late 14C "old palace", a somewhat isolated edifice set back from the other buildings. The spacious ground-floor hall, once the seat of the high court, has fine old beams and brackets decorated with scenes both religious and profane. The first floor was where the Parliament of

The Grote Markt and Stadhuis

Mechelen assembled, later to become the Grand Council. The **museum** has a fine collection of 16C painting and sculpture. *Tue-Sun, 10am-5pm. €2. Closed 1-2 Jan, 25-26 Dec.* ☎ *015 29 40 30 (Tourist Information Centre) or 015 21 16 02 (museum).*

St. Romboutskathedraal★★

8.30am-5.30pm (winter 4.30pm). ☎ *015 29 76 55.*

This Gothic building is remarkable for its grandiose tower which is as wide as the nave. Graceful pinnacles decorate the buttresses along the side aisles and elegant gables adorn the east end.

Tower★★★ – The tower, one of the finest in Belgium, forms the façade and porch; it measures 97m/318ft in height. It was designed to reach the extraordinary height of 167m/548ft, but the project was shelved in 1521. The Keldermans dynasty of architects directed the construction. The awesome proportions combine with powerful, yet subtle vertical lines to create an unforgettable impression. The tower houses two carillons.

Interior – Enter by way of the south portal, which opens beneath a tall window with Flamboyant tracery and a delicately arched pediment. The interior is surprisingly large (99m/325ft long, 28m/92ft high) but is nevertheless harmonious. The 13C central nave is 13m/43ft wide, and has six bays. 17C statues of the Apostles stand against stout cylindrical pillars to separate the bays. After the fire in 1342, the cathedral was embellished with an ambulatory and an apse featuring seven radiating chapels. The chapels in the north aisle were added between 1498 and 1502. Michel Vervoort's 18C pulpit displays the scene of St Norbert's conversion.

In the south transept is a poignant *Crucifixion* by Van Dyck. The sombre colours and the sorrowful faces of Jesus' mother Mary and of Mary Magadalene are particularly expressive. Lucas Fayd'herbe executed the black and white marble altar. Artus Quellin the Younger is said to have made the communion bench; this delicate work in white marble is in the Holy Sacrament chapel, at the end next to the tower. Cardinal Mercier's mausoleum is in the north aisle in a chapel near the transept; he died in 1926.

Leave from the door in the north transept. Go along Wollemarkt which leads to a little bridge.

Oud refugiehuis van de abdij van Sint-Truiden

From the bridge there is a delightful **view★** to the left of the 16C **Sint-Truiden abbey refuge**. The crow-stepped pediment and steeple stand out against tall trees, while the pink brick walls seem to plunge into the canal covered in aquatic plants. At the end of Schoutetstraat there is a tapestry factory

Go back to the bridge and into the covered passageway opposite.

St-Janskerk
Apr-Oct: 1.30-5.30pm; Nov-Mar: Tue-Sun 1.30-4.30pm. No charge. ☎ 015 29 40 37 (Tourist Information Centre).

This 15C church dedicated to St John has fine Baroque furnishings and, even more fascinating, a 1619 Rubens triptych, *The Adoration of the Magi*. The central panel is a remarkable composition in two parts, one dark, the other light. The subtle colours, the contrast between the gentle face of the Virgin Mary pictured in profile and the rugged features of the kings as they gaze wistfully at the fair-haired Infant make this an exceptional piece of work. Rubens' first wife, Isabella Brant, posed for the Virgin Mary's face.

Go round the north side of the church to Frederik de Merodestraat.

Hof van Busleyden
Dominated by its tower, this 16C brick mansion was built for one of Emperor Charles V's councillors. It stands at the back of a arcaded courtyard and houses the **Municipal Museum**. Adjacent to it is the **J. Denijn Royal Bell-Ringing School**.

Continue to Veemarkt and Blokstraat.

St-Pieter-en-Pauluskerk
This church, dedicated to St Peter and St Paul, has a lovely restored Baroque façade.

Go along Keizerstraat.

> ### THE BELLS OF MECHELEN
> In the Middle Ages Mechelen's bell-founders had already acquired a reputation for excellence, yet it was to an Amsterdam man, **Pieter Hemony**, that Mechelen turned in 1674 when it came to creating the carillon for the cathedral tower. In the late 19C the virtuoso carillon-player **Jef Denijn** made the chimes famous. He founded a school in 1922 and his students play throughout the world.
>
> The first carillon in the cathedral consisted of 49 chimes. A second set with the same number of chimes was added in 1981. Together the two sets of bells weigh 80t.

Paleis van Margaretha van Oostenrijk
Rombout Keldermans built this palace in the early 16C; it became the seat of the law courts in 1796. The buildings, although Renaissance in style, are clearly still influenced by Gothic ideas. They are laid out around a pretty arcaded courtyard.

Return to Grote Markt via Veemarkt and Befferstraat, then go along IJzerenleen.

IJzerenleen
This elongated square is named after the wrought-iron balustrades along it which protected the canal in the 16C. There are some beautifully restored façades lining the square.

Turn left on to Zoutwerf.

Zoutwerf
This quayside of the "Salt Wharf" is lined with several interesting buildings, notably "Salmon House", **Huis De Zalm**, built in the 16C for the fishmongers' guild. The pediment surmounting the door bears the carving of a golden salmon.

Take the 3rd street on the right ('t Plein).

Kerk van Onze -Lieve-Vrouw over de Dijle
Apr-Oct: 1.30-5.30pm; Nov-Mar: Tue-Sun 1.30-4.30pm. ☎ 015 29 40 37 (Tourist Information Centre).

This church contains a triptych by Rubens, *The Miraculous Draught of Fishes*.

Go along O.-L.-V.-straat, turn right into Guldenstraat, then into Van Beethovenstraat.

Haverwerf
This is the old "Oat Wharf". Three picturesque **old houses** stand near a little bridge opposite Vismarkt (Fish Market): St Joseph's House, with a scrolled gable; Devil's House, a timbered house with caryatids; and Paradise House, on which the tympana depict Adam and Eve.

Worth a Visit

Koninklijke Manufactuur van Wandtapijten Gaspard de Wit★
Guided tours (1hr 30min) Sat 10.30am. Closed public holidays, Jul, Christmas to New Year. €6. ☎ 0475 52 29 05.

The De Wit Royal Tapestry Manufactry is housed in the magnificent setting of the 15C refuge of Tongerlo Abbey. It is reached via a prettily laid-out garden. Several lovely ground-floor rooms form the background to to the display of a remarkable collection of old tapestries, an excellent introduction to the way in which this art has developed from the 16C to today. The attic, with a splendid timber roof, contains examples of modern tapestries, proof that the Manufactry is succeeding in its aim of preserving Flemish tapestry-making traditions.

But the emphasis is nevertheless on conservation and restoration of old tapestries, and the Manufactry has an excellent reputation for work of this kind at home and abroad. The guided tour leads through the workshops and there are demonstrations of the various stages in the making of a tapestry.

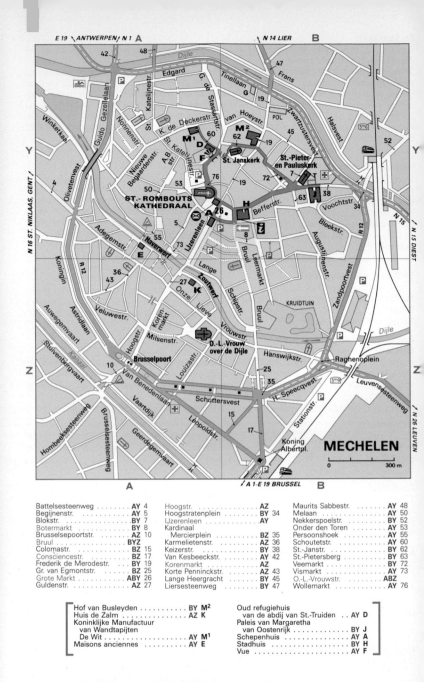

Battelsesteenweg	. . . .	**AY** 4
Begijnenstr.	. . . .	**AY** 5
Blokstr.	. . . .	**BY** 7
Botermarkt	. . . .	**BY** 8
Brusselsepoortstr.	. . . .	**AZ** 10
Bruul	. . . .	**BYZ**
Colomastr.	. . . .	**BZ** 15
Consciencestr.	. . . . .	**BZ** 17
Frederik de Merodestr.	. .	**BY** 19
Gr. van Egmontstr.	. . .	**BZ** 25
Grote Markt	. . . . . .	**ABY** 26
Guldenstr.	. . . .	**AZ** 27
Hoogstr.	. . . .	**AZ**
Hoogstratenplein	. . . .	**BY** 34
IJzerenleen	. . . .	**AY**
Kardinaal		
Mercierplein	. . . . .	**BZ** 35
Karmelietenstr.	. . . . .	**AZ** 36
Van Kesbeeckstr.	. . . .	**AY** 42
Keizerstr.	. . . .	**BY** 38
Korenmarkt	. . . .	**AZ**
Korte Penninckstr.	. . .	**AZ** 43
Lange Heergracht	. . . .	**BY** 45
Liersesteenweg	. . . . .	**BZ** 47
Maurits Sabbestr.	. . . .	**AY** 48
Melaan	. . . .	**AY** 50
Nekkerspoelstr.	. . . .	**BZ** 52
Onder den Toren	. . .	**AY** 53
Persoonshoek	. . . . .	**AY** 55
Schoutetstr.	. . . . . .	**AY** 60
St.-Janstr.	. . . .	**BY** 62
St.-Pietersberg	. . . . .	**BZ** 63
Veemarkt	. . . .	**BY** 72
Vismarkt	. . . .	**AY** 73
O.-L.-Vrouwstr.	. . . .	**ABZ**
Wollemarkt	. . . . . .	**AY** 76

Hof van Busleyden	. . . .	**BY** M²
Huis de Zalm	. . . .	**AZ** K
Koninklijke Manufactuur van Wandtapijten De Wit	. . . .	**AY** M¹
Maisons anciennes	. . . .	**AY** E
Oud refugiehuis van de abdij van St.-Truiden	. . **AY** D
Paleis van Margaretha van Oostenrijk	. . . .	**BY** J
Schepenhuis	. . . .	**AY** A
Stadhuis	. . . .	**BY** H
Vue	. . . .	**AY** F

Brusselsepoort

Tue-Sun 1pm (Sat, Sun and public holidays 10am)-5pm. Closed 1-2 Jan, 25-26 Dec. €2.
☎ 015 29 40 30 (Tourist Information Centre) or 015 27 44 25 (museum).
This is the only remaining trace of the 14C fortifications. The gate is flanked by
two towers with pepper-pot roofs dating from the 17C. The museum has displays
on local history and on the development of the city over time.

Excursions

Fort van Breendonk

12km/7.5mi W via Willebroek. 9.30am-6pm (Oct-Mar 5pm). Closed 1 Jan, 25 Dec, last
Sun in Aug €3. ☎ 03 886 62 09; www.breendonk.be
This fort, a national memorial, was built between 1906 and 1914 to complete
Antwerp's defences. Despite heavy bombardment in 1914, it was the last to sur-
render to the Germans. The Belgian Army chose it in May 1940 as its general

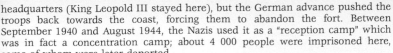

headquarters (King Leopold III stayed here), but the German advance pushed the troops back towards the coast, forcing them to abandon the fort. Between September 1940 and August 1944, the Nazis used it as a "reception camp" which was in fact a concentration camp; about 4 000 people were imprisoned here, some of whom were later deported.

A signposted tour, with recordings of survivors' accounts, takes visitors through the prisoners' rooms, the torture chamber, the huts used as living and sleeping quarters, the hostage execution enclosure and the gibbet used for prisoners sentenced to death. The documents in the small museum describe the two World Wars and life at Breendonk and other similar Nazi establishments.

FROM MECHELEN TO ELEWIJT
12km/7.5mi, leave by Leuvensesteenwe.

Muizen
The **Parc Zoologique de Planckendael**★★ is a vast zoological park covering an area of about 100 acres to the south. It is planted with flowers and trees and is home to nearly 1 000 animals. There are rare or endangered species here, aviaries of tropical birds, and lakes with large colonies of water fowl. ⅃ *Jan, Dec: 9am-4.30pm; Feb, mid-Oct. to end Nov: 9am-4.45pm; early Mar to mid-Mar, early Oct to mid-Oct: 9am-17.15pm; mid-Mar to end Jun, Sept: 9am-5.45pm; Jul-Aug: 9am-6.15pm; mid-Apr to Jun: Sun, Public holidays 9am-6.15pm. €13. ☎ 015 41 49 21.*

Hofstade
This immense recreation park covers an area of almost 150ha/371 acres. It includes two lakes and an ornithological reserve.

Elewijt
Kasteel Het Steen, to the west, is the castle where Rubens spent the last five years of his life (1635-40). It still has a pretty north façade with crow-stepped gables, as well as a 13C keep.

Kerbergen and Tremelo
23km/14.25mi E, leaving by Nekkerspoelstraat.

Keerbergen
This is a pleasant weekend and holiday venue in the Brabant Kempen region. Luxurious villas are tucked away amid the pine trees.

Tremelo
The **Pater Damiaanmuseum** is housed in the birthplace of **Father Damian** (1840-89), who died caring for Hawaii's lepers on Molokai Island. A collection of his personal belongings and an audio-visual presentation in several languages retrace his life. ⅃ *Guided tours (1hr) Sun 2-5pm (last admission 4.30pm); Jul-Aug: Tue-Sat 2-5.30pm. Closed end Dec to mid-Jan, Easter, Whitsun. €2.50. ☎ 016 53 05 19.*

La Meuse Namuroise★★

The Meuse rises high up on the Langres plateau in France at an altitude of 409m/1 342ft, then flows through Belgium and the southern Netherlands, travelling 950km/590mi before reaching the North Sea. The great river is at its most picturesque in the province of Namur, where it forces its way northward through a narrow valley before turning abruptly eastward at the town of Namur to flow along a more open vale towards Liège. The variety of landscapes along the Namur section of the river is a result of the types of rock through which it passes. Wooded slopes of schist alternate with limestones and sandstones; as the river cuts through the strata, the harder rocks form magnificent stretches of gorge, with spectacular cliffs, spurs and needles as well as deep caves.

Location
Namur – Michelin maps 716 H4, 5, I4 and 534 O21, P20, Q19.
In the heart of the province of Namur, this part of the valley of the Meuse is easily accessible on N 92 which runs along the river between Namur and Dinant, as well as by N 90 and N 959 which link Namur and Andenne.
🛈 *Avenue Reine Astrid 22, bte 2, 5000 Namur, ☎ 081 74 99 00; www.ftpn*

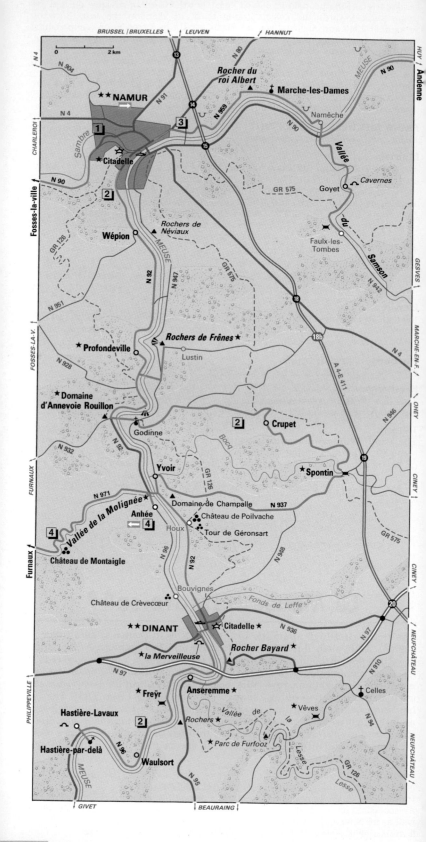

Tours

FROM NAMUR TO FOSSES-LA-VILLE ①

18km/11mi W.
Leave by ⑤ on town plan along N 90.

Floreffe

This **abbey** overlooking the River Sambre was founded in 1121 by the Premonstratensians and rebuilt in the 17C and 18C.

The main courtyard opens onto a terrace bordered with 18C buildings. A tower and 17C building with a portico can be seen beyond the garden. *Apr-Sept: guided tour (1hr) 1.30pm, 2.30pm, 3.30pm, 4.30pm, 5.30pm (additional tours Jul-Aug 10.30am, 11.30am. €2. ☏ 081 44 53 03.*

The **abbey church** (13C-18C), flanked by a tower, is 90m/295ft long. In the 18C, Laurent Dewez altered the interior in neo-Classical style. The immense chancel includes remarkable **choir stalls★** by Pieter Enderlin (1632-48), who carved some 40 figures, mostly representing the founders of religious orders, on the upper panels. The eight cherub musicians decorating the end-pieces are particularly noteworthy.

The 13C **mill-brewery** below the abbey has been turned into an inn.

Fosses-la-Ville

This town in the Entre-Sambre-et-Meuse region grew up around a monastery in the 7C. It was besieged on countless occasions, especially in the 17C.

St Feuillen collegiate church, which was rebuilt in the 18C, still has its late 10C Romanesque tower. The stalls were carved in 1524. The late 16C sculptures include an *Entombment* and a late 16C bust-reliquary of St Feuillen. A crypt at the east end of the church was added outside the main building in 1086. It is the only one of its kind still existing in Belgium.

"Le Petit Chapitre", next to the church, was once the summer residence of the Prince-Bishops of Liège. It is now a museum with a **collection of dolls**, 800 in total, all with individually tailored costumes. The figures represent characters taken from Belgian folklore, such as Till Eulenspiegel, Tchantchès, the Gilles of Binche, the **Chinels** and the participants in St Feuillen's impressive military parade which takes place every seven years on the last Sunday in September *(next parade in 2005)*.

FROM NAMUR TO HASTIÈRE-LAVAUX ②

80km/50mi – allow a day.
Leave Namur S on N 92.

This is one of the most romantic stretches of the Meuse, with sheer cliffs topped by castle ruins, evocative reminders of the valley's strategic importance as a well-trodden invasion route.

The population has settled along the course of the river, leaving the surrounding plateaus (Condroz to the east, Entre-Sambre-et-Meuse to the west) with few inhabitants. Straggling villages lie at the foot of the wild and rocky cliffs, while holiday homes, inns and cafés cluster by the waterside.

Wépion

This town is renowned for its strawberry farms. The impressive **Rochers de Néviaux** can be seen on the opposite bank.

Continue in the same direction.

Profondeville★

This charming tourist centre is pleasantly located in a meander of the Meuse opposite the Rochers de Frênes.

Cross the river on the next bridge and take the road towards Lustin.

Rochers de Frênes★

There is a beautiful **view★** of the Meuse Valley and Profondeville from the viewpoint at the top of these rocks *(access through the café)*.

Return to N 92.

Just short of Annevoie there is a pretty **view★** of Godinne priory, a charming 16C structure adjoining a 16C church with a Gothic chancel.

Domaine d'Annevoie-Rouillon★

The château and gardens of the Annevoie Estate are a fine example of 18C architecture and landscaping.

Gardens★★ – The estate has belonged to the Montpellier family since the 17C. It was in the late 18C that one of the members of the family conceived the idea of these gardens flowing with water, a synthesis of formal French and romantic Italian ideas, which would charm visitors with the sparkling diversity and imaginative design of their glades and fountains. It is pleasant to stroll beneath the fine old trees and admire the Buffet d'Eau (display of fountains opposite the house), the Petit Canal and, after a short climb, the Grand Canal, lined with lime trees. Besides these highlights there are also several strikingly original Baroque garden seats. *Early Apr-early Nov: 9.30am-5.30pm. €6.20. ☎ 082 61 11 78.*

Château– The original part of the building (1627) on the right can be recognised by the pattern in pink brick running just beneath the eaves. The castle was enlarged in 1775, the same year in which the gardens were created. Building and landscape complement one another in perfect harmony. *Not open to the public.*

Cross the river as you come into Godinne.

Annevoie gardens

Crupet

This village lies between two valleys and has a beautiful **manor house** (12C and 16C) surrounded by water. It is built in the form of a sturdy square tower with a bartizan on one side, a corner turret and a half-timbered overhanging gallery. The Carondelet family lived here until 1621, and their coat-of-arms can be seen on the pediment of the entrance porch. The tomb of these local lords is in **Crupet Church**, to the left of the entrance. The lords themselves are depicted in stiff ceremonial clothing.

Go through Durnal to Spontin.

Spontin★

Spontin, in the Bocq Valley, is well-known for its castle and its mineral water springs. The water supplies a bottling plant which produces 30 million bottles of sparkling and still mineral water annually as well as sodas and fruit syrups.

Château★ – The castle is enclosed by the waters of the River Bocq and is a remarkable example of Belgian medieval architecture, showing the development of a lordly residence from the 12C to the 17C. Starting life as a simple keep in the 12C, it was enlarged into a fortress in the 14C, then restored at the end of the 16C in Renaissance style and embellished with pink brickwork and pepper-pot roofs. The outbuildings were added in 1622, beyond the moat, and now close off the main courtyard. The old keep can be seen in another courtyard which also contains an elegant wrought-iron well canopy by Van Boeckel (19C). The austere rooms in the old main building, with their thick walls, sandstone floors, Gothic fireplaces and Louis XIII woodwork, form a sharp contrast with the apartments. The south part was decorated in neo-Gothic style in the 19C. *11am-4pm. €4. ☎ 083 69 90 55.*

Château de Spontin

Yvoir

Once a metalworking town, Yvoir is now a holiday resort with an island in the river which has been laid out as a **recreation centre**. *May-Sept: 9.30am-6pm. €1. ☎ 082 61 18 67.* It is possible to go caving and potholing nearby to the north. The **Domaine de Champalle** south of the town includes botanical gardens, a castle, and the Euro Butterfly Centre which has tropical greenhouses filled with hundreds of tropical butterflies, fresh-water and sea fish, and brightly-coloured birds.

Cross the Meuse and go towards Anhée.

The **Vallée de la Molignée**★ *(see Tour 4)* is soon reached.

Continue along N 92.

The ruins of the **Château de Poilvache** can be seen at a height of 125m/410ft above the Meuse, overlooking the vil-

lage of Houx. The people of Liège destroyed the castle in 1430 and it was then overrun by vegetation. According to legend it was built by the four Aymon sons. The 10C fortress was initially called Château d'Émeraude (literally "Emerald Castle") but was renamed Poilvache ("Cowhide") in the 14C, as a result of a ruse. The besieged occupants slipped out of the castle in search of cattle and were captured by the people of Dinant, some of whom then dressed up in the prisoners' clothes while others covered themselves with animal skins and hid themselves amid herds of cows. Their disguises enabled them to enter the castle. Further on the ruins of the **Tour de Géronsart** come into view.

Continue to Dinant, cross the river and take N 96 towards Bouvignes.

Bouvignes and Château de Crèvecoeur – *(see DINANT: excursions)*

Return to Dinant.

Dinant★★ – *(See DINANT)*

Take N 936 towards Philippeville.

Grotte La Merveilleuse★ – *(See DINANT)*

Return to Dinant and cross the river. Anseremme is on the east bank beyond Rocher Bayard.

Anseremme★ – *(see DINANT, tour 1)*

Follow N 96.

Château de Freÿr★

The estate is in a superb **setting**★★ beside the road running along the banks of the Meuse. The Classical buildings form a sharp contrast to the rough crags plunging down into the river on the opposite bank.

Château★ – The château was built from the 16C to the 18C, then restored in 1972. The style is Mosan Renaissance and Louis XV.

The tour takes visitors through a series of rooms with beautiful wood panelling and fireplaces, decorated with 17C and 18C furniture. Louis XIV was a guest here during the siege of Dinant in May 1675 and again in October for the signing of the Treaty of Freÿr. In 1785 the Governor of the Low Countries, Archduchess Marie-Christine, also stayed here.

A large entrance hall is decorated with paintings representing hunting scenes. The beautiful wrought-iron balustrade on the balcony took its inspiration from Place Stanislas in Nancy. *Early Apr to end Sept: guided tours (1hr 30min) Sat, Sun and public holidays, 11am, 2.30pm, 4pm (Jul-Aug, Tue-Sun); Oct-Mar: Sun 3pm. €6.* ☎ *082 22 22 00; www.freyr.be*

Gardens★ – The French-style gardens were designed in 1760 by the counts of Beaufort-Spontin using the principles defined by Le Nôtre. They run parallel to the river, laid out over three terraces decorated with pools. The lowest terrace is shaded by lime trees and has a collection of 33 **orange trees** in tubs, some of which are 300 years old. The other terraces include tall hedges that form a **maze**. At the highest point of the garden, near the Frédéric Salle pavillion with an interior decorated by the Moretti brothers, the view embraces the whole of the estate. The valley narrows beyond this point and splendid rugged cliffs plunge steeply into the Meuse on the opposite bank. These are the famous **Rochers de Freÿr**★.

Waulsort

This is a small tourist resort in a pleasant location. All that remains of the huge abbey founded here in the 11C is the abbot's palace.

Cross to the east bank.

Hastière-par-delà

The **Église Notre-Dame** stands "on the other side" *(par delà)* of the Meuse; it is in fact the remains of a priory in the Mosan Romanesque style (1033-35), except for the Gothic chancel. It has certain points in common with St Hadelin's in Celles, for example the large porch-tower, the pilaster strips, the nave with a wooden ceiling, and the great arches supported on square pillars. The 13C stalls were carved with a wide range of different motifs. The font dates from the 14C. The Romanesque **crypt** contains two Merovingian sarcophagi.

Return to the west bank.

Château de Freÿr.

Hastière-Lavaux

The **Grottes du Pont d'Arcole** *(Rue d'Anthée)* have five galleries with fascinating rock formations. The caves also include a deep well with an underground river running at its base. The upper gallery has delicate stalactites, some of them an extraordinarily pure white in colour. *Jul-Aug: guided tour (50min) 9am-6pm; from mid-Apr to end Sept: 10am-4pm; from early Oct to mid-Apr: Sat, Sun 10am-4pm. €5.* ☎ *081 64 44 01.*

FROM NAUMUR TO ANDENNE★ ③
35km/22mi

Downstream from Namur, the Meuse becomes wider and the valley broadens out. There are rock outcrops here and there, but in general the slopes are less dramatic. Limestone and dolomite are extracted in a number of quarries.
Leave Namur on N 959 and drive along the north bank of the Meuse.

Rocher du Roi Albert

Rocks rising 70m/230ft above the Meuse can be seen on the left. It was here that **King Albert I** fell to his death on 17 February 1934 while rock-climbing. A cross halfway up the face marks the place where his body was found. The surrounding forest has become a **national park**.

Marche-les-Dames

The Cistercians founded the **Abbaye Notre-Dame-du-Vivier** in the early 13C. It now accommodates the Little Sisters of Bethlehem. The abbey buildings date from the 13C and the 18C.
Cross the Meuse at Namêche and take N 942 towards Gesves.

Vallée du Samson

This is a fertile, picturesque valley.

Goyet

The **caverns** give an idea of the way of life in prehistoric cave dwellings; other caves nearby contain beautiful concretions. *Mar-Nov: guided tours (1hr 30min) Thur-Tue (daily during school holidays) 10am-5pm. €7.* ☎ *081 58 85 45.* A 19C **château** a short distance before Faulx-les-Tombes is a striking imitation of a medieval fortress.
Turn back and return to the Meuse Valley; follow it to Andenne.

Andenne

This little town grew up around the monastery founded in about 690 by St Begga, Charlemagne's great-great-great grandmother. The monastery became an aristocratic chapter of secular canonesses in the 11C.

The **War of the Cow** began in Andenne. A peasant had stolen a cow from a wealthy man in Ciney, and was recognised at the Andenne fair while he was trying to return the cow to its owner. He was arrested and hanged by the men of Ciney. The Count of Namur came to revenge his serf's death, aided by the people of Luxembourg, and they laid siege to the town. Liège's Prince-Bishop, sovereign of Ciney, called on Dinant for help. The war lasted for two years and devastated the Condroz region.

Collégiale Ste-Begge – This collegiate church was built in the 18C to plans by Dewez; it was designed to replace the monastery's seven churches. The church contains St Begga's Gothic blue stone tomb *(chapel north of the chancel)*. The church **museum** contains the canonesses' treasury consisting of paintings, sculptures, manuscripts and the finely worked reliquary of St Begga (c 1570-80). *Mid-Jul – mid-Aug: Sun 3pm-6.30pm; May-Oct: 1st Sun in month 3pm-6.30pm. Otherwise only by prior arrangement. €3. Apply to Mr R. Frennet, ☎ 085 84 13 44.*

THE VALLEY OF THE MOLIGNÉE★ ④
24km/15mi – About 4hr
Turn off N 96 on to N 971 by Anhée.

The Molignée is a small river that flows through a charming valley, wending its way between meadows and wooded slopes before it joins the Meuse. Villages of blue stone houses follow on from one another, and there are several abbeys on the hillsides.
Turn off N 96 on to N 971 by Anhée.

Château de Montaigle
This ruined fortress stands on an outcrop of rock. It was destroyed by the French in 1554.
Continue along N 971. Turn left at the old Falaën railway station.

Château-Ferme de Falaën
Jul-Aug: 1pm-8pm; Mar-Nov: Sat-Sun 1pm-8pm. €2.50. ☎ 082 69 96 26.
This 17C brick and limestone fortified farmhouse was once surrounded by a moat and defended by a drawbridge. It forms a square with a lofty tower at each corner. Inside there is a small and unusual **museum**, devoted to the subject of gastronomic brotherhoods, with temporary exhibitions.

Abbaye de Maredsous
9am-6pm. ☎ 082 69 82 84; www.maredsous.com
The Benedictines founded this abbey in 1872. It consists of a vast set of neo-Gothic buildings set on a wooded plateau overlooking a valley. Outside their hours of prayer, the monks engage in a wide range of activities (teaching, computer technology, theological research, hotel trade, bookshop). They also make the delicious Maredsous cheese.

Maredret
This village, which also has an abbey, specialises in crafts.

Ermeton-sur-Biert
The old castle overlooking this densely wooded area has become a convent.
Turn right beyond the station and go under the railway bridge.

Furnaux
The church has a magnificent **font**★ dating from about 1135-50. Four lions support the Mosan Romanesque basin, decorated with scenes from the Old and New Testaments, in particular the Baptism of Christ.

Mons★

Its importance proclaimed by the great belfry, Mons is both the capital of Hainaut province and the commercial hub of the Borinage mining region near the French border. Steep cobbled streets lined with elegant 17C and 18C residences lend the place a certain charm. Sculptor and architect Jacques du Brœucq (c 1510-84) was born here in the 16C, as was the musician Roland de Lassus (1532-94).

Location
Hainaut ℙ *– Population 91 187 – Michelin maps 716 E4 and 534 I20 – Plan of the built-up area in the current edition of the Red Guide Benelux.*
Mons is at the meeting-point of several main roads and just off the E 19/A 7 Paris-Brussels motorway.
🛈 *Grand-Place 22, ☎ 065 33 55 80; www.mons.be*
See also CANAL DU CENTRE and LE GRAND HORNU.

Background

The name 'Mons' is the Latin for "mount", and it was on the side of a hill that the town was founded. A settlement grew up around a convent founded in 650 by St Waudru at the foot of a fortress which later became the site of a castle built by the Counts of Hainaut.
The town reached the peak of its prosperity in the Middle Ages and during the reign of Emperor Charles V, due largely to its clothmaking activities. It was besieged several times because of its strategic position on the border with France. Louis XIV captured the town in 1691 after a three-week siege, and because of this the architectural style of most houses dates from this period.

In 1792 in **Jemappes** *(5km/3mi west)* the French General Dumouriez won a victory against the Austrians, temporarily making the country subject to rule from Paris.

In August 1914 it was at Mons that the British Expeditionary Force fought its first battle, holding up a much superior German force, which mistook the intense and rapid rifle fire of its marksmen for machine-guns. It was here too that the myth took hold of the "Angel of Mons", the appearance in the sky of a heavenly being giving heart to the British and terrifying their enemies.

In 1967, **SHAPE**, the Supreme Headquarters of the Allied Powers in Europe, moved from Paris to a site northeast of Mons. In 1971, the town acquired a state university with five faculties.

The Mons Ducasse – Mons is famous for its *ducasse,* the Procession of the Chariot of Gold which takes place on Holy Trinity Sunday (the Sunday after Whitsun). Brotherhoods and trade guilds together with folk in historic costume parade through the town, forming an escort for the reliquaries or statues of their patron saints. The march culminates in the appearance of St Waudru's processional chariot carrying her relics.

This procession is followed by the **Lumecon**, a medieval pageant enacting the battle during which St George slew the Dragon. The combat involves several characters and some strange animals known as *chinchins*. It is accompanied by traditional folk music and ends with the symbolic triumph of Good over Evil.

Directory

WHERE TO EAT

Chez Henry – *Rue du Havré 41 –* ☎ *065 35 23 06 – Closed Sun, Mon eve –* €16/25. Warm family atmosphere in this attractively rustic establishment with exposed beams and brick walls. Henry serves up the kind of straightforward, fortifying food that strikes a chord with everyone.

Alter Ego – *Rue de Nimy 6 –* ☎ *065 35 52 60 – closed mid-Jul – mid-Aug, Mon – €22/31.* Right by the Grand Place, a fine example of a classic bistro, with closely spaced tables, banquettes, lamps like bunches of grapes and a menu featuring good old-fashioned food.

WHERE TO STAY

Saint-Georges – *Rue des Clercs 15 –* ☎ *065 31 16 29 – www.saintgeorges.be –* €30/72. Having disposed of the dragon, St George – the province's patron saint – seems to have favoured this modest establishment with his name. It is located at the top of the town, right by the 17C belfry; bedrooms are fine for an overnight stay.

Infotel – *Rue d'Havré 32 –* ☎ *065 40 18 30 – hotelinfotel@infonie.be –* ◘ *– 20 rms: €67/89.* Just a step from the Grand-Place, right in the centre of town, a modern building where you can sleep in peace thanks to well-equipped rooms. Very useful courtyard car park.

TAKING A BREAK

Saey – *Grand'Place 12 –* ☎ *065 33 54 48 – 7.30am-10.30pm, Fri-Sat – midnight.* Combination of tea room, ice-cream parlour, bakers and delicatessen which has been a Mons institution since 1854. Outdoor seating on the Grand-Place.

L'Excelsior – *Grand-Place 29 –* ☎ *065 36 47 15 – 9.30am-midnight, -2am Sat, Sun.* Opened in 1922, this is one of the oldest café-restaurants in town, still with its copper-topped tables and its (now electrified) gaslights. Its speciality is a vegetable cocktail, but if that sounds too exotic, try the wines by the glass or the excellent choice of beers.

SHOPPING

H.Colson – *Rue des Fripiers 11 –* ☎ *065 36 33 74 – Tue-Sat 7am-1pm, 2pm-6pm, Sun 7am-1pm.* Patisserie famous for its local specialities which include lemon tart, *"Misérable"* (biscuit made with almonds and vanilla cream), and Mons macaroon (made with rice and almond paste)

Walking About

Start at Grand-Place.

Hôtel de Ville

9am-6.30pm (Fri 7pm). Closed 1 Jan (pm), 25 Dec ☎ *065 33 55 80.*

Dominating the spacious Grand-Place, Mons' town hall was built in 1458. When Charles the Bold died in 1477, construction was halted for lack of money. It was started again in the 16C but not completed until the 19C. The beautiful Gothic façade has a bell-tower, framed by two 17C pavilions with scrolled pediments.

Near the main door is the cast-iron figure of a monkey, known as the "Singe du Grand-Garde". Its origins remain a mystery. The monkey's head has been worn smooth by people stroking it for good luck. Note the 15C sculpted keystones in the porch. They are decorated with scenes symbolising the judicial functions of the town's aldermen.

MONS

The **interior** has rooms from many different periods, decorated with fine furniture, paintings and tapestries. The beams in the Gothic Room on the first floor are supported on beautiful carved corbels. The Gothic vaulting (17C) from the old St George's Chapel is in the next room; temporary exhibitions are held here.

Jardin du Mayeur

The Mayor's Garden was once the aldermen's orchard and farmyard. Nowadays it forms a pretty complement to the old buildings behind the town hall; one of them, the old pawnshop, is now home to the Musée du Centenaire. The "Joker's Fountain" represents a little boy spraying passers-by with water.

Beffroi★

The belfry was built at the highest point in the town on the charming square in front of the castle. From the square there are beautiful glimpses of the surrounding area, including the 11C-12C ruins of the outer walls of the **Château des Comtes de Hainaut** (12C) and the Counts' private chapel, dedicated to St Calixtus. Its crypt dates from the Romanesque period (11C).
The **belfry** (1662) is 87m/285ft high, with graceful onion domes and a traceried lantern tower. This is the only Baroque belfry in Belgium. There are 47 smaller bells and one 5t great bell in the carillon.
Go down Rue des Gades, then turn right into Rue des Clercs.

Collegiale Ste-Waudru★★

9am-6.30pm (Sun 7pm). Closed 1 Jan (p.m.), 25 Dec. ☎ 065 33 55 80 (Tourist Information Centre).
This impressive Brabant Gothic church was commissioned by the aristocratic chapter of St Waudru canonesses between 1450 and 1686, and was built under the direction of **Mathieu de Layens**. It stands on the very site once occupied by the modest monastery founded by St Waudru.
The exterior is impressive but somewhat squat, as the tower planned for the west front was never finished. It should have risen to a height of 190m/618ft but instead its top is on a line with the roof of the nave. There are 29 chapels around the church.

Interior – *Access by the south door.* The vast nave of three storeys (108m/354ft long) has clustered piers rising in a single sweep up to the brick vaulting. Jacques du Brœucq's 16C Italianate Renaissance alabaster **rood screen** was demolished in 1797, but the statues and low reliefs survived and are now distributed throughout the church.
Behind the west front, in front of the organ loft and its 18C instrument, is the **Car d'Or** (Chariot of Gold) built in 1781. It is used during the annual procession to carry St Waudru's 19C reliquary through the town.
Seven splendid **allegorical statues★** carved in alabaster by Du Brœucq are set out around the chancel. The four statues representing the Cardinal Virtues and the three representing the Theological Virtues are particularly graceful. There is also a superb statue of St Bartholomew (1574).

The clerestory windows in the chancel contain beautiful 16C and 17C stained glass, and include the five "imperial windows" presented by Maximilian of Austria. They were made by a master glass painter from Mons named Claix Eve.

In the first chapel on the south side of the ambulatory, there is a Gothic stone altarpiece called "Les Féries". The upper section dates from the 16C. The 12th chapel contains a beautiful black marble and alabaster altarpiece by Du Brœucq (1549), above which there is a lovely statue of Mary Magdalene surrounded by statuettes of the Evangelists. On the wall of the fourth chapel in the south aisle is a wonderful alabaster figure of Christ the Redeemer by the same artist.

Treasury – The church treasure is housed in the former chapterhouse and includes a number of interesting religious artefacts dating from the 13C to 19C. Among the items on display are church plate and gold and silver objects. A superb piece of jewellery that belonged to St Waudru and is known as the "Benoîte affique" dates from the Merovingian period. A small room next to the treasure house contains Jacques Du Brœucq's smaller sculptures. *Mar-Nov: Tue-Sun 1.30-6pm (Sun 5pm). Closed for the week of the Ducasse. €2.50. ☏ 065 33 55 80 (Tourist Information Centre) or 065 87 57 75.*

The Chariot of Gold in the Collégiale Ste-Waudru

Worth a Visit

Musée du Centenaire
Closed at time of going to press. For information ring. ☏ 065 33 55 80 (Tourist Information Centre).
This museum is mainly devoted to the First and Second World Wars, with other sections on archaeology and ceramics.

Musée du Folklore et de la Vie Montoise* (Maison Jean Lescarts)
Tue-Sun noon-6pm, Sun 10am-noon, 2-6pm. Closed 1-2 Jan, 25-26 Dec. €2.50. ☏ 065 31 43 57 ou 065 33 55 80 (Tourist Information Centre).
Reached by a flight of steps on the far side of a lapidary garden, the Folk Museum is housed in the Maison Jean Lescarts of 1636, a charming building which once served as a convent infirmary.
The museum illustrates local history and traditional life through furniture, simple decoration, various collections and a host of miscellaneous documents.

Musée des Beaux-Arts
Tue-Sun noon-6pm, Sun 10am-noon, 2pm-6pm. Closed 1-2 Jan, 25-26 Dec. €2.50. ☏ 065 40 53 06.
Works of art from the 16C to the present day are exhibited on a rota basis in the art gallery. Temporary exhibitions are also held in the museum.

Le Vieux Logis or Musées Chanoine-Puissant
Closed at time of going to press. ☏ 065 33 55 80 (Tourist Information Centre).
Before his death in 1934, Canon Puissant, a great art lover, installed extensive and wide-ranging collections of antique furniture, statues, gold and silverware and sketches in this little 16C house and in the nearby St Margaret's Chapel, a Romanesque building dating from the 13C. The chapel was once surrounded by the St Waudru parish graveyard (the "Attacat") and it was here that the Canon was buried.

Musée François Duesburg★

Entrance in Rue de la Houssière. Tue-Sun 1.30-6pm. Closed 1-2 Jan, 25-26 Dec. €4.
☎ *065 36 31 64.*

Housed in an old bank building, the museum's deliberately austere interior heightens the impact of the dazzling **collection of clocks★★** (1795-1815) made by the leading craftsmen of Paris. It was popular enthusiasm for writers such as Daniel Defoe *(Robinson Crusoe)*, Bernardin de Saint-Pierre *(Paul et Virginie)*, or Chateaubriand *(Atala)* and the influence of the philosopher Jean-Jacques Rousseau that provided them with their creative inspiration. Ten different craftsmen were needed to produce a single clock on which the bronze was either given a black patina or gilded. Note the superb "Paul et Virginie" clock said to have been commissioned in 1802 by Napoleon Bonaparte as a gift for the author whose work he so much admired.

The museum also houses a remarkable collection of porcelain from both Paris and Brussels, as well as paintings, engravings and books focusing on the same themes.

Mundaneum

Tue-Sun. 10am-6pm. €2.50. ☎ *065 31 53 43.*

Since 1998 this unusual museum, created by the famous designers Peeters and Schuiten, has housed the ambitious project developed by two lawyers from Brussels, P Otlet and H La Fontaine. In 1895, Otlet and La Fontaine founded the International Bibliography Office, creating a universal bibliographical register listing every book published around the world.

Excursions

Frameries

7km/4mi S.

The Parc d'Attractions Scientifiques (PASS) has been laid out on the site of the old Crachet coal mine and its slag heap. As well as creating new structures and spaces, the famous French architect has restored the old buildings which speak eloquently of the Borinage's rich industrial past. PASS introduces the evolution of science and technology with an array of techniques intended to make the subject entertaining. ♿ *Open school holidays 10am-6pm; term-time daily exc Wed 9am-5pm, Sat, Sun, public holidays 10am-6pm. Closed early to mid-Jan, Sept, 24, 25, 31 Dec. €12.50.* ☎ *070 22 22 52; www.pass.be*

Cuesmes

3.5km/2mi S. Leave from Grand-Place.

The **Maison de Van Gogh** stands in a pretty, rural setting of marshland. The great artist lived here with a family of miners, the Descrucqs, in 1879 and 1880. He had come to the Borinage district in December 1878 to preach the Gospel. It was here at Cuesmes that he began drawing the countryside and the life of miners. The ground-floor has reproductions of his works and there is an audio-visual presentation. *Tue-Sun 10am-6pm. Closed 1-2 Jan, 25-26 Dec. €2.50.* ☎ *065 35 56 11.*

Blaugies

20km/12.5mi SW on N 543, then turn right at Rieu-de-Bury.
There is a little 15C polychrome wooden altarpiece in the **church**, representing an *Entombment* with a heightened sense of movement. There is also a 12C font, with images of dragons biting bunches of grapes on one side.

Roisin

30km/18.5mi SW of Mons.
To the north of the village, near Le Caillou-qui-Bique, is the **Maison de Verhaeren**. This is where the great Belgian writer Emile Verhaeren lived with his wife Marthe from 1900 to 1916, during the last years of his life. The little **Musée Verhaeren** in the courtyard of the inn in Le Caillou includes a reconstruction of the poet's study. *Closed for renovation.* ☎ *065 36 04 64 (Tourist Information Centre).*

The PASS.

Ch. Bastin – J. Evrard/MICHELIN

Namur★★

Thanks to its strategic location commanding the confluence of the Sambre and Meuse, Namur was once a tactically important military base. Nowadays the enormous citadel spread over Champeau Hill still dominates the scene, while the town itself is a peaceful place of little squares and narrow streets which it is pleasure to explore. A popular tourist centre, Namur is also the political capital of Wallonia, home to the Walloon Parliament, whose seat is in Grognon, one of the city's oldest districts. Namur's university (Facultés Universitaires Notre-Dame-de-la-Paix), founded in 1831, maintains its excellent reputation.

Location
Namur 🅿 – *Population 104 994 – Michelin maps 716 H4 and 534 O20.*
Namur is midway between Charleroi and Liège on the great waterway of the Meuse. It is reached by road on the A 15/E 42 east-west motorway or the A 4/E 411 Brussels-Luxembourg motorway.
🄱 *Hôtel de ville,* ☎ *081 24 64 44 or Square Léopold,* ☎ *081 24 64 49; www.ville.namur.be*

Background

A city under siege – The history of the County of Namur is one of war and the city itself was frequently besieged. Even in Roman times, Julius Caesar attacked the Gaulish tribe of the Aduatuci here when they sought refuge here. In 1577 Don John of Austria captured the castle, and from the 17C onwards assaults followed thick and fast. One of the most decisive battles was in 1692, when a French army led by Louis XIV's great military engineer, Vauban, besieged the town. After its fall, witnessed by Louis himself, Vauban strengthened the fortifications, but Namur was captured again in 1695 by William III of Orange.

In 1746 the French attacked the city again. It was subsequently handed over to Austria, and Emperor Joseph II had the fortifications demolished.

The French Revolutionaries took Namur in 1792, but they were forced out by the Austrians the following year. The last siege, in 1794, returned the town to the French.

After the Battle of Waterloo in 1815, the French rearguard fought a valiant delaying action at Namur. The Dutch rebuilt the citadel in 1816.

In the late 19C Namur was surrounded by a ring of fortresses, which helped it to put up a heroic resistance against the invading German army in the opening weeks of the First World War. Nevertheless the town eventually fell, to suffer pillaging and wanton destruction. In the Second World War Namur was captured by the Germans in May 1940, and throughout the conflict suffered a number of air raids until 1944.

Directory

SIGHTSEEING

Guided tours – From May to September there are **individual guided tours** around the old parts of town, and on Sundays, the tourist information centre runs **themed tours**. For details ☎ 081 24 64 49. Visitors can also discover the city at their own pace thanks to an audio-tour. Tourist Information Centre ☎ 081 24 64 49.

Boat trips – There are 45-minute boat trips on the Sambre and Meuse in season. You can also cruise upstream to Wépion (1hr 45min) and Dinant (9hr). Starting-point at Grognon.

WHERE TO EAT

😄 **La Cava** – *Rue de la Monnaie 20* – ☎ *081 23 04 72* – ✍ *– €10/12.50.* Friendly Italian restaurant in the heart of the pedestrianised city centre close to Place d'Armes and the belfry. Meals are served beneath the vaults of a lovely old Gothic cellar dating from the 15C. Authentic Italian dishes.

😄 **La Cuve à Bière** – *Rue des Brasseurs 108* – ☎ *081 26 13 63* – *Closed Sun, Mon* – ✍ *– €13/25.* Once part of a brewery, this venerable old building is reached through a lovely little courtyard. Beer is still celebrated here, even in the "frothy" decor of the restaurant. Range of straightforward, copious meals.

😄 **Fenêtre sur cour** – *Rue du Président 35* – ☎ *081 23 09 08 – fenetre.sur.cour @skynet.be – Closed Sun, public holidays* – ✍ *– lunch €7.31 – €22.06/32.47.* Right in the busy town centre, this imposing mansion does indeed have a "window on the courtyard". Trendy atmoshere, traditional food, multiple-choice menu and daily specials fresh from the market.

😄😄 **Le Temps des Cerises** – *Rue des Brasseurs 22* – ☎ *081 22 53 26 – Closed Sun, Mon* – ✍ *– €25.79/33.47.* Long established here in the Street of the

Brewers, this friendly little bistro close to the Musée des Arts Anciens offers an assortment of traditional dishes as well as themed set meals which are changed five times a year.

Les Embrans – *Rue de la Tour 2 – ☎ 081 22 74 41 – Closed Carnival week, Easter fortnight, 3 weeks July, All Saints Day, Sun, Mon – lunch €20 – €26/38.* Restaurant-cum-fishmonger's opposite the theatre and just a step from the Oignes Priory Treasury. Extensive menu with plenty of mouthwatering seafood specialities attracting a faithful clientele.

Au Trois Petits Cochons – *Avenue de la Plante 4 – ☎ 081 22 70 10 – Closed early Mar – mid-Mar, Aug, Sat midday, Sun, Mon – €29.* At the foot of Namur's Citadel, right by the famous Pont de Jambes, this attractive little restaurant offers bistro-type cuisine adapted to contemporary tastes. Rustic interior, meals served in the courtyard in summer.

WHERE TO STAY

Les Tanneurs – *Rue des Tanneries 13 – ☎ 081 24 00 24 – info@tanneurs.com – ▣ – 30 rms: €38/217 – ☲ €7.* Comfortable hotel in a converted tannery consisting of a delightful group of 17C buildings. There's also a gastronomic restaurant and a friendly bistro serving grills. There are a few famous names in the visitors' book…

Grand Hotel de Flandre – *Place de la Station 14 – ☎ 081 23 18 68 –33 rms: €44.62/66.93 – ☲ €7.44.* Venerable establishment in a strategic location opposite the railway station. Simply furnished rooms somewhat in need of rejuvenation. Ask for one of the quieter ones to the rear of the building. Ground floor inn-restaurant.

Beau Vallon – *Chemin du Beau Vallon 38 – 5100 Wépion – ☎ 081 41 15 91 – ✉ – 5 rms: €23.50/55 ☲* This welcoming establishment built in local brick opens on to a park and is a quiet place to settle down for a while in this little strawberry-growing town just south of Namur. Impeccable rooms, lounge with blazing open fire on cold days.

La Ferme du Quartier – *Place Ste-Marguerite 4 – 5004 Bouge – ☎ 081 21 11 05 – Closed Jul, last week Dec, Sun eve – ▣ – 14 rms: €28/43 ☲ – restaurant €31.* This big 16C farmstead has been converted into a hotel. The rooms are small, quiet, and simply furnished. Traditional food served in a cheerful atmosphere.

New Hotel de Lives – *Chaussée de Liège 1178 – 5101 Lives-sur-Meuse – ☎ 081 58 05 13 – francis40@infonie.be – ▣ – 10 rms: €61/77 ☲* Massive riverbank inn between Namur and Andenne, not far from the Brussels-Luxembourg motorway. Somewhat faded rooms, but fine for an overnight stay. The ones at the back are quieter.

TAKING A BREAK

La Maison des Desserts – *Rue Haute-Marcelle 17 – ☎ 081 22 74 51 – Tue-Sun 8.30am-7pm.* Charming patisserie with a spacious tearoom and a luxuriant winter garden. This is the place to try Namur specialities such as Biétrumés (nut-filled caramels).

Brasserie Henry – *Place St-Aubain 3 – ☎ 081 22 02 04 – 8am-midnight, Fri, Sat – 1am.* Huge traditional brasserie in a splendid 19C town mansion. Come here for a bite or a cool glass of beer, especially when the sun comes out and you can enjoy the spacious summer terrace.

Panorama – *Route Merveilleuse 12 – ☎ 081 22 28 04 – winter: 11am-7pm; summer: 8.30am-midnight.* This café-restaurant established in Namur's medieval citadel deserves its name – the panorama over the town is outstanding. In summer there is a terrace overlooking the Meuse.

SHOPPING

La Cave de Wallonie – *Côté Terroirs – Rue de la Halle 6 – ☎ 081 22 06 83 – cavedewallonie@skynet.be – Mon midday-6pm; Tue-Sat 10am-12.30pm, 1.30pm-6pm.* Shop specialising in local products. There are liqueurs and fruit wines including the local aperitif called Florange, a wine flavoured with oranges and spices. Good, friendly advice given, so, if in doubt, feel free to ask.

Parfumerie Guy Delforge – *Citadelle Médiévale – ☎ 081 22 12 19 – Tue-Sat 9am-5.30pm, Sun 2.30pm-5.30pm.* Belgium's sole creative perfumer, Guy Delforge, sells his range of products based on 250 ingredients in the unusual setting of the medieval citadel. Workshop visits Saturday at 10.30am, other days by prior arrrangement.

ENTERTAINMENT

Théâtre Royal de Namur – *Place du Théâtre 2 – ☎ 081 226 026 – Mon-Sat 11am-6pm.* This lovely, recently restored theatre has a varied programme including classical concerts, opera, international variety shows, drama, and one-man shows.

EVENTS

Festivals – Every September, the **Fêtes de Wallonie** bring a variety of folk groups to Namur. The festivities include fights between *échasseurs*, historical figures clad in 17C costumes, who confront each other on stilts.

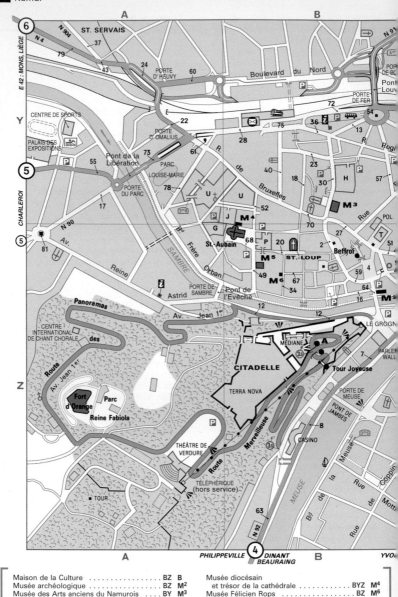

Worth a Visit

CITADEL★

Access via the Route Merveilleuse (1.5km/1mi) from the foot of the Citadel.

The Citadel and Route Merveilleuse

The **Tour Joyeuse**, a tower which once formed part of the Counts' castle, is on the right as this scenic "Road of Wonders" winds up towards the citadel.

At a hairpin bend close to the highest point of the road, a northeast-facing view-point affords a magnificent **panoramic view★★** of the valley of the Sambre and the Meuse. Not far from here, on the left, a narrow path leads back down to the town, giving another fine view over rooftops and church towers.

The road then reaches the **Donjon**, passing between two of the old castle's **towers** and crossing the moat separating the two main areas of the Citadel.

Fortifications

Late Mar-late Sept: guided tour 11am-5pm (mid-Apr – late May: Sat, Sun, public holidays). €6. ☎ 081 22 68 29; www.ville.namur.be

The late 15C and 16C Mediane bastion was reinforced in 1640 by the addition of another bastion, the Terra Nova, built by the Spanish. A wide moat separates them.

E 411 : BRUXELLES, ARLON
E 42 : MONS, LIÈGE

The tour reveals the complex defensive architecture of each bastion, from the outside as well as from the inside, with its two sets of underground works.

Fort d'Orange

Close to the **Parc d'Attractions Reine-Fabiola**, a local amusement park, this fort was built in 1691 to protect the Terra Nova bastion. The Dutch partly rebuilt it in 1816.

Route des Panoramas

This winding road heads down through the woods to the city centre.

TOWN CENTRE★

Cathédrale St-Aubain

This classical domed building was completed in 1751 by the Italian architect Pisoni. It stands on the site of the old collegiate church of St Aubain, founded in 1047. There are beautiful Baroque works of art inside, coming for the most part from the region's churches and abbeys. Note the Rubens School paintings above the choir stalls from Église St-Loup.

The old 18C bishop's palace is opposite the cathedral and is now used by the provincial administration.

The Citadel

Musée Diocésain et Trésor de la Cathédrale★

Visits by prior arrangement only €1.25. ☎ 081 44 42 85, 081 22 17 01 or 0476 97 23 24. www.ville.namur.be

Located to the right of the cathedral, the museum boasts a fine collection of religious objects: a priceless crown-reliquary in a case decorated with enamel discs (c 1210), a portable altar embellished with ivory plaques (12C), an arm-reliquary of St Adrian (c 1238), a statue of St Blaise (c 1260-80) in silver gilt, a Mosan statue of the Virgin Mary (c 1220) and a miniature triptych from a Paris workshop (early 14C) in enamelled and gilded silver, depicting a crucifixion scene.

Musée de Groesbeeck de Croix★

Tue-Sun 10am-midday, 1.30pm-5pm. Closed 25 Dec-1 Jan. €2. ☎ 081 23 75 10; www.ville.namur.be

This museum is accommodated in an elegant 18C Louis XV-style town house. The superb decoration of the rooms blends in harmoniously with the architecture; there are wonderful plaster ceilings, a monumental staircsae lit by a little lantern, and a room with gilded leather.

The museum also has many fine works of art (paintings, tapestries, sculptures, glass, gold and silverware, furniture, a 17C Ruckers harpsichord). Sumptuously decorated with old tiles, the kitchen has kept its enormous 18C stove. Finally, there is a delightful garden.

Musée Félicien Rops★

Due to re-open in 2004. Ring for details ☎ 081 22 01 10; www.namur.be

This fascinating museum is devoted to the famous painter, engraver and draughtsman Félicien Rops (1833-98). It contains a collection of lithographs, paintings, drawings and etchings (*Les Sataniques*), many of which have an erotic or a satirical theme.

Eglise St-Loup★

Guided tour Mon-Fri by prior arrangement with Mr Albert Henriette, ☎ 081 22 80 85 or 081 74 34 61.

This former Jesuit collegiate church is a remarkable Baroque building, built from 1621 to 1645 to plans by

Église St-Loup.

Pierre Huyssens. Ringed columns, surmounted by a red and white marble entablature, support superb sandstone vaulting richly decorated in high relief. Note also the lovely furnishings.

Musée des Arts Anciens et du Namurois★

Tue-Sun 10am-6pm. Closed 25 Dec-1 Jan. €1.24 or €2.48 during special exhibitions.
☎ 081 22 00 65; www.ville.namur.be

This museum is housed in the **Hôtel de Gaiffier d'Hestroy**, an elegant 17C mansion. It has a remarkable collection of works of art, sculptures and paintings made in the Namur region, dating from the Middle Ages to the Renaissance.

The collection of gold and silverware is particularly extensive and features religious objects in the Mosan style: most of these are reliquaries and 13C pyxes (small enamelled receptacles with conical lids in which the Eucharistic Host was kept after consecration). The outstanding paintings on wood, depicting the *Annunciation* and the *Visitation* were executed in c 1400 and unquestionably show Late Gothic influence. The *Crowning of the Virgin* (from northern France) has been adroitly superimposed on to a photographic background. Sculptures in stone and wood, including some fine retables, as well as beaten copper pieces bear witness to the high standard of artistic production in the Namur region. Note also the lovely examples of glassware, the display of stained glass, and the four fine landscape paintings by the early 16C artist Henri Blès.

Le Trésor du Prieuré d'Oignies aux Sœurs de Notre-Dame★★

Entrance at no 17 Rue Julie Billiart. Guided tour (50min) Tue-Sat, 10am-noon, 2pm-5pm, Sun 2pm-5pm. Closed public holidays, mid-Dec – late Dec. €1.50 ☎ 081 23 03 42;
www.ville.namur.be

The very rich Oignies Priory **treasury** is housed in one room; it was fortunately saved from the 1940 air raids. The display includes delicate early-13C Mosan gold and silverware by the monk **Hugo d'Oignies** including gospel books, reliquaries etc. The delicacy of his workmanship is remarkable, especially the medallions on a black background, the filigree and the leaf decoration on which tiny hunting scenes can be seen.

Beyond the theatre, the **Tour St-Jacques** comes into view on the left. The tower has an octagonal steeple and has been used as a **belfry** since the 18C.

Musée Archéologique★

Tue-Sun 10am- (Sat, Sun, public holidays 10.40am) 5pm. Closed 25 Dec-1 Jan. €2.
☎ 081 23 16 31; www.ville.namur.be

The Archaeology Museum is housed in what was once the meat market, a splendid 16C Mosan style building. The exhibitions display the results of digs carried out in the province. There are many magnificent examples of Roman and Merovingian antiquities.

Jewellery and glassware from the 1C to the 7C are represented through a series of stunning artefacts. The museum also features a model (1:600) of the city of Namur, a scaled-down replica of the one made by Larcher d'Aubancourt, royal engineer to Louis XIV.

To the rear of the museum is the **Maison de la Culture,** an arts centre built in 1964.

Excursion

Franc-Waret

12km.7.5mi NE. Leave by ② on the town plan on N 80.

The **château,** an imposing 18C building surrounded by a moat, is flanked by two wings set at right angles. To the rear, a turret and a square tower have survived from the castle's 16C predecessor

Nivelles*

The main attraction of this small and elegant town is its monumental collegiate church. In the 12C, walls were built round the town and a few of the towers have survived, such as the Tour Simone (in Rue Seutin). Nivelles was badly damaged in 1940 when the collegiate church, along with 500 houses, was set on fire, and has been carefully restored.

Location
Brabant Wallon – Population 23 714 – Michelin maps 716 G4 and 533 L19.
Nivelles is at the junction of several main roads and close to the A 7/E 19 Brussels-Mons motorway and the A 54 motorway to Charleroi.
🖪 *Place Albert I, ☎ 067 21 54 13; www.nivelles.be*

Background

The cradle of the **Carolingian** dynasty, Nivelles grew up around an abbey, founded in c 650 by Itta of Aquitaine, wife of Pepin the Elder, an ancestor of Charlemagne. Their daughter, St Gertrude, was the first Abbess of a mixed religious order that became a noble chapter of canonesses and canons in the 9C. All the canonesses were of noble birth and they soon began leading a life of luxury. The abbey remained extremely influential until its closure in 1798.

Local traditions – The **Tour de Sainte Gertrude** is a procession which takes place in autumn and which dates back to the 13C. It is held on the Sunday following Michaelmas, St Michael being the town's patron saint.
The procession follows a 14km/8.5mi route up hill and down dale; a 15C cart, drawn by six horses, carries the saint's reliquary.
As the procession wends its way back it is joined by giants (Argayon, Argayonne, their son Lolo and Godet the horse) as well as a group of canonesses in 17C dress.

Directory

Where to Stay

☞ **Ferme de Grambais** – *Chaussée de Braine-le-Comte 102 – ☎ 067 22 01 18 – ferme.de.grambais@proximedia.be – Closed early Jan-mid-Jan; restaurant Sun eve, Mon – 🅿 – 10 rms: €46/54 ☕ – restaurant €29.* In a countryside setting only five minutes from Nivelles, tranquil lodgings in old farm buildings laid out around a courtyard. Eat like a lord and sleep like a log.

☞ **La Ferme des Églantines chambre d'hôte** – *Chemin de Fontaine-l'Évêque 8 – ☎ 067 84 10 10 – ☐ – 5 rms: €49/57 ☕ – meals €20.* With a dream location deep in the countryside, this typical Brabant farmstead offers up-to-date rooms and a duplex. Attractive garden. Delicious light meals and a family atmosphere.

Speciality

Tarte al djote – This succulent cheese tart made with chard, herbs and onions is eaten hot and washed down with a glass of beer or red wine.

Worth a Visit

Collégiale Ste-Gertrude**

Daily except Sun a.m., 9am-5pm, guided tour (crypt, archæological basement, cloister treasury) 2pm, Sat, Sun 2pm, 3.30pm. ☎ 067 84 08 64 (Tourist Information Centre).
This great church was consecrated in 1046 in the presence of the Holy Roman Emperor Henry III. It is built in the variant of the Romanesque style known as Ottonian,and its layout, with a transept and chancel at each end of the nave, is an architectural expression of the Empire's double nature, representing the complementary elements of Emperor and Pope. The east chancel is built over a crypt with ribbed vaulting. The west chancel, representing Imperial authority, is part of the massive 12C fore-part of the building, usually referred to by its German name of "Westbau".
This Late Romanesque **Westbau** has five storeys accessible from two staircase towers and contains an apse, two gallery chapels (Chapelle de Ste Agathe and Chapelle de Ste Gertrude), a tiny space where prisoners were kept for short periods, a vast upper chamber (19m/63ft) called the "Imperial Hall", and an octagonal bell-tower. The two doorways are decorated with 12C Romanesque sculptures. On the south door is a carving of St Michael; on the north door is an illustration of the Story of Samson.
The highest transept gable on the south side of the church, called St Peter's Gable (Pignon St-Pierre), is decorated with Romanesque arcading.

Interior – The size and the simplicity are striking. The long nave (102m/331ft) was covered with ogive vaulting in the 17C and given a series of decorative features in the 18C. Restoration gave it back its original look while protecting it with a concrete ceiling made to look like wood. Note the graceful 15C painted wooden statue of the *Virgin of the Annunciation*★, the "Charles V" oak panel, the superb Renaissance choir stalls, a 16C marble and alabaster altarpiece attributed to the Dinant artist Thonon, and the 18C oak and marble pulpit representing the meeting between Jesus and the Woman of Samaria at Jacob's well by Laurent Delvaux. There are several other sculptures by the same artist.

In the east chancel, above St Gertrude's mausoleum, is a 16C brass chest. A modern reliquary (1982) by F Roulin has replaced the magnificent 13C reliquary of St Gertrude which was almost completely destroyed in the blaze following an air raid in May 1940. A

Ch. Bastin et J. Evrard/MICHELIN

Collégiale Ste-Gertrude

copy of the reliquary is displayed in the Imperial Hall, while fragments of the original one can be seen in the Chapelle Ste Gertrude. It is in this same chapel that you can see the "hole" of St Gertrude: legend has it that only those who have achieved "a state of grace" may pass through it. The gallery connecting Chapelle Ste Gertrude to Chapelle Ste Agathe affords a magnificent view of the imposing nave.

Crypt and archaeological basement – It was in the 11C crypt beneath the east chancel that pilgrims used to arrive to pray beneath St Gertrude's reliquary. The archaeological basement under the nave contains the ruins of the five churches, from the 7C to the 10C, which preceded the Romanesque one.

Cloisters – These 13C cloisters used to link the church to the monastery buildings which have now all disappeared. They serve as a reminder of the chapter of canons and canonesses who gradually replaced the monks and nuns of the early times. Only the north walk of the cloisters is still entirely authentic. In summer they are used as a venue for carillon concerts, while in winter they are home to a Christmas market.

Near the collegiate church is a statue of St Michael, one of the town's patron saints, the neo-Gothic Law Courts, and the **Porte de Saintes,** a gateway commemorating the twinning of Nivelles with the town of Saintes in France.

Musée Communal d'Archéologie, d'Art et d'Histoire
Rue de Bruxelles 27. Wed-Mon, 9.30am-noon, 2-5pm. Closed 1 Jan, Easter, 27 Sept. (Festival of Wallonia), Christmas. €1. ☎ 067 88 22 80.

This museum in an 18C house has fascinating collections of regional art and is the perfect way to round off a visit to the collegiate church. Particularly noteworthy are four limestone statues of Apostles from the Gothic rood screen in the church, a sumptuous 16C Brussels tapestry, and a beautiful collection of Baroque terracottas by the sculptor Laurent Delvaux (1696-1778). The three allegorical figures were designed for the semicircular façade of Charles of Lorraine's apartments in Brussels.

Archaeological collections covering the period between prehistoric and Gallo-Roman times are on the second floor.

Parc de la Dodaine
In the southern part of the town.

A flower-bedecked garden around a pond and a large lake are among the attractions of this park which also has a children's play area and sports facilities.

Following Avenue de la Tour-de-Guet west towards the motorway gives a view of the **Tourette**, a charming 17C square tower, on the right.

> ### "Jean de Nivelles"
> High on the belltower is the town's mascot, the jack-o'-the-clock known as "Jean de Nivelles"; the mechanical bellringer's historical namesake was a 15C nobleman who refused to take the field against the Duke of Burgundy, in defiance of his father and the king. Ever since, the proverbial "dog of Jean de Nivelles, which runs away when you call it", has been part of local fable.

Excursions

Ronquières
9km/5.25mi W on N 533.

This pleasant village is famous for its pretty view of the Charleroi Canal and its remarkable example of modern waterway technology.

The **Ronquières inclined plane★**, constructed in 1968, is 1 432m/4 698ft long. It makes it possible for boats to transfer easily across a change in the level of the canal of 67.58m/221ft. Two containers 91m/298ft long, filled with water, each with a 5 200t counterweight, can transport a 1 350t boat from one level to the other by running along a series of 236 rollers 70cm/28in in diameter. The scheme is completed upstream by a 300m/984ft aqueduct and a 150m/492ft **tower**.

An exhibition inside the tower includes a fascinating **audio-visual presentation** on inland navigation and a view of the winch room. The 11th floor commands a lovely view of the surrounding countryside. *Apr-Oct: 10am-7pm (last admission 5pm). €7. ☎ 065 36 04 64 (Hainaut provincial tourist office).*

The visit can be completed by a **boat trip** along the canal. *Departure from the foot of the canal reach. End Apr to early Sept: Daily (except Mon, Wed when not public holidays) noon, 2pm, 3.30pm, 5.30pm. €2.50. ☎ 065 36 04 64 (Hainaut provincial tourist office).*

Bois-Seigneur-Isaac
5km/3mi N on N 28.

The **abbey** here boasts a 16C Chapel of the Holy Blood with Baroque decoration. On the high altar note Laurent Delvaux's sculptures and low relief *(Entombment)*. The Gothic vaulted vestry still has a reliquary containing a piece of sacred cloth stained with Christ's Blood. It resulted from a miracle which occurred during the Eucharist in 1405 when blood flowed from a sacred wafer onto the altar cloth, and has since become an object of pilgrimage. The 18C **Château de Bois-Seigneur-Isaac** opposite the abbey is an enormous building which houses some valuable collections. *Guided tours (45min) last two Sun in Jun, First Sun in Jul, Sat, Sun during heritage week (journées du Patrimoine) 2pm-6pm. €4. ☎ 067 21 38 80.*

Braine-le-Château
12km/7mi N on N 28.

The castle, surrounded by water, is near a water mill (exhibitions). It belonged to the Counts of Hornes.

Maximilien de Hornes, Chamberlain to Emperor Charles V, had the **pillory** set up on the neighbouring market square in 1521. His alabaster mausoleum by Jean Mone can be seen in the church.

Seneffe★★
8km/5mi SW on N 27.

A long avenue leads to the **Château de Seneffe**, built between 1763 and 1768 to plans by Laurent Benoît Dewez for Count Depestre, a rich banker from Ath. The pediment of the sober neo-Classical facade bears the polychrome coat of arms of Depestre and his wife. The main building is flanked by two wings, each terminating in an elegant pavilion. The courtyard is bounded by a superb wrought-iron grille. The 22ha/54 acre park has a little Palladian theatre, an orangery, an ice-

Inside the Château de Seneffe.

house and a number of other buildings. Neglected for many years, the château has been restored and now houses important **gold and silverware collections** belonging to Belgium's Communauté Française.

The charm of the **interior** is not least due to its superb **parquet floors** made from precious woods. The little circular room next to the Salle de Compagnie and the Salle de Billard has a particularly splendid example. The walls of the rooms have sumptuous panelling and stucco work. The dedicated collector Claude d'Allemagne bequeathed some of his vast collections of silverware to the museum. Among the fine items on show are bowls, pots, chandeliers, book-bindings, and tableware including a number of pretty tureens (1766) by J-F Beghin with wonderfully engraved covers. In the Salle de Compagnie is a remarkable "windmill-bowl", with sails that revolve when a little pipe is blown into; the bowl itself was only filled on special occasions such as weddings, when it had to be emptied in one go. A monumental stairway with fine marquetry leads to the upper floor where changing exhibitions are held on a regular basis. *Tue-Sun 10am-6pm. Closed 1 Jan, 25 Dec. €4.96.* ☎ *064 55 69 13.*

Oostende ♨♨

OSTEND

Belgium's largest and most popular seaside resort, Ostend has a prestigious royal past, and was particularly favoured by King Leopold II. The seafront promenade stretches from the Casino-Kursaal of 1953 to the Thermae Palace Hotel. Nearby are the Royal and Venetian Galleries, a fine place for a stroll. The old fishermen's district is made up of a grid of narrow streets, bounded by the beach, the harbour mouth and the yacht harbour. The famous Ostend oysters are bred in the 80ha/198 acre Spuikom to the southeast.

Location
Westvlaanderen – Population 67 304 – Michelin maps 716 B2 and 533 C15 – Plan of the built-up area in the current edition of The Red Guide Benelux.
In the middle of Belgium's coastline, Ostend is reached from Bruges by the A 10 motorway and by the N 34 coast road.
🚹 *Monacoplein 2,* ☎ *059 70 11 99; www.toerisme-oostende.be*

Worth a Visit

Visserskaai
There is a virtually uninterrupted line of restaurants along this quayside. The fishing harbour can be seen from here, as can the large fish market on the far side of the harbour mouth, where the auctions of fish and shellfish make a fascinating spectacle.

Weststaketsel
This is one of the two piers flanking the harbour mouth or "havengeul". From here there is a view of the beach and the movement of the boats. At the far end, fishermen set up their dipping nets, square nets suspended on winches.

Noordzeeaquarium
The aquarium contains small tanks of North Sea fish and shellfish, as well as collections of shells. *Apr-May: 10am-noon, 2-5pm (Sat, Sun and public holidays 6pm); Jun-Sept: 10am-12.30pm, 2-6pm; Oct-Mar: Sat, Sun and public holidays 10am-12.30pm, 2-6pm. €2.* ☎ *059 32 16 69.*

Stedelijk Feest-en Kultuurpaleis
Ostend's Festival and Arts Centre overlooks Wapenplein, the town's main square. On the 2nd floor is the **Museum voor Schone Kunsten**. The town's fine arts museum has a collection of Romantic to Post-Impressionist Belgian paintings. On show are works by Ensor, Spilliaert, Musin and Van Rysselberghe. ♿ *Daily except Tue 2-5pm. Closed 1 Jan, 25 Dec. €2.* ☎ *059 80 53 35.*

Oostends Historisch Museum De Plate (Musée d'Histoire locale)
Mid-Jun to mid-Sept. and during school holidays: Wed-Mon 10am-noon, 2-5pm; midrest of the year: Sat 10am-noon, 2-5pm. Closed 1 Jan, 25 Dec. €2. ☎ *059 50 71 45; www.oostende.be*
Housed in the old royal palace, this museum is devoted to local history. Ostend's relationship with the sea is evoked by the reconstruction of a fishermen's café and a number of boat models. On the first floor is the room in which the much-loved first Louise-Marie, first Queen of the Belgians, passed away in October 1850.

Directory

WHERE TO EAT

Adelientje – *Bonenstraat 9 – ☎ 059 70 13 67 – Closed fortnight in Jun – €30*. Adelientje has been tickling tastebuds for more than 30 years with the harvest of the sea, appropriately enough, given the restaurant's location by the fish quay. Mussels aplenty in season, not forgetting the famous shrimp croquettes.

Fort Napoléon – *Vuurtorenweg – ☎ 059 33 21 60 – resto.fortnapoleon @skynet.be – Closed Mon exc school holidays – ⊟ – €35/58*. Contemporary bistro-type restaurant in an old fort guarding the approach to Ostend. Bright and airy dining room with glazed roof and summer terrace with a sand dune for company. A concept as original as it is fascinating.

WHERE TO STAY

't Atelier – *Veldbloemstraat 43 – ☎ 059 43 61 01 – ⊟ – 4 rms, 1 penthouse: €38/45* ☕ By the racecourse some 500m/0.3mi from the seafront, this pretty house has been converted into a B&B. Charming rooms and penthouse. The artist proprietor exhibits his work.

Cardiff – *St-Sebastiaanstraat 4 – ☎ 059 70 28 98 – Closed mid-Nov – mid-Dec, Tue out of season – ⊟ – 16 rms: €39/65* ☕ *– restaurant €14/24*. This small hotel is conveniently located close to the busy Wapenplein in a long traffic-free shopping street. Rooms have been given a completely new look. Cheerful dining room. Classic dishes.

Du Parc – *Marie-Joséplein 3 – ☎ 059 70 16 80 – hotel@duparcoostende.com – 44 rms: €57/76* ☕ Central, long-established hotel with contemporary, prettily refurbished rooms. Art Deco bar frequented by the cream of local society and a terrace which gets very popular as soon as the sun comes out.

TAKING A BREAK

Seafood stalls – *Visserskaai – from 11am*. Group of timber sheds by the fish market dispensing shrimps, anchovies, mussels and other types of seafood to take away. The fish soup is a great restorative when the weather turns cool.

Taverne James – *Galerie James Ensor 34 – ☎ 059 70 52 45 – Wed-Mon 9am-10pm*. This tavern tucked away in a shopping arcade is known for its traditional shrimp croquettes. The "James" from which it takes its name is James Ensor, the famous local painter of British descent. Somewhat faded decor, attractive terrace.

Café Botteltje – *Louisastraat 19 – ☎ 059 70 09 28 – www.hotelmarion.com – Mon 4.30pm, Tue, Thur, Sun 11.30am-1am, Fri 11.30am-2am, Sat 11.30am-3am*. This welcoming bistro is proud of its selection of beers and gins, one of the best along the coast. You can fight the cold by snuggling up to the open fireplace.

Café of the Hôtel du Parc – *Marie-Joséplein 3 – ☎ 059 51 13 05 – 8am-8pm – Closed 1st week Oct*. On the ground floor of one of Ostend's grand hotels (1932), this Art Deco café was once the haunt of holidaying artists and intellectuals. Good range of draught beers served as they should be, excellent hot chocolate and light meals. Terrace in summer.

ENTERTAINMENT & NIGHTLIFE

Den Artiest – *Kapucijnenstraat 13 – ☎ 059 80 88 89 – www.artiest.be – 4pm-4am*. Established within the walls of an old glassworks, this is a trendy place hosting a variety of events including live music and changing exhibitions. Spacious hall with glazed roof and gallery. Light meals. Festive ambience.

SHOPPING

Fish market – *Visserskaai – from 8am*. Array of stalls overflowing with the daily catch, mainly flat fish. Most of them are run by the wives of the fishermen.

EVENTS AND FESTIVALS

Festivals – In 1896 James Ensor was one of the promoters of the **"Dead Rat Ball"**, a name chosen in memory of a Montmartre café called Le Rat Mort.
This elegant annual event takes place on a Saturday in the Casino-Kursaal and is attended by enthusiastic crowds of people dressed up in costumes and masks centering on a particular theme.
Other unusual events held every year include the Blessing of the Sea with a historical procession and the **Theater aan Zee** Festival (music and drama in various locations around town).

James Ensorhuis

Jun-Sept: Wed-Mon 10am-noon, 2pm-5pm; Oct-May: Sat, Sun, public holidays 2pm-5pm. Closed 1 Jan, 25 Dec. €2. ☎ 059 80 53 35.
The inside of Ensor's home has been returned to its original state and turned into a museum. The entrance is through a seashell shop once run by his aunt and uncle. The artist's studio is on the second floor.

IJslandvaarder Amandine

Opposite the station. Mid-Apr – early Nov: 10am (Mon 2pm)-7pm. €2.50 ☎ 059 23 43 01.
In 1995 the *Amandine* undertook her final voyage to fish the seas off Iceland. Saved from being broken up and fully restored, this last of her kind now houses a small interactive museum. Photographs and audiovisual presentations give a good idea of what life was like aboard ship.

JAMES ENSOR (1860-1949)

Born in Ostend to an English father and a Flemish mother, this solitary genius rarely left his native town and was recognised only much later by his contemporaries as one of the greatest painters of the late 19C. Ensor painted initially in dark tones; later his palette brightened. Between 1883 and 1892 he used violent colours and a technique already tending towards Expressionism to illustrate macabre or satirical subjects which met with little public success. Ensor created an imaginary fantastic world of carnival, teeming with masked characters and skeletons, which paved the way for Surrealism.

L'Intrigue, James Ensor.

Museum voor Schone Kunsten, Antwerpen/BRIDGEMAN/GIRAUDON © ADAGP 2003

Opleidingszeilschip Mercator

Jul-Aug: 10am-6pm; Apr-Sept: 10am-12.30pm, 2-5.30pm; Oct-Mar: Sat, Sun 2-4.30pm. Closed 1 Jan, 25 Dec. €3.50. ☎ 059 70 56 54 or 02 720 01 39.

This white three-master, once an officers' training ship for the Belgian merchant navy, has been moored in the yacht harbour since 1964. Although still in working order, the *Mercator*, which 41 voyages across the world's seas in its career from 1932 to 1960, is now a floating museum. Photographs and other items recall her involvement in scientific missions, including bringing back gigantic Easter Island statues or the mortal remains of Father Damien.

St-Petrus-en-Pauluskerk

This church was built in 1905 in neo-Gothic style and contains the mausoleum of Queen Louise-Marie.

The **Peperbus**, the bell-tower of an 18C church destroyed by fire, stands nearby.

Provinciaal Museum voor Moderne Kunst

&. *Tue-Sun 10am-6pm. Closed 1 Jan, 25 Dec. €2.50 (€5 for exhibitions). ☎ 059 50 81 18; www.pmmk.be*

This museum exhibits Belgian paintings, sculptures, ceramics and graphic art on the various floors of a former cooperative. The collections *(exhibited in rotation)* give an idea of trends in modern and contemporary art.

Expressionism is represented by the Sint Martens-Latem artists. Among the more recent movements on display are abstract art, pop art and conceptual art. The museum also hosts temporary exhibitions with a national or international background.

Excursions

Stene

3km/2mi S by N 33.

The all white **St-Annakerk** has a prettily proportioned exterior and a rustic interior. Only the north aisle existed in the 14C. The nave and the south aisle were added in the 17C. Now restored, the presbytery to the south was added in 1764.

Raversijde

10km/6.3mi SW by the Koningsstraat.

Openluchtmuseum Atlantikwall – This open-air museum gives visitors an opportunity to explore trenches and bunkers used in the two World Wars. Begun by the German navy in 1915, the **Aachen battery**, thanks to its exceptional location, is one of the few remnants of the German coastal defences. It was designed to protect the port of Ostend and defend it from a possible landing by Allied forces. Those parts of the battery that have survived are artillery pieces, a muni-

OOSTENDE

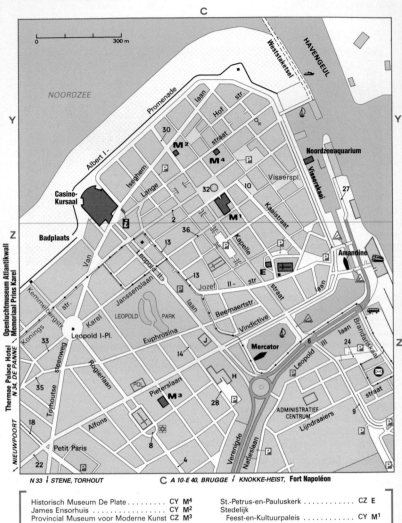

tions depot, an observation post and a control room. In 1941 the Germans returned to occupy the existing batteries along the coast. The **Saltzwedel Neu battery** was installed in the western part of the area. It formed part of the Atlantic Wall which stretched from Norway to Spain and was intended to deter an Allied invasion. Most of the bunkers are linked together by trenches or underground galleries. At the centre was the command post which issued orders to the various batteries. One of the bunkers still contained supplies when it was discovered, including crates filled with hand grenades, and gas masks. Another bunker has been reconstructed with equipment dating from the war to give an idea of the daily life of the troops. *Jul-Aug: guided tours 10.30am-6pm; early Apr to mid-Nov: 2pm-5pm (last admission 1hr before closing). €5.* ☎ 059 70 22 85.

Memoriaal Prins Karel – At the beginning of the 20C, King Leopold II purchased several plots of land in Raversijde. They form the heart of the present estate, which was extended first by Albert I, then by Prince Charles, who ruled as regent from 1944 to 1950. The villa within the grounds commemorates the prince, a more popular figure than his brother King Leopold III whose reputation had suffered because of his ambiguous behaviour during the German occupation and who felt unable to resume his throne at the end of the war.

The **Flemish Room** (Vlaamse Zaal), used during the war by the Germans as a mess hall, has an exhibition devoted to the prince-regent. Visitors can admire photographs and personal mementoes, as well as drawings executed by the Count

BASТIAN ZEVAROVI/WILHELIN

The beach at Ostend

of Flanders. In the **Prince's House**, which is of the utmost simplicity, note the two plaster sculptures attributed to Queen Elisabeth, an Empire-style armchair belonging to Napoleon, paintings and model trains. The Villa Goffinet houses changing exhibitions. *Jul-Aug: 10.30am-6pm; early April to mid-Nov: 2-5pm (last admission 1hr before. closing). €5. ☎ 059 70 22 85.*

Walraversijde – Here is a small archaeological exhibition of artefacts excavated since 1992 from the site of the medieval fishing village of Walraversijde.

Jabbeke
17km/10.5mi E by A 10-E 40. Leave the motorway at exit no 6.

Provinciaal Museum Constant Permeke★ – Permeke had this house, the Four Winds (Vier Winden), built in 1929 and he lived here for more than 20 years. The museum offers a comprehensive survey of the artist's work and contains practically all of his sculptures, some of which are displayed in the garden. *Tue-Sun. 10am-12.30pm, 1.30pm-6pm (Nov-Mar 5.30). Closed 1 Jan, 25 Dec. ☎ 050 91 12 88.*

CONSTANT PERMEKE, FLEMISH EXPRESSIONIST

The painter, sculptor and draughtsman Constant Permeke (1886-1952) belonged to the second Sint Martens-Latem School, together with Albert Servaes, the De Smet brothers and Frits van den Berghe. This group of artists took their name from a small village in the Leie region where they settled between 1905 and 1910. At the beginning of the First World War, Permeke was badly wounded and evacuated to England, where he painted his first great Expressionist works. His English landscapes can be likened to some of Ensor's thanks to his use of colour *(Harvest in Devonshire)*. Influenced by Cubism and African art, the artist gradually developed a more abstract style, especially in *About Permeke* (1922). This approach is also evidenced by many of his seascapes *(Large Seascape, 1935)* and landscapes. His huge, expressive portraits of fisherfolk *(Fisherman's Wife, 1921)* and peasants *(Peasant with Spade, 1930; The Sower, 1933)* show his close attachment to nature, exemplified by his use of warm, earthy hues. Towards the end of the 1930s, Permeke began producing nudes, some of which are quite outstanding *(The Three Graces, 1949)*. It was around the same time that he turned to sculpture *(Niobe, The Sower)*. Following his wife's death in 1948, he executed the poignant *Farewell*. At the end of his life, his palette lightened with works such as *Daily Bread and Breton Landscape*.

Gistel
9km/5.5mi S on N 33.

This little town is the scene of the annual **St Godeliva Procession**. The **church** houses the tomb of the saint, whose name means "beloved of God". Godeliva was married against her will to a lord called Bertulf, Lord of Gistel; she was later murdered and her body was thrown into a well in 1070.

Ten Putte Abbey *(3km/2mi W of Gistel)* was founded around this well. Enclosed by white walls, the abbey grounds have a charming garden which induces a contemplative mood. Visitors can see the well, the cellar where the saint is said to have been imprisoned, the corbelled chapel where she is believed to have accomplished a miracle, the abbey church, and a small museum dedicated to her memory.

Abbaye d'**Orval**★★

This abbey, tucked away in the Forest of Gaume, was founded in 1070 by Benedictines from Calabria in southern Italy. By the 12C it had become one of the most famous and richest Cistercian monasteries in Europe.

Location
Luxembourg – Maps 716 J 7 and 534 R 25.
The abbey is near the border with France, set in verdant countryside. N 88 and N 840 are the nearest main roads

Background

Legend and history – The name of the abbey (Orval means "Valley of Gold") and its coat of arms (in silver representing an azure stream from which a ring with three diamonds is emerging) recalls the legend of Countess Mathilda, Duchess of Lorraine. She was the abbey's protectress and she lost her wedding ring in a spring. It was miraculously returned to her by a trout.
The Église Notre-Dame was built at the end of the 12C in the Gothic style, with a few remaining traces of Romanesque architecture. It was altered in the 16C and the early 17C. The abbey had to be rebuilt in 1637 after being burned and pillaged by Maréchal de Chatillon's troops. The monastery was so prosperous in the 18C, however, that new construction was undertaken by the architect Dewez. No sooner had this work been finished than General Loyson's soldiers laid waste to it (1793). The abbey was sold in 1797.

The new monastery – The restoration of the monastery was undertaken in 1926 by Cistercian monks from the Abbaye de Sept-Fons in the Bourbonnais region (Auvergne, France). It was completed in 1948 and the new building was erected on the site of the earlier 18C buildings. It is plain yet elegant, built with a warm, golden stone. The layout follows the true Cistercian tradition.
The façade of the new abbey church, including a huge representation of the Virgin and Child, faces onto the retreatants' courtyard. It has a great purity of line.

Ruins
1hr. Follow the numbered tour. ♿ *Jun-Sept: 9.30am-6.30pm; Mar-Oct: 9.30-6pm; Nov-Feb: 10.30am-5.30pm. €3.50.* ☏ *061 32 51 06.*
After a film on monastery life *(20min)*, the tour takes visitors round the ruins dating from the Middle Ages to the 18C. The Gothic ruins of the **Église Notre-Dame** (Church of Our Lady) stand near the Mathilda Fountain, against a backdrop of trees and shrubs. The rose window in the north arm of the transept, the Romanesque capitals, and the Gothic and Renaissance pillars are remarkable. The tomb of Wenceslas, the first Duke of Luxembourg, is in the chancel. This chancel, with a flat Cistercian east end, was judged too small in the 17C, and an apse was added. The tour then visits the cloisters, which were rebuilt in the 14C, and the 18C undercroft. There is a garden of medicinal herbs in front of the monks' pharmacy, now a museum.

Oudenaarde★

This charming old Flemish town on the banks of the Scheldt has a particularly rich and sometimes turbulent history and a wealth of fine buildings. **Adriaen Brouwer**, whose paintings of Flemish peasant life recall those of Pieter Breughel, was born here c 1605. Famous for its tapestries in the past, today's Oudenaarde has a flourishing textile industry and is also known for "Oudenaards bruin", a dark beer once brewed by no fewer than 20 breweries.

Location
Oostvlaandern – Population 27 560 – Michelin maps 716 D3 and 533 G17 – Plan of the built-up area in the current edition of The Red Guide Benelux.
Set in the undulating countryside of the "Flemish Ardennes", Oudenaarde is easily reached from Ghent and Renaix on N 60. Access from Kortrijk and northern France by the A 14/E 17 motorway and N 459.
Stadhuis, Grote Markt 1, ☎ 055 31 72 51; www.oudenaarde.be

Background

Baldwin IV, Count of Flanders, built a fortress here in the early 11C. Oudenaarde was repeatedly attacked by the people of Ghent in the 14C and 15C; indeed they lost their famous cannon known as "Mad Meg" (Dulle Griet) here. The cannon is now in Ghent near the Vrijdagmarkt.
In 1521, Emperor Charles V besieged Oudenaarde during his conquest of the French enclave in the heart of his kingdom, the area around Tournai. While here, he fell in love with Johanna van den Geenst by whom he had a daughter, **Margaret of Parma**, who was to govern the Low Countries in the turbulent years of 1559 to 1568.
Oudenaarde suffered many other sieges, the most devastating being that inflicted by the French in 1684. The most famous date in the town's history, however, is 11 July 1708, when the Duke of Marlborough and Eugene of Savoy completely crushed the French army in one of the decisive battles of the War of the Spanish Succession.

Ch Bastin and J Evrard/MICHELIN

Oudenarde Town Hall

Walking About

Begin at Grote Markt

St-Walburgakerk
The east end of this large church rises just to the west of Oudenaarde's vast main square, Grote Markt. Its splendid tower is 90m/295ft high.

Huis van Margaretha van Parma
Margaret of Parma's House is on the southwest side of Grote Markt. It features tall crow-stepped dormer windows. To the left is the massive 11C Romanesque tower known as the **Boudewijnstoren**.

Begijnhof
The Beguine convent with its flower-filled parterres dates from the 13C. The simplicity of the chapel is very appealing.
Go along Kasteelstraat then turn left into Margaretha van Parmastraat. Cross the bridge and turn right on to Louise-Mariekaai.

OUDENAARDE

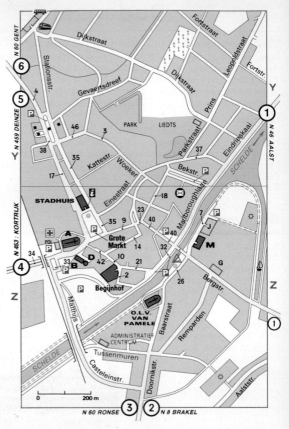

Boudewijnstoren	Z D	Huis van Margaretha van Parma	Z B
Huis de Lalaing en restauratieatelier	Z M	St.-Walburgakerk	Z A

Onze-Lieve-Vrouwekerk van Pamele*

Guided tours by prior arrangement with the Tourist Information Centre. ☎ 055 31 72 51.

A typical example of Scaldian, or Scheldt Gothic architecture, this lovely 13C church was built by Arnould de Binche. Inside, there are three aisles and a transept with an ambulatory, an unusual layout for a Belgian church. Two tombs, one from the early 16C and the other from the early 17C, can be seen at the rear of the west front.

Directory

WHERE TO EAT

☺🍴 **Wine and Dine CAFé** – *Hoogstraat 34 – ☎ 055 23 96 97 – info@derantere.be – Closed mid-Jul – mid-Aug – €32.* New restaurant with trendy decor – different levels, contemporary dark grey furniture and walls with brightly coloured paintings. Carefully prepared dishes and an animated ambience.

☺🍴 **Zwadderkotmolen** – *Zwadderkotstraat 2 – ☎ 055 49 84 95 – Closed 3 wks Sept, Christmas, 1 Jan, Tue, Wed – €36/52.* Five minutes from town on a country road, this friendly little restaurant is in an old mill; the mill machinery forms a fascinating feature of the gallery dominating the dining room. Cuisine of today. Summer terrace.

WHERE TO STAY

☺ **CESAR** – *Markt 6 – ☎ 055 30 13 81 – hotel.cesar@proximedia.be – 8 rms: €65/80 ☲ – restaurant €32.* In the heart of town, this hotel with its Victorian facade is full of character. Friendly family atmosphere, spacious, well-kept rooms, contemporary inn-restaurant and summer terrace with a fine view.

☺ **Host. La Pomme d'Or** – *Markt 62 – ☎ 055 31 19 00 – info@lapommedor.be – restaurant closed Mon – ☒ – 10 rms: €72/97 ☲* Pretty bedrooms with colour-coordinated fabrics, restaurant overlooking a swimming pool. Appetising classic menu with a local touch, and a good place to try the local brew.

Worth a Visit

Stadhuis★★★

Nov-Mar: guided tours (1hr 30min) Tue-Sat 9.30am-noon, 1.30pm-4pm, Sat 2pm-5pm; Apr-Oct: Tue-Sun 9am (Sat, Sun and public holidays 10am)-5.30pm. Closed 1-2 Jan, 24-26 Dec. €4. ☎ 055 31 72 51 (Tourist Information Centre).

Dominating the square, Oudenaarde's wonderful town hall was built 1525-30 by Hendrik van Pede, his design much influenced by other Belgian town halls such as those of Brussels and Leuven.

The town hall is built in Flamboyant Gothic style, but its spirit is already that of the Baroque. Lightness of line and rich yet exquisitely tasteful ornamentation contribute in large part to its charm.

Arcades support a projecting belfry, with a statue of an armed man on top, "Hanske de Krijger" ('the Warrior'). Graceful, slender steeples decorate the corners.

Inside, the municipal museum has a collection of furniture, sculpture and paintings, as well as a magnificent array of **silverware**. The **Council Chamber** by Van den Schelden boasts a lovely beautiful fireplace and a magnificent 16C oak doorway. The "listener" responsible for taking notes on the assembly's debates used to sit in the little lodge over the door. Note also some picturesque paintings *(The Five Senses)* by **Adriaen Brouwer**.

> ### OUDENAARDE TAPESTRIES
> During the 15C, high-warp tapestry began to replace Oudenaarde's declining cloth industry, and by the end of the century as many as 14 000 people were involved in tapestry-making. The town became a major centre for this craft in the 16C and 17C, specialising in *verdures*, in which flowers and plants form main themes of the composition.

The adjacent 14C **cloth hall** is now a concert venue and also houses a small **tapestry museum** with a number of "verdures" and other fine old tapestries.

The dolphin fountain in front of the building was a gift of the French King Louis XIV.

Huis de Lalaing and Restauratieatelier

Tue-Fri 9.30am-noon, 1.30-4pm. €1.25. ☎ 055 31 72 51 (Tourist Information Centre).

The Lalaing House owes its name to Philippe de Lalaing, the governor of the town under Charles V. Overlooking the Scheldt, the pretty building has white walls decorated in Rococo style and contains a workshop where old tapestries are restored and modern ones are woven.

Excursion

From Oudenaarde to Waregem

15km/9.3mi NW. Take N 459 towards Deinze.

In **Kruishoutem** the **Stichting (Foundation) Veranneman** *(Vandevoordeweg 2, on the Waregem road then to the left)* has a fine collection of contemporary art (Mathieu, Permeke, Vasarely, Hartung, Wunderlich, Mara, Raveel, Botero, Arman, Bram Bogart, Vic Gentils), as well as superb contemporary furniture made by Emiel Veranneman himself. The undulating park makes an impressive open-air setting for contemporary works by well-known Belgian and foreign sculptors. *Tue-Sat 2-6pm. Closed Aug, public holidays. €2.50. ☎ 09 383 52 87; www.gallery-veranneman.be*

Surrounded by its moat, the 17C **Château de Kruishoutem** has sturdy onion-domed corner towers and stands in the middle of a large park.

Take N 437.

Waregem – The Gaverbeek racecourse is where the Flanders Steeplechase takes place, one of the great crowd-pullers of the racing year.

De Panne ☼

Right on the border with France, the seaside resort of De Panne is particularly popular with French tourists. Its broad **beach**★ of fine sand is up to 250m/820ft wide at low tide and has no breakwaters, making it particularly suitable for sand-yachting. A section of the seemingly endless sand-dunes is protected as the Westhoek nature reserve, a paradise for lovers of solitary walks. Near the beach is the **memorial to King Leopold I**, marking the spot where Belgium's first sovereign landed in 1831 after travelling from England. As part of the tiny fragment of Belgium not occupied by Germany in the First World War, De Panne became the royal "capital"; in May 1940 its beach formed part of the Dunkirk perimeter from which 338 000 British and Allied soldiers were evacuated.

Location

Westvlaanderen – Population 9 760 – Michelin maps 716 A2 and 533 A16 – Town plan in the current edition of The Red Guide Benelux.

At the western extremity of the Belgian coast, only 21km/13mi from the French city of Dunkirk, and a 40min drive from Calais, De Panne is on N 34 and easily reached from the A 18/E 40 motorway (exit 1a).

🚹 *Zeelaan 21, ☎ 058 42 18 18; www.depanne.be*

Directory

WHERE TO EAT

🍽️🍷 **D'Oude Stove** – *Veurnestraat 309 – ☎ 058 42 01 05 – Closed Mon, Tue midday, 1 week Jan – €15/25.* Typical family restaurant away from the crowds, just opposite De Panne's swimming pool. Classic menu with a local touch, daily three-course specials chalked up on the board. Flemish bistro ambience and faithful clientele.

🍽️🍷 **Pauillac** – *Nieuwpoortlaan 55 – ☎ 058 42 25 86 – Pauillac@pandora.be – Closed late Nov – mid-Dec, Wed midday out of season exc school holidays, Wed eve mid-Nov – mid-Mar, Tue – €24.50/45.* Authentic traditional local cuisine, well-thought out menus, daily specials, friendly atmosphere, cheerful decor, flower-bedecked terrace in summer, altogether a great place for a meal!

WHERE TO STAY

🍷 **Cajou** – *Nieuwpoortlaan 42 – ☎ 058 41 13 13 03 – cajou.depanne @online.be – Closed Jan, 2 wks Dec; restaurant closed Sun eve, Mon exc public and school holidays – 🅿 – 32 rms: €42/72 ⌑ – restaurant €22/42.* Pleasant family hotel-restaurant just a step from the sea-dyke and close to a tram stop. Impeccable rooms, attractive dining room and small summer terrace at the front of the building. Fish dishes dominate the menu.

🍷 **Hotel Strandpark** – *Nieuwpoortlaan 151 – ☎ 058 42 02 22 – www.strandpark.be – Closed mid-Nov – Carnival exc Christmas school holidays – 🅿 – 57 rooms and studios: €56/63.* Tucked away among the sand-dunes, this seaside complex consists of a swarm of separate buildings with direct access to the beach. Family studios with kitchenette, lovely views, breakfast by arrangement. Note that the reception is not always staffed out of season.

Excursions

Westhoek

Part of the dunes to the west of De Panne form the Westhoek national nature reserve, which covers an area of 340ha/840 acres and extends up to the border. Visitors can explore the reserve on waymarked trails and there is also a programme of **guided walks**

Although marram grass and shrubs (dwarf willow, sea-buckthorn, common elder) cover most of the dunes, there is an open area in the middle that is sometimes called the Sahara.

Oosthoek

This nature reserve covers a 61-ha/150-acre area of dunes and woods southeast of De Panne. There is a visitor centre, called the "De Nachtegaal", with displays on the flora and fauna of the area and on the diverse landscapes to be found among the sanddunes.

Adinkerke
3km/1.75mi S.
The main attraction at Adinkerke is the 30ha/74-acre theme park **Plopsaland**, featuring the figures of Samson, together with Gert, his talking dog, and the imp Plop, all of them well-known favourites with Flemish children. *Apr-Oct: €19.75 (children under 1metre/c 3ft 3in: no charge). For more information call ☎ 058 42 02 02; www.plopsaland.be*

Sand-dunes at De Panne.

Philippeville

This pleasant little place began as a classic example of a Renaissance military town, built in haste in 1555 by Emperor Charles V after the nearby fortress of Mariembourghad fallen to the French the previous year. It was called Philippeville in honour of the Emperor's son, the future Philip II. Only a few underground passages and an old powder magazine survived the dismantling of the fortifications in 1860.

Location
Namur – Population 7 889 – Michelin maps 716 G5 and 534 M21.
In the Entre-Sambre-et-Meuse region, Philippeville can be reached on N 5 from Charleroi and N 97 from Dinant.
🛈 *Rue des Religieuses 2, ☎ 071 66 89 85; www.philippeville.be*

Worth a Visit

Underground passages
Jul-Aug: guided tour (1hr) 1.30-5.30pm; Sept-Jun by prior arrangement. Closed 21 Jul, Assumption, 25 Dec. €2.97. ☎ 071 66 89 85.
The old powder magazine, now the **Chapelle Notre-Dame-des-Remparts**, still has its thick walls which used to house a ventilation system.
Some of the 16C and 17C underground galleries, which extend for 10km/6.5mi under the town are open to visitors.

Excursion

Walcourt
13km/8mi N. Take N 40, then turn on to N 978 at Silenrieux.
Little Walcourt has been a fortified place since Gallo-Roman times. Nowadays the picturesque old town is famous for its annual procession in honour of Our Lady of Walcourt. The participants parade around the town (an event known as the **"Grand Tour"**), accompanied by an escort or **military march**, made up of men dressed as Napoleonic soldiers or zouaves, playing fifes and drums.

In the middle of the day, the "Jeu Scénique du Jardinet" takes place; enacted around a birch tree, it is a short play commemorating the miracle of the statue of the Virgin Mary which is said to have fled the basilica when it burned down in the 13C and to have been found later resting in a tree. Cresting a rise stands the 13C-16C **Basilique St-Materne★**, surmounted by an unusual-looking 17C bell-tower with an onion dome (rebuilt 1926).

The plain brick and grey stone **interior** is profusely furnished. The remarkable **rood screen★** (1531) is said to have been donated by Emperor Charles V. The structure is Gothic but its Renaissance decoration abounds with statues, medallions and ornamental foliage. The very simple stalls dating from the 16C have misericords carved with satirical motifs. The statue of Our Lady of Walcourt is in the north transept.

Housed in the presbytery, the **treasury★** has valuable works of art such as a 14C silver statue of the Virgin Mary, a little 13C turret-reliquary and, most outstanding of all, a 13C reliquary-cross with a delicate decoration typical of the style of the famous goldsmith Hugo d'Oignies. *Summer: 8am-6pm; Winter: 9am-4.30pm.* ☎ *071 61 13 66 (presbytery) or 071 61 25 26 (Tourist Information Centre).*

Poperinge

In the Middle Ages, Poperinge first became famous for cloth-making, then in the 15C turned to hop production. The gently undulating countryside around the town still has many hop-gardens, easily recognised by the regular lines of tall poles supporting the plants. Every three years in September the **Hop Festival** takes place with a picturesque procession. Captured by the Germans in 1914, Poperinge was swiftly retaken, to become the railhead and rest centre for this part of the Western Front. Still in use is Talbot House, the favourite meeting place for countless thousands of British troops, founded by the Revd P.B. Clayton of Toc H.

Location
Westvlaanderen – Population 19 258 – Michelin maps 716 B3 and 533 C17.
Between Ypres and the French border, the town is served by N 38.
🄱 *Grote Markt 1,* ☎ *057 34 66 76; www.poperinge.be*

Walking About

Grote Markt
Lined with outdoor cafés and restaurants in summer, Poperinge's attractive main square is dominated by the neo-Gothic town hall of 1911.
Cross the square to Vroonhof.

Hoofdkerk St.-Bertinus
This 15C hall-church has a particularly beautiful 17C rood screen, embellished with statues of Jesus and the Apostles. Note also the 18C pulpit and the richly decorated Baroque confessional.
From the square go along Gasthuisstraat, past Talbot House and the Hop Museum (see below). Continue along Casselstraat and turn right into St-Annastraat.

Weeuwhof
A little porch surmounted by a statue of the Virgin Mary leads into this 18C hospice, or "Widows' Courtyard", with picturesque cottages standing neatly around a flower garden.
Return to Casselstraat.

Onze-Lieve-Vrouwekerk
This 14C hall-church with a stone spire contains a wonderfully sculpted wooden communion pew.
Return to Grote Markt and go along G Gezellestraat, turning right into St-Janskruisstraat.

St-Janskerk
This church dedicated to St John has a massive tower similar to the bell-tower of St Bertin's. Inside, there is beautiful 18C woodwork and a much venerated statue of the Virgin Mary which is carried in an annual procession on the first Sunday of July.

Worth a Visit

Nationaal Hopmuseum
Gasthuisstraat 71.   Jul-Sept: 2-6pm; May-Jun: Sun, public holidays 2-6pm. €1.50.
☎ *057 34 66 76 or 057 34 66 77.*
The National Hop Museum is housed in an old public weighing station (stadsschaal) where, until 1968, the hops were weighed, selected, dried and pressed. Tools, machines, photographs and audio-visual presentations illustrate the cultivation and processing of hops.

Excursions

Lyssenthoek Military Cemetery
3km/1.75mi S.
More than 10 000 soldiers who perished in the First World War, many of them British, lie in this impressive, flower-bedecked cemetery.

Haringe
11km/6.75mi NW.
The interior of **St-Martinuskerk** has a certain rustic charm. The organ was made by the Ghent craftsman Van Peteghem in 1778.

Redu-Transinne

Lying in a magnificent undulating area of wooded countryside, this little village is home to a European space station for telemetry and remote satellite control. It is also a paradise for lovers of old books. About 30 second-hand booksellers have opened shops here, and in the summer and at weekends the village comes alive with crowds of people. Craft workers have also established themselves here, as have a number of restaurants.

Location
Luxembourg – Michelin maps 716 I5 and 534 P22.
The village is easily reached by the A 4/E 411 Brussels-Luxembourg motorway (exit 24) as well as on N 40.
ᴇ *Place de l'Esro 63,* ☎ *061 65 65 16.*

Worth a Visit

Euro Space Center★
Situated near E 411 motorway at exit 24. Apr-Sept: 10am-5pm; Oct-Mar: phone for details. €9.80. ☎ *061 65 64 65.*
The latest audio-visual techniques have been used to present the great adventure of space: there are films of space missions in the auditorium, an explanation of the future Columbus Space Laboratory in the holorama, a description of the history of astronomy and black holes in the planetarium, tours of several spaceships and rockets including full-scale models of Ariane 4 and 5, and to round off the visit, the thrills of the Space Show where moving seats give the audience the impression of being at the very centre of a spaceship battle. This is also a training centre for young people wishing to learn about space (courses lasting several days).

La Roche-en-Ardenne*

Long wooded spurs separated by deep valleys converge on this extremely popular summer resort, famed for the beauty of its **setting**★★ in a loop of the River Ourthe. La Roche is a splendid starting point for exploring the surrounding area with its wealth of recreational possibilities, which include an extensive network of waymarked footpaths.

Location
Luxembourg – Population 4 031 – Michelin maps 716 J5 and 534 S21 – Town plan in the current edition of The Red Guide Benelux.
In the heart of one of the loveliest parts of the Ardennes, La Roche-en-Ardenne is on N 89.
🖥 *Place du Marché 15,* ☎ *084 36 77 36; www.mid.be*

Directory

WHERE TO EAT
☺ **Le Fou du Roy** – *Rue Comte Th. D'Ursel 4 – 6940 Durbuy –* ☎ *086 21 08 68 – Closed Mon, Tue exc Jul, Aug – lunch €20 – €25.* Just a jester's hop, skip and jump from the bridge at Durbuy, the "King's Fool" is a pretty building in local style built against the walls of the castle. Delightful dining rooms one above the other and a hidden summer terrace. Wide-ranging menus featuring contemporary dishes.

☺☺ **Le Moulin** – *Place aux Foires 17 – 6940 Durbuy –* ☎ *086 21 29 70 – Closed 1st week Sept, 1st week Jan, Mon except public and school holidays – lunch €20 – €26/32.* In the heart of Durbuy, "the world's smallest town", this old mill has exchanged its waterwheel and millstones for pots and pans. Market-based cuisine served in a Mediterranean setting. Dine outside in fine weather.

WHERE TO STAY
☺☺ **Moulin de la Strument** – *Petite Strument 62 –* ☎ *084 41 15 07 – strument@skynet.be – closed Jan; restaurant closed Mon, Tue and Wed except public holidays, Jul-Aug –* 🅿 *– 8 rms: €65/71* ⌷ *– restaurant €26/35.*
Backing on to a dense forest of fir-trees, this big traditional building is a converted watermill. Friendly welcome, pleasant rooms, breakfast room with cheerful open fireplace, traditional food. The waterwheel still turns.

☺☺ **Les Tilleuls** – *Clos des Champs 11 – 6987 Hodister –* ☎ *084 47 71 31 – reservation@lestilleuls.be – Closed Jan; restaurant closed Sun eve, Mon and Tue out of season –* ✑ *– 8 rms: €55/72* ⌷ *– restaurant €34/52.* Deep in the countryside overlooking a bend in the river, this is a relaxing place to stay and to dine.
There is a spacious garden with a summer terrace and ornamental pool. Quiet rooms. Game specialities in season.

SHOPPING
Speciality – Everyone should try the famous delicacy known as "*Baisers de La Roche*" (La Roche kisses), meringues with a cream filling, which compete with the excellent local fruit tarts. The town's blue sandstone pottery is famous too.

Worth a Visit

Château
Access via a flight of stairs opposite the town hall. Jul-Aug: 10am-7pm; early Apr to mid-Nov 10am-noon, 2pm-5pm; mid-Nov to end Mar: 1.30-4.30pm, Sat, Sun 10am-noon, 1.30-4.30pm. €3.50. ☎ *084 36 77 36.*
Overlooking the town, the romantic ruins of this impressive 11C castle perch atop the rocky tree-clad spur known as the Deister.
The fortifications were strengthened after a French siege in 1680, but the castle was then demolished in the 18C on the orders of Emperor Joseph II.

Poterie-Musée Les grès de La Roche
Rue Rompré, via Place du Bronze. Jul-Aug: 10-noon, 1.30-5.30pm; Apr-Oct: Tue-Sun 10am-noon, 1.30-5.30pm; Nov-Mar: Sat, Sun and school holidays 10am-noon, 1.30-5.30pm. Closed Jan. €4. ☎ *084 41 18 78; www.mid.be/gdlr.*
The blue sandstone ware of La Roche is made here. The engraved design is highlighted in blue. The tour includes a visit to the old wood-burning kiln, the turning and decorating workshops as well as the factory museum.

Excursions

Chapelle Ste-Marguerite
Follow the River Ourthe towards Houffalize and take the road that climbs up to the left.
The chapel is on the Deister hill above the castle. A narrow path running along the crest of the spur climbs to a viewpoint with a superb **panorama**★★ over the town.

Parc "Nature et Santé" de Deister
Follow the road beyond the Chapelle de Ste-Marguerite to the top of the hill.
This 15ha/37 acre **forest park** on the Deister plateau is ideal for walks.

Houffalize
25km/15.5mi E on N 860.
This busy holiday place high up in the Ardennes (370m/1 214ft) has a lovely **setting**★ in the green valley of the eastern Ourthe. The town was destroyed during the **Battle of the Bulge** in 1944, and has since been rebuilt. The approaches from the south and the west afford pretty views over the slate rooftops.

Tours

THE UPPER OURTHE VALLEY★★
Round tour of 36km/22mi.
The eastern Ourthe, which rises near the village of Ourthe on the border with Luxembourg, and the western Ourthe, which rises at Ourt, a village south of St-Hubert, converge to form the River Ourthe near Nisramont. Upstream from La Roche-en-Ardenne, the river is more like a mountain brook, flowing vigorously through wild and beautiful countryside.
Leave La Roche-en-Ardenne to the SE on N 834 towards Bastogne.
The road climbs up to the plateau, from where there are clear views of the rolling countryside.
Turn left towards Nisramont. Cross the bridge over the Ourthe and turn left towards Nadrin.
A **marble sculpture** to the left of the road represents a stylised portico in the form of a menhir. This is the work of Portuguese sculptor Joao Charters de Almeida, created in 1991 on the occasion of the Europalia Portugal festival.
At Nadrin, turn left on to N 869. Leave the car at the Belvédère des Six Ourthe car park.

Belvédère des Six Ourthe★★
Closed Jan., Mar. €1. ☎ 084 44 41 93.
At the foot of the Hérou, a spur of schist 1 400m/4 593ft in length, there is a **tower** *(120 steps)* offering a panoramic view of the rugged and unspoiled countryside so typical of the Ardennes. The winding River Ourthe has cut a serpentine valley around wooded spurs, disappearing behind them and then reappearing again, giving the illusion of a series of lakes, hence the name of the viewpoint.

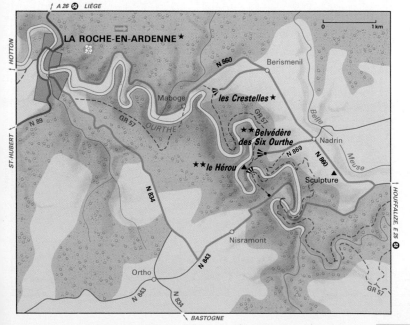

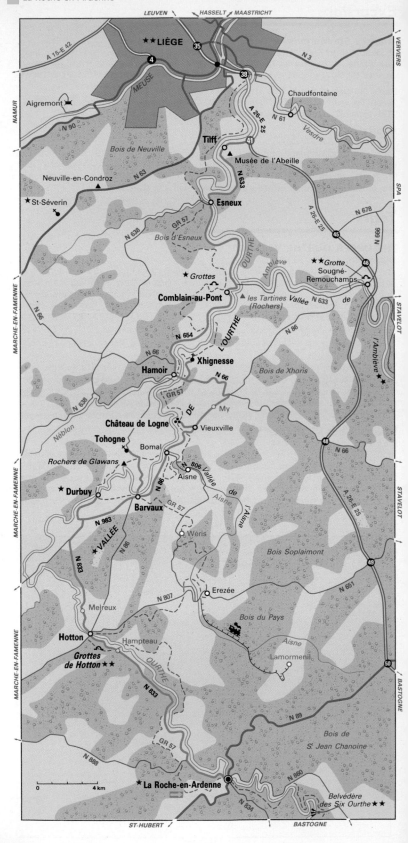

Le Hérou★★

Allow 30min there and back to have a view of the cliff.

This awesome outcrop, hidden beneath luxuriant vegetation, is crisscrossed by signposted footpaths, including the GR 57 long-distance route. The underlying rock suddenly appears in the form of a cliff dropping sharply down to the river to the east. The river at its foot runs through a wild landscape. This spot is popular with rock-climbing schools.

Return to Nadrin, then turn left towards Berismenil. Take the second turning to the left in Berismenil and head towards Crestelles.

Point de vue des Crestelles★

This is a remarkable viewpoint above a meander in the River Ourthe 200m/656ft below. It is a departure point for hang-gliding and paragliding.

Return to N 860. Go through Maboge (pretty view from the bridge), then return to La Roche-en-Ardenne.

LOWER OURTHE VALLEY★

95km/59mi – allow a day.

Between La Roche-en-Ardenne and Liège, the Ourthe flows through a delightful, tranquil valley, overlooked in places by rugged escarpments, while elsewhere the limestone has been hollowed out into caves.

The road follows the Ourthe to Melreux. After Hampteau, a path to the left leads to the Grottes de Hotton.

Grottes de Hotton★★

Jul-Aug: guided tours (1hr 15min) 10am-6pm (Apr-Oct 5pm), Nov-Mar: Sat, Sun and public holidays 2-3.30pm. €7. ☎ 084 46 60 46.

Some of these caves, which were formed by a river gradually cutting a course underground, was discovered between 1958 and 1964. Only the Grotte des Mille et Une Nuits (Cave of the Thousand and One Nights) at the end of the explored network is open to the public.

There is a great variety of concretions in the series of narrow chambers (temperature 12-16°C/54-61°F). The delicacy of their forms, ranging from strange, transparent macaroni-shapes to undulating draperies, is remarkable, but it is the splendour of their natural colours which is particularly striking. The calcite is pure white, dappled with red, brilliant orange, and delicate rose-pink from traces of iron. In the Galerie de l'Amitié (Friendship Gallery), this magical effect is accentuated by the clear reflections in the rock pools. The tour of the caves takes in a balcony 28m/92ft over a chasm, in which the roar of a distant waterfall (at the far end of the Spéléo-Club passageway) can be heard.

Hotton

The slate-roofed houses of this typical little town in the Famenne plain are strung out along the River Ourthe, which has an island midstream at this point. There is an 18C watermill upstream on the Érezée road. Downstream from the bridge is a dam.

Continue on N 833.

The imposing sandstone wall of **La Roche à Frêne** can be seen on the right. The road then runs through **Aisne**, the village after which the river is named, in which there are hot springs. Bomal lies at the confluence of the River Aisne and the River Ourthe.

Durbuy★

The road rejoins the Ourthe again near the tiny settlement of Durbuy, which lies among magnificent forests and is one of most attractive holiday places in the Ardennes. Given borough status in 1331, Durbuy was the world's smallest town with fewer than 400 inhabitants until it was merged with other communities in 1977. It has retained its old character with its maze of medieval streets, the 17C castle, the old bridge and the half-timbered corn market. The charming streets and stone houses, where many craftspeople and artists live, blend in well with the natural beauty of the site, at the foot of a spur of rock from which a spectacular geological fold, the Falize, can be seen.

Continue on N 983 to Barvaux.

Barvaux

This is another tourist centre in the Ourthe Valley. The river flows past the foot of the famous **Rochers de Glawans** downstream from here.

2km/1.3mi after Barvaux, turn left towards Tohogne.

Tohogne

This village has a well-restored **Romanesque church** with a number of fascinating works of art, including a 13C Mosan font and a 14C Calvary.

Return to N 86

Visitors with an interest in old trams or megalithic monuments should make a detour along the valley of the Aisne. In Bomal, take N 806 towards Aisne.

Aisne

This village which has given its name to the river has a number of hot springs. The gigantic sandstone wall known as the Roche à Frêne rears up on the left.

The road enters the valley of the Aisne.

Durbuy.

Erezée

The charming scenic tramway known as the **Tramway Touristique de l'Aisne** follows the Aisne through its rugged valley to the village of Forge. *Jul-Aug: Tue, Thur, Sat, Sun and public holidays 2pm, 3pm, 4pm and 5pm; end Mar to mid-Oct: Sat, Sun 2pm, 3pm, 4pm and 5pm. Journeys cost €6/10. ☎ 086 47 72 69.*
Take N 841 to Wéris.

Wéris

The charming 11C **church** dedicated to St Walburga in Wéris is built on slate columns. There is a 16C sculpted tabernacle to the right of the high altar. There are still several megaliths in Wéris, in particular a **dolmen** carved out of blocks of local pudding-stone *(northwest heading towards Barvaux, to the left not far from the road)*.
Return to Bomal via Barvaux.

Bomal

This little village is located at the confluence of the Aisne and the Ourthe. There is a fine **view★** of the valley, narrower here because of a rocky outcrop, beyond which the ruins of the Château de Logne can be seen.

Château de Logne

Jul-Aug: 10.30am-6.30pm; Apr-Oct: Sat, Sun 1-6pm (last admission 1hr before closing). €2.97. ☎ 086 21 20 33.
The castle was originally the property of the monks of Stavelot, then of the powerful La Marck family. A real "eagle's nest", it was one of the first fortresses designed for the age of firearms. It was destroyed in 1521 on the orders of Emperor Charles V. The objects excavated during digs within the walls are displayed at the **Ferme de la Bouverie** in Vieuxville. The village of Logne is a major centre for sports enthusiasts.
Turn left after My.

Hamoir

This is a small community on the banks of the Ourthe. A statue of the sculptor Jean Delcour stands in the central square; he was born here in 1627. The town hall is a charming 17C manor house, hidden in a pretty park on the left bank.
Round trip of 4km.2.5mi from Hamoir

Xhignesse

The Mosan Romanesque church of St Peter features a fine apse decorated with blind arcading surmounted by niches.
Continue on N 654.

Comblain-au-Pont

This small town lies at the confluence of the Ourthe and the Amblève, overlooked by an impressive cliff called the Tartines (Sandwiches) because the rocks appear to have been cut into slices.

The **Grotte de Comblain**★ is a cave 1km/0.75mi to the west on a little hill. *Easter-1 Nov: guided tours (1hr) 10am-5pm. €6.* ☎ *04 369 41 33.*
Continue in the same direction.

Esneux

This little town is built in tiers up a slope in a loop of the River Ourthe.
Follow N 633 to Tiliff.

Tilff

Tilff has a beekeeping museum, the **Musée de l'Abeille**, housed in an old farm which was once part of the local château. It has displays on the life of bees and the mysteries of beekeeping, collections of equipment and hives (in some the bees can be seen at work). *Jul-Aug: 10am-noon, 2-6pm; Apr-Sept: Sat, Sun and public holidays 10am-noon, 2-6pm. €2.,50.* ☎ *04 388 22 63.*

Liège★★ – *(See LIÈGE).*

Rochefort★

Overlooked by the ruins of its castle, this busy little town on the edge of the Lesse and Lomme national park is a good base for holidays and excursions into the surrounding countryside. The famous Trappist beer of Rochefort is made by the monks at the 13C Abbey of St Rémy, 2km/1.25mi from here. The famous marble quarries of St Rémy were also worked nearby (15C). In August 1792 the French general and friend of America, Lafayette, escaping the fury of the Parisian revolutionary mob, fled to Rochefort, where he stayed at the "Au Pélican" in Rue Jacquet.

Location

Namur – Population 11 767 – Michelin maps 716 I5 and 534 Q22.
On the edge of the Lesse and Lomme national park, Rochefort is served by the A 4/E 411 motorway (exit 22, then take N 911).
🚺 *Rue de Behogne 5,* ☎ *084 21 25 37; www.tourismerochefort.be*

Worth a Visit

Grotte de Lorette★

May-June: guided tour (45min/1hr) daily exc Wed 10am-11.30am, 12.30pm-5pm; July-Aug: 11am-5pm; Mar-Oct: daily exc Wed 10am, 11.30am, 1.30pm, 3pm, 4.30pm. €5.95. ☎ *084 21 20 80.*
This cave was originally hollowed out by the waters of the River Lomme and has a more rugged appearance than the one in Han. Its temperature is also lower (8°C/46°F).
The first concretions come into view at the end of a man-made corridor carved through a bed of non-porous marble. To the sound of background music, lights pick out an array of weird formations previously concealed in the shadows. The current course of the underground river and its successive riverbeds can be seen below. The little Hall of Arcades is hollowed out 80m/262ft beneath the Château de Beauregard.
The **Hall of the Sabbath** is the most impressive in terms of size, 65m/213ft by 125m/410ft. A glowing air balloon allowed to float up to the roof gives an idea of the height (85m/278ft). The tour returns via a man-made gallery opening onto a pretty view of the valley of the Lomme.

Excursions

Grupont

10km/6.25mi SE.
Grupont has a picturesque **Maison Espagnole,** also called the Burgomaster's House. Half-timbered and with jettied upper storeys, it dates from 1590.

Chevetogne

15km/9.3mi NW. Take N 949, then turn left on N 929.
Monastère de Chevetogne – An ecumenical community, celebrating the liturgy with Latin and Byzantine rites, settled here in 1939 in a 19C château. The **Eastern Orthodox Church** (1957) was built in the Novgorod Byzantine style. It is a square building with a vast narthex surmounted by a little cupola on a drum base. The walls and vaulting inside are covered with mural paintings. An effigy of Christ Pantocrator dominates the cupola. The iconostasis, which isolates the sanctuary, is decorated with icons. The monastery shop has lovely reproductions of Orthodox objets d'art.

Directory

WHERE TO EAT

◔◔ **Aux Menus Plaisirs** – *Rue du Manoir 2 – 6900 Marche-en-Famenne* – ☎ *084 31 38 71 – Closed Sun eve, Mon – lunch €20 – €26/39.* Finish off your day spent in the capital of the Famenne area by indulging in one of the "pleasurable menus" offered by this establishment, an old manor house with a delightful conservatory. Classic cuisine.

WHERE TO STAY

◔ **Le Vieux Logis** – *Rue Jacquet 71 – ☎ 084 21 10 24 – Closed Sun, mid-Jan – late Jan, mid-Sept – late Sept – 10 rms: €48/58:* The 17C "Old Lodgings" at the foot of the castle is a family hotel of character and an ideal place to stay when exploring the national park or the nearby caves.

Domaine Provincial Valéry Cousin★ – Full of trees and flowers, this vast recreation park is laid out around a château and a string of lakes. It has excellent sporting and leisure facilities and there are walks along signposted paths.

Lessive
6km/3.75mi SW, via Éprave.
The **Station Terrienne Belge de Télécommunications par Satellites** is set in the midst of woods south of the little village of Lessive. Equipped with three antennae and an impressively large radio relay tower, it has formed the link between satellites and the national telecommunications network since 1972.
The guided tour of the station ends with an exhibition on current and future communications technology, a museum on past telephone and telegraph communications, and a film of a satellite launch.

Château de Jannée
19km/12mi N on N 949, N 929 and N 4. Park: July-Aug: 10am-6pm. €2.50. ☎ 083 68 86 31.
The Château de Jannée, surrounded by its park, dates back to the 12C. Reconstructions in the 17C and 19C have given it its current appearance.

Tour

THE FAMENNE
12km/7.5mi NE on N 86.

Hargimont
The **Château de Jemeppe** was built in the 17C around a massive 13C keep.
Continue on N 86, then turn right onto a minor road.

Waha – This village has a charming sandstone **Romanesque church** dedicated to St Stephen. It was consecrated in the year 1050. There is a graceful 16C bell-tower on top of the 12C tower. The square shapes are superimposed in an imaginative way. The plain interior, with its massive pillars, houses some interesting works of art. Several gravestones can be seen in the porch. There is a beautiful Late Gothic (16C) Calvary over the rood beam. The font in the south aisle (1590) is decorated with four carved heads. The consecration stone dating from 1050 can be seen mounted on one of the

Waha – the Romanesque church.

pillars near the entrance to the chancel. Reliquaries, old books, missals and chasubles are exhibited in a display case. The church also has some beautiful statues of popular art: St Nicholas (15C), St Barbara (16C) and St Roch, in polychrome wood (17C).
Return to N 86.

Marche-en-Famenne
This is the capital of the Famenne. In 1577 Don John of Austria, Governor of the Low Countries, signed the Perpetual Edict here which confirmed the Pacification of Ghent (*see GENT*), freeing the country of Spanish troops.

Ronse

Ronse is set amid the gently rolling wooded hills of the Flemish Ardennes, near the border with French-speaking Wallonia, where the town is called Renaix. The Zotte Maandag (Mad Monday) festivities take place on the Saturday after Epiphany. The stars of this great popular festival are the masked characters called "Bommels". The Fiertel, a procession in honour of St Hermes, takes place on Trinity Sunday; the reliquary is carried along a route 32.6km/20.25mi long.

Location

Oostvlaanderen – Population 23 941 – Michelin maps 716 D3 and 533 G18.
Access to Ronse is by the A 8/E 429 Brussels-Tournai motorway. Leave at exit 31, then take N 60.
🛈 *Hoge Mote, De Biesestraat 2, ☎ 05 23 28 17.*

Worth a Visit

St.-Hermes Collegiaal

Mid-Apr – late Oct: Tue-Fri 10am-noon, 1.30pm-5pm, Sat, Sun and public holidays 10am-noon, 2.30pm-5.30pm; early Nov – mid-Apr by arrangement. €2.50. Information: Folklore Museum, Bruulplein (20m-65ft). ☎ 055 23 28 16.
The present church dates from the 15C and 16C. The south transept is devoted to the cult of St Hermes, a 3C martyr whose remains were presented by the Pope to Emperor Lothair.
The church stands above a vast and lovely Romanesque **crypt**★ (1089) with no fewer than 32 pillars. Despite restoration in the 13C and a 16C Gothic extension (16C) to the east end, the church has an overall harmony. Two side doors, which have been walled up, recall the original purpose of the building. Hermes was a famous and popular saint, drawing throngs of pilgrims, many in the belief that his relics had the power to cure mental illness.
The fine house (17C-18C) next to the church belonged to the Canon of the St Hermes chapter (Folk Museum).

Tour

FLEMISH ARDENNES

15km/9mi NW.
There is a pretty view of the town from the gardens north of Ronse (Parc de l'Arbre).
Take N 60 towards Oudenaarde, then turn left towards Kluisbergen at the top of the hill.
The **Hotondmolen** windmill stands to the right of the road near an inn, at an altitude of 150m/492ft. From the top of this squat building there is a vast panoramic view of the region and the Kluisberg *(viewing table). Wed-Mon 9am-midnight. Closed New Year. ☎ 055 21 33 05.*
Kluisberg – This hill, known as **Mont de l'Enclus** to French-speakers, rises to 141m/463ft. It lies exactly on the border between the French and Flemish-speaking regions and on the border between Oost-Vlaanderen and Hainaut. It is covered with pine woods and is very popular with visitors and holidaymakers.

St-Hubert★

This popular little upland resort stands at an altitude of 435m/1 427ft among the vast forests of the Ardennes. Its buildings cluster around the basilica, the site of pilgrimages to St Hubert, patron saint of hunters and butchers. St-Hubert was the birthplace of painter Pierre-Joseph Redouté (1759-1840), the "Raphael of Roses".

Location

Luxembourg – Population 5 737 – Michelin maps 716 J5 and 534 L22.
St-Hubert enjoys a privileged position in one of the country's loveliest regions. Access is by the A 4/E 411 Brussels-Arlon motorway. Leave at exit 25 and take N 89.
🛈 *Rue St-Gilles 12, ☎ 061 61 30 10.*

Background

The Legend of St Hubert – On Good Friday, in the year 683, **Hubert**, son-in-law of the Count of Leuven, was hunting in the forest, when his dogs raised a huge stag. The animal was almost at bay when it turned and a blinding image of Christ on the Cross appeared between its antlers. A voice then reproached St Hubert for his immoderate love of hunting, and told him to seek out his friend Lambert, Bishop of Tongres-Maastricht, to be instructed in prayer and ministry.

In Rome Hubert learned of Lambert's martyrdom and was offered the vacant bishopric by the Pope. Hubert refused it, protesting his unworthiness. An angel then descended from the heavens to give him the white stole that was the symbol of the Bishop's office, woven with gold by the Virgin Mary herself.

Once he had become Bishop of Maastricht, Hubert transferred the Episcopal See to Liège.

A town of hunters – Each year during the first weekend in September, the **International Days of Hunting and Nature** take place in St-Hubert. Hunting horns ring out from Saturday afternoon onwards. On Sunday, after a Solemn Mass and the blessing of the animals, a great historical procession takes place in the afternoon, recounting the history of the city and its abbey. More than 500 people in costume take part in the festivities. On **3 November**, St Hubert's Day, the Solemn Eucharist is followed by the blessing of animals and various festivities.

The opening of the Hunting Season at St-Hubert

Worth a Visit

Basilique St-Hubert★
Allow 30min. 9am-6pm (winter 5pm). ☎ *061 61 23 88.*
This old Benedictine abbey church was founded in the 7C. The relics of St Hubert were transferred here in the 9C, and have drawn crowds of pilgrims ever since. Several buildings have succeeded each other on this spot, and only the crypt remains of the original Romanesque church. The present Brabant Gothic church was rebuilt in 1526 after a fire (go round the south side of the church to see the Flamboyant Gothic section), but the façade was modified in the 18C. This explains why the two towers and the west front, on which the pediment depicts the miracle of St Hubert, are Baroque.

Interior★★ – The interior is impressive, being 25m/82ft high with five aisles. It has the typical layout of a pilgrimage church, with an ambulatory and radiating chapels. The first feature that strikes visitors is the colour of the stonework, a combination of pink, grey and ochre stone beneath brick vaulting dating from 1683.

Willem Geefs' St Hubert Mausoleum (1847) in the north transept depicts a slightly haughty, majestic figure. The lovely **stalls** (1733) in the chancel have panels depicting the lives of St Hubert *(right)* and St Benedict *(left)*. The statue of the Virgin Mary on the high altar is from the workshop of the Liège sculptor Delcour.

The Holy Stole woven with gold, dating from the 10C, is displayed in the south transept on the St Hubert altar. An altarpiece with 24 Limoges painted enamels based on Dürer's *Passion* is in the first chapel in the ambulatory. It was badly damaged by the Huguenots.

The Romanesque **crypt** under the chancel contains abbots' tombs. Their faces have been worn smooth by pilgrims' hands. The vaulting dates from the 16C.

Admire the Baroque organ before leaving the basilica.

Abbey Palace
On the left side of the square as you face the basilica.
Built in 1728, this palace with an elegant façade and a pediment decorated with foliage now houses the province's Cultural Affairs offices. There is some very beautiful wood panelling inside.

Directory

WHERE TO EAT

Le Cor de Chasse – *Avenue Nestor Martin 3* – ☎ *061 61 16 44* – *Closed early-mid Mar, early-mid Sep, Tue except Jul, Aug, Mon* – *lunch €10* – *€21/34* – *10 rms: €52/56* ☎ A venerable old inn close to St Gilles Church. In the hunting season, game is the great draw here, as you would guess from the inn sign. Small rooms and a lounge overlooking a little south-facing terrace.

WHERE TO STAY

du Luxembourg – *Place du Marché 7* – ☎ *061 61 10 93* – *Closed 1 week Jun, 1 week Jan, Thur except school holidays* – ▣ – *16 rms: €46/70* ☎ *restaurant €17/30*. Gracing the slope linking town hall and basilica, this establishment is full of provincial charm and has been welcoming travellers for more than a quarter of a century. Most of the very comfortable rooms have own facilities.

EVENTS AND FESTIVALS

Part of the Festival de Wallonie, St-Hubert's **Juillet Musical** (Musical July) is celebrated with concerts in the town and the nearby villages.

Excursions

Fourneau-St-Michel★★ – *(See FOURNEAU-ST-MICHEL)*

Game Park

2km/1.25mi N. May-Sept: Sat-Thur. 9am-6pm; Oct-Mar: 9am-4pm (Sat, Sun and public holidays 6pm). €3. ☎ 061 25 68 17.
Deer, moufflons (wild sheep) and wild boars can be observed along three signposted routes in this reserve. The road goes through beautiful beech and conifer forests named after King Albert and St Michael.

Val de Poix

9km/5.5mi to Smuid.
This peaceful valley is threaded by a little tributary of the Lomme. 3km/1.75mi from St-Hubert, to the left of the road by a small lake, there is an attractive old half-timbered house.

Vallée de la **Semois**★★

Rising near Arlon, the River Semois is a tributary of the Meuse, which it joins at Revin in France, where it is called the Semoy. Initially it runs through part of "Belgian Lorraine", then, downstream from Florenville, cuts through the schist outcrops of the Ardennes in a succession of striking meanders.

Location

Luxembourg-Namur –Michelin maps 716 H6, J7 and 534 P, Q, S, T24.
Close to the border with France, the Semois winds through a series of wonderfully wooded and picturesque landscapes. Access from Bouillon on N 89.

Tours

FROM CHINY TO BOUILLON★①

65km/40mi – about half a day.

Chiny

In winding its way past Chiny, the Semois penetrates the forested massif of the Ardennes for a short distance. The valley becomes deeper and narrower, and the wild scenery can only be seen from a boat.

Boat trip from Chiny to Lacuisine★

8km/5mi. Landing stage W of village, downstream from pont St-Nicolas (bridge).&. Jul-Aug: 9am-6pm; Apr-Oct: Sat, Sun 9am-6pm. €6.20. ☎ 0495 54 93 72.
The boat trip *(1hr 15min)* follows the gorge known as Paradise, past the Côte de l'Ecureuil ("Squirrel Hill") and Rocher du Pinco ("Pinco Rock") to the right and the Rocher du Hât to the left. The return trip can be made on foot *(45min)* through the woods, following the signposted paths *(route no 8)*.

Lacuisine

The river's turbulent waters calm down here, to flow gently through meadows and past an old watermill.

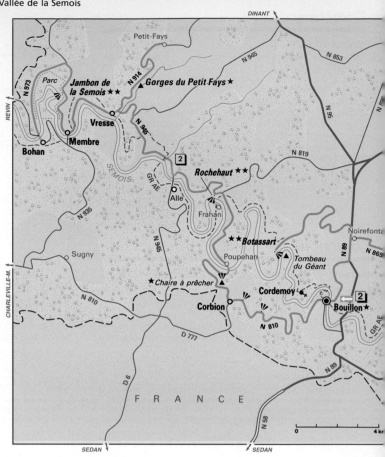

Viewpoint over the Semois Gorge★

2km/1.25mi N. Take the Neufchâteau road. Then 800m/0.5mi north of the fork for Martué, pass a narrow road on the left and take the path on the right.

Follow the white and orange markers in the woods *(15min)* to reach a promontory with a bench. There is a **view** down onto the wild wooded river banks, often covered with white flowers.

Continue to Florenville on N 85.

Florenville

High up on a sandstone outcrop near the French border, this little town is ideal as a touring centre.

From the terrace behind the east end of the church *(viewing table)* the Semois can be seen curving gently through a great sweep of well-farmed countryside.

The church was destroyed in 1940 and has been rebuilt. From the **viewpoint** at the top of the tower, there is a fine **view** over the rooftops of Florenville, the broad river valley, and the surrounding countryside *(220 steps)*. Jul-Aug: 10am-noon (Sun 11am), 2-6pm. Closed 15 Aug. €0.74. ☎ 061 31 12 29.

Take N 83

Chassepierre viewpoint★

5km/3mi from Florenville, this viewpoint (with its metal globe symbolising Peace) provides a lovely view over Chassepierre, one of the prettiest villages in Belgium, its slate-roofed houses converging on the onion-domed church (1702). The River Semois meanders through the plain not far away.

Continue on N 83. Beyond Ste-Cécile, turn right towards Herbeumont.

Before crossing the river, notice the old priory of Conques (18C) on the right of the road. In the Middle Ages this priory was a daughterhouse of Orval Abbey. It is now a hotel.

Take N 884 to Herbeumont.

Herbeumont

The ruins of the village's 12C castle stand on a bluff high above the river. It was destroyed by Louis XIV's troops.

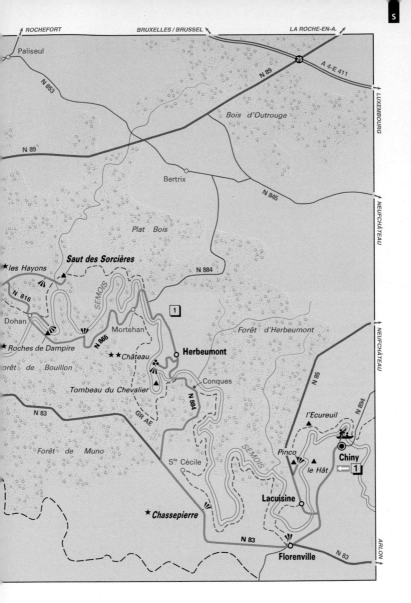

From the top, there is a spectacular **view★★** of the river's double meander encircling the **Tombeau du Chevalier**, a long wooded spur shaped like a medieval tomb, hence its name ("Knight's Tomb").

Follow the river in Mortehan. Then, before a right-hand bend as the road climbs, enjoy fine views of the wild undulating countryside. 2km/1.25mi on from a viewpoint near the **Roches de Dampire** (rocks), there is another **view★** of a beautiful loop in the River Semois.

2km/1.25mi beyond Dohan, take the road on the right to Les Hayons.

Just after Les Hayons, there is a pretty **glimpse★** of the River Semois and the valley in a great sweep of wooded countryside.

Saut des Sorcières

The "Witches' Leap" is in fact a series of little waterfalls between lakes.

Return to N 865. The road runs through Noirefontaine to Botassart.

Botassart

2km/1.25mi beyond this hamlet there is a remarkable **view★★** over one of the finest and most characteristic stretches of the Semois valley. The river forms a magnificent meander around a long wooded hill called **Tombeau du Géant** ("Giant's Tomb") because here again, like the Knight's Tomb, the hillsides resemble the sides of a sarcophagus.

Turn back to take the road down to Bouillon.

The Tombeau du Chevalier at Herbeumont.

FROM BOUILLON TO BOHAN★★ ②
53km/33mi – about half a day

Bouillon★ – *See BOUILLON.*
Leave Bouillon on the Corbion road, beyond the tunnel.
5km/3mi along the road there is a viewpoint with a fine prospect of Cordemoy Abbey. Then, 3km/1.75mi further on, enjoy the panoramic view of the wooded crests, notably the Giant's Tomb.
Follow N 810 to Corbion.

Corbion
Reached by a path, the aptly named **Chaire à Prêcher** is a natural viewpoint in the form of a pulpit. The panoramic **view★** takes in the village of Poupehan overlooking the Semois.
Take N 893

Rochehaut
There is a pretty **view★★** from this hilltop village. The river encircles a promontory surrounded by meadows. The houses of the village of Frahan are built in terraces up the hillside.
Alle, on the opposite bank, is situated at the neck of an old meander which has now been truncated by the course of the river.
Take the road on the right to Le Petit-Fays.

Gorges du Petit-Fays★
The road climbs up along the edge of this rugged gorge thickly covered in vegetation.
N 819 leads to Vresse-sur-Semois.

Vresse-sur-Semois
The road rejoins the Semois here, at its confluence with the Petit-Fays. Vresse was once an important centre of tobacco-growing. It is now popular with holidaymakers and artists. The **Musée du Tabac et du Folklore**, situated in the tourist and cultural centre describes the traditional cultivation and use of tobacco.
Typical wooden **tobacco-drying sheds** can be seen here and there on the way to Bohan.
Follow N 914 to Membre.

Membre
The 177ha/437 acre **Parc de Bohan-Membre** is near this village. This national park and nature reserve embraces many of the characteristic landscapes of the Semois valley, which can be appreciated by driving along the scenic road which runs around it.
In Membre turn right.
3km/1.75mi further on there is a beautiful **view★★** from the spot called **Jambon de la Semois**, a narrow wooded ridge.

Bohan
On a loop in the Semois, this little tourist centre is the last village in Belgium before the river crosses the border into France.

Sint-Niklaas

The capital of the intensively farmed Waasland, Sint-Niklaas is a workaday place best visited when its Thursday market, held here since the 16C, is in full swing. During the first week of September, the town plays host to the **Vredesfeesten (Festival of Peace)**, when a great many hot-air balloons are tethered on the main square, the largest in Belgium. Sint-Niklaas has a good number of Art Deco buildings to delight lovers of 20C architecture.

Location

Oostvlaanderen – Population 68 119 – Michelin maps 716 F2 and 533 J15.
Midway between Antwerp and Ghent, Sint-Niklaas is reached by the A 14/E 17 motorway (exit 15) and N 16.
🖪 *Grote Markt 45,* ☎ *03 777 26 81; www.sint-niklaas.be*

Walking About

Grote Markt

The country's largest market square covers an area of 3.19ha/7.8 acres. Some Flemish Renaissance houses stand at the east end of the square. From left to right they are the **Parochiehuis** (1663), which used to be the parish house and was then the town hall, the **Cipierage** (1662), once a prison, and next to the post office, the **Landhuis** (1637), formerly occupied by the Waasland administration.

St-Niklaaskerk (13C-18C) is set back from the square. The church contains statues by Lucas Fayd'herbe and a Crucifix attributed to Duquesnoy. *9am-11am.* ☎ *03 776 08 22*

The present town hall was built in neo-Gothic style between 1876 and 1878.

Parklaan leads to the lovely **municipal park**, in which a lake surrounds the much restored 16C **Walburg Castle**.

Worth a Visit

Mercatormuseum

Zamanstraat 49. &. *Thur-Sat 2pm (Sun 10am)-5pm. Closed 1-2 Jan, 25-26 Dec.* €2.50.
☎ *03 777 29 42.*
The Mercator Museum presents a survey of the art of cartography from Antiquity to the present day. The section devoted to the great geographer himself contains several valuable exhibits, including a terrestrial globe dating from 1541, a splendid celestial globe which has been beautifully restored (1551), the first edition of Mercator's Atlas (1585) and several Mercator-Hondius atlases.

GERARDUS MERCATOR

Gerhart Kremer – Geradus Mercator is his latinised name - was born in Rupelmonde, a small town south of Sint-Niklaas, in 1512. After studying at Leuven University, this gifted cartographer and mathematician published his first map of the Holy Land in 1537. In order to earn a living, Mercator applied himself to producing scientific instruments. In 1540 he brought out a detailed map of Flanders. His terrestrial globe divides the world into five continents: Europe, Asia, Africa, America and the South Pole. Besides these activities, Mercator was also commissioned to make a number of astronomical instruments by Charles V. Accused of heresy, he was imprisoned in Rupelmonde in 1544. Seven years later, in 1551, the cartographer produced a celestial globe featuring the 12 signs of the Zodiac and 39 constellations. It took him altogether 16 years to put the finishing touches to his map of Europe (1554). It was 15 years later that his famous planisphere saw the light of day. It was used in maritime navigation and based on a new concept in cartography known as orthomorphic projection or "Mercator's projection": the surface of the Earth is superimposed onto a cylinder, causing parallels and meridians to form a rectangular grid. His Atlas (the first volume came out in 1585) features a series of maps of France, Switzerland, the Netherlands, Germany, Italy and the Balkans. The very last tome was published in 1595. Mercator died in Duisburg, Germany, in 1594.

Collection Mercatormuseum

Mercator's Globe (1541)

Stedelijk Museum

Access by the Zwijgershoek car park on Zamanstraat. The Municipal Museum consists of a number of distinct collections.

Internationaal Ex-libriscentrum – Comparable to a library, this centre has a collection of nearly 140 000 ex-libris (16C-20C), drawn by 6 500 different artists of diverse origins. & *Visits by arrangement. €1.50.* ☎ *03 777 29 42.*

Afdeling Van Musiekdoos tot Grammofoon – This section of the museum, entitled "From Music Box to Gramophone" houses a remarkable collection including a wide range of cylindrical phonographs, record players and instruments producing mechanical music. The guided tour explains the development of these instruments and gives visitors the chance to hear some of them being played. *Apr-Sept: Tue-Sun 2pm (Sun 10am)-5pm. Closed 1-3 Jan, 25-26 Dec. €1.50.* ☎ *03 777 29 42.*

Cultuurhistorische Collecties – The **"Barbierama"** includes four hairdressing salons from the turn of the century (Art Nouveau and Classical styles) as well as many objects used in the past by barbers, surgeons and hairdressers. & *Apr-Sept: Tue-Sun 2pm (Sun 10am)-5pm. Closed 1-3 Jan, 25-26 Dec. €1.50.* ☎ *03 777 29 42.*

Boudelozaal – The Boudelo Room displays objects excavated during digs on the site of Baudelo Abbey, along with a collection of medieval tiles. Several reconstructed interiors illustrate daily life in the Middle Ages.

Salons voor Schone Kunsten

Stationsstraat 85. Thur-Sat 2pm (Sun, public holidays 10am)-5pm. Closed 1-3 Jan, 25-26 Dec. €1.50. ☎ *03 777 29 42.*

This superb town mansion was built for a textile manufacturer in 1928. The elegant salons are tastefully furnished and decorated with objets d'art from the 16C-20C. However, the museum stands out above all for its fine collection of paintings. The first salon has a number of works by famous artists: *Self-Portrait* by the Liège painter Lambert Lombard, a somewhat austere *Still-Life* by Willem Claeszoon. Heda, an *Emperor Nero Fleeing* attributed to Rubens and a pretty *Mountain Landscape* which Joos de Momper executed in collaboration with Sebastiaan Vrancx. Also on the ground floor are canvases by Evenepoel, Vogels, Laermans, Artan and J Stevens.

The first floor has works by local artists from the Waasland.

Tour

ALONG THE SCHELDT

Round trip of 35km/22mi.

Allow 2hr (not including tour of Kasteel van Bornem). Leave St.-Niklaas and head SE on N 16.

Temse

There is a fine prospect of the broad River Scheldt from the quayside of this industrial town. The river is spanned by a metal bridge, the longest in Belgium (365m/1 197ft long).

Follow N 16 and turn right after 5km/3mi towards Bornem. In the village follow signs to Kasteel van Bornem.

Kasteel van Bornem

Early Apr to mid-Oct: guided tour Sun 3.30pm, 6pm. €1.50. ☎ *064 31 08 08.*

This impressive neo-Gothic castle (1883-95) was designed by architect H Beyaert on the site of a fortress dating back to the 11C. The rooms open to the public contain family portraits, Chinese porcelain and antique furniture. The right wing is lived in by the Count of Bornem, John de Marnix de Sainte-Aldegonde. The most illustrious member of the Marnix family was **Philips Marnix van Sint-Aldegonde** (c 1538-98), a Calvinist writer and diplomat, and an ardent defender of William the Silent. He is said to be the author of the Dutch national anthem. A museum in the castle outbuildings houses a beautiful collection of European and American carriages.

Drive to St.-Amands via Zavelberg and Mariekerke.

St.Amands

This small town commands a magnificent **view★** of the Scheldt, which here forms a wide meander between lush green banks. Enjoy a pleasant stroll or bicycle ride along the dikes. A ferry will take you to Moerzeke, on the opposite bank.

Close to the river, the poet **Émile Verhaeren** (1855-1916) lies buried behind the church, next to his wife Marthe, in a black marble tomb. A few lines of verse taken from his *Hymn to the Scheldt* are engraved on the tombstone. The old ferryman's house (Het Veerhuis) has been reconstructed on the square, and on the riverside is a statue of the ferryman himself, the work of Mark Macken who inspired by Verhaeren's poem.

Verhaeren was a native of St.-Amands and his birthplace is situated at Verhaerenstraat 69. The De Leeuw House next door houses the **Provinciaal Museum Émile Verhaeren** *(first floor)*. Photographs, portraits, personal mementoes and various written documents illustrate the life and work of the great writer. The star exhibit is undoubtedly the small bronze bust of Verhaeren by Ossip Zadkine from the 1960s. & *Early Jul to mid-Sept: Daily (except Mon, Fri) noon-7pm; Apr-Oct: Sat, Sun and public holidays noon-7pm. No charge. ☎ 052 33 08 05.*

Take the road to Mariekerke again and follow the banks of the Scheldt towards Weert.

Before long the **road**★ runs along the banks of the Oude Schelde, an old arm of the Scheldt. The Kasteel van Bornem can be seen on the opposite bank. This is a picturesque, marshy area of poplars, willows and reedbeds, with orchards and fields bounded by drainage ditches. Asparagus-growing and basket-weaving are the principal activities of these wetlands. **Weert**, the main town, is very popular for Sunday outings.

The road joins N 16 which leads back to St-Niklaas.

Sint-Truiden

In the heart of a fruit-growing region famous for its apples, pears and cherries, this town grew up around an abbey founded in the 7C by St Trudo. Strategically located on the ancient highway running west from from Cologne, by the 13C Sint-Truiden had become a prosperous merchant town. Festivities take place in April when the fruit trees are in bossom.

Location

Limburg – Population 37 134 – Michelin maps 716 I3 and 533 Q17.
At the junction of N 3 and N 80, Sint-Truiden nestles among the gently undulating countryside of the Haspengouw plateau.
🛈 *Stadhuis, Grote Markt,* ☎ *011 70 18 18; www.sint-truiden.be*

Worth a Visit

Grote Markt

This vast square is dominated by the Gothic Collegiate Church of Our Lady with its 19C tower and by the town hall. This imposing but graceful building, its brick façade striped with bands of white stone, is flanked by a 17C belfry. The steps at the foot of the belfry date from 1596.

Behind the town hall is the massive Romanesque bell-tower of the town's old abbey.

April in the Haspengouw: fruit trees in blossom

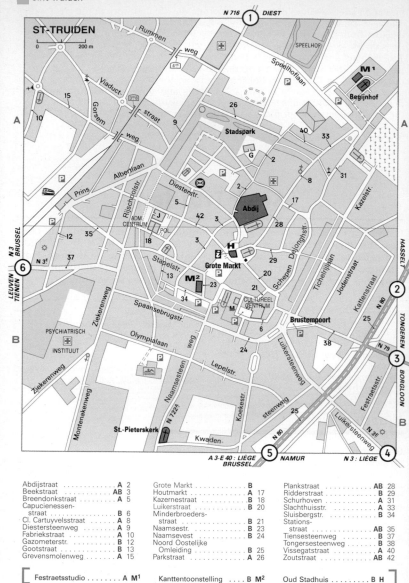

Abdij

Apr-Oct: Sat, Sun and public holidays 2-6pm. ☎ *011 70 18 18.*
Benedictines occupied this abbey until 1794. An 18C porch (on the pediment: St Trudo healing a blind woman) leads into the main courtyard. On the left, a late 18C building houses the Imperial Hall (Keizerszaal) with ceiling frescoes. The wall decoration and staircase are from later alterations. Now used for concerts, the 19C Academiezaal is particularly fine, thanks largely to its delicate stuccowork.

Begijnhof

The Beguine convent was founded in 1258. Its 16C, 17C and 18C buildings in characteristic Mosan style stand round a rectangular square, in the middle of which is a church.

Church – It dates from the 13C and 15C, and has 38 restored murals painted between the 13C and the 17C.

Studio Festraets – This contains most notably an **Astronomical Clock** built by one of the town's clockmakers. When the hour strikes, Death and a parade of medieval craftsmen make their appearance. & *Apr-Oct: Tue-Sun 1.45-4.45pm. No charge.* ☎ *011 70 18 18 (Tourist Information Centre).*

Brustempoort

These are the underground workings of the late medieval fortifications razed by the French in the late 17C. *Closed at time of going to press. Apply to the Tourist Information Centre,* ☎ *011 70 18 18.*

St-Pieterskerk
Dedicated to St Peter, this church is remarkable because of the contrasting colours in its walls (yellow ochre and brown). This late 12C building is a fine example of the Mosan Romanesque style. It has a wide doorway with a bell turret and is closed off by three apses, the main one bearing a gallery with colonnettes. Inside, the three aisles feature groined vaulting.

Kanttentoonstelling
The Ursuline convent that was once the refuge for Averbode Abbey now houses an exhibition of Sint-Truiden bobbin lace. *Sun 2pm-6pm. €1.50.* ☎ *011 68 23 56.*

Excursions

Borgloon
12km/7.5mi E on N 79 towards Tongeren.
This was once the main town in the county of Loon after which it is named. It has a charming 17C Mosan Renaissance town hall with arcades flanked by a tower. Note the statue of the Virgin Mary in a corner niche.

Close to Borgloon is the **Klooster van Kolen** *(Leave to the NE by the Kerniel road and before reaching Kerniel turn left).* This convent of the Belgian Croisiers Order is now occupied by Cistercian nuns.

The vestry contains the **reliquary of St Odile** (1292). The painted wood panels, of the Mosan School, depict the legend of the saint, which is identical to that of St Ursula. The panels were unfortunately cut up in the 19C. The vestry's mid-18C furnishings style were made in Liège and are remarkably elegant. It is also possible to visit the church, which was decorated in the 18C. *Tue-Sun 2pm (Sun 3pm)-5pm. Closed Maundy Thur, Good Fri, Easter Sat, 20 Aug, Dec-Feb (except Sun). €1.25.* ☎ *012 74 14 67.*

Kortenbos
6km/3.75mi NE on N 80 towards Hasselt.
The basilica church of Our Lady has a richly decorated Baroque interior. The nave has 17C oak panelling with integral confessionals with massive twisted columns.

Zepperen
3km/1.75mi E by ② on the town plan.
Sint-Genoveva, the church dedicated to St Genevieve, dates from the 15C and 16C and has a 12C tower at its entrance. Inside, in the south transept, there are several murals dating from 1509, representing the Last Judgement, St Christopher and the Life of St Genevieve.

Soignies ★

Narrow, winding streets converge on the famous abbey which was the reason for the town's existence and which was founded in c 650 by St Vincent Madelgaire. In honour of this saint, a great historical procession called the Grand Tour takes place on Whit Monday, covering a distance of 15km/9mi. Soignies is also known for its fine bluestone, a kind of granite, which led to the town becoming an important centre of stonemasonry.

Location
Hainaut – Population 24 572 – Michelin maps 716 F4 and 533 J19.
In the valley of the River Senne, Soignies is on N 6 and N 55.
🛈 *Rue du Lombard 2,* ☎ *067 34 73 76.*

Worth a Visit

Collégiale St-Vincent★★
Apr-Sept: 7.30am-6pm; Oct-Mar: 8am-5pm, Sun 2-6pm. ☎ *067 33 12 10.*
The construction of this great collegiate church began in c 965 with the two opposite ends, narthex and chancel, in Carolingian style, continued in the 11C in Scaldian Romanesque style, and was completed in the 13C with the construction of the Gothic west tower. The result is a forbidding building of sandstone ashlar, soberly decorated with pilaster-strips. Its layout in the shape of a Latin cross is arranged around the square transept crossing, which is decorated with pinnacles. Over the centuries, various sections have been added to the main building, including early 13C cloisters (of which only sections survive, with exposed timberwork) and the 15C Gothic St Hubert's Chapel. Both lie on the south side of the church.

Ch Bastin and J Evrard/MICHELIN

Interior of the Collégiale St-Vincent.

Interior *(entrance via the north aisle)* – The nave (20m/66ft high) is impressive with its alternating round and trefoil pillars, its vast galleries opening onto rounded arches of the same size, and its Romanesque rafters which replaced the Gothic vaulting during restoration in 1898 and were intended to return the church to its original appearance. Only the side aisles and the transept crossing have kept their original vaulting. The furnishings date mainly from the 17C and the Renaissance and Baroque styles predominate. This is evident in the ambo, a sort of rood screen concealing the chancel and set between the huge pillars behind the transept crossing. Its design, consisting of three flattened arches supporting a gallery, is Renaissance in style whereas its statues and decorative features are markedly Baroque. Note the superb statue of the Virgin Mary suckling the Infant Jesus in the niche on the south altar. It is made of painted white stone and dates from the 14C. Beyond the traceried door is the chancel, and behind the ambo gallery is a huge white marble low relief representing the Resurrection of Christ. Behind the high altar is a cupboard containing the St Vincent reliquary and the 19C reliquary containing the saint's head. Both of them can be brought down onto the high altar using an ingenious piece of machinery.

In the ambulatory on the south side of the chancel is a niche containing an 15C stone **Entombment** with expressive faces. The statue stands out against the remains of a painted background illustrating a scene from Christ's Passion.

Treasury – There are some 250 items in the church treasury including reliquaries, chalices, monstrances, church plate and vestments. They are displayed in the cloisters and the former chapterhouse, now a museum.

Near the church, the **old cemetery** (vieux cimetière) with its Romanesque/Gothic chapel *(access via Rue Henry-Leroy)* has been turned into a public park. It was once the last resting place of local people and is filled with gravestones and funerary monuments, the oldest of which date from the 14C. Note a 17C calvary and the Baroque gateway (at the end of the cemetery) which were part of the ornamentation of the church for 200 years.

Excursions

Horrues
4km/2.5mi NW on N 57.
The **church** dedicated to St Martin is a pretty little 12C Romanesque building with a 13C chancel. Like the collegiate church it was built in the local sandstone. An elegant 15C sculpted stone Gothic altarpiece depicting St Hubert's vision can be seen in the south aisle.

Ecaussinnes-Lalaing
15km/9mi E.
An impressive **castle** perched on a crag overlooks the town and the River Sennette. It was built in the 12C but was later partially modified and enlarged with square and round towers.

The vast rooms have period furniture, works of art, porcelain, glass and carved mantelpieces adorned with heraldic coats of arms.

The lovely **chapel** has a *Virgin and Child* attributed to the 14C Valenciennes artist Beauneveu. The kitchen still looks much as it did in the 15C. *Jul-Aug: Thur-Mon 10am-noon, 2pm-6pm; Apr-Oct: Sat, Sun and public holidays 10am-noon, 2-6pm. €5.* ☎ 067 44 24 90.

Since 1903 a festival supper for the unmarried, called the matrimonial meal, has been held on Whit Monday on the market square at the foot of the castle.

Le Rœulx
8km/5mi S on N 55. Closed for reconstruction at the time of going to press.

The **château** of the Princes of Cro, a resplendent successor to the 15C fortress, has an elegant, 18C Classical façade in brick and stone, with numerous windows. Many famous guests have stayed here, including Philip the Good, Emperor Charles V, Philip II, and Maria de Medici.

Inside there are rooms with groined vaulting which remain from the 15C and 16C building. The collections are interesting: antique furniture, historical mementoes, objets d'art, porcelain, and paintings by old masters such as Van Dyck and Van Loo. The vast park has some magnificent trees and a beautiful rose garden.

Spa ⚕

The mother of all spa towns, this famous inland watering place lies in one of the loveliest parts of the Ardennes, amid wooded hills which take on marvellous hues in the autumn. Its wealth of recreational and leisure facilities, its network of signposted footpaths and the many attractions of the surrounding countryside ensure its continuing popularity.

Location
Liège – Population 10 312 – Michelin maps 716 K4 and 534 U20 – Town plan in the current edition of The Red Guide Benelux.

In its gloriously leafy setting, Spa is just off the A 27/E 42 motorway. From exit 8, N 629 leads to the town centre.
🛈 *Place Royale 41, ☎ 087 79 53 53; www.spa-info.be*

Special Feature

A Sparkling Guest List – Spa's waters have been known since Roman times. From the 16C onwards, the town attracted huge crowds of *bobelins* (those taking the waters, from the Latin *bibulus*, meaning great drinker). Royalty such as Margaret of Valois, Christina of Sweden, Peter the Great (whose name was given to the oldest source, or *pouhon*), and writers such as Marmontel and Victor Hugo all came here.

During the First World War Kaiser Wilhelm II established himself here with his staff, and it was here that he abdicated in 1918. Two years later the Spa Conference brought the Allies and the Germans together in the Armistice Commission.

Spa Waters – Spa has a large number of springs. In addition to the Pouhon Pierre-le-Grand and the Pouhon Prince de Condé, there are also the Géronstère, Sauvenière, Fontaine de Groosbeek, Barisart, Tonnelet, and the only one to produce still water, Source de la Reine.

The still and sparkling waters contain iron and bicarbonates and are mostly used in the treatment of rheumatism and cardiac and respiratory problems.

I. Hendrik/GLOBAL PICTURES

The Spa Quarter – Spa has particularly fine examples of late 19C and early 20C **spa town architecture**, with numerous buildings in neo-Classical and Rococo style and much use of metal structures and large-scale painted frescoes. The finest examples are the **baths** built from 1862 to 1868, the **Casino**, a 1919 replacement for the 18C "Redoute", the elegant Galerie Léopold II of 1878 on Place Royale, and the Pouhon Pierre-le-Grand in its neo-Classical pavilion of 1880. &. *Apr-Oct: 10am-noon, 2-5.30pm; Nov-Mar: 1.30-5pm, Sat, Sun, public holidays 10am-noon, 1.30-5pm. Spa water: €0.20 per glass. ☎ 087 79 53 53 (Tourist Information Centre).*

Worth a Visit

Musée de la Ville d'eaux
Avenue Reine Astrid 77 B. Jul-Sept: 2.30-5.30pm; mid-Mar to end Dec: Sat, Sun 1.30-5.30pm. €2.50. ☎ 087 77 44 86

This museum occupies the main part of the royal villa which belonged to Queen Maria-Henrietta, a Habsburg princess and the second Queen of the Belgians, who died in Spa in 1902.

It has an extensive **collection of "jolités"★**, the painted wooden objects which are a speciality of Spa. There are also documents and furniture from the baths which evoke the town's illustrious past.

Musée Spadois du Cheval
In the stables of the Maria-Henrietta Villa. Same times and charges as the Musée de la Ville d'eaux.

The Spa Horse Museum recalls the town's equestrian past, when superb horses and fine carriages graced its streets and avenues and Europe's first horse races took place.

Excursions

Promenade des Artistes★
Leave on the Sauvenière road (N 62). The suburb of Neubois, where Kaiser Wilhelm II established his headquarters in 1918, is on the left. Turn right onto the Fontaines road at the crossroads by the **Source de la Sauvenière**. The **Source de la Reine** is in the woods on the left. About 1.3km/0.75mi on from the crossroads a little stream called the Picherotte flows down to Spa. The path which follows this steeply sloping little valley, scattered with rocks and shaded by magnificent trees, is called the Promenade des Artistes.

Continue along the Fontaines road to reach the **Source de la Géronstère**.

Maison de la Nature
6km/3.7mi S in Berinzenne. Jul-Aug: Sat 2-5pm; early Mar to mid-Nov: Wed, Sun 2-5pm. €2.50. ☎ 087 77 63 00.

In the depths of the town's forest, this museum in a restored farmhouse introduces visitors to various aspects of nature including vegetation, flora, geology and forestry work. The area's wildlife is also presented in large dioramas reproducing the animals' natural habitat in the Ardennes.

Sart
5km/3.25mi NE on N 629. The market square of this little place, overlooked by austere stone houses and a 15C church tower, is embellished with a *perron*, a symbol of liberty in the Liège region. *(see LIÈGE)*

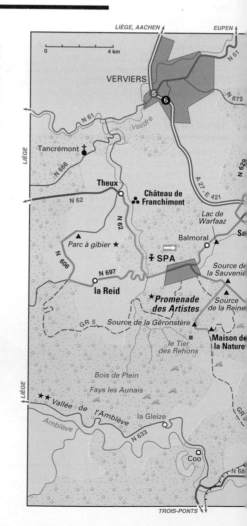

The Hogne valley
8km/5mi NW on N 62

Château de Franchimont – Set on a hill overlooking the Hoëgne Valley, the ruins of Franchimont (literally "Mount of the Franks") hark back to the Prince-Bishops of Liège who used the castle as their summer residence from the 16C onwards. It also recalls the 600 men who died trying to defend the approach to Liège from the forces of Charles the Bold in 1468.

The high and mighty walls of the keep were guarded by the pentagonal fortified enclosure with casemates at each corner.

There is a visitor centre and a small museum. On the right, a stairway leads to a panoramic viewpoint. *Apr-Sept: 9am-7pm; Oct-Mar: Sat, Sun 9am-7pm. €1.50.* ☎ *087 53 04 89.*

Theux – A 17C and 18C town hall and old houses surround the square, in which there is an 18C perron topped by a pine cone.

The **Église Saints-Hermès-et-Alexandre** is nearby. This church was preceded by a Merovingian chapel, then by a Carolingian church with a west tower, remains of which have been found. In c 1000 a Romanesque nave was built here, followed by a fortified tower a short time later. The chancel, dating from c 1500, is Gothic.

Note the sculpted Gothic stoops in the porch. The interior is unusual, with three arches separated by tall arches on pillars. This is the only hall-church with a flat Romanesque ceiling still in existence between the Loire and the Rhine. The ceiling in the nave was decorated in the 17C with 110 coffers painted with characters and scenes from the Life of Christ. The *Virgin Mary of Theux* (late 15C) is in a chapel on the north side of the chancel, and there is a fascinating Romanesque font with dragons and four heads on the corners.

La Reid
5km/3.25mi W on N 62, then take N 697.

A **Game Park★** (Parc à Gibier) has been laid out west of the village. It is in a beautiful forest setting, in which the main species of Ardennes wildlife are on show, as well as a few rare specimens of various origins.

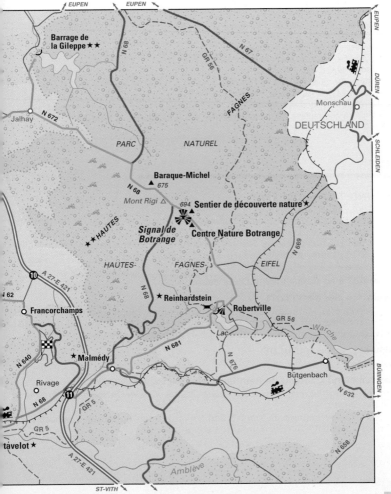

Directory

WHERE TO EAT

La Source de Barisart – *Route de Barisart 295 – ☎ 087 77 09 88 – p.servais@skynet.be – Closed mid-Mar – late Mar, early Oct – mid-Oct, Wed – lunch €19 – €20/27*. Tavern-restaurant in a 1970s building in a leafy setting. The dining room with its gallery is nevertheless rustic in style, and there is a spacious outdoor terrace for summer dining.

Rôtisserie du Porche – *Avenue Reine Astrid 48 – ☎ 087 77 33 10 – Closed Mon, Tue – ✄ – €23.55/39.91*. With its porte-cochère giving on to Spa's main avenue, this little restaurant has a landscaped terrace which is very popular on fine days. Long narrow dining room with exposed brickwork and tiled floor. Grills and casseroles.

WHERE TO EAT

Le Relais – *Place du Monument 22 – ☎ 087 77 11 08 – fr.viteux@skynet.be – Closed late Nov – mid-Dec – 12 rms: €55/67 ☕ – restaurant €17/38*. In the heart of the spa quarter, its facade a riot of flowers in summer, a human-scale establishment where a good night's sleep is guaranteed. Well-kept, functional rooms. Restaurant with emphasis on traditional dishes.

Le Menobu – *Rue du Menobu 546 – 4910 La Reid – ☎ 087 37 60 42 – menobu@spainto.be – restaurant closed 2 wks Jan, Tue, Wed exc public holidays out of season – 🄿 – 6 rms: €57/80 ☕ – restaurant €30*. Quiet inn on a country road close to the La Reid game park. The rooms to the rear have garden and countryside views. Inn-style restaurant and tea room. Outdoor dining in summer.

TAKING A BREAK

Le Clair Obscur – *Rue Delhasse 32 – ☎ 087 77 51 38 – Thur-Mon 5pm-2am*. Sample a range of French, Spanish and Australian wines in the bar of this wine restaurant established in a set of lovely vaulted cellars. Hushed atmosphere.

ENTERTAINMENT

Casino de Spa – *Rue Royale – ☎ 087 77 20 52 – 3pm-3am, Fri, Sat -4am*. Dating from 1763, this is reputed to be the world's oldest casino: gambling salon, bar, restaurant and shows. Further details from Tourist Information Centre.

LEISURE

The **Lac de Warfaaz** *(2.5km/1.5mi NE)* is popular with water sports enthusiasts. In addition, skiing and tobogganing are on offer at Le Thier des Raihons *(south)*.

EVENTS AND FESTIVALS

Among the many events, note the **Francofolies de Spa in July, the Theatre Festival in August, the Autumn Music Season**, and major temporary exhibitions. There is a Sunday morning flea market in the Galerie Léopold II.

Tour

A ROUND TRIP FROM SPA★

75km/47mi – allow 2hr.
Leave on N 62 SE in the direction of Malmédy.

Francorchamps

This village is known for the 7km-/4.3mi-long Spa-Francorchamps motor racing circuit, to the south. A small modern church is also interesting.

Take the motor racing circuit to Stavelot.

This **route★** goes through magnificent countryside.

Stavelot★ – *(See STAVELOT)*

From Stavelot to Malmédy take the Francorchamps motor racing circuit once more. It runs through very pretty scenery. To the left, the hills around the village of **Rivage** are still dotted with traditional half-timbered farmhouses.

Malmédy★ – *(See MALMÉDY)*

Follow N 681.

Robertville and Château de Reinhardstein★ – *(See MALMÉDY)*

After Robertville, the road crosses the Hautes-Fagnes plateau. In Jalhay, turn right to reach the Gileppe Dam.

Return to Spa by taking N 629 north and going through **Balmoral**, a suburb with luxurious villas half-concealed amid the green hills.

Stavelot★

This pleasant small town in the heart of the magnificent High Ardennes has many old houses, some of them half-timbered, as well as a number of charming little squares graced by fountains. The town grew up around an abbey, now superbly restored after three years of work. But Stavelot is most famous for its traditional carnival★★ which draws crowds of spectators every year.

Location
Liège – Population 6 501 – Michelin maps 716 K4 and 534 U20 – Local maps see Spa.
On the River Amblève, this old principality is served by the A 27 motorway (exit 11, than take N 68).
🚹 *Cour de l'Hôtel de Ville.* ☎ *080 86 27 06; www.stavelot.be*

Directory

WHERE TO EAT
🍽 **Val de la Cascade** – *Petit Coo 1 –* ☎ *080 68 40 78 – restaurant closed Tue, Wed except public holidays Oct-Mar –* 🅿 *– 20 rms: €57/73* ⊿*; restaurant €20/37.* Opposite the famous falls over which the waters of the Amblève cascade with a muted roar, plain but impeccable rooms and a restaurant with rustic decor. Copious traditional dishes, well-stocked cellar and summer terrace.

EVENTS AND FESTIVALS
Every year more than 1 500 people parade through Stavelot's streets during the extravagant Laetare Procession. The parade has a great many floats and is enlivened by hundreds of **Blancs-Moussis**, characters with long red noses and enormous white hooded costumes. Special events take place in the abbey during the summer months every year, notably the Vacances-Théâtre, the Festival of Music, and the Festival of Fairy Tale and Legend.

Walking About

Place St-Remacle
The **Fontaine du Perron** consists of a fountain and steps dating from 1769. Here, as in Liège, the fountain symbolises the town's independence.
Turn left at the bottom of the square.

Église St-Sébastien
9am-noon 2-6pm. ☎ *080 88 01 11.*
This church was built in the 18C. Its great pride is the monumental 13C **reliquary of St Remaclus★★**, of the Mosan School. Kept in the choir, it is made of gilded metal highlighted with filigree and enamels, and is flanked by statuettes of St Remaclus, St Lambert, and the Apostles (fashioned in a more archaic style). On the ends are statuettes of Christ and the Virgin Mary. On the top are scenes from the New Testament. In the church's Treasury is the 17C reliquary bust of St Poppo, the 11C abbot of Stavelot, in his right hand a model of the abbey church.
At the end of Place St-Remacle, up and to the right.

Ph. Gajic/MICHELIN

Reliquary of St Remaclus (detail)

Rue Haute
This is one of the most picturesque streets in Stavelot. It leads to a charming little square with an ancient fountain and several old half-timbered houses.

Worth a Visit

Old Abbey★
From the esplanade above the abbey there is a wonderful view down over the archaeological remains of its 11C church. Surrounding the cloister garden, the abbey buildings which were refurbished in the 18C are now occupied by a trio of museums.

Musée de la Principauté de Stavelot-Malmédy – *Ground floor.* Explanatory panels, audiovisual presentations, and 3D reconstructions evoke in a clear and captivating way key periods in the abbey's history. In the Middle Ages, under Abbot Wibald, the little principality was an important centre of Mosan culture, the works of art produced then being dispersed worldwide. & *Tue-Sun, 10am-6pm (last admission 4.30pm). Closed 1 Jan, mid-Lent, 25 Dec. €5.50.* ☎ *080 88 08 78; www.abbayedestavelot.be*

A LONG HISTORY

Founded around 650 by St Remaclus at the same time as Malmédy, Stavelot's abbey soon followed the Benedictine rule. Again like its rival Malmédy it became the seat of a little ecclesiastical principality, enjoying the same kind of political independence as the prince-bishops of Liège, bowing to no authority but that of the Holy Roman Empire. This enviable status came to an end in 1795 when it was attached to France.

Musée Guillaume Apollinaire – *1st floor.* This endearing little musuem invites visitors to explore the work of the great French poet. The "poetry room" offers the opportunity to actually hear some of his poems. & *Tue-Sun 10am-6pm (last admission 5.15pm). Closed 1 Jan, 25 Dec. €3.* ☎ *080 88 08 78.*

A FAMOUS GUEST

Guillaume Apollinaire (1880-1918) spent the summer of 1899 at Stavelot, staying in the Pension Constant, the present Hôtel Ô Mal Aimé, Rue Neuve 12. He fell head over heels in love with pretty "Marèye", Marie Dubois, and composed an acrostic poem in her honour in Walloon dialect: the original is now in the museum.

Musée du Circuit de Spa-Francorchamps – An exhibition in the vaulted undercroft of the old abbey describes the history of the motor racing circuit from 1896 to the present day. Racing cars and motorcycles, photographs, films and a model evoke great moments in the circuit's history. & *Tue-Sun 10am-6pm (last admission 5pm). Closed 1 Jan, mid-Carnival, 25 Dec. €4.* ☎ *080 88 08 78.*

Tour

THE AMBLÈVE VALLEY
46km/29mi – Allow 2 hr.

Leave Stavelot and head towards Trois-Ponts on N 68. The road skirts Trois-Ponts by the confluence of the Amblève and the Salm before reaching Coo.

The Amblève rises in the Hautes-Fagnes/Eifel nature park. Wild at first, it follows an erratic course, but later traces more gentle curves through a broad V-shaped valley between luxuriant green slopes.

Take N 633 to Coo

Coo

This lively holiday resort lies in a splendid mountain setting. It is well known for its magnificent **waterfall★**. In the 18C the River Amblève formed a long meander at this point, which erosion had worn into an almost full circle. Could the monks of Stavelot have had the idea of boring through the rock to complete the work that Nature had already begun? In any case, a waterfall eventually formed as a result of the drop in level.

There is a broad **panoramic view★** of the Amblève Valley from the tower built at the top of the Montagne de Lancre *(access by chairlift).* The Coo-Trois-Ponts electric-powered pumping stations can also be seen.

Leave Coo on N 633 towards La Gleize and Stoumont.

Shortly after **Stoumont**, a village perched high above the Amblève, the Congo viewpoint on the left gives a marvellous **prospect★** over the valley, so sparsely inhabited and thickly wooded here that in summer it resembles the tropical forest of Central Africa.

From Targnon the road follows the river until it flows into the Ourthe.

Just after Targnon, the N 645 on the left runs up the delightful **Lienne Valley**.

Continue on N 633.

Fonds de Quareux★

A little bridge under the railway line gives access to a footpath leading to the banks of the Amblève. The river rushes down here, foaming over enormous boulders of hard quartz which have broken away from the surrounding rocky massif.

Nonceveux

This community is on the south bank, tucked inside a meander. The north bank is very popular with holidaymakers in summer.

Follow the **Ninglinspo** torrent on foot *(15min; leave from the large car park on the right, just outside the town)* to reach the Chaudière, a natural basin of reddish stone with two small waterfalls.

Just before going under the Remouchamps viaduct, there is a glimpse of the Château de Montjardin on the left, perched amid the greenery and overlooking the river.

Continue towards Sougné-Remouchamps.

The waterfall at Coo

Sougné-Remouchamps

Remouchamps is a pleasant holiday location on the banks of the Amblève, where a Daisy Festival is held on the last weekend in June. Discovered in 1828 and opened to the public in 1912, its famous **caves**★★ were hollowed out of the rock by the Rubicon, a tributary of the Amblève. Visitors are taken on a fascinating tour, which ends with a boat trip. The last 80m/260ft of the gallery were blasted using dynamite. The circular entrance was once a prehistoric rock shelter. A wide corridor leads to a precipice from which a flight of steps descends to the river. Visitors pass a frozen waterfall and petrified rock pools *(gours)* in the Grand Gallery (20m/66ft high), then descend to the Rubicon beneath the vault of

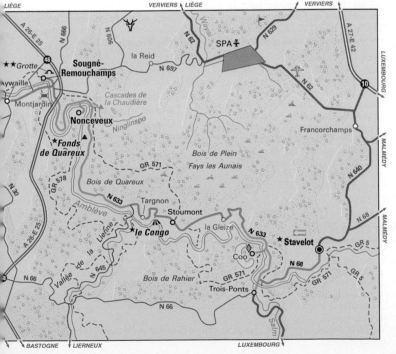

Ph. Gajic/MICHELIN

The Caves at Remouchamps.

sparkling stalactites. The tour takes them through the **"Cathedral"** measuring 100m/328ft by 40m/131ft with beautiful crystal concretions in three different colours, before reaching the Bridge of Titans. This is where the path goes down to the landing stage and the visit continues by boat for about 1km/0.75mi beneath strange, multicoloured rocks to the Precipice Chamber. *Feb-Nov: guided tour (1hr 15min) 9am-6pm; Dec, Jan: Sat, Sun and public holidays 10am-5pm. €8.50.* ☎ *04 360 90 70.*

In a commanding position downstream from **Aywaille**, there once stood the castle of Amblève, supposedly a residence of the Four Aymon Brothers.

Comblain-au-Pont and the confluence with the River Ourthe are soon reached.

Comblain-au-Pont – *(See LA-ROCHE-EN-ARDENNE, Lower Valley of the Ourthe).*

Thuin

Leafy Thuin enjoys a pretty setting★ overlooking the River Sambre. Picturesque alleyways link the upper and lower towns, and the riverside towpaths and attractive, undulating countryside make a pleasant change from the bustle of nearby Charleroi. Thuin was initially a possession of the Abbey of Lobbes, then was made part of the principality of Liège in 888. Bishop Notger fortified the town in the 10C. The St Roch military march takes place in May, as it has done for 350 years. A speciality of Thuin is the 'spantôle', a biscuit named after a cannon captured from the French in 1554.

Location

Hainaut – Population 14 589 – Michelin maps 716 F4 and 534 K20.
Midway between Charleroi and Beaumont and not far from the border with France, Thuin is a good base for exploring the attractive rural region known as the Thudinie. Crowning the promontory separating the Sambre from its tributary, the Bismelle, Thuin is reached by N 59 and N 559.
🛈 *Place Albert 2, ☎ 071 59 54 54; www.thuin.be*

Worth a Visit

Place du Chapitre
Dominated by the tall, square 17C belfry which once formed part of the town's collegiate church, the square offers a fine **view** over the winding Sambre Valley and the Lower Town with its port and barges. Further away across the Sambre the picturesque town of Lobbes can be seen, its collegiate church perched on a hilltop.

Not far from the square, in Grand-Rue, the post office is housed in the 16C refuge of Lobbes Abbey.

The St-Roch parade

Remparts du Midi

Follow the sign marked "Panorama" in Grand-Rue, then take a picturesque little street running along the 15C ramparts and passing the east end of the church.
On the left is the **Tour Notger**. This tower is all that remains of the ramparts built by the Prince-Bishop.

Hanging gardens

Drive out of the town on the Biesme road.
From the park on the right there is a pretty **view** of Thuin's ramparts, belfry and terraced gardens.

Écomusée de la Batellerie Thudo

On the right bank at the foot of the viaduct. Wed-Sun 10am-6pm. €2. ☎ 071 59 54 54.
On the banks of the Sambre in the bargees' quarter, this attractive little museum has been established aboard a barge built in Thuin in the 1950s. With a commentary supplied by former bargemen, it introduces visitors to boat-building and life on the river as it used to be. For many years Thuin's prosperity depended on its five boatyards and on inland navigation generally; as late as 1936, no fewer than 1 104 of the town's 5 000 inhabitants were boat people of one kind or another.

Excursion

Ragnies

3km S. This peaceful and picturesque little village has a pretty church dating originally from the 12C. The buildings of the old Ferme dè la Cour are now used by the **Distillerie de Bercée**, which produces a range of spirits using traditional methods, notably the famous Eau de Villé.

Tours

VALLEY OF THE SAMBRE

26km
Leave Thuin W on N 559.

Lobbes

Like the Abbaye d'Aulne, the riverside abbey at Lobbes was founded in the 7C by St Landelin. It was destroyed by the French in 1794.
The **Collégiale St-Ursmer** stands at the top of the hill, where it replaced a funerary church built by St Ursmer around 713. The present collegiate church dates back to the Carolingian period and was enlarged in the 11C. The chancel and crypt are Romanesque, as are the porch and the west tower, typical work of the Mosan School. A tower was added above the crossing in the 19C. Note the tombs of St Ursmer and St Erme in the crypt. The piers here were reworked in the 16C.
Take N 59 towards La Louvière, then turn right on a minor road towards Hourpes.

Abbaye d'Aulne★

Apr-Sept: Wed-Mon 11am-6.30pm. ☎ 071 51 52 98.

The imposing ruins of **Aulne Abbey** stand by the Sambre in a verdant setting. This monastery, founded in the 7C by St Landelin in a spot surrounded by alders (*aulnes* in French), was a daughter-house of Lobbes Abbey. A community of Cistercians from Clairvaux settled here in 1147. The abbey was burned down in 1794 and later restored to become the Herset Hospice in 1896; it was named after the founder, who was also the last abbot of Aulne.

Main courtyard – On the left are the stables and between them the 18C arcaded coach house. Next comes the 18C reception hall used by the Prince-Bishops of Liège. The guest quarters were at the back, where the abbot's palace stood before 1767; only a tower now remains.

Note, on the right, the late 18C arcades of the abbot's palace, as well as the west front of the church.

Église Abbatiale – The imposing 16C Gothic abbey church is hidden behind a Classical façade (1728). It still has its very beautiful chancel and transept; note the tracery in the window in the south transept. The north transept leads first to the vestry, then the 18C chapterhouse looking out on what little remains of the cloisters; both the vestry and chapterhouse had the monks' dormitories over them.

Take the path on the right to reach the part of the abbey where the elderly monks lived *(on the left)* and the infirmary *(at the end, on the right)*. There is a remarkable view of the majestically soaring lines of the church formed by the **east end** and **transept**★★ with their immense lancet windows.

Go back the same way towards the cloisters. On the right is one of the refectories dating from the 18C, with very pretty vaulting made of spherical bricks supported in the centre by flared columns. This was the everyday refectory, called the "lean" one because no meat was eaten here.

Continue in the same direction to Gozée.

As the road rises there is a fine view over the whole of the abbey site.

Gozée

It is worth taking a look at the **Zeupire Stone** *(on the left near a large café on the Beaumont road)*. This pink sandstone megalith weighs 20t and is thought to be the only surviving trace of an ancient cromlech.

Return the way you came and take N 59 to Thuin.

Tienen

On the Grande Gette river, Tienen lies between the open landscapes of the Hesbaye region and the Hageland ("hedge country"). A centre of cloth manufacture in the Middle Ages, the town now has the country's largest sugar refinery and is known in Belgium as "Sugartown".

Location

Vlaams Brabant – Population 31 481 – Michelin maps 716 H3 and 533 O18 – Town plan the current edition of The Red Guide Benelux.
Between Leuven and Sint-Truiden, Tienen is on the N 3 and near the E 40 (exit 25) which links Brussels and the Liège region.
🚪 *Grote Markt 4, ☎ 016 80 56 86; www.tienen.be*

Walking About

Onze-Lieve-Vrouw-ten-Poelkerk★

9am-4pm. ☎ 016 81 20 97.
The church was originally built by a pool, hence its name ("Our Lady of the Pool"). The pool was drained long ago, but one of the springs feeding it remains a place of pilgrimage. In Brabant Gothic style, its nave never completed, the great stone edifice stands on Tienen's spacious market square. The 13C chancel is plain and harmonious. The 14C transept has a square, onion-domed bell tower above it. The beautiful deep-set **doorways**★ by Jan van Osy date from 1360. Note the amusing little characters carved on the bases of the alcoves. The 14C statue of the Virgin Mary which used to decorate the central doorway was moved into the church and is now over the high altar.

From Grote Markt go along Peperstraat.

Wolmarkt

The restored Flemish Renaissance style **Van Ranst houses**, on the right at nos 19 and 21, are particularly outstanding.

Continue to the St.-Germanuskerk.

St-Germanuskerk

Built on the top of the hill, this church dedicated to St Germanus stands in the heart of the old town centre near the Veemarkt (cattle market). In the 12C and 13C it was a four-towered Romanesque basilica. Since the 16C the remains of the original forepart in typical Mosan Romanesque style have framed a massive tower, which had a carillon added to it in the 18C. The bells can be heard during **summer concerts**. The interior is Gothic. Near the central altar there is a copy of the Romanesque font now in the Musée du Cinquantenaire in Brussels. Note too the beautiful bronze lectern and, in a south chapel, the 15C *Miraculous Christ of the White Ladies*.

Worth a Visit

Stedelijk Museum Het Toreke

Tue-Sun 10am-5pm (last admission 4.30pm). Closed Christmas to New Year. €2.46. ☎ *016 80 56 86.*
Of modern design, Tienen's municipal museum is housed in a 16C prison in the courtyard of the old law courts. Archaeological finds from the Gallo-Roman period are presented in a fascinating way, while a new section is devoted to the history of the town since the 16C. Three themes are evoked: worship, traditional occupations, and popular festivals.

Excursion

Hakendover

4km W on N 3.
This ancient village is famous for its great procession of the Divine Redeemer. Accompanied by riders on horseback, the procession wends its way through the meadows and fields sown with seed which, despite being trampled down by the crowds, continue to produce good harvests.
The village church, **St-Salvatorskerk,** was founded in 690. It has retained a tower and part of the transept which are both Romanesque. The chancel was built in the 14C. The nave was enlarged in the 18C. A famous Brabant **altarpiece★** on the high altar is in wood and dates from 1400. It depicts in a lively yet elegant way the miraculous construction of the church, in 13 scenes. Three virgins undertook the construction of the church in the 7C but angels demolished it during the night. On the 13th day after Epiphany a crow showed the virgins where they should build the church. They took on 12 workers, and a 13th one, who was none other than Christ, came to join them. Thus was the church completed. *Visits by arrangement; contact Mr. Wouters, Van Oudenhovestraat 27, 3300 Hakendover,* ☎ *016 78 83 27.*

Tour

CROSSING THE LANGUAGE BORDER

13km/8mi SW on N 29.

Hoegaarden

Still just in Flemish Brabant, this town is well-known for its full-flavoured "white" beer.
There is a little Folklore Museum (Bier- en Streekmuseum) on the top floor of the 17C house known as **'t Nieuwhuys** *(Ernest Ourystraat 2), which* stands on the site of a Roman inn. The museum contains objects pertaining to local history. The old beer cellar is also open to visitors.

Jodoigne

In Walloon Brabant, Jodoigne was a fortress town in medieval times and is now an important agricultural centre.
The **Église St-Médard** was built in the late 12C, in a transitional style. The church is joined to the west by a massive square tower. The **apse** is harmonious, with a double row of arches in which the arcades are supported by colonnettes. The apse is flanked by two apsidal chapels isolated from the chancel. The chancel itself has slender colonnettes with capitals. Note the reliquary of St Médard in an alcove in the north transept, behind a grille.

Tongeren★

Together with Tournai, Tongeren is the oldest town in Belgium, originally laid out by the Romans, who suffered a humiliating defeat here at the hands of a great Gaulish chieftain, Ambiorix. It is in the **Haspengouw**, or Hesbaye in French, a gently undulating region of orchards, glorious with blossom in springtime.

Location

Limburg – Population 29 798 – Michelin maps 716 J3 and 533 R18.
Close to the linguistic border between Dutch and French and not far from the Netherlands, Tongeren is easily reached via the A 13/E 313 motorway between Liège and Hasselt. From exit 32 follow N 79.
🅱 *Stadhuisplein 9, ☎ 012 39 02 55; www.tongeren.be*

Walking About

Onze-Lieve-Vrouwebasiliek★★

Allow 2hr. 8am-noon, 1-6pm. ☎ 012 39 40 34.
A statue of Ambiorix (1866) stands in the market square. Pause to admire the impressive outline of the old church, a lovely Gothic building (13C-16C) with a striking unfinished tower-façade.
Interior – *Go along the south side of the church and enter through the little doorway.* There is a beautiful Romanesque painted wooden statue of Christ in the porch (11C). The 13C nave is supported by cylindrical pillars, which have capitals with crockets. The elegant triforium is crowned by a covered passageway. On the west side, beneath the rood screen, there is a beautiful copper door dating from 1711, and above it, an 18C Picard organ.
The finest works of art are in the chancel. The fine early-16C Antwerp wooden **altarpiece**★ on the high altar illustrates the Life of the Virgin Mary.
Note also the great paschal candlestick and the lectern, both of them made in 1372 by a Dinant coppersmith.
A miraculous **statue**★ of Our Lady of Tongeren, carved in walnut (1479), is in the north transept.
A series of digs have uncovered the remains of several medieval churches and a great many tombs. They will be gathered to form an archaeological exhibition open to visitors, which will be housed in the new treasury in the basement.

Ambiorix

TONGEREN

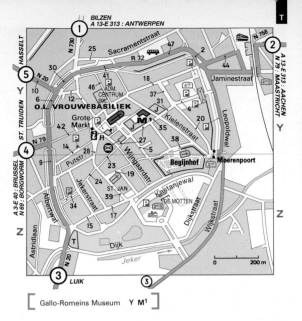

Gallo-Romeins Museum   Y M¹

A ROMAN CITY

Tongeren was originally a camp established by Caesar's lieutenants, Sabinus and Cotta. Their legions were massacred nearby by **Ambiorix**, the chief of the Eburones, who fomented a rebellion by part of Belgian Gaul against Caesar's armies in 54 BC. During the Roman occupation the developing town was called **Atuatuca-Tungrorum**, and became a staging-post on the frontier road running west from Cologne. It actually covered a much greater area at the time, as shown by the remains of the late 2C town walls covering a distance of 4.5km/3mi. Traces also exist on the Legioenenlaan to the west. The barbarian invasions in the late 3C were so hard on the community that, in the early 4C, it withdrew into a much smaller area surrounded by walls. Vestiges of these subsequent ramparts and a Roman tower built on the site of a 2C-3C Roman villa can be seen at Vrijthof, near the basilica. In the 4C Tongeren became the seat of a bishop, St Servais, but the see was subsequently moved to Maastricht for greater security. Gradually, under the protection of the principality of Liège, Tongeren began to prosper again. It organised an administrative system and built a third set of town walls in the 13C, of which some traces remain along Leopoldwal and 11 Novemberwal.

Treasury★★ – Among the treasures on show, note the 11C gospel-book covered with an ivory plaque (calvary scene), the 6C ivory diptych (St Paul), the 6C Merovingian gold clasp, the 14C monstrance-reliquary of St Ursula with an enamelled base, the reliquary-triptych of the Holy Cross (12C) in silver-gilt highlighted with enamelwork, a Head of Christ in wood (11C), the reliquary of the Martyrs of Trier (13C), and the reliquary of St Remaclus (15C), decorated with paintings.

Every seven years about 100 priests wearing centuries-old liturgical vestments carry the reliquaries from the treasury in a procession.

Cloisters★ – The charming cloisters have alternating single and double colonnettes. There are fascinating capitals on the row near the entrance. Gravestones have been set against the walls.

Follow Corversstraat and St-Catharinastraat to the Begijnhof

Begijnhof

Founded in the 13C, this convent was closed down during the French Revolution. The Onder de Linde courtyard to the west still has a certain charm with the gardens preceded by a rounded gateway. The Early Gothic **Catharinakerk** in the centre of the convent has fine furnishings and paintings. Adjoining the convent is the **Lakenmakerstoren**, a tower named after the Cloth Merchants' Guild whose role was to defend it. To the right of the tower is a chapel of 1701; to the left a 17C infirmary built in Mosan style. This imposing ensemble is prettily sited on the banks of the River Jeker, where graceful swans can be seen gliding on the peaceful waters.

Moerenpoort

May-Sept, Sat, Sun and public holidays 11am-5pm. €0.75. ☎ 012 39 02 55.
This 14C gate, once part of the medieval ramparts, is also the east entrance to the Beguine convent. It has been turned into a museum of local military history with a room devoted to town militias. There is a view of the Beguine convent, the town and the collegiate church from here.

Worth a Visit

Gallo-Romeins Museum★
& *9am (Mon noon)-5pm, Sat, Sun and public holidays 10am-6pm. Closed Christmas and New Year. €5: the price of the ticket includes a small guide to the museum.* ☎ *012 67 03 30.*

This modern Gallo-Roman Museum, attractively laid out, presents fine collections of archaeological artefacts dating from prehistory to the Middle Ages. An unusual exhibition space, recalling the strange interiors of Piranesi, centres on a mysterious dodecahedron, a Gallo-Roman object whose exact purpose has never been discovered. The basement contains prehistoric exhibits (terracotta fragments, figurines portraying divinities, glasswork, coins, jewellery) which testify to the town's past importance.

Gallo-Romeins Museum, Tongeren

Bronzework from the Roman era.

Note the superb sculpture of Jupiter defeating two men with serpents' tails and the fine bronze amphora depicting a young Nubian boy. The tour ends with the Merovingian collection.

Excursion

Alden Biesen
10km/6.25mi. Leave by ① on the town plan.
The **Commanderie Alden Biesen** (Old Rushes Commandery) north of **Rijkhoven** was founded by the Teutonic Order in 1220. The present buildings were erected or modified between the 16C and the 18C. The castle is an impressive four-sided building, flanked by towers and surrounded by a moat. The French King Louis XV attended a *Te Deum* in the church in 1747 to give thanks for victory at the Battle of Lawfeld (Lafelt) when the Austrians were defeated. There is a small exhibition in the gallery beside the church.

Tournai★★

Dominated by its huge cathedral, Tournai developed along the banks of the River Scheldt which divides it into two almost equal parts. The oldest town in Belgium (together with Tongeren), it has a prestigious history, during which it has been ruled by the Romans, Franks, English, French and Austrians. In its day Tournai was an artistic centre of great importance.

Location
Hainaut – Population 67 611 – Michelin maps 716 D4 and 533 F19.
The focal point of a mainly agricultural area, Tournai is not far from the French frontier and the great industrial conurbation of Lille-Roubaix. Access from Brussels on the A 8/E 429 motorway, from Lille on A 27/E 42.
🛈 *Vieux-Marché-aux-Poteries,* ☎ *069 22 20 45; www.tournai.be*

Background

The cradle of the French Monarchy – Tournai was already an important city in Roman times. In the 3C St Piat converted the town to Christianity. In the 5C it became the capital of a Frankish kingdom from which the Merovingian dynasty emerged. **King Clovis**, who conquered most of present-day France, was born here in 465 and made the city the seat of a bishop.

Later kings of France always considered Tournai as the cradle of their monarchy, and the city bears the royal fleur-de-lis in its coat of arms.

However, Tournai only became French in the late 12C, having been ruled during the previous centuries by the counts of Flanders and Hainaut. The 12C and 13C were great periods of construction. A few Romanesque houses, religious buildings and some parts of the second set of town walls have survived to the present day.

Tournai remained faithful to France during the Hundred Years War. The town, called the "Chambre du Roy" (King's Chamber), was isolated in a Belgium which supported the English cause. Joan of Arc invited the citizens of Tournai to come to Charles VII's coronation in Reims (1429), calling them *"gentilz loiaux Franchois"* ('noble, loyal Frenchmen'). When she was taken prisoner, Tournai sent her a purse of gold to ease her captivity.

Intense artistic activity – Already well known in the Merovingian period for its gold- and silversmiths, the city became a very important centre of art in the late Middle Ages. With the 13C reliquary of St Eleutherius, the craftsmen of Tournai once more proved their excellence in the field of metalwork, and in the 15C they were the respected rivals of the Mosan masters.

The use of local stone in building from the 12C onwards gave birth to a flourishing new school of sculpture. In the 15C fonts and funerary monuments were carved in the very finely grained grey-blue stone, or sometimes in imported white stone.

A contemporary of Van Eyck, the 15C artist **Robert Campin** (died in Tournai 1444) is thought by some scholars to be the Master of Flémalle, the anonymous artist responsible for a group of paintings only discovered around 1900. The charm of his art lies in his colours, the precision with which he depicts interiors and their furnishings, and the sense of serenity.

In more serious subjects a more dramatic mode of expression is evident, which brought Robert Campin closer to his student **Rogier Van der Weyden**. This artist was born in Tournai (1399-1464) and became the official painter of the city of Brussels in 1436.

The Belgian poet **Georges Rodenbach** was born in Tournai in 1855 but settled in Paris in 1887.

A much-disputed stronghold – From 1513 to 1519, Tournai was in the hands of King Henry VIII of England, who strengthened the defences of part of the city with a view to establishing a royal castle here. All that remains of his efforts is the keep now known as the **Tour Henri VIII**. The town then came under the rule of the Emperor Charles V and lost many of its privileges.

During a later period of religious strife, Tournai, under the heroic command of **Christine de Lalaing**, held out for two months in 1581 against Alexander Farnese. The town again became part of France during the reign of Louis XIV, from 1667 to 1709. The fortifications were reinforced and bastions added to the 13C ramparts by Vauban. Many brick and stone houses were built during this period, recognisable by their large windows and overhanging roofs.

A few of them are still standing despite the bombing of 1940, especially on Quai Notre-Dame. Tournai then became the seat of the Parliament of Flanders, representing the sovereign's justice. It fell into the hands of the Austrians after the signing of the Treaty of Utrecht (1713), was returned to the French after the 1745 **Battle of Fontenoy** (8km/5mi E), then was given back to the Austrians in 1748.

In the 18C, the copper and tapestry-making industries enjoyed a new lease of life. The porcelain from the factory founded in 1751 by François-Joseph Peterinck was very much in vogue at this time. Soft porcelain was made here with rich colours and a great variety of decoration, although the Chinese style was very popular. The works finally closed in 1891.

Highlight

CATHÉDRALE NOTRE-DAME★★★

For opening hours call ☎ 069 22 20 45 (Tourist Information Centre).

On UNESCO's World Heritage List, the most striking and unusual of Belgium's great churches stands in the centre of Tournai not far from the belfry. It served as a model, firstly for several churches in Tournai itself, then for religious buidings throughout the valley of the Scheldt, thereby giving birth to Scaldian art. The building's gigantic scale (134m/440ft long, 66m/216ft wide at the transept), together with the distinctive outline of its five massive towers, makes an unforgettable impression. The five **towers**, each one different, rise over the crossing. The oldest one, in the centre, is supported on the pillars of the crossing itself. Its purpose was to bring more light into the interior.

The nave and the arms of the transept, which have semicircular ends, date from the 12C. The slender Gothic chancel, which is taller than the nave and almost as long, replaced the Romanesque chancel in the 13C. This difference in style is evident both inside and outside the building.

Place PE Janson gives one of the best views of the whole of the cathedral.

Porte Mantile

This side door was so named to commemorate St Eleutherius' healing of blind Mantilius on this spot. The door still has some remarkable Romanesque carvings, especially on the string course running along the top (struggle between the Merovingian monarchs Sigebert and Chilpéric) and on the uprights (fight between Virtues and Vices).

Continue right round the east end of the church.

Directory

WHERE TO EAT

L'Écurie d'Ennetières – *Ruelle d'Ennetières 7* – ☎ *069 21 56 89 – Closed Carnival wk, 3 wks July, Mon and Tue eve – lunch 21€ – €29*. These old stables have been converted and are now a friendly inn-restaurant. Red brick walls, an array of marionettes, timber staircase and exposed beams produce a cheerful and lively atmosphere. Good solid food.

Le Pressoir – *Vieux Marché-aux-Poteries 2* – ☎ *069 22 35 13 – le.pressoir@infonie.be – Closed Carnival week, 3 wks Aug – lunch €25 – €29*. Attractive 18C building smothered in flowers for most of the year and looking onto cathedral and belfry. Traditional dishes, wines for the connoisseur and refined decor including antique furniture, old stone walls and high ceilings with exposed beams.

WHERE TO STAY

d'Alcantara – *Rue Bouchers St-Jacques 2* – ☎ *069 21 26 48 – hotelalcantara @hotmail.com – Closed Christmas –* 🅿 *– 15 rms: €72/104* ☑ In a central location, this old patrician house has been judiciously converted into a hotel. Spacious public rooms and bedrooms, attractive combination of historic elements and modern comforts. Stylish lounge and outdoor seating in the courtyard in summer.

Ferme du Sart – *Route de Grandmetz 13 –7911 Moustier* – ☎ *069 87 50 98 – detheux.xavier @worldonline.be – Closed mid-Jan - mid-Feb* – 🖅 *– 3 rms: €65/130* ☑ Close to the château at Moustier, this majestic 18C courtyard farmstead is reached through a monumental porch incorporating a carillon. The well-kept rooms are in an annexe. Breakfast features produce from the farm.

TAKING A BREAK

Le Contre-Quai – *Quai du Marché-au-Poisson 16* – ☎ *069 84 05 01 – 11am-1am, Sat-Mon from 5pm*. Quiet little bar on the banks of the Scheldt, favoured by local people and with a friendly atmosphere.

EVENTS AND FESTIVALS

Tournai is one of the Belgian towns where traditions are still very important. During the **Festival of the Nativity of Our Lady** (*second Sunday in September at 3pm*), which dates back to the Great Plague of 1090, the reliquary of St Eleutherius and certain items from cathedral treasury are carried in a procession.

The **Four Processions Days** combine publicity and folklore. There are giants representing figures who left their mark on the town's history such as the Merovingian ruler Childeric and King Louis XIV, a carnival parade, a procession of floral floats and a festival of military music.

Porte du Capitole

This Romanesque doorway resembles the Porte Mantile, except that it is unfortunately in very bad condition. Indeed, it is difficult to pick out the carvings of the end of the world on the string course. The archivolt is supported by two knights with a shield.

Go through the Fausse Porte or "False Doorway", the arch topped by St Vincent's Chapel, linking the cathedral with the Bishop's Palace.

West front

The west front is flanked by the Old Priory (18C) on one side and the Bishop's Palace on the other. It was altered in the 14C and masked by a **porch** which underwent alterations in the 16C. In it there are three tiers of sculptures. On the bottom row are 14C high reliefs, including three scenes depicting the story of Adam and Eve; above that are 16C low reliefs, with the Tournai procession to the left, and the conflict between Sigebert and his brother Chilpéric to the right; on the top row, there is a line of Apostles and saints dating from the 17C. There is a beautiful 14C statue of the Virgin Mary on the central pillar. It is venerated under the name of Our Lady of the Sick (Notre-Dame des Malades).

Interior

The nave is a vast structure of 10 bays. It is four storeys high and has great triple-rolled arches supported on short pillars with beautifully carved capitals. Above that, the galleries are surmounted by a triforium of round arches with a blind bay in the centre. The uppermost level is lit by tall clerestory windows. The 18C vaulting replaced a wooden ceiling. A rood screen made in 1572 cuts off the view along the nave.

The wall in the **south aisle** is covered with epitaphs.

Note the **capitals** on the pillars of the nave. They used to be painted. The carvings include plant decoration, animals, and human figures often in a rather whimsical style.

In the Chapelle St-Louis, or the Chapel of the Holy Sacrament, there is a *Crucifixion* by Jordaens as well as finely carved 18C wooden panels from an abbey (scenes from the lives of St Benedict and St Ghislain).

Crowned by a tall lantern, the **transept** is magnificent in size and splendour, creating the effect of a "cathedral within a cathedral".

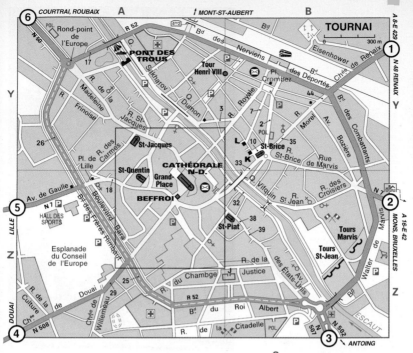

The layout is most unusual. Each transept ends in a semicircle surrounded by an ambulatory. The four-storey design echoes the design of the nave. The transept has traces of 12C frescoes and 16C stained-glass windows.

The frescoes in the **south transept** above the altar dedicated to Our Lady of Tournai represent Jerusalem the Heavenly City. The windows depict the struggle between Sigebert and his brother Chilpéric, Chilpéric according temporal power to the bishops of Tournai and, further up, episcopal privileges such as the tax on beer.

The **rood screen** is the work of Cornelis Floris II de Vriendt. It is a magnificent piece of Antwerp Renaissance art in variously coloured marble. The medallions and alabaster panels represent episodes from the Old and New Testaments.

The **chancel** (1243) is very long and has seven bays. Its delicacy contrasts with the somewhat austere solidity of the nave. French influence is very evident (Soissons).

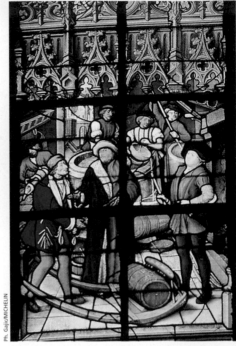

'The Tax on Beer', detail of a stained-glass window

The **ambulatory** ends in five radiating chapels. In the first chapel on the south side note the reliquary known as the "Maidens' Reliquary" (1572). In the next chapel there is a *Raising of Lazarus* by Pourbus the Elder and a painting by Coebergher. In the axial chapel there are *Scenes from the Life of the Virgin Mary* by Martin de Vos, a work that is somewhat Italian in style. Behind the rood screen in the first part of the chancel are the 18C canons' choir stalls and the sanctuary itself, with a high altar in Classical style (1727). In the chapels in the north ambulatory, there are gravestones by the Tournai School (14C-15C). Above the door leading into the reception room known as the "pilgrims' calefactory" (or 'heated room') is a painting of *Purgatory* (1635) by Rubens. Opposite it are three grisaille works by Piat Sauvage (18C), hung one above the other.

Traces of frescoes in the **north transept** depict the *Life and Martyrdom of St Margaret*. Here the stained-glass windows represent the separation of the Tournai diocese from the diocese of Noyon in France, to which it had been annexed in the 7C.

Among the capitals in the north aisle, note swans, imaginary animals, a woman being devoured by a monster and on the other side, visible only in the porch, Frédégonde and Chilpéric, and some birds drinking.

Treasury★★

The most prominent exhibits in this 15C vaulted chamber are two large reliquary chests dating from the 13C. The **Notre-Dame Reliquary** (1205) in silver and gilded copper, by Nicolas de Verdun, has marvellously formed relief figures beneath sumptuous arcading and medallions depicting the Passion of Christ, while the **St Eleutherius Reliquary** (1247) is decorated with a profusion of extraordinarily delicate statues of the Apostles set against a background of filigree, enamels and gems. Christ and St Eleutherius, who is holding the cathedral in his hand, are represented on the ends. Among the many valuable works, note in particular the *Seven Joys of Mary* (c 1546) by Pieter Pourbus, a reliquary of the True Cross called the *"Byzantine Cross"* of 5C or 6C oriental origin, an ivory reliquary chest called the *"Cologne Reliquary"* (13C) which still has traces of painting, a clasp for a cape decorated with the figure of a young woman symbolising the fortified town of Tournai (15C) and the imperial cloak worn by Charles V in the cathedral in 1531.

In the Chapelle du St-Esprit, the chapel dedicated to the Holy Spirit (17C), a long **tapestry** illustrates the Life of St Piat, the apostle of Tournai, and that of St Eleutherius, the first bishop of Tournai. It was woven in Arras and donated in 1402 by a former chaplain to the Duke of Burgundy. The 18C French Regency wood panelling in the chapterhouse has been elegantly and finely carved to depict the Life of St Ghislain.

Walking About

Grand-Place

This square is in fact triangular and is overlooked by the cathedral towers. At its centre there is a statue of Christine de Lalaing together with a fountain of unusual design. The belfry stands at one end, and the **Église St Quentin** at the other. In the circular chapel on the north side of the church is a 14C tomb and topped by a silver statue of Notre-Dame-de-la-Treille, carried in the procession which is held to celebrate the Feast of the Nativity.

The square was destroyed in 1940, but has had some beautiful structures rebuilt around it, such as the **Clothmakers' Hall** (1610) in a transitional style from Gothic to Baroque. Further to the right, there is a beautiful brick house dating from the Baroque period which used to be the tithe barn.

From Grand-Place go along Rue de l'Yser then Rue de la Tête d'Argent and turn left into Rue du Bourdon St-Jacques.

Église St-Jacques

Dedicated to St James, this church is built in Transitional style. The porch is surmounted by a massive square tower with turrets. An arcaded gallery runs along outside the nave; inside, this gallery forms an elegant traceried bridge over the crossing and is extended into the nave by a triforium.

Go along Rue du Cygne to the river. Cross the bridge and turn left.

Pont des Trous★

Part of the second set of town walls erected in the 13C, this old watergate was built to defend the entrance to the town from the River Scheldt that flows through it. From the neighbouring bridge (Boulevard Delwart) there is a fine **view★** of its three towers (rounded on this side, flat on the other) and of the cathedral. The watergate was raised 2.4m/8ft in 1948 to ease access for river traffic.

Go back the way you came and just before the Pont des Trous turn into Rue du Château.

Pont des Trous.

Tour Henri VIII

This massive 16C tower was built on the orders of Henry VIII during the English occupation of Tournai.

Go along Rue du Rempart and across Place Verte. Rue du Sondart leads to Rue Royale. Turn right, then immediately left, passing in front of a 13C/15C Gothic house.

Romanesque houses

Near the church dedicated to St Brice, two houses have kept their late-12C façades. They are a rare example of secular Scaldian Romanesque architecture, with windows divided by central colonnettes and aligned between two stone string courses.

Go along Rue des Puits d'Eau, cross the bridge and turn left. Take Rue Madame.

Église St-Piat

This 12C church was built on the site of a Merovingian basilica (6C). It was dedicated to St Piat, the first Christian missionary to Tournai, who founded the city's first church.

Go back the way you came, go along the riverside and over a small bridge. Take Rue St-Jean and then the first street on the right.

Tours Marvis and Tours St-Jean

These four towers, which were once part of the 13C fortifications, overlook pretty gardens on Boulevard Walter de Marvis.

Worth a Visit

Beffroi★

Tue-Sun 10am-noon, 2-5pm. €3. ☎ 069 22 20 45 (Tourist Information Centre).
This is the oldest belfry in Belgium, with foundations dating from the 12C. In 1294 the belfry was extended and strengthened by the addition of polygonal turrets.The upper sections were rebuilt after a fire in 1391. Until 1817, part of the belfry was used as a prison. A small exhibition and an audio-visual presentation evoke the history of this structure, which is now on the UNESCO World Heritage List.
From the first floor there is a view of the cathedral and, from the top of the tower (72m/236ft high, 256 steps), a fine **panorama** over the city. The 43-chime carillon gives beautiful **concerts**.

Musée des Beaux-Arts★

Apr-Oct: Wed-Mon 10am-1pm, 2-5.30pm; Nov-Mar: Wed-Mon 10am-noon (not Sun), 2-5pm. Closed 1-2 Jan, Good Fri, 1, 2, 11, 15 Nov, 24-26, 31 Dec. €3. ☎ 069 22 20 45 (Tourist Information Centre).
The Museum of Fine Arts was designed by the famous Art Nouveau architect **Victor Horta**, who gave it a star-shaped floor plan with all the rooms converging on the sculpture hall. This centralised layout and the huge glass roof is fronted by a curving façade surmounted by a bronze group by Guillaume Charlier called *Truth, Empress of the Arts*. In front of the left side of the museum is a sculpture of a woman by Georges Grard (20C). The museum houses works spanning the period between the 15C and the present day, in particular a collection of **Impressionist works** from the Brussels patron of the arts Henri van Cutsem.
Among the **old masters** the outstanding works are Rogier van der Weyden's *Virgin and Child*, Gossaert's *St Donatius*, and some delicate landscapes by Jan 'Velvet' Brueghel.
There is a fascinating display of all the known works by Rogier van der Weyden, using photographs in the same format as the original canvases.
From the 17C the gallery has canvases by Jordaens and a still life by Snyders. Two small pastoral scenes by Watteau represent the 18C. An entire room is devoted to the darkly Romantic historical paintings of the Tournai artist Louis Gallait (1810-87). 19C and 20C Belgian painting is well represented, with works by Henri De Braekeleer (Realism), Charles de Groux, Meunier, Joseph Stevens (an animal painter), Hippolyte Boulenger (landscape artist), Ensor and Émile Claus. Sculpture is not forgotten (works by Charlier, Rousseau and Van der Stappen).

Musée des Beaux-Arts

Ch. Bastin et J. Evrard/MICHELIN

Two of **Manet's** famous compositions stand out among the Impressionist works. They are *Argenteuil* (1874) and *At Father Lathuille's* (1879). Works by Seurat, Monet and Fantin-Latour are on display in the same room. The museum also has a large collection of drawings, including works by Van Gogh and Toulouse-Lautrec.

Opposite the art gallery is the courtyard of the **town hall** which stands on the site of the old Abbaye St-Martin (11C). The Romanesque crypt has survived. The **abbot's palace** (1763) was built to designs by Laurent Dewez. It has fine neo-Classical frontages.

Musée d'Histoire Naturelle

Apr-Oct: Wed-Mon 10am-1pm, 2-5.30pm; Nov-Mar: Wed-Mon 10am-noon (not Sun), 2-5pm. Closed 1-2 Jan, Good Fri, 1, 2, 11, 15 Nov, 24-26, 31 Dec. €2.50. ☎ 069 22 20 45 (Tourist Information Centre).

The Natural History Museum overlooks the courtyard of the town hall. Its neo-Classical interior resembles the natural history laboratories of the 19C. There are fine collections of stuffed animals in the main gallery. The square room at the end contains a series of dioramas, and watching a number of living creatures in the reptile house is a pleasant way to round off the visit (lizards, snakes, fish, tortoises etc).

Musée de la Tapisserie

  See Musée des Beaux-Arts. €2.50. ☎ 069 23 42 65.

The elegant façade of the Tapestry Museum overlooks Place Reine Astrid. The museum recalls a craft which flourished in Tournai from the 15C to the 18C, reaching a peak between 1450 and 1550; the small number of tapestries exhibited from this period demonstrate its main characteristics, which include variety in the subject matter (history, mythology, heraldry), bright colours and very elegant drawing. Numerous figures in 15C costume rival each other in magnificence in these lively, crowded compositions in which several scenes are superposed, as in the *Battle of Roncevalles* or *Famine in Jerusalem*. The high-warp **tapestry** of Tournai outdid the products from its rival Arras as well as from other Flemish workshops, being highly prized throughout Europe. The main features were the size of the tapestries, their lack of borders, the numerous figures depicted on them and the highly stylised manner.

A large part of the museum is given over to modern tapestry from the "Force Murale" group from the 1940s (Louis Delfour, Edmond Dubrunfaut and Roger Somville), as well as contemporary tapestry where the play of textures often has a sculptural quality.

Musée du Folklore

Take Réduit des Sions from Grand-Place to reach the Folk Museum. Apr-Oct: Wed-Mon 10am-1pm, 2-5.30pm; Nov-Mar: Wed-Mon 10am-noon (not Sun), 2-5pm. Closed 1-2 Jan, Good Fri, 1, 2, 11, 15 Nov, 24-26, 31 dec. €2.50. ☎ 069 22 40 69 (Tourist Information Centre).

The collections exhibited in the Spanish-style Maison tournaisienne ("Tournai House" with façades from 1673) bring to life the popular arts and traditions of Tournai and the surrounding area, as well as evoking everyday life. There are interesting reconstructions on the ground floor including an estaminet, a hosier's workshop with its knitting machine, and a room with life-size figures representing the craftsmen of days gone by. On the first floor note the Carnival Room and the pharmacy. On the second floor there is a model of 17C Tournai, a reproduction of one made for Louis XIV.

Nearby is the **Tour St-Georges**, part of the 11C and 12C town fortifications.

Musée d'Histoire et des Arts Décoratifs

Apr-Oct: Wed-Mon 10am-1pm, 2-5.30pm; Nov-Mar: Wed-Mon 10am-noon (not Sun), 2-5pm. Closed 1-2 Jan, Good Fri, 1, 2, 11, 15 Nov, 24-26, 31 Dec. €2. ☎ 069 33 23 53.

This museum has a large collection of porcelain from the royal and imperial works established in Tournai in the 18C. Note the service with bird-motifs based on the work of the 18C naturalist Georges Buffon, a commission for the Duc d'Orléans. On the first floor is a collection of Tournai coinage and some remarkable pieces of silver plate including a soup tureen and its very rare silver-gilt interior dating from 1787.

Musée d'Archéologie

Apr-Oct: Wed-Mon 10am-1pm, 2-5.30pm; Nov-Mar: Wed-Mon 10am-noon (not Sun), 2-5pm. Closed 1-2 Jan, Good Fri, 1, 2, 11, 15 Nov, 24-26, 31 Dec. €2. ☎ 069 22 16 72.

This museum occupies one of the pawnshops built by the Baroque architect Coeberger. On the ground floor there is a collection of Gallo-Roman exhibits uncovered during archaeological digs. Note the extensive collection of ceramics and glassware including a 4C baby's feeding bottle and a 3C-4C **Gallo-Roman lead sarcophagus★** found in 1989 beneath a street near the museum. There is also a **Roman well** dug out of the trunk of a hollow oak tree. The Merovingian section on the first floor contains objects found around the royal tomb of Childeric, which was discovered in 1653. Among the exhibits is the skeleton of one of the horses sacrificed during the funeral. The second floor is given over to prehistory and protohistory.

Excursions

Château d'Antoing
6km/3.75mi SE on N 507. Mid-May to end Sept: guided tour (2hr) Sun 3pm, 4pm. €3.
☎ *069 44 17 29.*
Traces of the 12C walls, the 15C keep and the Renaissance façade recall the ancient origins of this castle, rebuilt in the 19C in the neo-Gothic style. Some of the outbuildings were lent to the Jesuits when they were forced to leave France. Charles de Gaulle was a pupil here from 1907 to 1908. The **chapel** still has a rich collection of carved gravestones, particularly those of the De Melun family (early 15C). From the top of the **keep**, there is a beautiful **view** of the surrounding area. The rooms in the keep are open to visitors.

Mont-St-Aubert
6km/3.75mi N.
Very popular with visitors, this hill rises to a height of 149m/488ft. There is a fine **panoramic view**★ of the Flanders plain from the cemetery near the church. Tournai and the cathedral can just be seen to the south, behind the trees. The conurbation of Roubaix-Tourcoing can be seen on the horizon to the west.

Pierre Brunehault
10km/6.25mi on N 507; turn right on the way out of Hollain.
Near the ancient Roman road (or "Brunehault road") from Tournai to Bavay stands the Brunehault Stone, a trapezoidal menhir 4.5m/15ft high.

Leuze-en-Hainaut
13km/8mi E on N 7.
The vast **collegiate church** dedicated to St Peter was built in 1745 on the site of the old Gothic church destroyed by fire. The sobriety of the exterior is in stark contrast to the majesty of the interior. Note the beautiful 18C woodwork, especially the Louis XV panelling, the confessionals carved with various motifs, the pulpit under which St Peter in chains is represented, and the organ case.

Trois-Ponts

Close to Coo and Stavelot, Trois-Ponts is a picturesque Ardennes village, attractively situated at the confluence of the Salm and Amblève. Popular with visitors, it is an excellent starting point for exploring the riches of the surrounding countryside.

Location
Liège – Population 2 315 – Michelin maps 716 K4 and 534 U20.
In its riverside setting, this holiday village is on N 68 between Stavelot and Veilsalm.
🛈 *Place Communale 10,* ☎ *080 68 40 45.*

Excursions

VALLÉE DE LA SALM
13km/8mi to Vielsalm.
This picturesque valley was once a principality ruled by the Princes of Salm as a dependency of the Duchy of Luxembourg. The River Salm flows rapidly along a winding course through a deep steep-sided valley. The road, bordered by fine trees, runs alongside the river.

Grand-Halleux
The **Domaine de Monti** is nearby.
On the way out of Grand-Halleux, take a minor road on the left and follow signs to the Domaine de Monti.
This vast wooded estate is a wildlife park presenting the native fauna of the Ardennes, including stags, roe deer, fallow deer and wild boars. There are also mouflons, a type of wild sheep.
Take N 68.

Vielsalm
The Macralles (witches') Sabbath is on the evening of 20 July in a wood near the town. It is followed by the Bilberry Festival, which takes place the following day.
Anyone with time to spare should make a short diversion to Reuland. Continue on N 68, and at Bého turn on to N 827, then on to N 62.

Reuland

This pretty village is dominated by the ruins of its 11C castle. From the keep there is a superb **view★** of the white houses with their massive slate roofs clustering around the onion-domed church tower. Reuland is within the Hautes-Fagnes/Eifel nature park.

CIRCUIT DES PANORAMAS★

44km/27mi.
Detailed brochure available from the Tourist Information Centre

This signposted tourist route consists of two circular tours wending their way up hill and down dale and offering extensive panoramic views, now of the Amblève, now of the Salm. The scenic route known as the **"Boucle de Wanne"** to the southeast *(23km/14.5mi)* follows the lower course of the Salm. The road leaves the forest near Henumont, descends, then climbs again to Wanne amid pretty landscapes. Just before the village of Aisomont there is a dry ski slope (Val de Wanne) to the right. There then follows a descent to Trois-Ponts.

The **"Boucle de Basse-Bodeux"** *(21km/13mi)* is a winding route which climbs between the Salm and Baleur Valleys (towards Basse-Bodeux), then turns left towards Mont-de-Fosse. Beyond St-Jacques, Fosse and Reharmont, the scenic route crosses N 651 and goes on to Haute-Bodeux. Just before Basse-Bodeux, turn left. The road runs through a beautiful forest past the two reservoirs feeding the Coo/Trois-Ponts hydroelectric power station.

Return to Trois-Ponts by going down through the hamlet of Brume.

Turnhout

The main town of the Antwerp Kempen region, Turnhout's speciality is the production of playing cards. The town was part of the province of Brabant from the 12C to the 18C. Emperor Charles V made it a seigniory, which he gave to his sister Mary of Hungary. After the Treaty of Münster in 1648, Turnhout became a fiefdom held by the Orange-Nassau dynasty until 1753. The Battle of Turnhout in October 1789 during the Brabant Revolt brought Austrian rule to a temporary end. By 1790, however, the Austrians were back.

Location

Antwerpen – Population 38 518 – Michelin maps 716 H2 and 533 O15.
A stone's throw from the Dutch border, Turnhout is in the northeast of the province of Antwerpen. Access by motorway A 21/E 34 (exit 24).
🖪 *Grote Markt 44, ☎ 014 44 33 55; www.turnhout.be*

TURNHOUT

Baron Fr. Du Fourstr.	Y 2
Begijnenstr.	Y 4
Beekstr.	Z 3
Deken Adamsstr.	Z 5
Druivenstr.	Z 6
Gasthuisstr.	Z 7
Graatakker	Z 8
Guldensporenlei	Y 9
Hannuitstr.	Y 12
Hofpoort	Z 13
Kasteelstr.	Y 14
Koningin Elisabethlei	Y 16
Korte Gasthuisstr.	Z 17
Kwakkelstr.	Z 18
Mermansstr.	Z 19
Otterstr.	Z 21
Oude Vaartstr.	Y 22
Renier Sniedersstr.	Z 23
Sint Antoniusstr.	Z 25
Spoorwegstr.	Z 26
Veldstr.	Z 28
Victoriestr.	Z 29
Wezenstr.	Y 31

Cultuur- en ontmoetingscentrum		Y B
Kasteel „Hertogen van Brabant" (Gerechtshof)		Y J
Museum		Y M²
Nationaal Museum van de Speelkaart		Z M³
Taxandriamuseum		Y M¹

357

Walking About

Grote Markt

The focal point of the main square is the 15C-18C **St-Pieterskerk**. The church contains an interesting 19C pulpit, Baroque confessionals from 1740 and choir stalls dating from 1713, brought here from the old Corsendonk priory in Oud-Turnhout, east of the town.

The town hall was completed in 1961.

Go along Warandestraat, then turn immediately right into Begijnenstraat. The first street on the left leads to the castle of the Dukes of Brabant.

Kasteel Hertogen van Brabant

This solid, four-sided edifice surrounded by water dates from the 13C to 17C. In the Middle Ages it was a hunting lodge for the Dukes of Brabant, who came to hunt game in Kempen Forest. Mary of Hungary, who divided her time between Turnhout and Binche, turned it into a luxurious residence. The castle now houses the Law Courts.

An **arts centre**, De Warande, was built nearby in 1972.

Continue in the same direction.

Begijnhof

Probably founded in the 13C and rebuilt in the 16C and 17C after a fire, this charming precinct has houses arranged around a square overlooked by the Baroque church. It is now on the UNESCO World Heritage List.

In the house at no 56, there is a small **museum** devoted to life in the convent. &
Tue-Sun 2pm (Sun and public holidays 11am) -5pm. Closed 1, 2 Jan, 25, 26 Dec. €1.74.
☎ *014 43 63 35.*
Return to Grote Markt and go along Otterstraat, then by ③ on the town plan.

Windmolen

This pretty windmill, called "De Grote Bentel", was built in 1848 and has been restored.

Worth a Visit

Taxandria Museum

& *Tue-Sun 2pm (Sun and public holidays 11am)-5pm. Closed 1, 2 Jan, 25, 26 Dec.*
€1.74.

This museum, housed in a beautiful 16C town house, deals with the archaeology, history, art and folklore of the Kempen region, which was called Toxandria (Taxandria in Dutch) in Roman times.

There are extensive collections (note the bronze Bacchus dating from the Roman period) and a reconstruction of a traditional Kempen kitchen.

Playing cards

Nationaal Museum van de Speelkaart, Turnhout

Nationaal Museum van de Speelkaart

Tue-Sun 2pm (Sun and public holidays 11am)-5pm. Closed 1, 2 Jan, 25, 25 Dec. €2.23
(includes card game). ☎ *014 41 56 21.*

An old playing cards factory has been turned into a museum devoted to this industry which has existed in Turnhout since 1826. Besides the old machines used to make or print cards, there is an extensive collection of packs of cards from all over the world, the oldest dating from c 1500.

Excursions

Hoogstraten

18km/11mi NW on N 124.

A wide avenue planted with lime trees passes through this small town, overlooked by the magnificent tower (105m/344ft) of its church, **St-Catharinakerk**. The tower is built of brick with string courses of white stone. Rebuilt after being destroyed in 1944 it is still extraordinarily impressive.

The church was designed by Rombout Keldermans in the 16C.

Beautiful 16C stalls can be seen inside in the chancel. The tomb of Antoine de Lalaing and his spouse Elisabeth de Culembourg, by Jean Mone, is equally admirable. Note too the wonderful 14C-16C stained-glass windows and the display of tapestries. *Easter-All Saints Day: 9am-6pm. ☎ 03 340 19 55 (Tourist Information Centre).*

Probably founded at the end of the 14C, Hoogstraten's **begijnhof** was rebuilt after being burnt to the ground in 1506. It is a modest example of a Beguine convent, with small cottages surrounding a shaded lawn. The 17C Baroque church has an elegant porch.

Baarle-Hertog

14km/8.5mi N by N 119.

Baarle-Hertog is a Belgian enclave in Dutch territory. In the 12C the village of Baarle was divided into two. One part fell to the Duke of Brabant (Baarle-Hertog); the other was attached to the Breda seigniory and named **Baarle-Nassau** when Breda became the fiefdom of the Nassau family at the beginning of the 15C.

Each community now has its own town hall, church, police station, school and post office, and the border established in 1831 scrupulously respected community boundaries. However, except for the market square, which is definitely part of the Netherlands, the limits of the two territories are rather blurred.

The Belgian church can be recognised by its characteristic onion dome, but it is less clear to which country the houses belong. However, a close look at the plaques bearing the house numbers will help, since these are marked with the national colours.

Verviers

By Belgian standards, Verviers is a relatively new town, only having gained borough status in 1651. The demise of its once important textile industry led to years of decline, but the local economy is now growing again. Though there is little in the way of historic building, Verviers has several museums, and the leafy upper town is a well-to-do residential area. Famous natives include the violinist Henri Vieuxtemps (1820-81), and Henri Pirenne (1862-1935), author of a famous "History of Belgium" in seven volumes.

Location

Liège – Population 53 065 – Michelin map 716 K4 and 533 U19 – Plan of the built-up area in the current edition of The Red Guide Benelux.

On the banks of the River Vesdre close to the Hautes-Fagnes/Eifel nature reserve, Verviers is on the A 27/E 42 motorway (exit 4).

ℹ *Rue Xhavée 61, ☎ 087 33 02 13.*

Directory

Where to Eat

Chez Paul – *Place Albert I, 5 – ☎ 087 23 22 21 – Closed 1 wk Feb, mid-Jul – mid-Aug, Wed, Thur eve – €26/47.* This lovely neo-Classical residence in its tranquil parkland setting was once the meeting-place of local literary lions. Now the page has turned, and as a restaurant has an immaculate dining room in a Classical-contemporary style. There are also discreetly luxurious bedrooms and a summer terrace.

Where to Stay

des Ardennes – *Place de la Victoire 15 – ☎ 087 22 39 25 – 10 rms: €29/55 – ☕ €5.* No-frills establishment, conveniently close to the railway station. Functional rooms on three floors and ground floor café. Breakfast taken beneath the gaze of hunting trophies.

Specialities

Don't forget to try succulent **tarte au riz**, **gâteau de Verviers**, a sort of brioche, and **leftgot**, liver sausage with grapes.

VERVIERS

Centre touristique de la Laine et de la Mode	C M⁴
Hôtel de Ville	D H
Musée d'Archéologie et du Folklore	D M²
Musée des Beaux-Arts et de la Céramique	D M¹

Worth a Visit

Hôtel de Ville
This elegant 18C building stands on a hill. It has many windows and a **perron** in front of it.

Musée des Beaux-Arts et de la Céramique★
Open Mon, Wed, Sat 2pm-5pm, Sun 3pm-5pm
Established in an old 17C hospice for the elderly, this museum contains extensive collections of porcelain, Belgian and foreign glazed earthenware *(faïence)*, old Raeren sandstone pottery and paintings and sculptures from the 14C to the present day. Among the pictures is a *Landscape with St Christopher*, painted in bluish tones, and an attractive panel attributed to Pietro Lorenzetti. Engravings by artists from Liège from the 16C up to the present day are arranged in drawers. Upstairs, there is a collection of modern works (Tytgat, Magritte).

Musée d'Archéologie et du Folklore
This museum occupies an 18C town mansion, containing furniture in various styles (Louis XIII and Charles X). It also features a collection of Dutch furniture (in the Grand Salon) and mementoes of the violinist Henri Vieuxtemps. On the first floor, there is a Louis XV salon with furniture made in Liège. On the second floor is the collection of objects unearthed during digs in the region. An interesting **lace collection★** is displayed in drawers, with photographic enlargements making it possible to appreciate the delicacy of the work.

Église Notre-Dame
This church was rebuilt in the 18C. Since the 17C, pilgrims have come here to pray to the Black Madonna of the Recollects, a statue which was discovered in a strangely modified posture after an earthquake in 1692.

Centre touristique de la Laine et de la Mode
&. *Apr-Oct: 10am-6pm; Nov-Mar: Tue-Sun 10am-5pm. Closed 1 Jan, 25 Dec. €5.* ☎ 087 35 57 03.
Built at the beginning of the 19C, the attractively restored Dethier woollen factory now houses a fascinating museum depicting the town's prestigious past as a textile metropolis. An audio-guide introduces the visitor to the manufacturing process, while the second floor is dedicated to an exhibition of looms, tools and engravings, as well as audio-visual presentations on weaving, thread and cloth. An exhibition on the first floor traces the history of fashion from Antiquity to the present day through film extracts, models and cartoons.

Excursions

Limbourg★

7.5km/4.5mi E on N 61.

Perched on a rock high above the valley of the Vesdre, Limbourg was the capital of a duchy until the 13C. After the **Battle of Worringen** in 1288, it was annexed to Brabant and shared its fortunes until the end of the 18C. The town was a major stronghold and, as such, was besieged many times, notably by the French in 1675, Marlborough in 1703, and by the French again in 1748.

The town walls, the old Gothic church dedicated to St George, the quiet streets and the central paved square planted with lime trees, make a very picturesque scene.

Barrage de la Gileppe★★

13km/8mi E on N 61.

This dam was built on a tributary of the River Vesdre between 1869 and 1876, and increased in size between

Limbourg in bloom

1967 and 1971. Now 67m/220ft high and 320m/1 049ft long on a rock base of 235m/771ft, it has twice its original capacity, a total of 27 million m³/954 million cu ft. It supplies the region with water for both household and industrial purposes.

A stone lion dominates the crest of the dam, from where there is a splendid **view★★** of the wooded valley and the reservoir *(recreational activities are prohibited on the reservoir and its shores).*

FROM VERVIERS TO VAL-DIEU

15km/9.3mi N.

Leave on A 27/E 42. At Battice, take N 627, then turn right to Charneux. At Charneux, head for Thimister and turn left 1km/0.5mi after a small bridge.

Croix de Charneux

This great concrete cross was built on a hill 269m/882ft high, from which there is a fine view of the surrounding area. Nearby is the dome of an observation post (1932-35) belonging to the 19C Battice fort that formed part of the outer defences of Liège.

Continue north to Val-Dieu.

Barrage de la Gileppe

Abbaye du Val-Dieu

This abbey lies in the charming Berwinne Valley. The abbey was founded around 1216, and has been occupied by the Cistercians since 1844. The vast courtyard of the abbey farm is in front of the guest quarters (1732), to the left of which are the abbey buildings and church. Rebuilt in 1934, the church still has a Gothic chancel. There are beautiful Renaissance stalls inside.

FROM VERVIERS TO DEIGNÉ

11km/7mi SW.
Leave Verviers on N 61. At Pepinster take N 666.

Tancrémont

A pilgrimage chapel contains a lovely wooden **statue★** of Christ which is the object of great veneration. This statue was discovered buried in the earth around 1830. It depicts a crowned Christ in a robe that seems to be of Eastern influence, and is thought to date back to the 12C.

Banneux-Notre-Dame

This has been an international place of pilgrimage to Our Lady of the Poor since the eight apparitions to 11-year-old Mariette Beco during the winter of 1933. The Miraculous Spring, the Stations of the Cross and the chapels are dispersed throughout the neighbouring pine forest.

Deigné-Aywaille

The **Parc Safari du Monde Sauvage** is in Deigné. Hippopotamuses, zebras, camels, giraffes, buffaloes, rhinoceroses and gazelles roam free; their area of the park can be visited by car or on the little train *(departures hourly next to the farm)*. The section consisting of the enclosures and islets is visited on foot. The park also has a sea lion pool, a children's farm with a playground, an aviary of tropical birds and an auditorium in which visitors can watch films in 3-D.

Veurne★

The principal historic buildings of this charming little town are grouped around its magnificent market square. Their characteristic Flemish sumptuousness is tempered by a touch of Spanish solemnity, doubtless because they were mostly built during the prosperous reign of "Archdukes" Albert and Isabella. In 1914, during the Battle of the IJzer (Yser), Veurne was the headquarters of the Belgian army. Every July, the town stages the Procession of the Penitents★★, a striking demonstration of religious fervour.

Location

Westvlaanderen – Population 11 764 – Michelin maps 716 B2 and 533 B16.
Near the coast on the Flanders plain and not far from the French border, Veurne is reached from France and Bruges by the A 18/E 40 motorway and from Koksijde and Ypres by N 8.
🅱 *Grote Markt 29, ☎ 058 33 05 31; www.veurne.be*

Walking About

Allow 2hr

GROTE MARKT★★

Veurne's vast market square is surrounded by splendid public buildings and fine old houses with imposing gables, pediments and cornices, most of them dating from the early 17C.

Stadhuis

Currently closed for restoration.
☎ 058 33 05 31.
The town hall was built in 1596 *(left)* and 1612 *(right)* in Flemish Renaissance style, with a double pedimented façade and an elegant loggia. Towards the back of the building is a little onion-domed turret crowning a staircase.

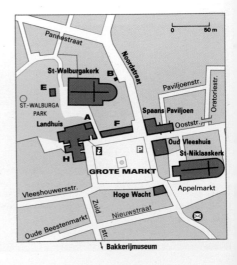

Directory

WHERE TO EAT

Olijfboom – *Noordstraat 3 – ☎ 058 31 70 77 – Closed 3 wks Sept, 3 wks Jan, Sun, Mon – €21/42.* This particular "Olive Tree" yields fine fruit in the shape of a welcoming dining room graced with modern works of art, a menu featuring contemporary cuisine, an interesting wine list, and, last but not least, reasonable prices.

Driekoningen – *Wulveringemstraat 40 – ☎ 058 29 90 12 – info@driekoningen.be – Closed early Mar – mid-Mar, 1 wk Jun, mid-Sept – early Oct, mid-Jan – early Feb, Mon eve, Tue lunchtime Oct-Mar, Tue eve, Wed – lunch €25 – €30/45.* Venerable inn (17C) in the heart of a delightful village in the back country south of Veurne. Attractive table settings, good range of classic dishes. Mostly patronised by your fellow-tourists in season.

WHERE TO STAY

de Loft – *Oude Vestingstraat 36 – ☎ 058 31 59 49 – deloft@pi.be – 8 rms: €52/62.* This "loft hotel" in what used to be a forge is close to the town centre but away from the crowds. Functional, bright rooms. For drinks and snacks there's a tearoom.

Landgoed de Kastanjeboom B&B – *Lekestraat 10 – 8433 Schore – ☎ 051 55 59 17 – de.kastanjeboom @belgacom.net – ☒ – 3 rms: €80 – meals €35.* This restored farm among the polders offers accommodation and meals alike. Cosy rooms, tranquil courtyard, breakfast room overlooking the countryside and outdoor dining in a charming "kitchen garden" setting in summer.

EVENTS AND FESTIVALS

A large flower market is held annually on Whit Monday. In August the "Anno 1900" Festival takes place, with events featuring old costumes and demonstrations of crafts from the past.

Every year the Sodality Brotherhood, founded in 1637, organises the **Procession of the Penitents** through the town. This very impressive pageant consists of floats portraying the Life and Death of Christ, followed by penitents dressed in sombre sackcloth robes with cowls over their heads. They walk barefoot and carry a heavy cross. The Sodality Brotherhood also follow the Stations of the Cross in the streets every Friday evening during Lent, every evening during Holy Week and on Maundy Thursday at midnight.

The walls inside are lined with magnificent **leather★** from Córdoba (reception room) or from Mechelen (council chamber and registry office). The collegiate room is embellished with blue velvet from Utrecht. Note also the 18C furniture, and paintings including a still life attributed to Paul de Vos. The courtroom of the old law courts, with direct access from the town hall, is also open to visitors.

Landhuis

Once the domain of a castellan (1618), the design for this building was inspired by the Stadhuis in Antwerp. Behind the part housing the old law courts stands the **belfry A** (1628), mainly Gothic in style but with a Baroque top section.

On the north side of the square, note the group of **five houses F** with beautiful gables adorned with heavy windows with pilasters.

Spaans Paviljoen

The 15C "Spanish Pavilion" on the corner of the square and Ooststraat was the town hall until 1586. It was the Spanish officers' quarters in the 17C.

Oud Vleeshuis

Built in 1615, the meat market has a pretty façade. It has been restored and now houses the local library.

Hoge Wacht

At the south end of the square, this arcaded house of 1636 would once have housed the town guards.

St Walburga's Church is reached via a narrow street to the right of the old law courts.

St-Walburgakerk

Apr-Sep: 8am-6pm. ☎ 058 33 05 31.

The first church on this site was destroyed by the Norsemen and rebuilt in the 12C in Romanesque style. A new building, on which work began in the 13C with ambitious plans, was never completed. Only the chancel was finished, and it is particularly impressive, being 27m/88ft in height with numerous flying buttresses. In the 14C the base of a tower **E** was built in the neighbouring square. The Romanesque part of the church was renovated in the 20C.

Inside the proportions are harmonious and impressive. Note the Flemish Renaissance stalls (1596), a pulpit by H Pulinx (1727) representing the vision of St John in Patmos, the 18C organ and rood screen and the 17C Flemish paintings. The fortress commissioned by Count Baldwin Iron Arm was built in the square west of the church.

Turn right into Pannestraat, then go along Noordstraat.

Noordstraat

In 1906 the Austrian poet **Rainer Maria Rilke** stayed in the old Inn of the Noble Rose (Die Nobele Rose, 1572), which is now a bank. Opposite, a small monument **B** commemorates the Nieuwpoort lock-keeper responsible in 1914 for the flooding of the polders which stemmed the advance of the German army.

Return to Grote Markt and cross it, turning left into Appelmarkt.

St-Niklaaskerk

8am-6pm. ☎ 058 33 05 31 (Tourist Information Centre).

This church dedicated to St Nicholas has a splendidly massive brick **tower** dating from the 13C and containing one of the oldest bells in Flanders, the Bomtje (1379). It is a hall-church, with three aisles of equal height inside. A fine triptych (1534) on the high altar represents the Crucifixion. Some scholars attribute it to Van Aemstel, brother-in-law of Pieter Coecke, whereas others believe it to be by Van Orley.

Excursions

Bakkerijmuseum

Albert I-laan 2, near the Veurne exit off motorway A 18/E 40. Apr-Sept: Mon-Thur, Fri (Jul-Aug) 10am-noon, 2pm-6pm, Sat, Sun, public holidays 2pm-6pm; Oct-Mar Sun-Thur 2pm-5pm. Closed 1 Jan, 25 Dec. €3. ☎ 058 31 38 97.

The Bakery Museum occupies a fine old building, the 17C Zuidgasthoeve. Outside, an model garden is used to demonstrate the various cereals used in the making of bread. There is also a small revolving mill. The main part of the building houses a rebuilt bakery and confectionery shop. The section "Bread as an Art Form" displays figurines made of chocolate, marzipan, and gingerbread. Other rooms contain various implements used for baking bread and *spekulaas* (small biscuit flavoured with brown sugar and cinnamon), and preparing ice cream and waffles, while the old stables house a cafeteria and an exhibition on bread from other countries. A third building displays little bread carts.

Lo

15km/9.3mi SE.

This little town still has a gateway flanked by turrets that was once part of the 14C ramparts. The beautiful 14C **hall church**, surmounted with a crocketed spire, was partly reconstructed in 1924. Inside there are fine 17C and 18C furnishings.

FROM VEURNE TO IZENBERGE

12km/7.5mi S on N 8.

Wulveringem

The manor house known as **Kasteel Beauvoorde** was built in the 16C and 17C on the site of a derelict castle. It is a charming building with crow-stepped gables, surrounded by water and hidden behind the great trees of the park. At the end of the 19C, Beauvoorde's last owner, Arthur Merghelynck, undertook a very thorough restoration. The interior has extensive collections of antique furniture and objets d'art (paintings, ceramics). The Knights' Hall has walls hung with gilded leather as well as fine 17C woodwork from a church in Oudenburg. *Jul-Aug: guided tour (1hr) daily exc Mon, Fri, 3pm, Sun 2.30pm, 4pm; June, Sept: Tue, Thur 3pm, Sun 2.30pm, 4pm. €3. ☎ 058 29 92 29.*

Izenberge

The **Bachten de Kupe** open-air museum consists of a number of re-erected buildings (shops, farm, an inn also serving as a village hall) which evoke traditional life in this part of Flanders. In the centre is a Gothic church, its interior graced with fine old woodwork, as well as a little 17C pilgrimage chapel. *Mid-Nov – late Mar: Mon-Fri 10.30am-5pm; early Apr – mid-Nov: Sat, Sun, public holidays 2pm-6pm. Closed Christmas, New Year. €3. ☎ 058 29 80 90.*

Villiers-la-Ville★★

In a lovely leafy setting, this tranquil little town is famous for the evocative ruins of its Cistercian abbey, the largest of its kind in Belgium. During the summer season, they are used as a venue for concerts and theatrical productions.

Location
Brabant Wallon – Population 9 116 – Michelin maps 716 G4 and 533 M19.
On the banks of the River Thyle, midway between Brussels and Charleroi, Villiers is reached by N 25, then N 275.
🚩 *Porte de Namur, Rue de l'Abbaye 53, ☎ 071 87 98 98.*

Directory

WHERE TO EAT
☺ **L'Auberge du Moulin** – *Rue de l'Abbaye 55 – ☎ 071 87 70 57 – auberge@cigalon.be – Closed Mar – €16/35.* This tavern-restaurant in the ancient watermill opposite the abbey is well-placed to satisfy appetites worked up by a conscientious tour of the ruins. Vast country-style dining room and good range of traditional dishes.

☺ **le Cigalon** – *Avenue Arsène Tournay 40 – ☎ 071 87 85 54 – cigalon@cigalon.be – Closed Mon – lunch €17 – €22/38.* Not far from the monastic ruins, this restaurant boasts Provencal-style decor. Good solid menu along with a fine selection of wines from France and Switzerland. Attractive shaded summer terrace.

Worth a Visit

Abbey Ruins★★
Apr-Oct: 10am-6pm; Nov-Mar: Wed-Mon 10am-5pm. Closed 1 Jan, 24, 25, 31 Dec. €3.80. ☎ 071 88 09 80.
The foundations of the abbey were laid by St Bernard as early as 1147, but the church and cloisters were only built between 1198 and 1209. Both the Spanish and the rebel noblemen known as Geuzen ransacked the convent in the 16C, and it was enclosed within fortifications in 1587. In 1789 the Austrians pillaged the buildings which were subsequently occupied by the French in 1795.
The 13C **watermill** across from the ruins has been turned into a restaurant.
Follow the signposted tour.
Main courtyard – The courtyard is lined with 18C buildings now in ruins. The abbots' palace is on the right.
Cloisters – The vast cloisters were altered in the 14C and again in the 16C. Solid but elegant, they have arches surmounted by an oculus.

Abbey Ruins

The surrounding buildings are set out in typical Cistercian fashion. To the east is the **chapterhouse**, which was refurbished in the 18C. Nearby is the 13C recumbent effigy of Gobert d'Aspremont. Above are the dormitories which were also renovated in the 18C. To the south are the calefactory (the one room that was heated), the refectory set at right angles to the cloisters and the kitchen. To the west is the undercroft with the lay-brothers' sleeping quarters above them. The abbey could accommodate up to 300 lay brothers in the 13C.

Church – The church was built in the early 13C but collapsed in 1884. Like most Cistercian establishments, its design was of a sober but very moving simplicity. The apse and transept were lit by oculi in the style of the Paris School, creating an unusual effect.

Leave the church by the west front and visit the 13C **brewery**, then go round the east end to see the 17C and 18C **abbey quarters**.

Église de la Visitation

Guided tour by prior arrangement with Animation Chrétienne et Tourisme, Rue du Sart 20, 1495 Villers-la-Ville, ☎ 071 87 72 85.

This church has two fine Brabant **altarpieces** from the 15C and 16C illustrating the Life of the Virgin Mary and the Life of the Infant Jesus. Other noteworthy features include a 17C pulpit, a *Christ Entombed* from 1607, portraits of the Abbots of Villers and the 17C funerary monuments of the Lords of Marbais. The 11 modern stained-glass windows are the work of F Crickx and G Massinon.

Virton

This attractive little place is the capital of the Gaume, the scenically varied, southernmost part of Belgium where the climate is milder than in the neighbouring Ardennes and where a distinctive dialect is spoken.

Location

Luxembourg – Population 11 038 – Michelin maps 716 J7 and 534 S25.
Bordering French Lorraine, picturesque Virton is set in pleasant undulating countryside. Access by the A 4/E 25 Namur-Arlon motorway (exit 29, then N 87) or from Montmédy in France by D 981 and N 871.
🄱 *Pavillon, Rue des Grasses Oies 2b, ☎ 063 57 89 04.*

Worth a Visit

Musée Gaumais

Rue d'Arlon. Apr-Nov and public holidays in spring and winter: Wed-Mon (June-Aug also Tue) 9.30am-noon, 2pm-6pm. €3. ☎ 063 57 03 15.

This Regional Museum is in the old Recollects' Convent, which has a jack-o'-the-clock. It specialises in local archaeology and ethnography. There are reconstructed interiors (traditional kitchen from the Gaume area) and craft workshops. Among the collections of industrial folk art, note the splendid examples of ornamental cast iron (firebacks and andirons), reminders that the Gaume was once widely reputed for its ironworks.

Excursions

Montauban

10km/6.25mi N. Take N 82 towards Arlon, then in Ethe turn left towards Buzenol.
South of **Buzenol**, near some old ironworks, by the stream there stands a wooded hill about 340m/1 115ft high. Easily defended, it was occupied in prehistoric times, the Roman period and the Middle Ages, and there are remains of fortifications from all these periods. The little **Musée des Sculptures romaines** has a number of Gallo-Roman low reliefs discovered on the site. The most famous one represents the front part of a *"vallus"*, the unique Celtic harvesting machine described by Pliny the Elder. A lifesize model was reconstructed based on a low relief in the Arlon Luxembourg Museum showing a man working a *vallus*.

FROM VIRTON TO TORGNY

9km/5.5mi S on the Montmédy road.
Turn right at Dampicourt.

Montquintin

The village is perched on a crest with an altitude of more than 300m/984ft. Near the church, a farm from 1765 contains the **Musée de la Vie Paysanne**, a Museum of Rural Life. The building itself is representative of traditional rural architecture and serves as a reminder of life in Gaume in bygone days. Besides the living quarters, it is possible to visit the barn and the cowshed with its hayloft and inspect old farm vehicles and implements. *July-Aug: 2pm-6pm; Mar-Oct on demand. €1.50.* ☎ *063 57 03 15.*
Return to the Malmédy road, then turn right towards Torgny.

Torgny

This pretty, flower-bedecked village is the southernmost locality in Belgium, with pantiled houses built of an almost golden stone. It stands on the open slopes of a valley where the remarkably mild climate permits the cultivation of vines.

De **Voerstreek**

The half-dozen villages of the Voerstreek constitute a little enclave of Dutch-speaking Limburg within the Walloon province of Liège. Known in French as Les Fourons, it is a lush green area of little river valleys, delightful wooded hillsides, fertile pastures and orchards, and has long been a bone of contention between Belgium's two main language communities.

Location

Limburg – Population 4 297 – Michelin maps 716 K3 and 533 T18.
In eastern Belgium, the area stretches for about 15km/9.5mi parallel to the border with the Netherlands to near Aachen in Germany. Access from Liège and Maastricht in the Netherlands by A 2 motorway.
🅑 *Kerkplein 212, 3798 's Gravenvoeren,* ☎ *04 381 07 36.*

Walking About

St-Martens-Voeren (Fouron-St-Martin)
The most outstanding features are the church with its Romanesque tower and a small 18C chateau, Het Veltmanshuis, now used as an arts centre.

St-Pieters-Voeren (Fouron-St-Pierre)
Near a lake are the superb buildings that once formed a **Commandery** belonging to the Teutonic Order. It was first constructed in 1242 but was rebuilt in the 17C.

Waterloo ★

It was at Waterloo on 18 June 1815 that the Allied Anglo-Dutch forces, under the command of the Duke of Wellington, and the Prussians, led by Field-Marshal Blücher, put an end to Napoleon's dreams of empire, thereby turning over a new page in European history.
Thou fatal Waterloo.
Millions of tongues record thee, and anew
Their children's lips shall echo them, and say –
"Here, where the sword united nations drew,
Our countrymen were warring on that day!"
And this is much, and all which will not pass away.
Lord Byron

Location

Brabant Wallon – Population 28 958 – Michelin maps 716 G 3 or 533 L 18.
To the south of Brussels, the field of battle and its various monuments are reached from the capital by N 5.
🅑 *Chaussée de Bruxelles 149,* ☎ *02 354 99 10.*

Background

The Battle – Napoleon's plan – Napoleon escaped from Elba, his first place of exile, in February 1815, landing in the south of France and gathering enthusiastic support on his march to Paris. The reinstated French King Louis XVIII fled ignominiously to Ghent, while the Allies who had thought Napoleon defeated for good assembled what forces they could. In Belgium these consisted of a Prussian army under Field Marshal Blücher and a mixed force commanded by the Duke of Wellington. To combat this threat, **Napoleon** ordered his army north, hoping to crush each army separately, before they had time to join forces. On 14 June he halted at Beaumont. Two days later, he won his last victory against Blücher at **Ligny**, northeast of Charleroi, a victory which nonetheless cost him dearly in loss of men and failed to rout the Prussian army. His Marshal Ney had meanwhile failed to defeat the British at Quatre-Bras.

Wellington withdrew to Waterloo where he intended to stand fast in defence of Brussels. On 17 June Napoleon set off to do battle with his old opponent, arriving on the Mont St-Jean plain and, as darkness fell, establishing his headquarters at the farm known as **Le Caillou**.

On 18 June bad weather delayed the arrival of some of the French troops, so the battle did not begin until almost noon, a delay which was to be a key factor in the final outcome.

The forces engage – While the French artillery and Napoleon's observation post were positioned near the **Cabaret de la Belle Alliance** coaching-inn, British and French troops fought each other until nightfall in bloody combat by the **Hougoumont** farmhouse. This was one of three farmhouses which were vital positions to be won by an army trying to gain possession of Mont St-Jean. After hours of fierce skirmishing, the French troops gave up the assault and retreated.

The focus of the battlefield then shifted to **La Haie Sainte**, a farm which was eventually won by the French after a vicious struggle, and then on to the farm at **La Papelotte**. At about 4pm, beneath a leaden sky, French troops plunged into the famous **Valley of the Sunken Road** *("chemin creux")*, in which sweeping French calvary charges led by Ney and General Kellermann were savagely battered by British fire, but nonetheless managed to inflict heavy losses on Wellington's troops, who were now in urgent need of reinforcement from their Prussian allies.

Napoleon was waiting for reinforcements of 30 000 men led by Marshal de Grouchy. They were expected to arrive from Wavre to the east. Blücher, however, having regrouped his troops and evaded Grouchy, skirted the French army's right flank to join the British army. The Prussian front guard then took the village of **Plancenoit** and began to put pressure on Napoleon's southeast flank.

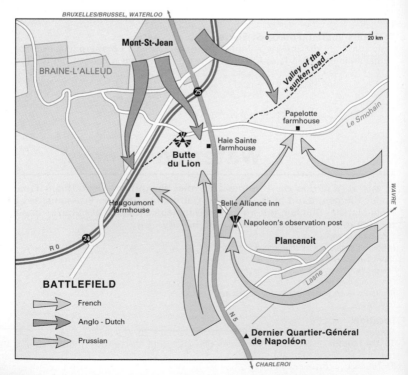

THE DUCHESS OF RICHMOND'S BALL

On 15 June 1815, the Duchess of Richmond gave a ball in Brussels. It has remained famous because it was during the evening that a letter arrived informing the Commander-in-Chief of the Allied forces, the Duke of Wellington, that Napoleon was now only 22km/14mi from the capital. It is said that the ballroom emptied in a mere 20min. Nobody knows exactly which of the private mansions in the town hosted the ball, but Lord Byron described the moment vividly:

"...Everything was joyous as a church bell pealing merrily after a wedding ceremony. Then came silence! Listen! A sinister noise resounded, like the knell of the funeral bell! The fearsome sound can still be heard. It is as if the clouds were acting as echoes. It seems to be coming nearer and more distinct with each passing minute. It is more and more terrifying. It is the brazen voice of battle beginning its clamour!..."

Surrounded, Napoleon finally sent his Imperial Guard to support Ney and engage with the British troops. The result was utter carnage on the "sunken road", as Wellington had had time to reorganise his defence strategy to include the Prussian reinforcements, and the Allied forces' fire shattered the closely packed ranks of Napoleon's Imperial Guard.

As night fell over the battlefield, littered with the bodies of 49 000 dead and wounded, the defeated French troops retreated, completely routed despite Ney's heroic efforts. Napoleon disappeared to Genappe under cover of darkness and Wellington joined Blücher at the **Belle Alliance Inn**.

Worth a Visit

THE BATTLEFIELD

In 1861, Victor Hugo stayed in the Hôtel des Colonnes in Mont St-Jean (it no longer exists) to write the chapter in *Les Misérables* describing the battle. Stendhal had already done so in the opening pages of his novel *The Charterhouse of Parma* (1839).

The physionomy of the battlefield has changed greatly since 1815 – a motorway and a main road now cross it – but the plain is nevertheless dotted with historic buildings and commemorative monuments.

Every year a historical re-enactment is held here, with more than 2 000 participants.

Visitor Centre

  Apr-Oct: 9.30am-6.30pm (Oct 5.30pm); Nov-Feb 10.30am-4pm; Mar: 10am-5pm. Closed 1 Jan, 25 Dec. €4.96. ☎ 02 385 19 12.

At the foot of the Butte du Lion, the centre has an audio-visual presentation which takes the audience into the very heart of events on 18 June 1815. A model situates the strategic points of the battle and depicts its main stages. The second part of the visit consists of a film evoking the battle itself.

Butte du Lion

Apr-Oct: 9.30am-6.30pm (Oct 5.30pm); Nov-Feb: 10.30am-4pm; Mar: 10am-5pm. Closed 1 Jan, 25 Dec. €1. ☎ 02 385 10 12.

This 45m/147ft-high mound was constructed in 1826 by the Kingdom of the Netherlands on the spot where the Prince of Orange was wounded fighting the Imperial Guard. A cast-iron lion weighing 28t stands at the top. Legend has it that the statue was made from the gunmetal of cannon captured on the battlefield, but this is in fact not true.

There is a good general view of the battlefield from the top. At the foot of the mound, to the south, the famous Valley of the Sunken Road has been largely levelled out, as the surrounding earth was taken to build the mound.

Panorama de la Bataille

Apr-Oct: 9.30am-6.30pm (Oct 5.30pm); Nov-Feb: 10.30am-4pm; Mar: 10am-5pm. Closed 1 Jan, 25 Dec. €2.73. ☎ 02 385 19 12.

This rotunda built in 1912 at the foot of the mound houses a grand panoramic painting 110m/360ft in circumference and 12m/39ft high, created by the French painter Dumoulin and five other artists. It represents a few of the most striking episodes in the battle at the precise moment when Ney sent his calvary along the "sunken path".

On the ground floor, there is a permanent exhibition of costumes, weapons and miscellaneous documents.

Musée de Personnages de Cire

  Apr-Sept: 9.30am-6.30pm; Oct: 10am-6pm; Nov-Mar: Sat, Sun, public holidays 10am-4.45pm. €1.75. ☎ 02 384 67 40.

This little Waxworks Museum stands almost opposite the Panorama. Its rather old-fashioned figures show Napoleon's last council of war with his staff at Le Caillou farm, and the three commanders of the Allied forces (the Prince of Orange, the Duke of Wellington and General Blücher).

Take N 5 towards Charleroi to Napoleon's headquarters.

Butte du Lion

Dernier Quartier-Général de Napoléon

  Apr-Oct, 10am-6.30pm; Nov-Mar: 1pm-5pm, Closed 1 Jan, 25 Dec. €2

On the southern edge of the battlefield, the old Le Caillou farm was Napoleon's headquarters on the eve of the combat. The Emperor's bedroom still contains one of his campbeds and other memorabilia including his bronze death mask. The other rooms contain the autographs of French generals involved in the 1815 campaign, maps, and relics from the battlefield. In the garden there is an ossuary dating from 1912, and the balcony from the Hôtel des Colonnes where Victor Hugo stayed in 1861. A memorial in the orchard recalls the final evening of the battalion of the Imperial Guard.

Continue on N 5 towards the town of Waterloo.

THE TOWN

The settlement of Waterloo originally grew up between the 15C and 17C   along the Genappe-Brussels road.

Wellington Museum

Chaussée de Bruxelles 147 (N 5). Apr-Sept: 9.30am-6.30pm; Oct-Mar: 10.30am-5pm. Closed 1 Jan, 25 Dec. €5. ☎ 02 354 78 06.

The inn where the **Duke of Wellington** set up his headquarters has been turned into a museum. There is the HQ itself, a museum illustrating the history of Waterloo and a library. The rooms, including Wellington's bedroom, display engravings, arms, paintings, documents and mementoes describing Europe in 1815.

Beyond the garden, the spacious, well-lit Map Room traces the course of the battle and has exhibits of special historic interest such as "La Suffisante", a gun cast in Douai (1813) and captured at Waterloo.

Église St-Joseph

Opposite the Wellington Museum. 8.30am-7pm. ☎ 02 354 00 11.

This church was originally no more than a forest chapel (1690) built to a central layout. It is still there but now forms the entrance to the new church. Inside numerous commemorative flagstones bear the names of officers and soldiers who fell at Waterloo.

Zoutleeuw★

A prosperous cloth town defended by sturdy walls in the Middle Ages, Zoutleeuw is now a sleepy little place, though it still boasts one of Belgium's most magnificent Gothic churches, its interior untouched by the iconoclasts of the 16C and the French Revolution. The town itself was pillaged by the French in 1678 and 1701, and its fortifications were demolished in the 18C.

Location
Vlaams-Brabant – Population 7 767 – Michelin maps 716 I 3 or 533 P 18.
On the border between Brabant and Limburg, Zoutleeuw is in the area known as the Hageland. Access by minor road off N 2 between Tienen and St-Truiden.
🛈 *Grote Markt 11,* ☎ *011 78 12 88; www.zoutleeuw.be*

Worth a Visit

St-Leonarduskerk
Apr-Sept: Tue-Sun 2pm-5pm; Oct: Sun 2pm-5pm. €1.25. Allow 45min. ☎ *011 78 12 88 (Tourist Information Centre).*
This splendid church dedicated to St Leonard was constructed over several centuries. The east end was built in the 13C, encircled by an external passage with colonnettes, as was the north arm of the transept. The nave and the south arm of the transept were built in the 14C.

In the 15C, Mathieu de Layens built the charming Late Gothic sacristy opposite the town hall. The 16C bell-tower, rebuilt in 1926, features a carillon with 39 chimes.

Spared the vandalism of 16C image-breakers and French Revolutionaries alike, the interior is a veritable museum of **religious art★★**.

In the nave hangs a "marianum", a double-sided statue of the Virgin Mary which dates from 1533. The wooden altarpiece of St Anne in the second chapel in the **south aisle** has painted panels (1565). Opposite there is a 16C gilded wooden triptych, also with painted panels, depicting the Glorification of the Holy Cross. The third chapel has a triptych by Pieter Aertsen (1575) with medallions representing the Seven Pains of the Virgin Mary. An 11C Romanesque crucifix surmounts the door leading into the sacristy.

The **south transept** has an altarpiece of c1478 recounting the Life of St Leonard. It is the finest work of the Brussels sculptor Arnould de Maeler. The figure of the saint placed in the centre of the altar is older (1300). The old St Leonard's Chapel at the end of the transept boasts a fine collection of 16C and 17C statues as well as a fascinating **treasury** (gold- and silverwork, copperware, and liturgical ornaments).

An exceptional series of 12C to 16C statues runs along the **ambulatory**.

In the **north transept** is the magnificent Avesne stone **tabernacle★★** of 1551, the pride of Zoutleeuw and the masterpiece of the Antwerp artist Cornelis Floris II de Vriendt. Standing 18m/59ft and nine tiers high, it is decorated with around 200 statues which are remarkably lifelike, both in their expressions and in the spontaneity of their poses. These Gothic characteristics are combined with decoration and composition showing Italian influence.

Scenes of Old Testament sacrifices decorate the base. Above them are episodes from the Garden of Eden, then, above the tabernacle alcove, the Last Supper and more scenes from the Old Testament. The upper tiers are decorated with a multitude of characters (the Virtues, the Fathers of the Church) with the Virgin Mary at the very top.

Near the tabernacle is a superb six-armed brass paschal chandelier made by Renier van Thienen in 1482. It incorporates a Calvary with figures of poignant simplicity.

Frans Floris, brother of Cornelis, is thought to be the creator of the triptych of *The Baptism of Christ*, opposite the tabernacle. Note the statues in the chapels in the **north aisle** and, in the second-last chapel (Lady Chapel), painted medallions representing the *Seven Joys of the Virgin Mary* by Pieter Aertsen (1554).

Stadhuis
Built 1530-38 during the reign of Emperor Charles V to plans attributed to the Mechelen-born architect Rombout Keldermans, this charming town hall marks the transition from Gothic to Renaissance. There is a traceried perron at the front. The façade is surmounted by a crow-stepped gable and includes tall basket-handle bays.

The **Drapers' Hall** to the right, with a brick façade striped with bands of white stone, dates from the 14C.

Vianden: the Château by night.

Grand Duchy
of Luxembourg

Berdorf

In the heart of Luxembourg's "Little Switzerland", Berdorf lies on the plateau which drops steeply to the Mullertal valley to the west and the valley of the Sûre to the northeast. As well as being a popular rock-climbing centre, the village is an excellent starting-point for walks in this part of the Germano-Luxembourg national park. In the church, the high altar rests on a block of stone with carvings of Roman date depicting the four divinities Minerva, Juno, Apollo and Hercules.

Location
Population 973 – Michelin maps 716 M6 and 717 X24 – Local map see PETITE SUISSE LUXEMBOURGEOISE.
In its leafy setting, Berdorf is 6km/4mi from Echternach by N 10 and CR 364.
🛈 *Rue Laach 7,* ☎ *79 06 43.*

Excursions

Berdorf is the starting point for numerous walks. The network of footpaths is shown on a noticeboard in the leisure centre next to the mini golf course.

Promenade B
This spectacular path runs along the lip of the plateau to the northwest of Berdorf before dropping down to Grundhof. It links several viewpoints that can also be reached from Berdorf by road, including:

Île du Diable★★ – *Turn left off the Mullerthal road and carry on towards the cemetery. Take the footpath on the left beyond the cemetery with the camp site on the right. Stroll through the attractive pinewood to reach the edge of the plateau (5min).*
There are **magnificent views** of the Mullerthal and beyond it of the wild wooded countryside around Beaufort.

Sieweschluff★ – *Take the Hammhof (Hamm farmhouse) road north, then turn left. Follow the F 2 path then the footpath leading to the plateau (10min).*
There is a marvellous **view** across the Sûre Valley and its wooded surroundings.

Kasselt★ – This 353m/1 158ft high promontory lies to the north of the Sieweschluff and affords an extensive **view** of the Sûre Valley. The river forms a meander here at the point where it is joined by its tributary the Ernz Noire. The view also encompasses the village of Grundhof.

Werschrumschluff★
2km/1.25mi S on the Mullerthal road.
The rock overhanging the road to the left is called the **pulpit** (Predigtstuhl in German, Predigstull in Lëtzebuergesch). From here it is possible to set off and explore the **Werschrumschluff**★, an immense gorge between two steep, rocky walls.

Clervaux★

Clervaux is a major tourist centre in a remarkable **setting**★★ in the heart of the thickly wooded Oesling region. The little town's slate-roofed buildings cluster around the church and the medieval castle on a promontory formed by the River Clerve, while rising above the trees on the hill to the west is the Abbey of the St-Maurice and St-Maur. Clervaux is within the Germano-Luxembourg nature park.

Location
Population 1 641 – Michelin maps 716 L5 and 717 V22.
In idyllic surroundings, Clervaux is close to the border with Belgium, and can be reached from Bastogne by N 874 and N 18. On the N 7 from Luxembourg city there are two viewpoints giving splendid panoramic **views**★★ over the town in its setting.
🛈 *Château (in season),* ☎ *92 93 95.*

Worth a Visit

Castle★
Dating originally from the 12C, the castle was substantially rebuilt in the 17C and restored after partial destruction during the Battle of the Bulge. It is flanked by a number of towers, including to the south the Burgundy Tower with its tiny belfry, and to the right the rather squat Brandenburg Tower.

Directory

In the Renaissance wing there is an **exhibition of models**★ of the various manor houses and fortresses in the Grand Duchy. *Early July to mid-Sept: 11am-6pm; May, Sun 11am-6pm; Jun, 1pm-5pm, Sun 11am-6pm; mid-Sept to end Apr, Sun 1pm-5pm. €1.25. ☎ 92 10 48-1.*

On the first and second floors there is an exhibition of black and white photographs entitled **The Family of Man**★. The work of Edward Steichen, the American photographer of Luxembourg origin, and devoted to the themes of birth, death and work among others, they present a poignant picture of humanity half a century ago. ♿ *mid-Apr to end Dec, daily (closed Mon mid-Sept to end Dec) 10am-6pm. Closed Christmas. €3.72. ☎ 52 24 24 23.*

The castle's south wing houses a little museum of the **Battle of the Bulge**. *Early July to mid-Sept: 11am-6pm; May, Sun 11am-6pm; Jun, 1pm-5pm, Sun 11am-6pm; mid-Sept to April, Sun 1-5pm. Closed Jan-Mar. €2.50. ☎ 92 10 48-1.*

Abbey of St-Maurice and St-Maur

This abbey was founded in 1909 by Benedictines from Solesmes, a French abbey in the Sarthe Valley. It consists of an array of neo-Romanesque buildings in brown schist, rebuilt in 1945.

The **abbey church** is fronted by a beautiful hexagonal tower in Burgundian Romanesque style, reminiscent of the "Holy Water" (Eau Bénite) bell-tower of the famous abbey at Cluny.

The interior, which has the austerity typical of Romanesque buildings, has stained-glass windows of exceptional luminosity. Near the entrance, on the left, there is a 15C *Pietà*. The high altar is by the French sculptor Kaeppelin. There are two finely worked 16C Rhenish altarpieces, still essentially Gothic in inspiration, facing each other in the arms of the transept.

An exhibition in the crypt explains monastic life as lived up to the present day.

Excursions

Vallée de la Clerve
11km/6.75mi S as far as Wilwerwiltz.
The river which gave Clervaux its name flows through this pleasant valley with its meadows and wooded slopes.

FROM CLERVAUX TO TROISVIERGES VIA HACHIVILLE
23km/14.25mi NW on N 18, N 12 and then a road on the left.

Hachiville
Close to the Belgian-Luxembourg border, Hachiville is a typical village of the Oesling region.

In the church there is an early 16C Brabant style **altarpiece**. It represents the *Joys and Sorrows of the Virgin Mary* in a series of attractive compositions.

The combined **chapel and hermitage** beside a spring in the woods 2km/1.25mi northwest has attracted pilgrims for 500 years.

From Hachiville return to N 12 and take this road to Troisvierges.

Troisvierges
This village is located on a plateau at an altitude of over 400m/1 312ft. The River Woltz (which becomes the Clerve at Clervaux) flows through the town. Troisvierges has an onion-domed **church** built by the Recollects in the 17C. The interior has fine Baroque furnishings including the pulpit and confessionals. The nave is separated from the chancel by two monumental altars. Niches in the left altarpiece contain statues of the three virgins Faith, Hope and Charity, which are venerated by pilgrims. *The Raising of the Cross* on the high altar is in the style of Rubens.

Diekirch

A commercial and cultural centre, Diekirch lies between the Gutland and Oesling regions; the Herrenberg (at a height of 394m/1 292ft) overlooking the town marks the first foothills of the Oesling. Diekirch is also an attractive tourist centre with a pedestrian precinct, green spaces along the banks of the Sûre, and surroundings waiting to be explored along the network of signposted footpaths. The town is well known for its brewery, which produces the famous Diekirch beer.

Location
Population 5 666 – Michelin maps 716 L6 and 717 V23.
In the lower valley of the River Sûre, Diekirch is reached from Luxembourg city by N 7.
🖪 *Esplanade 1, ☎ 80 30 23; www.diekirch.lu*

Worth a Visit

Museum
Place Guillaume, where the decanal church stands. Mid-Apr – late Oct: Fri-Wed 10am-noon, 2-6pm. €1.30. ☎ 80 30 23.
This little museum is situated behind the bandstand. Particularly worthy of note inside are the 3C **Roman mosaics**. The most remarkable (3.5 × 4.75m/11 × 15ft) has at its centre the head of the Medusa with two faces.

Église St-Laurent
Access on foot from the decanal church via the Esplanade and the fourth street on the right. Mid-Apr to end Oct: 10am-noon, 2-6pm. ☎ 80 30 23.
This little church dedicated to St Lawrence is hidden behind a ring of houses in the old district of the town. It has been a religious site since the 5C.
The Romanesque nave on the right was built over a Roman building. The nave on the left is Gothic and contains frescoes dating from the 15C (above the altar) and the 16C (in the chancel).
About 30 sarcophagi, mostly of Merovingian date, were found beneath the church in 1961 during archaeological digs.

Excursions

Deiwelselter
2km/1.25mi S on the Larochette road.
After a hairpin bend and before the Gilsdorf road, take Footpath D on the right. It leads through the woods to this little feature called the "Devil's Altar". The stones are said to have come from an ancient dolmen.
There are fine views of the town from the edge of the woods.

Brandenbourg
9km/5.5mi E on the Reisdorf road, then first left.
This charming village is in the valley of the Blees, a tributary of the Sûre, and is overlooked by the ruins of a 12C castle on the top of a hill.
A small Rural Life Museum has been set up in the **Maison Al Branebuurg.** It contains information on the region and a collection of everyday objects from times past. *Closed for building work. ☎ 80 38 03*

Echternach★

In delightful surroundings, the miniature capital of Luxembourg's "Little Switzerland" is a busy tourist centre. The town is dominated by the abbey founded in 698 by St Willibrord, a tireless missionary from northern England who evangelised the Frisians and built his largest monastery at Echternach where he died in 739. Some of the towers of the medieval walls still survive, in Rue des Redoutes, Rue Hoovelecker and Rue Brimmeyer (near a hospice).

Location
Population 4 367 – Michelin maps 716 M6 and 717 X24 – Local map see PETITE SUISSE LUXEMBOURGEOISE.
Right on the border with Germany, Echternach is at the junction of the N 10 and N 11.
🛈 *B.P. 30, ☎ 72 02 30; www.echternach.lu*

Directory

WHERE TO EAT
😊😊😊 **Au Vieux Moulin** – *Maison 6 – 6562 Lauterborn – ☎ 720 06 81 – Closed Jan, Mon, after 8.30pm – lunch €26 – €46/62.* Built on the site of an old mill, this characterful establishment attracts discriminating diners from a wide area. Appetising daily menu, attractive dining room, terrace, garden and lovely leafy surroundings. Well-kept guest rooms.

WHERE TO STAY
😊 **Le Petit Poète** – *Place du Marché 13 – ☎ 72 00 72 – lepetitpoete@vip.lu – Closed Dec-Jan, Tue out of season – 12 rms: €39/57 ⌷ – restaurant €22/38.* In the middle of town, in front of the old 15C law courts, this establishment offers rooms with plain but well thought-out decor on three floors. The café-cum-brasserie on the ground floor opens out on to the square and can get quite lively.

FESTIVALS AND EVENTS
Echternach is renowned for its "Dancing Procession". This unusual celebration dating back to the late Middle Ages is held in honour of St Willibrord and takes place on the Tuesday after Whit Monday. Linked to one another by white handkerchiefs, the dancers hop and skip through the streets, now moving forward, now back, to the sound of a polka.
At the beginning of the summer, during the Echternach International Festival, musical events take place in the basilica or in the Église St-Pierre-et-St-Paul.

Worth a Visit

Place du Marché★
Echternach's attractive market square is ringed by fine old houses. On one side stand the old Law Courts or **Dënzelt**, a charming 15C building with arcades, statues, and corner turrets. The Cross of Justice is a reconstruction of the original medieval cross.

Abbey★
This Benedictine monastery, which was of great cultural influence during the Middle Ages thanks to its famous scriptorium, was abandoned in 1797. The basilica and other buildings (1727-31) of the abbey form a majestic and harmonious group.
The **Basilique St Willibrord** was built in the 11C on the site of a Carolingian church, of which the crypt still exists. Largely destroyed in December 1944, it has been recon-

A. Kouprianoff/ MICHELIN

structed and retains its original charm. In the crypt, the stone sarcophagus containing the relics of St Willibrord is surmounted by a neo-Gothic reliquary. The cradle-vault of the chancel has traces of frescoes with scenes from the life of the Virgin Mary.

Musée de l'Abbaye –The abbey museum evokes Echternach's eventful past since Roman days, the personality of St Willibrord, and in particular the role of the abbey scriptorium, where the monks created superb illuminated manuscripts from the 9C to the 11C. An exhibition shows the different phases in the creation of these manuscripts and displays a number of facsimiles. The most famous was the *Codex Aureus Epternacensis*, a celebrated 11C gold gospel-book from Echternach that is now in the Germanic National Museum in Nuremberg. In the scriptorium, scribes laboured on scrupulous copies of sacred texts, while illuminators added sumptuous miniature paintings and elaborate lettering of the utmost delicacy. As Echternach's early monks were from the British Isles, the style of its scriptorium was characterised by abstract motifs and elaborate interlacing. *Jul-Aug: 10am-6pm; end Mar to end Oct, 10am-noon, 2-5pm (Jun 6pm). €2.* ☎ *72 95 37.*

In the square opposite the abbey there is a lovely orangery with statues of the Seasons. To the northeast, a pretty park extends as far as the Sûre, on the banks of which stands a graceful Louis XV-style pavilion.

Villa Romaine

1km/0.5mi on N11/E 29, towards Luxembourg city. Leave Echternach on Rue de Luxembourg and follow signs indicating Lac/See. The remains of a large Roman villa dating from the 1C can be seen here on the edge of the town. The villa was originally symmetrical, but was then enlarged and modified over the course of the following three centuries.

Excursion

Wolfschlucht/Gorge du Loup★★

45min on foot there and back. By car, drive along Rue André Duscher from Place du Marché and turn right towards Troosknepchen after the cemetery. The footpath leaves from Rue Emersinde near the bus station.

The route follows Footpath B up to the pavilion at the **Troosknepchen viewpoint** from which there are fine **views★** of Echternach in the valley below. Continue on Footpath B, through a beech forest to the Wolfschlucht/Gorge du Loup (Wolf Gorge). A great pointed rock to the left of the entrance to the gorge is known as Cleopatra's Needle. A flight of steps crosses this dark, impressive cleft between two jagged, sheer walls of rock 50m/164ft high. At the end of the gorge, a flight of steps to the right leads to the **Bildscheslay viewpoint** from which there is a pretty view of the Sûre flowing through lush countryside.

Vallée de l'Eisch★

The River Eisch wends its way in meanders through meadows, forests and between high, wooded walls of rock. A drive along the riverside road reveals six castles; originally there were seven, hence the valley's other name of "Vallée des Sept Châteaux". Between Koerich and Mersch there is also a footpath and cycleway.

Location

Michelin maps 716 K6-L6 and 717 U25-V24.
The valley cuts through attractive countryside with a number of charming little villages. Access from Luxembourg city by N 6 and CR 110.
🛈 *Hôtel de Ville (Castle), 7501 Mersch;* ☎ *32 50 23.*

Tour

26km/16mi – allow 1hr 30min

Koerich

On its hilltop, the church has lovely Baroque furnishings, particularly in the chancel. By the river there are the ruins of a medieval castle which was altered during the Renaissance period (note the fireplace).
Take CR 110 and turn right on to CR 105 where the road divides.

Septfontaines

This is a picturesque village clinging to the slopes which drop steeply down towards the River Eisch. Above it are the ruins of the **castle** (13C-15C).

The **church** contains an interesting *Entombment*.

A number of elegantly carved stones from a Baroque Stations of the Cross have been set up in the churchyard.

At the foot of the castle are the seven springs (*fontaines* in French) which gave their name to the village.

Continue on CR 105

Ansembourg

This little place has two **castles**. On the hillside there is a 12C castle that was altered in the 16C and 18C, and in the valley, a 17C castle that was once the residence of the owner of the local iron smelting plant, with a turreted doorway and beautiful 18C gardens. The **Château de Hollenfels** can be seen a little further on, on top of a ridge. It was enlarged in the 18C around a 13C keep and is now a youth hostel.

After the bridge over the Eisch, take the minor road on the right.

Hunnebour

At the foot of a high rocky ridge is the Hunnebour, a spring in a restful shady **setting★**.

Continue along CR 105.

Mersch

The medieval **castle** has been extensively restored. It is a tall square building in front of which there is a gateway with small turrets. Nearby is the onion-domed **Tour St-Michel**, all that is left of a church which has since disappeared.

Esch-sur-Alzette

Esch-sur-Alzette, the Grand Duchy's second largest town, is also the capital of the "red earth" district which owes its name to its deposits of iron ore. Once the country's main iron and steel production centre, this cosmopolitan place (more than one-third of the inhabitants are foreigners) is also an important commercial centre. The Rue d'Alzette in the middle of town is lined by fine residences built in Art Nouveau and Art Deco style.

Location

Population 24 564 – Michelin maps 716 K7 and 717 U26 – Town plan in the current edition of The Red Guide Benelux.

To the south of Luxembourg city and just a stone's throw from the border with France, Esch-sur-Alzette is reached from the capital by the A4 motorway and from France by D 16. It is also close to the east-west A 13 motorway.

🛈 *Hôtel de ville, ☎ 54 73 83.*

Directory

WHERE TO EAT

Bec Fin – *Place Norbert Metz 15 – ☎ 54 33 22 – lunch €22 – Closed 1st wk Sept, 1st wk Jan, Sun eve, Mon – €38.* This restaurant on a square bordered by the ring road stands out because of its charming appearance. Tasty, classic cuisine, served in pleasant traditional surroundings. There aren't many tables, so book ahead if you can.

WHERE TO STAY

De Foetz – *Rue Avenir 1 – 3895 Foetz – ☎ 57 25 45 – hfoetz@pt.lu – Closed school holidays, Christmas; restaurant closed Sun –*

🅿 *– 40 rms: €42/62 ⊊ – restaurant €22.* Modern hotel to be found in the shopping centre at Foetz, just to the north of Esch-sur-Alzette. Functional, practical rooms. Well-considered classic dishes in the restaurant.

Acacia – *Rue de la Libération 10 – ☎ 54 10 61 – hacacia@pt.lu – Closed Christmas-New Year; restaurant closed Sun and public holidays – 23 rms: €62/84 ⊊ – restaurant €55.* Establishment run by the same family for 25 years. Conveniently close to the station for rail travellers. Small, functional rooms. Dining room with splendid open fireplace. Traditional dishes.

Worth a Visit

Parc de la ville
Take the Dudelange road, then the first road on the right after the tunnel.
This vast flower-bedecked park covers an area of 57ha/140 acres. It is laid out in terraces on a hill overlooking the town to the east of the station. There is a small game reserve at the top (402m/1 318ft in altitude) in the **Galgenberg** open-air centre.

Musée de la Résistance
Place de la Résistance. Thur, Sat, Sun and public holidays 3-6pm. No charge. ☎ *54 84 72.*
This little museum was built in 1956 in the town centre to commemorate the heroism of the Luxembourg people and their resistance to the occupying forces (1940-44). The work in the mines and factories, the general strike of 1942, the struggle of the underground movement and the deportations are described through low reliefs, frescoes, statues and documents.

Excursions

Rumelange
6km/3.75mi SE on N 33.
This mining community near the French border features a fascinating mining museum, the **Musée National des Mines**. Parts of the iron mines worked on both sides of the border until 1958 are open to the public. The tour of 900m/0.5mi of galleries (temperature: 12ºC/53ºF), part of which is on a small train, gives an insight into the various extraction processes and the development of techniques and materials used since the mine was first opened. *Mid-Apr to end Oct; guided tours (2hr) 2-5pm; Nov to mid-Apr: second Sun of the month 2-5pm. €4.96.* ☎ *56 56 88.*

Rodange
12km/7mi NW. Take N 31 towards Differdange, then N 5.
Rodange is a small industrial town. A little tourist train *(from 2km/1.25mi S of the church on the Lasauvage road, as far as "Bois de Rodange")* pulled by century-old steam engines, travels about 6km/3.75mi through the **Fond de Gras Valley** overlooked by the Titelberg. A railcar operates a shuttle service between the road and the old Fond de Gras station. Once an iron-ore mine, this has become the starting point for the train ride. *Departures from Petange May-Sept, Sun and public holidays. Closed 23 Jun. 1st Class round trip €9; 2nd Class round trip €6.* ☎ *31 90 69.*

Bascharage
14km/8.5mi NW on A 13 or CR 110.
The **Brasserie Nationale** in this town makes a type of lager mostly consumed locally.
In the **Taillerie Luxembourgeoise de Pierres Précieuses** *(Rue de la Continentale, east of the station)* precious stones from all five continents are cut and polished. The stonecutters can be seen at work, and there is a large exhibition of minerals and jewels. *Guided tours (30min) Tue-Sat, 8.30am (Sat 8am)-noon, 1-5pm. Closed public holidays.* ☎ *50 90 32.*

Larochette★

In the valley of the Ernz Blanche river, this little town is dominated by sandstone crags, from one of which rise the ruins of two castles. Larochette makes an excellent starting point for exploring the surrounding countryside with its deep woods and extensive network of footpaths.

Location

Population 1 416 – Michelin maps 716 L6 and 717 W24.
On the edge of the Grand Duchy's Little Switzerland, Larochette is linked to Diekirch by N 14 and to Mersch by N 8.
🛈 *Hôtel de Ville, ☎ 83 76 76.*

Worth a Visit

Castles

Access via the Nommern road. Mid-Apr to Oct, 10am-6pm. €1.50. ☎ 268 70 206.
The ruins on the rocky plateau are all that remains of a pair of medieval strongholds. The 14C Palais des Créhange overlooks the town while the even older Palais des Hombourg rises above the road to Mersch.

Excursion

ROUND TRIP

12km/7.5mi – allow 30min.
Take the road towards Nommern.
The road emerges from the conifer forest revealing a heathland nature reserve on the left. From it rises the **Champignon**, a splendid mushroom-shaped block of sandstone.There are fine views as the roads drops down to **Nommern**.
At Nommern take the Larochette road.
The Circuit auto-pédestre no 2 (Motorists' Walk no 2) leaves from a left-hand bend in the road. It leads through the forest to the magnificent **Nommerlayen★**, an array of extraordinary sandstone formations in a wide variety of shapes.
Return to Larochette on N 8.

Luxembourg★★

The first impressions of the capital of the Grand Duchy are unexpected, built as it is on a plateau crisscrossed by ravines, which are spanned by innumerable bridges. Cross one, and Luxembourg comes across as a quiet country town; arrive by a different one and the city takes on the daunting aspect of a military bastion, or is revealed as a modern hub of business and seat of government. Its squares, with their elegant façades painted in pastel colours, could be the backdrop for a theatre production and numerous viewpoints disclose vistas of lush green valleys. Yet for all its apparent tranquillity, behind the scenes there is all the liveliness and activity to be expected of a capital city.

Location

Population 78 290 – Michelin maps 716 L7 and 717 V25.
The city is an important road junction, reached from Arlon in Belgium by the E 25 motorway which continues south to Thionville in France.
🛈 *Place d'Armes, BP 181, ☎ 22 28 09; www.Luxembourg-city.lu*

Background

The history of the city is closely connected with that of the country itself.
In Roman times, Luxembourg was situated at the intersection of two important roads, one from Trier to Reims via Arlon (now Grand-Rue), and the other linking Metz to Aachen. The sandstone outcrop now known as the Rocher de Bock had already been fortified. In the 10C, Count Sigefroi (from the Moselle), who styled himself Count of Luxembourg, built a castle near the upper town, on the Bock. A first defensive wall was erected around the upper town, then reinforced with a second the following century.

Sightseeing

Guided tours – Between April and October (Mon, Wed, Sat and Sun the rest of the year), the Tourist Information Centre offers guided tours of the old city centre, known as "City Promenades" starting at 2pm. In addition there are several other tours which can be carried out either with a guide or independently, in which case the appropriate brochure should be obtained from the TIC. Among them, the *Circuit Wenzel* goes through the old parts of town while the *Circuit Mansfeld* takes the visitor on an historic exploration of the Clausen district.

Tourist train – The little Petrusse Express is a "street train" which takes visitors round the lower town and the Pétrusse valley (Mar-Oct). Starting-point and tickets in Place de la Constitution.

Where to Eat

☞ **Il Cherubino** – *Rue Notre-Dame 10 –* ☏ *47 17 94 – Closed Sat eve, Sun –* ✂ *–* €20/32. Diners are greeted by a cherub at this little establishment just a few steps away from the old Jesuit college and the Cathedral. Tempting choice of Italian dishes and wines and authentic Italian atmosphere.

☞ **Caves Gourmandes** – *Rue Eau 32 –* ☏ *46 11 24 – Closed lunchtime Sat, Sun –* lunch €20 – €24/50. Gourmets flock to these vaulted cellars tucked away in a little street in the city centre, not far from the Grand-Ducal palace. Tasty dishes much influenced by the cuisine of southwestern France.

Where to Stay

☞ **Trust Inn** – *Rue de Neudorf 679 (the road to Trier) –* ☏ *423 05 11 – trustinn@pt.lu –* ▣ *– 7 rms:* €55/79 ⌑ This little hotel has charming bedrooms, in which breakfast is served (there is no separate breakfast room). Good sound-proofing keeps out the traffic noise in this busy position. Friendly reception.

☞ **Vasco da Gamma** – *Rue Joseph Junck 27 –* ☏ *49 30 70 –* ✂ *– 28 rms:* €59.49/81.80 ⌑ *– restaurant* €13.39/39.66. Conveniently located for the railway station, albeit in an area of slightly dubious character. Decor evokes the life of the celebrated explorer. Decent bedrooms. Portuguese and Mediterranean dishes in the restaurant.

☞☞ **Sieweburen** – *Rue Septfontaines 36 – 2534 Rollingergrund –* ☏ *44 23 56 – Closed mid-Dec – mid-Jan; restaurant closed Wed –* ▣ *– 14 rms:* €80/110 ⌑ *– restaurant* €26. Only a few minutes drive from town, this large timber-framed house is set in quiet, leafy surroundings. Impeccable rooms, some with mansard windows. Restaurant meals to suit everyone's taste and a selection of French and local wines.

☞☞ **Casanova** – *Place Guillaume II 10 –* ☏ *22 04 93 –* ✂ *– 17 rms:* €85/110 ⌑ *– restaurant* €24.55/39.65. This city centre establishment is on the square dominated by the equestrian statue of King William II. Contemporary, comfortable rooms which have recently been restored to their pristine state. Inn-restaurant with outdoor seating in fine weather.

Taking a Break

Namur – *Rue des Capucins 27 –* ☏ *22 34 08.* "By Appointment to the Ducal Court", this establishment founded in 1863 is a must for lovers of sweet things. Patisserie, chocolates, sweets and home-made ice cream prepared with loving care and with an eye to beauty as well as taste. Straightforward street-level tearoom and a more select atmosphere on the first floor.

Caves vinicoles de Wormeldange – *Route du Vin 115 – 5482 Wormeldange – May-Aug: 10am-5pm; Sept-Apr by appointment; Wäistuff May-Oct: 11am-8pm, Sat-Sun and public holidays 10.30am-8pm; Nov-Apr: Sat 3pm-8pm, Sun and public holidays 10.30am-12.30pm, 3pm-8pm.* The Poll-Fabaire sparkling wine cellars were established here in 1930. Explanations of how the product is made are followed by a tasting in the traditional Luxembourg "Wäistuff". Afternoon "wine-dance" on Sundays.

Brasserie Mansfeld – *Rue de la Tour Jacob 3 –* ☏ *43 34 86 – Tue-Sun 10am-1am.* This splendid country-style brasserie overlooking the Alzette is one of the city's most attractive places in which to enjoy a drink in the open air. Cosmopolitan clientele.

Tavern "Wëlle Mann" – *Rue Wiltheim 12 –* ☏ *47 17 83 – Tue-Sun 10am-7pm.* Traditional, long-established inn right by the National Museum, featuring a wonderful carved dresser and a superb ceramic fresco. Panoramic terrace overlooking the luxuriant valley of the Alzette.

Entertainment

Utopolis – *Avenue J-F Kennedy 45 –* ☏ *22 46 11 – www.pt.lu/infoweb/cinema/index.htm.* This vast complex next to a huge shopping centre in the rapidly developing Kirchberg area has a hi-tech cinema around which are grouped a range of leisure facilites, including themed bars and restaurants, a "Bistropolis" and a "Coyote Café" as well as boutiques.

Shopping

The streets around the Place d'Armes (including Grand-Rue, Rue des Capucins and Rue Chimay) are closed to traffic and are particularly suitable for browsing and window-shopping. The area around the railway station also provides many opportunities. Bear in mind that many shops are closed Monday morning.

Events and Festivals

The traditional folk festival of **Emais'chen**, when young lovers exchange terracotta ware sold especially for the occasion, takes place on Easter Monday on Place du Musée. In spring, the **Printemps Musical-Festival de Luxembourg** offers a wide variety of concerts, ranging from jazz to classical music. From the end of August onwards, on Place du Glacis, there is the big **Schueberfouer** fair and market which dates back to 1340.

In the 12C the city, along with the Count of Luxembourg, came under the rule of Henry V the Blind, Count of Namur. His grandson **Henry VII** became **Holy Roman Emperor** in 1308. The House of Luxembourg held the imperial throne until 1437. In 1346 the son of Emperor Henry VII, **John the Blind**, King of Bohemia and Count of Luxembourg, was killed fighting in the French ranks against the English at the Battle of Crécy. In the 14C a third line of defences was built around the upper town, while the lower towns were also fortified.

A strategic prize – In the 15C, Luxembourg fell into the hands of the House of Burgundy. It next passed to Emperor Charles V (in 1555) who fortified the city, then to Philip II.

The city came under French rule in 1684, after being skilfully besieged by **Vauban**, who went on to strengthen its fortifications. Having fallen once more into the hands of the Spaniards in 1698, it was occupied by the French again in 1701, who were in turn succeeded by the Austrians from 1714 to 1795. In spite of heavy reinforcement of its fortifications and the building of casemates, the city surrendered to a French Revolutionary force in 1795 and was incorporated into France. After the defeat of Napoleon, the Duchy was raised to a **Grand Duchy** by the Congress of Vienna. It was accountable to the German Confederation but belonged to the house of Orange-Nassau and was governed by William I, King of the Netherlands. As a result, the city was occupied by a Prussian garrison which did not leave Luxembourg until 1867. Once the country's neutrality had been declared in the Treaty of London, the three rings of fortifications were dismantled.

Despite its neutrality, Luxembourg was invaded by Germany in 1914 and again in 1940. It was liberated by American forces under General Patton on 10 September 1944.

A truly European city – In 1952 Luxembourg became the headquarters of the ECSC, the European Coal and Steel Community, the organisation which was to pave the way for an ever-closer association of the countries of Europe. When the European Economic Community (or Common Market) was formed in 1957, the city was chosen (together with Strasbourg) as the alternating home of the **General Secretariat of the European Parliament**.

In 1966 the 22-storey European Centre was completed on the Kirchberg plateau. This building was intended to bring the various departments of the General Secretariat of the European Parliament together under one roof.

Since 1967, when the executive councils of the three bodies of the ECSC, EURATOM and EEC merged to form a single commission with its headquarters in Brussels, many institutions have been set up on the Kirchberg. They include the European Investment Bank, departments of the Commission of the European Union (in particular the Statistics Department), the European School, the European Court of Justice (founded in 1952) and the Court of Auditors of the European Union. The Official Publications Office for the European Union is established in the city district known as Luxembourg-Gare.

Since 1965 the Council of Ministers, the main decision-making body within the European Union, has held its sessions in Luxembourg three times a year (in April, June and October). There are currently about 7 000 European civil servants in Luxembourg.

A MAGNIFICENT SETTING

The city and fortifications are perched on top of a sandstone bluff with precipitous sides, skirted by two rivers, the Alzette and the Pétrusse. The old town is separated from the modern one to the south by the deep gorge of the Pétrusse, which is spanned by bridges such as the famous **Pont Adolphe** (1899-1903), built in a bold, impressive style. To the north, it is linked to the Kirchberg plateau by the red-painted **Pont Grande-Duchesse Charlotte** (1964) spanning the Alzette. There are three districts in the valleys – Grund, Clausen and Pfaffenthal. Marvellous **views** of the city in all its varied guises can be enjoyed from every bend along the clifftop roads and promenades.

In the high season there is floodlighting, which shows off the city in its setting to full advantage.

The old quarters of the city and its extensive defences were given UNESCO World Heritage status in 1994.

Walking About

THE OLD TOWN★★

Allow half a day
Set off from Place d'Armes.

Place d'Armes

This shaded square is the lively centre of the city. In high season the cafés spill onto the pavements. Behind the bandstand is a column in honour of **Michel Lentz**, the author of the Luxembourg national anthem, and **Edmond de la Fontaine**, the local writer and composer. The main feature of the square is the **Palais Municipal**, built in 1907, which houses the tourist information centre. In a

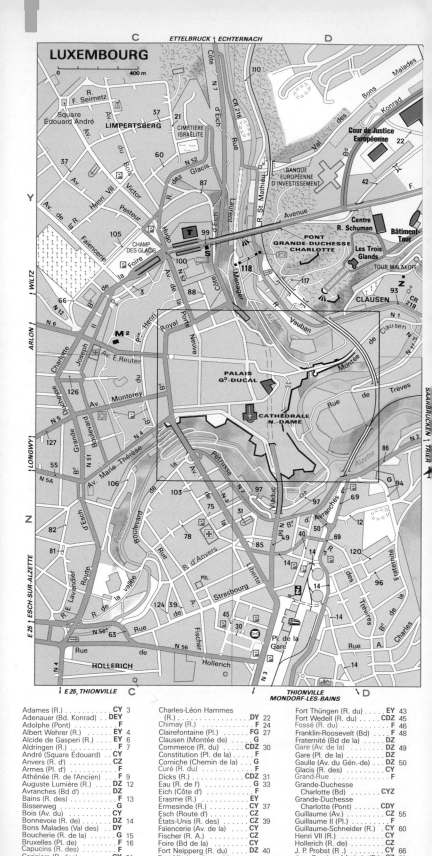

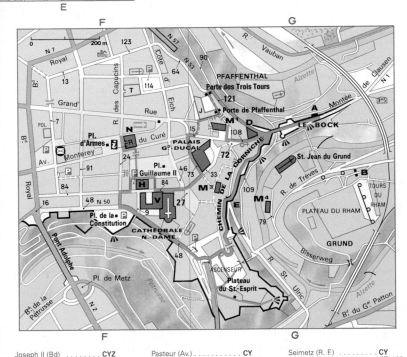

Ancien collège des Jésuites . . . . F V
Bâtiment J. Monnet . . . . EY
Cathédrale Notre-Dame . . . . F
Centre Robert Schuman . . . . DY
Conseil d'État . . . . G D
Cour de Justice Européenne . . . . . . DY
« Dent Creuse » . . . . G A
Hémicycle . . . . EY
Hôtel de ville . . . . F H
Le Bock . . . . G
Les Trois Glands . . . . DY
Maison natale de R. Schuman . . . . . DY Z
Monument Robert Schuman . . . . . . CY S
Musée J.-P. Pescatore . . . . CY M²
Musée National d'Histoire et d'Art . . G M¹
Musée d'Histoire de la Ville
  de Luxembourg . . . . G M³
Natur Musée . . . . G M⁴
Palais Grand-Ducal . . . . G
Palais municipal . . . . F N
Plateau du Saint-Esprit . . . . G
Porte Pfaffenthal . . . . G
Porte de Grund . . . . G E
Porte des Trois Tours . . . . G
Saint-Jean du Grund . . . . G
Théâtre municipal . . . . CY T
Tour Jacob . . . . G B

Place d'Armes

building on the corner of the square, on Rue du Curé, a **model** of the Luxembourg fortress is on show. *School holidays 10am-5pm. €1.49.* ☎ *22 28 09*
From Rue du Curé, a delightful passageway leads to Place Guillaume II.

Place Guillaume II
The equestrian statue of William II of the Netherlands (1792-1849), Grand Duke of Luxembourg, stands in the centre of the square. The **town hall**, in the local architectural style, was begun in 1830.
Go along Rue Chimay which leads to Place de la Constitution.

Place de la Constitution
This former bastion on the Beck, which includes a commemorative obelisk, affords marvellous **views**★★ of the Pont Adolphe and the Pétrusse gorge, now laid out as gardens. The entrance to the Pétrusse casemates is to be found here.
Take Boulevard Roosevelt to Plateau St-Esprit.
Boulevard Roosevelt is lined with the buildings of the **old Jesuit college**, including the new section of the cathedral.

Plateau St-Esprit
The impressive citadel designed by Vauban contains the monument to National Solidarity. There are **views**★★ from the top of the citadel across the Pétrusse and Alzette valleys, the Rham plateau and the lower town of Grund with its church.
From Plateau St-Esprit go down to the car park. To get from here to the Chemin de la Corniche and the Grund district, use the steps or the lift in a nerby modern building.

Chemin de la Corniche★★
This has been called "the most beautiful balcony in Europe" because of its **views**★★. You first go past the old building in which the State Archives are kept, before following the old ramparts along the edge of the Alzette escarpment, and reaching the enormous gateway known as the **Porte de Grund** (1632). The elegant façades of houses belonging to the nobility line this route, which overlooks the Grund and the spire of the Church of St-Jean-du-Grund in the valley below.

Le Bock
This spur of rock used to be linked to the town by a drawbridge (now the Pont du Château). It has been smoothed off somewhat by the construction of the road up from Clausen (Montée de Clausen).
The Bock formed the foundation of Luxembourg Castle, now in ruins, which was built in the 10C, demolished in 1555 and converted into a small fort in the 17C. Destroyed in 1684 when the town was besieged by the French, it was rebuilt by Vauban.
In 1745 the Austrians strengthened the fortifications and built the casemates. The Bock was razed in 1875. The only thing left standing is the tower called **Dent Creuse** ("hollow tooth").
From the top of the ruins there are **views**★★ of the Rham plateau which was the site of a Gallo-Roman villa. To the left is the huge square gate, known as **Tour Jacob** or Dinselpuert. This was the Trier gateway and formed part of the 14C defences. The buildings on the right are the barracks built by Vauban (hospices). At the foot of the Bock, on the north side, is the old St-Esprit convent (17C).

Casemates du Bock★★

Mar-Oct, 10am-5pm. €1.74. ☎ *22 28 09.*

In 1745, this defensive labyrinth was dug out of the sandstone outcrop on which the city is built. The section open to the public is a minute part of a network of 23km/14mi of underground passages which linked the various sections of the fortress and served as a shelter during the Second World War. The "archaeological crypt" contains remains of the fortress and an audio-visual presentation of its history. Some of the openings have views of the gorge and Rham district.

On the right of the entrance to the upper town a **monument** has been built to commemorate visits to Luxembourg by famous people, most notably Goethe in 1792. Nearby is the porticoed building housing the **Council of State**.

Go along Rue Sigefroi to Place du Marché.

Place du Marché

Once the intersection of Roman roads and formerly also the fish market, this square is surrounded by old houses. The one described as "Sous les Piliers" ("under the pillars") has Flamboyant Gothic style windows and, above a Renaissance portico, a niche in the same style containing a statue of St Anne and the Virgin Mary and Child. Further along on the left there is a picturesque house with a projecting turret.

Boulevard Victor Thorn

This boulevard affords **views**★ of the Alzette Valley, spanned by the Pont Vauban, and the huddle of the Pfaffenthal suburbs. Above the valley, the Pont Grande-Duchesse Charlotte connects the city with the Kirchberg plateau and the European Centre. The **Trois Glands** fort can be seen through a gap in the trees.

Porte des Trois Tours

Built on the site of the second set of town walls, this gate is in fact flanked by two, not three, towers.

The city centre is entered through the first **Porte de Pfaffenthal** (17C).

Go along Rue de la Boucherie and Rue du Marché aux Herbes to Place Clairefontaine.

Place Clairefontaine

A memorial to Grand Duchess Charlotte stands in this attractive square.

Cathédrale Notre-Dame★

The cathedral dates from the 17C and was originally a Jesuit church. Its delicate spires were added in the 20C. On the north side there is a fascinating **doorway** decorated with Renaissance and Baroque motifs.

The building is a good example of a hall-church, all three of its aisles being of the same height. The style is basically Gothic, although the pillars are decorated with unusual arabesques in relief, and the gallery above the entrance is very delicately worked in a style that is half Renaissance and half Baroque. On the left of the nave there is a gallery reserved for the Grand Ducal family. The neo-Gothic choir was added in the 20C. The miraculous statue of the Comforter of the Afflicted (national patron saint since 1678) is the object of particular devotion. A pilgrimage is held here during the third week after Easter.

Leave the cathedral by the door on the south side of the chancel to get to the treasury chapel and the **crypt**. The treasury chapel contains the cenotaph of John the Blind, killed at Crécy in 1346. The tomb was made in 1688 and depicts an *Entombment*. The crypt houses some fascinating works by modern artists. It was in the cathedral that Josephine Charlotte of Belgium married Jean de Luxembourg in 1953. He went on to become Grand Duke in 1964 following the abdication of his mother, Grand Duchess Charlotte. The Jesuit School adjacent to the cathedral is now the National Library (Bibliothèque Nationale).

From the cathedral return to Place d'Armes.

THE KIRCHBERG

Allow 30min – building works in progress.

Crossed by a motorway and home to a number of European institutions, the Kirchberg plateau has undergone considerable development (hotel, European School etc). The Parc des Expositions (exhibition centre) is beyond the plateau at the end of the motorway.

Before crossing the bridge leading to the Kirchberg, note the **Municipal Theatre** on the left. It was built in 1964 and has a long façade with windows arranged in a geometric pattern.

To the right of the road leading onto the bridge, there is a monument to the French statesman of Luxembourg origin, Robert Schuman, designed by Robert Lentz.

Pont Grande-Duchesse Charlotte★

Boldly painted in red, this steel structure over the Alzette was completed in 1966; it measures over 350m/1 148ft long.

Take the second road on the right after the bridge, towards the European Centre.

European Centre

The 22-storey building, completed in 1965, is occupied by the General Secretariat of the European Parliament. The Council of Ministers holds sessions here for three months every year. Additional space was created by a smaller building, the **Centre Robert Schuman**. A third structure, the **Hémicycle**, was finished in 1980 and is used as a conference centre.

Take the road which leads into the woods behind the European Centre to get to the Trois Glands.

Les Trois Glands

Once part of the city's outer ring of defences, the massive 18C Fort Thüngen is also known as the Three Acorns (*glands* in French) because of the acorn-shaped decorations crowning its drum-like towers.

Turn left at the end of the lawn.

A small viewpoint overlooks Clausen and its church. To the left is the turreted house in which Robert Schuman was born. To the right, there is a **view★** of the city, the Bock, and the Rham district with its tower blocks.

Return to the European Centre and go under the motorway to reach the European Court of Justice.

European Court of Justice

The dark-brown painted steel structure of the four-storey European Court, built in 1970, stands on a vast terrace, on which there are two sculptures by Henry Moore and Lucien Wercollier.

The nearby **Bâtiment Jean Monnet**, with its walls of smoked glass, houses the administration offices.

Worth a Visit

Musée national d'Histoire et d'Art★

Tue-Sun 10am-5pm. Closed 1 Jan, 1 Nov, 25 Dec. €5. ☎ 47 93 30-1; www.mnha.lu

Gallo-Roman collection★ – This particularly rich collection is to be found mainly on the ground floor. Digs carried out in the south of the country (at Dalheim and on the Titelberg) revealed that the area was densely populated in Roman times. The exhibits are well displayed and include bronzes, terracotta and delicate glassware.

The numerous funerary monuments may be compared with those in Trier and Arlon. The little house-shaped stones, which may have contained urns, and the stones carved with the four divinities were widespread in the south of Luxembourg. The Merovingian period has left a legacy of weapons and beautiful jewellery. The **Salle des Médailles** or treasury displays rare items from all historical periods, including the remarkable **bronze mask of Hellange** dating from the 1C.

Fine art collection – A range of religious sculptures (11C-18C) is laid out in various rooms in this section, as well as in the Gallo-Roman section and in the rooms devoted to Luxembourg Life.

Musée national d'Histoire et d'Art, Luxembourg

A fireback (1586)

Most of the works displayed in the **Ancient Art** section (3rd floor) come from three collections – the Edmond Reiffers Collection (Italian paintings from the 13C-16C), the Wilhelmy-Hoffmann Collection (Northern European Schools and Flemish works from the 16C-17C; note a *Charity* by Cranach the Elder and a copy of the Hachiville altarpiece) and the Bentick-Thyssen Collection (temporary exhibition).

The **Modern Art** section (1st and 2nd floor) includes sculptures by Rodin, Maillol, Lobo, and Hadju, canvases and figurative or abstract tapestries by the Paris School (Bertholle, Bissière, Borès, Chastel, Estève, Fautrier, Gilioli, Lurçat, Pignon, Soulages, Tàpies, Veira da Silva) and works by the Luxembourg Expressionist Joseph Kutter (1894-1941).

Luxembourg Life section (decorative arts, folk art and tradition)★★ – *Access via the first floor of the Musée d'Histoire et d'Art.*

Displayed in four old town residences, this outstanding section of the museum gives an insight into life in Luxembourg from the 16C to the 20C. The interiors are decorated with beautiful furniture, Boch faience (Septfontaines), Nospelt pottery, pewterware, and a large collection of paintings under glass.

Firebacks are on display in the vaulted cellars, part of which is devoted to the viti-culture of the Moselle Valley, famed for its white and sparkling wines.

Palais Grand-Ducal★

Mid-Jul to end Aug: guided tours (50min) Mon-Fri pm, Sat am. For further information contact the Tourist Information Centre. Individual visitors should buy their tickets from the Tourist Information Centre on Place d'Armes. €5.50. ☎ 22 28 09.

The left wing, formerly the town hall, dates back to the 16C. Graceful turrets flank its façade, which is decorated with geometric patterns in low relief.

The right wing, known as La Balance, was added in 1741, and the rear wing, which has a view of the garden, in 1891. The building (1859) on the right of La Balance is the lower House of Parliament. Since 1895, most official functions have been held in this palace. A collection of well-preserved weapons is kept in the guard-room. The main staircase, with a charming balustrade decorated with the monogram of Adelaide-Marie, wife of Grand Duke Adolf, leads off to the suites.

The former Room of the Nobles, also known as the **Salon des Rois**, where por-traits of all the past Grand Dukes are hung, is used for official audiences. In the dining room there are four tapestries which were a gift from Napoleon after his stay at the palace in 1804. They illustrate the story of Telemachus.

Musée d'Histoire de la Ville de Luxembourg★

Tue-Sun 10am-6pm (Thur 8pm). Closed 1 Jan, 1 Nov, 25 Dec. €2.40. ☎ 47 96 45 00.

Laid out in a highly original and stimulating way, the city's history museum occu-pies four recently restored houses dating from the 17C, 18C and 19C. The original buildings are believed to date back to the Middle Ages; in the 18C they were used as a refuge for the Abbaye d'Orval.

The museum presents a fascinating survey of the city's history from its early days up to the present through a host of exhibits: audio-visual presentations, ancient documents, interactive terminals, handwritten maps, seals, weapons, paintings and helmets, including a splendid engraved 16C helmet. Note the six maplewood mod-els (on a scale of 1:666) which show how the city has evolved over time. The exhi-bition focuses heavily on Luxembourg as a fortress-town, much fought-over by the European powers. Other areas of activity are evoked, such as the economy (includ-ing ARBED, Luxembourg's giant steel company), politics (independence in 1890), religion (Marian cult) and art (the town has always been a thriving cultural centre).

The upper floors illustrate the remarkable social changes that have taken place since the 19C, including the emergence of the modern bourgeoisie, new leisure activities, free schooling and daily life in the capital.

Casemates de la Pétrusse

Entrance on Place de la Constitution. Open summer, Easter and Whitsun holidays: guided tours (50min) 11am-4pm. €1.75. ☎ 22 28 09.

This extensive network of underground passages opening onto the Pétrusse Valley was created in 1746 by the Austrians to improve defences on the southern side of the plateau.

Villa Vauban

Open for temporary exhibitions Tue-Sun 10am-6pm (Thur 8pm). Closed 1 Jan, 1 Nov, 25 Dec. €2.50. ☎ 47 96 30 61.

The sophisticated 19C interior of the Villa Vauban makes a fine setting for a col-lection of Belgian, Dutch and French painting from the 17C up to the present day. After a number of paintings attributed to Canaletto (Room 3), note among the Flemish canvases works from the 17C by David Teniers the Younger *(Interior, The Smoker).*

The extensive 17C Dutch collection includes several genre paintings (Gérard Dou's *Empirical*, Jan Steen's *Festival of Kings*) and a Van de Capelle seascape. 19C French painting is represented notably by a Delacroix *(Young Turk Stroking his Horse)* and a Courbet *(Seascape).*

The museum also organises temporary exhibitions.

THE SUBURBS

A drive along the right bank of the Alzette through the suburbs of lower Grund, Pfaffenthal and Clausen reveals a completely different side of the city. These are working-class districts, with little houses and breweries still producing local beers. There are also very different views of the old town and its fortifications from these districts at the bottom of the ravines.

Natur Musée

 ♿ *Tue-Sun 10am-6pm. Closed 1 Jan, 1 Nov, 24, 25, 31 Dec. €4.50.* ☎ *46 22 33-1.*

The 14C Hospice St-Jean stands in a wonderful setting at the heart of the ancient district of Grund and forms part of the UNESCO World Heritage site. The buildings house the Musée National d'Histoire Naturelle (National Museum of Natural History). The original premises were used first as an asylum and an orphanage and were later converted into a women's prison in the 19C. On the ground floor, interactive terminals and educational displays provide information on the human body and its subtle workings, the development of the human being from fertilisation to birth, and the position occupied by the human species in the world. Dioramas, interactive screens and a collection of stuffed animals enlighten visitors on the various regions of the Grand Duchy.

The first floor explains the different planets of our solar system and the Big Bang phenomenon and explores the links between humanity and the animal world.

Église St-Jean-du-Grund

This church dedicated to St John belonged to the Benedictine Abbey in Munster until the French Revolution. The present building dates from 1705.

The outstanding features of the interior are the three Flemish Baroque altarpieces in the chancel. Note also the Stations of the Cross in 16C Limoges enamel made by Leonard Limosin, the 18C organ, the Gothic font and, in a chapel to the left of the nave, a graceful *Black Virgin and Child* of the Cologne School, carved in c 1360 and the object of great veneration.

Excursions

Military Cemeteries

5km/3mi E. Leave via Boulevard du Général Patton.

The American Cemetery at **Hamm**, just outside the capital, is one of 13 American Second World War cemeteries in Europe. It recalls the Grand Duchy of Luxembourg's gratitude to its liberators. This imposing 20ha/50 acre cemetery is in woods, overlooked by a memorial chapel built in 1960, and contains 5 076 graves. Opposite the white crosses arranged in a curve stands General Patton's grave, identical in design to all the others.

Further to the east *(access via the Contern road)* is the **Sandweiler German Cemetery**, inaugurated in 1955. It comes into sight at a bend in the forest road. Broad lawns, on which trees have been planted and short crosses made of dark Black Forest granite arranged in groups of five, cover an area of 4ha/9.8 acres. A monumental cross stands over the common grave in which 4 829 soldiers out of the 10 885 buried in this cemetery have been laid to rest.

From Luxembourg to Bettembourg

15km/9.3mi S, towards Thionville.

Hespérange is a picturesque town on the banks of the Alzette. Above it are the ruins of a 13C-14C castle, among which small homes with tiny front gardens have been built.

Bettembourg has a large recreation park, the **Parc Merveilleux**. The 30ha/74 acre grounds have animals and numerous attractions for children, in particular reconstructions of fairy-tale scenes. ♿ *End Mar to mid-Oct: 9.30am-6pm. €6.* ☎ *51 10 48 24.*

From Luxembourg to Junglinster

13km/8mi N, towards Echternach.

A lovely drive through the heart of a thick forest leads to Eisenborn, on the banks of the River Ernz Blanche. **Bourglinster**, a picturesque village at the foot of an old restored castle, is to the right.

Junglinster has a charming 18C church with rendered stonework enhanced by pastel paintings. It is surrounded by an old **cemetery** with 19C crosses that have a faintly archaic look.

Mondorf-les-Bains ★

Close to the border with France, Mondorf is a popular spa town whose warm (24°C) waters are used to treat rheumatism and liver and stomach complaints. The spa establishment with its modern facilities lies to the east of the old town; it is reached via the Avenue des Bains which is graced by a number of lovely Art Nouveau edifices.

Location

Population 3 292 – Michelin maps 716 L7 and 717 W25.
In the southeast of the country and right next to the small town of Mondorff just across the border in France, Mondorf-les-Bains is linked to the Moselle valley by N 16 and to Thionville in France by D 1.
🛈 *Avenue des Bains 26, ☎ 66 75 75; www.mondorf-info-lu.*

Directory

WHERE TO STAY

Grand-Chef – *Avenue des Bains 36 – ☎ 66 80 12 – granchef@pt.lu – mid-Mar – late Nov – restaurant closed Wed lunchtime exc public holidays –* 🅿 *– 35 rms: €61/95* ⌂ *– restaurant €21/36.* Next to Mondorf's spa establishment, this venerable private hotel offers spacious, comfortable bedrooms, elegant public spaces and a welcoming bar. Extensive park with a lake.

TAKING A BREAK

Propriété viticole Schumacher-Knepper – *Route du Vin 28 – 5495 Wintrange – ☎ 66 40 08 – www.schumacher knepper.lu – by arrangement.* This estate on the Wine Route welcomes visitors with an informative guided tour around its cellars and invites them to a tasting of its products, which include the sparkling wine Alexandre de Musset.

Worth a Visit

Park★

By the spa buildings, this 36ha/88 acre park, with lovely trees and shrubs and colourful flowerbeds, extends over a hillside, offering pretty views of the local countryside. The new pavilion for the Kind spring (1963) is in the centre of the park.

Église St-Michel

8am-6pm. This pink pebble-dashed church stands on a hill overlooking the old town. It was built in 1764 and is surrounded by a cemetery. Inside it has sumptuous Louis XV **furnishings★**. The organ loft carved with musical emblems, the confessionals, the altars and the remarkable pulpit are all in perfect harmony with the stuccowork and *trompe-l'œil* frescoes painted by Weiser (1766), an artist born in Bohemia.

Vallée de la **Moselle luxembourgeoise**★

Running through the Grand Duchy from Schengen on the French border to Wasserbillig, the River Moselle, from the Latin name Mosella or "little Meuse", separates Luxembourg from Germany, at times reaching a width of 100m/109yd. The main attractions of the route along this valley are the hillsides carpeted with vines, the pretty wine villages, and a certain special quality of the light which enhances the attractiveness of this lovely landscape still further.

Location
Michelin maps 716 M6 and 717 X25-26.
Access from Mondorf-les-Bains by CR 152 and from Luxembourg city by N 2/E 29.

Background

A vast programme of engineering works completed in 1964 improved the navigability of the Moselle, making it accessible to vessels of 3 200t from its confluence with the Rhine at Koblenz upstream as far as Thionville in France.
Installations along the Luxembourg section of the river include dams at Grevenmacher and Stadtbredimus, each with a lock and a hydroelectric plant. All structures were built at water level so as not to disfigure the surrounding countryside.

Tour

THE WINE ROAD
46km/29mi – allow half a day
Take N 10 which runs along the Moselle for the whole of the route.

Schengen
With its extensive vineyards and its wine-cellars, Schengen is the prime winegrowing area of the Luxembourg Moselle region, but the name of this border village is perhaps more famous for the treaty signed here aboard the pleasure steamer *Marie-Astrid* on 14 June 1985. Providing for the abolition of internal bor-

Directory

SIGHTSEEING
Rambles – The Moselle footpath runs for about 40km/25mi along the river bank from the Stromberg, a hill south of Schengen, to Wasserbillig.
Boat trips – A boat trip along the Moselle between Wasserbillig and Schengen is a marvellous way to enjoy the valley landscape with its vineyards and wine-villages.

WHERE TO EAT
⊜ **Pavillon St Martin** – *Route de Stadtbredimus 53 – 5570 Remich – ☎ 23 66 91 02 – Closed mid-Dec – late Jan, Mon – ☑ – €24/44.* Lazing by the riverbank, this restaurant with its outdoor seating combines tradition and variety, offering everything from a vintner's snack to *coq au riesling* and bountiful salads. Local wines make a fine accompaniment.
⊜⊜ **Côté Moselle** – *Route du vin 3 –5445 Schengen – ☎ 266 66 21 – Closed Tue out of season – ☑ – lunch €10 – €34.50/40.50.* In a modern building in a new part of Schengen this brasserie offers a range of uncomplicated dishes, served in fine weather on a landscaped terrace with a view towards the river.

WHERE TO STAY
⊜ **L'Écluse** – *Route du Vin 29 – 5450 Stadtbredimus – ☎ 236 19 11 – restaurant closed Christmas fortnight, fortnight in June, Wed lunchtime, Thur – ▣ – 16 rms: €45/60 ☑ – restaurant €22/35.* Small family establishment overlooking one of the locks on the river. Fairly compact, functional rooms, some with balconies. A well-lit conservatory houses the restaurant. Attractive terrace and garden.
⊜ **de l'Esplanade** – *Esplanade 5 – 5533 Remich – ☎ 23 66 91 71 – esplanade@pt.lu – Closed Dec-Jan, Mon exc mid-June – mid-Aug – 18 rms: €51/73 ☑ – restaurant €16/37.* Just a step from Remich town centre and overlooking the Moselle. Soberly decorated small bedrooms, some with a view of the river. Classic decor in the dining room which opens onto a canopied outdoor terrace.

SPECIALITIES
Moselle wines – Wines from the vineyards of the Luxembourg section of the Moselle can be tasted in the main wine cooperatives. There are white wines, from the Rivaner, Auxerrois, Pinot blanc, Pinot gris, Riesling, Traminer and Elbling varieties, and few rosé and sparkling wines.

Luxembourg Moselle Valley

ders between the countries concerned and the setting up of a common external border, the **Schengen Agreement** was initially signed by representatives of Luxembourg, Germany, France, Belgium and the Netherlands, and its scope has since been extended to other countries of the European Union.

Remerschen

Set back slightly from the river, this town is at the foot of the vine-clad slopes of the Kapberg. A steep flight of steps rises past Stations of the Cross to a Calvary.

Schwebsange

In a garden to the right of the road are a 15C winepress and a fruit-crushing machine.

More winepresses can be seen by the church, as can the charming fountain known as the **Fontaine des Enfants aux Raisins**, around which the annual Wine Festival takes place.

Schwebsange also boasts the Grand Duchy's only marina.

Bech-Kleinmacher

The old wine-growers' houses, "A Possen" (1617) and "Muedelshaus", have been turned into the **Musée Folklorique et Viticole**.

Small rooms with rustic furniture (kitchen with an open fire) serve as reminders of life in the past. Traditional activities are presented in workshops and other features include a dairy, a wine museum and a wine cellar complete with a grape-crushing vat. *May-Oct: Tue-Sun 2-7pm; Mar-Dec, Fri-Sun 2-7pm. Closed 25 Dec. €4.* ☏ *23 69 73 53.*

Take the Wellenstein road which runs past the front of the museum.

Wellenstein

On the approach to this attractive village with its 70ha/172 acres of vineyards are the Grand Duchy's largest **wine cooperatives**. ♿ *May-Aug: guided tours (1hr) Tue-Fri 9am-noon, Sat 11am-6pm, Sun, public holidays 2-7pm. €1.75.* ☏ *23 6966-1.*

The road climbs the **Scheuerberg** (views of the vineyards) then descends to Remich (views of the Moselle).

In Remich, return to the Moselle.

Remich

The town of Remich has several wine cellars. The **Caves St-Martin** to the north of the town, which have been hollowed out of the rock, specialise in the production of sparkling wines. ♿ *Feb-Nov: guided tours (1hr) 10am-noon, 1.30-6pm. €2.55.* ☏ *23 69 97 74.*

The river bank at Remich has been laid out as a long promenade.

Stadtbredimus

Large wine cooperatives.

Shortly after Stadtbredimus, take the Greiveldange road on the left.

As the road climbs the hill there are fine **views★** of the Moselle's meandering course, the steep vine-clad Luxembourg slopes and, on the German side towards Palzem, a more gently undulating countryside which is also planted with vineyards.

Beyond **Greiveldange**, which has a large wine cooperative, return to the valley.

Ehnen

This wine-growing village still has an old quarter with cobbled streets, as well as a round church, built in 1826 and flanked with a Romanesque tower.

A vintner's home has been turned into the **Musée du Vin**. Tools used until the 1960s are on show here, and photographs give a pleasant illustration of the cultivation of vines and production of Moselle wine in days gone by. Related professions, such as coopering are also mentioned, and the tour ends with a wine-tasting session. *Apr-Oct: Tue-Sun. 9.30-11.30am, 2-5pm. €3.* ☎ *76 00 26.*

Wormeldange

This is the main town in the Luxembourg Riesling area. There are large **wine cooperatives** near the exit of the town, on the left. *May-Oct: guided tours (1hr) Mon-Sat 1-6pm. Closed public holidays. €2.* ☎ *23 69 66-1; www.vinsmoselle.lu.*

High up on the spot known as **Koeppchen**, where an old castle once stood, is a chapel dedicated to St Donat. From here there is a fine view of the river and of Wormeldange.

Machtum

This small village lies on a bend in the river. A winepress and a fruit-crusher are on display on a lawn.

The bend straightens out to reveal the vast **Grevenmacher dam** with its lock and power station.

Grevenmacher

Surrounded by vineyards and orchards, this little town is a major wine-growing centre with cooperative wine cellars and a private cellar. The **wine cooperatives** are in the north of the town *(Rue des Caves).*& *May-Aug: guided tours (1hr) Mon-Sat 10am-5pm. €1,75.* ☎ *23 69 66-1.* South of the bridge are the **Caves Bernard-Massard**, founded in 1921. They produce a sparkling wine using the champagne method. The tour of the lower cellars ends with a documentary film on the Grand Duchy of Luxembourg, the Moselle, wine-growing and the production of sparkling wine. & *Apr-Oct: guided tours (1hr) 9.30am-6pm. €2.50.* ☎ *750 54 51.*

Mertert

This busy commercial port is linked to Wasserbillig by a riverside footpath.

Wasserbillig

Situated at the confluence of the Moselle and the Sûre, this town on the border with Germany is an important road junction, tourist centre and starting point for boat trips.

Petite Suisse
Luxembourgeoise★★★

The natural attractions of the area known as Luxembourg's Little Switzerland include lovely forests of beech, hornbeam, pine, birch and oak, rich, damp pastures, stretches of heathland with bracken, bilberry and mosses, and foaming streams tumbling along in their boulder-strewn beds. Deep in the woodland, strange rock formations contribute their own special note to the charm of this romantic landscape.

Location

Michelin maps 716 L6 – M6 and 717 X24.

Part of the Germano-Luxembourg national park, Little Switzerland is bounded by Echternach, Beaufort, Larochette and Consdorf. Access from Echternach by N 10.

🖪 *Porte St-Willibrord, Parvis de la Basilique – Echternach –* ☎ *72 02 30; www.echternach.lu*

Tour

34km/21mi from Echternach – allow 1 day

Echternach★ – *(See ECHTERNACH)*

From Echternach take N 10 towards Diekirch.

The road follows the course of the River Sûre and passes close to the Gorge du Loup/Wolfschlucht.

Turn immediately left towards Berdorf.

About 1km/0.5mi on from the fork the road is joined by **Footpath B** which goes down from the Wolfschlucht into the Aesbach Valley.

Directory

Where to Eat

⊜⊜ **Le Cigalon** – *Rue Ernz Noire 1 – 6245 Müllerthal – ☎ 79 94 95 – le cigalon@internet.lu – hotel closed Jan-Feb; restaurant closed Mar – €27/49.* Nestling in the forest, an establishment in which both bedrooms and restaurant are imbued with a Provençal spirit ("Cigalon" means "cicada"). Lovely terrace and grounds with views of the verdant surroundings. Fitness room.

⊜⊜⊜ **Reilander Millen** – *On the Juglinster-Müllerthal road – 7639 Reuland – ☎ 83 72 52 – Closed 3 wks around Carnival, mid-Aug – mid-Sept, Mon and Sat lunchtime – lunch €12 – €45/55.* An 18C mill and a leafy valley form the setting for this restaurant. Meals are served in a pretty, country-style dining room. The menu is not large, but very appetising, and changes with the seasons. Good range of wines.

Where to Stay

⊜ **de la Station** – *Route d'Echternach 10 – 6250 Scheidgen – ☎ 79 08 91 –info@hoteldelastation.pt.lu – early April – mid-Mar – restaurant closed Mon, Tue –* P *– 25 rms: €47/75 ☕ – restaurant €43.* A good place to stay, with well-kept rooms and countryside views. Good soundproofing takes care of the noise from the road. Pleasantly shaded garden. Dining room in typical local style.

Le Perekop

This is a rock about 40m/131ft high, which overhangs the road on the right and looks like a set of ruins. A flight of steps in a crevice leads up to the top, where there is a view of the surrounding woods.

Walk★★ – At Le Perekop **Footpath B** (Echternach to Grundhof) runs along at road level. The stretch running west along the River Aesbach to where the path diverges *(30min)* is among the most attractive in the area. Note the rocks worn down by erosion. They include the Tour Malakoff and, further on, the Chipkapass. When the road leaves the woods, Berdorf comes into view ahead on the plateau.

Berdorf – *(See BERDORF)*

From Berdorf take the Müllerthal road.

Not far along on the left is the **Predigstuhl**, a pulpit-shaped rock which partially conceals the **Werschrumschluff★** behind it.

The road slopes steeply down into the Müllerthal Valley.

At Vugelsmullen (or Vogelsmuhle) in the Müllerthal, take a right turn immediately followed by a left towards Beaufort.

Beaufort

Set on a rise, this small town produces a blackcurrant liqueur called Cassero.

Château de Beaufort★

Apr-Oct, 9am-6pm. €2. ☎ 83 60 02.

The romantic-looking ruins of this fortress (12C-16C) stand in a wooded valley near a lake. In 1871, Victor Hugo wrote of the castle, "It comes into sight round a bend, at the foot of a gorge in a forest; it's like a vision. It's magnificent." The old

Rock formations in Luxembourg's Petite Suisse

Ph. Gajic/MICHELIN

SHAPELY SANDSTONE

Forming part of one of the escarpments ("côtes") of the Gutland, the calcareous Luxembourg sandstone has been sculpted by the erosive forces of Nature with amazing results. Erosion has worn grooves into the rocks, often making them look like tumble-down walls. Once water had eroded it, the sandstone plateau broke up, fissures appeared between the sedimentary layers, and huge blocks (diaclases) broke away and began to slide downhill towards the valley on their bed of argillaceous limestone.

Numerous signposted footpaths invite you to explore "Little Switzerland" and discover the springs, ravines and gullies of this fascinating landscape.

castle consists of a huge, towering keep linked to a fortress. Restorations in 1930 tidied it up and made it more accessible. The neighbouring castle was built by the lord of Beaufort in 1647. The footpath from the west side of the lake leads towards the Hallerbach waterfall.

Return to Vogelsmuhle by car. Just before the hamlet, a small road branches off to the right along the Müllerthal. About 300m/328yd along this road, leave the car and take the footpath leading to the Hallerbach (allow 30min return on foot).

Hallerbach★

The river can be seen through the woods tumbling down through mossy boulders and forming charming little waterfalls *(allow 30min return on foot)*.

Return to Vogelsmuhle and turn right.

Müllerthal★★★

This is the name given to the valley of the **Ernz Noire**. Interrupted now and then by cascades, the river flows between banks carpeted with meadows and backing onto wooded slopes. Spectacular outcrops of sandstone can be seen rising from the trees.

Continue, then turn left towards Consdorf.

To get back to the top of the plateau the road follows a little valley with attractive rock formations jutting out here and there along its sides.

Consdorf

This village on the edge of the woods is very popular during the summer months.

Scheidgen

A popular holiday place.

Return to Echternach via Lauterborn.

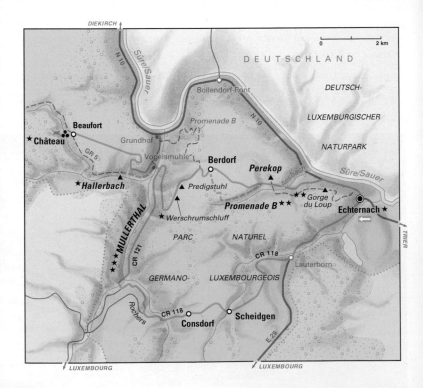

Rindschleiden*

This peaceful little hamlet tucked away in its leafy valley is famous for its parish church which possesses a remarkably complete set of frescoes. In a garden nearby is the miraculous well of St Willibrord, the object of an annual pilgrimage. By its side stands an old 15C font.

Location
Michelin maps 716 fold 18 and 717 U23 – Local map see VALLÉE DE LA SÛRE.
Rindschleiden is on the CR 308 to the south of Esch-sur-Sûre.

Worth a Visit

Parish Church*
The church is Romanesque in origin. Its chancel was altered in the Late Gothic period, while the nave was enlarged in the 16C and given three vaults of equal height.
Inside, all the vaulting and the walls of the chancel are covered with **frescoes**. Dating from the early 15C (chancel) and 16C (nave), they were only discovered and restored in 1952. They depict a multitude of figures in clear colours outlined in black; there are saints, royal personages, and a variety of religious scenes.
Note also the 17C and 18C wooden statues as well as some fine examples of carving in stone: a 15C Eucharistic Cabinet surmounted by an oculus, keystones, capitals and 16C statues on the springers of the vaulting.

Vallée de la **Sûre**★★

The River Sûre rises high up in the Belgian Ardennes, then flows eastward across Luxembourg to its confluence with the Our at Wallendorf. From here it turns southeast, forming the border with Germany as far as Wasserbillig where it joins the Moselle. One way of exploring the valley of this fascinating river with its verdant banks and rocky outcrops is to walk the signposted footpaths which follow much of its course.

Location
Michelin maps 716 K6 – L6 – M6 and 717 folds 3, 4.
In the heart of the Luxembourg Ardennes, the valley of the Sûre can be reached by N 15 which links Bastogne in Belgium with Ettelbruck.
Maison du Parc, Route de Lultzhausen 15, 9650 Esch-sur-Sûre, ☎ 899 33 11; www.naturpark-sure.lu

Tour

UPPER VALLEY★★ 1
68km/42mi – allow half a day
This is the most beautiful stretch of the Sûre, where the river cuts deeply into the ancient massif of the Oesling.
The valley through which the road runs is also followed by the Haute-Sûre footpath linking Martelange on the border to Ettelbruck, 60km/37mi away.

Hochfels*
From the chalet on this 460m/1 509ft summit there is a **bird's-eye view** of the winding valley and its wooded slopes.
The route passes through the village of Boulaide and crosses the Sûre at **Pont-Misère**. It then climbs, giving fine **views** over the Haute-Sûre lake downstream from the bridge as well as back to the Hochfels and Boulaide.

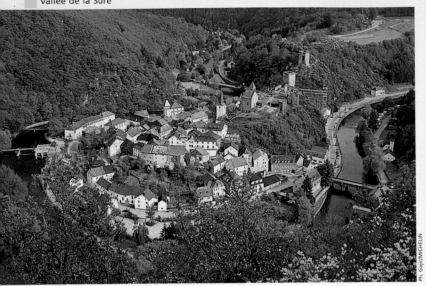

Esch-sur-Sûre

Insenborn

This place on the **Lac de la Haute-Sûre**★ is popular for water sports *(sailing, windsurfing, boating, swimming, fishing, diving)*, which are permitted upstream of Lultzhausen.

From Insenborn to Esch-sur-Sûre the road runs along the shore of the lake. There are remarkable **viewpoints**★ over the green, winding river banks covered with broom and bristling with firs.

Barrage d'Esch-sur-Sûre

At the base of this 48m/157ft high dam, which has a capacity of 62 million m^3/2 190 million cu ft, there is a hydroelectric plant. Two secondary dams have been built to control flooding – Bavigne *(northwest)* and Pont-Misère *(upstream)*.

There is a good **view**★ of the lake from the Kaundorf road, on a bend 800m/0.5mi beyond the dam.

Esch-sur-Sûre★

With its slate-roofed houses stepping up the hillside, this picturesque village is almost completely encircled by a meander in the Sûre. Guarding the landward approach, on top of the crags dropping steeply to the river, are the ruins of a castle.

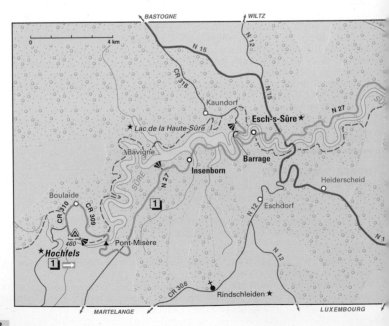

There is a fine view of the ruins and of the village in its setting from the round watchtower on the hilltop beyond the castle. The castle itself dates back to the 10C and was demolished in 1795. The village still has some traces of its medieval walls.

On the way downstream towards Göbelsmuhle there are occasional views down to the Sûre in its thickly wooded gorge.

Having entered the Haute-Sûre national park and passed through Göbelsmuhle, the road comes within sight of the Château de Bourscheidon its hilltop site.

After Lipperscheid take the road on the left.

Point de Vue de Grenglay★★
15min return on foot, via a path signposted "Point de Vue".

From the lip of this impressive escarpment there is a fine **view** of the Château de Bourscheid on its promontory high above the river.

Return to N 27 and turn right towards Château de Bourscheid.

Château de Bourscheid★
Apr, 11am-5pm; May-Jun, 10am-6pm; Jul-Sept: 10am-7pm; Oct, 11am-4pm; Nov-Mar, Sat, Sun and public holidays 11am-4pm. €3. ☎ 99 05 70.

Built from the local brown-coloured schist, the **ruins★** of this castle crown a spectacular site 155m/508ft above the Sûre. An 11C keep and a Gothic fireplace remain from the upper castle or fortress. The lower part of the castle, including the gabled residence known as the Stolzembourg Mansion, was built in the 14C and altered many times since. In the 19C it fell into ruin, but it has been restored since 1972 and is now a museum displaying objects found during digs at the castle (pottery, architectural fragments). It is also used to host temporary exhibitions. On the ground floor are reproductions of drawings of the castle.

There are fine **views★** of the surrounding area from the keep and towers.

Just to the left of the entrance to a camp site about 800m/0.5mi beyond the castle, a **viewpoint★★** gives a superb perspective over the ruins and the valley.

Return to the valley.

From here the river descends southwards towards Erpeldange through a lush **landscape★** of trees and meadows.

THE LOWER VALLEY★ ②
57km/35mi – allow half a day

The lower course of the Sûre is less austere and more pastoral. After emerging from the Ardennes massif, the river flows between gentler slopes and wider fields. The road stays close to the river nearly all the way to its confluence with the Moselle.

Beyond Erpeldange, on the far side of the bridge towards Ettelbruck, there is a memorial to General Patton.

Ettelbruck
This is a road and railway junction at the confluence of the Sûre and the Alzette, as well as a commercial and agricultural centre.

Diekirch – *(See DIEKIRCH)*
Take N 17, then N 19 towards Reisdorf.

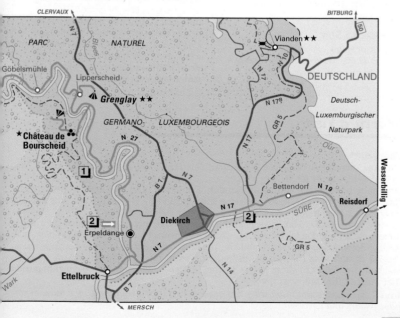

Reisdorf

This charming village stands at the entrance to the pretty valley of the Ernz Blanche. Shortly after the village, near Wallendorf, the River Our flows into the Sûre.
Take the N 10 to Echternach.

Echternach★ – (See ECHTERNACH)
Continue on N 10.

Barrage de Rosport

Downstream from Rosport, the Sûre forms a gigantic loop. The river is held back by a large dam, whose hydroelectric power station is fed by a pressure pipe leading from the entrance to the meander, the flow of the river being thereby artificially accelerated by the enhanced gradient.
At **Wasserbillig** the Sûre flows into the Moselle.

Vianden★★

This picturesque little town has a remarkable setting★★ on the River Our. Clinging to the slopes, its old houses are dominated by the romantic outline of the imposing castle of the Counts of Vianden. Victor Hugo stayed here in May 1871 after being expelled from Belgium.

Location
Population 1 501 – Michelin maps 716 L6 and 717 W23.
On the border with Germany, Vianden is reached by N 10 along the River Our from Clervaux, by N 17 from Diekirch, and by B 50 from Bitburg in Germany. There are fine views of the town and its surroundings from the heights to the west; the road up to Mont St-Nicholas for example leads to a viewpoint (also accessible by chairlift and via a path from the castle) affording a superb **panorama★★★** over town, castle and valley.
🚹 *Rue du Vieux Marché 1, ☎ 83 42 57.*

Directory

WHERE TO EAT
☺ **Auberge Aal Veinen "Beim Hunn"** – *Grand-Rue 114 – ☎ 83 43 68 – ahahn@pt.lu – Closed late Nov – early Dec, Mon eve, Tue exc July-Sept – lunch €9 – €15/27.* This typical inn stands at the foot of Vianden's castle. It boasts a grill restaurant with a cheerful countryside atmosphere and a number of bedrooms with solid wooden furnishings.

WHERE TO STAY
☺ **Victor Hugo** – *Rue Victor Hugo 1 – ☎ 83 41 60 – www.hotel-victor-hugo.lu – ⊟ – 14 rms: €45 – restaurant €33.* The sign is a reminder that the author of *Les* *Misérables* spent time in Vianden. Range of dishes catering for everyone's taste. The brasserie-style dining room is extended in fine weather onto an attractive terrace.
Heintz – *Grand-Rue 55 – ☎ 83 41 55 – hoheintz@pt.lu – mid-Apr – early Nov – restaurant closed Wed and Thur lunchtime exc July-Aug – ⊡ – 26 rms: €51/74 – restaurant €22/30.* This traditional hostelry next to the town's Trinitarian Church has long been in the same family ownership. The rooms to the rear have balconies with hill views. In fine weather the garden and terrace will tempt you to linger.

Worth a Visit

Château★★
Mar-Apr, 10am-5pm; May-Oct, 10am-6pm; Nov-Feb, 10am-4pm. Closed 1 Jan, 2 Nov, 25 Dec. €4.50. ☎ 84 92 91.
Originally built by the counts of Vianden, the castle then belonged to the Orange-Nassau family from 1417, except for a short period in the early 19C, when it was bought by a speculator who left it in a severely damaged state.
In 1977 Grand Duke Jean gave it to the State of Luxembourg, and since then it has undergone a remarkable restoration, which has given it back its late 18C appearance. Archaeological digs have revealed the presence of a small fortress constructed in the 5C as well as a first set of walls dating from the 9C. The counts of Vianden reached the height of their power in the 12C and 13C, and it is from this period that most of the buildings date.
Tour – *Signs and room numbering help visitors find their way through the maze of corridors, stairs and terraces.*

The castle consists of the 12C Petit Palais and the imposing Grand Palais. The Romanesque rooms of the Petit Palais have Gothic windows (Armoury and Byzantine Room). An archeological exhibition illustrates the various stages in the construction of the castle. The chapel consists of a 10-sided base from the Carolingian period surmounted by a hexagonal upper storey with polychrome colonettes. The Grand Palais includes the huge **Knight's Hall** and, above it, the Counts' Hall with a lovely collection of tapestries.

There are fine **views★** of the valley of the Our and the town from the sentry-walk and the garden.

Musée d'Art Rustique
Grand-Rue 98. Mid-Apr to early Oct, Tue-Sun 11am-5pm €2.50. ☎ 83 45 91.
Vianden's Museum of Rustic Art is housed in an old town mansion. The delightful interior is typical of the area and is filled with country-style furnishings, among them a fine array of firebacks and a collection of dolls.

Église des Trinitaires
Grand-Rue. This Gothic abbey church with two aisles dates from the 13C. In the north aisle is a medieval tomb with the recumbent figure of Maria of Vianden. The pretty cloisters, also of 13C date, have been restored.

Bridge over the Our
From this bridge, which is protected by a statue of St John of Nepomuk, patron saint of bridges, there is a pleasant **view** of the town and castle.

Maison de Victor Hugo
Jul, Aug, Easter and Christmas holidays, Tue-sun 10am-6pm.
Already familiar with Vianden after several previous journeys, the exiled **Victor Hugo** stayed here from 8 June to 22 August 1871. The house has been turned into a museum and displays a number of his drawings and letters. A bust by Rodin of the great French author can be seen opposite the house.

Excursion

DAM AND POWER STATION
Allow 2hr

Barrage de Lohmühle
1km/0.75mi N. The course of the River Our above Vianden has been transformed by a massive hydro-electric power scheme, a joint German-Luxembourg venture consisting of upper and lower reservoirs linked by pipes driven through the mountain. The Lohmühle dam holds back the 10 million m^3/107 million cu ft of water of the 8km/5mi long lower reservoir. On the west bank at the foot of the dam stands the **Église Neuve** (New Church), built in 1770 in the old plague victims' district.

Hydroelectric Pumping Station
5km/3mi N of the dam, beyond Bivels.
Hollowed out of the rock, the machine room controls the flow of water between the lower reservoir and the upper reservoir at Mont St-Nicolas. When demand for electricity is low, water from the lower reservoir is pumped into the upper reservoir, then released at times of peak consumption.
Annual energy production can reach 1 600 million kilowatts.
The **visitors' gallery** has fascinating models and illuminated displays.

Bassins Supérieurs du Mont St-Nicolas
5km/3mi W on the Diekirch road, then right.
Beyond the crossroads there is a striking **view★★** of Vianden and its castle. The **upper basins**, surrounded by 4.6km/2.75mi of dikes, form an artificial lake, 14-35m/45-114ft deep and with a capacity of 6.6 million m^3/71 million cu ft. A flight of steps leads to one section of the dike. There is a **view** of the reservoir and its water draw-down tower, which is linked to the bank by a footbridge.
From below the reservoir there is a fine **view★** of the deep, well cultivated valley of the Our and of the Eifel uplands in Germany.

Tour

VALLEY OF THE OUR★★
20km/12.5mi, ending at Dasburg in Germany.
The River Our marks the border between Germany and the Grand Duchy all the way from Ouren in Belgium to Wallendorf, where it joins the Sûre. The river has cut a deep and winding valley through the ancient rocks of the massif, sometimes barely squeezing its way between sheer cliffs.
Head N from Vianden.
The road runs initially along the crest of the **Lohmühle dam** *(See "excursion").*

Bivels

This village lies in a remarkable **setting★** in the centre of an enormous meander of the Our.

Hydroelectric Pumping Station

(See "excursion").

Stolzembourg

The romantic ruins of a castle are perched on a hilltop above the village.

Dasburg

A charming little place attractively sited on the German side of the river.

Wiltz

High up on the Oesling plateau (315m/1 033ft) little Wiltz is famous as an international scouting centre. The lower town extends along the banks of the River Wiltz, while the picturesque upper town is squeezed onto a spur of rock between the church and the castle.
Every year the castle gardens make a pretty setting for a European Festival of Open-Air Theatre and Music.

Location

Population 4 277 – Michelin maps 716 K6 and 717 U23.
In the valley of the River Wiltz in the heart of the Luxembourg Ardennes, the town is reached from Ettelbruck and from Bastogne in Belgium by N 15, then N 26 or N 12.
🛈 *Château,* ☎ *95 74 44.*

Worth a Visit

Église Décanale

This 16C church in the lower town was extended and restored in the 20C.
Its two Gothic aisles contain the tombstones of the lords of Wiltz. A beautiful Louis XV grille closes off the Counts' Chapel.
On the climb to the upper town, note a **monument** on the left, recalling that it was at Wiltz that the first general strike against the German occupation began in September 1942.

Château

The château of the Counts of Wiltz still has a square 13C tower, which was altered in 1722. The main wing dates from 1631. It has now been turned into an old people's home. The amphitheatre created in 1954 at the foot of the main staircase is where the festival events take place.

Croix de Justice

Dating from the 16C, this "Cross of Justice" replaced a medieval cross symbolising the rights granted to the town (justice, freedom, trade).
Note the statues of the Virgin Mary and St John of Nepomuk who is said to have saved the town from fire.

Monument Notre-Dame de Fatima

Access via the Noertrange road, CR 329, to the west.
The road passes a brewery whose copper vats can be seen. There is a fine **view** from the monument (1952) of the town's white-walled, slate-roofed buildings stepping up the hillside.
The shrine is a pilgrimage site for Luxembourg's comparatively large Portuguese community.

Excursion

Vallée de la Wiltz

11km/6.75mi E on N 25 ending at Kautenbach.
This pretty, winding valley runs between wooded hillsides.

Index

Luxembourg